BOLLINGEN SERIES XIX

衛禮賢譯解

董作賓題

The I Ching

OR

BOOK OF CHANGES

The Richard Wilhelm Translation
rendered into English by Cary F. Baynes

Foreword by C. G. Jung

Preface to the Third Edition
by Hellmut Wilhelm

BOLLINGEN SERIES XIX

PRINCETON UNIVERSITY PRESS

THIS WORK IS THE NINETEENTH IN A SERIES OF BOOKS SPONSORED
BY BOLLINGEN FOUNDATION

First Edition, in two volumes, 1950
Second Edition, in one volume, 1961
*Third Edition, reset in new format, with a preface by Hellmut
Wilhelm, and an index, 1967*
twenty-second printing, 1987
twenty-fourth printing, 1990
twenty-seventh printing, 1997

Library of Congress Catalogue Card Number: 67-24740
ISBN-13: 978-0-691-09750-3
ISBN-10: 0-691-09750-X

Designed by Bert Clarke
Printed in the U.S.A.

40   39   38   37   36   35   34   33

NOTE ON THE CHINESE TITLE PAGE

The two large Chinese characters read *Chou I*, "Changes of Chou," alternative
name of the "Book of Changes" (cf. pp. *lviii–lix*). The characters at the right
read *Wei Li-hsien i-chieh*, "Translated and annotated by Richard Wilhelm";
those on the left, *Tung Tso-pin t'i*, "Calligraphy by Tung Tso-pin." The seal is
that of Tung Tso-pin.

CONTENTS

BOOK I: THE TEXT

PART I

*[Alternative English versions of the names of some of the hexagrams are given in square brackets.—C.F.B.]

Contents

PART II

BOOK II: THE MATERIAL

PART I

A. *Underlying Principles*

Contents

B. *Detailed Discussion*

PART II

The Structure of the Hexagrams

viii

BOOK III: THE COMMENTARIES

PART I

PART II

Appendixes

Indexes

Preface to the Third Edition

It is with delight and not without a certain pride that I see this translation of the Book of Changes presented in a new edition. The fact of its widespread and continuing acceptance stands as a justification of my father's conviction, the propagation of which he took as his calling, that the overwhelming importance of the Book within the history and the system of Chinese thought would be borne out when tested against general, and not only specifically Chinese, human conditions and against general, and not only specifically Chinese, processes of the human mind.

Since the appearance of my father's work and its English rendering by Cary F. Baynes, two of the earlier translations have also experienced a revival: the one by de Harlez, originally published in 1889, now issued with added commentaries taken in part from my father[1]; and the one by Legge, originally published in 1882, now in two editions, one in paperback,[2] and one with added remarks by Ch'u Chai and Winberg Chai.[3] Two independent new translations have been published, one by Yüan Kuang, originally in French and later also in German,[4] and the simplified English version by my friend John Blofeld.[5]

1. *Le Livre des mutations*, texte primitif traduit du chinois par Charles de Harlez, présenté et annoté par Raymond de Becker (Paris, 1959).

2. Dover Publications, New York, 1963.

3. *I Ching: Book of Changes*, translated by James Legge, edited with introduction and Study Guide by Ch'u Chai and Winberg Chai (New Hyde Park, New York, 1964).

4. Le Maître Yüan-kuang, *Méthode pratique de Divination Chinoise par le "Yi-king"* (Paris, 1950); Meister Yüan-kuang, *I Ging: Praxis chinesischer Weissagung*, translated by Fritz Werle (Munich, 1951).

5. John Blofeld, *The Book of Change*: a new translation of the ancient Chinese I Ching . . . with detailed instruction for its practical use in divination (London and New York, 1965).

It will be recalled that my father began his translation more than half a century ago and that he worked on it together with one of the foremost Chinese scholars of the period, Lao Nai-hsüan. Lao was, of course, in complete possession of the traditional *I Ching* lore, but he was also one of the most modern-minded personalities of his age. It was he who, in the context of late Imperial China, promoted institutional, legal, educational, and even language reforms of an amazingly progressive hue. Even though the tradition was for him a live concern, he was not just a tradition-bound interpreter; the concept of change, also in his own time, was part of his credo. It was his openness to the development of the traditional potential in terms of his own period that made the co-operation between him and my father so easy and so fruitful.

Much scholarship both in China and abroad has been devoted since then to a number of questions concerning the history and meaning of the text, and it might be of interest here to recapitulate briefly some of the new insights. Several lines of investigation have been followed. One of them has been the exploitation of hitherto unknown comparative material, specifically the inscribed oracle bones, which had not yet been subjected to research at the time my father worked on the Book. A second one has emerged from more advanced methods of philology and textual comparison, and a third one finally from a more advanced structural analysis of the texts themselves and of their prosodic and euphonic aspects. Taken together, these studies have added a great deal to the understanding and appreciation of the meaningful growth of the text over the centuries and to an elucidation of specific images employed in the texts.

Thus it is now widely maintained that the older layers of the text, as we know them today, assumed their present form in the century before Confucius, and that in them earlier versions of the text have been added to or even changed. Attempts have been made to reconstruct what might have been the original versions, which would be characterized by a pristine beauty of structure and euphony, in line with or superior to other texts of early Chou times. They would furthermore be characterized by a much more exclusive use of imagery as a means of expression and would be innocent of expository statements such as we find in the texts today. Attempts to differentiate an (earlier) layer of images from a (later) layer of concepts cannot, however, be called successful, and it now appears that the intimate interplay between image and concept was one of the original features of the text. The range of fields from which these images were taken must have been practically unlimited. Some of them came without doubt from the then current mythology, others from the then existing poetry (at times passages are taken over literally into the Book), others from religious and social institutions; still others seem to reflect the recognition of the archetypal configurations of specific moments in history. Many of the images used can, however, not (or not yet) be thus elucidated, and the postulate still stands unshaken that much of the imagery of the Book derives from the intuition of its original authors.

To these pristine texts there must then have been added at a very early time the so-called diviners' formulae, which spell out the divinatory message implied in the images. These were both short statements about the propitiousness or otherwise of a given situation and somewhat more elaborate formulae of advice cast in a wording that involves fixed but never stereotyped imagery.

The latest discernible additions to, and changes of, the older layers of the text must have taken place, as mentioned, during the century preceding Confucius. These changes reflect a reinterpretation of the original images and concepts more intimate and more sophisticated than those of the diviners' formulae. They mirror a new stage in the development of the human mind, a higher degree of self-realization, and they are expressed in ideas and positions not available to the earlier period. Most obvious among these additions is the idea of the "superior man," *chün-tzu*, a term which meant an aristocrat in early Chou China. Some of these changes are quite incisive. Taken together, however, they represent a growth in awareness, rather than a falsification, of the original import of the Book.

The later layers of the Book, the so-called Ten Wings, have, as is recalled, been attributed to Confucius by the orthodox tradition. It can now be shown that some of the wording of at least one of them, the *Wên-Yen* (Commentary on the Words of the Text), and some of the material of at least one other, the *Shuo Kua* (Discussion of the Trigrams), were already available in pre-Confucian times. Most of the rest, however, is now generally assumed to be much later than Confucius. The Confucian school is responsible for much of what is in the Ten Wings of today, and some of this might remotely reflect traditions preserved in this school which go back to Confucius himself. The present reading of those passages in the Wings which are attributed to Confucius cannot have been written in Confucius' own time nor in the time immediately following. Some of the ideas expressed in these passages have, however, retained, even in their more modern garb, a specifically Confucian ring.[6] Other parts of the Wings must be very late Chou and possibly even post-Chou.

In addition to the endeavors outlined above, recent scholarship has concerned itself with other aspects of the Book which cannot be dealt with here. The most prominent among these is the purity of the Book's system, which already amazed Leibniz, and another concerns apocryphal writings which were connected with the Book and which reflect, among other things, a developed interest in prognostication and "portentology," called to life by the political battles of the day rather than by an understanding of the Book's own message.

Reference has been made to recent Chinese scholarship regarding the Book of Changes. This renewed interest in the Book is fundamentally different, of course, from the one that produced the abundance of *I Ching* studies during Imperial times. The Book is no longer considered part of Holy Writ but is submitted to the same type of analysis as any other ancient text would be. The results have been highly rewarding. There is, however, evidence of a continued strain of reverence which has by now overcome—or more cautiously: is about to overcome—the fashion of the earlier republican times to see in the Book only a conglomerate of superstition or, at the least, murk. Everybody knows, of course, that a host of problems still remains unsolved; but sober scholarship gradually recognizes again that what has been dealt with in the Book is a unique

---

6. I cannot make myself take seriously the claim that Confucius did not know the Book of Changes.

manifestation of the human mind. The more emotionally inclined have proceeded to regard the Book again as one of the
most treasured parts of the Chinese tradition. To the extent
that opinions can be expressed, this is true even in the context
of Communist China. Kuo Mo-jo, who until his recent purge
was the foremost cultural official of Communist China, devoted
himself to the Book extensively, particularly in his earlier
years. And when, in the early 1960's, the ideological reins
were somewhat relaxed and it was possible for a time to
deal with matters of intellectual concern, the two issues which
engendered nationwide discussions were the ethical system of
Confucius and the Book of Changes. By now these discussions
have been curtailed, but the phenomenon persists: whenever
the rare chance of expression is given, the Book emerges as
one of the foremost concerns of Chinese intellectuals even
under the specific set of circumstances prevailing on mainland
China.

When this new edition was being prepared, the editors gave
much thought to the question whether a rearrangement of
the contents of the Book might facilitate its use for the non-
Chinese reader. The final decision was to leave unchanged the
arrangement which my father had chosen. This decision was
based not only on the conviction that books, too, are organisms
which should undergo incisive operations only in dire emer-
gencies; the more important consideration was that the present
arrangement is the most meaningful and the easiest to handle.
In the traditional Chinese editions the presentation of the text
is not uniform. The problem of arrangement pertains particularly to the text of certain of the Ten Wings which might
either be divided up among the hexagrams or be read as a
continuous text. The second alternative has points in its favor.
One of the Wings, the book *Tsa Kua* (Miscellaneous Notes on
the Hexagrams), which discusses the hexagrams one by one
(or rather in pairs), does not coincide in sequence with the
hexagrams in the main text. The particular curve of development thus gets lost when this book is divided up among the
hexagrams. Nor is this all. The *Tsa Kua*, when read in its own
sequence, is an accomplished poem with a firm prosodic structure and a consistent rhyme system. The same is true of the

Small Images, the commentaries on the line texts, found in the third book of this translation. Thus here we have early examples of didactic Chinese poetry the features of which are lost when these texts are divided up among the hexagrams.

These considerations notwithstanding, my father chose, after much hesitation, to employ a modified form of the first alternative for the arrangement of his translation. (See the chart opposite: "The Major Divisions of the Material.") He furthermore chose to distinguish systematically (again, with one modification) between the older layers of the texts and the material of the Ten Wings. In this way he arrived at a division into three "books": the (old) Text, the Material, and the Commentaries (contained in the Ten Wings). Book I gives the older layers of the text, the Judgments pertaining to the hexagrams as a whole, and the line texts. To these he added the so-called Great Images, which appear for each hexagram under the caption "The Image." These do, of course, belong to the Wings. Their inclusion here reflects my father's special approach to the Book. Of a later date, these texts reflect a more advanced interpretation and understanding of the situation represented in the individual hexagrams. In frequently surprising statements they formulate succinctly the reaction of the "superior man" to the specific configuration of imagery offered by the system of the line structure. They are thus not to be considered commentaries on specific passages of the older texts (as the so-called Small Images and the *Wên Yen* are); they constitute a third and independent approach, in addition to the judgments and the line texts, to the situations entailed by the hexagrams.

To the translation of these three types of classical texts, my father added his own elucidative remarks (in this as in other editions, printed in smaller type). These remarks are based on a careful reading of the later (postclassical) commentatory literature, on his discussions with Lao and other friends and experts, on the modern scholarly literature then available, and on his own understanding and interpretation of the passages and situations involved.

Book II contains the translations of the more systematic among the Ten Wings, specifically, the *Shuo Kua* (Discussion of the Trigrams) and the *Ta Chuan* (The Great Treatise), the

The Major Divisions of the Material

THE TEXT   bk. I, pp. 3 *ff*.

THE TEN WINGS

1, 2.   *T'uan Chuan*: Commentary on the Decision   bk. III, under the individual hexagrams

3, 4.   *Hsiang Chuan*: Commentary on the Images   bks. I, III, under the individual hexagrams

5, 6.   *Ta Chuan*: The Great Treatise [Great Commentary]   bk. II, pp. 280 *ff*.
                    or
      Hsi Tz'u Chuan: Commentary on the Appended Judgments

7.   *Wên Yen*: Commentary on the Words of the Text   bk. III, under hexagrams 1 and 2

8.   *Shuo Kua*: Discussion of the Trigrams   bk. II, pp. 262 *ff*.

9.   *Hsü Kua*: Sequence of the Hexagrams   bk. III, under the individual hexagrams

10.   *Tsa Kua*: Miscellaneous Notes on the Hexagrams   bk. III, under the individual hexagrams

translated passages again being elucidated by my father's own remarks. To these translations is appended an essay from my father's own hand, "The Structure of the Hexagrams." (Another, "On Consulting the Oracle," has been transposed to the end of the volume for this edition.)

Book III, finally, is again arranged in the sequence of the hexagrams. It repeats the basic translations found in Book I and arranges under them those books and passages from the Ten Wings that are considered commentatory to the texts. These include passages found in the Great Treatise, which are repeated here under the caption "Appended Judgments," a term which is the rendering of an alternate name of this treatise, *Hsi Tz'u*. Here again, my father's own remarks (in smaller type) are added to the translations, dealing in this case not so much with general considerations as with technical and systematic aspects, the principles and concepts of which are discussed in the above-mentioned essay on "The Structure of the Hexagrams."

HELLMUT WILHELM

Seattle, December 1966

I am grateful to Wallace K. Snider for discovering several typographical errors and an interesting textual error on page 530: in the first line of the Note, hexagram I (27) should be cited rather than I (42).

H. W.

Seattle, April 1968

Foreword

Since I am not a sinologue, a foreword to the Book of Changes from my hand must be a testimonial of my individual experience with this great and singular book. It also affords me a welcome opportunity to pay tribute again to the memory of my late friend, Richard Wilhelm. He himself was profoundly aware of the cultural significance of his translation of the *I Ching*, a version unrivaled in the West.

If the meaning of the Book of Changes were easy to grasp, the work would need no foreword. But this is far from being the case, for there is so much that is obscure about it that Western scholars have tended to dispose of it as a collection of "magic spells," either too abstruse to be intelligible, or of no value whatsoever. Legge's translation of the *I Ching*, up to now the only version available in English, has done little to make the work accessible to Western minds.[1] Wilhelm, however, has made every effort to open the way to an understanding of the symbolism of the text. He was in a position to do this because he himself was taught the philosophy and the use of the *I Ching* by the venerable sage Lao Nai-hsüan; moreover, he had over a period of many years put the peculiar technique of the oracle into practice. His grasp of the living meaning of

---

1. Legge makes the following comment on the explanatory text for the individual lines: "According to our notions, a framer of emblems should be a good deal of a poet, but those of the *Yi* only make us think of a dryasdust. Out of more than three hundred and fifty, the greater number are only grotesque" (*The Sacred Books of the East*, XVI: *The Yi King*, 2nd edn., Oxford: Clarendon Press, 1899, p. 22). Of the "lessons" of the hexagrams, the same author says: "But why, it may be asked, why should they be conveyed to us by such an array of lineal figures, and in such a farrago of emblematic representations" (ibid., p. 25). However, we are nowhere told that Legge ever bothered to put the method to a practical test.

C. G. Jung

the text gives his version of the *I Ching* a depth of perspective that an exclusively academic knowledge of Chinese philosophy could never provide.

I am greatly indebted to Wilhelm for the light he has thrown upon the complicated problem of the *I Ching*, and for insight as regards its practical application as well. For more than thirty years I have interested myself in this oracle technique, or method of exploring the unconscious, for it has seemed to me of uncommon significance. I was already fairly familiar with the *I Ching* when I first met Wilhelm in the early nineteen twenties; he confirmed for me then what I already knew, and taught me many things more.

I do not know Chinese and have never been in China. I can assure my reader that it is not altogether easy to find the right access to this monument of Chinese thought, which departs so completely from our ways of thinking. In order to understand what such a book is all about, it is imperative to cast off certain prejudices of the Western mind. It is a curious fact that such a gifted and intelligent people as the Chinese has never developed what we call science. Our science, however, is based upon the principle of causality, and causality is considered to be an axiomatic truth. But a great change in our standpoint is setting in. What Kant's *Critique of Pure Reason* failed to do, is being accomplished by modern physics. The axioms of causality are being shaken to their foundations: we know now that what we term natural laws are merely statistical truths and thus must necessarily allow for exceptions. We have not sufficiently taken into account as yet that we need the laboratory with its incisive restrictions in order to demonstrate the invariable validity of natural law. If we leave things to nature, we see a very different picture: every process is partially or totally interfered with by chance, so much so that under natural circumstances a course of events absolutely conforming to specific laws is almost an exception.

The Chinese mind, as I see it at work in the *I Ching*, seems to be exclusively preoccupied with the chance aspect of events. What we call coincidence seems to be the chief concern of this peculiar mind, and what we worship as causality passes almost unnoticed. We must admit that there is something to be said for the immense importance of chance. An incalculable amount

xxii

of human effort is directed to combating and restricting the nuisance or danger represented by chance. Theoretical considerations of cause and effect often look pale and dusty in comparison to the practical results of chance. It is all very well to say that the crystal of quartz is a hexagonal prism. The statement is quite true in so far as an ideal crystal is envisaged. But in nature one finds no two crystals exactly alike, although all are unmistakably hexagonal. The actual form, however, seems to appeal more to the Chinese sage than the ideal one. The jumble of natural laws constituting empirical reality holds more significance for him than a causal explanation of events that, moreover, must usually be separated from one another in order to be properly dealt with.

The manner in which the *I Ching* tends to look upon reality seems to disfavor our causalistic procedures. The moment under actual observation appears to the ancient Chinese view more of a chance hit than a clearly defined result of concurring causal chain processes. The matter of interest seems to be the configuration formed by chance events in the moment of observation, and not at all the hypothetical reasons that seemingly account for the coincidence. While the Western mind carefully sifts, weighs, selects, classifies, isolates, the Chinese picture of the moment encompasses everything down to the minutest nonsensical detail, because all of the ingredients make up the observed moment.

Thus it happens that when one throws the three coins, or counts through the forty-nine yarrow stalks, these chance details enter into the picture of the moment of observation and form a part of it—a part that is insignificant to us, yet most meaningful to the Chinese mind. With us it would be a banal and almost meaningless statement (at least on the face of it) to say that whatever happens in a given moment possesses inevitably the quality peculiar to that moment. This is not an abstract argument but a very practical one. There are certain connoisseurs who can tell you merely from the appearance, taste, and behavior of a wine the site of its vineyard and the year of its origin. There are antiquarians who with almost uncanny accuracy will name the time and place of origin and the maker of an *objet d'art* or piece of furniture on merely looking at it. And there are even astrologers who can tell you, without any previous knowledge of your nativity, what the position of sun and moon was and what zodiacal sign rose above the horizon in the moment of your birth. In the face of such facts, it must be admitted that moments can leave long-lasting traces.

In other words, whoever invented the *I Ching* was convinced that the hexagram worked out in a certain moment coincided with the latter in quality no less than in time. To him the hexagram was the exponent of the moment in which it was cast—even more so than the hours of the clock or the divisions of the calendar could be—inasmuch as the hexagram was understood to be an indicator of the essential situation prevailing in the moment of its origin.

This assumption involves a certain curious principle that I have termed synchronicity,[2] a concept that formulates a point of view diametrically opposed to that of causality. Since the latter is a merely statistical truth and not absolute, it is a sort of working hypothesis of how events evolve one out of another, whereas synchronicity takes the coincidence of events in space and time as meaning something more than mere chance, namely, a peculiar interdependence of objective events among themselves as well as with the subjective (psychic) states of the observer or observers.

The ancient Chinese mind contemplates the cosmos in a way comparable to that of the modern physicist, who cannot deny that his model of the world is a decidedly psychophysical structure. The microphysical event includes the observer just as much as the reality underlying the *I Ching* comprises subjective, i.e., psychic conditions in the totality of the momentary situation. Just as causality describes the sequence of events, so synchronicity to the Chinese mind deals with the coincidence of events. The causal point of view tells us a dramatic story about how *D* came into existence: it took its origin from *C*, which existed before *D*, and *C* in its turn had a father, *B*, etc. The synchronistic view on the other hand tries to produce an equally meaningful picture of coincidence. How does it happen that *A'*, *B'*, *C'*, *D'*, etc., appear all in the same moment and

2. [Cf. "Synchronicity: An Acausal Connecting Principle," *The Structure and Dynamics of the Psyche* (Coll. Works of C. G. Jung, vol. 8).]

in the same place? It happens in the first place because the physical events A' and B' are of the same quality as the psychic events C' and D', and further because all are the exponents of one and the same momentary situation. The situation is assumed to represent a legible or understandable picture.

Now the sixty-four hexagrams of the *I Ching* are the instrument by which the meaning of sixty-four different yet typical situations can be determined. These interpretations are equivalent to causal explanations. Causal connection is statistically necessary and can therefore be subjected to experiment. Inasmuch as situations are unique and cannot be repeated, experimenting with synchronicity seems to be impossible under ordinary conditions.[3] In the *I Ching*, the only criterion of the validity of synchronicity is the observer's opinion that the text of the hexagram amounts to a true rendering of his psychic condition. It is assumed that the fall of the coins or the result of the division of the bundle of yarrow stalks is what it necessarily must be in a given "situation," inasmuch as anything happening in that moment belongs to it as an indispensable part of the picture. If a handful of matches is thrown to the floor, they form the pattern characteristic of that moment. But such an obvious truth as this reveals its meaningful nature only if it is possible to read the pattern and to verify its interpretation, partly by the observer's knowledge of the subjective and objective situation, partly by the character of subsequent events. It is obviously not a procedure that appeals to a critical mind used to experimental verification of facts or to factual evidence. But for someone who likes to look at the world at the angle from which ancient China saw it, the *I Ching* may have some attraction.

My argument as outlined above has of course never entered a Chinese mind. On the contrary, according to the old tradition, it is "spiritual agencies," acting in a mysterious way, that make the yarrow stalks give a meaningful answer.[4] These powers form, as it were, the living soul of the book. As the

---

3. Cf. J. B. Rhine, *The Reach of the Mind* (New York and London, 1928).

4. They are *shên*, that is "spirit-like." "Heaven produced the 'spirit-like things' " (Legge, p. 41).

latter is thus a sort of animated being, the tradition assumes that one can put questions to the *I Ching* and expect to receive intelligent answers. Thus it occurred to me that it might interest the uninitiated reader to see the *I Ching* at work. For this purpose I made an experiment strictly in accordance with the Chinese conception: I personified the book in a sense, asking its judgment about its present situation, i.e., my intention to present it to the Western mind.

Although this procedure is well within the premises of Taoist philosophy, it appears exceedingly odd to us. However, not even the strangeness of insane delusions or of primitive superstition has ever shocked me. I have always tried to remain unbiased and curious—*rerum novarum cupidus*. Why not venture a dialogue with an ancient book that purports to be animated? There can be no harm in it, and the reader may watch a psychological procedure that has been carried out time and again throughout the millennia of Chinese civilization, representing to a Confucius or a Lao-tse both a supreme expression of spiritual authority and a philosophical enigma. I made use of the coin method, and the answer obtained was hexagram 50, Ting, THE CALDRON.

In accordance with the way my question was phrased, the text of the hexagram must be regarded as though the *I Ching* itself were the speaking person. Thus it describes itself as a caldron, that is, as a ritual vessel containing cooked food. Here the food is to be understood as spiritual nourishment. Wilhelm says about this:

The *ting*, as a utensil pertaining to a refined civilization, suggests the fostering and nourishing of able men, which redounded to the benefit of the state. . . . Here we see civilization as it reaches its culmination in religion. The *ting* serves in offering sacrifice to God. . . . The supreme revelation of God appears in prophets and holy men. To venerate them is true veneration of God. The will of God, as revealed through them, should be accepted in humility.

Keeping to our hypothesis, we must conclude that the *I Ching* is here testifying concerning itself.

When any of the lines of a given hexagram have the value of six or nine, it means that they are specially emphasized and hence important in the interpretation. [5] In my hexagram the "spiritual agencies" have given the emphasis of a nine to the lines in the second and in the third place. The text says:

> Nine in the second place means:
> There is food in the *ting*.
> My comrades are envious,
> But they cannot harm me.
> Good fortune.

Thus the *I Ching* says of itself: "I contain (spiritual) nourishment." Since a share in something great always arouses envy, the chorus of the envious [6] is part of the picture. The envious want to rob the *I Ching* of its great possession, that is, they seek to rob it of meaning, or to destroy its meaning. But their enmity is in vain. Its richness of meaning is assured; that is, it is convinced of its positive achievements, which no one can take away. The text continues:

> Nine in the third place means:
> The handle of the *ting* is altered.
> One is impeded in his way of life.
> The fat of the pheasant is not eaten.
> Once rain falls, remorse is spent.
> Good fortune comes in the end.

The handle [German *Griff*] is the part by which the *ting* can be grasped [*gegriffen*]. Thus it signifies the concept [7] (*Begriff*) one has of the *I Ching* (the *ting*). In the course of time this concept has apparently changed, so that today we can no longer grasp (*begreifen*) the *I Ching*. Thus "one is impeded in his way of life." We are no longer supported by the wise counsel and deep insight of the oracle; therefore we no

---

5. See the explanation of the method in Wilhelm's text, p. 721.

6. For example, the *invidi* ("the envious") are a constantly recurring image in the old Latin books on alchemy, especially in the *Turba philosophorum* (eleventh or twelfth century).

7. From the Latin *concipere*, "to take together," e.g., in a vessel: *concipere* derives from *capere*, "to take," "to grasp."

longer find our way through the mazes of fate and the obscurities of our own natures. The fat of the pheasant, that is, the best and richest part of a good dish, is no longer eaten. But when the thirsty earth finally receives rain again, that is, when this state of want has been overcome, "remorse," that is, sorrow over the loss of wisdom, is ended, and then comes the longed-for opportunity. Wilhelm comments: "This describes a man who, in a highly evolved civilization, finds himself in a place where no one notices or recognizes him. This is a severe block to his effectiveness." The *I Ching* is complaining, as it were, that its excellent qualities go unrecognized and hence lie fallow. It comforts itself with the hope that it is about to regain recognition.

The answer given in these two salient lines to the question I put to the *I Ching* requires no particular subtlety of interpretation, no artifices, no unusual knowledge. Anyone with a little common sense can understand the meaning of the answer; it is the answer of one who has a good opinion of himself, but whose value is neither generally recognized nor even widely known. The answering subject has an interesting notion of itself: it looks upon itself as a vessel in which sacrificial offerings are brought to the gods, ritual food for their nourishment. It conceives of itself as a cult utensil serving to provide spiritual nourishment for the unconscious elements or forces ("spiritual agencies") that have been projected as gods—in other words, to give these forces the attention they need in order to play their part in the life of the individual. Indeed, this is the original meaning of the word *religio*—a careful observation and taking account of (from *relegere*[8]) the numinous.

The method of the *I Ching* does indeed take into account the hidden individual quality in things and men, and in one's own unconscious self as well. I have questioned the *I Ching* as one questions a person whom one is about to introduce to friends: one asks whether or not it will be agreeable to him. In answer the *I Ching* tells me of its religious significance, of the fact that at present it is unknown and misjudged, of its hope of being restored to a place of honor—this last obviously

---

8. This is the classical etymology. The derivation of *religio* from *religare*, "bind to," originated with the Church Fathers.

with a sidelong glance at my as yet unwritten foreword,[9] and above all at the English translation. This seems a perfectly understandable reaction, such as one could expect also from a person in a similar situation.

But how has this reaction come about? Because I threw three small coins into the air and let them fall, roll, and come to rest, heads up or tails up as the case might be. This odd fact that a reaction that makes sense arises out of a technique seemingly excluding all sense from the outset, is the great achievement of the *I Ching*. The instance I have just given is not unique; meaningful answers are the rule. Western sinologues and distinguished Chinese scholars have been at pains to inform me that the *I Ching* is a collection of obsolete "magic spells." In the course of these conversations my informant has sometimes admitted having consulted the oracle through a fortune teller, usually a Taoist priest. This could be "only nonsense" of course. But oddly enough, the answer received apparently coincided with the questioner's psychological blind spot remarkably well.

I agree with Western thinking that any number of answers to my question were possible, and I certainly cannot assert that another answer would not have been equally significant. However, the answer received was the first and only one; we know nothing of other possible answers. It pleased and satisfied me. To ask the same question a second time would have been tactless and so I did not do it: "the master speaks but once." The heavy-handed pedagogic approach that attempts to fit irrational phenomena into a preconceived rational pattern is anathema to me. Indeed, such things as this answer should remain as they were when they first emerged to view, for only then do we know what nature does when left to herself undisturbed by the meddlesomeness of man. One ought not to go to cadavers to study life. Moreover, a repetition of the experiment is impossible, for the simple reason that the original situation cannot be reconstructed. Therefore in each instance there is only a first and single answer.

To return to the hexagram itself. There is nothing strange in the fact that all of Ting, THE CALDRON, amplifies the themes

---

9. I made this experiment before I actually wrote the foreword.

announced by the two salient lines.[10] The first line of the hexagram says:

> A *ting* with legs upturned.
>
> Furthers removal of stagnating stuff.
>
> One takes a concubine for the sake of her son.
>
> No blame.

A *ting* that is turned upside down is not in use. Hence the *I Ching* is like an unused caldron. Turning it over serves to remove stagnating matter, as the line says. Just as a man takes a concubine when his wife has no son, so the *I Ching* is called upon when one sees no other way out. Despite the quasi-legal status of the concubine in China, she is in reality only a somewhat awkward makeshift; so likewise the magic procedure of the oracle is an expedient that may be utilized for a higher purpose. There is no blame, although it is an exceptional recourse.

The second and third lines have already been discussed. The fourth line says:

> The legs of the *ting* are broken.
>
> The prince's meal is spilled
>
> And his person is soiled.
>
> Misfortune.

Here the *ting* has been put to use, but evidently in a very clumsy manner, that is, the oracle has been abused or misinterpreted. In this way the divine food is lost, and one puts oneself to shame. Legge translates as follows: "Its subject will be made to blush for shame." Abuse of a cult utensil such as the *ting* (i.e., the *I Ching*) is a gross profanation. The *I Ching* is evidently insisting here on its dignity as a ritual vessel and protesting against being profanely used.

The fifth line says:

> The *ting* has yellow handles, golden carrying rings.
>
> Perseverance furthers.

---

10. The Chinese interpret only the changing lines in the hexagram obtained by use of the oracle. I have found all the lines of the hexagram to be relevant in most cases.

The *I Ching* has, it seems, met with a new, correct (yellow) understanding, that is, a new concept (*Begriff*) by which it can be grasped. This concept is valuable (golden). There is indeed a new edition in English, making the book more accessible to the Western world than before.

The sixth line says:

> The *ting* has rings of jade.
> Great good fortune.
> Nothing that would not act to further.

Jade is distinguished for its beauty and soft sheen. If the carrying rings are of jade, the whole vessel is enhanced in beauty, honor, and value. The *I Ching* expresses itself here as being not only well satisfied but indeed very optimistic. One can only await further events and in the meantime remain content with the pleasant conclusion that the *I Ching* approves of the new edition.

I have shown in this example as objectively as I can how the oracle proceeds in a given case. Of course the procedure varies somewhat according to the way the question is put. If for instance a person finds himself in a confusing situation, he may himself appear in the oracle as the speaker. Or, if the question concerns a relationship with another person, that person may appear as the speaker. However, the identity of the speaker does not depend entirely on the manner in which the question is phrased, inasmuch as our relations with our fellow beings are not always determined by the latter. Very often our relations depend almost exclusively on our own attitudes, though we may be quite unaware of this fact. Hence, if an individual is unconscious of his role in a relationship, there may be a surprise in store for him; contrary to expectation, he himself may appear as the chief agent, as is sometimes unmistakably indicated by the text. It may also occur that we take a situation too seriously and consider it extremely important, whereas the answer we get on consulting the *I Ching* draws attention to some unsuspected other aspect implicit in the question.

Such instances might at first lead one to think that the oracle is fallacious. Confucius is said to have received only one inappropriate answer, i.e., hexagram 22, GRACE—a thoroughly aesthetic hexagram. This is reminiscent of the advice given to Socrates by his daemon—"You ought to make more music"—whereupon Socrates took to playing the flute. Confucius and Socrates compete for first place as far as reasonableness and a pedagogic attitude to life are concerned; but it is unlikely that either of them occupied himself with "lending grace to the beard on his chin," as the second line of this hexagram advises. Unfortunately, reason and pedagogy often lack charm and grace, and so the oracle may not have been wrong after all.

To come back once more to our hexagram. Though the *I Ching* not only seems to be satisfied with its new edition, but even expresses emphatic optimism, this still does not foretell anything about the effect it will have on the public it is intended to reach. Since we have in our hexagram two yang lines stressed by the numerical value nine, we are in a position to find out what sort of prognosis the *I Ching* makes for itself. Lines designated by a six or a nine have, according to the ancient conception, an inner tension so great as to cause them to change into their opposites, that is, yang into yin, and vice versa. Through this change we obtain in the present instance hexagram 35, Chin, PROGRESS.

The subject of this hexagram is someone who meets with all sorts of vicissitudes of fortune in his climb upward, and the text describes how he should behave. The *I Ching* is in this same situation: it rises like the sun and declares itself, but it is rebuffed and finds no confidence—it is "progressing, but in sorrow." However, "one obtains great happiness from one's ancestress." Psychology can help us to elucidate this obscure passage. In dreams and fairy tales the grandmother, or ancestress, often represents the unconscious, because the latter in a man contains the feminine component of the psyche. If the *I Ching* is not accepted by the conscious, at least the unconscious meets it halfway, and the *I Ching* is more closely connected with the unconscious than with the rational attitude of consciousness. Since the unconscious is often represented in dreams by a feminine figure, this may be the explanation here. The feminine person might be the translator, who has given the book her maternal care, and this might easily appear to the *I Ching* as a "great happiness." It anticipates general under-

standing, but is afraid of misuse—"Progress like a hamster."
But it is mindful of the admonition, "Take not gain and loss to
heart." It remains free of "partisan motives." It does not thrust
itself on anyone.

The *I Ching* therefore faces its future on the American
book market calmly and expresses itself here just about as any
reasonable person would in regard to the fate of so controversial
a work. This prediction is so very reasonable and full of common
sense that it would be hard to think of a more fitting answer.

All of this happened before I had written the foregoing
paragraphs. When I reached this point, I wished to know the
attitude of the *I Ching* to the new situation. The state of things
had been altered by what I had written, inasmuch as I myself
had now entered upon the scene, and I therefore expected to
hear something referring to my own action. I must confess that
I had not been feeling too happy in the course of writing this
foreword, for, as a person with a sense of responsibility toward
science, I am not in the habit of asserting something I cannot
prove or at least present as acceptable to reason. It is a dubious
task indeed to try to introduce to a critical modern public a
collection of archaic "magic spells," with the idea of making
them more or less acceptable. I have undertaken it because I
myself think that there is more to the ancient Chinese way of
thinking than meets the eye. But it is embarrassing to me that
I must appeal to the good will and imagination of the reader,
inasmuch as I have to take him into the obscurity of an age-old
magic ritual. Unfortunately I am only too well aware of the
arguments that can be brought against it. We are not even
certain that the ship that is to carry us over the unknown seas
has not sprung a leak somewhere. May not the old text be corrupt? Is Wilhelm's translation accurate? Are we not self-
deluded in our explanations?

The *I Ching* insists upon self-knowledge throughout. The
method by which this is to be achieved is open to every kind of
misuse, and is therefore not for the frivolous-minded and im-
mature; nor is it for intellectualists and rationalists. It is appropriate only for thoughtful and reflective people who like to
think about what they do and what happens to them—a pre-
dilection not to be confused with the morbid brooding of the
hypochondriac. As I have indicated above, I have no answer to

the multitude of problems that arise when we seek to harmonize the oracle of the *I Ching* with our accepted scientific canons. But needless to say, nothing "occult" is to be inferred. My position in these matters is pragmatic, and the great disciplines that have taught me the practical usefulness of this viewpoint are psychotherapy and medical psychology. Probably in no other field do we have to reckon with so many unknown quantities, and nowhere else do we become more accustomed to adopting methods that work even though for a long time we may not know why they work. Unexpected cures may arise from questionable therapies and unexpected failures from allegedly reliable methods. In the exploration of the unconscious we come upon very strange things, from which a rationalist turns away with horror, claiming afterward that he did not see anything. The irrational fullness of life has taught me never to discard anything, even when it goes against all our theories (so short-lived at best) or otherwise admits of no immediate explanation. It is of course disquieting, and one is not certain whether the compass is pointing true or not; but security, certitude, and peace do not lead to discoveries. It is the same with this Chinese mode of divination. Clearly the method aims at self-knowledge, though at all times it has also been put to superstitious use.

I of course am thoroughly convinced of the value of self-knowledge, but is there any use in recommending such insight, when the wisest of men throughout the ages have preached the need of it without success? Even to the most biased eye it is obvious that this book represents one long admonition to careful scrutiny of one's own character, attitude, and motives. This attitude appeals to me and has induced me to undertake the foreword. Only once before have I expressed myself in regard to the problem of the *I Ching*: this was in a memorial address in tribute to Richard Wilhelm.[11] For the rest I have maintained a discreet silence. It is by no means easy

11. [Cf. R. Wilhelm and C. G. Jung, *The Secret of the Golden Flower*, tr. Cary F. Baynes (London and New York, 1931; new edn., revised, 1962), in which this address appears as an appendix. The book did not appear in English until a year after Wilhelm's death. The address is also in *The Spirit in Man, Art, and Literature* (Coll. Works of C. G. Jung, vol. 15).]

to feel one's way into such a remote and mysterious mentality as that underlying the *I Ching*. One cannot easily disregard such great minds as Confucius and Lao-tse, if one is at all able to appreciate the quality of the thoughts they represent; much less can one overlook the fact that the *I Ching* was their main source of inspiration. I know that previously I would not have dared to express myself so explicitly about so uncertain a matter. I can take this risk because I am now in my eighth decade, and the changing opinions of men scarcely impress me any more; the thoughts of the old masters are of greater value to me than the philosophical prejudices of the Western mind.

I do not like to burden my reader with these personal considerations; but, as already indicated, one's own personality is very often implicated in the answer of the oracle. Indeed, in formulating my question I even invited the oracle to comment directly on my action. The answer was hexagram 29, K'an, THE ABYSMAL. Special emphasis is given to the third place by the fact that the line is designated by a six. This line says:

> Forward and backward, abyss on abyss.
> In danger like this, pause at first and wait,
> Otherwise you will fall into a pit in the abyss.
> Do not act in this way.

Formerly I would have accepted unconditionally the advice, "Do not act in this way," and would have refused to give my opinion of the *I Ching*, for the sole reason that I had none. But now the counsel may serve as an example of the way in which the *I Ching* functions. It is a fact that if one begins to think about it, the problems of the *I Ching* do represent "abyss on abyss," and unavoidably one must "pause at first and wait" in the midst of the dangers of limitless and uncritical speculation; otherwise one really will lose his way in the darkness. Could there be a more uncomfortable position intellectually than that of floating in the thin air of unproved possibilities, not knowing whether what one sees is truth or illusion? This is the dreamlike atmosphere of the *I Ching*, and in it one has nothing to rely upon except one's own so fallible subjective judgment. I cannot but admit that this line represents very appropriately the feelings with which I wrote the foregoing passages. Equally fitting is the comforting beginning of this hexagram—"If you are sincere, you have success in your heart"—for it indicates that the decisive thing here is not the outer danger but the subjective condition, that is, whether one believes oneself to be "sincere" or not.

The hexagram compares the dynamic action in this situation to the behavior of flowing water, which is not afraid of any dangerous place but plunges over cliffs and fills up the pits that lie in its course (K'an also stands for water). This is the way in which the "superior man" acts and "carries on the business of teaching."

K'an is definitely one of the less agreeable hexagrams. It describes a situation in which the subject seems in grave danger of being caught in all sorts of pitfalls. Just as in interpreting a dream one must follow the dream text with utmost exactitude, so in consulting the oracle one must hold in mind the form of the question put, for this sets a definite limit to the interpretation of the answer. The first line of the hexagram notes the presence of the danger: "In the abyss one falls into a pit." The second line does the same, then adds the counsel: "One should strive to attain small things only." I apparently anticipated this advice by limiting myself in this foreword to a demonstration of how the *I Ching* functions in the Chinese mind, and by renouncing the more ambitious project of writing a psychological commentary on the whole book.

The fourth line says:

> A jug of wine, a bowl of rice with it;
> Earthen vessels
> Simply handed in through the window.
> There is certainly no blame in this.

Wilhelm makes the following comment here:

Although as a rule it is customary for an official to present certain introductory gifts and recommendations before he is appointed, here everything is simplified to the utmost. The gifts are insignificant, there is no one to sponsor him, he introduces himself; yet all this need not be humiliating if only there is the honest intention of mutual help in danger.

It looks as if the book were to some degree the subject of this line.

The fifth line continues the theme of limitation. If one studies the nature of water, one sees that it fills a pit only to the rim and then flows on. It does not stay caught there:

> The abyss is not filled to overflowing,
>
> It is filled only to the rim.

But if, tempted by the danger, and just because of the uncertainty, one were to insist on forcing conviction by special efforts, such as elaborate commentaries and the like, one would only be mired in the difficulty, which the top line describes very accurately as a tied-up and caged-in condition. Indeed, the last line often shows the consequences that result when one does not take the meaning of the hexagram to heart.

In our hexagram we have a six in the third place. This yin line of mounting tension changes into a yang line and thus produces a new hexagram showing a new possibility or tendency. We now have hexagram 48, Ching, THE WELL. The water hole no longer means danger, however, but rather something beneficial, a well:

> Thus the superior man encourages the people at
>   their work,
>
> And exhorts them to help one another.

The image of people helping one another would seem to refer to the reconstruction of the well, for it is broken down and full of mud. Not even animals drink from it. There are fishes living in it, and one can shoot these, but the well is not used for drinking, that is, for human needs. This description is reminiscent of the overturned and unused *ting* that is to receive a new handle. Moreover, this well, like the *ting*, is cleaned. But no one drinks from it:

> This is my heart's sorrow,
>
> For one might draw from it.

The dangerous water hole or abyss pointed to the *I Ching*, and so does the well, but the latter has a positive meaning: it contains the waters of life. It should be restored to use. But one has no concept (*Begriff*) of it, no utensil with which to carry the water; the jug is broken and leaks. The *ting* needs new handles and carrying rings by which to grasp it, and so also the well must be newly lined, for it contains "a clear, cold spring from which one can drink." One may draw water from it, because "it is dependable."

It is clear that in this prognosis the speaking subject is again the *I Ching*, representing itself as a spring of living water. The preceding hexagram described in detail the danger confronting the person who accidentally falls into the pit within the abyss. He must work his way out of it, in order to discover that it is an old, ruined well, buried in mud, but capable of being restored to use again.

I submitted two questions to the method of chance represented by the coin oracle, the second question being put after I had written my analysis of the answer to the first. The first question was directed, as it were, to the *I Ching*: what had it to say about my intention to write a foreword? The second question concerned my own action, or rather the situation in which I was the acting subject who had discussed the first hexagram. To the first question the *I Ching* replied by comparing itself to a caldron, a ritual vessel in need of renovation, a vessel that was finding only doubtful favor with the public. To the second question the reply was that I had fallen into a difficulty, for the *I Ching* represented a deep and dangerous water hole in which one might easily be mired. However, the water hole proved to be an old well that needed only to be renovated in order to be put to useful purposes once more.

These four hexagrams are in the main consistent as regards theme (vessel, pit, well); and as regards intellectual content, they seem to be meaningful. Had a human being made such replies, I should, as a psychiatrist, have had to pronounce him of sound mind, at least on the basis of the material presented. Indeed, I should not have been able to discover anything delirious, idiotic, or schizophrenic in the four answers. In view of the *I Ching*'s extreme age and its Chinese origin, I cannot consider its archaic, symbolic, and flowery language abnormal. On the contrary, I should have had to congratulate this hypothetical person on the extent of his insight into my unexpressed state of doubt. On the other hand, any person of clever and versatile mind can turn the whole thing around and show how

I have projected my subjective contents into the symbolism of the hexagrams. Such a critique, though catastrophic from the standpoint of Western rationality, does no harm to the function of the *I Ching*. On the contrary, the Chinese sage would smilingly tell me: "Don't you see how useful the *I Ching* is in making you project your hitherto unrealized thoughts into its abstruse symbolism? You could have written your foreword without ever realizing what an avalanche of misunderstanding might be released by it."

The Chinese standpoint does not concern itself as to the attitude one takes toward the performance of the oracle. It is only we who are puzzled, because we trip time and again over our prejudice, viz., the notion of causality. The ancient wisdom of the East lays stress upon the fact that the intelligent individual realizes his own thoughts, but not in the least upon the way in which he does it. The less one thinks about the theory of the *I Ching*, the more soundly one sleeps.

It would seem to me that on the basis of this example an unprejudiced reader would now be in a position to form at least a tentative judgment on the operation of the *I Ching*.[12] More cannot be expected from a simple introduction. If by means of this demonstration I have succeeded in elucidating the psychological phenomenology of the *I Ching*, I shall have carried out my purpose. As to the thousands of questions, doubts, and criticisms that this singular book stirs up—I cannot answer these. The *I Ching* does not offer itself with proofs and results; it does not vaunt itself, nor is it easy to approach. Like a part of nature, it waits until it is discovered. It offers neither facts nor power, but for lovers of self-knowledge, of wisdom—if there be such—it seems to be the right book. To one person its spirit appears as clear as day; to another, shadowy as twilight; to a third, dark as night. He who is not pleased by it does not have to use it, and he who is against it is not obliged to find it true. Let it go forth into the world for the benefit of those who can discern its meaning.

C. G. Jung

Zurich, 1949

12. The reader will find it helpful to look up all four of these hexagrams in the text and to read them together with the relevant commentaries.

Translator's Note

A translation of a translation is likely to evoke the questioning protest: Why risk the danger of a double distortion of a text? In the case of Richard Wilhelm's version of the *I Ching*, the answer is simple and ready to hand. However many other translations of this book may appear, and whatever their excellence, Wilhelm's will remain unique, both by reason of his relation to the *I Ching* and because of the background out of which his translation grew. Unlike any other translator of this ancient work, he did not envisage the learned world as his only audience, and therefore addressed himself to the difficult task of making the *I Ching* intelligible to the lay reader. He wished to bring this first philosophy, this first effort of men to place themselves in the cosmos, out of the domain of specialists in philology and to put it into the hands of individuals anywhere who, like the authors of the *I Ching*, are concerned with their relation to the universe and to their fellow men.

No less unique than this purpose of Wilhelm's with regard to his translation were the circumstances that enabled him to carry it out. Long residence in China, mastery of both the spoken and the written language, and close association with the cultural leaders of the day, made it possible for him to understand the Chinese classics from the standpoint of the Chinese themselves. In translating the *I Ching* he was guided by a scholar of the old school, one of the last of his kind, who knew thoroughly the great field of commentary literature that has grown up around the book in the course of the ages.

Quite naturally also, it was Wilhelm's particular wish to have his translation appear in English, widening by so much the circle of its readers. It is clear that in desiring thus to make available to many people the wisdom that he himself had found in the *I Ching*, Wilhelm presupposed in his readers a degree of spiritual integrity that, together with the essential dignity of the book, would preclude the use of the oracle for trivial purposes, or its exploitation by charlatans of whatever type. Time alone will show whether his faith was justified.

I was studying analytical psychology in Zurich when Dr. Jung asked me to undertake the rendering of the German version into English. The translation was to have had Wilhelm's supervision; this, it was thought, would compensate my ignorance of Chinese. But his death in 1930 came long before I was ready to submit a manuscript to him. As I proceeded with the translation, I found that one very real compensation for my lack of Chinese remained, namely, the access to its philosophy afforded me through my growing knowledge of the work of Jung. This gave me a key to the archetypal world of the *I Ching*.

The second world war and attendant circumstances beyond my personal control brought many long interruptions to my undertaking. But in the end the delays worked wholly to the advantage of the translation. Shortly after the manuscript had gone to press, Dr. Hellmut Wilhelm, who like his father has devoted much time to the study of the *I Ching*, left his home in Peiping to continue his work in sinology in the United States. I had already had expert advice from him by letter, and had always hoped that by some unexpected turn of fate it would be possible for him to criticize my translation, since he alone knew his father's work sufficiently well to take the latter's place. It was now my great good fortune to go over the proofs with him while he checked the translation against the Chinese text—using the very volumes that had accompanied Richard Wilhelm "on many a journey, halfway round the globe."

With Dr. Wilhelm's arrival, a question arose as to whether it would be wise to rewrite certain passages of the translation to conform them to findings of modern scholarship that were not available to Richard Wilhelm when he did his work. Dr. Wilhelm decided that the book should be left as his father wrote it, because in no instance was the proposed change of more than minor importance with respect to the work as a whole.

In the parts of the German text that render the Chinese, I have tried to be as literal in my translation as possible, in order to establish a guideline in the highly allusive and symbolic language. (One need only compare passages in Wilhelm's version with the same passages as rendered by Legge in order to see how completely different two interpretations of the same Chinese sentence may be.) When I have deviated from this rule, it has been in the few places where Dr. Wilhelm pointed out that a paraphrase is needed to cover the Chinese meaning.

The great age and unbroken continuity of Chinese culture are wonderful to contemplate; to keep this perspective before the reader's mind, I have given, where possible, dates for the works and authors mentioned by Wilhelm. All footnotes added by me are inclosed in square brackets.

Wherever the English names of the hexagrams appear in the body of the text, they are printed in small capitals; in this way they can be distinguished from trigrams of the same name. The Chinese characters for the names of the hexagrams have been rewritten for this edition. I have to thank Dr. Shih Yu-chung for this contribution. Wade's system of transliteration has been used in putting the German version of Chinese words into their English equivalents. The excellent key to the hexagrams was brought to my notice by Carol Fisher Baumann.

The Chinese title page is from the hand of Professor Tung Tso-pin of the Academia Sinica.

There are few sentences in this translation that were not discussed again and again before they took final form, and the work as a whole has been revised many times. For aid in the early stages of my undertaking I am indebted to Emma Jung and to Frieda Hauswirth. Later, when I returned to this country, I received very great assistance from Dr. Erla Roda-kiewicz and from my daughter, Ximena de Angulo. For help at that time on matters of style I am also grateful to Elizabeth M. Brown and to Mary E. Strong. Dr. Wilfrid Lay, who learned Chinese for the sole purpose of reading the *I Ching*, brought to my attention a number of points that I would otherwise have missed. Dr. George H. Danton read the manuscript two years before it reached its finished form, and gave me valuable suggestions. For the final truing up of the translation with the German text, and for rescuing it from the ever-present threat of translator's English, I cannot give praise and appreciation enough to my editor, Renée Darmstadter.

Accuracy and intelligibility have been the goals set for this translation, but it must prove itself in a still more vital test. If the reader is drawn out of the accustomed framework of his thought to view the world in a new perspective, if his imagination is stimulated and his psychological insight deepened, he will know that Wilhelm's *I Ching* has been faithfully reproduced.

CARY F. BAYNES

Morris, Connecticut, 1949

Translator's Note for the Third Edition

This edition presents the *I Ching* in an entirely new format, more compact as a book, and clearer in its typographical distinctions. Professor Hellmut Wilhelm, of the Far Eastern and Russian Institute in the University of Washington (Seattle), has contributed a preface to the new edition, in which he comments on recent research and on other translations of the Book of Changes and elucidates the principles that guided his father's work. Professor Wilhelm has approved the editors' additions, rearrangements of some of the secondary material, and revisions of bibliographical information in footnotes. The rearrangements consist in placing a chart, "The Major Divisions of the Material," adjacent to the new preface, with which it is interrelated; and moving a section "On Consulting the Oracle" to the end of the volume, for convenience. An index of the hexagrams by pattern has been taken over from the German edition, and a general index has been compiled.

As I remarked in a Translator's Note to the second edition, I am indebted to Professor Wilhelm also for an explanatory note concerning the Chinese title page, and to Mr. R. F. C. Hull, the translator of the Collected Works of C. G. Jung, for having called my attention to an error of translation in Jung's foreword. With minor changes, the foreword was published in 1958 in *Psychology and Religion: West and East* (Collected Works of C. G. Jung, vol. 11).

The Western student of the *I Ching* is always grateful for aid in the understanding of the Book. He will find such aid in two works of Professor Hellmut Wilhelm published since the first edition of the English version of the *I Ching* in 1950: *Change: Eight Lectures on the I Ching* (New York: Bollingen Series LXII, and London, 1960) and "The Concept of Time in the Book of Changes," in *Man and Time* (Papers from the Eranos Yearbooks, 3; New York: Bollingen Series XXX, and London, 1957).

C. F. B.

Morris, Connecticut, January 1967

Preface

This translation of the Book of Changes was begun nearly ten years ago. After the Chinese revolution,[1] when Tsingtao became the residence of a number of the most eminent scholars of the old school, I met among them my honored teacher Lao Nai-hsüan. I am indebted to him not only for a deeper understanding of the Great Learning,[2] the Doctrine of the Mean,[3] and the Book of Mencius, but also because he first opened my mind to the wonders of the Book of Changes. Under his experienced guidance I wandered entranced through this strange and yet familiar world. The translation of the text was made after detailed discussion. Then the German version was retranslated into Chinese and it was only after the meaning of the text had been fully brought out that we considered our version to be truly a translation.

While we were in the midst of this work, the horror of the world war broke in upon us. The Chinese scholars were scattered to the four winds, and Mr. Lao left for Ch'ü-fou, the home of Confucius, to whose family he was related. The translation of the Book of Changes was laid aside, although during the siege of Tsingtao, when I was in charge of the Chinese Red Cross, not a day passed on which I did not devote some time to the study of ancient Chinese wisdom. It was a curious coincidence that in the encampment outside the city, the besieging Japanese commander, General Kamio, was reading the Book of Mencius in his moments of relaxation, while I, a German, was similarly delving into Chinese wisdom in my free hours. Happiest of all, however, was an old Chinese who

---

1. [1911.]
2. [*Ta Hsüeh.*]
3. [*Chung Yung.*]

was so wholly absorbed in his sacred books that not even a grenade falling at his side could disturb his calm. He reached out for it—it was a dud—then drew back his hand and, remarking that it was very hot, forthwith returned to his books.

Tsingtao was captured. Despite all sorts of other tasks, I again found time for intensive work on the translation, but the teacher with whom I had begun the work was now far away, and it was impossible for me to leave Tsingtao. In the midst of my perplexities, it made me very happy to receive a letter from Mr. Lao saying that he was ready to go on with our interrupted studies. He came, and the translation was brought to completion. Those were rare hours of inspiration that I spent with my aged master. When the work in its essential features was almost finished, fate called me back to Germany. In the meantime my venerable master departed this world.

Habent sua fata libelli. In Germany I seemed to be as far removed as possible from ancient Chinese wisdom, although in Europe also many a word of counsel from the mysterious book has here and there fallen on fertile soil. Hence my joy and surprise were great indeed when in the house of a good friend in Friedenau, I found the Book of Changes—and in a beautiful edition for which I had hunted in vain through all the bookshops of Peking. My friend moreover proved a friend indeed, in making this happy find my permanent possession. Since then the book has accompanied me on many a journey, halfway round the globe.

I came back to China. New tasks claimed me. In Peking a wholly new world, with other people and other interests, opened up before me. Nonetheless, here too help soon came to hand in many ways, and in the warm days of a Peking summer the work was finally brought to conclusion. Recast again and again, the text has at last attained a form that—though it falls far short of my wish—makes it possible for me to give the book to the world. May the same joy in pure wisdom be the part of those who read the translation as was mine while I worked upon it.

RICHARD WILHELM

Peking, in the summer of 1923

Introduction

The Book of Changes—*I Ching* in Chinese—is unquestionably one of the most important books in the world's literature. Its origin goes back to mythical antiquity, and it has occupied the attention of the most eminent scholars of China down to the present day. Nearly all that is greatest and most significant in the three thousand years of Chinese cultural history has either taken its inspiration from this book, or has exerted an influence on the interpretation of its text. Therefore it may safely be said that the seasoned wisdom of thousands of years has gone into the making of the *I Ching*. Small wonder then that both of the two branches of Chinese philosophy, Confucianism and Taoism, have their common roots here. The book sheds new light on many a secret hidden in the often puzzling modes of thought of that mysterious sage, Lao-tse, and of his pupils, as well as on many ideas that appear in the Confucian tradition as axioms, accepted without further examination.

Indeed, not only the philosophy of China but its science and statecraft as well have never ceased to draw from the spring of wisdom in the *I Ching*, and it is not surprising that this alone, among all the Confucian classics, escaped the great burning of the books under Ch'in Shih Huang Ti.[1] Even the commonplaces of everyday life in China are saturated with its influence. In going through the streets of a Chinese city, one will find, here and there at a street corner, a fortune teller sitting behind a neatly covered table, brush and tablet at hand, ready to draw from the ancient book of wisdom pertinent counsel and information on life's minor perplexities. Not only that, but the very signboards adorning the houses—perpendicular wooden panels done in gold on black lacquer—are covered with in-

---

1. [213 B.C.]

scriptions whose flowery language again and again recalls thoughts and quotations from the *I Ching*. Even the policy makers of so modern a state as Japan, distinguished for their astuteness, do not scorn to refer to it for counsel in difficult situations.

In the course of time, owing to the great repute for wisdom attaching to the Book of Changes, a large body of occult doctrines extraneous to it—some of them possibly not even Chinese in origin—have come to be connected with its teachings. The Ch'in and Han dynasties[2] saw the beginning of a formalistic natural philosophy that sought to embrace the entire world of thought in a system of number symbols. Combining a rigorously consistent, dualistic yin-yang doctrine with the doctrine of the "five stages of change" taken from the Book of History,[3] it forced Chinese philosophical thinking more and more into a rigid formalization. Thus increasingly hairsplitting cabalistic speculations came to envelop the Book of Changes in a cloud of mystery, and by forcing everything of the past and of the future into this system of numbers, created for the *I Ching* the reputation of being a book of unfathomable profundity. These speculations are also to blame for the fact that the seeds of a free Chinese natural science, which undoubtedly existed at the time of Mo Ti[4] and his pupils, were killed, and replaced by a sterile tradition of writing and reading books that was wholly removed from experience. This is the reason why China has for so long presented to Western eyes a picture of hopeless stagnation.

Yet we must not overlook the fact that apart from this mechanistic number mysticism, a living stream of deep human wisdom was constantly flowing through the channel of this book into everyday life, giving to China's great civilization that ripeness of wisdom, distilled through the ages, which we wistfully admire in the remnants of this last truly autochthonous culture.

---

2. [Beginning in the last half of the third century B.C. and ending about A.D. 220.]

3. [*Shu Ching*, the oldest of the Chinese classics. Modern scholarship has placed most of the records contained in the *Shu Ching* near the first millennium B.C., though formerly a much greater age was ascribed to the earliest of them.]

4. [Fifth and fourth centuries B.C.]

What is the Book of Changes actually? In order to arrive at an understanding of the book and its teachings, we must first of all boldly strip away the dense overgrowth of interpretations that have read into it all sorts of extraneous ideas. This is equally necessary whether we are dealing with the superstitions and mysteries of old Chinese sorcerers or the no less superstitious theories of modern European scholars who try to interpret all historical cultures in terms of their experience of primitive savages. [5] We must hold here to the fundamental principle that the Book of Changes is to be explained in the light of its own content and of the era to which it belongs. With this the darkness lightens perceptibly and we realize that this book, though a very profound work, does not offer greater difficulties to our understanding than any other book that has come down through a long history from antiquity to our time.

1. THE USE OF THE BOOK OF CHANGES

The Book of Oracles

At the outset, the Book of Changes was a collection of linear signs to be used as oracles. [6] In antiquity, oracles were everywhere in use; the oldest among them confined themselves to the answers yes and no. This type of oracular pronouncement is likewise the basis of the Book of Changes. "Yes" was indicated by a simple unbroken line (———), and "No" by a broken line (— —). However, the need for greater differentiation seems to have been felt at an early date, and the single lines were combined in pairs:

$$\equiv\quad\equiv\equiv\quad\equiv\equiv\quad\equiv\equiv$$

To each of these combinations a third line was then added. In

---

5. We might mention here, because of its oddity, the grotesque and amateurish attempt on the part of Rev. Canon McClatchie, M.A., to apply the key of "comparative mythology" to the *I Ching*. His book was published in 1876 under the title, *A Translation of the Confucian Yi King or the Classic of Changes, with Notes and Appendix*.

6. From the discussion here presented, it will become self-evident that the Book of Changes was not a lexicon, as has been assumed in many quarters.

this way the eight trigrams[7] came into being. These eight trigrams were conceived as images of all that happens in heaven and on earth. At the same time, they were held to be in a state of continual transition, one changing into another, just as transition from one phenomenon to another is continually taking place in the physical world. Here we have the fundamental concept of the Book of Changes. The eight trigrams are symbols standing for changing transitional states; they are images that are constantly undergoing change. Attention centers not on things in their state of being—as is chiefly the case in the Occident—but upon their movements in change. The eight trigrams therefore are not representations of things as such but of their tendencies in movement.

These eight images came to have manifold meanings. They represented certain processes in nature corresponding with their inherent character. Further, they represented a family consisting of father, mother, three sons, and three daughters, not in the mythological sense in which the Greek gods peopled Olympus, but in what might be called an abstract sense, that is, they represented not objective entities but functions.

A brief survey of these eight symbols that form the basis of the Book of Changes yields the following classification:

	Name	Attribute	Image	Family Relationship
☰	Ch'ien	the Creative	strong	heaven	father
☷	K'un	the Receptive	devoted, yielding	earth	mother
☳	Chên	the Arousing	inciting movement	thunder	first son
☵	K'an	the Abysmal	dangerous	water	second son
☶	Kên	Keeping Still	resting	mountain	third son

7. [*Zeichen*, meaning sign, is used by Wilhelm to denote the linear figures in the *I Ching*, those of three lines as well as those of six lines. The Chinese word for both types of signs is *kua*. To avoid ambiguity, the precedent established by Legge (*The Sacred Books of the East*, XVI: *The Yi King*) has been adopted throughout: the term "trigram" is used for the sign consisting of three lines, and "hexagram" for the sign consisting of six lines.]

l

	Name	*Attribute*	*Image*	*Family Relationship*
☴ Sun	the Gentle	penetrating	wind, wood	first daughter
☲ Li	the Clinging	light-giving	fire	second daughter
☱ Tui	the Joyous	joyful	lake	third daughter

The sons represent the principle of movement in its various stages—beginning of movement, danger in movement, rest and completion of movement. The daughters represent devotion in its various stages—gentle penetration, clarity and adaptability, and joyous tranquillity.

In order to achieve a still greater multiplicity, these eight images were combined with one another at a very early date, whereby a total of sixty-four signs was obtained. Each of these sixty-four signs consists of six lines, either positive or negative. Each line is thought of as capable of change, and whenever a line changes, there is a change also of the situation represented by the given hexagram. Let us take for example the hexagram K'un, THE RECEPTIVE, earth:

It represents the nature of the earth, strong in devotion; among the seasons it stands for late autumn, when all the forces of life are at rest. If the lowest line changes, we have the hexagram Fu, RETURN:

The latter represents thunder, the movement that stirs anew within the earth at the time of the solstice; it symbolizes the return of light.

As this example shows, all of the lines of a hexagram do not necessarily change; it depends entirely on the character of a given line. A line whose nature is positive, with an increasing dynamism, turns into its opposite, a negative line, whereas a positive line of lesser strength remains unchanged. The same principle holds for the negative lines.

More definite information about those lines which are to be considered so strongly charged with positive or negative energy that they move, is given in book II in the Great Commentary (pt. I, chap. IX), and in the special section on the use of the oracle at the end of book III. Suffice it to say here that positive lines that move are designated by the number 9, and negative lines that move by the number 6, while non-moving lines, which serve only as structural matter in the hexagram, without intrinsic meaning of their own, are represented by the number 7 (positive) or the number 8 (negative). Thus, when the text reads, "Nine at the beginning means . . ." this is the equivalent of saying: "When the positive line in the first place is represented by the number 9, it has the following meaning. . . ." If, on the other hand, the line is represented by the number 7, it is disregarded in interpreting the oracle. The same principle holds for lines represented by the numbers 6 and 8 [8] respectively.

We may obtain the hexagram named in the example above —K'un, THE RECEPTIVE—in the following form:

8 at the top	— —
8 in the fifth place	— —
8 in the fourth place	— —
8 in the third place	— —
8 in the second place	— —
6 at the beginning	— —

Hence the five upper lines are not taken into account; only the 6 at the beginning has an independent meaning, and by its transformation into its opposite, the situation K'un, THE RECEPTIVE,

becomes the situation Fu, RETURN:

---

8. [For this reason, the numbers 7 and 8 never appear in the portion of the text dealing with the meanings of the individual lines.]

In this way we have a series of situations symbolically expressed by lines, and through the movement of these lines the situations can change one into another. On the other hand, such change does not necessarily occur, for when a hexagram is made up of lines represented by the numbers 7 and 8 only, there is no movement within it, and only its aspect as a whole is taken into consideration.

In addition to the law of change and to the images of the states of change as given in the sixty-four hexagrams, another factor to be considered is the course of action. Each situation demands the action proper to it. In every situation, there is a right and a wrong course of action. Obviously, the right course brings good fortune and the wrong course brings misfortune. Which, then, is the right course in any given case? This question was the decisive factor. As a result, the *I Ching* was lifted above the level of an ordinary book of soothsaying. If a fortune teller on reading the cards tells her client that she will receive a letter with money from America in a week, there is nothing for the woman to do but wait until the letter comes—or does not come. In this case what is foretold is fate, quite independent of what the individual may do or not do. For this reason fortune telling lacks moral significance. When it happened for the first time in China that someone, on being told the auguries for the future, did not let the matter rest there but asked, "What am I to do?" the book of divination had to become a book of wisdom.

It was reserved for King Wên, who lived about 1150 B.C., and his son, the Duke of Chou, to bring about this change. They endowed the hitherto mute hexagrams and lines, from which the future had to be divined as an individual matter in each case, with definite counsels for correct conduct. Thus the individual came to share in shaping fate. For his actions intervened as determining factors in world events, the more decisively so, the earlier he was able with the aid of the Book of Changes to recognize situations in their germinal phases. The germinal phase is the crux. As long as things are in their beginnings they can be controlled, but once they have grown to their full consequences they acquire a power so overwhelming that man stands impotent before them. Thus the Book of Changes became a book of divination of a very special kind.

The hexagrams and lines in their movements and changes mysteriously reproduced the movements and changes of the macrocosm. By the use of yarrow stalks,[9] one could attain a point of vantage from which it was possible to survey the condition of things. Given this perspective, the words of the oracle would indicate what should be done to meet the need of the time.

The only thing about all this that seems strange to our modern sense is the method of learning the nature of a situation through the manipulation of yarrow stalks. This procedure was regarded as mysterious, however, simply in the sense that the manipulation of the yarrow stalks makes it possible for the unconscious in man to become active. All individuals are not equally fitted to consult the oracle. It requires a clear and tranquil mind, receptive to the cosmic influences hidden in the humble divining stalks. As products of the vegetable kingdom, these were considered to be related to the sources of life. The stalks were derived from sacred plants.

The Book of Wisdom

Of far greater significance than the use of the Book of Changes as an oracle is its other use, namely, as a book of wisdom. Laotse[10] knew this book, and some of his profoundest aphorisms were inspired by it. Indeed, his whole thought is permeated with its teachings. Confucius[11] too knew the Book of Changes and devoted himself to reflection upon it. He probably wrote down some of his interpretative comments and imparted others to his pupils in oral teaching. The Book of Changes as edited and annotated by Confucius is the version that has come down to our time.

If we inquire as to the philosophy that pervades the book, we can confine ourselves to a few basically important concepts. The underlying idea of the whole is the idea of change. It is

---

9. [The stalks come from the plant known to us as common yarrow, or milfoil (*Achillea millefolium*).]

10. [Second half of fifth century B.C.]

11. [551–479 B.C.]

related in the Analects[12] that Confucius, standing by a river, said: "Everything flows on and on like this river, without pause, day and night." This expresses the idea of change. He who has perceived the meaning of change fixes his attention no longer on transitory individual things but on the immutable, eternal law at work in all change. This law is the tao[13] of Lao-tse, the course of things, the principle of the one in the many. That it may become manifest, a decision, a postulate, is necessary. This fundamental postulate is the "great primal beginning" of all that exists, *t'ai chi*—in its original meaning, the "ridgepole." Later Chinese philosophers devoted much thought to this idea of a primal beginning. A still earlier beginning, *wu chi*, was represented by the symbol of a circle. Under this conception, *t'ai chi* was represented by the circle divided into the light and the dark, yang and yin, ◉.[14]

This symbol has also played a significant part in India and Europe. However, speculations of a gnostic-dualistic character are foreign to the original thought of the *I Ching*; what it posits is simply the ridgepole, the line. With this line, which in itself represents oneness, duality comes into the world, for the line at the same time posits an above and a below, a right and left, front and back—in a word, the world of the opposites.

These opposites became known under the names yin and yang and created a great stir, especially in the transition period between the Ch'in and Han dynasties, in the centuries just before our era, when there was an entire school of yin-yang doctrine. At that time, the Book of Changes was much in use as a book of magic, and people read into the text all sorts of things not originally there. This doctrine of yin and yang,

---

12. *Lun Yü*, IX, 16. [This book comprises conversations of Confucius and his disciples.]

13. [Here, as throughout the book, Wilhelm uses the German word *Sinn* ("meaning") in capitals (*SINN*) for the Chinese word *tao* (see p. 297 and n. 1). The reasons that led Wilhelm to choose *SINN* to represent *tao* (see p. XIV of the introduction to his translation of Lao-tse: *Tao Te King: Das Buch des Alten von Sinn und Leben*, 3rd edn., Düsseldorf and Cologne, 1952) have no relation to the English word "meaning." Therefore in the English rendering, "tao" has been used wherever *SINN* occurs.]

14. [Known as *t'ai chi t'u*, "the supreme ultimate." See R. Wilhelm, *A Short History of Chinese Civilization*, tr. by J. Joshua (London, 1929), p. 249.]

of the female and the male as primal principles, has naturally also attracted much attention among foreign students of Chinese thought. Following the usual bent, some of these have predicated in it a primitive phallic symbolism, with all the accompanying connotations.

To the disappointment of such discoverers it must be said that there is nothing to indicate this in the original meaning of the words yin and yang. In its primary meaning yin is "the cloudy," "the overcast," and yang means actually "banners waving in the sun,"[15] that is, something "shone upon," or bright. By transference the two concepts were applied to the light and dark sides of a mountain or of a river. In the case of a mountain the southern is the bright side and the northern the dark side, while in the case of a river seen from above, it is the northern side that is bright (yang), because it reflects the light, and the southern side that is in shadow (yin). Thence the two expressions were carried over into the Book of Changes and applied to the two alternating primal states of being. It should be pointed out, however, that the terms yin and yang do not occur in this derived sense either in the actual text of the book or in the oldest commentaries. Their first occurrence is in the Great Commentary, which already shows Taoistic influence in some parts. In the Commentary on the Decision the terms used for the opposites are "the firm" and "the yielding," not yang and yin.

However, no matter what names are applied to these forces, it is certain that the world of being arises out of their change and interplay. Thus change is conceived of partly as the continuous transformation of the one force into the other and partly as a cycle of complexes of phenomena, in themselves connected, such as day and night, summer and winter. Change is not meaningless—if it were, there could be no knowledge of it—but subject to the universal law, tao.

The second theme fundamental to the Book of Changes is its theory of ideas. The eight trigrams are images not so much

15. Cf. the noteworthy discussions of Liang Ch'i-ch'ao in the Chinese journal *The Endeavor*, July 15 and 22, 1923, also the English essay by B. Schindler, "The Development of the Chinese Conceptions of Supreme Beings," *Asia Major*, Hirth Anniversary Volume (London: Probsthain, n.d.), pp. 298–366.

of objects as of states of change. This view is associated with the concept expressed in the teachings of Lao-tse, as also in those of Confucius, that every event in the visible world is the effect of an "image," that is, of an idea in the unseen world. Accordingly, everything that happens on earth is only a reproduction, as it were, of an event in a world beyond our sense perception; as regards its occurrence in time, it is later than the suprasensible event. The holy men and sages, who are in contact with those higher spheres, have access to these ideas through direct intuition and are therefore able to intervene decisively in events in the world. Thus man is linked with heaven, the suprasensible world of ideas, and with earth, the material world of visible things, to form with these a trinity of the primal powers.

This theory of ideas is applied in a twofold sense. The Book of Changes shows the images of events and also the unfolding of conditions *in statu nascendi.* Thus, in discerning with its help the seeds of things to come, we learn to foresee the future as well as to understand the past. In this way the images on which the hexagrams are based serve as patterns for timely action in the situations indicated. Not only is adaptation to the course of nature thus made possible, but in the Great Commentary (pt. II, chap. II), an interesting attempt is made to trace back the origin of all the practices and inventions of civilization to such ideas and archetypal images. Whether or not the hypothesis can be made to apply in all specific instances, the basic concept contains a truth. [16]

The third element fundamental to the Book of Changes are the judgments. The judgments clothe the images in words, as it were; they indicate whether a given action will bring good fortune or misfortune, remorse or humiliation. The judgments make it possible for a man to make a decision to desist from a course of action indicated by the situation of the moment but harmful in the long run. In this way he makes himself independent of the tyranny of events. In its judgments, and in the

16. Cf. the extremely important discussions of Hu Shih in *The Development of the Logical Method in Ancient China* (2nd edn., New York: Paragon, 1963), and the even more detailed discussion in the first volume of his history of philosophy [*Chung-kuo chê-hsüeh-shih ta-kang*; not available in translation].

interpretations attached to it from the time of Confucius on, the Book of Changes opens to the reader the richest treasure of Chinese wisdom; at the same time it affords him a comprehensive view of the varieties of human experience, enabling him thereby to shape his life of his own sovereign will into an organic whole and so to direct it that it comes into accord with the ultimate tao lying at the root of all that exists.

2. THE HISTORY OF THE BOOK OF CHANGES

In Chinese literature four holy men are cited as the authors of the Book of Changes, namely, Fu Hsi, King Wên, the Duke of Chou, and Confucius. Fu Hsi is a legendary figure representing the era of hunting and fishing and of the invention of cooking. The fact that he is designated as the inventor of the linear signs of the Book of Changes means that they have been held to be of such antiquity that they antedate historical memory. Moreover, the eight trigrams have names that do not occur in any other connection in the Chinese language, and because of this they have even been thought to be of foreign origin. At all events, they are not archaic characters, as some have been led to believe by the half accidental, half intentional resemblances to them appearing here and there among ancient characters.[17]

The eight trigrams are found occurring in various combinations at a very early date. Two collections belonging to antiquity are mentioned: first, the Book of Changes of the Hsia dynasty,[18] called *Lien Shan*, which is said to have begun with the hexagram Kên, KEEPING STILL, mountain; second, the Book of Changes dating from the Shang dynasty,[19] entitled *Kuei Ts'ang*, which began with the hexagram K'un, THE RECEPTIVE. The latter circumstance is mentioned in passing by Confucius himself as a historical fact. It is difficult to say whether the names of the sixty-four hexagrams were then in existence, and if so, whether they were the same as those in the present Book of Changes.

---

17. Question has centered especially upon the trigram K'an (☵), which resembles the character for water, *shui* (〳〵).

18. [According to tradition, 2205–1766 B.C.]

19. [According to tradition, 1766–1150 B.C.]

According to general tradition, which we have no reason to challenge, the present collection of sixty-four hexagrams originated with King Wên,[20] progenitor of the Chou dynasty. He is said to have added brief judgments to the hexagrams during his imprisonment at the hands of the tyrant Chou Hsin. The text pertaining to the individual lines originated with his son, the Duke of Chou. This form of the book, entitled the Changes of Chou (*Chou I*), was in use as an oracle throughout the Chou period, as can be proven from a number of the ancient historical records.

This was the status of the book at the time Confucius came upon it. In his old age he gave it intensive study, and it is highly probable that the Commentary on the Decision (*T'uan Chuan*) is his work. The Commentary on the Images also goes back to him, though less directly. A third treatise, a very valuable and detailed commentary on the individual lines, compiled by his pupils or by their successors, in the form of questions and answers, survives only in fragments.[21]

Among the followers of Confucius, it would appear, it was principally Pu Shang (Tzŭ Hsia) who spread the knowledge of the Book of Changes. With the development of philosophical speculation, as reflected in the Great Learning (*Ta Hsüeh*) and the Doctrine of the Mean (*Chung Yung*),[22] this type of phi-

---

20. [King Wên was the head of a western state that suffered oppression from the house of Shang (Yin). He was given the title of king posthumously by his son Wu, who overthrew Chou Hsin, took possession of the Shang realm, and became the first ruler of the Chou dynasty, which in traditional chronology is dated 1150–249 B.C.]

21. Some are in the section known as the *Wên Yen* [Commentary on the Words of the Text], some in the *Ta Chuan* [Great Commentary]. [Cf. p. *xix*.]

22. [The Great Learning presents the Confucian principles concerning the education of the "superior man," based on the view that innate within man are the qualities that when developed guide him to a personal and a social ethic. The Doctrine of the Mean shows that the "way of the superior man" leads to harmony between heaven, man, and earth. Both of these works belong to the school of thought led by Tzŭ-ssŭ, grandson of Confucius. They originally formed part of the *Li Chi*, the Book of Rites. Under the titles *Ta Hsio* and *Kung Yung* they can be found as bks. 39 and 28 in Legge's translation of the Book of Rites (*The Sacred Books of the East*, XXVII: *The Li Ki*, Oxford, 1885).]

losophy exercised an ever increasing influence upon the interpretation of the Book of Changes. A literature grew up around
the book, fragments of which—some dating from an early and
some from a later time—are to be found in the so-called Ten
Wings. They differ greatly with respect to content and intrinsic
value.

The Book of Changes escaped the fate of the other classics
at the time of the famous burning of the books under the
tyrant Ch'in Shih Huang Ti. Hence, if there is anything in
the legend that the burning alone is responsible for the muti-
lation of the texts of the old books, the *I Ching* at least should
be intact; but this is not the case. In reality it is the vicissitudes
of the centuries, the collapse of ancient cultures, and the change
in the system of writing that are to be blamed for the damage
suffered by all ancient works.

After the Book of Changes had become firmly established as
a book of divination and magic in the time of Ch'in Shih Huang
Ti, the entire school of magicians (*fang shih*) of the Ch'in and
Han dynasties made it their prey. And the yin-yang doctrine,
which was probably introduced through the work of Tsou
Yen,[23] and later promoted by Tung Chung Shu, Liu Hsin, and
Liu Hsiang,[24] ran riot in connection with the interpretation of
the *I Ching*.

The task of clearing away all this rubbish was reserved for a
great and wise scholar, Wang Pi,[25] who wrote about the meaning of the Book of Changes as a book of wisdom, not as a book
of divination. He soon found emulation, and the teachings of
the yin-yang school of magic were displaced, in relation to the
book, by a philosophy of statecraft that was gradually developing. In the Sung[26] period, the *I Ching* was used as a basis for
the *t'ai chi t'u* doctrine—which was probably not of Chinese
origin—until the appearance of the elder Ch'êng Tzŭ's[27] very
good commentary. It had become customary to separate the
old commentaries contained in the Ten Wings and to place
them with the individual hexagrams to which they refer. Thus

---

23. [Fourth century B.C.]
24. [All three are Han scholars.]
25. [A.D. 226–249.]
26. [A.D. 960–1279.]
27. [Ch'êng Hao, A.D. 1032–1085.]

the book became by degrees entirely a textbook relating to statecraft and the philosophy of life. Then Chu Hsi[28] attempted to rehabilitate it as a book of oracles; in addition to a short and precise commentary on the *I Ching*, he published an introduction to his investigations concerning the art of divination.

The critical-historical school of the last dynasty also took the Book of Changes in hand. However, because of their opposition to the Sung scholars and their preference for the Han commentators, who were nearer in point of time to the compilation of the Book of Changes, they were less successful here than in their treatment of the other classics. For the Han commentators were in the last analysis sorcerers, or were influenced by theories of magic. A very good edition was arranged in the K'ang Hsi [29] period, under the title *Chou I Chê Chung*; it presents the text and the wings separately and includes the best commentaries of all periods. This is the edition on which the present translation is based.

3. THE ARRANGEMENT OF THE TRANSLATION

An exposition of the principles that have been followed in the translation of the Book of Changes should be of essential help to the reader.

The translation of the text has been given as brief and concise a form as possible, in order to preserve the archaic impression that prevails in the Chinese. This has made it all the more necessary to present not only the text but also digests of the most important Chinese commentaries. These digests have been made as succinct as possible and afford a survey of the outstanding contributions made by Chinese scholarship toward elucidation of the book. Comparisons with Occidental writings,[30] which frequently suggested themselves, as well as

---

28. [A.D. 1130–1200.]

29. [A.D. 1662–1722.]

30. [A number of footnote quotations from German poetry, chiefly passages from Goethe, have been omitted in the English rendering because their poetic suggestiveness disappears in translation.]

views of my own, have been introduced as sparingly as possible and have invariably been expressly identified as such. The reader may therefore regard the text and the commentary as genuine renditions of Chinese thought. Special attention is called to this fact because many of the fundamental truths presented are so closely parallel to Christian tenets that the impression is often really striking.

In order to make it as easy as possible for the layman to understand the *I Ching*, the texts of the sixty-four hexagrams, together with pertinent interpretations, are presented in book I. The reader will do well to begin by reading this part with his attention fixed on its main ideas and without allowing himself to be distracted by the imagery. For example, he should follow through the idea of the Creative in its step-by-step development—as delineated in masterly fashion in the first hexagram—taking the dragons for granted for the moment. In this way he will gain an idea of what Chinese wisdom has to say about the conduct of life.

The second and third books explain why all these things are as they are. Here the material essential to an understanding of the structure of the hexagrams has been brought together, but only so much of it as is absolutely necessary, and as far as possible only the oldest material, as preserved in the Ten Wings, is presented. So far as has been feasible, these commentaries have been broken down and apportioned to the relevant parts of the text, in such a way as to afford a better understanding of them—their essential content having been made available earlier in the commentary summaries in book I. Therefore, for one who would plumb the depths of wisdom in the Book of Changes, the second and third books are indispensable. On the other hand, the Western reader's power of comprehension ought not to be burdened at the outset with too much that is unfamiliar. Consequently it has not been possible to avoid a certain amount of repetition, but such reiteration will be of help in obtaining a thorough understanding of the book. It is my firm conviction that anyone who really assimilates the essence of the Book of Changes will be enriched thereby in experience and in true understanding of life.

R. W.

Book I

THE TEXT

PART I

乾

1. *Ch'ien / The Creative*

☰ *above*	CH'IEN	THE CREATIVE, HEAVEN
☰ *below*	CH'IEN	THE CREATIVE, HEAVEN

The first hexagram is made up of six unbroken lines. These unbroken lines stand for the primal power, which is light-giving, active, strong, and of the spirit. The hexagram is consistently strong in character, and since it is without weakness, its essence is power or energy. Its image is heaven. Its energy is represented as unrestricted by any fixed conditions in space and is therefore conceived of as motion. Time is regarded as the basis of this motion. Thus the hexagram includes also the power of time and the power of persisting in time, that is, duration.

The power represented by the hexagram is to be interpreted in a dual sense—in terms of its action on the universe and of its action on the world of men. In relation to the universe, the hexagram expresses the strong, creative action of the Deity. In relation to the human world, it denotes the creative action of the holy man or sage, of the ruler or leader of men, who through his power awakens and develops their higher nature.[1]

---

1. The hexagram is assigned to the fourth month, May–June, when the light-giving power is at its zenith, i.e., before the summer solstice has marked the beginning of the year's decline. [The German text reads "April–May"; this is obviously a slip, for the first month of the Chinese lunar year extends approximately from the beginning of February to the beginning of March. New Year is a variable date, falling around February 5. Two or three other slips of this sort occurring later in the book have been similarly corrected, but without special mention.]

3

THE JUDGMENT

THE CREATIVE works sublime success,
Furthering[2] through perseverance.

According to the original meaning, the attributes [sublimity, potentiality of success, power to further, perseverance] are paired. When an individual draws this oracle, it means that success will come to him from the primal depths of the universe and that everything depends upon his seeking his happiness and that of others in one way only, that is, by perseverance in what is right.

The specific meanings of the four attributes became the subject of speculation at an early date. The Chinese word here rendered by "sublime" means literally "head," "origin," "great." This is why Confucius says in explaining it: "Great indeed is the generating power of the Creative; all beings owe their beginning to it. This power permeates all heaven."[3] For this attribute inheres in the other three as well.

The beginning of all things lies still in the beyond in the form of ideas that have yet to become real. But the Creative furthermore has power to lend form to these archetypes of ideas. This is indicated in the word success, and the process is represented by an image from nature: "The clouds pass and the rain does its work, and all individual beings flow into their forms."[4]

Applied to the human world, these attributes show the great man the way to notable success: "Because he sees with great clarity causes and effects, he completes the six steps at the right time and mounts toward heaven on them at the right time, as though on six dragons." The six steps are the six different positions given in the hexagram, which are represented

---

2. [The German word used here is *fördernd*, literally rendered by "furthering." It occurs again and again as a key word in Wilhelm's rendering of the Chinese text. To avoid extreme awkwardness, the phrase "is favorable" is occasionally used as an alternative.]

3. [This quotation and those following are from commentary material on this hexagram appearing in bk. III. It will be noted here, as well as in a number of other instances, that the wording of the passages is not identical in the two books.]

4. Cf. Gen. 2 : 1 ff., where the development of the different creatures is also attributed to the fall of rain.

later by the dragon symbol. Here it is shown that the way to success lies in apprehending and giving actuality to the way of the universe [tao], which, as a law running through end and beginning, brings about all phenomena in time. Thus each step attained forthwith becomes a preparation for the next. Time is no longer a hindrance but the means of making actual what is potential.

The act of creation having found expression in the two attributes sublimity and success, the work of conservation is shown to be a continuous actualization and differentiation of form. This is expressed in the two terms "furthering" (literally, "creating that which accords with the nature of a given being") and "persevering" (literally, "correct and firm"). "The course of the Creative alters and shapes beings until each attains its true, specific nature, then it keeps them in conformity with the Great Harmony. Thus does it show itself to further through perseverance."

In relation to the human sphere, this shows how the great man brings peace and security to the world through his activity in creating order: "He towers high above the multitude of beings, and all lands are united in peace."

Another line of speculation goes still further in separating the words "sublime," "success," "furthering," "perseverance," and parallels them with the four cardinal virtues in humanity. To sublimity, which, as the fundamental principle, embraces all the other attributes, it links love. To the attribute success are linked the mores,[5] which regulate and organize the

---

5. ["Mores" is the word chosen to render the German word *Sitte*, when the latter refers, as in the present instance, to what the Chinese know as *li*. However, neither "mores" nor any other available English word, such as "manners" or "customs," conveys an adequate idea of what *li* stood for in ancient China, because none of them necessarily denotes anything more than behavior growing out of and regulated by tradition. The ideas for which *li* stands seem to have had their origin in a religious attitude to life and in ethical principles developing out of that attitude. On the religious side *li* meant the observance with true piety of the ritual through which the "will of heaven" was interpreted and made to prevail on earth. On the moral side it meant the sense of propriety—understood to be innate in man—that, through training, makes possible right relationships in personal life and in society. *Li* was the cornerstone upon which Confucius built in his effort to bring order out of chaos in his era (see *The Sacred Books of the*

expressions of love and thereby make them successful. The attribute furthering is correlated with justice, which creates the conditions in which each receives that which accords with his being, that which is due him and which constitutes his happiness. The attribute perseverance is correlated with wisdom, which discerns the immutable laws of all that happens and can therefore bring about enduring conditions. These speculations, already broached in the commentary called *Wên Yen*,[6] later formed the bridge connecting the philosophy of the "five stages (elements) of change," as laid down in the Book of History (*Shu Ching*) with the philosophy of the Book of Changes, which is based solely on the polarity of positive and negative principles. In the course of time this combination of the two systems of thought opened the way for an increasingly intricate number symbolism.[7]

THE IMAGE

The movement of heaven is full of power.

Thus the superior man makes himself strong and
untiring.

Since there is only one heaven, the doubling of the trigram Ch'ien, of which heaven is the image, indicates the movement of heaven. One complete revolution of heaven makes a day, and the repetition of the trigram means that each day is followed by another. This creates the idea of time. Since it is the same heaven moving with untiring power, there is also created

---

East, XXVII: *The Li Ki*). Obedience to the code of *li* was entirely self-imposed as regards the "superior man," who in feudal times was always a man of rank. The conduct of the "inferior man"—the lower-class individual—was governed by law.]

6. [See p. 259. The text of the *Wên Yen* (Commentary on the Words of the Text) appears in bk. III.]

7. The Creative causes the beginning and begetting of all beings, and can therefore be designated as heaven, radiant energy, father, ruler. It is a question whether the Chinese personified the Creative, as the Greeks conceived it in Zeus. The answer is that this problem is not the main one for the Chinese. The divine-creative principle is suprapersonal and makes itself perceptible only through its all-powerful activity. It has, to be sure, an external aspect, which is heaven, and heaven, like all that lives, has a spiritual consciousness, God, the Supreme Ruler. But all this is summed up as the Creative.

the idea of duration both in and beyond time, a movement that never stops nor slackens, just as one day follows another in an unending course. This duration in time is the image of the power inherent in the Creative.

With this image as a model, the sage learns how best to develop himself so that his influence may endure. He must make himself strong in every way, by consciously casting out all that is inferior and degrading. Thus he attains that tirelessness which depends upon consciously limiting the fields of his activity.

THE LINES

Nine at the beginning[8] means:
Hidden dragon. Do not act.

In China the dragon has a meaning altogether different from that given it in the Western world. The dragon is a symbol of the electrically charged, dynamic, arousing force that manifests itself in the thunderstorm. In winter this energy withdraws into the earth; in the early summer it becomes active again, appearing in the sky as thunder and lightning. As a result the creative forces on earth begin to stir again.

Here this creative force is still hidden beneath the earth and therefore has no effect. In terms of human affairs, this symbolizes a great man who is still unrecognized. Nonetheless he remains true to himself. He does not allow himself to be influenced by outward success or failure, but confident in his strength, he bides his time. Hence it is wise for the man who consults the oracle and draws this line to wait in the calm

---

8. The lines are counted from the bottom up, i.e., the lowest is taken as the first. If the person consulting the oracle draws a seven, this is important in relation to the structure of the hexagram as a whole, because it is a strong line, but inasmuch as it does not move [change] it has no meaning as an individual line. On the other hand, if the questioner draws a nine, the line is a moving one, and a special meaning is attached to it; this must be considered separately. The same principle applies in respect to all the other strong lines [and also as regards moving and nonmoving weak lines, i.e., sixes and eights]. The two lowest lines in each hexagram stand for the earth, the two in the middle for the world of man, and the upper two for heaven. [Further details as to the meaning of the nines and sixes are given on p. 722.]

strength of patience. The time will fulfill itself. One need not fear lest strong will should not prevail; the main thing is not to expend one's powers prematurely in an attempt to obtain by force something for which the time is not yet ripe.

> Nine in the second place means:
> Dragon appearing in the field.
> It furthers one to see the great man.

Here the effects of the light-giving power begin to manifest themselves. In terms of human affairs, this means that the great man makes his appearance in his chosen field of activity. As yet he has no commanding position but is still with his peers. However, what distinguishes him from the others is his seriousness of purpose, his unqualified reliability, and the influence he exerts on his environment without conscious effort. Such a man is destined to gain great influence and to set the world in order. Therefore it is favorable to see him.

> Nine in the third place means:
> All day long the superior man is creatively active.
> At nightfall his mind is still beset with cares.
> Danger. No blame.

A sphere of influence opens up for the great man. His fame begins to spread. The masses flock to him. His inner power is adequate to the increased outer activity.[9] There are all sorts of things to be done, and when others are at rest in the evening, plans and anxieties press in upon him. But danger lurks here at the place of transition from lowliness to the heights. Many a great man has been ruined because the masses flocked to him and swept him into their course. Ambition has destroyed his integrity. However, true greatness is not impaired by temptations. He who remains in touch with the time that is dawning,

---

9. [The upper trigram is considered to be "outside," the lower "inside" (see p. 357). This distinction underlies the constant juxtaposition, to be observed throughout bks. I and III, of inner, mental states and external actions or events, of subjective and objective experiences. From this also arise the frequent comparisons between ability and position, form and content, outer adornment and inner worth.]

and with its demands, is prudent enough to avoid all pitfalls, and remains blameless.

> Nine in the fourth place means:
> Wavering flight over the depths.
> No blame.

A place of transition has been reached, and free choice can enter in. A twofold possibility is presented to the great man: he can soar to the heights and play an important part in the world, or he can withdraw into solitude and develop himself. He can go the way of the hero or that of the holy sage who seeks seclusion. There is no general law to say which of the two is the right way. Each one in this situation must make a free choice according to the inner law of his being. If the individual acts consistently and is true to himself, he will find the way that is appropriate for him. This way is right for him and without blame.

> ○ Nine in the fifth place[10] means:
> Flying dragon in the heavens.
> It furthers one to see the great man.

Here the great man has attained the sphere of the heavenly beings. His influence spreads and becomes visible throughout the whole world. Everyone who sees him may count himself blessed. Confucius says about this line:

Things that accord in tone vibrate together. Things that have affinity in their inmost natures seek one another. Water flows to what is wet, fire turns to what is dry. Clouds (the breath of heaven) follow the dragon, wind (the breath of earth) follows the tiger. Thus the sage arises, and all creatures follow him with their eyes. What is born of heaven feels related to what is above. What is born of earth feels related to what is below. Each follows its kind.

> Nine at the top means:
> Arrogant dragon will have cause to repent.

---

10. [The circle indicates that this line is a governing ruler of the hexagram. Constituting rulers are marked by a square. For explanation of governing and constituting rulers, see p. 364.]

When a man seeks to climb so high that he loses touch with the rest of mankind, he becomes isolated, and this necessarily leads to failure. This line warns against titanic aspirations that exceed one's power. A precipitous fall would follow.

> When all the lines are nines, it means:
> There appears a flight of dragons without heads.
> Good fortune.

When all the lines are nines, it means that the whole hexagram is in motion and changes into the hexagram K'un, THE RECEPTIVE, whose character is devotion. The strength of the Creative and the mildness of the Receptive unite. Strength is indicated by the flight of dragons, mildness by the fact that their heads are hidden. This means that mildness in action joined to strength of decision brings good fortune.

坤

2. K'un / The Receptive

☷☷ *above* K'UN THE RECEPTIVE, EARTH
below K'UN THE RECEPTIVE, EARTH

This hexagram is made up of broken lines only. The broken line represents the dark, yielding, receptive primal power of yin. The attribute of the hexagram is devotion; its image is the earth. It is the perfect complement of THE CREATIVE—the complement, not the opposite,[1] for the Receptive does not combat the Creative but completes it. It represents nature in contrast to spirit, earth in contrast to heaven, space as against time, the female-maternal as against the male-paternal. However, as applied to human affairs, the principle of this complementary relationship is found not only in the relation between man and woman, but also in that between prince and

1. [Hexagrams that are opposites in structure are not necessarily opposites in meaning.]

minister and between father and son. Indeed, even in the individual this duality appears in the coexistence of the spiritual world and the world of the senses.

But strictly speaking there is no real dualism here, because there is a clearly defined hierarchic relationship between the two principles. In itself of course the Receptive is just as important as the Creative, but the attribute of devotion defines the place occupied by this primal power in relation to the Creative. For the Receptive must be activated and led by the Creative; then it is productive of good. Only when it abandons this position and tries to stand as an equal side by side with the Creative, does it become evil. The result then is opposition to and struggle against the Creative, which is productive of evil to both.

THE JUDGMENT

THE RECEPTIVE brings about sublime success,
Furthering through the perseverance of a mare.
If the superior man undertakes something and tries
    to lead,
He goes astray;
But if he follows, he finds guidance.
It is favorable to find friends in the west and south,
To forego friends in the east and north.
Quiet perseverance brings good fortune.

The four fundamental aspects of the Creative—"sublime success, furthering through perseverance"—are also attributed to the Receptive. Here, however, the perseverance is more closely defined: it is that of a mare. The Receptive connotes spatial reality in contrast to the spiritual potentiality of the Creative. The potential becomes real and the spiritual becomes spatial through a specifically qualifying definition. Thus the qualification, "of a mare," is here added to the idea of perseverance. The horse belongs to earth just as the dragon belongs to heaven. Its tireless roaming over the plains is taken as a symbol of the vast expanse of the earth. This is the symbol chosen because the mare combines the strength and swiftness of the horse with the gentleness and devotion of the cow.

11

Only because nature in its myriad forms corresponds with the myriad impulses of the Creative can it make these impulses real. Nature's richness lies in its power to nourish all living things; its greatness lies in its power to give them beauty and splendor. Thus it prospers all that lives. It is the Creative that begets things, but they are brought to birth by the Receptive. Applied to human affairs, therefore, what the hexagram indicates is action in conformity with the situation. The person in question is not in an independent position, but is acting as an assistant. This means that he must achieve something. It is not his task to try to lead—that would only make him lose the way—but to let himself be led. If he knows how to meet fate with an attitude of acceptance, he is sure to find the right guidance. The superior man lets himself be guided; he does not go ahead blindly, but learns from the situation what is demanded of him and then follows this intimation from fate.

Since there is something to be accomplished, we need friends and helpers in the hour of toil and effort, once the ideas to be realized are firmly set. The time of toil and effort is indicated by the west and the south, for west and south symbolize the place where the Receptive works for the Creative, as nature does in summer and autumn. If in that situation one does not mobilize all one's powers, the work to be accomplished will not be done. Hence to find friends there means to find guidance. But in addition to the time of toil and effort, there is also a time of planning, and for this we need solitude. The east symbolizes the place where a man receives orders from his master, and the north the place where he reports on what he has done. At that time he must be alone and objective. In this sacred hour he must do without companions, so that the purity of the moment may not be spoiled by factional hates and favoritism.

THE IMAGE

The earth's condition is receptive devotion.
Thus the superior man who has breadth of character
Carries the outer world.

Just as there is only one heaven, so too there is only one earth.

In the hexagram of heaven the doubling of the trigram implies duration in time, but in the hexagram of earth the doubling connotes the solidity and extension in space by virtue of which the earth is able to carry and preserve all things that live and move upon it. The earth in its devotion carries all things, good and evil, without exception. In the same way the superior man gives to his character breadth, purity, and sustaining power, so that he is able both to support and to bear with people and things.

THE LINES

Six at the beginning means:
When there is hoarfrost underfoot,
Solid ice is not far off.

Just as the light-giving power represents life, so the dark power, the shadowy, represents death. When the first hoarfrost comes in the autumn, the power of darkness and cold is just at its beginning. After these first warnings, signs of death will gradually multiply, until, in obedience to immutable laws, stark winter with its ice is here.

In life it is the same. After certain scarcely noticeable signs of decay have appeared, they go on increasing until final dissolution comes. But in life precautions can be taken by heeding the first signs of decay and checking them in time.

○ Six in the second place means:
Straight, square, great.
Without purpose,
Yet nothing remains unfurthered.

The symbol of heaven is the circle, and that of earth is the square. Thus squareness is a primary quality of the earth. On the other hand, movement in a straight line, as well as magnitude, is a primary quality of the Creative. But all square things have their origin in a straight line and in turn form solid bodies. In mathematics, when we discriminate between lines, planes, and solids, we find that rectangular planes result from straight lines, and cubic magnitudes from rectangular planes. The Receptive accommodates itself to the qualities of the Creative and makes them its own. Thus a square develops out of a straight line and a cube out of a square. This is compliance with the laws of the Creative; nothing is taken away, nothing added. Therefore the Receptive has no need of a special purpose of its own, nor of any effort; yet everything turns out as it should.

Nature creates all beings without erring: this is its straightness. It is calm and still: this is its foursquareness. It tolerates all creatures equally: this is its greatness. Therefore it attains what is right for all without artifice or special intentions. Man achieves the height of wisdom when all that he does is as self-evident as what nature does.

> Six in the third place means:
> Hidden lines.
> One is able to remain persevering.
> If by chance you are in the service of a king,
> Seek not works, but bring to completion.

If a man is free of vanity he is able to conceal his abilities and keep them from attracting attention too soon; thus he can mature undisturbed. If conditions demand it, he can also enter public life, but that too he does with restraint. The wise man gladly leaves fame to others. He does not seek to have credited to himself things that stand accomplished, but hopes to release active forces; that is, he completes his works in such a manner that they may bear fruit for the future.

> Six in the fourth place means:
> A tied-up sack. No blame, no praise.

The dark element opens when it moves and closes when at rest.[2] The strictest reticence is indicated here. The time is dangerous, because any degree of prominence leads either to the enmity of irresistible antagonists if one challenges them or to misconceived recognition if one is complaisant. Therefore a man ought to maintain reserve, be it in solitude or in the turmoil of the world, for there too he can hide himself so well that no one knows him.

---

2. [See p. 301, sec. 2.]

Six in the fifth place means:

A yellow lower garment brings supreme good fortune.

Yellow is the color of the earth and of the middle; it is the symbol of that which is reliable and genuine. The lower garment is inconspicuously decorated—the symbol of aristocratic reserve. When anyone is called upon to work in a prominent but not independent position, true success depends on the utmost discretion. A man's genuineness and refinement should not reveal themselves directly; they should express themselves only indirectly as an effect from within.

Six at the top means:

Dragons fight in the meadow.

Their blood is black and yellow.

In the top place the dark element should yield to the light. If it attempts to maintain a position to which it is not entitled and to rule instead of serving, it draws down upon itself the anger of the strong. A struggle ensues in which it is overthrown, with injury, however, to both sides. The dragon, symbol of heaven, comes to fight the false dragon that symbolizes the inflation of the earth principle. Midnight blue is the color of heaven; yellow is the color of the earth. Therefore, when black and yellow blood flow, it is a sign that in this unnatural contest both primal powers suffer injury.[3]

When all the lines are sixes, it means:

Lasting perseverance furthers.

When nothing but sixes appears, the hexagram of THE RECEPTIVE changes into the hexagram of THE CREATIVE. By holding fast to what is right, it gains the power of enduring. There is indeed no advance, but neither is there retrogression.

---

3. While the top line of THE CREATIVE indicates titanic pride and forms a parallel to the Greek legend of Icarus, the top line of THE RECEPTIVE presents a parallel to the myth of Lucifer's rebellion against God, or to the battle between the powers of darkness and the gods of Valhalla, which ended with the Twilight of the Gods.

屯

3. *Chun / Difficulty at the Beginning*

☵	*above* K'AN	THE ABYSMAL, WATER
☳	*below* CHÊN	THE AROUSING, THUNDER

The name of the hexagram, Chun, really connotes a blade of grass pushing against an obstacle as it sprouts out of the earth— hence the meaning, "difficulty at the beginning." The hexagram indicates the way in which heaven and earth bring forth individual beings. It is their first meeting, which is beset with difficulties. The lower trigram Chên is the Arousing; its motion is upward and its image is thunder. The upper trigram K'an stands for the Abysmal, the dangerous. Its motion is downward and its image is rain. The situation points to teeming, chaotic profusion; thunder and rain fill the air. But the chaos clears up. While the Abysmal sinks, the upward movement eventually passes beyond the danger. A thunderstorm brings release from tension, and all things breathe freely again.

THE JUDGMENT

DIFFICULTY AT THE BEGINNING works supreme
    success,
Furthering through perseverance.
Nothing should be undertaken.
It furthers one to appoint helpers.

Times of growth are beset with difficulties. They resemble a first birth. But these difficulties arise from the very profusion of all that is struggling to attain form. Everything is in motion: therefore if one perseveres there is a prospect of great success, in spite of the existing danger. When it is a man's fate to undertake such new beginnings, everything is still unformed, dark.

Hence he must hold back, because any premature move might bring disaster. Likewise, it is very important not to remain alone; in order to overcome the chaos he needs helpers. This is not to say, however, that he himself should look on passively at what is happening. He must lend his hand and participate with inspiration and guidance.

THE IMAGE

Clouds and thunder:
The image of DIFFICULTY AT THE BEGINNING.
Thus the superior man
Brings order out of confusion.

Clouds and thunder are represented by definite decorative lines; this means that in the chaos of difficulty at the beginning, order is already implicit. So too the superior man has to arrange and organize the inchoate profusion of such times of beginning, just as one sorts out silk threads from a knotted tangle and binds them into skeins. In order to find one's place in the infinity of being, one must be able both to separate and to unite.

THE LINES

○ Nine at the beginning means:
Hesitation and hindrance.
It furthers one to remain persevering.
It furthers one to appoint helpers.

If a person encounters a hindrance at the beginning of an enterprise, he must not try to force advance but must pause and take thought. However, nothing should put him off his course; he must persevere and constantly keep the goal in sight. It is important to seek out the right assistants, but he can find them only if he avoids arrogance and associates with his fellows in a spirit of humility. Only then will he attract those with whose help he can combat the difficulties.

Six in the second place means:
Difficulties pile up.
Horse and wagon part.

> He is not a robber;
> He wants to woo when the time comes.
> The maiden is chaste,
> She does not pledge herself.
> Ten years—then she pledges herself.

We find ourselves beset by difficulties and hindrances. Suddenly there is a turn of affairs, as if someone were coming up with a horse and wagon and unhitching them. This event comes so unexpectedly that we assume the newcomer to be a robber. Gradually it becomes clear that he has no evil intentions but seeks to be friendly and to offer help. But this offer is not to be accepted, because it does not come from the right quarter. We must wait until the time is fulfilled; ten years is a fulfilled cycle of time. Then normal conditions return of themselves, and we can join forces with the friend intended for us.

Using the image of a betrothed girl who remains true to her lover in face of grave conflicts, the hexagram gives counsel for a special situation. When in times of difficulty a hindrance is encountered and unexpected relief is offered from a source unrelated to us, we must be careful and not take upon ourselves any obligations entailed by such help; otherwise our freedom of decision is impaired. If we bide our time, things will quiet down again, and we shall attain what we have hoped for. [1]

> Six in the third place means:
> Whoever hunts deer without the forester
> Only loses his way in the forest.
> The superior man understands the signs of the time
> And prefers to desist.
> To go on brings humiliation.

---

[1]. A different translation is possible here, which would result in a different interpretation:

> Difficulties pile up.
> Horse and wagon turn about.
> If the robber were not there,
> The wooer would come.
> The maiden is faithful, she does not pledge herself.
> Ten years—then she pledges herself.

If a man tries to hunt in a strange forest and has no guide, he loses his way. When he finds himself in difficulties he must not try to steal out of them unthinkingly and without guidance. Fate cannot be duped; premature effort, without the necessary guidance, ends in failure and disgrace. Therefore the superior man, discerning the seeds of coming events, prefers to renounce a wish rather than to provoke failure and humiliation by trying to force its fulfillment.

> Six in the fourth place means:
> Horse and wagon part.
> Strive for union.
> To go brings good fortune.
> Everything acts to further.

We are in a situation in which it is our duty to act, but we lack sufficient power. However, an opportunity to make connections offers itself. It must be seized. Neither false pride nor false reserve should deter us. Bringing oneself to take the first step, even when it involves a certain degree of self-abnegation, is a sign of inner clarity. To accept help in a difficult situation is not a disgrace. If the right helper is found, all goes well.

> ○ Nine in the fifth place means:
> Difficulties in blessing.
> A little perseverance brings good fortune.
> Great perseverance brings misfortune.

An individual is in a position in which he cannot so express his good intentions that they will actually take shape and be understood. Other people interpose and distort everything he does. He should then be cautious and proceed step by step. He must not try to force the consummation of a great undertaking, because success is possible only when general confidence already prevails. It is only through faithful and conscientious work, unobtrusively carried on, that the situation gradually clears up and the hindrance disappears.

> Six at the top means:
> Horse and wagon part.
> Bloody tears flow.

The difficulties at the beginning are too great for some persons. They get stuck and never find their way out; they fold their hands and give up the struggle. Such resignation is the saddest of all things. Therefore Confucius says of this line: "Bloody tears flow: one should not persist in this."

漾

4. *Mêng / Youthful Folly*

above KÊN	KEEPING STILL, MOUNTAIN
below K'AN	THE ABYSMAL, WATER

In this hexagram we are reminded of youth and folly[1] in two different ways. The image of the upper trigram, Kên, is the mountain, that of the lower, K'an, is water; the spring rising at the foot of the mountain is the image of inexperienced youth. Keeping still is the attribute of the upper trigram; that of the lower is the abyss, danger. Stopping in perplexity on the brink of a dangerous abyss is a symbol of the folly of youth. However, the two trigrams also show the way of overcoming the follies of youth. Water is something that of necessity flows on. When the spring gushes forth, it does not know at first where it will go. But its steady flow fills up the deep place blocking its progress, and success is attained.

THE JUDGMENT

YOUTHFUL FOLLY has success.

It is not I who seek the young fool;

---

1. ["Fool" and "folly" as used in this hexagram should be understood to mean the immaturity of youth and its consequent lack of wisdom, rather than mere stupidity. Parsifal is known as the "pure fool" not because he was dull-witted but because he was inexperienced.]

The young fool seeks me.
At the first oracle I inform him.
If he asks two or three times, it is importunity.
If he importunes, I give him no information.
Perseverance furthers.

In the time of youth, folly is not an evil. One may succeed in spite of it, provided one finds an experienced teacher and has the right attitude toward him. This means, first of all, that the youth himself must be conscious of his lack of experience and must seek out the teacher. Without this modesty and this interest there is no guarantee that he has the necessary receptivity, which should express itself in respectful acceptance of the teacher. This is the reason why the teacher must wait to be sought out instead of offering himself. Only thus can the instruction take place at the right time and in the right way.

A teacher's answer to the question of a pupil ought to be clear and definite like that expected from an oracle; thereupon it ought to be accepted as a key for resolution of doubts and a basis for decision. If mistrustful or unintelligent questioning is kept up, it serves only to annoy the teacher. He does well to ignore it in silence, just as the oracle gives one answer only and refuses to be tempted by questions implying doubt.

Given in addition a perseverance that never slackens until the points are mastered one by one, real success is sure to follow. Thus the hexagram counsels the teacher as well as the pupil.

THE IMAGE

A spring wells up at the foot of the mountain:
The image of YOUTH.
Thus the superior man fosters his character
By thoroughness in all that he does.

A spring succeeds in flowing on and escapes stagnation by filling up all the hollow places in its path. In the same way character is developed by thoroughness that skips nothing but, like water, gradually and steadily fills up all gaps and so flows onward.

THE LINES

Six at the beginning means:
To make a fool develop
It furthers one to apply discipline.
The fetters should be removed.
To go on in this way brings humiliation.

Law is the beginning of education. Youth in its inexperience
is inclined at first to take everything carelessly and playfully.
It must be shown the seriousness of life. A certain measure of
taking oneself in hand, brought about by strict discipline, is a
good thing. He who plays with life never amounts to anything.
However, discipline should not degenerate into drill. Continuous drill has a humiliating effect and cripples a man's powers.

○ Nine in the second place means:
To bear with fools in kindliness brings good fortune.
To know how to take women
Brings good fortune.
The son is capable of taking charge of the household.

These lines picture a man who has no external power, but who
has enough strength of mind to bear his burden of responsibility. He has the inner superiority and strength that enable him
to tolerate with kindliness the shortcomings of human folly.
The same attitude is owed to women as the weaker sex. One
must understand them and give them recognition in a spirit
of chivalrous consideration. Only this combination of inner
strength with outer reserve enables one to take on the responsibility of directing a larger social body with real success.

Six in the third place means:
Take not a maiden who, when she sees a man of
bronze,
Loses possession of herself.
Nothing furthers.

A weak, inexperienced man, struggling to rise, easily loses his
own individuality when he slavishly imitates a strong person-

ality of higher station. He is like a girl throwing herself away when she meets a strong man. Such a servile approach should not be encouraged, because it is bad both for the youth and the teacher. A girl owes it to her dignity to wait until she is wooed. In both cases it is undignified to offer oneself, and no good comes of accepting such an offer.

> Six in the fourth place means:
> Entangled folly brings humiliation.

For youthful folly it is the most hopeless thing to entangle itself in empty imaginings. The more obstinately it clings to such unreal fantasies, the more certainly will humiliation overtake it.

Often the teacher, when confronted with such entangled folly, has no other course but to leave the fool to himself for a time, not sparing him the humiliation that results. This is frequently the only means of rescue.

> O Six in the fifth place means:
> Childlike folly brings good fortune.

An inexperienced person who seeks instruction in a childlike and unassuming way is on the right path, for the man devoid of arrogance who subordinates himself to his teacher will certainly be helped.

> Nine at the top means:
> In punishing folly
> It does not further one
> To commit transgressions.
> The only thing that furthers
> Is to prevent transgressions.

Sometimes an incorrigible fool must be punished. He who will not heed will be made to feel. This punishment is quite different from a preliminary shaking up. But the penalty should not be imposed in anger; it must be restricted to an objective guarding against unjustified excesses. Punishment is never an end in itself but serves merely to restore order.

This applies not only in regard to education but also in regard to the measures taken by a government against a populace guilty of transgressions. Governmental interference should always be merely preventive and should have as its sole aim the establishment of public security and peace.

5. *Hsü / Waiting (Nourishment[1])*

above	K'AN	THE ABYSMAL, WATER
below	CH'IEN	THE CREATIVE, HEAVEN

All beings have need of nourishment from above. But the gift of food comes in its own time, and for this one must wait. This hexagram shows the clouds in the heavens, giving rain to refresh all that grows and to provide mankind with food and drink. The rain will come in its own time. We cannot make it come; we have to wait for it. The idea of waiting is further suggested by the attributes of the two trigrams—strength within, danger in front.[2] Strength in the face of danger does not plunge ahead but bides its time, whereas weakness in the face of danger grows agitated and has not the patience to wait.

THE JUDGMENT

WAITING. If you are sincere,

You have light and success.

Perseverance brings good fortune.

It furthers one to cross the great water.

Waiting is not mere empty hoping. It has the inner certainty of reaching the goal. Such certainty alone gives that light

1. [In the German translation, this secondary name does not appear in bk. I. See p. 410.]

2. [The upper trigram is considered to be in front of the lower. See p. 357.]

which leads to success. This leads to the perseverance that brings good fortune and bestows power to cross the great water.

One is faced with a danger that has to be overcome. Weakness and impatience can do nothing. Only a strong man can stand up to his fate, for his inner security enables him to endure to the end. This strength shows itself in uncompromising truthfulness [with himself]. It is only when we have the courage to face things exactly as they are, without any sort of self-deception or illusion, that a light will develop out of events, by which the path to success may be recognized. This recognition must be followed by resolute and persevering action. For only the man who goes to meet his fate resolutely is equipped to deal with it adequately. Then he will be able to cross the great water—that is to say, he will be capable of making the necessary decision and of surmounting the danger.

THE IMAGE

Clouds rise up to heaven:
The image of WAITING.
Thus the superior man eats and drinks,
Is joyous and of good cheer.

When clouds rise in the sky, it is a sign that it will rain. There is nothing to do but to wait until the rain falls. It is the same in life when destiny is at work. We should not worry and seek to shape the future by interfering in things before the time is ripe. We should quietly fortify the body with food and drink and the mind with gladness and good cheer. Fate comes when it will, and thus we are ready.

THE LINES

Nine at the beginning means:
Waiting in the meadow.
It furthers one to abide in what endures.
No blame.

The danger is not yet close. One is still waiting on the open plain. Conditions are still simple, yet there is a feeling of something impending. One must continue to lead a regular life as long as possible. Only in this way does one guard against a premature waste of strength, keep free of blame and error that would become a source of weakness later on.

> Nine in the second place means:
> Waiting on the sand.
> There is some gossip.
> The end brings good fortune.

The danger gradually comes closer. Sand is near the bank of the river, and the water means danger. Disagreements crop up. General unrest can easily develop in such times, and we lay the blame on one another. He who stays calm will succeed in making things go well in the end. Slander will be silenced if we do not gratify it with injured retorts.

> Nine in the third place means:
> Waiting in the mud
> Brings about the arrival of the enemy.

Mud is no place for waiting, since it is already being washed by the water of the stream. Instead of having gathered strength to cross the stream at one try, one has made a premature start that has got him no farther than the muddy bank. Such an unfavorable position invites enemies from without, who naturally take advantage of it. Caution and a sense of the seriousness of the situation are all that can keep one from injury.

> Six in the fourth place means:
> Waiting in blood.
> Get out of the pit.

The situation is extremely dangerous. It is of utmost gravity now—a matter of life and death. Bloodshed seems imminent. There is no going forward or backward; we are cut off as if in a pit. Now we must simply stand fast and let fate take its course. This composure, which keeps us from aggravating the trouble by anything we might do, is the only way of getting out of the dangerous pit.

○ Nine in the fifth place means:

　Waiting at meat and drink.

　Perseverance brings good fortune.

Even in the midst of danger there come intervals of peace when things go relatively well. If we possess enough inner strength, we shall take advantage of these intervals to fortify ourselves for renewed struggle. We must know how to enjoy the moment without being deflected from the goal, for perseverance is needed to remain victorious.

This is true in public life as well; it is not possible to achieve everything all at once. The height of wisdom is to allow people enough recreation to quicken pleasure in their work until the task is completed. Herein lies the secret of the whole hexagram. It differs from Chien, OBSTRUCTION (39), in the fact that in this instance, while waiting, we are sure of our cause and therefore do not lose the serenity born of inner cheerfulness.

　Six at the top means:

　One falls into the pit.

　Three uninvited guests arrive.

　Honor them, and in the end there will be good
　　fortune.

The waiting is over; the danger can no longer be averted. One falls into the pit and must yield to the inevitable. Everything seems to have been in vain. But precisely in this extremity things take an unforeseen turn. Without a move on one's own part, there is outside intervention. At first one cannot be sure of its meaning: is it rescue or is it destruction? A person in this situation must keep his mind alert and not withdraw into himself with a sulky gesture of refusal, but must greet the new turn with respect. Thus he ultimately escapes the danger, and all goes well. Even happy turns of fortune often come in a form that at first seems strange to us.

次

6. *Sung / Conflict*

	above	CH'IEN	THE CREATIVE, HEAVEN
	below	K'AN	THE ABYSMAL, WATER

The upper trigram, whose image is heaven, has an upward movement; the lower trigram, water, in accordance with its nature, tends downward. Thus the two halves move away from each other, giving rise to the idea of conflict.

The attribute of the Creative is strength, that of the Abysmal is danger, guile. Where cunning has force before it, there is conflict.

A third indication of conflict, in terms of character, is presented by the combination of deep cunning within and fixed determination outwardly. A person of this character will certainly be quarrelsome.

THE JUDGMENT

CONFLICT. You are sincere
And are being obstructed.
A cautious halt halfway brings good fortune.
Going through to the end brings misfortune.
It furthers one to see the great man.
It does not further one to cross the great water.

Conflict develops when one feels himself to be in the right and runs into opposition. If one is not convinced of being in the right, opposition leads to craftiness or high-handed encroachment but not to open conflict.

If a man is entangled in a conflict, his only salvation lies in being so clear-headed and inwardly strong that he is always ready to come to terms by meeting the opponent halfway. To carry on the conflict to the bitter end has evil effects even when one is in the right, because the enmity is then perpetuated. It is important to see the great man, that is, an impartial man whose authority is great enough to terminate the conflict amicably or assure a just decision. In times of strife, crossing the great water is to be avoided, that is, dangerous enterprises are not to be begun, because in order to be successful they require concerted unity of forces. Conflict within weakens the power to conquer danger without.

THE IMAGE

Heaven and water go their opposite ways:
The image of CONFLICT.
Thus in all his transactions the superior man
Carefully considers the beginning.

The image indicates that the causes of conflict are latent in the opposing tendencies of the two trigrams. Once these opposing tendencies appear, conflict is inevitable. To avoid it, therefore, everything must be taken carefully into consideration in the very beginning. If rights and duties are exactly defined, or if, in a group, the spiritual trends of the individuals harmonize, the cause of conflict is removed in advance.

THE LINES

Six at the beginning means:
If one does not perpetuate the affair,
There is a little gossip.
In the end, good fortune comes.

While a conflict is in the incipient stage, the best thing to do is to drop the issue. Especially when the adversary is stronger, it is not advisable to risk pushing the conflict to a decision. It may come to a slight dispute, but in the end all goes well.

Nine in the second place means:
One cannot engage in conflict;
One returns home, gives way.

> The people of his town,
> Three hundred households,
> Remain free of guilt.

In a struggle with an enemy of superior strength, retreat is no disgrace. Timely withdrawal prevents bad consequences. If, out of a false sense of honor, a man allowed himself to be tempted into an unequal conflict, he would be drawing down disaster upon himself. In such a case a wise and conciliatory attitude benefits the whole community, which will then not be drawn into the conflict.

> Six in the third place means:
> To nourish oneself on ancient virtue induces
>   perseverance.
> Danger. In the end, good fortune comes.
> If by chance you are in the service of a king,
> Seek not works.

This is a warning of the danger that goes with an expansive disposition. Only that which has been honestly acquired through merit remains a permanent possession. It can happen that such a possession may be contested, but since it is really one's own, one cannot be robbed of it. Whatever a man possesses through the strength of his own nature cannot be lost. If one enters the service of a superior, one can avoid conflict only by not seeking works for the sake of prestige. It is enough if the work is done: let the honor go to the other.

> Nine in the fourth place means:
> One cannot engage in conflict.
> One turns back and submits to fate,
> Changes one's attitude,
> And finds peace in perseverance.
> Good fortune.

This refers to a person whose inner attitude at first lacks peace. He does not feel content with his situation and would like to improve it through conflict. In contrast to the situation of the nine in the second place, he is dealing with a weaker opponent and might therefore succeed. But he cannot carry on the fight, because, since right is not on his side, he cannot justify the conflict to his conscience. Therefore he turns back and accepts his fate. He changes his mind and finds lasting peace in being at one with eternal law. This brings good fortune.

○ Nine in the fifth place means:
　　To contend before him
　　Brings supreme good fortune.

This refers to an arbiter in a conflict who is powerful and just, and strong enough to lend weight to the right side. A dispute can be turned over to him with confidence. If one is in the right, one attains great good fortune.

　　Nine at the top means:
　　Even if by chance a leather belt is bestowed on one,
　　By the end of a morning
　　It will have been snatched away three times.

Here we have someone who has carried a conflict to the bitter end and has triumphed. He is granted a decoration, but his happiness does not last. He is attacked again and again, and the result is conflict without end.

師

7. *Shih | The Army*

above	K'UN	THE RECEPTIVE, EARTH
below	K'AN	THE ABYSMAL, WATER

This hexagram is made up of the trigrams K'an, water, and K'un, earth, and thus it symbolizes the ground water stored up in the earth. In the same way military strength is stored up in the mass of the people—invisible in times of peace but always ready for use as a source of power. The attributes of the two trigrams are danger inside and obedience outside. This points to the nature of an army, which at the core is dangerous, while discipline and obedience must prevail outside.

Of the individual lines, the one that controls the hexagram is the strong nine in the second place, to which the other lines, all yielding, are subordinate. This line indicates a commander, because it stands in the middle of one of the two trigrams. But since it is in the lower rather than the upper trigram, it represents not the ruler but the efficient general, who maintains obedience in the army by his authority.

THE JUDGMENT

THE ARMY. The army needs perseverance
And a strong man.
Good fortune without blame.

An army is a mass that needs organization in order to become a fighting force. Without strict discipline nothing can be accomplished, but this discipline must not be achieved by force. It requires a strong man who captures the hearts of the people and awakens their enthusiasm. In order that he may develop his abilities he needs the complete confidence of his ruler, who must entrust him with full responsibility as long as the war lasts. But war is always a dangerous thing and brings with it destruction and devastation. Therefore it should not be resorted to rashly but, like a poisonous drug, should be used as a last recourse.

The justifying cause of a war, and clear and intelligible war aims, ought to be explained to the people by an experienced leader. Unless there is a quite definite war aim to which the people can consciously pledge themselves, the unity and strength of conviction that lead to victory will not be forthcoming. But the leader must also look to it that the passion of war and the delirium of victory do not give rise to unjust acts that will not meet with general approval. If justice and perseverance are the basis of action, all goes well.

THE IMAGE

In the middle of the earth is water:
The image of THE ARMY.
Thus the superior man increases his masses
By generosity toward the people.

Ground water is invisibly present within the earth. In the same way the military power of a people is invisibly present in the masses. When danger threatens, every peasant becomes a soldier; when the war ends, he goes back to his plow. He who is generous toward the people wins their love, and a people living under a mild rule becomes strong and powerful. Only a people economically strong can be important in military power. Such power must therefore be cultivated by improving the economic condition of the people and by humane government. Only when there is this invisible bond between government and people, so that the people are sheltered by their government as ground water is sheltered by the earth, is it possible to wage a victorious war.

THE LINES

Six at the beginning means:
An army must set forth in proper order.
If the order is not good, misfortune threatens.

At the beginning of a military enterprise, order is imperative. A just and valid cause must exist, and the obedience and co-ordination of the troops must be well organized, otherwise the result is inevitably failure.

○ Nine in the second place means:
In the midst of the army.
Good fortune. No blame.
The king bestows a triple decoration.

The leader should be in the midst of his army, in touch with it, sharing good and bad with the masses he leads. This alone makes him equal to the heavy demands made upon him. He needs also the recognition of the ruler. The decorations he receives are justified, because there is no question of personal preferment here: the whole army, whose center he is, is honored in his person.

> Six in the third place means:
> Perchance the army carries corpses in the wagon.
> Misfortune.

Here we have a choice of two explanations. One points to defeat because someone other than the chosen leader interferes with the command; the other is similar in its general meaning, but the expression, "carries corpses in the wagon," is interpreted differently. At burials and at sacrifices to the dead it was customary in China for the deceased to whom the sacrifice was made to be represented by a boy of the family, who sat in the dead man's place and was honored as his representative. On the basis of this custom the text is interpreted as meaning that a "corpse boy" is sitting in the wagon, or, in other words, that authority is not being exercised by the proper leaders but has been usurped by others. Perhaps the whole difficulty clears up if it is inferred that there has been an error in copying. The character *fan*, meaning "all," may have been misread as *shih*, which means "corpse." Allowing for this error, the meaning would be that if the multitude assumes leadership of the army (rides in the wagon), misfortune will ensue.

> Six in the fourth place means:
> The army retreats. No blame.

In face of a superior enemy, with whom it would be hopeless to engage in battle, an orderly retreat is the only correct procedure, because it will save the army from defeat and disintegration. It is by no means a sign of courage or strength to insist upon engaging in a hopeless struggle regardless of circumstances.

> O Six in the fifth place means:
> There is game in the field.
> It furthers one to catch it.
> Without blame.

Let the eldest lead the army.
The younger transports corpses;
Then perseverance brings misfortune.

Game is in the field—it has left its usual haunts in the forest and is devastating the fields. This points to an enemy invasion. Energetic combat and punishment are here thoroughly justified, but they must not degenerate into a wild melee in which everyone fends for himself. Despite the greatest degree of perseverance and bravery, this would lead to misfortune. The army must be directed by an experienced leader. It is a matter of waging war, not of permitting the mob to slaughter all who fall into their hands; if they do, defeat will be the result, and despite all perseverance there is danger of misfortune.

Six at the top means:
The great prince issues commands,
Founds states, vests families with fiefs.
Inferior people should not be employed.

The war has ended successfully, victory is won, and the king divides estates and fiefs among his faithful vassals. But it is important that inferior people should not come into power. If they have helped, let them be paid off with money, but they should not be awarded lands or the privileges of rulers, lest power be abused.

比

8. *Pi / Holding Together* [*Union*]

☰☰	*above* K'AN	THE ABYSMAL, WATER
☷☷	*below* K'UN	THE RECEPTIVE, EARTH

The waters on the surface of the earth flow together wherever they can, as for example in the ocean, where all the rivers come together. Symbolically this connotes holding together and the laws that regulate it. The same idea is suggested by the fact that all the lines of the hexagram except the fifth, the place of the ruler, are yielding. The yielding lines hold together because they are influenced by a man of strong will in the leading position, a man who is their center of union. Moreover, this strong and guiding personality in turn holds together with the others, finding in them the complement of his own nature.

THE JUDGMENT

HOLDING TOGETHER brings good fortune.
Inquire of the oracle once again
Whether you possess sublimity, constancy, and
   perseverance;
Then there is no blame.
Those who are uncertain gradually join.
Whoever comes too late
Meets with misfortune.

What is required is that we unite with others, in order that all may complement and aid one another through holding together. But such holding together calls for a central figure around whom other persons may unite. To become a center of influence holding people together is a grave matter and fraught with great responsibility. It requires greatness of spirit, consistency, and strength. Therefore let him who wishes to gather others about him ask himself whether he is equal to the undertaking, for anyone attempting the task without a real calling for it only makes confusion worse than if no union at all had taken place.

But when there is a real rallying point, those who at first are hesitant or uncertain gradually come in of their own accord. Late-comers must suffer the consequences, for in holding together the question of the right time is also important. Relationships are formed and firmly established according to definite inner laws. Common experiences strengthen these ties, and he who comes too late to share in these basic experiences must suffer for it if, as a straggler, he finds the door locked.

If a man has recognized the necessity for union and does not feel strong enough to function as the center, it is his duty to become a member of some other organic fellowship.

THE IMAGE

On the earth is water:
The image of HOLDING TOGETHER.
Thus the kings of antiquity
Bestowed the different states as fiefs
And cultivated friendly relations
With the feudal lords.

Water fills up all the empty places on the earth and clings fast to it. The social organization of ancient China was based on this principle of the holding together of dependents and rulers. Water flows to unite with water, because all parts of it are subject to the same laws. So too should human society hold together through a community of interests that allows each individual to feel himself a member of a whole. The central power of a social organization must see to it that every member finds that his true interest lies in holding together with it, as was the case in the paternal relationship between king and vassals in ancient China.

THE LINES

Six at the beginning means:
Hold to him in truth and loyalty;
This is without blame.
Truth, like a full earthen bowl:
Thus in the end
Good fortune comes from without.

Fundamental sincerity is the only proper basis for forming relationships. This attitude, symbolized by a full earthen bowl, in which the content is everything and the empty form nothing, shows itself not in clever words but through the strength of what lies within the speaker. This strength is so great that it has power to attract good fortune to itself from without.

> Six in the second place means:
> Hold to him inwardly.
> Perseverance brings good fortune.

If a person responds perseveringly and in the right way to the behests from above that summon him to action, his relations with others are intrinsic and he does not lose himself. But if a man seeks association with others as if he were an obsequious office hunter, he throws himself away. He does not follow the path of the superior man, who never loses his dignity.

> Six in the third place means:
> You hold together with the wrong people.

We are often among people who do not belong to our own sphere. In that case we must beware of being drawn into false intimacy through force of habit. Needless to say, this would have evil consequences. Maintaining sociability without intimacy is the only right attitude toward such people, because otherwise we should not be free to enter into relationship with people of our own kind later on.

> Six in the fourth place means:
> Hold to him outwardly also.
> Perseverance brings good fortune.

Here the relations with a man who is the center of union are well established. Then we may, and indeed we should, show our attachment openly. But we must remain constant and not allow ourselves to be led astray.

> ○ Nine in the fifth place means:
> Manifestation of holding together.
> In the hunt the king uses beaters on three sides only
> And foregoes game that runs off in front.
> The citizens need no warning.
> Good fortune.

In the royal hunts of ancient China it was customary to drive up the game from three sides, but on the fourth the animals had a chance to run off. If they failed to do this they had to pass through a gate behind which the king stood ready to shoot. Only animals that entered here were shot; those that ran off in front were permitted to escape. This custom accorded with a kingly attitude; the royal hunter did not wish to turn the chase into a slaughter, but held that the kill should consist only of those animals which had so to speak voluntarily exposed themselves.

There is depicted here a ruler, or influential man, to whom people are attracted. Those who come to him he accepts, those who do not come are allowed to go their own way. He invites none, flatters none—all come of their own free will. In this way there develops a voluntary dependence among those who hold to him. They do not have to be constantly on their guard but may express their opinions openly. Police measures are not necessary, and they cleave to their ruler of their own volition. The same principle of freedom is valid for life in general. We should not woo favor from people. If a man cultivates within himself the purity and the strength that are necessary for one who is the center of a fellowship, those who are meant for him come of their own accord.

> Six at the top means:
> He finds no head for holding together.
> Misfortune.

The head is the beginning. If the beginning is not right, there is no hope of a right ending. If we have missed the right moment for union and go on hesitating to give complete and full devotion, we shall regret the error when it is too late.

9. *Hsiao Ch'u / The Taming Power of the Small*

☴	*above*	SUN	THE GENTLE, WIND
☰	*below*	CH'IEN	THE CREATIVE, HEAVEN

This hexagram means the force of the small—the power of the shadowy—that restrains, tames, impedes. A weak line in the fourth place, that of the minister, [1] holds the five strong lines in check. In the Image it is the wind blowing across the sky. The wind restrains the clouds, the rising breath of the Creative, and makes them grow dense, but as yet is not strong enough to turn them to rain. The hexagram presents a configuration of circumstances in which a strong element is temporarily held in leash by a weak element. It is only through gentleness that this can have a successful outcome.

THE JUDGMENT

THE TAMING POWER OF THE SMALL
Has success.
Dense clouds, no rain from our western region.

This image refers to the state of affairs in China at the time when King Wên, who came originally from the west, was in the east at the court of the reigning tyrant Chou Hsin. The moment for action on a large scale had not yet arrived. King Wên could only keep the tyrant somewhat in check by friendly persuasion. Hence the image of many clouds, promising moisture and blessing to the land, although as yet no rain falls. The situation is not unfavorable; there is a prospect of ultimate success, but there are still obstacles in the way, and we can merely take preparatory measures. Only through the small

---

1. [See p. 360.]

means of friendly persuasion can we exert any influence. The time has not yet come for sweeping measures. However, we may be able, to a limited extent, to act as a restraining and subduing influence. To carry out our purpose we need firm determination within and gentleness and adaptability in external relations.

THE IMAGE

The wind drives across heaven:
The image of THE TAMING POWER OF THE SMALL.
Thus the superior man
Refines the outward aspect of his nature.

The wind can indeed drive the clouds together in the sky; yet, being nothing but air, without solid body, it does not produce great or lasting effects. So also an individual, in times when he can produce no great effect in the outer world, can do nothing except refine the expression of his nature in small ways.

THE LINES

Nine at the beginning means:
Return to the way.
How could there be blame in this?
Good fortune.

It lies in the nature of a strong man to press forward. In so doing he encounters obstructions. Therefore he returns to the way suited to his situation, where he is free to advance or to retreat. In the nature of things this will bring good fortune, for it is wise and reasonable not to try to obtain anything by force.

Nine in the second place means:
He allows himself to be drawn into returning.
Good fortune.

One would like to press forward, but before going farther one sees from the example of others like oneself that this way is blocked. In such a case, if the effort to push forward is not in harmony with the time,[2] a reasonable and resolute man will

2. [See p. 359 for an explanation of what is meant by the "time."]

41

not expose himself to a personal rebuff, but will retreat with others of like mind. This brings good fortune, because he does not needlessly jeopardize himself.

> Nine in the third place means:
> The spokes burst out of the wagon wheels.
> Man and wife roll their eyes.

Here an attempt is made to press forward forcibly, in the consciousness that the obstructing power is slight. But since, under the circumstances, power actually lies with the weak, this sudden offensive is doomed to failure. External conditions hinder the advance, just as loss of the wheel spokes stops the progress of a wagon. We do not yet heed this hint from fate, hence there are annoying arguments like those of a married couple. Naturally this is not a favorable state of things, for though the situation may enable the weaker side to hold its ground, the difficulties are too numerous to permit of a happy result. In consequence even the strong man cannot so use his power as to exert the right influence on those around him. He experiences a rebuff where he expected an easy victory, and he thus compromises his dignity.

> □ Six in the fourth place means:
> If you are sincere, blood vanishes and fear gives way.
> No blame.

If one is in the difficult and responsible position of counselor to a powerful man, one should restrain him in such a way that right may prevail. Therein lies a danger so great that the threat of actual bloodshed may arise. Nonetheless, the power of disinterested truth is greater than all these obstacles. It carries such weight that the end is achieved, and all danger of bloodshed and all fear disappear.

> ○ Nine in the fifth place means:
> If you are sincere and loyally attached,
> You are rich in your neighbor.

Loyalty leads to firm ties because it means that each partner complements the other. In the weaker person loyalty consists

42

in devotion, in the stronger it consists in trustworthiness. This relation of mutual reinforcement leads to a true wealth that is all the more apparent because it is not selfishly hoarded but is shared with friends. Pleasure shared is pleasure doubled.

> Nine at the top means:
> The rain comes, there is rest.
> This is due to the lasting effect of character.
> Perseverance brings the woman into danger.
> The moon is nearly full.
> If the superior man persists,
> Misfortune comes.

Success is at hand. The wind has driven up the rain. A fixed standpoint has been reached. This has come about through the cumulation of small effects produced by reverence for a superior character. But a success thus secured bit by bit calls for great caution. It would be a dangerous illusion for anyone to think he could presume upon it. The female principle, the weak element that has won the victory, should never persist in vaunting it—that would lead to danger. The dark power in the moon is strongest when the moon is almost full. When it is full and directly opposite the sun, its waning is inevitable. Under such circumstances one must be content with what has been achieved. To advance any further, before the appropriate time has come, would lead to misfortune.

10. Lü / Treading [Conduct]

above	CH'IEN	THE CREATIVE, HEAVEN
below	TUI	THE JOYOUS, LAKE

The name of the hexagram means on the one hand the right way of conducting oneself. Heaven, the father, is above, and the lake, the youngest daughter, is below. This shows the difference between high and low, upon which composure, correct social conduct, depends. On the other hand, the word for the name of the hexagram, TREADING,[1] means literally treading upon something. The small and cheerful [Tui] treads upon the large and strong [Ch'ien]. The direction of movement of the two primary trigrams is upward. The fact that the strong treads on the weak is not mentioned in the Book of Changes, because it is taken for granted. For the weak to take a stand against the strong is not dangerous here, because it happens in good humor [Tui] and without presumption, so that the strong man is not irritated but takes it all in good part.

THE JUDGMENT

TREADING. Treading upon the tail of the tiger.
It does not bite the man. Success.

The situation is really difficult. That which is strongest and that which is weakest are close together. The weak follows behind the strong and worries it. The strong, however, acquiesces and does not hurt the weak, because the contact is in good humor and harmless.

In terms of a human situation, one is handling wild, intractable people. In such a case one's purpose will be achieved if one behaves with decorum. Pleasant manners succeed even with irritable people.

44

THE IMAGE

Heaven above, the lake below:
The image of TREADING.
Thus the superior man discriminates between high
    and low,
And thereby fortifies the thinking of the people.

Heaven and the lake show a difference of elevation that inheres in the natures of the two, hence no envy arises. Among mankind also there are necessarily differences of elevation; it is impossible to bring about universal equality. But it is important that differences in social rank should not be arbitrary and unjust, for if this occurs, envy and class struggle are the inevitable consequences. If, on the other hand, external differences in rank correspond with differences in inner worth, and if inner worth forms the criterion of external rank, people acquiesce and order reigns in society.

THE LINES

Nine at the beginning means:
Simple conduct. Progress without blame.

The situation is one in which we are still not bound by any obligations of social intercourse. If our conduct is simple, we remain free of them. We can quietly follow our predilections as long as we are content and make no demands on people.

The meaning of the hexagram is not standstill but progress. A man finds himself in an altogether inferior position at the start. However, he has the inner strength that guarantees progress. If he can be content with simplicity, he can make progress without blame. When a man is dissatisfied with modest circumstances, he is restless and ambitious and tries to advance, not for the sake of accomplishing anything worth while, but merely in order to escape from lowliness and poverty by dint of his conduct. Once his purpose is achieved, he is certain to become arrogant and luxury-loving. Therefore blame attaches to his progress. On the other hand, a man who

1. [*Auftreten*, the German word used for the name of the hexagram, means both "treading" and "conduct."]

45

is good at his work is content to behave simply. He wishes to make progress in order to accomplish something. When he attains his goal, he does something worth while, and all is well.

> Nine in the second place means:
> Treading a smooth, level course.
> The perseverance of a dark man[2]
> Brings good fortune.

The situation of a lonely sage is indicated here. He remains withdrawn from the bustle of life, seeks nothing, asks nothing of anyone, and is not dazzled by enticing goals. He is true to himself and travels through life unassailed, on a level road. Since he is content and does not challenge fate, he remains free of entanglements.

> ☐ Six in the third place means:
> A one-eyed man is able to see,
> A lame man is able to tread.
> He treads on the tail of the tiger.
> The tiger bites the man.
> Misfortune.
> Thus does a warrior act on behalf of his great prince.

A one-eyed man can indeed see, but not enough for clear vision. A lame man can indeed tread, but not enough to make progress. If in spite of such defects a man considers himself strong and consequently exposes himself to danger, he is inviting disaster, for he is undertaking something beyond his strength. This reckless way of plunging ahead, regardless of the adequacy of one's powers, can be justified only in the case of a warrior battling for his prince.

> Nine in the fourth place means:
> He treads on the tail of the tiger.
> Caution and circumspection
> Lead ultimately to good fortune.

---

2. [See explanation of this line in bk. III, pp. 437–38.]

This text refers to a dangerous enterprise. The inner power to carry it through is there, but this inner power is combined with hesitating caution in one's external attitude. This line contrasts with the preceding line, which is weak within but outwardly presses forward. Here one is sure of ultimate success, which consists in achieving one's purpose, that is, in overcoming danger by going forward.

○ Nine in the fifth place means:
Resolute conduct.
Perseverance with awareness of danger.

This refers to the ruler of the hexagram as a whole. One sees that one has to be resolute in conduct. But at the same time one must remain conscious of the danger connected with such resoluteness, especially if it is to be persevered in. Only awareness of the danger makes success possible.

Nine at the top means:
Look to your conduct and weigh the favorable signs.
When everything is fulfilled, supreme good fortune comes.

The work is ended. If we want to know whether good fortune will follow, we must look back upon our conduct and its consequences. If the effects are good, then good fortune is certain. No one knows himself. It is only by the consequences of his actions, by the fruit of his labors, that a man can judge what he is to expect.

11. *T'ai* / Peace

☷ *above* K'UN   THE RECEPTIVE, EARTH
☰ *below* CH'IEN   THE CREATIVE, HEAVEN

The Receptive, which moves downward, stands above; the Creative, which moves upward, is below. Hence their influences meet and are in harmony, so that all living things bloom and prosper. This hexagram belongs to the first month (February–March), at which time the forces of nature prepare the new spring.

THE JUDGMENT

PEACE. The small departs,
The great approaches.
Good fortune. Success.

This hexagram denotes a time in nature when heaven seems to be on earth. Heaven has placed itself beneath the earth, and so their powers unite in deep harmony. Then peace and blessing descend upon all living things.

In the world of man it is a time of social harmony; those in high places show favor to the lowly, and the lowly and inferior in their turn are well disposed toward the highly placed. There is an end to all feuds.

Inside, at the center, in the key position, is the light principle; the dark principle is outside. Thus the light has a powerful influence, while the dark is submissive. In this way each receives its due. When the good elements of society occupy a central position and are in control, the evil elements come under their influence and change for the better. When the spirit of heaven rules in man, his animal nature also comes under its influence and takes its appropriate place.

The individual lines enter the hexagram from below and leave it again at the top. Here the small, weak, and evil elements are about to take their departure, while the great, strong, and good elements are moving up. This brings good fortune and success.

THE IMAGE

Heaven and earth unite: the image of PEACE.

Thus the ruler

Divides and completes the course of heaven and
    earth;

He furthers and regulates the gifts of heaven and
    earth,

And so aids the people.

Heaven and earth are in contact and combine their influences, producing a time of universal flowering and prosperity. This stream of energy must be regulated by the ruler of men. It is done by a process of division. Thus men divide the uniform flow of time into the seasons, according to the succession of natural phenomena, and mark off infinite space by the points of the compass. In this way nature in its overwhelming profusion of phenomena is bounded and controlled. On the other hand, nature must be furthered in her productiveness. This is done by adjusting the products to the right time and the right place, which increases the natural yield. This controlling and furthering activity of man in his relation to nature is the work on nature that rewards him.

THE LINES

Nine at the beginning means:

When ribbon grass is pulled up, the sod comes with it.

Each according to his kind.

Undertakings bring good fortune.

In times of prosperity every able man called to fill an office draws like-minded people along with him, just as in pulling

49

up ribbon grass one always pulls up a bunch of it, because the stalks are connected by their roots. In such times, when it is possible to extend influence widely, the mind of an able man is set upon going out into life and accomplishing something.

○ Nine in the second place means:

Bearing with the uncultured in gentleness,

Fording the river with resolution,

Not neglecting what is distant,

Not regarding one's companions:

Thus one may manage to walk in the middle.

In times of prosperity it is important above all to possess enough greatness of soul to bear with imperfect people. For in the hands of a great master no material is unproductive; he can find use for everything. But this generosity is by no means laxity or weakness. It is during times of prosperity especially that we must always be ready to risk even dangerous undertakings, such as the crossing of a river, if they are necessary. So too we must not neglect what is distant but must attend scrupulously to everything. Factionalism and the dominance of cliques are especially to be avoided. Even if people of like mind come forward together, they ought not to form a faction by holding together for mutual advantage; instead, each man should do his duty. These are four ways in which one can overcome the hidden danger of a gradual slackening that always lurks in any time of peace. And that is how one finds the middle way for action.

Nine in the third place means:

No plain not followed by a slope.

No going not followed by a return.

He who remains persevering in danger

Is without blame.

Do not complain about this truth;

Enjoy the good fortune you still possess.

Everything on earth is subject to change. Prosperity is followed by decline: this is the eternal law on earth. Evil can indeed be held in check but not permanently abolished. It always returns. This conviction might induce melancholy, but it should not; it ought only to keep us from falling into illusion when good fortune comes to us. If we continue mindful of the danger, we remain persevering and make no mistakes. As long as a man's inner nature remains stronger and richer than anything offered by external fortune, as long as he remains inwardly superior to fate, fortune will not desert him.

> Six in the fourth place means:
> He flutters down, not boasting of his wealth,
> Together with his neighbor,
> Guileless and sincere.

In times of mutual confidence, people of high rank come in close contact with the lowly quite simply and without boasting of their wealth. This is not due to the force of circumstances but corresponds with their inmost sentiment. The approach is made quite spontaneously, because it is based on inner conviction.

> ○ Six in the fifth place means:
> The sovereign I
> Gives his daughter in marriage.
> This brings blessing
> And supreme good fortune.

The sovereign I is T'ang the Completer.[1] By his decree the imperial princesses, although higher in rank than their husbands, had to obey them like all other wives. Here too we are shown a truly modest union of high and low that brings happiness and blessings.

> Six at the top means:
> The wall falls back into the moat.
> Use no army now.

---

1. [This refers to Ch'êng T'ang, the first of the Shang rulers, whose reign is thought to have begun in 1766 B.C. However, modern Chinese scholarship no longer accepts the identification of the Emperor I (1191–1155 B.C., according to tradition) with T'ang, and holds that the daughter mentioned was given to King Wên's father, or perhaps to King Wên himself.]

Make your commands known within your own town.
Perseverance brings humiliation.

The change alluded to in the middle of the hexagram has begun to take place. The wall of the town sinks back into the moat from which it was dug. The hour of doom is at hand. When matters have come to this pass, we should submit to fate and not try to stave it off by violent resistance. The one recourse left us is to hold our own within our intimate circle. Should we persevere in trying to resist the evil in the usual way, our collapse would only be more complete, and humiliation would be the result.

12. *P'i / Standstill* [*Stagnation*]

above	CH'IEN	THE CREATIVE, HEAVEN
below	K'UN	THE RECEPTIVE, EARTH

This hexagram is the opposite of the preceding one. Heaven is above, drawing farther and farther away, while the earth below sinks farther into the depths. The creative powers are not in relation. It is a time of standstill and decline. This hexagram is linked with the seventh month (August–September), when the year has passed its zenith and autumnal decay is setting in.

THE JUDGMENT

STANDSTILL. Evil people do not further
The perseverance of the superior man.
The great departs; the small approaches.

Heaven and earth are out of communion and all things are benumbed. What is above has no relation to what is below, and on earth confusion and disorder prevail. The dark power is within, the light power is without. Weakness is within, harshness without. Within are the inferior, and without are the superior. The way of inferior people is in ascent; the way of superior people is on the decline. But the superior people do not allow themselves to be turned from their principles. If the possibility of exerting influence is closed to them, they nevertheless remain faithful to their principles and withdraw into seclusion.

THE IMAGE

Heaven and earth do not unite:

The image of STANDSTILL.

Thus the superior man falls back upon his inner
     worth

In order to escape the difficulties.

He does not permit himself to be honored with
     revenue.

When, owing to the influence of inferior men, mutual mistrust prevails in public life, fruitful activity is rendered impossible, because the fundaments are wrong. Therefore the superior man knows what he must do under such circumstances; he does not allow himself to be tempted by dazzling offers to take part in public activities. This would only expose him to danger, since he cannot assent to the meanness of the others. He therefore hides his worth and withdraws into seclusion.

THE LINES

Six at the beginning means:

When ribbon grass is pulled up, the sod comes with it.

Each according to his kind.

Perseverance brings good fortune and success.

The text is almost the same as that of the first line of the preceding hexagram, but with a contrary meaning. In the latter a man is drawing another along with him on the road to an official career; here a man is drawing another with him into retirement from public life. This is why the text says here,

"Perseverance brings good fortune and success," and not "Undertakings bring good fortune." If it becomes impossible to make our influence count, it is only by retirement that we spare ourselves humiliation. Success in a higher sense can be ours, because we know how to safeguard the value of our personalities.

☐ Six in the second place means:
  They bear and endure;
  This means good fortune for inferior people.
  The standstill serves to help the great man to attain
    success.

Inferior people are ready to flatter their superiors in a servile way. They would also endure the superior man if he would put an end to their confusion. This is fortunate for them. But the great man calmly bears the consequences of the standstill. He does not mingle with the crowd of the inferior; that is not his place. By his willingness to suffer personally he insures the success of his fundamental principles.

  Six in the third place means:
  They bear shame.

Inferior people who have risen to power illegitimately do not feel equal to the responsibility they have taken upon themselves. In their hearts they begin to be ashamed, although at first they do not show it outwardly. This marks a turn for the better.

  Nine in the fourth place means:
  He who acts at the command of the highest
  Remains without blame.
  Those of like mind partake of the blessing.

The time of standstill is nearing the point of change into its opposite. Whoever wishes to restore order must feel himself called to the task and have the necessary authority. A man who sets himself up as capable of creating order according to his own judgment could make mistakes and end in failure. But the man who is truly called to the task is favored by the conditions of the time, and all those of like mind will share in his blessing.

○ Nine in the fifth place means:
　Standstill is giving way.
　Good fortune for the great man.
"What if it should fail, what if it should fail?"
　In this way he ties it to a cluster of mulberry shoots.

The time undergoes a change. The right man, able to restore order, has arrived. Hence "Good fortune." But such periods of transition are the very times in which we must fear and tremble. Success is assured only through greatest caution, which asks always, "What if it should fail?" When a mulberry bush is cut down, a number of unusually strong shoots sprout from the roots. Hence the image of tying something to a cluster of mulberry shoots is used to symbolize the way of making success certain. Confucius says about this line:

Danger arises when a man feels secure in his position. Destruction threatens when a man seeks to preserve his worldly estate. Confusion develops when a man has put everything in order. Therefore the superior man does not forget danger in his security, nor ruin when he is well established, nor confusion when his affairs are in order. In this way he gains personal safety and is able to protect the empire.

Nine at the top means:
　The standstill comes to an end.
　First standstill, then good fortune.

The standstill does not last forever. However, it does not cease of its own accord; the right man is needed to end it. This is the difference between a state of peace and a state of stagnation. Continuous effort is necessary to maintain peace: left to itself it would change into stagnation and disintegration. The time of disintegration, however, does not change back automatically to a condition of peace and prosperity; effort must be put forth in order to end it. This shows the creative attitude that man must take if the world is to be put in order.

同人

13. *T'ung Jên / Fellowship with Men*

above	CH'IEN	THE CREATIVE, HEAVEN
below	LI	THE CLINGING, FLAME

The image of the upper trigram Ch'ien is heaven, and that of
the lower, Li, is flame. It is the nature of fire to flame up to
heaven. This gives the idea of fellowship. It is the second line
that, by virtue of its central character, unites the five strong
lines around it. This hexagram forms a complement to Shih,
THE ARMY (7). In the latter, danger is within and obedience
without—the character of a warlike army, which, in order to
hold together, needs one strong man among the many who
are weak. Here, clarity is within and strength without—the
character of a peaceful union of men, which, in order to hold
together, needs one yielding nature among many firm persons.

THE JUDGMENT

FELLOWSHIP WITH MEN in the open.
Success.
It furthers one to cross the great water.
The perseverance of the superior man furthers.

True fellowship among men must be based upon a concern
that is universal. It is not the private interests of the individual
that create lasting fellowship among men, but rather the goals
of humanity. That is why it is said that fellowship with men
in the open succeeds. If unity of this kind prevails, even difficult and dangerous tasks, such as crossing the great water,
can be accomplished. But in order to bring about this sort of
fellowship, a persevering and enlightened leader is needed—

a man with clear, convincing, and inspiring aims and the strength to carry them out. (The inner trigram means clarity; the outer, strength.)

THE IMAGE

Heaven together with fire:
The image of FELLOWSHIP WITH MEN.
Thus the superior man organizes the clans
And makes distinctions between things.

Heaven has the same direction of movement as fire, yet it is different from fire. Just as the luminaries in the sky serve for the systematic division and arrangement of time, so human society and all things that really belong together must be organically arranged. Fellowship should not be a mere mingling of individuals or of things—that would be chaos, not fellowship. If fellowship is to lead to order, there must be organization within diversity.

THE LINES

Nine at the beginning means:
Fellowship with men at the gate.
No blame.

The beginning of union among people should take place before the door. All are equally close to one another. No divergent aims have yet arisen, and one makes no mistakes. The basic principles of any kind of union must be equally accessible to all concerned. Secret agreements bring misfortune.

O Six in the second place means:
Fellowship with men in the clan.
Humiliation.

There is danger here of formation of a separate faction on the basis of personal and egotistic interests. Such factions, which are exclusive and, instead of welcoming all men, must condemn one group in order to unite the others, originate from low motives and therefore lead in the course of time to humiliation.

Nine in the third place means:
He hides weapons in the thicket;
He climbs the high hill in front of it.
For three years he does not rise up.

Here fellowship has changed about to mistrust. Each man distrusts the other, plans a secret ambush, and seeks to spy on his fellow from afar. We are dealing with an obstinate opponent whom we cannot come at by this method. Obstacles standing in the way of fellowship with others are shown here. One has mental reservations for one's own part and seeks to take his opponent by surprise. This very fact makes one mistrustful, suspecting the same wiles in his opponent and trying to ferret them out. The result is that one departs further and further from true fellowship. The longer this goes on, the more alienated one becomes.

Nine in the fourth place means:
He climbs up on his wall; he cannot attack.
Good fortune.

Here the reconciliation that follows quarrel moves nearer. It is true that there are still dividing walls on which we stand confronting one another. But the difficulties are too great. We get into straits, and this brings us to our senses. We cannot fight, and therein lies our good fortune.

○ Nine in the fifth place means:
Men bound in fellowship first weep and lament,
But afterward they laugh.
After great struggles they succeed in meeting.

Two people are outwardly separated, but in their hearts they are united. They are kept apart by their positions in life. Many difficulties and obstructions arise between them and cause them grief. But, remaining true to each other, they allow nothing to separate them, and although it costs them a severe struggle to overcome the obstacles, they will succeed. When they come together their sadness will change to joy. Confucius says of this:

Life leads the thoughtful man on a path of many windings.
Now the course is checked, now it runs straight again.
Here winged thoughts may pour freely forth in words,
There the heavy burden of knowledge must be shut away in
  silence.
But when two people are at one in their inmost hearts,
They shatter even the strength of iron or of bronze.
And when two people understand each other in their inmost
  hearts,
Their words are sweet and strong, like the fragrance of
  orchids.

Nine at the top means:
Fellowship with men in the meadow.
No remorse.

The warm attachment that springs from the heart is lacking
here. We are by this time actually outside of fellowship with
others. However, we ally ourselves with them. The fellowship
does not include all, but only those who happen to dwell near
one another. The meadow is the pasture at the entrance to
the town. At this stage, the ultimate goal of the union of mankind has not yet been attained, but we need not reproach ourselves. We join the community without separate aims of our
own.

大有

14. *Ta Yu / Possession in Great Measure*

	above	LI	THE CLINGING, FLAME
	below	CH'IEN	THE CREATIVE, HEAVEN

The fire in heaven above shines far, and all things stand out in
the light and become manifest. The weak fifth line occupies
the place of honor, and all the strong lines are in accord with it.

All things come to the man who is modest and kind in a high position.[1]

THE JUDGMENT

POSSESSION IN GREAT MEASURE.
Supreme success.

The two trigrams indicate that strength and clarity unite. Possession in great measure is determined by fate and accords with the time. How is it possible that the weak line has power to hold the strong lines fast and to possess them? It is done by virtue of unselfish modesty. The time is favorable—a time of strength within, clarity and culture without. Power is expressing itself in a graceful and controlled way. This brings supreme success and wealth.[2]

THE IMAGE

Fire in heaven above:
The image of POSSESSION IN GREAT MEASURE.
Thus the superior man curbs evil and furthers good,
And thereby obeys the benevolent will of heaven.

The sun in heaven above, shedding light over everything on earth, is the image of possession on a grand scale. But a possession of this sort must be administered properly. The sun brings both evil and good into the light of day. Man must combat and curb the evil, and must favor and promote the good. Only in this way does he fulfill the benevolent will of God, who desires only good and not evil.

THE LINES

Nine at the beginning means:
No relationship with what is harmful;
There is no blame in this.

---

1. The meaning of this hexagram parallels the saying of Jesus: "Blessed are the meek: for they shall inherit the earth."

2. It might be supposed that HOLDING TOGETHER (8) would be a more favorable hexagram than POSSESSION IN GREAT MEASURE, because in the former one strong individual gathers five weak ones around him. But the judgment added in the present hexagram,

> If one remains conscious of difficulty,
> One remains without blame.

Great possession that is still in its beginnings and that has not yet been challenged brings no blame, since there has been no opportunity to make mistakes. Yet there are many difficulties to be overcome. It is only by remaining conscious of these difficulties that one can keep inwardly free of possible arrogance and wastefulness, and thus in principle overcome all cause for blame.

> Nine in the second place means:
> A big wagon for loading.
> One may undertake something.
> No blame.

Great possession consists not only in the quantity of goods at one's disposal, but, first and foremost, in their mobility and utility, for then they can be used in undertakings, and we remain free of embarrassment and mistakes. The big wagon, which will carry a heavy load and in which one can journey far, means that there are at hand able helpers who give their support and are equal to their task. One can load great responsibility upon such persons, and this is necessary in important undertakings.

> Nine in the third place means:
> A prince offers it to the Son of Heaven.
> A petty man cannot do this.

A magnanimous, liberal-minded man should not regard what he possesses as his exclusive personal property, but should place it at the disposal of the ruler or of the people at large. In so doing, he takes the right attitude toward his possession, which as private property can never endure. A petty man is incapable

---

"Supreme success," is much the more favorable. The reason is that in the eighth hexagram the men held together by the powerful ruler are only simple subordinate persons, while here those who stand as helpers at the side of the mild ruler are strong and able individuals.

of this. He is harmed by great possessions, because instead of sacrificing them, he would keep them for himself. [3]

> Nine in the fourth place means:
> He makes a difference
> Between himself and his neighbor.
> No blame.

This characterizes the position of a man placed among rich and powerful neighbors. It is a dangerous position. He must look neither to the right nor to the left, and must shun envy and the temptation to vie with others. In this way he remains free of mistakes. [4]

> O Six in the fifth place means:
> He whose truth is accessible, yet dignified,
> Has good fortune.

The situation is very favorable. People are being won not by coercion but by unaffected sincerity, so that they are attached to us in sincerity and truth. However, benevolence alone is not sufficient at the time of POSSESSION IN GREAT MEASURE. For insolence might begin to spread. Insolence must be kept in bounds by dignity; then good fortune is assured.

> Nine at the top means:
> He is blessed by heaven.
> Good fortune.
> Nothing that does not further.

In the fullness of possession and at the height of power, one remains modest and gives honor to the sage who stands outside

---

3. This offers the same dictum about possessions as that found in the words of the Bible: "Whosoever shall seek to save his life shall lose it; and whosoever shall lose his life shall preserve it" [Luke 17:33].

4. Another generally accepted translation of the line is as follows:
> He does not rely on his abundance.
> No blame.

This would mean that the individual avoids mistakes because he possesses as if he possessed nothing.

the affairs of the world. By this means one puts oneself under the beneficent influence descending from heaven, and all goes well. Confucius says of this line:

To bless means to help. Heaven helps the man who is devoted; men help the man who is true. He who walks in truth and is devoted in his thinking, and furthermore reveres the worthy, is blessed by heaven. He has good fortune, and there is nothing that would not further.

謙

15. *Ch'ien* / *Modesty*

	above	K'UN	THE RECEPTIVE, EARTH
	below	KÊN	KEEPING STILL, MOUNTAIN

This hexagram is made up of the trigrams Kên, Keeping Still, mountain, and K'un. The mountain is the youngest son of the Creative, the representative of heaven on earth. It dispenses the blessings of heaven, the clouds and rain that gather round its summit, and thereafter shines forth radiant with heavenly light. This shows what modesty is and how it functions in great and strong men. K'un, the earth, stands above. Lowliness is a quality of the earth: this is the very reason why it appears in this hexagram as exalted, by being placed above the mountain. This shows how modesty functions in lowly, simple people: they are lifted up by it.

THE JUDGMENT

MODESTY creates success.

The superior man carries things through.

It is the law of heaven to make fullness empty and to make full what is modest; when the sun is at its zenith, it must, according to the law of heaven, turn toward its setting, and at its nadir it rises toward a new dawn. In obedience to the same law, the moon when it is full begins to wane, and when empty of light it waxes again. This heavenly law works itself out in the fates of men also. It is the law of earth to alter the full and to contribute to the modest. High mountains are worn down by the waters, and the valleys are filled up. It is the law of fate to undermine what is full and to prosper the modest. And men also hate fullness and love the modest.

The destinies of men are subject to immutable laws that must fulfill themselves. But man has it in his power to shape his fate, according as his behavior exposes him to the influence of benevolent or of destructive forces. When a man holds a high position and is nevertheless modest, he shines with the light of wisdom; if he is in a lowly position and is modest, he cannot be passed by. Thus the superior man can carry out his work to the end without boasting of what he has achieved.

THE IMAGE

Within the earth, a mountain:

The image of MODESTY.

Thus the superior man reduces that which is too much,

And augments that which is too little.

He weighs things and makes them equal.

The wealth of the earth in which a mountain is hidden is not visible to the eye, because the depths are offset by the height of the mountain. Thus high and low complement each other, and the result is the plain. Here an effect that it took a long time to achieve, but that in the end seems easy of accomplishment and self-evident, is used as the image of modesty. The superior man does the same thing when he establishes order in the world; he equalizes the extremes that are the source of social discontent and thereby creates just and equable conditions.[1]

---

1. This hexagram offers a number of parallels to the teachings of the Old and the New Testament, e.g., "And whosoever shall exalt himself shall be abased; and he that shall humble himself shall be exalted" [Matt. 23:12]; "Every valley shall be exalted, and every

THE LINES

Six at the beginning means:
A superior man modest about his modesty
May cross the great water.
Good fortune.

A dangerous enterprise, such as the crossing of a great stream, is made much more difficult if many claims and considerations have to be taken into account. On the other hand, the task is easy if it is attended to quickly and simply. Therefore the unassuming attitude of mind that goes with modesty fits a man to accomplish even difficult undertakings: he imposes no demands or stipulations but settles matters easily and quickly. Where no claims are put forward, no resistances arise.

Six in the second place means:
Modesty that comes to expression.
Perseverance brings good fortune.

"Out of the fullness of the heart the mouth speaketh." When a man's attitude of mind is so modest that this expresses itself in his outward behavior, it is a source of good fortune to him. For the possibility of exerting a lasting influence arises of itself, and no one can interfere.

O Nine in the third place means:
A superior man of modesty and merit
Carries things to conclusion.
Good fortune.

This is the center of the hexagram, where its secret is disclosed. A distinguished name is readily earned by great achievements. If a man allows himself to be dazzled by fame, he will soon be criticized, and difficulties will arise. If, on the

_____

mountain and hill shall be made low: and the crooked shall be made straight, and the rough places plain" [Isa. 40 : 4]; "God resisteth the proud, but giveth grace unto the humble" [Jas. 4 : 6]. The concept of the Last Judgment in the Parsee religion shows similar features. The Greek notion of the jealousy of the gods might be mentioned in connection with the third of the biblical passages here cited.

contrary, he remains modest despite his merit, he makes himself beloved and wins the support necessary for carrying his work through to the end.

> Six in the fourth place means:
> Nothing that would not further modesty
> In movement.

Everything has its proper measure. Even modesty in behavior can be carried too far. Here, however, it is appropriate, because the place between a worthy helper below and a kindly ruler above carries great responsibility. The confidence of the man in superior place must not be abused nor the merits of the man in inferior place concealed. There are officials who indeed do not strive for prominence; they hide behind the letter of the ordinances, decline all responsibility, accept pay without giving its equivalent in work, and bear empty titles. This is the opposite of what is meant here by modesty. In such a position, modesty is shown by interest in one's work.

> Six in the fifth place means:
> No boasting of wealth before one's neighbor.
> It is favorable to attack with force.
> Nothing that would not further.

Modesty is not to be confused with weak good nature that lets things take their own course. When a man holds a responsible position, he must at times resort to energetic measures. In doing so he must not try to make an impression by boasting of his superiority but must make certain of the people around him. The measures taken should be purely objective and in no way personally offensive. Thus modesty manifests itself even in severity.

> Six at the top means:
> Modesty that comes to expression.
> It is favorable to set armies marching
> To chastise one's own city and one's country.

A person who is really sincere in his modesty must make it show in reality. He must proceed with great energy in this.

When enmity arises nothing is easier than to lay the blame on another. A weak man takes offense perhaps, and draws back, feeling self-pity; he thinks that it is modesty that keeps him from defending himself. Genuine modesty sets one to creating order and inspires one to begin by disciplining one's own ego and one's immediate circle. Only through having the courage to marshal one's armies against oneself, will something forceful really be achieved. [2]

---

2. There are not many hexagrams in the Book of Changes in which all the lines have an exclusively favorable meaning, as in the hexagram of MODESTY. This shows how great a value Chinese wisdom places on this virtue.

16. *Yü | Enthusiasm*

above	CHÊN	THE AROUSING, THUNDER
below	K'UN	THE RECEPTIVE, EARTH

The strong line in the fourth place, that of the leading official, meets with response and obedience from all the other lines, which are all weak. The attribute of the upper trigram, Chên, is movement; the attributes of K'un, the lower, are obedience and devotion. This begins a movement that meets with devotion and therefore inspires enthusiasm, carrying all with it. Of great importance, furthermore, is the law of movement along the line of least resistance, which in this hexagram is enunciated as the law for natural events and for human life.

THE JUDGMENT

ENTHUSIASM. It furthers one to install helpers
And to set armies marching.

The time of ENTHUSIASM derives from the fact that there is at hand an eminent man who is in sympathy with the spirit of the people and acts in accord with it. Hence he finds universal and willing obedience. To arouse enthusiasm it is necessary for a man to adjust himself and his ordinances to the character of those whom he has to lead. The inviolability of natural laws rests on this principle of movement along the line of least resistance. These laws are not forces external to things but represent the harmony of movement immanent in them. That is why the celestial bodies do not deviate from their orbits and why all events in nature occur with fixed regularity. It is the same with human society: only such laws as are rooted in popular sentiment can be enforced, while laws violating this sentiment merely arouse resentment.

Again, it is enthusiasm that enables us to install helpers for the completion of an undertaking without fear of secret opposition. It is enthusiasm too that can unify mass movements, as in war, so that they achieve victory.

THE IMAGE

Thunder comes resounding out of the earth:
The image of ENTHUSIASM.
Thus the ancient kings made music
In order to honor merit,
And offered it with splendor
To the Supreme Deity,
Inviting their ancestors to be present.

When, at the beginning of summer, thunder—electrical energy—comes rushing forth from the earth again, and the first thunderstorm refreshes nature, a prolonged state of tension is resolved. Joy and relief make themselves felt. So too, music has power to ease tension within the heart and to loosen the grip of obscure emotions. The enthusiasm of the heart expresses itself involuntarily in a burst of song, in dance and rhythmic movement of the body. From immemorial times the inspiring effect of the invisible sound that moves all hearts, and draws them together, has mystified mankind.

Rulers have made use of this natural taste for music; they elevated and regulated it. Music was looked upon as something serious and holy, designed to purify the feelings of men. It fell to music to glorify the virtues of heroes and thus to construct a bridge to the world of the unseen. In the temple men drew near to God with music and pantomimes (out of this later the theater developed). Religious feeling for the Creator of the world was united with the most sacred of human feelings, that of reverence for the ancestors. The ancestors were invited to these divine services as guests of the Ruler of Heaven and as representatives of humanity in the higher regions. This uniting of the human past with the Divinity in solemn moments of religious inspiration established the bond between God and man. The ruler who revered the Divinity in revering his ancestors became thereby the Son of Heaven, in whom the heavenly and the earthly world met in mystical contact.

These ideas are the final summation of Chinese culture. Confucius has said of the great sacrifice at which these rites were performed: "He who could wholly comprehend this sacrifice could rule the world as though it were spinning on his hand."

THE LINES

Six at the beginning means:
Enthusiasm that expresses itself
Brings misfortune.

A man in an inferior position has aristocratic connections about which he boasts enthusiastically. This arrogance inevitably invites misfortune. Enthusiasm should never be an egotistic emotion; it is justified only when it is a general feeling that unites one with others.

Six in the second place means:
Firm as a rock. Not a whole day.
Perseverance brings good fortune.

This describes a person who does not allow himself to be misled by any illusions. While others are letting themselves be dazzled by enthusiasm, he recognizes with perfect clarity the first signs of the time. Thus he neither flatters those above nor neglects those beneath him; he is as firm as a rock. When the first sign of discord appears, he knows the right moment for withdrawing and does not delay even for a day. Perseverance in such conduct will bring good fortune. Confucius says about this line:

To know the seeds, that is divine indeed. In his association with those above him, the superior man does not flatter. In his association with those beneath him, he is not arrogant. For he knows the seeds. The seeds are the first imperceptible beginning of movement, the first trace of good fortune (or misfortune) that shows itself. The superior man perceives the seeds and immediately takes action. He does not wait even a whole day. In the Book of Changes it is said: "Firm as a rock. Not a whole day. Perseverance brings good fortune."

Firm as a rock, what need of a whole day?
The judgment can be known.
The superior man knows what is hidden and what is evident.
He knows weakness, he knows strength as well.
Hence the myriads look up to him.

> Six in the third place means:
> Enthusiasm that looks upward creates remorse.
> Hesitation brings remorse.

This line is the opposite of the preceding one: the latter bespeaks self-reliance, while here there is enthusiastic looking up to a leader. If a man hesitates too long, this also will bring remorse. The right moment for approach must be seized: only then will he do the right thing.

> ○ Nine in the fourth place means:
> The source of enthusiasm.
> He achieves great things.
> Doubt not.
> You gather friends around you
> As a hair clasp gathers the hair.

This describes a man who is able to awaken enthusiasm through his own sureness and freedom from hesitation. He attracts people because he has no doubts and is wholly sincere. Owing to his confidence in them he wins their enthusiastic co-operation and attains success. Just as a clasp draws the hair together and holds it, so he draws men together by the support he gives them.

Six in the fifth place means:
Persistently ill, and still does not die.

Here enthusiasm is obstructed. A man is under constant pressure, which prevents him from breathing freely. However, this pressure has its advantage—it prevents him from consuming his powers in empty enthusiasm. Thus constant pressure can actually serve to keep one alive.

Six at the top means:
Deluded enthusiasm.
But if after completion one changes,
There is no blame.

It is a bad thing for a man to let himself be deluded by enthusiasm. But if this delusion has run its course, and he is still capable of changing, he is freed of error. A sober awakening from false enthusiasm is quite possible and very favorable.

17. *Sui / Following*

above	TUI	THE JOYOUS, LAKE
below	CHÊN	THE AROUSING, THUNDER

The trigram Tui, the Joyous, whose attribute is gladness, is above; Chên, the Arousing, which has the attribute of movement, is below. Joy in movement induces following. The Joyous is the youngest daughter, while the Arousing is the eldest son. An older man defers to a young girl and shows her consideration. By this he moves her to follow him.

THE JUDGMENT

FOLLOWING has supreme success.
Perseverance furthers. No blame.

In order to obtain a following one must first know how to adapt oneself. If a man would rule he must first learn to serve, for only in this way does he secure from those below him the joyous assent that is necessary if they are to follow him. If he has to obtain a following by force or cunning, by conspiracy or by creating factions, he invariably arouses resistance, which obstructs willing adherence. But even joyous movement can lead to evil consequences, hence the added stipulation, "Perseverance furthers"—that is, consistency in doing right—together with "No blame." Just as we should not ask others to follow us unless this condition is fulfilled, so it is only under this condition that we can in turn follow others without coming to harm.

The thought of obtaining a following through adaptation to the demands of the time is a great and significant idea; this is why the appended judgment is so favorable.

THE IMAGE

Thunder in the middle of the lake:
The image of FOLLOWING.
Thus the superior man at nightfall
Goes indoors for rest and recuperation.

In the autumn electricity withdraws into the earth again and rests. Here it is the thunder in the middle of the lake that serves as the image—thunder in its winter rest, not thunder in motion. The idea of following in the sense of adaptation to the demands of the time grows out of this image. Thunder in the middle of the lake indicates times of darkness and rest. Similarly, a superior man, after being tirelessly active all day, allows himself rest and recuperation at night. No situation can become favorable until one is able to adapt to it and does not wear himself out with mistaken resistance.

THE LINES

○ Nine at the beginning means:
The standard is changing.
Perseverance brings good fortune.
To go out of the door in company
Produces deeds.

There are exceptional conditions in which the relation between
leader and followers changes. It is implicit in the idea of
following and adaptation that if one wants to lead others, one
must remain accessible and responsive to the views of those
under him. At the same time, however, he must have firm
principles, so that he does not vacillate where there is only a
question of current opinion. Once we are ready to listen to the
opinions of others, we must not associate exclusively with
people who share our views or with members of our own party;
instead, we must go out and mingle freely with all sorts of
people, friends or foes. That is the only way to achieve
something.

Six in the second place means:
If one clings to the little boy,
One loses the strong man.

In friendships and close relationships an individual must make
a careful choice. He surrounds himself either with good or
with bad company; he cannot have both at once. If he throws
himself away on unworthy friends he loses connection with
people of intellectual power who could further him in the good.

Six in the third place means:
If one clings to the strong man,
One loses the little boy.
Through following one finds what one seeks.
It furthers one to remain persevering.

When the right connection with distinguished people has been
found, a certain loss naturally ensues. A man must part company with the inferior and superficial. But in his heart he will
feel satisfied, because he will find what he seeks and needs for

the development of his personality. The important thing is to remain firm. He must know what he wants and not be led astray by momentary inclinations.

> Nine in the fourth place means:
> Following creates success.
> Perseverance brings misfortune.
> To go one's way with sincerity brings clarity.
> How could there be blame in this?

It often happens, when a man exerts a certain amount of influence, that he obtains a following by condescension toward inferiors. But the people who attach themselves to him are not honest in their intentions. They seek personal advantage and try to make themselves indispensable through flattery and subservience. If one becomes accustomed to such satellites and cannot do without them, it brings misfortune. Only when a man is completely free from his ego, and intent, by conviction, upon what is right and essential, does he acquire the clarity that enables him to see through such people, and become free of blame.

> ○ Nine in the fifth place means:
> Sincere in the good. Good fortune.

Every man must have something he follows—something that serves him as a lodestar. He who follows with conviction the beautiful and the good may feel himself strengthened by this saying.

> Six at the top means:
> He meets with firm allegiance
> And is still further bound.
> The king introduces him
> To the Western Mountain.

This refers to a man, an exalted sage, who has already put the turmoil of the world behind him. But a follower appears who understands him and is not to be put off. So the sage comes back into the world and aids the other in his work. Thus there develops an eternal tie between the two.

The allegory is chosen from the annals of the Chou dynasty. The rulers of this dynasty honored men who had served them well by awarding them a place in the royal family's temple of ancestors on the Western Mountain. In this way they were regarded as sharing in the destiny of the ruling family.

18. *Ku* / *Work on What Has Been Spoiled* [*Decay*]

above	KÊN	KEEPING STILL, MOUNTAIN
below	SUN	THE GENTLE, WIND

The Chinese character *ku* represents a bowl in whose contents worms are breeding. This means decay. It has come about because the gentle indifference of the lower trigram has come together with the rigid inertia of the upper, and the result is stagnation. Since this implies guilt, the conditions embody a demand for removal of the cause. Hence the meaning of the hexagram is not simply "what has been spoiled" but "work on what has been spoiled."

THE JUDGMENT

WORK ON WHAT HAS BEEN SPOILED
Has supreme success.
It furthers one to cross the great water.
Before the starting point, three days.
After the starting point, three days.

What has been spoiled through man's fault can be made good again through man's work. It is not immutable fate, as in the time of STANDSTILL, that has caused the state of corruption, but rather the abuse of human freedom. Work toward improving conditions promises well, because it accords with the possibilities of the time. We must not recoil from work and danger—symbolized by crossing of the great water—but must take hold energetically. Success depends, however, on proper deliberation. This is expressed by the lines, "Before the starting point, three days. After the starting point, three days." We must first know the causes of corruption before we can do away with them; hence it is necessary to be cautious during the time before the start. Then we must see to it that the new way is safely entered upon, so that a relapse may be avoided; therefore we must pay attention to the time after the start. Decisiveness and energy must take the place of the inertia and indifference that have led to decay, in order that the ending may be followed by a new beginning.

THE IMAGE

The wind blows low on the mountain:
The image of DECAY.
Thus the superior man stirs up the people
And strengthens their spirit.

When the wind blows low on the mountain, it is thrown back and spoils the vegetation. This contains a challenge to improvement. It is the same with debasing attitudes and fashions; they corrupt human society. To do away with this corruption, the superior man must regenerate society. His methods likewise must be derived from the two trigrams, but in such a way that their effects unfold in orderly sequence. The superior man must first remove stagnation by stirring up public opinion, as the wind stirs everything, and must then strengthen and tranquillize the character of the people, as the mountain gives tranquillity and nourishment to all that grows in its vicinity.

THE LINES

Six at the beginning means:
Setting right what has been spoiled by the father.
If there is a son,
No blame rests upon the departed father.
Danger. In the end good fortune.

Rigid adherence to tradition has resulted in decay. But the decay has not yet penetrated deeply and so can still be easily remedied. It is as if a son were compensating for the decay his father allowed to creep in. Then no blame attaches to the father. However, one must not overlook the danger or take the matter too lightly. Only if one is conscious of the danger connected with every reform will everything go well in the end.

Nine in the second place means:
Setting right what has been spoiled by the mother.
One must not be too persevering.

This refers to mistakes that as a result of weakness have brought about decay—hence the symbol, "what has been spoiled by the mother." In setting things right in such a case, a certain gentle consideration is called for. In order not to wound, one should not attempt to proceed too drastically.

Nine in the third place means:
Setting right what has been spoiled by the father.
There will be a little remorse. No great blame.

This describes a man who proceeds a little too energetically in righting the mistakes of the past. Now and then, as a result, minor discords and annoyances will surely develop. But too much energy is better than too little. Therefore, although he may at times have some slight cause for regret, he remains free of any serious blame.

Six in the fourth place means:
Tolerating what has been spoiled by the father.
In continuing one sees humiliation.

This shows the situation of someone too weak to take measures against decay that has its roots in the past and is just beginning to manifest itself. It is allowed to run its course. If this continues, humiliation will result.

○ Six in the fifth place means:
Setting right what has been spoiled by the father.
One meets with praise.

77

An individual is confronted with corruption originating from neglect in former times. He lacks the power to ward it off alone, but with able helpers he can at least bring about a thorough reform, if he cannot create a new beginning, and this also is praiseworthy.

> Nine at the top means:
> He does not serve kings and princes,
> Sets himself higher goals.

Not every man has an obligation to mingle in the affairs of the world. There are some who are developed to such a degree that they are justified in letting the world go its own way and in refusing to enter public life with a view to reforming it. But this does not imply a right to remain idle or to sit back and merely criticize. Such withdrawal is justified only when we strive to realize in ourselves the higher aims of mankind. For although the sage remains distant from the turmoil of daily life, he creates incomparable human values for the future.[1]

---

1. Goethe's attitude after the Napoleonic wars is an example of this in European history.

19. *Lin / Approach*

above	K'UN	THE RECEPTIVE, EARTH
below	TUI	THE JOYOUS, LAKE

The Chinese word *lin* has a range of meanings that is not exhausted by any single word of another language. The ancient explanations in the Book of Changes give as its first meaning, "becoming great." What becomes great are the two strong lines growing into the hexagram from below; the light-giving power expands with them. The meaning is then further extended to include the concept of approach, especially the approach of what is strong and highly placed in relation to what is lower. Finally the meaning includes the attitude of condescension of a man in high position toward the people, and in general the setting to work on affairs. This hexagram is linked with the twelfth month (January–February), when, after the winter solstice, the light power begins to ascend again.

THE JUDGMENT

APPROACH has supreme success.
Perseverance furthers.
When the eighth month comes,
There will be misfortune.

The hexagram as a whole points to a time of joyous, hopeful progress. Spring is approaching. Joy and forbearance bring high and low nearer together. Success is certain. But we must work with determination and perseverance to make full use of the propitiousness of the time. And one thing more: spring does not last forever. In the eighth month the aspects are reversed. Then only two strong, light lines are left; these do not advance but are in retreat (see next hexagram). We must take heed of this change in good time. If we meet evil before it becomes reality—before it has even begun to stir—we can master it.

THE IMAGE

The earth above the lake:
The image of APPROACH.
Thus the superior man is inexhaustible
In his will to teach,
And without limits
In his tolerance and protection of the people.

The earth borders upon the lake from above.[1] This symbolizes the approach and condescension of the man of higher position to those beneath him. The two parts of the image indicate what his attitude toward these people will be. Just as the lake is

---

1. [See the two trigrams.]

inexhaustible in depth, so the sage is inexhaustible in his readiness to teach mankind, and just as the earth is boundlessly wide, sustaining and caring for all creatures on it, so the sage sustains and cares for all people and excludes no part of humanity.

THE LINES

○ Nine at the beginning means:
  Joint approach.
  Perseverance brings good fortune.

The good begins to prevail and to find response in influential circles. This in turn is an incentive to men of ability. It is well to join this upward trend, but we must not let ourselves be carried away by the current of the time; we must adhere perseveringly to what is right. This brings good fortune.

○ Nine in the second place means:
  Joint approach.
  Good fortune.
  Everything furthers.

When the stimulus to approach comes from a high place, and when a man has the inner strength and consistency that need no admonition, good fortune will ensue. Nor need the future cause any concern. He is well aware that everything earthly is transitory, and that a descent follows upon every rise, but need not be confused by this universal law of fate. Everything serves to further. Therefore he will travel the paths of life swiftly, honestly, and valiantly.

  Six in the third place means:
  Comfortable approach.
  Nothing that would further.
  If one is induced to grieve over it,
  One becomes free of blame.

Things are going well for a man: he achieves power and influence. But in this lies the danger that he may relax, and confident of his position, allow the easygoing, careless mood to show itself in his dealings with other people. This would inevitably be harmful. But there is possibility of a change of mood. If he regrets his mistaken attitude and feels the responsibility of an influential position, he frees himself of faults.

> Six in the fourth place means:
> Complete approach.
> No blame.

While the three lower lines indicate rise to power and influence, the three upper lines show the attitude of persons in higher position toward those of lower rank for whom they procure influence. Here is shown the open-minded approach of a person of high rank to a man of ability whom he draws into his own circle, regardless of class prejudice. This is very favorable.

> Six in the fifth place means:
> Wise approach.
> This is right for a great prince.
> Good fortune.

A prince, or anyone in a leading position, must have the wisdom to attract to himself people of ability who are expert in directing affairs. His wisdom consists both in selecting the right people and in allowing those chosen to have a free hand without interference from him. For only through such self-restraint will he find the experts needed to satisfy all of his requirements.

> Six at the top means:
> Greathearted approach.
> Good fortune. No blame.

A sage who has put the world behind him and who in spirit has already withdrawn from life may, under certain circumstances, decide to return once more to the here and now and to approach other men. This means great good fortune for the men whom he teaches and helps. And for him this greathearted humbling of himself is blameless.

觀

20. *Kuan / Contemplation (View)*

above	SUN	THE GENTLE, WIND
below	K'UN	THE RECEPTIVE, EARTH

A slight variation of tonal stress gives the Chinese name for this hexagram a double meaning. It means both contemplating and being seen, in the sense of being an example. These ideas are suggested by the fact that the hexagram can be understood as picturing a type of tower characteristic of ancient China.

A tower of this kind commanded a wide view of the country; at the same time, when situated on a mountain, it became a landmark that could be seen for miles around. Thus the hexagram shows a ruler who contemplates the law of heaven above him and the ways of the people below, and who, by means of good government, sets a lofty example to the masses.

This hexagram is linked with the eighth month (September –October). The light-giving power retreats and the dark power is again on the increase. However, this aspect is not material in the interpretation of the hexagram as a whole.

THE JUDGMENT

CONTEMPLATION. The ablution has been made,
But not yet the offering.
Full of trust they look up to him.

The sacrificial ritual in China began with an ablution and a libation by which the Deity was invoked, after which the sacrifice was offered. The moment of time between these two ceremonies is the most sacred of all, the moment of deepest inner concentration. If piety is sincere and expressive of real faith, the contemplation of it has a transforming and awe-inspiring effect on those who witness it.

Thus also in nature a holy seriousness is to be seen in the fact that natural occurrences are uniformly subject to law. Contemplation of the divine meaning underlying the workings of the universe gives to the man who is called upon to influence others the means of producing like effects. This requires that power of inner concentration which religious contemplation develops in great men strong in faith. It enables them to apprehend the mysterious and divine laws of life, and by means of profoundest inner concentration they give expression to these laws in their own persons. Thus a hidden spiritual power emanates from them, influencing and dominating others without their being aware of how it happens.

THE IMAGE

The wind blows over the earth:
The image of CONTEMPLATION.
Thus the kings of old visited the regions of the world,
Contemplated the people,
And gave them instruction.

When the wind blows over the earth it goes far and wide, and the grass must bend to its power. These two occurrences find confirmation in the hexagram. The two images are used to symbolize a practice of the kings of old; in making regular journeys the ruler could, in the first place, survey his realm and make certain that none of the existing usages of the people escaped notice; in the second, he could exert influence through which such customs as were unsuitable could be changed.

All of this points to the power possessed by a superior personality. On the one hand, such a man will have a view of the real sentiments of the great mass of humanity and therefore cannot be deceived; on the other, he will impress the people so profoundly, by his mere existence and by the impact of his personality, that they will be swayed by him as the grass by the wind.

THE LINES

Six at the beginning means:
Boylike contemplation.
For an inferior man, no blame.
For a superior man, humiliation.

This means contemplation from a distance, without comprehension. A man of influence is at hand, but his influence is not understood by the common people. This matters little in the case of the masses, for they benefit by the actions of the ruling sage whether they understand them or not. But for a superior man it is a disgrace. He must not content himself with a shallow, thoughtless view of prevailing forces; he must contemplate them as a connected whole and try to understand them.

Six in the second place means:
Contemplation through the crack of the door.
Furthering for the perseverance of a woman.

Through the crack of the door one has a limited outlook; one looks outward from within. Contemplation is subjectively limited. One tends to relate everything to oneself and cannot put oneself in another's place and understand his motives. This is appropriate for a good housewife. It is not necessary for her to be conversant with the affairs of the world. But for a man who must take active part in public life, such a narrow, egotistic way of contemplating things is of course harmful.

Six in the third place means:
Contemplation of my life
Decides the choice
Between advance and retreat.

This is the place of transition. We no longer look outward to receive pictures that are more or less limited and confused, but direct our contemplation upon ourselves in order to find a guideline for our decisions. This self-contemplation means the overcoming of naïve egotism in the person who sees everything solely from his own standpoint. He begins to reflect and in this way acquires objectivity. However, self-knowledge does not mean preoccupation with one's own thoughts; rather, it means concern about the effects one creates. It is only the effects our lives produce that give us the right to judge whether what we have done means progress or regression.

> Six in the fourth place means:
> Contemplation of the light of the kingdom.
> It furthers one to exert influence as the guest
>   of a king.

This describes a man who understands the secrets by which a kingdom can be made to flourish. Such a man must be given an authoritative position, in which he can exert influence. He should be, so to speak, a guest—that is, he should be honored and allowed to act independently, and should not be used as a tool.

> ○ Nine in the fifth place means:
> Contemplation of my life.
> The superior man is without blame.

A man in an authoritative position to whom others look up must always be ready for self-examination. The right sort of self-examination, however, consists not in idle brooding over oneself but in examining the effects one produces. Only when these effects are good, and when one's influence on others is good, will the contemplation of one's own life bring the satisfaction of knowing oneself to be free of mistakes.

> ○ Nine at the top means:
> Contemplation of his life.
> The superior man is without blame.

While the preceding line represents a man who contemplates himself, here in the highest place everything that is personal, related to the ego, is excluded. The picture is that of a sage who stands outside the affairs of the world. Liberated from his ego, he contemplates the laws of life and so realizes that knowing how to become free of blame is the highest good.

85

噬嗑

21. Shih Ho / Biting Through

```
═══   above   LI    THE CLINGING, FIRE
═══   below   CHÊN  THE AROUSING, THUNDER
```

This hexagram represents an open mouth (cf. hexagram 27) with an obstruction (in the fourth place) between the teeth. As a result the lips cannot meet. To bring them together one must bite energetically through the obstacle. Since the hexagram is made up of the trigrams for thunder and for lightning, it indicates how obstacles are forcibly removed in nature. Energetic biting through overcomes the obstacle that prevents joining of the lips; the storm with its thunder and lightning overcomes the disturbing tension in nature. Recourse to law and penalties overcomes the disturbances of harmonious social life caused by criminals and slanderers. The theme of this hexagram is a criminal lawsuit, in contradistinction to that of Sung, CONFLICT (6), which refers to civil suits.

THE JUDGMENT

BITING THROUGH has success.
It is favorable to let justice be administered.

When an obstacle to union arises, energetic biting through brings success. This is true in all situations. Whenever unity cannot be established, the obstruction is due to a talebearer and traitor who is interfering and blocking the way. To prevent permanent injury, vigorous measures must be taken at once. Deliberate obstruction of this sort does not vanish of its own accord. Judgment and punishment are required to deter or obviate it.

However, it is important to proceed in the right way. The hexagram combines Li, clarity, and Chên, excitement. Li is yielding, Chên is hard. Unqualified hardness and excitement would be too violent in meting out punishment; unqualified clarity and gentleness would be too weak. The two together create the just measure. It is of moment that the man who makes the decisions (represented by the fifth line) is gentle by nature, while he commands respect by his conduct in his position.

THE IMAGE

Thunder and lightning:
The image of BITING THROUGH.
Thus the kings of former times made firm the laws
Through clearly defined penalties.

Penalties are the individual applications of the law. The laws specify the penalties. Clarity prevails when mild and severe penalties are clearly differentiated, according to the nature of the crimes. This is symbolized by the clarity of lightning. The law is strengthened by a just application of penalties. This is symbolized by the terror of thunder. This clarity and severity have the effect of instilling respect; it is not that the penalties are ends in themselves. The obstructions in the social life of man increase when there is lack of clarity in the penal codes and slackness in executing them. The only way to strengthen the law is to make it clear and to make penalties certain and swift.

THE LINES[1]

Nine at the beginning means:
His feet are fastened in the stocks,
So that his toes disappear.
No blame.

If a sentence is imposed the first time a man attempts to do

---

1. Apart from the meaning of the hexagram as a whole, the single lines are explained as follows: the persons represented by the first and the top line suffer punishment, the others inflict it (see the corresponding lines in hexagram 4, Mêng, YOUTHFUL FOLLY).

wrong, the penalty is a mild one. Only the toes are put in the stocks. This prevents him from sinning further and thus he becomes free of blame. It is a warning to halt in time on the path of evil.

> Six in the second place means:
> Bites through tender meat,
> So that his nose disappears.
> No blame.

It is easy to discriminate between right and wrong in this case; it is like biting through tender meat. But one encounters a hardened sinner, and, aroused by anger, one goes a little too far. The disappearance of the nose in the course of the bite signifies that indignation blots out finer sensibility. However, there is no great harm in this, because the penalty as such is just.

> Six in the third place means:
> Bites on old dried meat
> And strikes on something poisonous.
> Slight humiliation. No blame.

Punishment is to be carried out by someone who lacks the power and authority to do so. Therefore the culprits do not submit. The matter at issue is an old one—as symbolized by salted game—and in dealing with it difficulties arise. This old meat is spoiled: by taking up the problem the punisher arouses poisonous hatred against himself, and in this way is put in a somewhat humiliating position. But since punishment was required by the time, he remains free of blame.

> Nine in the fourth place means:
> Bites on dried gristly meat.
> Receives metal arrows.
> It furthers one to be mindful of difficulties
> And to be persevering.
> Good fortune.

There are great obstacles to be overcome, powerful opponents are to be punished. Though this is arduous, the effort succeeds. But it is necessary to be hard as metal and straight as an arrow to surmount the difficulties. If one knows these difficulties and remains persevering, he attains good fortune. The difficult task is achieved in the end.

○ Six in the fifth place means:
  Bites on dried lean meat.
  Receives yellow gold.
  Perseveringly aware of danger.
  No blame.

The case to be decided is indeed not easy but perfectly clear. Since we naturally incline to leniency, we must make every effort to be like yellow gold—that is, as true as gold and as impartial as yellow, the color of the middle [the mean]. It is only by remaining conscious of the dangers growing out of the responsibility we have assumed that we can avoid making mistakes.

  Nine at the top means:
  His neck is fastened in the wooden cangue,
  So that his ears disappear.
  Misfortune.

In contrast to the first line, this line refers to a man who is incorrigible. His punishment is the wooden cangue, and his ears disappear under it—that is to say, he is deaf to warnings. This obstinacy leads to misfortune.[2]

---

2. It should be noted here that there is an alternative interpretation of this hexagram, based on the idea, "Above, light (the sun); below, movement." In this interpretation the hexagram symbolizes a market below, full of movement, while the sun is shining in the sky above. The allusion to meat suggests that it is a food market. Gold and arrows are articles of trade. The disappearance of the nose means the vanishing of smell, that is, the person in question is not covetous. The idea of poison points to the dangers of wealth, and so on throughout.

Confucius says in regard to the nine at the beginning in this hexagram: "The inferior man is not ashamed of unkindness and does not shrink from injustice. If no advantage beckons he makes no effort. If

22. Pi / Grace

☶	*above* KÊN	KEEPING STILL, MOUNTAIN
☲	*below* LI	THE CLINGING, FIRE

This hexagram shows a fire that breaks out of the secret depths of the earth and, blazing up, illuminates and beautifies the mountain, the heavenly heights. Grace—beauty of form—is necessary in any union if it is to be well ordered and pleasing rather than disordered and chaotic.

THE JUDGMENT

GRACE has success.

In small matters

It is favorable to undertake something.

Grace brings success. However, it is not the essential or fundamental thing; it is only the ornament and must therefore be used sparingly and only in little things. In the lower trigram of fire a yielding line comes between two strong lines and makes them beautiful, but the strong lines are the essential content and the weak line is the beautifying form. In the upper trigram

---

he is not intimidated he does not improve himself, but if he is made to behave correctly in small matters he is careful in large ones. This is fortunate for the inferior man."

On the subject of the nine at the top Confucius says: "If good does not accumulate, it is not enough to make a name for a man. If evil does not accumulate, it is not strong enough to destroy a man. Therefore the inferior man thinks to himself, 'Goodness in small things has no value,' and so neglects it. He thinks, 'Small sins do no harm,' and so does not give them up. Thus his sins accumulate until they can no longer be covered up, and his guilt becomes so great that it can no longer be wiped out."

of the mountain, the strong line takes the lead, so that here again the strong element must be regarded as the decisive factor. In nature we see in the sky the strong light of the sun; the life of the world depends on it. But this strong, essential thing is changed and given pleasing variety by the moon and the stars. In human affairs, aesthetic form comes into being when traditions exist that, strong and abiding like mountains, are made pleasing by a lucid beauty. By contemplating the forms existing in the heavens we come to understand time and its changing demands. Through contemplation of the forms existing in human society it becomes possible to shape the world.[1]

THE IMAGE

Fire at the foot of the mountain:
The image of GRACE.
Thus does the superior man proceed
When clearing up current affairs.
But he dare not decide controversial issues in
    this way.

The fire, whose light illuminates the mountain and makes it pleasing, does not shine far; in the same way, beautiful form suffices to brighten and to throw light upon matters of lesser moment, but important questions cannot be decided in this way. They require greater earnestness.

THE LINES

Nine at the beginning means:
He lends grace to his toes, leaves the carriage,
    and walks.

---

1. This hexagram shows tranquil beauty—clarity within, quiet without. This is the tranquillity of pure contemplation. When desire is silenced and the will comes to rest, the world-as-idea becomes manifest. In this aspect the world is beautiful and removed from the struggle for existence. This is the world of art. However, contemplation alone will not put the will to rest absolutely. It will awaken again, and then all the beauty of form will appear to have been only a brief moment of exaltation. Hence this is still not the true way of redemption. For this reason Confucius felt very uncomfortable when once, on consulting the oracle, he obtained the hexagram of GRACE.

A beginner in a subordinate place must take upon himself the labor of advancing. There might be an opportunity of surreptitiously easing the way—symbolized by the carriage—but a self-contained man scorns help gained in a dubious fashion. He thinks it more graceful to go on foot than to drive in a carriage under false pretenses.

○ Six in the second place means:
   Lends grace to the beard on his chin.

The beard is not an independent thing; it moves only with the chin. The image therefore means that form is to be considered only as a result and attribute of content. The beard is a superfluous ornament. To devote care to it for its own sake, without regard for the inner content of which it is an ornament, would bespeak a certain vanity.

   Nine in the third place means:
   Graceful and moist.
   Constant perseverance brings good fortune.

This represents a very charming life situation. One is under the spell of grace and the mellow mood induced by wine. This grace can adorn, but it can also swamp us. Hence the warning not to sink into convivial indolence but to remain constant in perseverance. Good fortune depends on this.

   Six in the fourth place means:
   Grace or simplicity?
   A white horse comes as if on wings.
   He is not a robber,
   He will woo at the right time.

An individual is in a situation in which doubts arise as to which is better—to pursue the grace of external brilliance, or to return to simplicity. The doubt itself implies the answer. Confirmation comes from the outside; it comes like a white winged horse. The white color indicates simplicity. At first it may be disappointing to renounce comforts that might have been obtained, yet one finds peace of mind in a true relationship with the friend who courts him. The winged horse is the symbol of the thoughts that transcend all limits of space and time.

> Six in the fifth place means:
> Grace in hills and gardens.
> The roll of silk is meager and small.
> Humiliation, but in the end good fortune.

A man withdraws from contact with people of the lowlands, who seek nothing but magnificence and luxury, into the solitude of the heights. There he finds an individual to look up to, whom he would like to have as a friend. But the gifts he has to offer are poor and few, so that he feels ashamed. However, it is not the material gifts that count, but sincerity of feeling, and so all goes well in the end.

> ○ Nine at the top means:
> Simple grace. No blame.

Here at the highest stage of development all ornament is discarded. Form no longer conceals content but brings out its value to the full. Perfect grace consists not in exterior ornamentation of the substance, but in the simple fitness of its form.

剥

23. *Po / Splitting Apart*

above	KÊN	KEEPING STILL, MOUNTAIN
below	K'UN	THE RECEPTIVE, EARTH

The dark lines are about to mount upward and overthrow the last firm, light line by exerting a disintegrating influence on it. The inferior, dark forces overcome what is superior and strong, not by direct means, but by undermining it gradually and imperceptibly, so that it finally collapses.

The lines of the hexagram present the image of a house, the top line being the roof, and because the roof is being shattered the house collapses. The hexagram belongs to the ninth month (October–November). The yin power pushes up ever more powerfully and is about to supplant the yang power altogether.

THE JUDGMENT

SPLITTING APART. It does not further one
To go anywhere.

This pictures a time when inferior people are pushing forward and are about to crowd out the few remaining strong and superior men. Under these circumstances, which are due to the time, it is not favorable for the superior man to undertake anything.

The right behavior in such adverse times is to be deduced from the images and their attributes. The lower trigram stands for the earth, whose attributes are docility and devotion. The upper trigram stands for the mountain, whose attribute is stillness. This suggests that one should submit to the bad time and remain quiet. For it is a question not of man's doing but of time conditions, which, according to the laws of heaven, show an alternation of increase and decrease, fullness and emptiness. It is impossible to counteract these conditions of the time. Hence it is not cowardice but wisdom to submit and avoid action.

THE IMAGE

The mountain rests on the earth:
The image of SPLITTING APART.
Thus those above can ensure their position
Only by giving generously to those below.

The mountain rests on the earth. When it is steep and narrow, lacking a broad base, it must topple over. Its position is strong only when it rises out of the earth broad and great, not proud and steep. So likewise those who rule rest on the broad foundation of the people. They too should be generous and benevolent, like the earth that carries all. Then they will make their position as secure as a mountain is in its tranquillity.

THE LINES

Six at the beginning means:
The leg of the bed is split.
Those who persevere are destroyed.
Misfortune.

Inferior people are on the rise and stealthily begin their destructive burrowing from below in order to undermine the place where the superior man rests. Those followers of the ruler who remain loyal are destroyed by slander and intrigue. The situation bodes disaster, yet there is nothing to do but wait.

Six in the second place means:
The bed is split at the edge.
Those who persevere are destroyed.
Misfortune.

The power of the inferior people is growing. The danger draws close to one's person; already there are clear indications, and rest is disturbed. Moreover, in this dangerous situation one is as yet without help or friendly advances from above or below. Extreme caution is necessary in this isolation. One must adjust to the time and promptly avoid the danger. Stubborn perseverance in maintaining one's standpoint would lead to downfall.

Six in the third place means:
He splits with them. No blame.

An individual finds himself in an evil environment to which he is committed by external ties. But he has an inner relationship with a superior man, and through this he attains the stability to free himself from the way of the inferior people around him. This brings him into opposition to them of course, but that is not wrong.

Six in the fourth place means:
The bed is split up to the skin.
Misfortune.

Here the disaster affects not only the resting place but even the occupant. No warning or other comment is added. Misfortune has reached its peak: it can no longer be warded off.

> Six in the fifth place means:
> A shoal of fishes. Favor comes through the court
>   ladies.
> Everything acts to further.

Here, in immediate proximity to the strong, light-giving principle at the top, the nature of the dark force undergoes a change. It no longer opposes the strong principle by means of intrigues but submits to its guidance. Indeed, as the head of the other weak lines, it leads all of these to the strong line, just as a princess leads her maids-in-waiting like a shoal of fishes to her husband and thus gains his favor. Inasmuch as the lower element thus voluntarily places itself under the higher, it attains happiness and the higher also receives its due. Therefore all goes well.

> ○ Nine at the top means:
> There is a large fruit still uneaten.
> The superior man receives a carriage.
> The house of the inferior man is split apart.

Here the splitting apart reaches its end. When misfortune has spent itself, better times return. The seed of the good remains, and it is just when the fruit falls to the ground that good sprouts anew from its seed. The superior man again attains influence and effectiveness. He is supported by public opinion as if in a carriage. But the inferior man's wickedness is visited upon himself. His house is split apart. A law of nature is at work here. Evil is not destructive to the good alone but inevitably destroys itself as well. For evil, which lives solely by negation, cannot continue to exist on its own strength alone. The inferior man himself fares best when held under control by a superior man.

復

24. *Fu / Return (The Turning Point)*

	above	K'UN	THE RECEPTIVE, EARTH
	below	CHÊN	THE AROUSING, THUNDER

The idea of a turning point arises from the fact that after the dark lines have pushed all of the light lines upward and out of the hexagram, another light line enters the hexagram from below. The time of darkness is past. The winter solstice brings the victory of light. This hexagram is linked with the eleventh month, the month of the solstice (December–January).

THE JUDGMENT

RETURN. Success.
Going out and coming in without error.
Friends come without blame.
To and fro goes the way.
On the seventh day comes return.
It furthers one to have somewhere to go.

After a time of decay comes the turning point. The powerful light that has been banished returns. There is movement, but it is not brought about by force. The upper trigram K'un is characterized by devotion; thus the movement is natural, arising spontaneously. For this reason the transformation of the old becomes easy. The old is discarded and the new is introduced. Both measures accord with the time; therefore no harm results. Societies of people sharing the same views are formed. But since these groups come together in full public knowledge and are in harmony with the time, all selfish separatist tendencies are excluded, and no mistake is made.

The idea of RETURN is based on the course of nature. The movement is cyclic, and the course completes itself. Therefore it is not necessary to hasten anything artificially. Everything comes of itself at the appointed time. This is the meaning of heaven and earth.

All movements are accomplished in six stages, and the seventh brings return. Thus the winter solstice, with which the decline of the year begins, comes in the seventh month after the summer solstice; so too sunrise comes in the seventh double hour after sunset. Therefore seven is the number of the young light, and it arises when six, the number of the great darkness, is increased by one. In this way the state of rest gives place to movement.

THE IMAGE

Thunder within the earth:
The image of THE TURNING POINT.
Thus the kings of antiquity closed the passes
At the time of solstice.
Merchants and strangers did not go about,
And the ruler
Did not travel through the provinces.

The winter solstice has always been celebrated in China as the resting time of the year—a custom that survives in the time of rest observed at the new year. In winter the life energy, symbolized by thunder, the Arousing, is still underground. Movement is just at its beginning; therefore it must be strengthened by rest, so that it will not be dissipated by being used prematurely. This principle, i.e., of allowing energy that is renewing itself to be reinforced by rest, applies to all similar situations. The return of health after illness, the return of understanding after an estrangement: everything must be treated tenderly and with care at the beginning, so that the return may lead to a flowering.

THE LINES

○ Nine at the beginning means:
Return from a short distance.

No need for remorse.
Great good fortune.

Slight digressions from the good cannot be avoided, but one must turn back in time, before going too far. This is especially important in the development of character; every faintly evil thought must be put aside immediately, before it goes too far and takes root in the mind. Then there is no cause for remorse, and all goes well.

Six in the second place means:
Quiet return. Good fortune.

Return always calls for a decision and is an act of self-mastery. It is made easier if a man is in good company. If he can bring himself to put aside pride and follow the example of good men, good fortune results.

Six in the third place means:
Repeated return. Danger. No blame.

There are people of a certain inner instability who feel a constant urge to reverse themselves. There is danger in continually deserting the good because of uncontrolled desires, then turning back to it again because of a better resolution. However, since this does not lead to habituation in evil, a general inclination to overcome the defect is not wholly excluded.

Six in the fourth place means:
Walking in the midst of others,
One returns alone.

A man is in a society composed of inferior people, but is connected spiritually with a strong and good friend, and this makes him turn back alone. Although nothing is said of reward and punishment, this return is certainly favorable, for such a resolve to choose the good brings its own reward.

Six in the fifth place means:
Noblehearted return. No remorse.

When the time for return has come, a man should not take shelter in trivial excuses, but should look within and examine himself. And if he has done something wrong he should make a noblehearted resolve to confess his fault. No one will regret having taken this road.

> Six at the top means:
> Missing the return. Misfortune.
> Misfortune from within and without.
> If armies are set marching in this way,
> One will in the end suffer a great defeat,
> Disastrous for the ruler of the country.
> For ten years
> It will not be possible to attack again.

If a man misses the right time for return, he meets with misfortune. The misfortune has its inner cause in a wrong attitude toward the world. The misfortune coming upon him from without results from this wrong attitude. What is pictured here is blind obstinacy and the judgment that is visited upon it.

无妄

25. *Wu Wang / Innocence (The Unexpected)*

═══	*above* CH'IEN	THE CREATIVE, HEAVEN
══ ══	*below* CHÊN	THE AROUSING, THUNDER

Ch'ien, heaven, is above; Chên, movement, is below. The lower trigram Chên is under the influence of the strong line it has received from above, from heaven. When, in accord with this, movement follows the law of heaven, man is innocent and without guile. His mind is natural and true, unshadowed by reflection or ulterior designs. For wherever conscious purpose is to be seen, there the truth and innocence of nature have been lost. Nature that is not directed by the spirit is not true but degenerate nature. Starting out with the idea of the natural, the train of thought in part goes somewhat further and thus the hexagram includes also the idea of the unintentional or unexpected.

THE JUDGMENT

INNOCENCE. Supreme success.
Perseverance furthers.
If someone is not as he should be,
He has misfortune,
And it does not further him
To undertake anything.

Man has received from heaven a nature innately good, to guide him in all his movements. By devotion to this divine spirit within himself, he attains an unsullied innocence that leads him to do right with instinctive sureness and without any ulterior thought of reward and personal advantage. This instinctive certainty brings about supreme success and "furthers through perseverance." However, not everything instinctive is nature in this higher sense of the word, but only that which is right and in accord with the will of heaven. Without this quality of rightness, an unreflecting, instinctive way of acting brings only misfortune. Confucius says about this: "He who departs from innocence, what does he come to? Heaven's will and blessing do not go with his deeds."

THE IMAGE

Under heaven thunder rolls:
All things attain the natural state of innocence.
Thus the kings of old,
Rich in virtue, and in harmony with the time,
Fostered and nourished all beings.

In springtime when thunder, life energy, begins to move again under the heavens, everything sprouts and grows, and all beings receive from the creative activity of nature the childlike innocence of their original state. So it is with the good rulers of mankind: drawing on the spiritual wealth at their command, they take care of all forms of life and all forms of culture and do everything to further them, and at the proper time.

THE LINES

O Nine at the beginning means:
Innocent behavior brings good fortune.

The original impulses of the heart are always good, so that we may follow them confidently, assured of good fortune and achievement of our aims.

Six in the second place means:
If one does not count on the harvest while plowing,
Nor on the use of the ground while clearing it,
It furthers one to undertake something.

We should do every task for its own sake as time and place demand and not with an eye to the result. Then each task turns out well, and anything we undertake succeeds.

Six in the third place means:
Undeserved misfortune.
The cow that was tethered by someone
Is the wanderer's gain, the citizen's loss.

Sometimes undeserved misfortune befalls a man at the hands of another, as for instance when someone passes by and takes a tethered cow along with him. His gain is the owner's loss. In all transactions, no matter how innocent, we must accommodate ourselves to the demands of the time, otherwise unexpected misfortune overtakes us.

Nine in the fourth place means:
He who can be persevering
Remains without blame.

We cannot lose what really belongs to us, even if we throw it away. Therefore we need have no anxiety. All that need concern us is that we should remain true to our own natures and not listen to others.

O Nine in the fifth place means:
  Use no medicine in an illness
  Incurred through no fault of your own.
  It will pass of itself.

An unexpected evil may come accidentally from without. If it does not originate in one's own nature or have a foothold there, one should not resort to external means to eradicate it, but should quietly let nature take its course. Then improvement will come of itself.

  Nine at the top means:
  Innocent action brings misfortune.
  Nothing furthers.

When, in a given situation, the time is not ripe for further progress, the best thing to do is to wait quietly, without ulterior designs. If one acts thoughtlessly and tries to push ahead in opposition to fate, success will not be achieved.

大畜

26. *Ta Ch'u / The Taming Power of the Great*

☰☰	*above* KÊN	KEEPING STILL, MOUNTAIN
	below CH'IEN	THE CREATIVE, HEAVEN

The Creative is tamed by Kên, Keeping Still. This produces great power, a situation in contrast to that of the ninth hexagram, Hsiao Ch'u, THE TAMING POWER OF THE SMALL, in which the Creative is tamed by the Gentle alone. There one weak line must tame five strong lines, but here four strong lines are restrained by two weak lines; in addition to a minister, there is a prince, and the restraining power therefore is far stronger.

The hexagram has a threefold meaning, expressing different aspects of the concept "holding firm." Heaven within the mountain gives the idea of holding firm in the sense of holding together; the trigram Kên, which holds the trigram Ch'ien still, gives the idea of holding firm in the sense of holding back; the third idea is that of holding firm in the sense of caring for and nourishing. This last is suggested by the fact that a strong line at the top, which is the ruler of the hexagram, is honored and tended as a sage. The third of these meanings also attaches specifically to this strong line at the top, which represents the sage.

THE JUDGMENT

THE TAMING POWER OF THE GREAT.
Perseverance furthers.
Not eating at home brings good fortune.
It furthers one to cross the great water.

To hold firmly to great creative powers and store them up, as set forth in this hexagram, there is need of a strong, clear-headed man who is honored by the ruler. The trigram Ch'ien points to strong creative power; Kên indicates firmness and truth. Both point to light and clarity and to the daily renewal of character. Only through such daily self-renewal can a man continue at the height of his powers. Force of habit helps to keep order in quiet times; but in periods when there is a great storing up of energy, everything depends on the power of the personality. However, since the worthy are honored, as in the case of the strong personality entrusted with leadership by the ruler, it is an advantage not to eat at home but rather to earn one's bread by entering upon public office. Such a man is in harmony with heaven; therefore even great and difficult undertakings, such as crossing the great water, succeed.

THE IMAGE

Heaven within the mountain:
The image of THE TAMING POWER OF THE GREAT.
Thus the superior man acquaints himself with many
    sayings of antiquity
And many deeds of the past,
In order to strengthen his character thereby.

Heaven within the mountain points to hidden treasures. In the words and deeds of the past there lies hidden a treasure that men may use to strengthen and elevate their own characters. The way to study the past is not to confine oneself to mere knowledge of history but, through application of this knowledge, to give actuality to the past.

THE LINES

Nine at the beginning means:
Danger is at hand. It furthers one to desist.

A man wishes to make vigorous advance, but circumstances present an obstacle. He sees himself held back firmly. If he should attempt to force an advance, it would lead him into misfortune. Therefore it is better for him to compose himself and to wait until an outlet is offered for release of his stored-up energies.

Nine in the second place means:
The axletrees are taken from the wagon.

Here advance is checked just as in the third line of THE TAMING POWER OF THE SMALL (9). However, in the latter the restraining force is slight; thus a conflict arises between the propulsive and the restraining movement, as a result of which the spokes fall out of the wagon wheels, while here the restraining force is absolutely superior; hence no struggle takes place. One submits and removes the axletrees from the wagon —in other words, contents himself with waiting. In this way energy accumulates for a vigorous advance later on.

Nine in the third place means:
A good horse that follows others.
Awareness of danger,
With perseverance, furthers.
Practice chariot driving and armed defense daily.
It furthers one to have somewhere to go.

The way opens; the hindrance has been cleared away. A man is in contact with a strong will acting in the same direction as his own, and goes forward like one good horse following another. But danger still threatens, and he must remain aware of it, or he will be robbed of his firmness. Thus he must acquire skill on the one hand in what will take him forward, and on the other in what will protect him against unforeseen attacks. It is good in such a pass to have a goal toward which to strive.

Six in the fourth place means:
The headboard of a young bull.
Great good fortune.

This line and the one following it are the two that tame the forward-pushing lower lines. Before a bull's horns grow out, a headboard is fastened to its forehead, so that later when the horns appear they cannot do harm. A good way to restrain wild force is to forestall it. By so doing one achieves an easy and a great success.

O Six in the fifth place means:
The tusk of a gelded boar.
Good fortune.

Here the restraining of the impetuous forward drive is achieved in an indirect way. A boar's tusk is in itself dangerous, but if the boar's nature is altered, the tusk is no longer a menace. Thus also where men are concerned, wild force should not be combated directly; instead, its roots should be eradicated.

O Nine at the top means:
One attains the way of heaven. Success.

The time of obstruction is past. The energy long dammed up by inhibition forces its way out and achieves great success. This refers to a man who is honored by the ruler and whose principles now prevail and shape the world.

頤

27. *I* / *The Corners of the Mouth (Providing Nourishment)*

above KÊN   KEEPING STILL, MOUNTAIN
below CHÊN THE AROUSING, THUNDER

This hexagram is a picture of an open mouth; above and below are the firm lines of the lips, and between them the opening. Starting with the mouth, through which we take food for nourishment, the thought leads to nourishment itself. Nourishment of oneself, specifically of the body, is represented in the three lower lines, while the three upper lines represent nourishment and care of others, in a higher, spiritual sense.

THE JUDGMENT

THE CORNERS OF THE MOUTH.
Perseverance brings good fortune.
Pay heed to the providing of nourishment
And to what a man seeks
To fill his own mouth with.

In bestowing care and nourishment, it is important that the right people should be taken care of and that we should attend to our own nourishment in the right way. If we wish to know what anyone is like, we have only to observe on whom he bestows his care and what sides of his own nature he cultivates and nourishes. Nature nourishes all creatures. The great man fosters and takes care of superior men, in order to take care of all men through them. Mencius says about this:

If we wish to know whether anyone is superior or not, we need only observe what part of his being he regards as especially important. The body has superior and inferior, important and unimportant parts. We must not injure important parts for the sake of the unimportant, nor must we injure the superior parts for the sake of the inferior. He who cultivates the inferior parts of his nature is an inferior man. He who cultivates the superior parts of his nature is a superior man.[1]

THE IMAGE

At the foot of the mountain, thunder:

The image of PROVIDING NOURISHMENT.

Thus the superior man is careful of his words

And temperate in eating and drinking.

"God comes forth in the sign of the Arousing"[2]: when in the spring the life forces stir again, all things come into being anew. "He brings to perfection in the sign of Keeping Still": thus in the early spring, when the seeds fall to earth, all things are made ready. This is an image of providing nourishment through movement and tranquillity. The superior man takes it as a pattern for the nourishment and cultivation of his character. Words are a movement going from within outward. Eating and drinking are movements from without inward. Both kinds of movement can be modified by tranquillity. For tranquillity keeps the words that come out of the mouth from exceeding proper measure, and keeps the food that goes into the mouth from exceeding its proper measure. Thus character is cultivated.

THE LINES

Nine at the beginning means:

You let your magic tortoise go,

---

1. Book of Mencius, bk. VI, sec. A, 14. [Mencius lived from 389 to 305 B.C.]

2. [See p. 268, sec. 5.]

> And look at me with the corners of your mouth
>   drooping.
> Misfortune.

The magic tortoise is a creature possessed of such supernatural powers that it lives on air and needs no earthly nourishment. The image means that a man fitted by nature and position to live freely and independently renounces this self-reliance and instead looks with envy and discontent at others who are outwardly in better circumstances. But such base envy only arouses derision and contempt in those others. This has bad results.

> Six in the second place means:
> Turning to the summit for nourishment,
> Deviating from the path
> To seek nourishment from the hill.
> Continuing to do this brings misfortune.

Normally a person either provides his own means of nourishment or is supported in a proper way by those whose duty and privilege it is to provide for him. If, owing to weakness of spirit, a man cannot support himself, a feeling of uneasiness comes over him; this is because in shirking the proper way of obtaining a living, he accepts support as a favor from those in higher place. This is unworthy, for he is deviating from his true nature. Kept up indefinitely, this course leads to misfortune.

> Six in the third place means:
> Turning away from nourishment.
> Perseverance brings misfortune.
> Do not act thus for ten years.
> Nothing serves to further.

He who seeks nourishment that does not nourish reels from desire to gratification and in gratification craves desire. Mad pursuit of pleasure for the satisfaction of the senses never brings one to the goal. One should never (ten years is a complete cycle of time) follow this path, for nothing good can come of it.

> Six in the fourth place means:
> Turning to the summit
> For provision of nourishment
> Brings good fortune.
> Spying about with sharp eyes
> Like a tiger with insatiable craving.
> No blame.

In contrast to the six in the second place, which refers to a man bent exclusively on his own advantage, this line refers to one occupying a high position and striving to let his light shine forth. To do this he needs helpers, because he cannot attain his lofty aim alone. With the greed of a hungry tiger he is on the lookout for the right people. Since he is not working for himself but for the good of all, there is no wrong in such zeal.

> ○ Six in the fifth place means:
> Turning away from the path.
> To remain persevering brings good fortune.
> One should not cross the great water.

A man may be conscious of a deficiency in himself. He should be undertaking the nourishment of the people, but he has not the strength to do it. Thus he must turn from his accustomed path and beg counsel and help from a man who is spiritually his superior but undistinguished outwardly. If he maintains this attitude of mind perseveringly, success and good fortune are his. But he must remain aware of his dependence. He must not put his own person forward nor attempt great labors, such as crossing the great water.

> ○ Nine at the top means:
> The source of nourishment.
> Awareness of danger brings good fortune.
> It furthers one to cross the great water.

This describes a sage of the highest order, from whom emanate all influences that provide nourishment for others. Such a position brings with it heavy responsibility. If he remains conscious of this fact, he has good fortune and may confidently undertake even great and difficult labors, such as crossing the great water. These undertakings bring general happiness for him and for all others.

大過

28. Ta Kuo / Preponderance of the Great

| | above | TUI | THE JOYOUS, LAKE |
| | below | SUN | THE GENTLE, WIND, WOOD |

This hexagram consists of four strong lines inside and two weak lines outside. When the strong are outside and the weak inside, all is well and there is nothing out of balance, nothing extraordinary in the situation. Here, however, the opposite is the case. The hexagram represents a beam that is thick and heavy in the middle but too weak at the ends. This is a condition that cannot last; it must be changed, must pass, or misfortune will result.

THE JUDGMENT

PREPONDERANCE OF THE GREAT.
The ridgepole sags to the breaking point.
It furthers one to have somewhere to go.
Success.

The weight of the great is excessive. The load is too heavy for the strength of the supports. The ridgepole, on which the whole roof rests, sags to the breaking point, because its supporting ends are too weak for the load they bear. It is an exceptional time and situation; therefore extraordinary measures are demanded. It is necessary to find a way of transition as

111

quickly as possible, and to take action. This promises success. For although the strong element is in excess, it is in the middle, that is, at the center of gravity, so that a revolution is not to be feared. Nothing is to be achieved by forcible measures. The problem must be solved by gentle penetration to the meaning of the situation (as is suggested by the attribute of the inner trigram, Sun); then the change-over to other conditions will be successful. It demands real superiority; therefore the time when the great preponderates is a momentous time.

THE IMAGE

The lake rises above the trees:
The image of PREPONDERANCE OF THE GREAT.
Thus the superior man, when he stands alone,
Is unconcerned,
And if he has to renounce the world,
He is undaunted.

Extraordinary times when the great preponderates are like floodtimes when the lake rises over the treetops. But such conditions are temporary. The two trigrams indicate the attitude proper to such exceptional times: the symbol of the trigram Sun is the tree, which stands firm even though it stands alone, and the attribute of Tui is joyousness, which remains undaunted even if it must renounce the world.

THE LINES

Six at the beginning means:
To spread white rushes underneath.
No blame.

When a man wishes to undertake an enterprise in extraordinary times, he must be extraordinarily cautious, just as when setting a heavy thing down on the floor, one takes care to put rushes under it, so that nothing will break. This caution, though it may seem exaggerated, is not a mistake. Exceptional enterprises cannot succeed unless utmost caution is observed in their beginnings and in the laying of their foundations.

○ Nine in the second place means:
A dry poplar sprouts at the root.
An older man takes a young wife.
Everything furthers.

Wood is near water; hence the image of an old poplar sprouting at the root. This means an extraordinary reanimation of the processes of growth. In the same way, an extraordinary situation arises when an older man marries a young girl who suits him. Despite the unusualness of the situation, all goes well.

From the point of view of politics, the meaning is that in exceptional times one does well to join with the lowly, for this affords a possibility of renewal.

Nine in the third place means:
The ridgepole sags to the breaking point.
Misfortune.

This indicates a type of man who in times of preponderance of the great insists on pushing ahead. He accepts no advice from others, and therefore they in turn are not willing to lend him support. Because of this the burden grows, until the structure of things bends or breaks. Plunging willfully ahead in times of danger only hastens the catastrophe.

○ Nine in the fourth place means:
The ridgepole is braced. Good fortune.
If there are ulterior motives, it is humiliating.

Through friendly relations with people of lower rank, a responsible man succeeds in becoming master of the situation. But if, instead of working for the rescue of the whole, he were to misuse his connections to obtain personal power and success, it would lead to humiliation.

Nine in the fifth place means:
A withered poplar puts forth flowers.
An older woman takes a husband.
No blame. No praise.

A withered poplar that flowers exhausts its energies thereby and only hastens its end. An older woman may marry once more, but no renewal takes place. Everything remains barren. Thus, though all the amenities are observed, the net result is only the anomaly of the situation.

Applied to politics, the metaphor means that if in times of insecurity we give up alliance with those below us and keep up only the relationships we have with people of higher rank, an unstable situation is created.

> Six at the top means:
> One must go through the water.
> It goes over one's head.
> Misfortune. No blame.

Here is a situation in which the unusual has reached a climax. One is courageous and wishes to accomplish one's task, no matter what happens. This leads into danger. The water rises over one's head. This is the misfortune. But one incurs no blame in giving up one's life that the good and the right may prevail. There are things that are more important than life.

坎

29. *K'an / The Abysmal (Water)*

☵	*above*	K'AN	THE ABYSMAL, WATER
☵	*below*	K'AN	THE ABYSMAL, WATER

This hexagram consists of a doubling of the trigram K'an. It is one of the eight hexagrams in which doubling occurs. The trigram K'an means a plunging in. A yang line has plunged in between two yin lines and is closed in by them like water in a ravine. The trigram K'an is also the middle son. The Receptive has obtained the middle line of the Creative, and thus K'an develops. As an image it represents water, the water that comes from above and is in motion on earth in streams and rivers, giving rise to all life on earth.

In man's world K'an represents the heart, the soul locked up within the body, the principle of light inclosed in the dark —that is, reason. The name of the hexagram, because the trigram is doubled, has the additional meaning, "repetition of danger." Thus the hexagram is intended to designate an objective situation to which one must become accustomed, not a subjective attitude. For danger due to a subjective attitude means either foolhardiness or guile. Hence too a ravine is used to symbolize danger; it is a situation in which a man is in the same pass as the water in a ravine, and, like the water, he can escape if he behaves correctly.

THE JUDGMENT

The Abysmal repeated.
If you are sincere, you have success in your heart,
And whatever you do succeeds.

Through repetition of danger we grow accustomed to it. Water sets the example for the right conduct under such circumstances. It flows on and on, and merely fills up all the places through which it flows; it does not shrink from any dangerous spot nor from any plunge, and nothing can make it lose its own essential nature. It remains true to itself under all conditions. Thus likewise, if one is sincere when confronted with difficulties, the heart can penetrate the meaning of the situation. And once we have gained inner mastery of a problem, it will come about naturally that the action we take will succeed. In danger all that counts is really carrying out all that has to be done—thoroughness—and going forward, in order not to perish through tarrying in the danger.

Properly used, danger can have an important meaning as a protective measure. Thus heaven has its perilous height protecting it against every attempt at invasion, and earth has its mountains and bodies of water, separating countries by their dangers. Thus also rulers make use of danger to protect themselves against attacks from without and against turmoil within.

THE IMAGE

Water flows on uninterruptedly and reaches its goal:
The image of the Abysmal repeated.
Thus the superior man walks in lasting virtue
And carries on the business of teaching.

Water reaches its goal by flowing continually. It fills up every depression before it flows on. The superior man follows its example; he is concerned that goodness should be an established attribute of character rather than an accidental and isolated occurrence. So likewise in teaching others everything depends on consistency, for it is only through repetition that the pupil makes the material his own.

THE LINES

Six at the beginning means:
Repetition of the Abysmal.
In the abyss one falls into a pit.
Misfortune.

By growing used to what is dangerous, a man can easily allow it to become part of him. He is familiar with it and grows used to evil. With this he has lost the right way, and misfortune is the natural result.

○ Nine in the second place means:
The abyss is dangerous.
One should strive to attain small things only.

When we are in danger we ought not to attempt to get out of it immediately, regardless of circumstances; at first we must content ourselves with not being overcome by it. We must calmly weigh the conditions of the time and be satisfied with small gains, because for the time being a great success cannot be attained. A spring flows only sparingly at first, and tarries for some time before it makes its way into the open.

Six in the third place means:
Forward and backward, abyss on abyss.

In danger like this, pause at first and wait,
Otherwise you will fall into a pit in the abyss.
Do not act in this way.

Here every step, forward or backward, leads into danger. Escape is out of the question. Therefore we must not be misled into action, as a result of which we should only bog down deeper in the danger; disagreeable as it may be to remain in such a situation, we must wait until a way out shows itself.

Six in the fourth place means:
A jug of wine, a bowl of rice[1] with it;
Earthen vessels
Simply handed in through the window.
There is certainly no blame in this.

In times of danger ceremonious forms are dropped. What matters most is sincerity. Although as a rule it is customary for an official to present certain introductory gifts and recommendations before he is appointed, here everything is simplified to the utmost. The gifts are insignificant, there is no one to sponsor him, he introduces himself; yet all this need not be humiliating if only there is the honest intention of mutual help in danger.

Still another idea is suggested. The window is the place through which light enters the room. If in difficult times we want to enlighten someone, we must begin with that which is in itself lucid and proceed quite simply from that point on.

○ Nine in the fifth place means:
The abyss is not filled to overflowing,
It is filled only to the rim.
No blame.

Danger comes because one is too ambitious. In order to flow out of a ravine, water does not rise higher than the lowest point of the rim. So likewise a man when in danger has only to proceed along the line of least resistance; thus he reaches

---

1. The usual translation, "two bowls of rice," has been corrected on the basis of Chinese commentaries.

the goal. Great labors cannot be accomplished in such times; it is enough to get out of the danger.

> Six at the top means:
> Bound with cords and ropes,
> Shut in between thorn-hedged prison walls:
> For three years one does not find the way.
> Misfortune.

A man who in the extremity of danger has lost the right way and is irremediably entangled in his sins has no prospect of escape. He is like a criminal who sits shackled behind thorn-hedged prison walls.

30. *Li / The Clinging, Fire*

☲	*above* LI	THE CLINGING, FIRE
☲	*below* LI	THE CLINGING, FIRE

This hexagram is another double sign. The trigram Li means "to cling to something," "to be conditioned," "to depend or rest on something," and also "brightness." A dark line clings to two light lines, one above and one below—the image of an empty space between two strong lines, whereby the two strong lines are made bright. The trigram represents the middle daughter. The Creative has incorporated the central line of the Receptive, and thus Li develops. As an image, it is fire. Fire has no definite form but clings to the burning object and thus is bright. As water pours down from heaven, so fire flames up from the earth. While K'an means the soul shut within the body, Li stands for nature in its radiance.

THE JUDGMENT

THE CLINGING. Perseverance furthers.

It brings success.

Care of the cow brings good fortune.

What is dark clings to what is light and so enhances the brightness of the latter. A luminous thing giving out light must have
within itself something that perseveres; otherwise it will in
time burn itself out. Everything that gives light is dependent
on something to which it clings, in order that it may continue
to shine.

Thus sun and moon cling to heaven, and grain, grass, and
trees cling to the earth. So too the twofold clarity of the
dedicated man clings to what is right and thereby can shape
the world. Human life on earth is conditioned and unfree,
and when man recognizes this limitation and makes himself
dependent upon the harmonious and beneficent forces of the
cosmos, he achieves success. The cow is the symbol of extreme
docility. By cultivating in himself an attitude of compliance
and voluntary dependence, man acquires clarity without sharp-
ness and finds his place in the world.[1]

THE IMAGE

That which is bright rises twice:

The image of FIRE.

Thus the great man, by perpetuating this brightness,

Illumines the four quarters of the world.

Each of the two trigrams represents the sun in the course of a
day. The two together represent the repeated movement of
the sun, the function of light with respect to time. The great
man continues the work of nature in the human world.
Through the clarity of his nature he causes the light to spread

---

1. It is a noteworthy and curious coincidence that fire and care of
the cow are connected here just as in the Parsee religion. [According
to the Parsee belief the Divine Light, or Fire, was manifested in the
mineral, vegetable, and animal worlds before it appeared in human
form. Its animal incarnation was the cow, and Ahura-Mazda was
nourished on her milk.]

farther and farther and to penetrate the nature of man ever more deeply.

THE LINES

Nine at the beginning means:
The footprints run crisscross.
If one is seriously intent, no blame.

It is early morning and work begins. The mind has been closed to the outside world in sleep; now its connections with the world begin again. The traces of one's impressions run crisscross. Activity and haste prevail. It is important then to preserve inner composure and not to allow oneself to be swept along by the bustle of life. If one is serious and composed, he can acquire the clarity of mind needed for coming to terms with the innumerable impressions that pour in. It is precisely at the beginning that serious concentration is important, because the beginning holds the seed of all that is to follow.

O Six in the second place means:
Yellow light. Supreme good fortune.

Midday has come; the sun shines with a yellow light. Yellow is the color of measure and mean. Yellow light is therefore a symbol of the highest culture and art, whose consummate harmony consists in holding to the mean.

Nine in the third place means:
In the light of the setting sun,
Men either beat the pot and sing
Or loudly bewail the approach of old age.
Misfortune.

Here the end of the day has come. The light of the setting sun calls to mind the fact that life is transitory and conditional. Caught in this external bondage, men are usually robbed of their inner freedom as well. The sense of the transitoriness of life impels them to uninhibited revelry in order to enjoy life while it lasts, or else they yield to melancholy and spoil the precious time by lamenting the approach of old age. Both attitudes are wrong. To the superior man it makes no difference whether death comes early or late. He cultivates himself, awaits his allotted time, and in this way secures his fate.

> Nine in the fourth place means:
> Its coming is sudden;
> It flames up, dies down, is thrown away.

Clarity of mind has the same relation to life that fire has to wood. Fire clings to wood, but also consumes it. Clarity of mind is rooted in life but can also consume it. Everything depends upon how the clarity functions. Here the image used is that of a meteor or a straw fire. A man who is excitable and restless may rise quickly to prominence but produces no lasting effects. Thus matters end badly when a man spends himself too rapidly and consumes himself like a meteor.

○ Six in the fifth place means:
> Tears in floods, sighing and lamenting.
> Good fortune.

Here the zenith of life has been reached. Were there no warning, one would at this point consume oneself like a flame. Instead, understanding the vanity of all things, one may put aside both hope and fear, and sigh and lament: if one is intent on retaining his clarity of mind, good fortune will come from this grief. For here we are dealing not with a passing mood, as in the nine in the third place, but with a real change of heart.

> Nine at the top means:
> The king uses him to march forth and chastise.
> Then it is best to kill the leaders
> And take captive the followers. No blame.

It is not the purpose of chastisement to impose punishment blindly but to create discipline. Evil must be cured at its roots. To eradicate evil in political life, it is best to kill the ringleaders and spare the followers. In educating oneself it is best to root out bad habits and tolerate those that are harmless. For asceticism that is too strict, like sentences of undue severity, fails in its purpose.

PART II

31. *Hsien / Influence (Wooing)*

above	TUI	THE JOYOUS, LAKE
below	KÊN	KEEPING STILL, MOUNTAIN

The name of the hexagram means "universal," "general," and in a figurative sense "to influence," "to stimulate." The upper trigram is Tui, the Joyous; the lower is Kên, Keeping Still. By its persistent, quiet influence, the lower, rigid trigram stimulates the upper, weak trigram, which responds to this stimulation cheerfully and joyously. Kên, the lower trigram, is the youngest son; the upper, Tui, is the youngest daughter. Thus the universal mutual attraction between the sexes is represented. In courtship, the masculine principle must seize the initiative and place itself below the feminine principle.

Just as the first part of book I begins with the hexagrams of heaven and earth, the foundations of all that exists, the second part begins with the hexagrams of courtship and marriage, the foundations of all social relationships.

THE JUDGMENT

Influence. Success.

Perseverance furthers.

To take a maiden to wife brings good fortune.

The weak element is above, the strong below; hence their powers attract each other, so that they unite. This brings about success, for all success depends on the effect of mutual attraction. By keeping still within while experiencing joy without, one can prevent the joy from going to excess and hold it within proper bounds. This is the meaning of the added

admonition, "Perseverance furthers," for it is perseverance
that makes the difference between seduction and courtship;
in the latter the strong man takes a position inferior to that of
the weak girl and shows consideration for her. This attraction
between affinities is a general law of nature. Heaven and earth
attract each other and thus all creatures come into being.
Through such attraction the sage influences men's hearts, and
thus the world attains peace. From the attractions they exert
we can learn the nature of all beings in heaven and on earth.

THE IMAGE

A lake on the mountain:
The image of influence.
Thus the superior man encourages people to
    approach him
By his readiness to receive them.

A mountain with a lake on its summit is stimulated by the
moisture from the lake. It has this advantage because its
summit does not jut out as a peak but is sunken. The image
counsels that the mind should be kept humble and free, so
that it may remain receptive to good advice. People soon give
up counseling a man who thinks that he knows everything
better than anyone else.

THE LINES

Six at the beginning means:
The influence shows itself in the big toe.

A movement, before it is actually carried out, shows itself first
in the toes. The idea of an influence is already present, but it
is not immediately apparent to others. As long as the intention
has no visible effect, it is of no importance to the outside world
and leads neither to good nor to evil.

Six in the second place means:
The influence shows itself in the calves of the legs.
Misfortune.
Tarrying brings good fortune.

In movement, the calf of the leg follows the foot; by itself it can neither go forward nor stand still. Since the movement is not self-governed, it bodes ill. One should wait quietly until one is impelled to action by a real influence. Then one remains uninjured.

> Nine in the third place means:
> The influence shows itself in the thighs.
> Holds to that which follows it.
> To continue is humiliating.

Every mood of the heart influences us to movement. What the heart desires, the thighs run after without a moment's hesitation; they hold to the heart, which they follow. In the life of man, however, acting on the spur of every caprice is wrong and if continued leads to humiliation. Three considerations suggest themselves here. First, a man should not run precipitately after all the persons whom he would like to influence, but must be able to hold back under certain circumstances. As little should he yield immediately to every whim of those in whose service he stands. Finally, where the moods of his own heart are concerned, he should never ignore the possibility of inhibition, for this is the basis of human freedom.

> ○ Nine in the fourth place means:
> Perseverance brings good fortune.
> Remorse disappears.
> If a man is agitated in mind,
> And his thoughts go hither and thither,
> Only those friends
> On whom he fixes his conscious thoughts
> Will follow.

Here the place of the heart is reached. The impulse that springs from this source is the most important of all. It is of particular concern that this influence be constant and good; then, in spite of the danger arising from the great susceptibility of the human heart, there will be no cause for remorse. When the quiet power of a man's own character is at work, the effects produced are right. All those who are receptive to the vibrations of such a spirit will then be influenced. Influence over others should not express itself as a conscious and willed effort to manipulate them. Through practicing such conscious incitement, one becomes wrought up and is exhausted by the eternal stress and strain. Moreover, the effects produced are then limited to those on whom one's thoughts are consciously fixed.

○ Nine in the fifth place means:
  The influence shows itself in the back of the neck.
  No remorse.

The back of the neck is the most rigid part of the body. When the influence shows itself there, the will remains firm and the influence does not lead to confusion. Hence remorse does not enter into consideration here. What takes place in the depths of one's being, in the unconscious, can neither be called forth nor prevented by the conscious mind. It is true that if we cannot be influenced ourselves, we cannot influence the outside world.

  Six at the top means:
  The influence shows itself in the jaws, cheeks, and
    tongue.

The most superficial way of trying to influence others is through talk that has nothing real behind it. The influence produced by such mere tongue wagging must necessarily remain insignificant. Hence no indication is added regarding good or bad fortune.

恒

32. *Hêng* / *Duration*

☰☰ *above* CHÊN THE AROUSING, THUNDER
☰☰ *below* SUN THE GENTLE, WIND

The strong trigram Chên is above, the weak trigram Sun below. This hexagram is the inverse of the preceding one. In the latter we have influence, here we have union as an enduring condition. The two images are thunder and wind, which are likewise constantly paired phenomena. The lower trigram indicates gentleness within; the upper, movement without.

In the sphere of social relationships, the hexagram represents the institution of marriage as the enduring union of the sexes. During courtship the young man subordinates himself to the girl, but in marriage, which is represented by the coming together of the eldest son and the eldest daughter, the husband is the directing and moving force outside, while the wife, inside, is gentle and submissive.

THE JUDGMENT

DURATION. Success. No blame.
Perseverance furthers.
It furthers one to have somewhere to go.

Duration is a state whose movement is not worn down by hindrances. It is not a state of rest, for mere standstill is regression. Duration is rather the self-contained and therefore self-renewing movement of an organized, firmly integrated whole, taking place in accordance with immutable laws and beginning anew at every ending. The end is reached by an inward movement, by inhalation, systole, contraction, and this movement turns into a new beginning, in which the movement is directed outward, in exhalation, diastole, expansion.

Heavenly bodies exemplify duration. They move in their fixed orbits, and because of this their light-giving power endures. The seasons of the year follow a fixed law of change and transformation, hence can produce effects that endure.

So likewise the dedicated man embodies an enduring meaning in his way of life, and thereby the world is formed. In that which gives things their duration, we can come to understand the nature of all beings in heaven and on earth.

THE IMAGE

Thunder and wind: the image of DURATION.
Thus the superior man stands firm
And does not change his direction.

Thunder rolls, and the wind blows; both are examples of extreme mobility and so are seemingly the very opposite of duration, but the laws governing their appearance and subsidence, their coming and going, endure. In the same way the independence of the superior man is not based on rigidity and immobility of character. He always keeps abreast of the time and changes with it. What endures is the unswerving directive, the inner law of his being, which determines all his actions.

THE LINES

Six at the beginning means:
Seeking duration too hastily brings misfortune persistently.
Nothing that would further.

Whatever endures can be created only gradually by long-continued work and careful reflection. In the same sense Lao-tse says: "If we wish to compress something, we must first let it fully expand." He who demands too much at once is acting precipitately, and because he attempts too much, he ends by succeeding in nothing.

○ Nine in the second place means:
Remorse disappears.

The situation is abnormal. A man's force of character is greater than the available material power. Thus he might be afraid of allowing himself to attempt something beyond his strength. However, since it is the time of DURATION, it is possible for him to control his inner strength and so to avoid excess. Cause for remorse then disappears.

> Nine in the third place means:
> He who does not give duration to his character
> Meets with disgrace.
> Persistent humiliation.

If a man remains at the mercy of moods of hope or fear aroused by the outer world, he loses his inner consistency of character. Such inconsistency invariably leads to distressing experiences. These humiliations often come from an unforeseen quarter. Such experiences are not merely effects produced by the external world, but logical consequences evoked by his own nature.

> Nine in the fourth place means:
> No game in the field.

If we are in pursuit of game and want to get a shot at a quarry, we must set about it in the right way. A man who persists in stalking game in a place where there is none may wait forever without finding any. Persistence in search is not enough. What is not sought in the right way is not found.

> Six in the fifth place means:
> Giving duration to one's character through perseverance.
> This is good fortune for a woman, misfortune for a man.

A woman should follow a man her whole life long, but a man should at all times hold to what is his duty at the given moment. Should he persistently seek to conform to the woman, it would be a mistake for him. Accordingly it is altogether right for a woman to hold conservatively to tradition, but a man must always be flexible and adaptable and allow himself to be guided solely by what his duty requires of him at the moment.

> Six at the top means:
> Restlessness as an enduring condition brings mis-
> fortune.

There are people who live in a state of perpetual hurry without ever attaining inner composure. Restlessness not only prevents all thoroughness but actually becomes a danger if it is dominant in places of authority.

33. *Tun / Retreat*

☰	*above* CH'IEN	THE CREATIVE, HEAVEN
☶	*below* KÊN	KEEPING STILL, MOUNTAIN

The power of the dark is ascending. The light retreats to security, so that the dark cannot encroach upon it. This retreat is a matter not of man's will but of natural law. Therefore in this case withdrawal is proper; it is the correct way to behave in order not to exhaust one's forces.[1]

In the calendar this hexagram is linked with the sixth month (July–August), in which the forces of winter are already showing their influence.

THE JUDGMENT

RETREAT. Success.

In what is small, perseverance furthers.

---

1. The idea expressed by this hexagram is similar to that in the saying of Jesus: "But I say unto you, That ye resist not evil" (Matt. 5:39).

Conditions are such that the hostile forces favored by the time are advancing. In this case retreat is the right course, and it is through retreat that success is achieved. But success consists in being able to carry out the retreat correctly. Retreat is not to be confused with flight. Flight means saving oneself under any circumstances, whereas retreat is a sign of strength. We must be careful not to miss the right moment while we are in full possession of power and position. Then we shall be able to interpret the signs of the time before it is too late and to prepare for provisional retreat instead of being drawn into a desperate life-and-death struggle. Thus we do not simply abandon the field to the opponent; we make it difficult for him to advance by showing perseverance in single acts of resistance. In this way we prepare, while retreating, for the counter-movement. Understanding the laws of a constructive retreat of this sort is not easy. The meaning that lies hidden in such a time is important.

THE IMAGE

Mountain under heaven: the image of RETREAT.
Thus the superior man keeps the inferior man at a
    distance,
Not angrily but with reserve.

The mountain rises up under heaven, but owing to its nature it finally comes to a stop. Heaven on the other hand retreats upward before it into the distance and remains out of reach. This symbolizes the behavior of the superior man toward a climbing inferior; he retreats into his own thoughts as the inferior man comes forward. He does not hate him, for hatred is a form of subjective involvement by which we are bound to the hated object. The superior man shows strength (heaven) in that he brings the inferior man to a standstill (mountain) by his dignified reserve.

THE LINES

☐ Six at the beginning means:
    At the tail in retreat. This is dangerous.
    One must not wish to undertake anything.

Since the hexagram is the picture of something that is retreating, the lowest line represents the tail and the top line the head. In a retreat it is advantageous to be at the front. Here one is at the back, in immediate contact with the pursuing enemy. This is dangerous, and under such circumstances it is not advisable to undertake anything. Keeping still is the easiest way of escaping from the threatening danger.

☐ Six in the second place means:
   He holds him fast with yellow oxhide.
   No one can tear him loose.

Yellow is the color of the middle. It indicates that which is correct and in line with duty. Oxhide is strong and not to be torn.

While the superior men retreat and the inferior press after them, the inferior man represented here holds on so firmly and tightly to the superior men that the latter cannot shake him off. And because he is in quest of what is right and so strong in purpose, he reaches his goal. [2] Thus the line confirms what is said in the Judgment: "In what is small"—here equivalent to "in the inferior man"—"perseverance furthers."

   Nine in the third place means:
   A halted retreat
   Is nerve-wracking and dangerous.
   To retain people as men- and maidservants
   Brings good fortune.

When it is time to retreat it is both unpleasant and dangerous to be held back, because then one no longer has freedom of action. In such a case the only expedient is to take into one's service, so to speak, those who refuse to let one go, so that one may at least keep one's initiative and not fall helplessly under their domination. But even with this expedient the situation is far from satisfactory—for what can one hope to accomplish with such servants?

---

2. A similar idea is suggested in the story of Jacob's battle with the angel of Peniel: "I will not let thee go, except thou bless me" (Gen. 32 : 26).

Nine in the fourth place means:
Voluntary retreat brings good fortune to the
    superior man
And downfall to the inferior man.

In retreating the superior man is intent on taking his departure willingly and in all friendliness. He easily adjusts his mind to retreat, because in retreating he does not have to do violence to his convictions. The only one who suffers is the inferior man from whom he retreats, who will degenerate when deprived of the guidance of the superior man.

○ Nine in the fifth place means:
Friendly retreat. Perseverance brings good fortune.

It is the business of the superior man to recognize in time that the moment for retreat has come. If the right moment is chosen, the retreat can be carried out within the forms of perfect friendliness, without the necessity of disagreeable discussions. Yet, for all the observance of amenities, absolute firmness of decision is necessary if one is not to be led astray by irrelevant considerations.

Nine at the top means:
Cheerful retreat. Everything serves to further.

The situation is unequivocal. Inner detachment has become an established fact, and we are at liberty to depart. When one sees the way ahead thus clearly, free of all doubt, a cheerful mood sets in, and one chooses what is right without further thought. Such a clear path ahead always leads to the good.

大壯

34. *Ta Chuang* / The Power of the Great

above	CHÊN	THE AROUSING, THUNDER
below	CH'IEN	THE CREATIVE, HEAVEN

The great lines, that is, the light, strong lines, are powerful. Four light lines have entered the hexagram from below and are about to ascend higher. The upper trigram is Chên, the Arousing; the lower is Ch'ien, the Creative. Ch'ien is strong, Chên produces movement. The union of movement and strength gives the meaning of THE POWER OF THE GREAT. The hexagram is linked with the second month (March–April).

THE JUDGMENT

THE POWER OF THE GREAT. Perseverance furthers.

The hexagram points to a time when inner worth mounts with great force and comes to power. But its strength has already passed beyond the median line, hence there is danger that one may rely entirely on one's own power and forget to ask what is right. There is danger too that, being intent on movement, we may not wait for the right time. Therefore the added statement that perseverance furthers. For that is truly great power which does not degenerate into mere force but remains inwardly united with the fundamental principles of right and of justice. When we understand this point—namely, that greatness and justice must be indissolubly united—we understand the true meaning of all that happens in heaven and on earth.

THE IMAGE

Thunder in heaven above:
The image of THE POWER OF THE GREAT.

Thus the superior man does not tread upon paths
That do not accord with established order.

Thunder—electrical energy—mounts upward in the spring.
The direction of this movement is in harmony with that of the
movement of heaven. It is therefore a movement in accord
with heaven, producing great power. However, true greatness
depends on being in harmony with what is right. Therefore in
times of great power the superior man avoids doing anything
that is not in harmony with the established order.

THE LINES

Nine at the beginning means:
Power in the toes.
Continuing brings misfortune.
This is certainly true.

The toes are in the lowest place and are ready to advance. So
likewise great power in lowly station is inclined to effect advance by force. This, if carried further, would certainly lead
to misfortune, and therefore by way of advice a warning is
added.

Nine in the second place means:
Perseverance brings good fortune.

The premise here is that the gates to success are beginning to
open. Resistance gives way and we forge ahead. This is the
point at which, only too easily, we become the prey of exuber-
ant self-confidence. This is why the oracle says that perseverance (i.e., perseverance in inner equilibrium, without
excessive use of power) brings good fortune.

Nine in the third place means:
The inferior man works through power.
The superior man does not act thus.
To continue is dangerous.
A goat butts against a hedge
And gets its horns entangled.

Making a boast of power leads to entanglements, just as a goat entangles its horns when it butts against a hedge. Whereas an inferior man revels in power when he comes into possession of it, the superior man never makes this mistake. He is conscious at all times of the danger of pushing ahead regardless of circumstances, and therefore renounces in good time the empty display of force.

○ Nine in the fourth place means:

Perseverance brings good fortune.

Remorse disappears.

The hedge opens; there is no entanglement.

Power depends upon the axle of a big cart.

If a man goes on quietly and perseveringly working at the removal of resistances, success comes in the end. The obstructions give way and all occasion for remorse arising from excessive use of power disappears.

Such a man's power does not show externally, yet it can move heavy loads, like a big cart whose real strength lies in its axle. The less that power is applied outwardly, the greater its effect.

Six in the fifth place means:

Loses the goat with ease.

No remorse.

The goat is noted for hardness outwardly and weakness within. Now the situation is such that everything is easy; there is no more resistance. One can give up a belligerent, stubborn way of acting and will not have to regret it.

Six at the top means:

A goat butts against a hedge.

It cannot go backward, it cannot go forward.

Nothing serves to further.

If one notes the difficulty, this brings good fortune.

If we venture too far we come to a deadlock, unable either to advance or to retreat, and whatever we do merely serves to complicate things further. Such obstinacy leads to insuperable difficulties. But if, realizing the situation, we compose ourselves and decide not to continue, everything will right itself in time.

35. *Chin / Progress*

	above	LI	THE CLINGING, FIRE
	below	K'UN	THE RECEPTIVE, EARTH

The hexagram represents the sun rising over the earth. It is therefore the symbol of rapid, easy progress, which at the same time means ever widening expansion and clarity.

THE JUDGMENT

PROGRESS. The powerful prince
Is honored with horses in large numbers.
In a single day he is granted audience three times.

As an example of progress, this pictures a time when a powerful feudal lord rallies the other lords around the sovereign and pledges fealty and peace. The sovereign rewards him richly and invites him to a closer intimacy.

A twofold idea is set forth here. The actual effect of the progress emanates from a man who is in a dependent position and whom the others regard as their equal and are therefore willing to follow. This leader has enough clarity of vision not to abuse his great influence but to use it rather for the benefit of his ruler. His ruler in turn is free of all jealousy, showers presents on the great man, and invites him continually to his court. An enlightened ruler and an obedient servant—this is the condition on which great progress depends.

THE IMAGE

The sun rises over the earth:
The image of PROGRESS.
Thus the superior man himself
Brightens his bright virtue.

The light of the sun as it rises over the earth is by nature clear. The higher the sun rises, the more it emerges from the dark mists, spreading the pristine purity of its rays over an ever widening area. The real nature of man is likewise originally good, but it becomes clouded by contact with earthly things and therefore needs purification before it can shine forth in its native clarity.[1]

THE LINES

Six at the beginning means:
Progressing, but turned back.
Perseverance brings good fortune.
If one meets with no confidence, one should remain
     calm.
No mistake.

At a time when all elements are pressing for progress, we are still uncertain whether in the course of advance we may not meet with a rebuff. Then the thing to do is simply to continue in what is right; in the end this will bring good fortune. It may be that we meet with no confidence. In this case we ought not to try to win confidence regardless of the situation, but should remain calm and cheerful and refuse to be roused to anger. Thus we remain free of mistakes.

Six in the second place means:
Progressing, but in sorrow.
Perseverance brings good fortune.
Then one obtains great happiness from one's
     ancestress.

---

1. This is the theme dealt with in detail in the Great Learning, *Ta Hsüeh* [*The Chinese Classics*, I: *Confucian Analects*, etc., tr. James Legge, 2nd edn., Oxford, 1893, pp. 355–81].

Progress is halted; an individual is kept from getting in touch with the man in authority with whom he has a connection. When this happens, he must remain persevering, although he is grieved; then with a maternal gentleness the man in question will bestow great happiness upon him. This happiness comes to him—and is well deserved—because in this case mutual attraction does not rest on selfish or partisan motives but on firm and correct principles.

Six in the third place means:
All are in accord. Remorse disappears.

A man strives onward, in association with others whose backing encourages him. This dispels any cause for regret over the fact that he does not have enough independence to triumph un-aided over every hostile turn of fate.

Nine in the fourth place means:
Progress like a hamster.
Perseverance brings danger.

In times of progress it is easy for strong men in the wrong places to amass great possessions. But such conduct shuns the light. And since times of progress are also always times in which dubious procedures are inevitably brought to light, perseverance in such action always leads to danger.

O Six in the fifth place means:
Remorse disappears.
Take not gain and loss to heart.
Undertakings bring good fortune.
Everything serves to further.

The situation described here is that of one who, finding himself in an influential position in a time of progress, remains gentle and reserved. He might reproach himself for lack of energy in making the most of the propitiousness of the time and obtaining all possible advantage. However, this regret passes away. He must not take either loss or gain to heart; they are minor considerations. What matters much more is the fact that in this way he has assured himself of opportunities for successful and beneficent influence.

138

Nine at the top means:
Making progress with the horns is permissible
Only for the purpose of punishing one's own city.
To be conscious of danger brings good fortune.
No blame.
Perseverance brings humiliation.

Making progress with lowered horns—i.e., acting on the offensive—is permissible, in times like those referred to here, only in dealing with the mistakes of one's own people. Even then we must bear in mind that proceeding on the offensive may always be dangerous. In this way we avoid the mistakes that otherwise threaten, and succeed in what we set out to do. On the other hand, perseverance in such overenergetic behavior, especially toward persons with whom there is no close connection, will lead to humiliation.

明夷

36. *Ming I / Darkening of the Light*

	above	K'UN	THE RECEPTIVE, EARTH
	below	LI	THE CLINGING, FIRE

Here the sun has sunk under the earth and is therefore darkened. The name of the hexagram means literally "wounding of the bright"; hence the individual lines contain frequent references to wounding. The situation is the exact opposite of that in the foregoing hexagram. In the latter a wise man at the head of affairs has able helpers, and in company with them makes progress; here a man of dark nature is in a position of authority and brings harm to the wise and able man.

THE JUDGMENT

DARKENING OF THE LIGHT. In adversity
It furthers one to be persevering.

One must not unresistingly let himself be swept along by unfavorable circumstances, nor permit his steadfastness to be
shaken. He can avoid this by maintaining his inner light, while
remaining outwardly yielding and tractable. With this attitude
he can overcome even the greatest adversities.

In some situations indeed a man must hide his light, in
order to make his will prevail in spite of difficulties in his immediate environment. Perseverance must dwell in inmost
consciousness and should not be discernible from without.
Only thus is a man able to maintain his will in the face of
difficulties.

THE IMAGE

The light has sunk into the earth:
The image of DARKENING OF THE LIGHT.
Thus does the superior man live with the great mass:
He veils his light, yet still shines.

In a time of darkness it is essential to be cautious and reserved.
One should not needlessly awaken overwhelming enmity by
inconsiderate behavior. In such times one ought not to fall in
with the practices of others; neither should one drag them
censoriously into the light. In social intercourse one should
not try to be all-knowing. One should let many things pass,
without being duped.

THE LINES

Nine at the beginning means:
Darkening of the light during flight.
He lowers his wings.
The superior man does not eat for three days
On his wanderings.
But he has somewhere to go.
The host has occasion to gossip about him.

With grandiose resolve a man endeavors to soar above all obstacles, but thus encounters a hostile fate. He retreats and evades the issue. The time is difficult. Without rest, he must hurry along, with no permanent abiding place. If he does not want to make compromises within himself, but insists on remaining true to his principles, he suffers deprivation. Nevertheless he has a fixed goal to strive for, even though the people with whom he lives do not understand him and speak ill of him.

○ Six in the second place means:
   Darkening of the light injures him in the left thigh.
   He gives aid with the strength of a horse.
   Good fortune.

Here the Lord of Light is in a subordinate place and is wounded by the Lord of Darkness. But the injury is not fatal; it is only a hindrance. Rescue is still possible. The wounded man gives no thought to himself; he thinks only of saving the others who are also in danger. Therefore he tries with all his strength to save all that can be saved. There is good fortune in thus acting according to duty.

   Nine in the third place means:
   Darkening of the light during the hunt in the south.
   Their great leader is captured.
   One must not expect perseverance too soon.

It seems as if chance were at work. While the strong, loyal man is striving eagerly and in good faith to create order, he meets the ringleader of the disorder, as if by accident, and seizes him. Thus victory is achieved. But in abolishing abuses one must not be too hasty. This would turn out badly because the abuses have been in existence so long.

   Six in the fourth place means:
   He penetrates the left side of the belly.
   One gets at the very heart of the darkening of the light,
   And leaves gate and courtyard.

We find ourselves close to the commander of darkness and so discover his most secret thoughts. In this way we realize that there is no longer any hope of improvement, and thus we are enabled to leave the scene of disaster before the storm breaks.

○ Six in the fifth place means:
   Darkening of the light as with Prince Chi.
   Perseverance furthers.

Prince Chi lived at the court of the evil tyrant Chou Hsin, who, although not mentioned by name, furnishes the historical example on which this whole situation is based. Prince Chi was a relative of the tyrant and could not withdraw from court; therefore he concealed his true sentiments and feigned insanity. Although he was held a slave, he did not allow external misery to deflect him from his convictions.

This provides a teaching for those who cannot leave their posts in times of darkness. In order to escape danger, they need invincible perseverance of spirit and redoubled caution in their dealings with the world.

□ Six at the top means:
   Not light but darkness.
   First he climbed up to heaven,
   Then he plunged into the depths of the earth.

Here the climax of the darkening is reached. The dark power at first held so high a place that it could wound all who were on the side of good and of the light. But in the end it perishes of its own darkness, for evil must itself fall at the very moment when it has wholly overcome the good, and thus consumed the energy to which it owed its duration.

家人

37. *Chia Jên* / *The Family* [*The Clan*]

above	SUN	THE GENTLE, WIND
below	LI	THE CLINGING, FIRE

This hexagram represents the laws obtaining within the family. The strong line at the top represents the father, the lowest the son. The strong line in the fifth place represents the husband, the yielding second line the wife. On the other hand, the two strong lines in the fifth and the third place represent two brothers, and the two weak lines correlated with them in the fourth and the second place stand for their respective wives. Thus all the connections and relationships within the family find their appropriate expression. Each individual line has the character according with its place. The fact that a strong line occupies the sixth place—where a weak line might be expected—indicates very clearly the strong leadership that must come from the head of the family. The line is to be considered here not in its quality as the sixth but in its quality as the top line. THE FAMILY shows the laws operative within the household that, transferred to outside life, keep the state and the world in order. The influence that goes out from within the family is represented by the symbol of the wind created by fire.

THE JUDGMENT

THE FAMILY. The perseverance of the woman furthers.

The foundation of the family is the relationship between husband and wife. The tie that holds the family together lies in the loyalty and perseverance of the wife. Her place is within (second line), while that of the husband is without (fifth line). It is in accord with the great laws of nature that husband and wife take their proper places. Within the family a strong authority is needed; this is represented by the parents. If the father is really a father and the son a son, if the elder brother fulfills his position, and the younger fulfills his, if the husband is really a husband and the wife a wife, then the family is in order. When the family is in order, all the social relationships of mankind will be in order.

Three of the five social relationships are to be found within the family—that between father and son, which is the relation of love, that between husband and wife, which is the relation of chaste conduct, and that between elder and younger brother, which is the relation of correctness. The loving reverence of the son is then carried over to the prince in the form of faithfulness to duty; the affection and correctness of behavior existing between the two brothers are extended to a friend in the form of loyalty, and to a person of superior rank in the form of deference. The family is society in embryo; it is the native soil on which performance of moral duty is made easy through natural affection, so that within a small circle a basis of moral practice is created, and this is later widened to include human relationships in general.

THE IMAGE

Wind comes forth from fire:
The image of THE FAMILY.
Thus the superior man has substance in his words
And duration in his way of life.

Heat creates energy: this is signified by the wind stirred up by the fire and issuing forth from it. This represents influence working from within outward. The same thing is needed in the regulation of the family. Here too the influence on others must proceed from one's own person. In order to be capable of producing such an influence, one's words must have power, and this they can have only if they are based on something real, just as flame depends on its fuel. Words have influence only when they are pertinent and clearly related to definite circumstances. General discourses and admonitions have no effect whatsoever. Furthermore, the words must be supported by one's entire conduct, just as the wind is made effective by its duration. Only firm and consistent conduct will make such an impression on others that they can adapt and conform to it. If words and conduct are not in accord and not consistent, they will have no effect.

THE LINES

Nine at the beginning means:
Firm seclusion within the family.
Remorse disappears.

The family must form a well-defined unit within which each member knows his place. From the beginning each child must be accustomed to firmly established rules of order, before ever its will is directed to other things. If we begin too late to enforce order, when the will of the child has already been overindulged, the whims and passions, grown stronger with the years, offer resistance and give cause for remorse. If we insist on order from the outset, occasions for remorse may arise —in general social life these are unavoidable—but the remorse always disappears again, and everything rights itself. For there is nothing more easily avoided and more difficult to carry through than "breaking a child's will."

O Six in the second place means:
She should not follow her whims.
She must attend within to the food.
Perseverance brings good fortune.

The wife must always be guided by the will of the master of the house, be he father, husband, or grown son. Her place is within the house. There, without having to look for them, she has great and important duties. She must attend to the nourishment of her family and to the food for the sacrifice. In this way she becomes the center of the social and religious life of the family, and her perseverance in this position brings good fortune to the whole house.

In relation to general conditions, the counsel given here is to seek nothing by means of force, but quietly to confine one-self to the duties at hand.

> Nine in the third place means:
> When tempers flare up in the family,
> Too great severity brings remorse.
> Good fortune nonetheless.
> When woman and child dally and laugh,
> It leads in the end to humiliation.

In the family the proper mean between severity and indulgence ought to prevail. Too great severity toward one's own flesh and blood leads to remorse. The wise thing is to build strong dikes within which complete freedom of movement is allowed each individual. But in doubtful instances too great severity, despite occasional mistakes, is preferable, because it preserves discipline in the family, whereas too great weakness leads to disgrace.

> Six in the fourth place means:
> She is the treasure of the house.
> Great good fortune.

It is upon the woman of the house that the well-being of the family depends. Well-being prevails when expenditures and income are soundly balanced. This leads to great good fortune. In the sphere of public life, this line refers to the faithful steward whose measures further the general welfare.

> ○ Nine in the fifth place means:
> As a king he approaches his family.
> Fear not.
> Good fortune.

A king is the symbol of a fatherly man who is richly endowed in mind. He does nothing to make himself feared; on the contrary, the whole family can trust him, because love governs their intercourse. His character of itself exercises the right influence.

Nine at the top means:
His work commands respect.
In the end good fortune comes.

In the last analysis, order within the family depends on the character of the master of the house. If he cultivates his personality so that it works impressively through the force of inner truth, all goes well with the family. In a ruling position one must of his own accord assume responsibility.

38. *K'uei* / Opposition

above	LI	THE CLINGING, FLAME
below	TUI	THE JOYOUS, LAKE

This hexagram is composed of the trigram Li above, i.e., flame, which burns upward, and Tui below, i.e., the lake, which seeps downward. These two movements are in direct contrast. Furthermore, Li is the second daughter and Tui the youngest daughter, and although they live in the same house they belong to different men; hence their wills are not the same but are divergently directed.

THE JUDGMENT

OPPOSITION. In small matters, good fortune.

When people live in opposition and estrangement they cannot carry out a great undertaking in common; their points of view diverge too widely. In such circumstances one should above all not proceed brusquely, for that would only increase the existing opposition; instead, one should limit oneself to producing gradual effects in small matters. Here success can still be expected, because the situation is such that the opposition does not preclude all agreement.

In general, opposition appears as an obstruction, but when it represents polarity within a comprehensive whole, it has also its useful and important functions. The oppositions of heaven and earth, spirit and nature, man and woman, when reconciled, bring about the creation and reproduction of life. In the world of visible things, the principle of opposites makes possible the differentiation by categories through which order is brought into the world.

THE IMAGE

Above, fire; below, the lake:
The image of OPPOSITION.
Thus amid all fellowship
The superior man retains his individuality.

The two elements, fire and water, never mingle but even when in contact retain their own natures. So the cultured man is never led into baseness or vulgarity through intercourse or community of interests with persons of another sort; regardless of all commingling, he will always preserve his individuality.

THE LINES

Nine at the beginning means:
Remorse disappears.
If you lose your horse, do not run after it;
It will come back of its own accord.
When you see evil people,
Guard yourself against mistakes.

Even in times when oppositions prevail, mistakes can be avoided, so that remorse disappears. When opposition begins to manifest itself, a man must not try to bring about unity by force, for by so doing he would only achieve the contrary, just as a horse goes farther and farther away if one runs after it. If it is one's own horse, one can safely let it go; it will come back of its own accord. So too when someone who belongs with us is momentarily estranged because of a misunderstanding, he will return of his own accord if we leave matters to him. On the other hand, it is well to be cautious when evil men who do not belong with us force themselves upon us, again as the result of a misunderstanding. Here the important thing is to avoid mistakes. We must not try to shake off these evil men by force; this would give rise to real hostility. We must simply endure them. They will eventually withdraw of their own accord.

○ Nine in the second place means:
> One meets his lord in a narrow street.
> No blame.

As a result of misunderstandings, it has become impossible for people who by nature belong together to meet in the correct way. This being so, an accidental meeting under informal circumstances may serve the purpose, provided there is an inner affinity between them.

> Six in the third place means:
> One sees the wagon dragged back,
> The oxen halted,
> A man's hair and nose cut off.
> Not a good beginning, but a good end.

Often it seems to a man as though everything were conspiring against him. He sees himself checked and hindered in his progress, insulted and dishonored.[1] However, he must not let himself be misled; despite this opposition, he must cleave to the man with whom he knows he belongs. Thus, notwithstanding the bad beginning, the matter will end well.

> Nine in the fourth place means:
> Isolated through opposition,
> One meets a like-minded man
> With whom one can associate in good faith.
> Despite the danger, no blame.

If a man finds himself in a company of people from whom he is separated by an inner opposition, he becomes isolated. But if

---

1. Cutting off of the hair and nose was a severe and degrading punishment.

149

in such a situation a man meets someone who fundamentally, by the very law of his being, is kin to him, and whom he can trust completely, he overcomes all the dangers of isolation. His will achieves its aim, and he becomes free of faults.

○ Six in the fifth place means:
　　Remorse disappears.
　　The companion bites his way through the wrappings.
　　If one goes to him,
　　How could it be a mistake?

Coming upon a sincere man, one fails to recognize him at first because of the general estrangement. However, he bites his way through the wrappings that are causing the separation. When such a companion thus reveals himself in his true character, it is one's duty to go to meet him and to work with him.

　　Nine at the top means:
　　Isolated through opposition,
　　One sees one's companion as a pig covered with dirt,
　　As a wagon full of devils.
　　First one draws a bow against him,
　　Then one lays the bow aside.
　　He is not a robber; he will woo at the right time.
　　As one goes, rain falls; then good fortune comes.

Here the isolation is due to misunderstanding; it is brought about not by outer circumstances but by inner conditions. A man misjudges his best friends, taking them to be as unclean as a dirty pig and as dangerous as a wagon full of devils. He adopts an attitude of defense. But in the end, realizing his mistake, he lays aside the bow, perceiving that the other is approaching with the best intentions for the purpose of close union. Thus the tension is relieved. The union resolves the tension, just as falling rain relieves the sultriness preceding a thunderstorm. All goes well, for just when opposition reaches its climax it changes over to its antithesis.

39. *Chien / Obstruction*

	above	K'AN	THE ABYSMAL, WATER
	below	KÊN	KEEPING STILL, MOUNTAIN

The hexagram pictures a dangerous abyss lying before us and a steep, inaccessible mountain rising behind us. We are surrounded by obstacles; at the same time, since the mountain has the attribute of keeping still, there is implicit a hint as to how we can extricate ourselves. The hexagram represents obstructions that appear in the course of time but that can and should be overcome. Therefore all the instruction given is directed to overcoming them.

THE JUDGMENT

OBSTRUCTION. The southwest furthers.
The northeast does not further.
It furthers one to see the great man.
Perseverance brings good fortune.

The southwest is the region of retreat, the northeast that of advance. Here an individual is confronted by obstacles that cannot be overcome directly. In such a situation it is wise to pause in view of the danger and to retreat. However, this is merely a preparation for overcoming the obstructions. One must join forces with friends of like mind and put himself under the leadership of a man equal to the situation: then one will succeed in removing the obstacles. This requires the will to persevere just when one apparently must do something that leads away from his goal. This unswerving inner purpose brings good fortune in the end. An obstruction that lasts only for a time is useful for self-development. This is the value of adversity.

THE IMAGE

Water on the mountain:
The image of OBSTRUCTION.
Thus the superior man turns his attention to himself
And molds his character.

Difficulties and obstructions throw a man back upon himself. While the inferior man seeks to put the blame on other persons, bewailing his fate, the superior man seeks the error within himself, and through this introspection the external obstacle becomes for him an occasion for inner enrichment and education.

THE LINES

Six at the beginning means:
Going leads to obstructions,
Coming meets with praise.

When one encounters an obstruction, the important thing is to reflect on how best to deal with it. When threatened with danger, one should not strive blindly to go ahead, for this only leads to complications. The correct thing is, on the contrary, to retreat for the time being, not in order to give up the struggle but to await the right moment for action.

Six in the second place means:
The king's servant is beset by obstruction upon
    obstruction,
But it is not his own fault.

Ordinarily it is best to go around an obstacle and try to overcome it along the line of least resistance. But there is one instance in which a man must go out to meet the trouble, even though difficulty piles upon difficulty: this is when the path of duty leads directly to it—in other words, when he cannot act of his own volition but is duty bound to go and seek out danger in the service of a higher cause. Then he may do it without compunction, because it is not through any fault of his that he is putting himself in this difficult situation.

> Nine in the third place means:
> Going leads to obstructions;
> Hence he comes back.

While the preceding line shows the official compelled by duty to follow the way of danger, this line shows the man who must act as father of a family or as head of his kin. If he were to plunge recklessly into danger, it would be a useless act, because those entrusted to his care cannot get along by themselves. But if he withdraws and turns back to his own, they welcome him with great joy.

> Six in the fourth place means:
> Going leads to obstructions,
> Coming leads to union.

This too describes a situation that cannot be managed single-handed. In such a case the direct way is not the shortest. If a person were to forge ahead on his own strength and without the necessary preparations, he would not find the support he needs and would realize too late that he has been mistaken in his calculations, inasmuch as the conditions on which he hoped he could rely would prove to be inadequate. In this case it is better, therefore, to hold back for the time being and to gather together trustworthy companions who can be counted upon for help in overcoming the obstructions.

> ○ Nine in the fifth place means:
> In the midst of the greatest obstructions,
> Friends come.

Here we see a man who is called to help in an emergency. He should not seek to evade the obstructions, no matter how dangerously they pile up before him. But because he is really called to the task, the power of his spirit is strong enough to attract helpers whom he can effectively organize, so that through the well-directed co-operation of all participants the obstruction is overcome.

> Six at the top means:
> Going leads to obstructions,
> Coming leads to great good fortune.
> It furthers one to see the great man.

This refers to a man who has already left the world and its tumult behind him. When the time of obstructions arrives, it might seem that the simplest thing for him to do would be to turn his back upon the world and take refuge in the beyond. But this road is barred to him. He must not seek his own salvation and abandon the world to its adversity. Duty calls him back once more into the turmoil of life. Precisely because of his experience and inner freedom, he is able to create something both great and complete that brings good fortune. And it is favorable to see the great man in alliance with whom one can achieve the work of rescue.

解

40. *Hsieh / Deliverance*

above	CHÊN	THE AROUSING, THUNDER
below	K'AN	THE ABYSMAL, WATER

Here the movement goes out of the sphere of danger. The obstacle has been removed, the difficulties are being resolved. Deliverance is not yet achieved; it is just in its beginning, and the hexagram represents its various stages.

THE JUDGMENT

DELIVERANCE. The southwest furthers.
If there is no longer anything where one has to go,
Return brings good fortune.
If there is still something where one has to go,
Hastening brings good fortune.

This refers to a time in which tensions and complications begin to be eased. At such times we ought to make our way back to ordinary conditions as soon as possible; this is the meaning of "the southwest." These periods of sudden change have great importance. Just as rain relieves atmospheric tension, making all the buds burst open, so a time of deliverance from burdensome pressure has a liberating and stimulating effect on life. One thing is important, however: in such times we must not overdo our triumph. The point is not to push on farther than is necessary. Returning to the regular order of life as soon as deliverance is achieved brings good fortune. If there are any residual matters that ought to be attended to, it should be done as quickly as possible, so that a clean sweep is made and no retardations occur.

THE IMAGE

Thunder and rain set in:
The image of DELIVERANCE.
Thus the superior man pardons mistakes
And forgives misdeeds.

A thunderstorm has the effect of clearing the air; the superior man produces a similar effect when dealing with mistakes and sins of men that induce a condition of tension. Through clarity he brings deliverance. However, when failings come to light, he does not dwell on them; he simply passes over mistakes, the unintentional transgressions, just as thunder dies away. He forgives misdeeds, the intentional transgressions, just as water washes everything clean.

THE LINES

Six at the beginning means:
Without blame.

In keeping with the situation, few words are needed. The hindrance is past, deliverance has come. One recuperates in peace and keeps still. This is the right thing to do in times when difficulties have been overcome.

○ Nine in the second place means:
One kills three foxes in the field

> And receives a yellow arrow.
> Perseverance brings good fortune.

The image is taken from the hunt. The hunter catches three cunning foxes and receives a yellow arrow as a reward. The obstacles in public life are the designing foxes who try to influence the ruler through flattery. They must be removed before there can be any deliverance. But the struggle must not be carried on with the wrong weapons. The yellow color points to measure and mean in proceeding against the enemy; the arrow signifies the straight course. If one devotes himself wholeheartedly to the task of deliverance, he develops so much inner strength from his rectitude that it acts as a weapon against all that is false and low.

> Six in the third place means:
> If a man carries a burden on his back
> And nonetheless rides in a carriage,
> He thereby encourages robbers to draw near.
> Perseverance leads to humiliation.

This refers to a man who has come out of needy circumstances into comfort and freedom from want. If now, in the manner of an upstart, he tries to take his ease in comfortable surroundings that do not suit his nature, he thereby attracts robbers. If he goes on thus he is sure to bring disgrace upon himself. Confucius says about this line:

Carrying a burden on the back is the business of a common man; a carriage is the appurtenance of a man of rank. Now, when a common man uses the appurtenance of a man of rank, robbers plot to take it away from him. If a man is insolent toward those above him and hard toward those below him, robbers plot to attack him. Carelessness in guarding things tempts thieves to steal. Sumptuous ornaments worn by a maiden are an enticement to rob her of her virtue.

> Nine in the fourth place means:
> Deliver yourself from your great toe.
> Then the companion comes,
> And him you can trust.

In times of standstill it will happen that inferior people attach themselves to a superior man, and through force of daily habit they may grow very close to him and become indispensable, just as the big toe is indispensable to the foot because it makes walking easier. But when the time of deliverance draws near, with its call to deeds, a man must free himself from such chance acquaintances with whom he has no inner connection. For otherwise the friends who share his views, on whom he could really rely and together with whom he could accomplish something, mistrust him and stay away.

○ Six in the fifth place means:

If only the superior man can deliver himself,

It brings good fortune.

Thus he proves to inferior men that he is in earnest.

Times of deliverance demand inner resolve. Inferior people cannot be driven off by prohibitions or any external means. If one desires to be rid of them, he must first break completely with them in his own mind; they will see for themselves that he is in earnest and will withdraw.

Six at the top means:

The prince shoots at a hawk on a high wall.

He kills it. Everything serves to further.

The hawk on a high wall is the symbol of a powerful inferior in a high position who is hindering the deliverance. He withstands the force of inner influences, because he is hardened in his wickedness. He must be forcibly removed, and this requires appropriate means. Confucius says about this line:

The hawk is the object of the hunt; bow and arrow are the tools and means. The marksman is man (who must make proper use of the means to his end). The superior man contains the means in his own person. He bides his time and then acts. Why then should not everything go well? He acts and is free. Therefore all he has to do is to go forth, and he takes his quarry. This is how a man fares who acts after he has made ready the means.

損

41. *Sun / Decrease*

	above	KÊN	KEEPING STILL, MOUNTAIN
	below	TUI	THE JOYOUS, LAKE

This hexagram represents a decrease of the lower trigram in favor of the upper, because the third line, originally strong, has moved up to the top, and the top line, originally weak, has replaced it.[1] What is below is decreased to the benefit of what is above. This is out-and-out decrease. If the foundations of a building are decreased in strength and the upper walls are strengthened, the whole structure loses its stability. Likewise, a decrease in the prosperity of the people in favor of the government is out-and-out decrease. And the entire theme of the hexagram is directed to showing how this shift of wealth can take place without causing the sources of wealth in the nation and its lower classes to fail.

THE JUDGMENT

DECREASE combined with sincerity
Brings about supreme good fortune
Without blame.
One may be persevering in this.
It furthers one to undertake something.
How is this to be carried out?
One may use two small bowls for the sacrifice.

---

1. [The present hexagram and the following one, INCREASE, are regarded as formed by changes in T'ai, PEACE (11), and P'i, STAND-STILL (12), respectively. See p. 596.]

158

Decrease does not under all circumstances mean something bad. Increase and decrease come in their own time. What matters here is to understand the time and not to try to cover up poverty with empty pretense. If a time of scanty resources brings out an inner truth, one must not feel ashamed of simplicity. For simplicity is then the very thing needed to provide inner strength for further undertakings. Indeed, there need be no concern if the outward beauty of the civilization, even the elaboration of religious forms, should have to suffer because of simplicity. One must draw on the strength of the inner attitude to compensate for what is lacking in externals; then the power of the content makes up for the simplicity of form. There is no need of presenting false appearances to God. Even with slender means, the sentiment of the heart can be expressed. [2]

THE IMAGE

At the foot of the mountain, the lake:
The image of DECREASE.
Thus the superior man controls his anger
And restrains his instincts.

The lake at the foot of the mountain evaporates. In this way it decreases to the benefit of the mountain, which is enriched by its moisture. The mountain stands as the symbol of a stubborn strength that can harden into anger. The lake is the symbol of unchecked gaiety that can develop into passionate drives at the expense of the life forces. Therefore decrease is necessary; anger must be decreased by keeping still, the instincts must be curbed by restriction. By this decrease of the lower powers of the psyche, the higher aspects of the soul are enriched.

THE LINES

Nine at the beginning means:
Going quickly when one's tasks are finished
Is without blame.
But one must reflect on how much one may decrease
    others.

_____
2. Cf. the story of the widow's mite in the Gospel of Luke.

It is unselfish and good when a man, after completing his own urgent tasks, uses his strength in the service of others, and without bragging or making much of it, helps quickly where help is needed. But the man in a superior position who is thus aided must weigh carefully how much he can accept without doing the helpful servant or friend real harm. Only where such delicacy of feeling exists can one give oneself unconditionally and without hesitation.

> Nine in the second place means:
> Perseverance furthers.
> To undertake something brings misfortune.
> Without decreasing oneself,
> One is able to bring increase to others.

A high-minded self-awareness and a consistent seriousness with no forfeit of dignity are necessary if a man wants to be of service to others. He who throws himself away in order to do the bidding of a superior diminishes his own position without thereby giving lasting benefit to the other. This is wrong. To render true service of lasting value to another, one must serve him without relinquishing oneself.

□ Six in the third place means:
> When three people journey together,
> Their number decreases by one.
> When one man journeys alone,
> He finds a companion.

When there are three people together, jealousy arises. One of them will have to go. A very close bond is possible only between two people. But when one man is lonely, he is certain to find a companion who complements him.

> Six in the fourth place means:
> If a man decreases his faults,
> It makes the other hasten to come and rejoice.
> No blame.

A man's faults often prevent even well-disposed people from coming closer to him. His faults are sometimes reinforced by the environment in which he lives. But if in humility he can bring himself to the point of giving them up, he frees his well-disposed friends from an inner pressure and causes them to approach the more quickly, and there is mutual joy.

○ Six in the fifth place means:

Someone does indeed increase him.

Ten pairs of tortoises cannot oppose it.

Supreme good fortune.

If someone is marked out by fate for good fortune, it comes without fail. All oracles—as for instance those that are read from the shells of tortoises—are bound to concur in giving him favorable signs. He need fear nothing, because his luck is ordained from on high.

□ Nine at the top means:

If one is increased without depriving others,

There is no blame.

Perseverance brings good fortune.

It furthers one to undertake something.

One obtains servants

But no longer has a separate home.

There are people who dispense blessings to the whole world. Every increase in power that comes to them benefits the whole of mankind and therefore does not bring decrease to others. Through perseverance and zealous work a man wins success and finds helpers as they are needed. But what he accomplishes is not a limited private advantage; it is a public good and available to everyone.

42. I / Increase

above	SUN	THE GENTLE, WIND
below	CHÊN	THE AROUSING, THUNDER

The idea of increase is expressed in the fact that the strong lowest line of the upper trigram has sunk down and taken its place under the lower trigram. This conception also expresses the fundamental idea on which the Book of Changes is based. To rule truly is to serve.

A sacrifice of the higher element that produces an increase of the lower is called an out-and-out increase: it indicates the spirit that alone has power to help the world.

THE JUDGMENT

INCREASE. It furthers one
To undertake something.
It furthers one to cross the great water.

Sacrifice on the part of those above for the increase of those below fills the people with a sense of joy and gratitude that is extremely valuable for the flowering of the commonwealth. When people are thus devoted to their leaders, undertakings are possible, and even difficult and dangerous enterprises will succeed. Therefore in such times of progress and successful development it is necessary to work and make the best use of the time. This time resembles that of the marriage of heaven and earth, when the earth partakes of the creative power of heaven, forming and bringing forth living beings. The time of INCREASE does not endure, therefore it must be utilized while it lasts.

THE IMAGE

Wind and thunder: the image of INCREASE.
Thus the superior man:
If he sees good, he imitates it;
If he has faults, he rids himself of them.

While observing how thunder and wind increase and strength-
en each other, a man can note the way to self-increase and self-
improvement. When he discovers good in others, he should
imitate it and thus make everything on earth his own. If he
perceives something bad in himself, let him rid himself of it.
In this way he becomes free of evil. This ethical change represents the most important increase of personality.

THE LINES

☐ Nine at the beginning means:
It furthers one to accomplish great deeds.
Supreme good fortune. No blame.

If great help comes to a man from on high, this increased
strength must be used to achieve something great for which he
might otherwise never have found energy, or readiness to take
responsibility. Great good fortune is produced by selflessness,
and in bringing about great good fortune, he remains free of
reproach.

○ Six in the second place means:
Someone does indeed increase him;
Ten pairs of tortoises cannot oppose it.
Constant perseverance brings good fortune.
The king presents him before God.
Good fortune.

A man brings about real increase by producing in himself the
conditions for it, that is, through receptivity to and love of the
good. Thus the thing for which he strives comes of itself, with
the inevitability of natural law. Where increase is thus in
harmony with the highest laws of the universe, it cannot be
prevented by any constellation of accidents. But everything

depends on his not letting unexpected good fortune make him heedless; he must make it his own through inner strength and steadfastness. Then he acquires meaning before God and man, and can accomplish something for the good of the world.

> Six in the third place means:
> One is enriched through unfortunate events.
> No blame, if you are sincere
> And walk in the middle,
> And report with a seal to the prince.

A time of blessing and enrichment has such powerful effects that even events ordinarily unfortunate must turn out to the advantage of those affected by them. These persons become free of error, and by acting in harmony with truth they gain such inner authority that they exert influence as if sanctioned by letter and seal.

> □ Six in the fourth place means:
> If you walk in the middle
> And report to the prince,
> He will follow.
> It furthers one to be used
> In the removal of the capital.

It is important that there should be men who mediate between leaders and followers. These should be disinterested people, especially in times of increase, since the benefit is to spread from the leader to the people. Nothing of this benefit should be held back in a selfish way; it should really reach those for whom it is intended. This sort of intermediary, who also exercises a good influence on the leader, is especially important in times when it is a matter of great undertakings, decisive for the future and requiring the inner assent of all concerned.

> ○ Nine in the fifth place means:
> If in truth you have a kind heart, ask not.
> Supreme good fortune.
> Truly, kindness will be recognized as your virtue.

True kindness does not count upon nor ask about merit and gratitude but acts from inner necessity. And such a truly kind heart finds itself rewarded in being recognized, and thus the beneficent influence will spread unhindered.

> Nine at the top means:
> He brings increase to no one.
> Indeed, someone even strikes him.
> He does not keep his heart constantly steady.
> Misfortune.

The meaning here is that through renunciation those in high place should bring increase to those below. By neglecting this duty and helping no one, they in turn lose the furthering influence of others and soon find themselves alone. In this way they invite attacks. An attitude not permanently in harmony with the demands of the time will necessarily bring misfortune with it. Confucius says about this line:

The superior man sets his person at rest before he moves; he composes his mind before he speaks; he makes his relations firm before he asks for something. By attending to these three matters, the superior man gains complete security. But if a man is brusque in his movements, others will not co-operate. If he is agitated in his words, they awaken no echo in others. If he asks for something without having first established relations, it will not be given to him. If no one is with him, those who would harm him draw near.

夫

43. *Kuai / Break-through (Resoluteness)*

above	TUI	THE JOYOUS, LAKE
below	CH'IEN	THE CREATIVE, HEAVEN

This hexagram signifies on the one hand a break-through after a long accumulation of tension, as a swollen river breaks through its dikes, or in the manner of a cloudburst. On the other hand, applied to human conditions, it refers to the time when inferior people gradually begin to disappear. Their influence is on the wane; as a result of resolute action, a change in conditions occurs, a break-through. The hexagram is linked with the third month [April–May].

THE JUDGMENT

BREAK-THROUGH. One must resolutely make the
     matter known
At the court of the king.
It must be announced truthfully. Danger.
It is necessary to notify one's own city.
It does not further to resort to arms.
It furthers one to undertake something.

Even if only one inferior man is occupying a ruling position in a city, he is able to oppress superior men. Even a single passion still lurking in the heart has power to obscure reason. Passion and reason cannot exist side by side—therefore fight without quarter is necessary if the good is to prevail.

In a resolute struggle of the good against evil, there are, however, definite rules that must not be disregarded, if it is to succeed. First, resolution must be based on a union of strength and friendliness. Second, a compromise with evil is not possible; evil must under all circumstances be openly discredited. Nor must our own passions and shortcomings be glossed over. Third, the struggle must not be carried on directly by force. If evil is branded, it thinks of weapons, and if we do it the favor of fighting against it blow for blow, we lose in the end because thus we ourselves get entangled in hatred and passion. Therefore it is important to begin at home, to be on guard in our own persons against the faults we have branded. In this way, finding no opponent, the sharp edges of the weapons of evil become dulled. For the same reasons we should not combat our own faults directly. As long as we wrestle with them, they continue victorious. Finally, the best way to fight evil is to make energetic progress in the good.

THE IMAGE

The lake has risen up to heaven:
The image of BREAK-THROUGH.
Thus the superior man
Dispenses riches downward
And refrains from resting on his virtue.

When the water of a lake has risen up to heaven, there is reason to fear a cloudburst. Taking this as a warning, the superior man forestalls a violent collapse. If a man were to pile up riches for himself alone, without considering others, he would certainly experience a collapse. For all gathering is followed by dispersion. Therefore the superior man begins to distribute while he is accumulating. In the same way, in developing his character he takes care not to become hardened in obstinacy but to remain receptive to impressions by help of strict and continuous self-examination.

THE LINES

Nine at the beginning means:
Mighty in the forward-striding toes.
When one goes and is not equal to the task,
One makes a mistake.

In times of a resolute advance, the beginning is especially difficult. We feel inspired to press forward but resistance is still strong; therefore we ought to gauge our own strength and venture only so far as we can go with certainty of success. To plunge blindly ahead is wrong, because it is precisely at the beginning that an unexpected setback can have the most disastrous results.

Nine in the second place means:
A cry of alarm. Arms at evening and at night.
Fear nothing.

Readiness is everything. Resolution is indissolubly bound up with caution. If an individual is careful and keeps his wits about him, he need not become excited or alarmed. If he is watchful at all times, even before danger is present, he is armed when danger approaches and need not be afraid. The superior man is on his guard against what is not yet in sight and on the alert for what is not yet within hearing; therefore he dwells in the midst of difficulties as though they did not exist. If a man develops his character, people submit to him of their own accord. If reason triumphs, the passions withdraw of themselves. To be circumspect and not to forget one's armor is the right way to security.

Nine in the third place means:
To be powerful in the cheekbones
Brings misfortune.
The superior man is firmly resolved.
He walks alone and is caught in the rain.
He is bespattered,
And people murmur against him.
No blame.

Here we have a man in an ambiguous situation. While all others are engaged in a resolute fight against all that is inferior, he alone has a certain relationship with an inferior man. If he were to show strength outwardly and turn against this man before the time is ripe, he would only endanger the entire situation, because the inferior man would too quickly have recourse to countermeasures. The task of the superior man becomes extremely difficult here. He must be firmly resolved within himself and, while maintaining association with the inferior man, avoid any participation in his vileness. He will of course be misjudged. It will be thought that he belongs to the party of the inferior man. He will be lonely because no one will understand him. His relations with the inferior man will sully him in the eyes of the multitude, and they will turn against him, grumbling. But he can endure this lack of appreciation and makes no mistake, because he remains true to himself.

> Nine in the fourth place means:
> There is no skin on his thighs,
> And walking comes hard.
> If a man were to let himself be led like a sheep,
> Remorse would disappear.
> But if these words are heard
> They will not be believed.

Here a man is suffering from inner restlessness and cannot abide in his place. He would like to push forward under any circumstances, but encounters insuperable obstacles. Thus his situation entails an inner conflict. This is due to the obstinacy with which he seeks to enforce his will. If he would desist from this obstinacy, everything would go well. But this advice, like so much other good counsel, will be ignored. For obstinacy makes a man unable to hear, for all that he has ears.

> ○ Nine in the fifth place means:
> In dealing with weeds,
> Firm resolution is necessary.
> Walking in the middle
> Remains free of blame.

Weeds always grow back again and are difficult to exterminate. So too the struggle against an inferior man in a high position demands firm resolution. One has certain relations with him, hence there is danger that one may give up the struggle as hopeless. But this must not be. One must go on resolutely and not allow himself to be deflected from his course. Only in this way does one remain free of blame.

☐ Six at the top means:
　No cry.
　In the end misfortune comes.

Victory seems to have been achieved. There remains merely a remnant of the evil resolutely to be eradicated as the time demands. Everything looks easy. Just there, however, lies the danger. If we are not on guard, evil will succeed in escaping by means of concealment, and when it has eluded us new misfortunes will develop from the remaining seeds, for evil does not die easily. So too in dealing with the evil in one's own character, one must go to work with thoroughness. If out of carelessness anything were to be overlooked, new evil would arise from it.

姤

44. *Kou / Coming to Meet*

above	CH'IEN	THE CREATIVE, HEAVEN
below	SUN	THE GENTLE, WIND

This hexagram indicates a situation in which the principle of darkness, after having been eliminated, furtively and unexpectedly obtrudes again from within and below. Of its own accord the female principle comes to meet the male. It is an unfavorable and dangerous situation, and we must understand and promptly prevent the possible consequences.

　The hexagram is linked with the fifth month [June–July], because at the summer solstice the principle of darkness gradually becomes ascendant again.

THE JUDGMENT

COMING TO MEET. The maiden is powerful.
One should not marry such a maiden.

The rise of the inferior element is pictured here in the image of a bold girl who lightly surrenders herself and thus seizes power. This would not be possible if the strong and light-giving element had not in turn come halfway. The inferior thing seems so harmless and inviting that a man delights in it; it looks so small and weak that he imagines he may dally with it and come to no harm.

The inferior man rises only because the superior man does not regard him as dangerous and so lends him power. If he were resisted from the first, he could never gain influence.

The time of COMING TO MEET is important in still another way. Although as a general rule the weak should not come to meet the strong, there are times when this has great significance. When heaven and earth come to meet each other, all creatures prosper; when a prince and his official come to meet each other, the world is put in order. It is necessary for elements predestined to be joined and mutually dependent to come to meet one another halfway. But the coming together must be free of dishonest ulterior motives, otherwise harm will result.

THE IMAGE

Under heaven, wind:
The image of COMING TO MEET.
Thus does the prince act when disseminating his
    commands
And proclaiming them to the four quarters of heaven.

The situation here resembles that in hexagram 20, Kuan, CONTEMPLATION (VIEW). In the latter the wind blows over the earth, here it blows under heaven; in both cases it goes everywhere. There the wind is on the earth and symbolizes the ruler taking note of the conditions in his kingdom; here the wind blows from above and symbolizes the influence exercised by the ruler through his commands. Heaven is far from the things of earth, but it sets them in motion by means of the wind. The ruler is far from his people, but he sets them in motion by means of his commands and decrees.

THE LINES

☐ Six at the beginning means:

It must be checked with a brake of bronze.

Perseverance brings good fortune.

If one lets it take its course, one experiences misfortune.

Even a lean pig has it in him to rage around.

If an inferior element has wormed its way in, it must be energetically checked at once. By consistently checking it, bad effects can be avoided. If it is allowed to take its course, misfortune is bound to result; the insignificance of that which creeps in should not be a temptation to underrate it. A pig that is still young and lean cannot rage around much, but after it has eaten its fill and become strong, its true nature comes out if it has not previously been curbed.

○ Nine in the second place means:

There is a fish in the tank. No blame.

Does not further guests.

The inferior element is not overcome by violence but is kept under gentle control. Then nothing evil is to be feared. But care must be taken not to let it come in contact with those further away, because once free it would unfold its evil aspects unchecked.

Nine in the third place means:

There is no skin on his thighs,

And walking comes hard.

If one is mindful of the danger,

No great mistake is made.

There is a temptation to fall in with the evil element offering itself—a very dangerous situation. Fortunately circumstances prevent this; one would like to do it, but cannot. This leads to painful indecision in behavior. But if we gain clear insight into the danger of the situation, we shall at least avoid more serious mistakes.

> Nine in the fourth place means:
> No fish in the tank.
> This leads to misfortune.

Insignificant people must be tolerated in order to keep them well disposed. Then we can make use of them if we should need them. If we become alienated from them and do not meet them halfway, they turn their backs on us and are not at our disposal when we need them. But this is our own fault.

> ○ Nine in the fifth place means:
> A melon covered with willow leaves.
> Hidden lines.
> Then it drops down to one from heaven.

The melon, like the fish, is a symbol of the principle of darkness. It is sweet but spoils easily and for this reason is protected with a cover of willow leaves. This is a situation in which a strong, superior, well-poised man tolerates and protects the inferiors in his charge. He has the firm lines of order and beauty within himself but he does not lay stress upon them. He does not bother his subordinates with outward show or tiresome admonitions but leaves them quite free, putting his trust in the transforming power of a strong and upright personality. And behold! Fate is favorable. His inferiors respond to his influence and fall to his disposition like ripe fruit.

> Nine at the top means:
> He comes to meet with his horns.
> Humiliation. No blame.

When a man has withdrawn from the world, its tumult often becomes unbearable to him. There are many people who in a noble pride hold themselves aloof from all that is low and rebuff it brusquely wherever it comes to meet them. Such persons are reproached for being proud and distant, but since active duties no longer hold them to the world, this does not greatly matter. They know how to bear the dislike of the masses with composure.

茻

45. Ts'ui / Gathering Together [Massing]

<table>
<tr><td>≡≡</td><td>above</td><td>TUI</td><td>THE JOYOUS, LAKE</td></tr>
<tr><td>≡≡</td><td>below</td><td>K'UN</td><td>THE RECEPTIVE, EARTH</td></tr>
</table>

This hexagram is related in form and meaning to Pi, HOLD-
ING TOGETHER (8). In the latter, water is over the earth; here
a lake is over the earth. But since the lake is a place where
water collects, the idea of gathering together is even more
strongly expressed here than in the other hexagram. The same
idea also arises from the fact that in the present case it is two
strong lines (the fourth and the fifth) that bring about the
gathering together, whereas in the former case one strong
line (the fifth) stands in the midst of weak lines.

THE JUDGMENT

GATHERING TOGETHER. Success.
The king approaches his temple.
It furthers one to see the great man.
This brings success. Perseverance furthers.
To bring great offerings creates good fortune.
It furthers one to undertake something.

The gathering together of people in large communities is
either a natural occurrence, as in the case of the family, or an
artificial one, as in the case of the state. The family gathers
about the father as its head. The perpetuation of this gathering
in groups is achieved through the sacrifice to the ancestors, at
which the whole clan is gathered together. Through the collective piety of the living members of the family, the ancestors

become so integrated in the spiritual life of the family that it cannot be dispersed or dissolved.

Where men are to be gathered together, religious forces are needed. But there must also be a human leader to serve as the center of the group. In order to be able to bring others together, this leader must first of all be collected within himself. Only collective moral force can unite the world. Such great times of unification will leave great achievements behind them. This is the significance of the great offerings that are made. In the secular sphere likewise there is need of great deeds in the time of GATHERING TOGETHER.

THE IMAGE

Over the earth, the lake:
The image of GATHERING TOGETHER.
Thus the superior man renews his weapons
In order to meet the unforeseen.

If the water in the lake gathers until it rises above the earth, there is danger of a break-through. Precautions must be taken to prevent this. Similarly where men gather together in great numbers, strife is likely to arise; where possessions are collected, robbery is likely to occur. Thus in the time of GATHERING TOGETHER we must arm promptly to ward off the unexpected. Human woes usually come as a result of unexpected events against which we are not forearmed. If we are prepared, they can be prevented.

THE LINES

Six at the beginning means:
If you are sincere, but not to the end,
There will sometimes be confusion, sometimes
    gathering together.
If you call out,
Then after one grasp of the hand you can laugh again.
Regret not. Going is without blame.

The situation is this: People desire to gather around a leader to whom they look up. But they are in a large group, by which they allow themselves to be influenced, so that they waver in their decision. Thus they lack a firm center around which to gather. But if expression is given to this need, and if they call for help, one grasp of the hand from the leader is enough to turn away all distress. Therefore they must not allow themselves to be led astray. It is undoubtedly right that they should attach themselves to this leader.

> Six in the second place means:
> Letting oneself be drawn
> Brings good fortune and remains blameless.
> If one is sincere,
> It furthers one to bring even a small offering.

In the time of GATHERING TOGETHER, we should make no arbitrary choice of the way. There are secret forces at work, leading together those who belong together. We must yield to this attraction; then we make no mistakes. Where inner relationships exist, no great preparations and formalities are necessary. People understand one another forthwith, just as the Divinity graciously accepts a small offering if it comes from the heart.

> Six in the third place means:
> Gathering together amid sighs.
> Nothing that would further.
> Going is without blame.
> Slight humiliation.

Often a man feels an urge to unite with others, but the individuals around him have already formed themselves into a group, so that he remains isolated. The whole situation proves untenable. Then he ought to choose the way of progress, resolutely allying himself with a man who stands nearer to the center of the group, and can help him to gain admission to the closed circle. This is not a mistake, even though at first his position as an outsider is somewhat humiliating.

> O Nine in the fourth place means:
> Great good fortune. No blame.

This describes a man who gathers people around him in the name of his ruler. Since he is not striving for any special advantages for himself but is working unselfishly to bring about general unity, his work is crowned with success, and everything becomes as it should be.

○ Nine in the fifth place means:
    If in gathering together one has position,
    This brings no blame.
    If there are some who are not yet sincerely in
        the work,
    Sublime and enduring perseverance is needed.
    Then remorse disappears.

When people spontaneously gather around a man, it is only a good. It gives him a certain influence that can be altogether useful. But of course there is also the possibility that many may gather around him not because of a feeling of confidence but merely because of his influential position. This is certainly to be regretted. The only means of dealing with such people is to gain their confidence through steadfastness and intensified, unswerving devotion to duty. In this way secret mistrust will gradually be overcome, and there will be no occasion for regret.

    Six at the top means:
    Lamenting and sighing, floods of tears.
    No blame.

It may happen that an individual would like to ally himself with another, but his good intentions are misunderstood. Then he becomes sad and laments. But this is the right course. For it may cause the other person to come to his senses, so that the alliance that has been sought and so painfully missed is after all achieved.

升

46. Shêng / Pushing Upward

≡≡ *above* K'UN THE RECEPTIVE, EARTH
≡ *below* SUN THE GENTLE, WIND, WOOD

The lower trigram, Sun, represents wood, and the upper, K'un, means the earth. Linked with this is the idea that wood in the earth grows upward. In contrast to the meaning of Chin, PROGRESS (35), this pushing upward is associated with effort, just as a plant needs energy for pushing upward through the earth. That is why this hexagram, although it is connected with success, is associated with effort of the will. In PROGRESS the emphasis is on expansion; PUSHING UPWARD indicates rather a vertical ascent—direct rise from obscurity and lowliness to power and influence.

THE JUDGMENT

PUSHING UPWARD has supreme success.
One must see the great man.
Fear not.
Departure toward the south
Brings good fortune.

The pushing upward of the good elements encounters no obstruction and is therefore accompanied by great success. The pushing upward is made possible not by violence but by modesty and adaptability. Since the individual is borne along by the propitiousness of the time, he advances. He must go to see authoritative people. He need not be afraid to do this, because success is assured. But he must set to work, for activity (this is the meaning of "the south") brings good fortune.

THE IMAGE

Within the earth, wood grows:
The image of PUSHING UPWARD.
Thus the superior man of devoted character
Heaps up small things
In order to achieve something high and great.

Adapting itself to obstacles and bending around them, wood in the earth grows upward without haste and without rest. Thus too the superior man is devoted in character and never pauses in his progress.

THE LINES

☐ Six at the beginning means:
Pushing upward that meets with confidence
Brings great good fortune.

This is the situation at the beginning of ascent. Just as wood draws strength for its upward push from the root, which in itself is in the lowest place, so the power to rise comes from this low and obscure station. But there is a spiritual affinity with the rulers above, and this solidarity creates the confidence needed to accomplish something.

Nine in the second place means:
If one is sincere,
It furthers one to bring even a small offering.
No blame.

Here a strong man is presupposed. It is true that he does not fit in with his environment, inasmuch as he is too brusque and pays too little attention to form. But as he is upright in character, he meets with response, and his lack of outward form does no harm. Here uprightness is the outcome of sound qualities of character, whereas in the corresponding line of the preceding hexagram it is the result of innate humility.

Nine in the third place means:
One pushes upward into an empty city.

All obstructions that generally block progress fall away here. Things proceed with remarkable ease. Unhesitatingly one follows this road, in order to profit by one's success. Seen from without, everything seems to be in the best of order. However, no promise of good fortune is added. It is a question how long such unobstructed success can last. But it is wise not to yield to such misgivings, because they only inhibit one's power. Instead, the point is to profit by the propitiousness of the time.

> Six in the fourth place means:
> The king offers him Mount Ch'i.
> Good fortune. No blame.

Mount Ch'i is in western China, the homeland of King Wên, whose son, the Duke of Chou, added the words to the individual lines. The pronouncement takes us back to a time when the Chou dynasty was coming into power. At that time King Wên introduced his illustrious helpers to the god of his native mountain, and they received their places in the halls of the ancestors by the side of the ruler. This indicates a stage in which pushing upward attains its goal. One acquires fame in the sight of gods and men, is received into the circle of those who foster the spiritual life of the nation, and thereby attains a significance that endures beyond time.

> O Six in the fifth place means:
> Perseverance brings good fortune.
> One pushes upward by steps.

When a man is advancing farther and farther, it is important for him not to become intoxicated by success. Precisely when he experiences great success it is necessary to remain sober and not to try to skip any stages; he must go on slowly, step by step, as though hesitant. Only such calm, steady progress, overleaping nothing, leads to the goal.

> Six at the top means:
> Pushing upward in darkness.
> It furthers one
> To be unremittingly persevering.

He who pushes upward blindly deludes himself. He knows only advance, not retreat. But this means exhaustion. In such a case it is important to be constantly mindful that one must be conscientious and consistent and must remain so. Only thus does one become free of blind impulse, which is always harmful.

囲

47. *K'un* / *Oppression* (*Exhaustion*)

☰	*above*	TUI	THE JOYOUS, LAKE
☵	*below*	K'AN	THE ABYSMAL, WATER

The lake is above, water below; the lake is empty, dried up.[1] Exhaustion is expressed in yet another way: at the top, a dark line is holding down two light lines; below, a light line is hemmed in between two dark ones. The upper trigram belongs to the principle of darkness, the lower to the principle of light. Thus everywhere superior men are oppressed and held in restraint by inferior men.

THE JUDGMENT

OPPRESSION. Success. Perseverance.
The great man brings about good fortune.
No blame.
When one has something to say,
It is not believed.

Times of adversity are the reverse of times of success, but they can lead to success if they befall the right man. When a strong man meets with adversity, he remains cheerful despite all danger, and this cheerfulness is the source of later successes; it

---

1. [Literally, "exhausted."]

is that stability which is stronger than fate. He who lets his spirit be broken by exhaustion certainly has no success. But if adversity only bends a man, it creates in him a power to react that is bound in time to manifest itself. No inferior man is capable of this. Only the great man brings about good fortune and remains blameless. It is true that for the time being outward influence is denied him, because his words have no effect. Therefore in times of adversity it is important to be strong within and sparing of words.

THE IMAGE

There is no water in the lake:
The image of EXHAUSTION.
Thus the superior man stakes his life
On following his will.

When the water has flowed out below, the lake must dry up and become exhausted. That is fate. This symbolizes an adverse fate in human life. In such times there is nothing a man can do but acquiesce in his fate and remain true to himself. This concerns the deepest stratum of his being, for this alone is superior to all external fate.

THE LINES

Six at the beginning means:
One sits oppressed under a bare tree
And strays into a gloomy valley.
For three years one sees nothing.

When adversity befalls a man, it is important above all things for him to be strong and to overcome the trouble inwardly. If he is weak, the trouble overwhelms him. Instead of proceeding on his way, he remains sitting under a bare tree and falls ever more deeply into gloom and melancholy. This makes the situation only more and more hopeless. Such an attitude comes from an inner delusion that he must by all means overcome.

○ Nine in the second place means:
One is oppressed while at meat and drink.

The man with the scarlet knee bands is just coming.
It furthers one to offer sacrifice.
To set forth brings misfortune.
No blame.

This pictures a state of inner oppression. Externally, all is well, one has meat and drink. But one is exhausted by the commonplaces of life, and there seems to be no way of escape. Then help comes from a high place. A prince—in ancient China princes wore scarlet knee bands—is in search of able helpers. But there are still obstructions to be overcome. Therefore it is important to meet these obstructions in the invisible realm by offerings and prayer. To set forth without being prepared would be disastrous, though not morally wrong. Here a disagreeable situation must be overcome by patience of spirit.

Six in the third place means:
A man permits himself to be oppressed by stone,
And leans on thorns and thistles.
He enters his house and does not see his wife.
Misfortune.

This shows a man who is restless and indecisive in times of adversity. At first he wants to push ahead, then he encounters obstructions that, it is true, mean oppression only when recklessly dealt with. He butts his head against a wall and in consequence feels himself oppressed by the wall. Then he leans on things that have in themselves no stability and that are merely a hazard for him who leans on them. Thereupon he turns back irresolutely and retires into his house, only to find, as a fresh disappointment, that his wife is not there. Confucius says about this line:

If a man permits himself to be oppressed by something that ought not to oppress him, his name will certainly be disgraced. If he leans on things upon which one cannot lean, his life will certainly be endangered. For him who is in disgrace and danger, the hour of death draws near; how can he then still see his wife?

> Nine in the fourth place means:
> He comes very quietly, oppressed in a golden
>   carriage.
> Humiliation, but the end is reached.

A well-to-do man sees the need of the lower classes and would like very much to be of help. But instead of proceeding with speed and energy where there is need, he begins in a hesitant and measured way. Then he encounters obstructions. Powerful and wealthy acquaintances draw him into their circle; he has to do as they do and cannot withdraw from them. Hence he finds himself in great embarrassment. But the trouble is transitory. The original strength of his nature offsets the mistake he has made, and the goal is reached.

> ○ Nine in the fifth place means:
> His nose and feet are cut off.
> Oppression at the hands of the man with the purple
>   knee bands.
> Joy comes softly.
> It furthers one to make offerings and libations.

An individual who has the good of mankind at heart is oppressed from above and below (this is the meaning of the cutting off of nose and feet). He finds no help among the people whose duty it would be to aid in the work of rescue (ministers wore purple knee bands). But little by little, things take a turn for the better. Until that time, he should turn to God, firm in his inner composure, and pray and offer sacrifice for the general well-being.

> Six at the top means:
> He is oppressed by creeping vines.
> He moves uncertainly and says, "Movement brings
>   remorse."
> If one feels remorse over this and makes a start,
> Good fortune comes.

A man is oppressed by bonds that can easily be broken. The distress is drawing to an end. But he is still irresolute; he is still

influenced by the previous condition and fears that he may
have cause for regret if he makes a move. But as soon as he
grasps the situation, changes this mental attitude, and makes
a firm decision, he masters the oppression.

井

48. *Ching / The Well*

above	K'AN	THE ABYSMAL, WATER
below	SUN	THE GENTLE, WIND, WOOD

Wood is below, water above. The wood goes down into the earth
to bring up water. The image derives from the pole-and-
bucket well of ancient China. The wood represents not the
buckets, which in ancient times were made of clay, but rather
the wooden poles by which the water is hauled up from the
well. The image also refers to the world of plants, which lift
water out of the earth by means of their fibers.

The well from which water is drawn conveys the further
idea of an inexhaustible dispensing of nourishment.

THE JUDGMENT

THE WELL. The town may be changed,
But the well cannot be changed.
It neither decreases nor increases.
They come and go and draw from the well.
If one gets down almost to the water
And the rope does not go all the way,
Or the jug breaks, it brings misfortune.

In ancient China the capital cities were sometimes moved,
partly for the sake of more favorable location, partly because of
a change in dynasties. The style of architecture changed in the

course of centuries, but the shape of the well has remained the same from ancient times to this day. Thus the well is the symbol of that social structure which, evolved by mankind in meeting its most primitive needs, is independent of all political forms. Political structures change, as do nations, but the life of man with its needs remains eternally the same—this cannot be changed. Life is also inexhaustible. It grows neither less nor more; it exists for one and for all. The generations come and go, and all enjoy life in its inexhaustible abundance.

However, there are two prerequisites for a satisfactory political or social organization of mankind. We must go down to the very foundations of life. For any merely superficial ordering of life that leaves its deepest needs unsatisfied is as ineffectual as if no attempt at order had ever been made. Carelessness—by which the jug is broken—is also disastrous. If for instance the military defense of a state is carried to such excess that it provokes wars by which the power of the state is annihilated, this is a breaking of the jug.

This hexagram applies also to the individual. However men may differ in disposition and in education, the foundations of human nature are the same in everyone. And every human being can draw in the course of his education from the inexhaustible wellspring of the divine in man's nature. But here likewise two dangers threaten: a man may fail in his education to penetrate to the real roots of humanity and remain fixed in convention—a partial education of this sort is as bad as none—or he may suddenly collapse and neglect his self-development.

THE IMAGE

Water over wood: the image of THE WELL.
Thus the superior man encourages the people at
    their work,
And exhorts them to help one another.

The trigram Sun, wood, is below, and the trigram K'an, water, is above it. Wood sucks water upward. Just as wood as an organism imitates the action of the well, which benefits all parts of the plant, the superior man organizes human society, so that, as in a plant organism, its parts co-operate for the benefit of the whole.

THE LINES

Six at the beginning means:
One does not drink the mud of the well.
No animals come to an old well.

If a man wanders around in swampy lowlands, his life is sub-
merged in mud. Such a man loses all significance for mankind.
He who throws himself away is no longer sought out by others.
In the end no one troubles about him any more.

Nine in the second place means:
At the wellhole one shoots fishes.
The jug is broken and leaks.

The water itself is clear, but it is not being used. Thus the well
is a place where only fish will stay, and whoever comes to it,
comes only to catch fish. But the jug is broken, so that the fish
cannot be kept in it.

This describes the situation of a person who possesses good
qualities but neglects them. No one bothers about him. As a
result he deteriorates in mind. He associates with inferior men
and can no longer accomplish anything worth while.

Nine in the third place means:
The well is cleaned, but no one drinks from it.
This is my heart's sorrow,
For one might draw from it.
If the king were clear-minded,
Good fortune might be enjoyed in common.

An able man is available. He is like a purified well whose water
is drinkable. But no use is made of him. This is the sorrow of
those who know him. One wishes that the prince might learn
about it; this would be good fortune for all concerned.

Six in the fourth place means:
The well is being lined. No blame.

True, if a well is being lined with stone, it cannot be used while
the work is going on. But the work is not in vain; the result is

that the water stays clear. In life also there are times when a man must put himself in order. During such a time he can do nothing for others, but his work is nonetheless valuable, because by enhancing his powers and abilities through inner development, he can accomplish all the more later on.

○ Nine in the fifth place means:

In the well there is a clear, cold spring

From which one can drink.

A well that is fed by a spring of living water is a good well. A man who has virtues like a well of this sort is born to be a leader and savior of men, for he has the water of life. Nevertheless, the character for "good fortune" is left out here. The all-important thing about a well is that its water be drawn. The best water is only a potentiality for refreshment as long as it is not brought up. So too with leaders of mankind: it is all-important that one should drink from the spring of their words and translate them into life.

Six at the top means:

One draws from the well

Without hindrance.

It is dependable.

Supreme good fortune.

The well is there for all. No one is forbidden to take water from it. No matter how many come, all find what they need, for the well is dependable. It has a spring and never runs dry. Therefore it is a great blessing to the whole land. The same is true of the really great man, whose inner wealth is inexhaustible; the more that people draw from him, the greater his wealth becomes.

革

49. *Ko / Revolution (Molting)*

above	TUI	THE JOYOUS, LAKE
below	LI	THE CLINGING, FIRE

The Chinese character for this hexagram means in its original sense an animal's pelt, which is changed in the course of the year by molting. From this the word is carried over to apply to the "moltings" in political life, the great revolutions connected with changes of governments.

The two trigrams making up the hexagram are the same two that appear in K'uei, OPPOSITION (38), that is, the two younger daughters, Li and Tui. But while there the elder of the two daughters is above, and what results is essentially only an opposition of tendencies, here the younger daughter is above. The influences are in actual conflict, and the forces combat each other like fire and water (lake), each trying to destroy the other. Hence the idea of revolution.

THE JUDGMENT

REVOLUTION. On your own day
You are believed.
Supreme success,
Furthering through perseverance.
Remorse disappears.

Political revolutions are extremely grave matters. They should be undertaken only under stress of direst necessity, when there is no other way out. Not everyone is called to this task, but only the man who has the confidence of the people, and even he only when the time is ripe. He must then proceed in the right way, so that he gladdens the people and, by enlightening them, prevents excesses. Furthermore, he must be quite free of selfish aims and must really relieve the need of the people. Only then does he have nothing to regret.

Times change, and with them their demands. Thus the seasons change in the course of the year. In the world cycle also there are spring and autumn in the life of peoples and nations, and these call for social transformations.

THE IMAGE

Fire in the lake: the image of REVOLUTION.
Thus the superior man
Sets the calendar in order
And makes the seasons clear.

Fire below and the lake above combat and destroy each other. So too in the course of the year a combat takes place between the forces of light and the forces of darkness, eventuating in the revolution of the seasons. Man masters these changes in nature by noting their regularity and marking off the passage of time accordingly. In this way order and clarity appear in the apparently chaotic changes of the seasons, and man is able to adjust himself in advance to the demands of the different times.

THE LINES

Nine at the beginning means:
Wrapped in the hide of a yellow cow.

Changes ought to be undertaken only when there is nothing else to be done. Therefore at first the utmost restraint is necessary. One must become firm in one's mind, control one-self—yellow is the color of the mean, and the cow is the symbol of docility—and refrain from doing anything for the time being, because any premature offensive will bring evil results.

Six in the second place means:
When one's own day comes, one may create
    revolution.
Starting brings good fortune. No blame.

When we have tried in every way to bring about reforms, but without success, revolution becomes necessary. But such a thoroughgoing upheaval must be carefully prepared. There must be available a man who has the requisite abilities and who possesses public confidence. To such a man we may well turn. This brings good fortune and is not a mistake. The first thing to be considered is our inner attitude toward the new condition that will inevitably come. We have to go out to meet it, as it were. Only in this way can it be prepared for.

> Nine in the third place means:
> Starting brings misfortune.
> Perseverance brings danger.
> When talk of revolution has gone the rounds
>   three times,
> One may commit himself,
> And men will believe him.

When change is necessary, there are two mistakes to be avoided. One lies in excessive haste and ruthlessness, which bring disaster. The other lies in excessive hesitation and conservatism, which are also dangerous. Not every demand for change in the existing order should be heeded. On the other hand, repeated and well-founded complaints should not fail of a hearing. When talk of change has come to one's ears three times, and has been pondered well, he may believe and acquiesce in it. Then he will meet with belief and will accomplish something.[1]

> Nine in the fourth place means:
> Remorse disappears. Men believe him.
> Changing the form of government brings good
>   fortune.

Radical changes require adequate authority. A man must have inner strength as well as influential position. What he does must correspond with a higher truth and must not spring from

---

1. Cf. Goethe's tale, "Das Märchen," in which the phrase, "The hour has come!" is repeated three times before the great transformation begins.

arbitrary or petty motives; then it brings great good fortune. If a revolution is not founded on such inner truth, the results are bad, and it has no success. For in the end men will support only those undertakings which they feel instinctively to be just.

○ Nine in the fifth place means:
  The great man changes like a tiger.
  Even before he questions the oracle
  He is believed.

A tigerskin, with its highly visible black stripes on a yellow ground, shows its distinct pattern from afar. It is the same with a revolution brought about by a great man: large, clear guiding lines become visible, understandable to everyone. Therefore he need not first consult the oracle, for he wins the spontaneous support of the people.

  Six at the top means:
  The superior man changes like a panther.
  The inferior man molts in the face.
  Starting brings misfortune.
  To remain persevering brings good fortune.

After the large and fundamental problems are settled, certain minor reforms, and elaborations of these, are necessary. These detailed reforms may be likened to the equally distinct but relatively small marks of the panther's coat. As a consequence, a change also takes place among the inferior people. In conformity with the new order, they likewise "molt." This molting, it is true, does not go very deep, but that is not to be expected. We must be satisfied with the attainable. If we should go too far and try to achieve too much, it would lead to unrest and misfortune. For the object of a great revolution is the attainment of clarified, secure conditions ensuring a general stabilization on the basis of what is possible at the moment.

鼎

50. *Ting* / *The Caldron*

```
═══ ═══   above   LI    THE CLINGING, FIRE
═════════ below   SUN   THE GENTLE, WIND, WOOD
```

The six lines construct the image of Ting, THE CALDRON;
at the bottom are the legs, over them the belly, then come the
ears (handles), and at the top the carrying rings. At the same
time, the image suggests the idea of nourishment. The *ting*,
cast of bronze, was the vessel that held the cooked viands in
the temple of the ancestors and at banquets. The head of the
family served the food from the *ting* into the bowls of the
guests.[1]

THE WELL (48) likewise has the secondary meaning of giving nourishment, but rather more in relation to the people.
The *ting*, as a utensil pertaining to a refined civilization, suggests the fostering and nourishing of able men, which redounded to the benefit of the state.[2]

This hexagram and THE WELL are the only two in the Book
of Changes that represent concrete, man-made objects. Yet
here too the thought has its abstract connotation.

Sun, below, is wood and wind; Li, above, is flame. Thus together they stand for the flame kindled by wood and wind,
which likewise suggests the idea of preparing food.

---

1. [There are beautiful examples of the *ting* in most of our mu-
seums, where they are classified as ritual vessels. The German word
used by Wilhelm for *ting* is *Tiegel*, meaning literally "caldron" and,
in another sense, "crucible." Since this characteristic Chinese vessel
is unique in form, so different from either a caldron or a crucible in the
usual sense, the word *ting* has been retained wherever feasible here.]

2. Cf. the other three hexagrams dealing with nourishment, viz.,
hexagrams 5, 27, 48.

THE JUDGMENT

THE CALDRON. Supreme good fortune.
Success.

While THE WELL relates to the social foundation of our life, and this foundation is likened to the water that serves to nourish growing wood, the present hexagram refers to the cultural superstructure of society. Here it is the wood that serves as nourishment for the flame, the spirit. All that is visible must grow beyond itself, extend into the realm of the invisible. Thereby it receives its true consecration and clarity and takes firm root in the cosmic order.

Here we see civilization as it reaches its culmination in religion. The *ting* serves in offering sacrifice to God. The highest earthly values must be sacrificed to the divine. But the truly divine does not manifest itself apart from man. The supreme revelation of God appears in prophets and holy men. To venerate them is true veneration of God. The will of God, as revealed through them, should be accepted in humility; this brings inner enlightenment and true understanding of the world, and this leads to great good fortune and success.

THE IMAGE

Fire over wood:
The image of THE CALDRON.
Thus the superior man consolidates his fate
By making his position correct.

The fate of fire depends on wood; as long as there is wood below, the fire burns above. It is the same in human life; there is in man likewise a fate that lends power to his life. And if he succeeds in assigning the right place to life and to fate, thus bringing the two into harmony, he puts his fate on a firm footing. These words contain hints about the fostering of life as handed on by oral tradition in the secret teachings of Chinese yoga.

THE LINES

Six at the beginning means:
A *ting* with legs upturned.

Furthers removal of stagnating stuff.

One takes a concubine for the sake of her son.

No blame.

If a *ting* is turned upside down before being used, no harm is done—on the contrary, this clears it of refuse. A concubine's position is lowly, but because she has a son she comes to be honored.

These two metaphors express the idea that in a highly developed civilization, such as that indicated by this hexagram, every person of good will can in some way or other succeed. No matter how lowly he may be, provided he is ready to purify himself, he is accepted. He attains a station in which he can prove himself fruitful in accomplishment, and as a result he gains recognition.

Nine in the second place means:

There is food in the *ting*.

My comrades are envious,

But they cannot harm me.

Good fortune.

In a period of advanced culture, it is of the greatest importance that one should achieve something significant. If a man concentrates on such real undertakings, he may indeed experience envy and disfavor, but that is not dangerous. The more he limits himself to his actual achievements, the less harm can the envious inflict on him.

Nine in the third place means:

The handle of the *ting* is altered.

One is impeded in his way of life.

The fat of the pheasant is not eaten.

Once rain falls, remorse is spent.

Good fortune comes in the end.

The handle is the means for lifting up the *ting*. If the handle is altered, the *ting* cannot be lifted up and used, and, sad to say, the delicious food in it, such as pheasant fat, cannot be eaten by anyone.

This describes a man who, in a highly evolved civilization, finds himself in a place where no one notices or recognizes him. This is a severe block to his effectiveness. All of his good qualities and gifts of mind thus needlessly go to waste. But if he will only see to it that he is possessed of something truly spiritual, the time is bound to come, sooner or later, when the difficulties will be resolved and all will go well. The fall of rain symbolizes here, as in other instances, release of tension.

> Nine in the fourth place means:
> The legs of the *ting* are broken.
> The prince's meal is spilled
> And his person is soiled.
> Misfortune.

A man has a difficult and responsible task to which he is not adequate. Moreover, he does not devote himself to it with all his strength but goes about with inferior people; therefore the execution of the work fails. In this way he also incurs personal opprobrium.

Confucius says about this line: "Weak character coupled with honored place, meager knowledge with large plans, limited powers with heavy responsibility, will seldom escape disaster."

> ○ Six in the fifth place means:
> The *ting* has yellow handles, golden carrying rings.
> Perseverance furthers.

Here we have, in a ruling position, a man who is approachable and modest in nature. As a result of this attitude he succeeds in finding strong and able helpers who complement and aid him in his work. Having achieved this attitude, which requires constant self-abnegation, it is important for him to hold to it and not to let himself be led astray.

> ○ Nine at the top means:
> The *ting* has rings of jade.
> Great good fortune.
> Nothing that would not act to further.

In the preceding line the carrying rings are described as golden, to denote their strength; here they are said to be of jade. Jade is notable for its combination of hardness with soft luster. This counsel, in relation to the man who is open to it, works greatly to his advantage. Here the counsel is described in relation to the sage who imparts it. In imparting it, he will be mild and pure, like precious jade. Thus the work finds favor in the eyes of the Deity, who dispenses great good fortune, and becomes pleasing to men, wherefore all goes well.

51. *Chên* / *The Arousing (Shock, Thunder)*

above	CHÊN	THE AROUSING, THUNDER
below	CHÊN	THE AROUSING, THUNDER

The hexagram Chên represents the eldest son, who seizes rule with energy and power. A yang line develops below two yin lines and presses upward forcibly. This movement is so violent that it arouses terror. It is symbolized by thunder, which bursts forth from the earth and by its shock causes fear and trembling.

THE JUDGMENT

SHOCK brings success.
Shock comes—oh, oh!
Laughing words—ha, ha!
The shock terrifies for a hundred miles,
And he does not let fall the sacrificial spoon and
    chalice.

The shock that comes from the manifestation of God within the depths of the earth makes man afraid, but this fear of God is good, for joy and merriment can follow upon it.

When a man has learned within his heart what fear and trembling mean, he is safeguarded against any terror produced by outside influences. Let the thunder roll and spread terror a hundred miles around: he remains so composed and reverent in spirit that the sacrificial rite is not interrupted. This is the spirit that must animate leaders and rulers of men—a profound inner seriousness from which all outer terrors glance off harmlessly.

THE IMAGE

Thunder repeated: the image of SHOCK.
Thus in fear and trembling
The superior man sets his life in order
And examines himself.

The shock of continuing thunder brings fear and trembling. The superior man is always filled with reverence at the manifestation of God; he sets his life in order and searches his heart, lest it harbor any secret opposition to the will of God. Thus reverence is the foundation of true culture.

THE LINES

O Nine at the beginning means:
Shock comes—oh, oh!
Then follow laughing words—ha, ha!
Good fortune.

The fear and trembling engendered by shock come to an individual at first in such a way that he sees himself placed at a disadvantage as against others. But this is only transitory. When the ordeal is over, he experiences relief, and thus the very terror he had to endure at the outset brings good fortune in the long run.

Six in the second place means:
Shock comes bringing danger.
A hundred thousand times
You lose your treasures
And must climb the nine hills.

Do not go in pursuit of them.

After seven days you will get them back again.

This pictures a situation in which a shock endangers a man and he suffers great losses. Resistance would be contrary to the movement of the time and for this reason unsuccessful. Therefore he must simply retreat to heights inaccessible to the threatening forces of danger. He must accept his loss of property without worrying too much about it. When the time of shock and upheaval that has robbed him of his possessions has passed, he will get them back again without going in pursuit of them.

> Six in the third place means:
> Shock comes and makes one distraught.
> If shock spurs to action
> One remains free of misfortune.

There are three kinds of shock—the shock of heaven, which is thunder, the shock of fate, and, finally, the shock of the heart. The present hexagram refers less to inner shock than to the shock of fate. In such times of shock, presence of mind is all too easily lost: the individual overlooks all opportunities for action and mutely lets fate take its course. But if he allows the shocks of fate to induce movement within his mind, he will overcome these external blows with little effort.

> Nine in the fourth place means:
> Shock is mired.

Movement within the mind depends for its success partly on circumstances. If there is neither a resistance that might be vigorously combated, nor yet a yielding that permits of victory —if, instead, everything is tough and inert like mire—movement is crippled.

> Six in the fifth place means:
> Shock goes hither and thither.
> Danger.
> However, nothing at all is lost.
> Yet there are things to be done.

This is a case not of a single shock but of repeated shocks with no breathing space between. Nonetheless, the shock causes no loss, because one takes care to stay in the center of movement and in this way to be spared the fate of being helplessly tossed hither and thither.

> Six at the top means:
> Shock brings ruin and terrified gazing around.
> Going ahead brings misfortune.
> If it has not yet touched one's own body
> But has reached one's neighbor first,
> There is no blame.
> One's comrades have something to talk about.

When inner shock is at its height, it robs a man of reflection and clarity of vision. In such a state of shock it is of course impossible to act with presence of mind. Then the right thing is to keep still until composure and clarity are restored. But this a man can do only when he himself is not yet infected by the agitation, although its disastrous effects are already visible in those around him. If he withdraws from the affair in time, he remains free of mistakes and injury. But his comrades, who no longer heed any warning, will in their excitement certainly be displeased with him. However, he must not take this into account.

艮

52. Kên / Keeping Still, Mountain

☶	*above*	KÊN	KEEPING STILL, MOUNTAIN
	below	KÊN	KEEPING STILL, MOUNTAIN

The image of this hexagram is the mountain, the youngest son of heaven and earth. The male principle is at the top, because it strives upward by nature; the female principle is below, since the direction of its movement is downward. Thus there is rest because the movement has come to its normal end.

In its application to man, the hexagram turns upon the problem of achieving a quiet heart. It is very difficult to bring quiet to the heart. While Buddhism strives for rest through an ebbing away of all movement in nirvana, the Book of Changes holds that rest is merely a state of polarity that always posits movement as its complement. Possibly the words of the text embody directions for the practice of yoga.

THE JUDGMENT

KEEPING STILL. Keeping his back still
So that he no longer feels his body.
He goes into his courtyard
And does not see his people.
No blame.

True quiet means keeping still when the time has come to keep still, and going forward when the time has come to go forward. In this way rest and movement are in agreement with the demands of the time, and thus there is light in life.

The hexagram signifies the end and the beginning of all movement. The back is named because in the back are located all the nerve fibers that mediate movement. If the movement of these spinal nerves is brought to a standstill, the ego, with its restlessness, disappears as it were. When a man has thus become calm, he may turn to the outside world. He no longer sees in it the struggle and tumult of individual beings, and therefore he has that true peace of mind which is needed for understanding the great laws of the universe and for acting in harmony with them. Whoever acts from these deep levels makes no mistakes.

THE IMAGE

Mountains standing close together:
The image of KEEPING STILL.
Thus the superior man

> Does not permit his thoughts
> To go beyond his situation.

The heart thinks constantly. This cannot be changed, but the movements of the heart—that is, a man's thoughts—should restrict themselves to the immediate situation. All thinking that goes beyond this only makes the heart sore.

THE LINES

> Six at the beginning means:
> Keeping his toes still.
> No blame.
> Continued perseverance furthers.

Keeping the toes still means halting before one has even begun to move. The beginning is the time of few mistakes. At that time one is still in harmony with primal innocence. Not yet influenced by obscuring interests and desires, one sees things intuitively as they really are. A man who halts at the beginning, so long as he has not yet abandoned truth, finds the right way. But persisting firmness is needed to keep one from drifting irresolutely.

> Six in the second place means:
> Keeping his calves still.
> He cannot rescue him whom he follows.
> His heart is not glad.

The leg cannot move independently; it depends on the movement of the body. If a leg is suddenly stopped while the whole body is in vigorous motion, the continuing body movement will make one fall.

The same is true of a man who serves a master stronger than himself. He is swept along, and even though he may himself halt on the path of wrongdoing, he can no longer check the other in his powerful movement. Where the master presses forward, the servant, no matter how good his intentions, cannot save him.

> Nine in the third place means:
> Keeping his hips still.

Making his sacrum stiff.
Dangerous. The heart suffocates.

This refers to enforced quiet. The restless heart is to be subdued by forcible means. But fire when it is smothered changes into acrid smoke that suffocates as it spreads.

Therefore, in exercises in meditation and concentration, one ought not to try to force results. Rather, calmness must develop naturally out of a state of inner composure. If one tries to induce calmness by means of artificial rigidity, meditation will lead to very unwholesome results.

Six in the fourth place means:
Keeping his trunk still.
No blame.

As has been pointed out above in the comment on the Judgment, keeping the back at rest means forgetting the ego. This is the highest stage of rest. Here this stage has not yet been reached: the individual in this instance, though able to keep the ego, with its thoughts and impulses, in a state of rest, is not yet quite liberated from its dominance. Nonetheless, keeping the heart at rest is an important function, leading in the end to the complete elimination of egotistic drives. Even though at this point one does not yet remain free from all the dangers of doubt and unrest, this frame of mind is not a mistake, as it leads ultimately to that other, higher level.

Six in the fifth place means:
Keeping his jaws still.
The words have order.
Remorse disappears.

A man in a dangerous situation, especially when he is not adequate to it, is inclined to be very free with talk and presumptuous jokes. But injudicious speech easily leads to situations that subsequently give much cause for regret. However, if a man is reserved in speech, his words take ever more definite form, and every occasion for regret vanishes.

○ Nine at the top means:
    Noblehearted keeping still.
    Good fortune.

This marks the consummation of the effort to attain tranquillity. One is at rest, not merely in a small, circumscribed way in regard to matters of detail, but one has also a general resignation in regard to life as a whole, and this confers peace and good fortune in relation to every individual matter.

53. *Chien / Development (Gradual Progress)*

	above	SUN	THE GENTLE, WIND, WOOD
	below	KÊN	KEEPING STILL, MOUNTAIN

This hexagram is made up of Sun (wood, penetration) above, i.e., without, and Kên (mountain, stillness) below, i.e., within. A tree on a mountain develops slowly according to the law of its being and consequently stands firmly rooted. This gives the idea of a development that proceeds gradually, step by step. The attributes of the trigrams also point to this: within is tranquillity, which guards against precipitate actions, and without is penetration, which makes development and progress possible.

THE JUDGMENT

DEVELOPMENT. The maiden
Is given in marriage.
Good fortune.
Perseverance furthers.

The development of events that leads to a girl's following a man to his home proceeds slowly. The various formalities must be disposed of before the marriage takes place. This principle of gradual development can be applied to other situations as well; it is always applicable where it is a matter of correct relationships of co-operation, as for instance in the appointment of an official. The development must be allowed to take its proper course. Hasty action would not be wise. This is also true, finally, of any effort to exert influence on others, for here too the essential factor is a correct way of development through cultivation of one's own personality. No influence such as that exerted by agitators has a lasting effect.

Within the personality too, development must follow the same course if lasting results are to be achieved. Gentleness that is adaptable, but at the same time penetrating, is the outer form that should proceed from inner calm.

The very gradualness of the development makes it necessary to have perseverance, for perseverance alone prevents slow progress from dwindling to nothing.

THE IMAGE

On the mountain, a tree:
The image of DEVELOPMENT.
Thus the superior man abides in dignity and virtue,
In order to improve the mores.

The tree on the mountain is visible from afar, and its development influences the landscape of the entire region. It does not shoot up like a swamp plant; its growth proceeds gradually. Thus also the work of influencing people can be only gradual. No sudden influence or awakening is of lasting effect. Progress must be quite gradual, and in order to obtain such progress in public opinion and in the mores of the people, it is necessary for the personality to acquire influence and weight. This comes about through careful and constant work on one's own moral development.

THE LINES

Six at the beginning means:
The wild goose gradually draws near the shore.

The young son is in danger.
There is talk. No blame.

All the individual lines in this hexagram symbolize the gradual flight of the wild goose. The wild goose is the symbol of conjugal fidelity, because it is believed that this bird never takes another mate after the death of the first.

The initial line suggests the first resting place in the flight of water birds from the water to the heights. The shore is reached. The situation is that of a lonely young man who is just starting out to make his way in life. Since no one comes to help him, his first steps are slow and hesitant, and he is surrounded by danger. Naturally he is subjected to much criticism. But these very difficulties keep him from being too hasty, and his progress is successful.

○ Six in the second place means:
The wild goose gradually draws near the cliff.
Eating and drinking in peace and concord.
Good fortune.

The cliff is a safe place on shore. The development has gone a step further. The initial insecurity has been overcome, and a safe position in life has been found, giving one enough to live on. This first success, opening up a path to activity, brings a certain joyousness of mood, and one goes to meet the future reassured.

It is said of the wild goose that it calls to its comrades whenever it finds food; this is the symbol of peace and concord in good fortune. A man does not want to keep his good luck for himself only, but is ready to share it with others.

Nine in the third place means:
The wild goose gradually draws near the plateau.
The man goes forth and does not return.
The woman carries a child but does not bring it forth.
Misfortune.
It furthers one to fight off robbers.

The high plateau is dry and unsuitable for the wild goose. If it goes there, it has lost its way and gone too far. This is contrary to the law of development.

It is the same in human life. If we do not let things develop quietly but plunge of our own choice too rashly into a struggle, misfortune results. A man jeopardizes his own life, and his family perishes thereby. However, this is not at all necessary; it is only the result of transgressing the law of natural development. If one does not willfully provoke a conflict, but confines himself to vigorously maintaining his own position and to warding off unjustified attacks, all goes well.

> Six in the fourth place means:
> The wild goose gradually draws near the tree.
> Perhaps it will find a flat branch. No blame.

A tree is not a suitable place for a wild goose. But if it is clever, it will find a flat branch on which it can get a footing. A man's life too, in the course of its development, often brings him into inappropriate situations, in which he finds it difficult to hold his own without danger. Then it is important to be sensible and yielding. This enables him to discover a safe place in which life can go on, although he may be surrounded by danger.

> ○ Nine in the fifth place means:
> The wild goose gradually draws near the summit.
> For three years the woman has no child.
> In the end nothing can hinder her.
> Good fortune.

The summit is a high place. In a high position one easily becomes isolated. One is misjudged by the very person on whom one is dependent—the woman by her husband, the official by his superior. This is the work of deceitful persons who have wormed their way in. The result is that relationships remain sterile, and nothing is accomplished. But in the course of further development, such misunderstandings are cleared away, and reconciliation is achieved after all.

Nine at the top means:
The wild goose gradually draws near the cloud
heights.
Its feathers can be used for the sacred dance.
Good fortune.

Here life comes to its end. A man's work stands completed.
The path rises high toward heaven, like the flight of wild
geese when they have left the earth far behind. There they
fly, keeping to the order of their flight in strict formation.
And if their feathers fall, they can serve as ornaments in the
sacred dance pantomimes performed in the temples. Thus the
life of a man who has perfected himself is a bright light for
the people of the earth, who look up to him as an example.

歸 妹

54. *Kuei Mei / The Marrying Maiden*

| | *above* | CHÊN | THE AROUSING, THUNDER |
| | *below* | TUI | THE JOYOUS, LAKE |

Above we have Chên, the eldest son, and below, Tui, the
youngest daughter. The man leads and the girl follows him in
gladness. The picture is that of the entrance of the girl into
her husband's house. In all, there are four hexagrams depict-
ing the relationship between husband and wife. Hsien,
INFLUENCE (31), describes the attraction that a young couple
have for each other; Hêng, DURATION (32), portrays the
permanent relationships of marriage; Chien, DEVELOPMENT
(53), reflects the protracted, ceremonious procedures attending
the arrangement of a proper marriage; finally, Kuei Mei,

THE MARRYING MAIDEN, shows a young girl under the guidance of an older man who marries her.[1]

THE JUDGMENT

THE MARRYING MAIDEN.
Undertakings bring misfortune.
Nothing that would further.

A girl who is taken into the family, but not as the chief wife, must behave with special caution and reserve. She must not take it upon herself to supplant the mistress of the house, for that would mean disorder and lead to untenable relationships.

The same is true of all voluntary relationships between human beings. While legally regulated relationships evince a fixed connection between duties and rights, relationships based on personal inclination depend in the long run entirely on tactful reserve.

Affection as the essential principle of relatedness is of the greatest importance in all relationships in the world. For the union of heaven and earth is the origin of the whole of nature. Among human beings likewise, spontaneous affection is the all-inclusive principle of union.

THE IMAGE

Thunder over the lake:
The image of THE MARRYING MAIDEN.
Thus the superior man
Understands the transitory
In the light of the eternity of the end.

---

1. In China, monogamy is formally the rule, and every man has but one official wife. This marriage, which is less the concern of the two participants than of their families, is contracted with strict observance of forms. But the husband retains the right also to indulge his more personal inclinations. Indeed, it is the most gracious duty of a good wife to be helpful to him in this respect. In this way the relationship that develops becomes a beautiful and open one, and the girl who enters the family at the husband's wish subordinates herself modestly to the wife as a younger sister. Of course it is a most difficult and delicate matter, requiring tact on the part of all concerned. But

Thunder stirs the water of the lake, which follows it in shimmering waves. This symbolizes the girl who follows the man of her choice. But every relationship between individuals bears within it the danger that wrong turns may be taken, leading to endless misunderstandings and disagreements. Therefore it is necessary constantly to remain mindful of the end. If we permit ourselves to drift along, we come together and are parted again as the day may determine. If on the other hand a man fixes his mind on an end that endures, he will succeed in avoiding the reefs that confront the closer relationships of people.

THE LINES

Nine at the beginning means:
The marrying maiden as a concubine.
A lame man who is able to tread.
Undertakings bring good fortune.

The princes of ancient China maintained a fixed order of rank among the court ladies, who were subordinated to the queen as are younger sisters to the eldest. Frequently they came from the family of the queen, who herself led them to her husband.

The meaning is that a girl entering a family with the consent of the wife will not rank outwardly as the equal of the latter but will withdraw modestly into the background. However, if she understands how to fit herself into the pattern of things, her position will be entirely satisfactory, and she will feel sheltered in the love of the husband to whom she bears children.

The same meaning is brought out in the relationships between officials. A man may enjoy the personal friendship of a prince and be taken into his confidence. Outwardly this man must keep tactfully in the background behind the official ministers of state, but, although he is hampered by this status, as if he were lame, he can nevertheless accomplish something through the kindliness of his nature.

---

under favorable circumstances this represents the solution of a problem for which European culture has failed to find an answer. Needless to say, the ideal set for woman in China is achieved no oftener than is the European ideal.

Nine in the second place means:
A one-eyed man who is able to see.
The perseverance of a solitary man furthers.

Here the situation is that of a girl married to a man who has disappointed her. Man and wife ought to work together like a pair of eyes. Here the girl is left behind in loneliness; the man of her choice either has become unfaithful or has died. But she does not lose the inner light of loyalty. Though the other eye is gone, she maintains her loyalty even in loneliness.

☐ Six in the third place means:
The marrying maiden as a slave.
She marries as a concubine.

A girl who is in a lowly position and finds no husband may, in some circumstances, still win shelter as a concubine.

This pictures the situation of a person who longs too much for joys that cannot be obtained in the usual way. He enters upon a situation not altogether compatible with self-esteem. Neither judgment nor warning is added to this line; it merely lays bare the actual situation, so that everyone may draw a lesson from it.

Nine in the fourth place means:
The marrying maiden draws out the allotted time.
A late marriage comes in due course.

The girl is virtuous. She does not wish to throw herself away, and allows the customary time for marriage to slip by. However, there is no harm in this; she is rewarded for her purity and, even though belatedly, finds the husband intended for her.

○ Six in the fifth place means:
The sovereign I gave his daughter in marriage.
The embroidered garments of the princess
Were not as gorgeous

> As those of the servingmaid.
> The moon that is nearly full
> Brings good fortune.

The sovereign I is T'ang the Completer. This ruler decreed that the imperial princesses should be subordinated to their husbands in the same manner as other women (cf. hexagram 11, six in the fifth place). The emperor does not wait for a suitor to woo his daughter but gives her in marriage when he sees fit. Therefore it is in accord with custom for the girl's family to take the initiative here.

We see here a girl of aristocratic birth who marries a man of modest circumstances and understands how to adapt herself with grace to the new situation. She is free of all vanity of outer adornment, and forgetting her rank in her marriage, takes a place below that of her husband, just as the moon, before it is quite full, does not directly face the sun.

☐ Six at the top means:

> The woman holds the basket, but there are no
>   fruits in it.
> The man stabs the sheep, but no blood flows.
> Nothing that acts to further.

At the sacrifice to the ancestors, the woman had to present harvest offerings in a basket, while the man slaughtered the sacrificial animal with his own hand. Here the ritual is only superficially fulfilled; the woman takes an empty basket and the man stabs a sheep slaughtered beforehand—solely to preserve the forms. This impious, irreverent attitude bodes no good for a marriage.

55. Fêng / Abundance [Fullness]

| | above | CHÊN | THE AROUSING, THUNDER |
| | below | LI | THE CLINGING, FLAME |

Chên is movement; Li is flame, whose attribute is clarity. Clarity within, movement without—this produces greatness and abundance. The hexagram pictures a period of advanced civilization. However, the fact that development has reached a peak suggests that this extraordinary condition of abundance cannot be maintained permanently.

THE JUDGMENT

ABUNDANCE has success.
The king attains abundance.
Be not sad.
Be like the sun at midday.

It is not given to every mortal to bring about a time of outstanding greatness and abundance. Only a born ruler of men is able to do it, because his will is directed to what is great. Such a time of abundance is usually brief. Therefore a sage might well feel sad in view of the decline that must follow. But such sadness does not befit him. Only a man who is inwardly free of sorrow and care can lead in a time of abundance. He must be like the sun at midday, illuminating and gladdening everything under heaven.

THE IMAGE

Both thunder and lightning come:
The image of ABUNDANCE.

> Thus the superior man decides lawsuits
> And carries out punishments.

This hexagram has a certain connection with Shih Ho, BITING THROUGH (21), in which thunder and lightning similarly appear together, but in the reverse order. In BITING THROUGH, laws are laid down; here they are applied and enforced. Clarity [Li] within makes it possible to investigate the facts exactly, and shock [Chên] without ensures a strict and precise carrying out of punishments.

THE LINES

> Nine at the beginning means:
> When a man meets his destined ruler,
> They can be together ten days,
> And it is not a mistake.
> Going meets with recognition.

To bring about a time of abundance, a union of clarity with energetic movement is needed. Two individuals possessed of these two attributes are suited to each other, and even if they spend an entire cycle of time together during the period of abundance, it will not be too long, nor is it a mistake. Therefore one may go forth, in order to make one's influence felt; it will meet with recognition.

> Six in the second place means:
> The curtain is of such fullness
> That the polestars can be seen at noon.
> Through going one meets with mistrust and hate.
> If one rouses him through truth,
> Good fortune comes.

It often happens that plots and party intrigues, which have the darkening effect of an eclipse of the sun, come between a ruler intent on great achievement and the man who could effect great undertakings. Then, instead of the sun, we see the northern stars in the sky. The ruler is overshadowed by a party that has usurped power. If a man at such a time were to try to take energetic measures, he would encounter only mistrust and envy, which would prohibit all movement. The essential thing then is to hold inwardly to the power of truth, which in the end is so strong that it exerts an invisible influence on the ruler, so that all goes well.

> Nine in the third place means:
> The underbrush is of such abundance
> That the small stars can be seen at noon.
> He breaks his right arm. No blame.

The image is that of a progressive covering over of the sun. Here the eclipse reaches totality, therefore even the small stars can be seen at noon.

In the sphere of social relationships, this means that the prince is now so eclipsed that even the most insignificant persons can push themselves into the foreground. This makes it impossible for an able man, though he might be the right hand of the ruler, to undertake anything. It is as though his arm were broken, but he is not to blame for being thus hindered in action.

> Nine in the fourth place means:
> The curtain is of such fullness
> That the polestars can be seen at noon.
> He meets his ruler, who is of like kind.
> Good fortune.

Here the darkness is already decreasing, therefore interrelated elements come together. Here too the complement must be found—the necessary wisdom to complement joy of action. Then everything will go well. The complementary factor postulated here is the reverse of the one in the first line. In the latter, wisdom is to be complemented by energy, while here energy is complemented by wisdom.

> ○ Six in the fifth place means:
> Lines are coming,
> Blessing and fame draw near.
> Good fortune.

The ruler is modest and therefore open to the counsel of able men. Thus he is surrounded by men who suggest to him the lines of action. This brings blessing, fame, and good fortune to him and all the people.

> Six at the top means:
> His house is in a state of abundance.
> He screens off his family.
> He peers through the gate
> And no longer perceives anyone.
> For three years he sees nothing.
> Misfortune.

This describes a man who because of his arrogance and obstinacy attains the opposite of what he strives for. He seeks abundance and splendor for his dwelling. He wishes at all odds to be master in his house, which so alienates his family that in the end he finds himself completely isolated.

56. *Lü / The Wanderer*

	above	LI	THE CLINGING, FIRE
	below	KÊN	KEEPING STILL, MOUNTAIN

The mountain, Kên, stands still; above it fire, Li, flames up and does not tarry. Therefore the two trigrams do not stay together. Strange lands and separation are the wanderer's lot.

THE JUDGMENT

THE WANDERER. Success through smallness.
Perseverance brings good fortune
To the wanderer.

When a man is a wanderer and stranger, he should not be gruff nor overbearing. He has no large circle of acquaintances, therefore he should not give himself airs. He must be cautious and reserved; in this way he protects himself from evil. If he is obliging toward others, he wins success.

A wanderer has no fixed abode; his home is the road. Therefore he must take care to remain upright and steadfast, so that he sojourns only in the proper places, associating only with good people. Then he has good fortune and can go his way unmolested.

THE IMAGE

Fire on the mountain:
The image of THE WANDERER.
Thus the superior man
Is clear-minded and cautious
In imposing penalties,
And protracts no lawsuits.

When grass on a mountain takes fire, there is bright light. However, the fire does not linger in one place, but travels on to new fuel. It is a phenomenon of short duration. This is what penalties and lawsuits should be like. They should be a quickly passing matter, and must not be dragged out indefinitely. Prisons ought to be places where people are lodged only temporarily, as guests are. They must not become dwelling places.

THE LINES

Six at the beginning means:
If the wanderer busies himself with trivial things,
He draws down misfortune upon himself.

A wanderer should not demean himself or busy himself with inferior things he meets with along the way. The humbler and more defenseless his outward position, the more should he preserve his inner dignity. For a stranger is mistaken if he hopes to find a friendly reception through lending himself to jokes and buffoonery. The result will be only contempt and insulting treatment.

Six in the second place means:
The wanderer comes to an inn.
He has his property with him.
He wins the steadfastness[1] of a young servant.

The wanderer here described is modest and reserved. He does not lose touch with his inner being, hence he finds a resting place. In the outside world he does not lose the liking of other people, hence all persons further him, so that he can acquire property. Moreover, he wins the allegiance of a faithful and trustworthy servant—a thing of inestimable value to a wanderer.

Nine in the third place means:
The wanderer's inn burns down.
He loses the steadfastness of his young servant.
Danger.

A truculent stranger does not know how to behave properly. He meddles in affairs and controversies that do not concern him; thus he loses his resting place. He treats his servant with aloofness and arrogance; thus he loses the man's loyalty. When a stranger in a strange land has no one left on whom he can rely, the situation becomes very dangerous.

Nine in the fourth place means:
The wanderer rests in a shelter.
He obtains his property and an ax.
My heart is not glad.

This describes a wanderer who knows how to limit his desires outwardly, though he is inwardly strong and aspiring. Therefore he finds at least a place of shelter in which he can stay. He also succeeds in acquiring property, but even with this he is not secure. He must be always on guard, ready to defend himself with arms. Hence he is not at ease. He is persistently conscious of being a stranger in a strange land.

---

1. [Literally, "perseverance."]

○ Six in the fifth place means:
  He shoots a pheasant.
  It drops with the first arrow.
  In the end this brings both praise and office.

Traveling statesmen were in the habit of introducing themselves to local princes with the gift of a pheasant. Here the
wanderer wants to enter the service of a prince. To this end
he shoots a pheasant, killing it at the first shot. Thus he finds
friends who praise and recommend him, and in the end the
prince accepts him and confers an office upon him.

Circumstances often cause a man to seek a home in foreign
parts. If he knows how to meet the situation and how to
introduce himself in the right way, he may find a circle of
friends and a sphere of activity even in a strange country.

  Nine at the top means:
  The bird's nest burns up.
  The wanderer laughs at first,
  Then must needs lament and weep.
  Through carelessness he loses his cow.
  Misfortune.

The picture of a bird whose nest burns up indicates loss of
one's resting place. This misfortune may overtake the bird if
it is heedless and imprudent when building its nest. It is the
same with a wanderer. If he lets himself go, laughing and
jesting, and forgets that he is a wanderer, he will later have
cause to weep and lament. For if through carelessness a man
loses his cow—i.e., his modesty and adaptability—evil will
result.

巽

57. *Sun / The Gentle*
(The Penetrating, Wind)

	above	SUN	THE GENTLE, WIND, WOOD
	below	SUN	THE GENTLE, WIND, WOOD

Sun is one of the eight doubled trigrams. It is the eldest daughter and symbolizes wind or wood; it has for its attribute gentleness, which nonetheless penetrates like the wind or like growing wood with its roots.

The dark principle, in itself rigid and immovable, is dissolved by the penetrating light principle, to which it subordinates itself in gentleness. In nature, it is the wind that disperses the gathered clouds, leaving the sky clear and serene. In human life it is penetrating clarity of judgment that thwarts all dark hidden motives. In the life of the community it is the powerful influence of a great personality that uncovers and breaks up those intrigues which shun the light of day.

THE JUDGMENT

THE GENTLE. Success through what is small.

It furthers one to have somewhere to go.

It furthers one to see the great man.

Penetration produces gradual and inconspicuous effects. It should be effected not by an act of violation but by influence that never lapses. Results of this kind are less striking to the eye than those won by surprise attack, but they are more enduring and more complete. If one would produce such effects, one must have a clearly defined goal, for only when the penetrating influence works always in the same direction can the object be attained. Small strength can achieve its purpose only by subordinating itself to an eminent man who is capable of creating order.

THE IMAGE

Winds following one upon the other:
The image of THE GENTLY PENETRATING.
Thus the superior man
Spreads his commands abroad
And carries out his undertakings.

The penetrating quality of the wind depends upon its cease-lessness. This is what makes it so powerful; time is its instrument. In the same way the ruler's thought should penetrate the soul of the people. This too requires a lasting influence brought about by enlightenment and command. Only when the command has been assimilated by the people is action in accordance with it possible. Action without preparation of the ground only frightens and repels.

THE LINES

☐ Six at the beginning means:
In advancing and in retreating,
The perseverance of a warrior furthers.

Inborn gentleness is often carried to the point of indecisiveness. One does not feel strong enough to advance resolutely. A thousand doubts crop up; one is, however, not minded to with-draw but drifts indecisively to and fro. In such a situation, a military decisiveness is the proper thing, so that one resolutely does what order demands. Resolute discipline is far better than irresolute license.

Nine in the second place means:
Penetration under the bed.
Priests and magicians are used in great number.
Good fortune. No blame.

At times one has to deal with hidden enemies, intangible in-fluences that slink into dark corners and from this hiding affect people by suggestion. In instances like this, it is necessary to trace these things back to the most secret recesses, in order to determine the nature of the influences to be dealt with. This is the task of the priests; removing the influences is the task of the magicians. The very anonymity of such plotting requires an especially vigorous and indefatigable effort, but this is well worth while. For when such elusive influences are brought into the light and branded, they lose their power over people.

> Nine in the third place means:
> Repeated penetration. Humiliation.

Penetrating reflection must not be pushed too far, lest it cripple the power of decision. After a matter has been thoroughly pondered, it is essential to form a decision and to act. Repeated deliberation brings fresh doubts and scruples, and thereby humiliation, because one shows oneself unable to act.

> ☐ Six in the fourth place means:
> Remorse vanishes.
> During the hunt
> Three kinds of game are caught.

When a responsible position and accumulated experience lead one to combine innate modesty with energetic action, great success is assured. The three kinds of animals referred to served for offerings to the gods, for feasting guests, and for everyday consumption. When the catch answered all three purposes, the hunt was considered especially successful.

> ○ Nine in the fifth place means:
> Perseverance brings good fortune.
> Remorse vanishes.
> Nothing that does not further.
> No beginning, but an end.
> Before the change, three days.
> After the change, three days.
> Good fortune.

In the situation described in Ku, WORK ON WHAT HAS BEEN
SPOILED (18), an entirely new point of departure must be set
up, whereas here it is only a question of reforms. The beginning
has not been good, but the moment has been reached when a
new direction can be taken. Change and improvement are
called for. Such steps must be undertaken with steadfastness,
that is, with a firm and correct attitude of mind; then they
will succeed, and remorse will disappear. But it must be re-
membered that such improvements require careful consideration. Before a change is made, it must be pondered over again
and again. After the change is made, it is necessary to note
carefully for some time after how the improvements bear the
test of actuality. Such careful work is accompanied by good
fortune.

> Nine at the top means:
> Penetration under the bed.
> He loses his property and his ax.
> Perseverance brings misfortune.

A man's understanding is sufficiently penetrating. He follows
up injurious influences into the most secret corners. But he no
longer has the strength to combat them decisively. In this case
any attempt to penetrate into the personal domain of darkness
would only bring harm.

兆

58. *Tui | The Joyous, Lake*

above	TUI	THE JOYOUS, LAKE
below	TUI	THE JOYOUS, LAKE

This hexagram, like Sun, is one of the eight formed by doubling
of a trigram. The trigram Tui denotes the youngest daughter;
it is symbolized by the smiling lake, and its attribute is joyous-

ness. Contrary to appearances, it is not the yielding quality of the top line that accounts for joy here. The attribute of the yielding or dark principle is not joy but melancholy. However, joy is indicated by the fact that there are two strong lines within, expressing themselves through the medium of gentleness.

True joy, therefore, rests on firmness and strength within, manifesting itself outwardly as yielding and gentle.

THE JUDGMENT

THE JOYOUS. Success.
Perseverance is favorable.

The joyous mood is infectious and therefore brings success. But joy must be based on steadfastness if it is not to degenerate into uncontrolled mirth. Truth and strength must dwell in the heart, while gentleness reveals itself in social intercourse. In this way one assumes the right attitude toward God and man and achieves something. Under certain conditions, intimidation without gentleness may achieve something momentarily, but not for all time. When, on the other hand, the hearts of men are won by friendliness, they are led to take all hardships upon themselves willingly, and if need be will not shun death itself, so great is the power of joy over men.

THE IMAGE

Lakes resting one on the other:
The image of THE JOYOUS.
Thus the superior man joins with his friends
For discussion and practice.

A lake evaporates upward and thus gradually dries up; but when two lakes are joined they do not dry up so readily, for one replenishes the other. It is the same in the field of knowledge. Knowledge should be a refreshing and vitalizing force. It becomes so only through stimulating intercourse with congenial friends with whom one holds discussion and practices application of the truths of life. In this way learning becomes many-sided and takes on a cheerful lightness, whereas there is always something ponderous and one-sided about the learning of the self-taught.

THE LINES

Nine at the beginning means:
Contented joyousness. Good fortune.

A quiet, wordless, self-contained joy, desiring nothing from without and resting content with everything, remains free of all egotistic likes and dislikes. In this freedom lies good fortune, because it harbors the quiet security of a heart fortified within itself.

○ Nine in the second place means:
Sincere joyousness. Good fortune.
Remorse disappears.

We often find ourselves associating with inferior people in whose company we are tempted by pleasures that are inappropriate for the superior man. To participate in such pleasures would certainly bring remorse, for a superior man can find no real satisfaction in low pleasures. When, recognizing this, a man does not permit his will to swerve, so that he does not find such ways agreeable, not even dubious companions will venture to proffer any base pleasures, because he would not enjoy them. Thus every cause for regret is removed.

□ Six in the third place means:
Coming joyousness. Misfortune.

True joy must spring from within. But if one is empty within and wholly given over to the world, idle pleasures come streaming in from without. This is what many people welcome as diversion. Those who lack inner stability and therefore need amusement, will always find opportunity of indulgence. They attract external pleasures by the emptiness of their natures. Thus they lose themselves more and more, which of course has bad results.

Nine in the fourth place means:
Joyousness that is weighed is not at peace.
After ridding himself of mistakes a man has joy.

Often a man finds himself weighing the choice between various kinds of pleasures, and so long as he has not decided which kind he will choose, the higher or the lower, he has no inner peace. Only when he clearly recognizes that passion brings suffering, can he make up his mind to turn away from the lower pleasures and to strive for the higher. Once this decision is sealed, he finds true joy and peace, and inner conflict is overcome.

○ Nine in the fifth place means:

Sincerity toward disintegrating influences is dangerous.

Dangerous elements approach even the best of men. If a man permits himself to have anything to do with them, their disintegrating influence acts slowly but surely, and inevitably brings dangers in its train. But if he recognizes the situation and can comprehend the danger, he knows how to protect himself and remains unharmed.

☐ Six at the top means:

Seductive joyousness.

A vain nature invites diverting pleasures and must suffer accordingly (cf. the six in the third place). If a man is unstable within, the pleasures of the world that he does not shun have so powerful an influence that he is swept along by them. Here it is no longer a question of danger, of good fortune or misfortune. He has given up direction of his own life, and what becomes of him depends upon chance and external influences.

漢

Huan / Dispersion [*Dissolution*]

☴	*above* SUN	THE GENTLE, WIND
☵	*below* K'AN	THE ABYSMAL, WATER

Wind blowing over water disperses it, dissolving it into foam
and mist. This suggests that when a man's vital energy is
dammed up within him (indicated as a danger by the attribute
of the lower trigram), gentleness serves to break up and dissolve the blockage.

THE JUDGMENT

DISPERSION. Success.
The king approaches his temple.
It furthers one to cross the great water.
Perseverance furthers.

The text of this hexagram resembles that of Ts'ui, GATHERING
TOGETHER (45). In the latter, the subject is the bringing
together of elements that have been separated, as water collects in lakes upon the earth. Here the subject is the dispersing
and dissolving of divisive egotism. DISPERSION shows the way,
so to speak, that leads to gathering together. This explains the
similarity of the two texts.

Religious forces are needed to overcome the egotism that
divides men. The common celebration of the great sacrificial
feasts and sacred rites, which gave expression simultaneously
to the interrelation and social articulation of family and state,
was the means employed by the great rulers to unite men. The
sacred music and the splendor of the ceremonies aroused a
strong tide of emotion that was shared by all hearts in unison,

and that awakened a consciousness of the common origin of all creatures. In this way disunity was overcome and rigidity dissolved. A further means to the same end is co-operation in great general undertakings that set a high goal for the will of the people; in the common concentration on this goal, all barriers dissolve, just as, when a boat is crossing a great stream, all hands must unite in a joint task.

But only a man who is himself free of all selfish ulterior considerations, and who perseveres in justice and steadfastness, is capable of so dissolving the hardness of egotism.

THE IMAGE

The wind drives over the water:
The image of DISPERSION.
Thus the kings of old sacrificed to the Lord
And built temples.

In the autumn and winter, water begins to freeze into ice. When the warm breezes of spring come, the rigidity is dissolved, and the elements that have been dispersed in ice floes are reunited. It is the same with the minds of the people. Through hardness and selfishness the heart grows rigid, and this rigidity leads to separation from all others. Egotism and cupidity isolate men. Therefore the hearts of men must be seized by a devout emotion. They must be shaken by a religious awe in face of eternity—stirred with an intuition of the One Creator of all living beings, and united through the strong feeling of fellowship experienced in the ritual of divine worship.

THE LINES

Six at the beginning means:
He brings help with the strength of a horse.
Good fortune.

It is important that disunion should be overcome at the outset, before it has become complete—that the clouds should be dispersed before they have brought storm and rain. At such times when hidden divergences in temper make themselves felt and lead to mutual misunderstandings, we must take quick and vigorous action to dissolve the misunderstandings and mutual distrust.

☐ Nine in the second place means:
  At the dissolution
  He hurries to that which supports him.
  Remorse disappears.

When an individual discovers within himself the beginnings of alienation from others, of misanthropy and ill humor, he must set about dissolving these obstructions. He must rouse himself inwardly, hasten to that which supports him. Such support is never found in hatred, but always in a moderate and just judgment of men, linked with good will. If he regains this unobstructed outlook on humanity, while at the same time all saturnine ill humor is dissolved, all occasion for remorse disappears.

  Six in the third place means:
  He dissolves his self. No remorse.

Under certain circumstances, a man's work may become so difficult that he can no longer think of himself. He must set aside all personal desires and disperse whatever the self gathers about it to serve as a barrier against others. Only on the basis of a great renunciation can he obtain the strength for great achievements. By setting his goal in a great task outside himself, he can attain this standpoint.

☐ Six in the fourth place means:
  He dissolves his bond with his group.[1]
  Supreme good fortune.
  Dispersion leads in turn to accumulation.
  This is something that ordinary men do not think of.

When we are working at a task that affects the general welfare, we must leave all private friendships out of account. Only by rising above party interests can we achieve something decisive.

----

1. [Literally, in the German, "He dissolves himself from his group."]

He who has the courage thus to forego what is near wins what is afar. But in order to comprehend this standpoint, one must have a wide view of the interrelationships of life, such as only unusual men attain.

○ Nine in the fifth place means:
>His loud cries are as dissolving as sweat.
>Dissolution! A king abides without blame.

In times of general dispersion and separation, a great idea provides a focal point for the organization of recovery. Just as an illness reaches its crisis in a dissolving sweat, so a great and stimulating idea is a true salvation in times of general deadlock. It gives the people a rallying point—a man in a ruling position who can dispel misunderstandings.

>Nine at the top means:
>He dissolves his blood.
>Departing, keeping at a distance, going out,
>Is without blame.

The idea of the dissolving of a man's blood means the dispersion of that which might lead to bloodshed and wounds, i.e., avoidance of danger. But here the thought is not that a man avoids difficulties for himself alone, but rather that he rescues his kin —helps them to get away before danger comes, or to keep at a distance from an existing danger, or to find a way out of a danger that is already upon them. In this way he does what is right.

節

60. *Chieh / Limitation*

	above	K'AN	THE ABYSMAL, WATER
	below	TUI	THE JOYOUS, LAKE

A lake occupies a limited space. When more water comes into it, it overflows. Therefore limits must be set for the water. The image shows water below and water above, with the firmament between them as a limit.

The Chinese word for limitation really denotes the joints that divide a bamboo stalk. In relation to ordinary life it means the thrift that sets fixed limits upon expenditures. In relation to the moral sphere it means the fixed limits that the superior man sets upon his actions—the limits of loyalty and disinterestedness.

THE JUDGMENT

LIMITATION. Success.
Galling limitation must not be persevered in.

Limitations are troublesome, but they are effective. If we live economically in normal times, we are prepared for times of want. To be sparing saves us from humiliation. Limitations are also indispensable in the regulation of world conditions. In nature there are fixed limits for summer and winter, day and night, and these limits give the year its meaning. In the same way, economy, by setting fixed limits upon expenditures, acts to preserve property and prevent injury to the people.

But in limitation we must observe due measure. If a man should seek to impose galling limitations upon his own nature, it would be injurious. And if he should go too far in imposing limitations on others, they would rebel. Therefore it is necessary to set limits even upon limitation.

THE IMAGE

Water over lake: the image of LIMITATION.
Thus the superior man
Creates number and measure,
And examines the nature of virtue and correct
   conduct.

A lake is something limited. Water is inexhaustible. A lake can contain only a definite amount of the infinite quantity of water; this is its peculiarity. In human life too the individual achieves significance through discrimination and the setting of limits. Therefore what concerns us here is the problem of clearly defining these discriminations, which are, so to speak, the backbone of morality. Unlimited possibilities are not suited to man; if they existed, his life would only dissolve in the boundless. To become strong, a man's life needs the limitations ordained by duty and voluntarily accepted. The individual attains significance as a free spirit only by surrounding himself with these limitations and by determining for himself what his duty is.

THE LINES

Nine at the beginning means:
Not going out of the door and the courtyard
Is without blame.

Often a man who would like to undertake something finds himself confronted by insurmountable limitations. Then he must know where to stop. If he rightly understands this and does not go beyond the limits set for him, he accumulates an energy that enables him, when the proper time comes, to act with great force. Discretion is of prime importance in preparing the way for momentous things. Concerning this, Confucius says:

Where disorder develops, words are the first steps. If the prince is not discreet, he loses his servant. If the servant is not discreet, he loses his life. If germinating things are not handled with discretion, the perfecting of them is impeded. Therefore the superior man is careful to maintain silence and does not go forth.

> Nine in the second place means:
> Not going out of the gate and the courtyard
> Brings misfortune.

When the time for action has come, the moment must be quickly seized. Just as water first collects in a lake without flowing out, yet is certain to find an outlet when the lake is full, so it is in the life of man. It is a good thing to hesitate so long as the time for action has not come, but no longer. Once the obstacles to action have been removed, anxious hesitation is a mistake that is bound to bring disaster, because one misses one's opportunity.

> Six in the third place means:
> He who knows no limitation
> Will have cause to lament.
> No blame.

If an individual is bent only on pleasures and enjoyment, it is easy for him to lose his sense of the limits that are necessary. If he gives himself over to extravagance, he will have to suffer the consequences, with accompanying regret. He must not seek to lay the blame on others. Only when we realize that our mistakes are of our own making will such disagreeable experiences free us of errors.

> Six in the fourth place means:
> Contented limitation. Success.

Every limitation has its value, but a limitation that requires persistent effort entails a cost of too much energy. When, however, the limitation is a natural one (as for example, the limitation by which water flows only downhill), it necessarily leads to success, for then it means a saving of energy. The energy that otherwise would be consumed in a vain struggle with the object, is applied wholly to the benefit of the matter in hand, and success is assured.

○ Nine in the fifth place means:
 Sweet limitation brings good fortune.
 Going brings esteem.

The limitation must be carried out in the right way if it is to be effective. If we seek to impose restrictions on others only, while evading them ourselves, these restrictions will always be resented and will provoke resistance. If, however, a man in a leading position applies the limitation first to himself, demanding little from those associated with him, and with modest means manages to achieve something, good fortune is the result. Where such an example occurs, it meets with emulation, so that whatever is undertaken must succeed.

 Six at the top means:
 Galling limitation.
 Perseverance brings misfortune.
 Remorse disappears.

If one is too severe in setting up restrictions, people will not endure them. The more consistent such severity, the worse it is, for in the long run a reaction is unavoidable. In the same way, the tormented body will rebel against excessive asceticism. On the other hand, although ruthless severity is not to be applied persistently and systematically, there may be times when it is the only means of safeguarding against guilt and remorse. In such situations ruthlessness toward oneself is the only means of saving one's soul, which otherwise would succumb to irresolution and temptation.

中孚

61. *Chung Fu / Inner Truth*

above	SUN	THE GENTLE, WIND
below	TUI	THE JOYOUS, LAKE

The wind blows over the lake and stirs the surface of the water.
Thus visible effects of the invisible manifest themselves. The
hexagram consists of firm lines above and below, while it is
open in the center. This indicates a heart free of prejudices
and therefore open to truth. On the other hand, each of the
two trigrams has a firm line in the middle; this indicates the
force of inner truth in the influences they represent.

The attributes of the two trigrams are: above, gentleness,
forbearance toward inferiors; below, joyousness in obeying
superiors. Such conditions create the basis of a mutual confidence that makes achievements possible.

The character *fu* ("truth") is actually the picture of a
bird's foot over a fledgling. It suggests the idea of brooding. An
egg is hollow. The light-giving power must work to quicken it
from outside, but there must be a germ of life within, if life is
to be awakened. Far-reaching speculations can be linked with
these ideas.

THE JUDGMENT

INNER TRUTH. Pigs and fishes.
Good fortune.
It furthers one to cross the great water.
Perseverance furthers.

Pigs and fishes are the least intelligent of all animals and therefore the most difficult to influence. The force of inner truth

must grow great indeed before its influence can extend to such creatures. In dealing with persons as intractable and as difficult to influence as a pig or a fish, the whole secret of success depends on finding the right way of approach. One must first rid oneself of all prejudice and, so to speak, let the psyche of the other person act on one without restraint. Then one will establish contact with him, understand and gain power over him. When a door has thus been opened, the force of one's personality will influence him. If in this way one finds no obstacles insurmountable, one can undertake even the most dangerous things, such as crossing the great water, and succeed.

But it is important to understand upon what the force of inner truth depends. This force is not identical with simple intimacy or a secret bond. Close ties may exist also among thieves; it is true that such a bond acts as a force but, since it is not invincible, it does not bring good fortune. All association on the basis of common interests holds only up to a certain point. Where the community of interest ceases, the holding together ceases also, and the closest friendship often changes into hate. Only when the bond is based on what is right, on steadfastness, will it remain so firm that it triumphs over everything.

THE IMAGE

Wind over lake: the image of INNER TRUTH.
Thus the superior man discusses criminal cases
In order to delay executions.

Wind stirs water by penetrating it. Thus the superior man, when obliged to judge the mistakes of men, tries to penetrate their minds with understanding, in order to gain a sympathetic appreciation of the circumstances. In ancient China, the entire administration of justice was guided by this principle. A deep understanding that knows how to pardon was considered the highest form of justice. This system was not without success, for its aim was to make so strong a moral impression that there was no reason to fear abuse of such mildness. For it sprang not from weakness but from a superior clarity.

THE LINES

Nine at the beginning means:
Being prepared brings good fortune.
If there are secret designs, it is disquieting.

The force of inner truth depends chiefly on inner stability and preparedness. From this state of mind springs the correct attitude toward the outer world. But if a man should try to cultivate secret relationships of a special sort, it would deprive him of his inner independence. The more reliance he places on the support of others, the more uneasy and anxious he will become as to whether these secret ties are really tenable. In this way inner peace and the force of inner truth are lost.

Nine in the second place means:
A crane calling in the shade.
Its young answers it.
I have a good goblet.
I will share it with you.

This refers to the involuntary influence of a man's inner being upon persons of kindred spirit. The crane need not show itself on a high hill. It may be quite hidden when it sounds its call; yet its young will hear its note, will recognize it and give answer. Where there is a joyous mood, there a comrade will appear to share a glass of wine.

This is the echo awakened in men through spiritual attraction. Whenever a feeling is voiced with truth and frankness, whenever a deed is the clear expression of sentiment, a mysterious and far-reaching influence is exerted. At first it acts on those who are inwardly receptive. But the circle grows larger and larger. The root of all influence lies in one's own inner being: given true and vigorous expression in word and deed, its effect is great. The effect is but the reflection of something that emanates from one's own heart. Any deliberate intention of an effect would only destroy the possibility of producing it. Confucius says about this line:

The superior man abides in his room. If his words are well spoken, he meets with assent at a distance of more than a thousand miles. How much more then from near by! If the superior man abides in his room and his words are not well spoken, he meets with contradiction at a distance of more than a thousand miles. How much more then from near by! Words go forth from one's own person and exert their influence on men. Deeds are born close at hand and become visible far away. Words and deeds are the hinge and bowspring of the superior man. As hinge and bowspring move, they bring honor or disgrace. Through words and deeds the superior man moves heaven and earth. Must one not, then, be cautious?

☐ Six in the third place means:
   He finds a comrade.
   Now he beats the drum, now he stops.
   Now he sobs, now he sings.

Here the source of a man's strength lies not in himself but in his relation to other people. No matter how close to them he may be, if his center of gravity depends on them, he is inevitably tossed to and fro between joy and sorrow. Rejoicing to high heaven, then sad unto death—this is the fate of those who depend upon an inner accord with other persons whom they love. Here we have only the statement of the law that this is so. Whether this condition is felt to be an affliction or the supreme happiness of love, is left to the subjective verdict of the person concerned.

☐ Six in the fourth place means:
   The moon nearly at the full.
   The team horse goes astray.
   No blame.

To intensify the power of inner truth, a man must always turn to his superior, from whom he can receive enlightenment as the moon receives light from the sun. However, this requires a certain humility, like that of the moon when it is not yet quite full. At the moment when the moon becomes full and stands directly opposite the sun, it begins to wane. Just as on the one hand we must be humble and reverent when face to face with the source of enlightenment, so likewise must we on the other renounce factionalism among men. Only by pursuing one's course like a horse that goes straight ahead without looking sidewise at its mate, can one retain the inner freedom that helps one onward.

○ Nine in the fifth place means:
He possesses truth, which links together.
No blame.

This describes the ruler who holds all elements together by the power of his personality. Only when the strength of his character is so ample that he can influence all who are subject to him, is he as he needs to be. The power of suggestion must emanate from the ruler. It will firmly knit together and unite all his adherents. Without this central force, all external unity is only deception and breaks down at the decisive moment.

Nine at the top means:
Cockcrow penetrating to heaven.
Perseverance brings misfortune.

The cock is dependable. It crows at dawn. But it cannot itself fly to heaven. It just crows. A man may count on mere words to awaken faith. This may succeed now and then, but if persisted in, it will have bad consequences.

小過

62. *Hsiao Kuo* / *Preponderance of the Small*

☳	*above*	CHÊN	THE AROUSING, THUNDER
☶	*below*	KÊN	KEEPING STILL, MOUNTAIN

While in the hexagram Ta Kuo, PREPONDERANCE OF THE GREAT (28), the strong lines preponderate and are within, inclosed between weak lines at the top and bottom, the present hexagram has weak lines preponderating, though here again they are on the outside, the strong lines being within. This indeed is the basis of the exceptional situation indicated by the hexagram. When strong lines are outside, we have the hexagram I, PROVIDING NOURISHMENT (27), or Chung Fu, INNER TRUTH (61); neither represents an exceptional state. When strong elements within preponderate, they necessarily enforce their will. This creates struggle and exceptional conditions in general. But in the present hexagram it is the weak element that perforce must mediate with the outside world. If a man occupies a position of authority for which he is by nature really inadequate, extraordinary prudence is necessary.

THE JUDGMENT

PREPONDERANCE OF THE SMALL. Success.

Perseverance furthers.

Small things may be done; great things should not be done.

The flying bird brings the message:

It is not well to strive upward,

It is well to remain below.

Great good fortune.

Exceptional modesty and conscientiousness are sure to be rewarded with success; however, if a man is not to throw himself away, it is important that they should not become empty form and subservience but be combined always with a correct dignity in personal behavior. We must understand the demands of the time in order to find the necessary offset for its deficiencies and damages. In any event we must not count on great success, since the requisite strength is lacking. In this lies the importance of the message that one should not strive after lofty things but hold to lowly things.

The structure of the hexagram gives rise to the idea that this message is brought by a bird. In Ta Kuo, PREPONDERANCE OF THE GREAT (28), the four strong, heavy lines within, supported only by two weak lines without, give the image of a sagging ridgepole. Here the supporting weak lines are both outside and preponderant; this gives the image of a soaring bird. But a bird should not try to surpass itself and fly into the sun; it should descend to the earth, where its nest is. In this way it gives the message conveyed by the hexagram.

THE IMAGE

Thunder on the mountain:

The image of PREPONDERANCE OF THE SMALL.

Thus in his conduct the superior man gives preponderance to reverence.

In bereavement he gives preponderance to grief.

In his expenditures he gives preponderance to thrift.

Thunder on the mountain is different from thunder on the plain. In the mountains, thunder seems much nearer; outside the mountains, it is less audible than the thunder of an ordinary storm. Thus the superior man derives an imperative from this image: he must always fix his eyes more closely and more directly on duty than does the ordinary man, even though this might make his behavior seem petty to the outside world. He is exceptionally conscientious in his actions. In bereavement emotion means more to him than ceremoniousness. In all his personal expenditures he is extremely simple and unpretentious. In comparison with the man of the masses, all this makes him stand out as exceptional. But the essential significance of his attitude lies in the fact that in external matters he is on the side of the lowly.

THE LINES

Six at the beginning means:

The bird meets with misfortune through flying.

A bird ought to remain in the nest until it is fledged. If it tries to fly before this, it invites misfortune. Extraordinary measures should be resorted to only when all else fails. At first we ought to put up with traditional ways as long as possible; otherwise we exhaust ourselves and our energy and still achieve nothing.

○ Six in the second place means:

She passes by her ancestor

And meets her ancestress.

> He does not reach his prince
> And meets the official.
> No blame.

Two exceptional situations are instanced here. In the temple of ancestors, where alternation of generations prevails, the grandson stands on the same side as the grandfather. Hence his closest relations are with the grandfather. The present line designates the grandson's wife, who during the sacrifice passes by the ancestor and goes toward the ancestress. This unusual behavior is, however, an expression of her modesty. She ventures rather to approach the ancestress, for she feels related to her by their common sex. Hence here deviation from the rule is not a mistake.

Another image is that of the official who, in compliance with regulation, first seeks an audience with his prince. If he is not successful in this, he does not try to force anything but goes about conscientious fulfillment of his duty, taking his place among the other officials. This extraordinary restraint is likewise not a mistake in exceptional times. (The rule is that every official should first have an audience with the prince by whom he is appointed. Here the appointment is made by the minister.)

> Nine in the third place means:
> If one is not extremely careful,
> Somebody may come up from behind and strike him.
> Misfortune.

At certain times extraordinary caution is absolutely necessary. But it is just in such life situations that we find upright and strong personalities who, conscious of being in the right, disdain to hold themselves on guard, because they consider it petty. Instead, they go their way proud and unconcerned. But this self-confidence deludes them. There are dangers lurking for which they are unprepared. Yet such danger is not unavoidable; one can escape it if he understands that the time demands that he pay especial attention to small and insignificant things.

> Nine in the fourth place means:
> No blame. He meets him without passing by.

Going brings danger. One must be on guard.
Do not act. Be constantly persevering.

Hardness of character is tempered by yielding position,[1] so that no mistakes are made. The situation here calls for extreme caution; one must make no attempt of one's own initiative to reach the desired end. And if one were to go on, endeavoring to force his way to the goal, he would be endangered. Therefore one must be on guard and not act but continue inwardly to persevere.

○ Six in the fifth place means:
Dense clouds,
No rain from our western territory.
The prince shoots and hits him who is in the cave.

As a high place is pictured here, the image of a flying bird has become that of flying clouds. But dense as the clouds are, they race across the sky and give no rain. Similarly, in exceptional times there may be a born ruler who is qualified to set the world in order, but who cannot achieve anything or confer blessing on the people because he stands alone and has no helpers. In such times a man must seek out helpers with whose aid he can carry out the task. But these helpers must be modestly sought out in the retirement to which they have withdrawn. It is not their fame nor their great names but their genuine achievements that are important. Through such modesty the right man is found, and the exceptional task is carried out in spite of all difficulties.

Six at the top means:
He passes him by, not meeting him.
The flying bird leaves him.
Misfortune.
This means bad luck and injury.

If one overshoots the goal, one cannot hit it. If a bird will not come to its nest but flies higher and higher, it eventually falls into the hunter's net. He who in times of extraordinary

---

1. [See pp. 360 f.]

salience of small things does not know how to call a halt, but restlessly seeks to press on and on, draws upon himself misfortune at the hands of gods and men, because he deviates from the order of nature.

既濟

63. *Chi Chi* / *After Completion*

☰☰	*above*	K'AN	THE ABYSMAL, WATER
☰☰	*below*	LI	THE CLINGING, FIRE

This hexagram is the evolution of T'ai, PEACE (11). The transition from confusion to order is completed, and everything is in its proper place even in particulars. The strong lines are in the strong places, the weak lines in the weak places. This is a very favorable outlook, yet it gives reason for thought. For it is just when perfect equilibrium has been reached that any movement may cause order to revert to disorder. The one strong line that has moved to the top, thus effecting complete order in details, is followed by the other lines, each moving according to its nature, and thus suddenly there arises again the hexagram P'i, STANDSTILL (12).

Hence the present hexagram indicates the conditions of a time of climax, which necessitate the utmost caution.

THE JUDGMENT

AFTER COMPLETION. Success in small matters.
Perseverance furthers.
At the beginning good fortune,
At the end disorder.

The transition from the old to the new time is already accomplished. In principle, everything stands systematized, and it is only in regard to details that success is still to be achieved.

In respect to this, however, we must be careful to maintain the right attitude. Everything proceeds as if of its own accord, and this can all too easily tempt us to relax and let things take their course without troubling over details. Such indifference is the root of all evil. Symptoms of decay are bound to be the result. Here we have the rule indicating the usual course of history. But this rule is not an inescapable law. He who understands it is in position to avoid its effects by dint of unremitting perseverance and caution.

THE IMAGE

Water over fire: the image of the condition
In AFTER COMPLETION.
Thus the superior man
Takes thought of misfortune
And arms himself against it in advance.

When water in a kettle hangs over fire, the two elements stand in relation and thus generate energy (cf. the production of steam). But the resulting tension demands caution. If the water boils over, the fire is extinguished and its energy is lost. If the heat is too great, the water evaporates into the air. These elements here brought into relation and thus generating energy are by nature hostile to each other. Only the most extreme caution can prevent damage. In life too there are junctures when all forces are in balance and work in harmony, so that everything seems to be in the best of order. In such times only the sage recognizes the moments that bode danger and knows how to banish it by means of timely precautions.

THE LINES

Nine at the beginning means:
He brakes his wheels.
He gets his tail in the water.
No blame.

In times following a great transition, everything is pressing forward, striving in the direction of development and progress. But this pressing forward at the beginning is not good; it overshoots the mark and leads with certainty to loss and collapse. Therefore a man of strong character does not allow himself to be infected by the general intoxication but checks his course in time. He may indeed not remain altogether untouched by the disastrous consequences of the general pressure, but he is hit only from behind like a fox that, having crossed the water, at the last minute gets its tail wet. He will not suffer any real harm, because his behavior has been correct.

> ○ Six in the second place means:
>> The woman loses the curtain of her carriage.
>> Do not run after it;
>> On the seventh day you will get it.

When a woman drove out in her carriage, she had a curtain that hid her from the glances of the curious. It was regarded as a breach of propriety to drive on if this curtain was lost. Applied to public life, this means that a man who wants to achieve something is not receiving that confidence of the authorities which he needs, so to speak, for his personal protection. Especially in times "after completion" it may happen that those who have come to power grow arrogant and conceited and no longer trouble themselves about fostering new talent.

This as a rule results in office seeking. If a man's superiors withhold their trust from him, he will seek ways and means of getting it and of drawing attention to himself. We are warned against such an unworthy procedure: "Do not seek it." Do not throw yourself away on the world, but wait tranquilly and develop your personal worth by your own efforts. Times change. When the six stages of the hexagram have passed, the new era dawns. That which is a man's own cannot be permanently lost. It comes to him of its own accord. He need only be able to wait.

> Nine in the third place means:
> The Illustrious Ancestor
> Disciplines the Devil's Country.
> After three years he conquers it.
> Inferior people must not be employed.

"Illustrious Ancestor" is the dynastic title of the Emperor Wu Ting of the Yin dynasty. [1] After putting his realm in order with a strong hand, he waged long colonial wars for the subjection of the Huns who occupied the northern borderland with constant threat of incursions.

The situation described is as follows. After times of completion, when a new power has arisen and everything within the country has been set in order, a period of colonial expansion almost inevitably follows. Then as a rule long-drawn-out struggles must be reckoned with. For this reason, a correct colonial policy is especially important. The territory won at such bitter cost must not be regarded as an almshouse for people who in one way or another have made themselves impossible at home, but who are thought to be quite good enough for the colonies. Such a policy ruins at the outset any chance of success. This holds true in small as well as in large matters, because it is not only rising states that carry on a colonial policy; the urge to expand, with its accompanying dangers, is part and parcel of every ambitious undertaking.

> Six in the fourth place means:
> The finest clothes turn to rags.
> Be careful all day long.

In a time of flowering culture, an occasional convulsion is bound to occur, uncovering a hidden evil within society and at first causing a great sensation. But since the situation is favorable on the whole, such evils can easily be glossed over and concealed from the public. Then everything is forgotten and peace apparently reigns complacently once more. However, to the thoughtful man such occurrences are grave omens that he does not neglect. This is the only way of averting evil consequences.

> Nine in the fifth place means:
> The neighbor in the east who slaughters an ox
> Does not attain as much real happiness
> As the neighbor in the west
> With his small offering.

---

1. [Wu Ting reigned from 1324 to 1266 B.C.]

Religious attitudes are likewise influenced by the spiritual atmosphere prevailing in times after completion. In divine worship the simple old forms are replaced by an ever more elaborate ritual and an ever greater outward display. But inner seriousness is lacking in this show of magnificence; human caprice takes the place of conscientious obedience to the divine will. However, while man sees what is before his eyes, God looks into the heart. Therefore a simple sacrifice offered with real piety holds a greater blessing than an impressive service without warmth.

> Six at the top means:
> He gets his head in the water. Danger.

Here in conclusion another warning is added. After crossing a stream, a man's head can get into the water only if he is so imprudent as to turn back. As long as he goes forward and does not look back, he escapes this danger. But there is a fascination in standing still and looking back on a peril overcome. However, such vain self-admiration brings misfortune. It leads only to danger, and unless one finally resolves to go forward without pausing, one falls a victim to this danger.

未濟

64. *Wei Chi* / Before Completion

above	LI	THE CLINGING, FLAME
below	K'AN	THE ABYSMAL, WATER

This hexagram indicates a time when the transition from disorder to order is not yet completed. The change is indeed prepared for, since all the lines in the upper trigram are in relation to those in the lower.[1] However, they are not yet in

---

1. [See p. 362.]

their places. While the preceding hexagram offers an analogy to autumn, which forms the transition from summer to winter, this hexagram presents a parallel to spring, which leads out of winter's stagnation into the fruitful time of summer. With this hopeful outlook the Book of Changes comes to its close.

THE JUDGMENT

BEFORE COMPLETION. Success.
But if the little fox, after nearly completing the
    crossing,
Gets his tail in the water,
There is nothing that would further.

The conditions are difficult. The task is great and full of responsibility. It is nothing less than that of leading the world out of confusion back to order. But it is a task that promises success, because there is a goal that can unite the forces now tending in different directions. At first, however, one must move warily, like an old fox walking over ice. The caution of a fox walking over ice is proverbial in China. His ears are constantly alert to the cracking of the ice, as he carefully and circumspectly searches out the safest spots. A young fox who as yet has not acquired this caution goes ahead boldly, and it may happen that he falls in and gets his tail wet when he is almost across the water. Then of course his effort has been all in vain. Accordingly, in times "before completion," deliberation and caution are the prerequisites of success.

THE IMAGE

Fire over water:
The image of the condition before transition.
Thus the superior man is careful
In the differentiation of things,
So that each finds its place.

When fire, which by nature flames upward, is above, and water, which flows downward, is below, their effects take opposite directions and remain unrelated. If we wish to achieve an effect, we must first investigate the nature of the forces in question and ascertain their proper place. If we can bring these forces to bear in the right place, they will have the desired effect, and completion will be achieved. But in order to handle external forces properly, we must above all arrive at the correct standpoint ourselves, for only from this vantage can we work correctly.

THE LINES

Six at the beginning means:
He gets his tail in the water.
Humiliating.

In times of disorder there is a temptation to advance oneself as rapidly as possible in order to accomplish something tangible. But this enthusiasm leads only to failure and humiliation if the time for achievement has not yet arrived. In such a time it is wise to spare ourselves the opprobrium of failure by holding back. [2]

Nine in the second place means:
He brakes his wheels.
Perseverance brings good fortune.

Here again the time to act has not yet come. But the patience needed is not that of idle waiting without thought of the morrow. Kept up indefinitely, this would not lead to any success. Instead, an individual must develop in himself the strength that will enable him to go forward. He must have a vehicle, as it were, to effect the crossing. But he must for the time being use the brakes. Patience in the highest sense means putting brakes on strength. Therefore he must not fall asleep and lose sight of the goal. If he remains strong and steadfast in his resolve, all goes well in the end.

Six in the third place means:
Before completion, attack brings misfortune.
It furthers one to cross the great water.

---

2. Note how this situation differs from that in the first line of the preceding hexagram.

The time of transition has arrived, but one lacks the strength to complete the transition. If one should attempt to force it, disaster would result, because collapse would then be unavoidable. What is to be done? A new situation must be created; one must engage the energies of able helpers and in this fellowship take the decisive step—cross the great water. Then completion will become possible.

> Nine in the fourth place means:
> Perseverance brings good fortune.
> Remorse disappears.
> Shock, thus to discipline the Devil's Country.
> For three years, great realms are awarded.

Now it is the time of struggle. The transition must be completed. We must make ourselves strong in resolution; this brings good fortune. All misgivings that might arise in such grave times of struggle must be silenced. It is a question of a fierce battle to break and to discipline the Devil's Country, the forces of decadence. But the struggle also has its reward. Now is the time to lay the foundations of power and mastery for the future.

> ○ Six in the fifth place means:
> Perseverance brings good fortune.
> No remorse.
> The light of the superior man is true.
> Good fortune.

The victory has been won. The power of steadfastness has not been routed. Everything has gone well. All misgivings have been overcome. Success has justified the deed. The light of a superior personality shines forth anew and makes its influence felt among men who have faith in it and rally around it. The new time has arrived, and with it good fortune. And just as the sun shines forth in redoubled beauty after rain, or as a forest grows more freshly green from charred ruins after a fire, so the new era appears all the more glorious by contrast with the misery of the old.

> Nine at the top means:
> There is drinking of wine
> In genuine confidence. No blame.
> But if one wets his head,
> He loses it, in truth.

Before completion, at the dawning of the new time, friends foregather in an atmosphere of mutual trust, and the time of waiting is passed in conviviality. Since the new era is hard on the threshold, there is no blame in this. But one must be careful in all this to keep within proper bounds. If in his exuberance a man gets drunk, he forfeits the favorableness of the situation through his intemperance.

NOTE. The hexagram AFTER COMPLETION represents a gradual transition from a time of ascent past a peak of culture to a time of standstill. The hexagram BEFORE COMPLETION represents a transition from chaos to order. This hexagram comes at the end of the Book of Changes. It points to the fact that every end contains a new beginning. Thus it gives hope to men. The Book of Changes is a book of the future.

Book II

THE MATERIAL

Introduction

The text forming the nucleus of the Book of Changes has been presented in the first part of this work (bk. I). In that portion the chief concern has been to bring to light the spiritual aspect of the book, the wisdom concealed under its frequently odd forms. What our commentary offers is a summary of what has been said and thought in connection with the hexagrams and the lines in the course of many centuries by China's most distinguished philosophers. However, the reader will often be assailed by the thought: Why is it all like this? Why are these images, frequently so startling, coupled with the hexagrams and the lines? From what depths of consciousness do they come? Are they purely arbitrary creations or do they follow definite laws? Moreover, how does it happen that, in a given case, the image used is connected with the particular thought? Is it not mere caprice to seek a profound philosophy where, according to all appearances, only a grotesque fantasy is at play?

The second part (bks. II, III) is meant to answer these questions, as far as possible. It is intended to disclose the material out of which that world of ideas arose—to present the body corresponding with that spirit. We see that a hidden connection actually exists, that even apparently arbitrary images have, in one way or another, a basis in the structure of the hexagrams, when our understanding of it goes deep enough.

The oldest commentaries, which as a rule combine structural interpretation of the hexagrams with philosophical explanations, go back to Confucius himself or at least to his circle. Their philosophical content has already been utilized in the first portion of the work (bk. I). Here they are used again, in conjunction with the text material, apart from which they are unintelligible, and explained in their technical aspect. This

technical side is indispensable for a complete understanding
of the book, and no Chinese commentator omits it. Nonetheless,
it has seemed advisable to separate it at the beginning
from the philosophical aspect, in order that the Western reader
should not be too much bewildered by unaccustomed matter.
I do not regret the unavoidable repetitions. The Book of
Changes is a work that represents thousands of years of slow
organic growth, and that can be assimilated only through
prolonged reflection and meditation. And in the course of this,
the apparent repetition serves constantly to open up new
perspectives. The material presented in the second portion of
our translation consists chiefly of what has come to be known
as the Ten Wings. These ten wings, or expositions, contain in
substance the oldest commentary literature relating to the
Book of Changes.

The first of the commentaries [FIRST and SECOND WING] is
called *T'uan Chuan*. Actually, *t'uan* means the boar's head
offered at sacrifices; by reason of similarity of sound, the word
took on the additional meaning of "decision." The judgments
pertaining to the individual hexagrams were called *t'uan*,
"decisions," or *tz'u*, "judgments," or *hsi tz'u*, "appended
judgments." These judgments or decisions are attributed to
King Wên of Chou (*ca.* 1150 B.C.), and this premise regarding
their origin has on the whole not been questioned. The *T'uan
Chuan*, or Commentary on the Decision,[1] gives exact interpretations
of King Wên's decisions [judgments], on the basis
of the structure and the other elements of the hexagrams.
This commentary is an extremely thorough and valuable piece
of work and throws much light upon the inner organization of
the hexagrams of the *I Ching*. The Chinese ascribe it to
Confucius. I see no reason for doubting this ascription, inasmuch
as it is well known that Confucius devoted much thought
to the Book of Changes, and since the views expressed in this
commentary nowhere conflict with his views. The commentary
is made up of two parts, corresponding with parts I and II of
the text of the *I Ching*, and forms the first two wings or expositions.
In this translation the commentary has been divided and

---

1. [See bk. III, under the individual hexagrams.]

each comment has been placed with the hexagram to which it pertains. [2]

The THIRD and the FOURTH WING are formed by the so-called *Hsiang Chuan*, Commentary on the Images. This commentary is also made up of two parts corresponding with the two divisions of the text. In its present form it consists of the so-called Great Images, [3] which refer to the images associated with the two trigrams in each hexagram; from these the commentary in each case deduces the meaning of the hexagram as a whole, and from this contemplation in turn draws conclusions applicable to the life of man.

The whole range of ideas contained in this commentary places it in proximity to the Great Learning, *Ta Hsüeh*, [4] and hence in very close proximity to Confucius as well.

Besides the Great Images, this commentary contains also the Small Images. [5] These are very brief references to the Duke of Chou's comments on the individual lines of the hexagrams. However, they do not deal in any way with images, and it must have been owing to some misapprehension, or perhaps to chance, that this commentary on the text of the individual lines found its way into the Commentary on the Images. This commentary on the lines contains only brief

2. James Legge stresses the opinion that a real understanding of the *I Ching* becomes possible only when the commentary material is separated from the text (*The Sacred Books of the East*, XVI: *The Yi King*, 2nd edn., Oxford, 1899). Accordingly he carefully separates the ancient commentaries from the text, and then supplies with it the commentaries of the Sung period [A.D. 960–1279]. Legge does not say why he holds the Sung period to be more closely related to the original text than Confucius [551–479 B.C.]. What he does is to follow with meticulous literalness the edition called *Chou I Chê Chung*, belonging to the K'ang Hsi period [1662–1722], which I also have used. The rendering is very inferior to Legge's other translations. For example, he does not take the trouble to translate the names of the hexagrams—a task of course not easy but by so much the more necessary. In other respects also, definite misconceptions occur.

3. [Bks. I, III, under the individual hexagrams: passages entitled "The Image."]

4. [See p. *lix*, n. 22.]

5. [This section of the commentary appears in bk. III apportioned to the respective hexagrams under the heading *b* in the passages entitled "The Lines."]

suggestions, mostly in rhyme. It may be that the Small Images are mnemonic phrases taken from a more detailed commentary. It is certain that they are very old and originated with the Confucian school, but I should not like to say definitely how close the connection with Confucius himself may be.

These commentaries [Great Images, Small Images] have also been divided and apportioned to the hexagrams to which they refer.

The FIFTH and the SIXTH WING constitute a treatise that presents many difficulties. It is entitled *Hsi Tz'u*, or *Ta Chuan*, and likewise has two parts.[6] The title *Ta Chuan* occurs in Ssŭ-ma Ch'ien[7] and means Great Commentary, or Great Treatise. As regards the title *Hsi Tz'u*, Appended Judgments,[8] Chu Hsi says:

The appended judgments are the judgments originally made by King Wên and the Duke of Chou and appended by them to the hexagrams and their lines; they make up the present text of the book. The section before us is the commentary in which Confucius explains the appended judgments, at the same time giving a general introduction to the whole text of the complete work.[9]

The lack of clarity in the definition is immediately apparent. If the "appended judgments" are really the comments of King Wên and the Duke of Chou on the hexagrams and the lines, we should expect from a "commentary on the appended judgments" a discussion of the judgments in question and not a treatise on the work in general. But we have a commentary[10] dealing with the decisions [judgments] on the hexagrams, that is, with the text of King Wên. On the other hand, there is no detailed commentary on the Duke of Chou's judgments

---

6. [See below, pp. 280 ff., and also bk. III, where passages are repeated as "Appended Judgments."]

7. [Famous historian known in China as the "father of history." Born about 145 B.C., died 86 B.C.]

8. [The full title is *Hsi Tz'u Chuan*, Commentary on the Appended Judgments.]

9. [Chu Hsi (A.D. 1130–1200) was the author of commentaries on most of the Chinese classics. His interpretations remained the generally accepted standard until the middle of the seventeenth century.]

10. [*T'uan Chuan*: First Wing, Second Wing.]

on the lines. What we have are only the brief catch phrases that go under the obviously incorrect title of Small Images. It is true that there are also fragments of another such commentary, or rather, of a number of such commentaries. Several of these fragments—referring to the first two hexagrams—are contained in the *Wên Yen* (Commentary on the Words of the Text), which will be further discussed below. Explanations of single lines do occur, scattered here and there in the Commentary on the Appended Judgments [*Hsi Tz'u Chuan*]. Thus it is highly probable that two quite different things appear together in what is today known as *Hsi Tz'u Chuan*: first, a collection of essays on the Book of Changes in general, probably constituting what Ssŭ-ma Ch'ien called the Great Commentary, *Ta Chuan*; second, scattered among these, and cursorily arranged according to standpoints, fragments of a commentary on the judgments appended to the individual lines. There is much evidence to show that these fragments are derived from the same source as the collection of commentaries known as *Wên Yen*.

It is quite evident that the treatises known as *Hsi Tz'u* or *Ta Chuan* were not set down by Confucius, because many passages in them are cited as sayings of the Master.[11] Of course this commentary does contain traditional material of the Confucian school, dating from various periods.

The so-called SEVENTH WING, named *Wên Yen* (Commentary on the Words of the Text), is a very important section. It is the remnant of a commentary on the Book of Changes—or rather of a whole series of such commentaries—and contains very valuable material deriving from the Confucian school. Unfortunately it does not go beyond the second hexagram, K'un.

The *Wên Yen* (in the present translation divided between

---

11. This commentary moreover places the origin of the Book of Changes in "middle antiquity." This term belongs to an arrangement of historical periods according to which the epoch of the Spring and Autumn Annals [*Ch'un Ch'iu*, a chronological list of events that occurred in the state of Lu between 722 and 481 B.C., edited by Confucius], which closes with Confucius, is called "later antiquity." It is obvious that this arrangement of periods could not have been utilized by Confucius himself.

Ch'ien and K'un[12]) contains in all four different commentaries on the hexagram Ch'ien, THE CREATIVE. In the translation they have been designated as *a*, *b*, *c*, *d*. Commentary *a* of this series belongs to the same stratum as the fragments found scattered through the *Hsi Tz'u Chuan*. The text is given with the appended question, "What does this mean?" This is like the form used in the *Kung Yang*, a commentary on the *Ch'un Ch'iu*. Commentaries *b* and *c* contain brief remarks on the individual lines, in the style of the Small Images. Commentary *d*, like *a*, again deals with the judgment on the hexagram as a whole and with the individual lines, but in a freer manner than *a*.

Only one commentary on the second hexagram, K'un, survives in the *Wên Yen*. It is related in character to *a*, although it represents a different stratum (the text is placed after the explanations by the Master). The same stratum is likewise represented in the *Hsi Tz'u Chuan*.

The EIGHTH WING, *Shuo Kua*, Discussion of the Trigrams, contains material of great antiquity in explanation of the eight primary trigrams.[13] Probably it embodies many fragments antedating Confucius and treated in commentary by him or by his school.

The NINTH WING, *Hsü Kua*, the Sequence—or Order—of the Hexagrams, offers a rather unconvincing explanation of the present sequence of the hexagrams. It is interesting only because the names of the hexagrams are sometimes given peculiar interpretations that are undoubtedly based on ancient tradition. This commentary, which of course has nothing to do with Confucius, has likewise been divided and apportioned to the individual hexagrams, under the heading "The Sequence."[14]

The last [TENTH] wing, *Tsa Kua*, Miscellaneous Notes on the Hexagrams, is made up of definitions of the hexagrams in mnemonic verses, for the most part contrasting them in pairs.

---

12. [Bk. III, under hexagrams 1 and 2.]
13. [See below, pp. 262 ff.]
14. [Bk. III, under the individual hexagrams.]

However, the order followed in the *Tsa Kua* differs essentially from the arrangement in the present Book of Changes. These definitions have also been separated and placed with the respective hexagrams under the heading "Miscellaneous Notes."[15]

In the pages following there appear, first, translations of the *Shuo Kua*, Discussion of the Trigrams, and of the *Hsi Tz'u Chuan*, Commentary on the Appended Judgments, more correctly called *Ta Chuan*, Great Commentary. Then follows some material on the structure of the hexagrams, derived from various sources, that is important for the understanding of the second portion of the work.

---

15. [Bk. III, under the individual hexagrams.]

Shuo Kua / Discussion of the Trigrams[1]

1. In ancient times the holy sages made the Book of Changes thus:

They invented the yarrow-stalk oracle in order to lend aid in a mysterious way to the light of the gods. To heaven they assigned the number three and to earth the number two; from these they computed the other numbers.

They contemplated the changes in the dark and the light and established the hexagrams in accordance with them. They brought about movements in the firm and the yielding, and thus produced the individual lines.

They put themselves in accord with tao and its power, and in conformity with this laid down the order of what is right. By thinking through the order of the outer world to the end, and by exploring the law of their nature to the deepest core, they arrived at an understanding of fate.

This first section refers to the Book of Changes as a whole and to the fundamental principles underlying it. The original purpose of the hexagrams was to consult destiny. As divine beings do not give direct expression to their knowledge, a means had to be found by which they could make themselves intelligible. Suprahuman intelligence has from the beginning

---

1. [Eighth Wing.]

made use of three mediums of expression—men, animals, and plants, in each of which life pulsates in a different rhythm. Chance came to be utilized as a fourth medium; the very absence of an immediate meaning in chance permitted a deeper meaning to come to expression in it. The oracle was the outcome of this use of chance. The Book of Changes is founded on the plant oracle as manipulated by men with mediumistic powers.

The established language for communication with suprahuman intelligences was based on numbers and their symbolism. The fundamental principles of the world are heaven and earth, spirit and matter. Earth is the derived principle; therefore the number two is assigned to it. Heaven is the ultimate unity; yet it includes the earth within itself, and is therefore assigned the number three. The number one could not be used, as it is too abstract and rigid and does not include the idea of the manifold. Following out this conception, the uneven numbers were assigned to the world of heaven, the even numbers to the world of earth.

The hexagrams, consisting of six lines each, are, so to speak, representations of actual conditions in the world, and of the combinations of the light-giving, heavenly power and the dark, earthly power that occur in these situations. Within the hexagrams, however, it is always possible for the individual lines to change and regroup themselves; just as world situations continually change and reconstitute themselves, so out of each hexagram there arises a new one. The process of change is to be observed in the lines that move, and the end result in the new hexagram thus formed.

In addition to its use as an oracle, the Book of Changes also serves to further intuitive understanding of conditions in the world, penetration to the uttermost depths of nature and spirit. The hexagrams give complete images of conditions and relationships existing in the world; the individual lines treat particular situations as they change within these general conditions. The Book of Changes is in harmony with tao and its power (natural law and moral law). Therefore it can lay down the rules of what is right for each person. The ultimate meaning of the world—fate, the world as it is, how it has come to be so through creative decision (*ming*)—can be apprehended by going down to the ultimate sources in the world of outer experience and of inner experience. Both paths lead to the same goal. (Cf. the first chapter of Lao-tse.)

2. In ancient times the holy sages made the Book of Changes thus:

Their purpose was to follow the order of their nature and of fate. Therefore they determined the tao of heaven and called it the dark and the light. They determined the tao of the earth and called it the yielding and the firm. They determined the tao of man and called it love[2] and rectitude. They combined these three fundamental powers and doubled them; therefore in the Book of Changes a sign is always formed by six lines.

The places are divided into the dark and the light. The yielding and the firm occupy these by turns. Therefore the Book of Changes has six places, which constitute the linear figures.

This section deals with the elements of the individual hexagrams and their interrelation with the cosmic process. Just as in the heavens, evening and morning make a day through the alternation of dark and light (yin and yang), so the alternating even and uneven places in the hexagrams are respectively designated as dark and light. The first, third, and fifth places are light; the second, fourth, and sixth are dark. Furthermore, just as on earth all beings are formed from both firm and yielding elements, so the individual lines are firm, i.e., undivided, or yielding, i.e., divided. In correspondence with these two basic powers in heaven and on earth, there exist in man the polarities of love and rectitude—love being related to the light principle and rectitude to the dark. These human attributes, because they belong to the category of the subjective, not of the objective, are not represented specifically in the places and lines of the hexagrams. The trinity of world

---

2. [In the sense of humane feeling.]

principles, however, does come to expression in the hexagram as a whole and in its parts. These three principles are differentiated as subject (man), object having form (earth), and content (heaven). The lowest place in the trigram is that of earth; the middle place belongs to man and the top place to heaven. In correspondence with the principle of duality in the universe, the original three-line signs are doubled; thus in the hexagrams there are two places each for earth, for man, and for heaven. The two lowest places are those of the earth, the third and fourth are those of man, and the two at the top are those of heaven.

A fully rounded concept of the universe is expressed here, directly related to that expressed in the Doctrine of the Mean.[3]

All the ideas set forth in this first chapter link it to the collection of essays on the meaning and structure of the hexagrams called the Appended Judgments,[4] and are not connected with what follows here.

CHAPTER II

3. Heaven and earth determine the direction. The forces of mountain and lake are united. Thunder and wind arouse each other. Water and fire do not combat each other. Thus are the eight trigrams intermingled.

Counting that which is going into the past depends on the forward movement. Knowing that which is to come depends on the backward movement. This is why the Book of Changes has backward-moving numbers.

Here, in what is probably a very ancient saying, the eight primary trigrams are named in a sequence of pairs that, according to tradition, goes back to Fu Hsi—that is to say, it was

---

3. [See p. *lix*, n. 22.]

4. [I.e., the *Ta Chuan* or *Hsi Tz'u Chuan*, given as the Great Treatise or Great Commentary on pp. 280 ff.]

already in existence at the time of the compilation of the Book of Changes under the Chou dynasty. It is called the Sequence of Earlier Heaven, or the Primal Arrangement.[1] The different trigrams are correlated with the cardinal points, as shown in the accompanying diagram [fig. 1]. (It is to be noted that the Chinese place south at the top.)

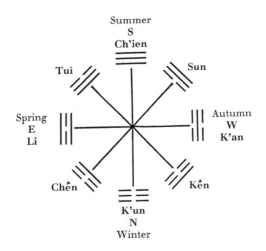

Fig. 1. Sequence of Earlier Heaven, or Primal Arrangement

Ch'ien, heaven, and K'un, earth, determine the north-south axis. Then follows the axis Kên-Tui, mountain and lake. Their forces are interrelated in that the wind blows from the mountain to the lake, and the clouds and mists rise from the lake to the mountain. Chên, thunder, and Sun, wind, strengthen each other when they appear. Li, fire, and K'an, water, are irreconcilable opposites in the phenomenal world. In the primal relationships, however, their effects do not conflict; on the contrary, they balance each other.

When the trigrams intermingle, that is, when they are in motion, a double movement is observable: first, the usual clockwise movement, cumulative and expanding as time goes

---

1. [Literally, "Before-the-World Sequence."]

on, and determining the events that are passing; second, an opposite, backward movement, folding up and contracting as time goes on, through which the seeds of the future take form. To know this movement is to know the future. In figurative terms, if we understand how a tree is contracted into a seed, we understand the future unfolding of the seed into a tree.

> 4. Thunder brings about movement, wind brings about dispersion, rain brings about moisture, the sun brings about warmth, Keeping Still brings about standstill, the Joyous brings about pleasure, the Creative brings about rulership, the Receptive brings about shelter.

Here again the forces for which the eight primary trigrams stand are presented in terms of their effects in nature. The first four are referred to by their images, the last four by their names, because only the first four indicate in their images natural forces at work throughout time, while the last four point to conditions that come about in the course of the year.

Thus we have first a forward-moving (rising) line, in which the forces of the preceding year take effect. According to section 3, following this line leads to knowledge of the past, which is present as a latent cause in the effects it produces. In the second group, named not according to the images (phenomena) but according to the attributes of the trigrams, a backward movement sets in (a jump from Li in the east back to Kên in the northwest). Along this line the forces of the coming year develop, and following it leads to knowledge of the future, which is being prepared as an effect by its causes—like seeds that, in contracting, consolidate.

Within the Primal Arrangement the forces always take effect as pairs of opposites. Thunder, the electrically charged force, awakens the seeds of the old year. Its opposite, the wind, dissolves the rigidity of the winter ice. The rain moistens the seeds, enabling them to germinate, while its opposite, the sun, provides the necessary warmth. Hence the saying: "Water and fire do not combat each other." Then come the backward-moving forces. Keeping Still stops further expansion; germination begins. Its opposite, the Joyous, brings about the joys of the harvest. Finally there come into play the directing forces —the Creative, representing the great law of existence, and the Receptive, representing shelter in the womb, into which everything returns after completing the cycle of life.

As in the course of the year, so in human life we find ascending and backward-moving lines of force from which the present and the future can be deduced.

> 5. God comes forth in the sign of the Arousing; he brings all things to completion in the sign of the Gentle; he causes creatures to perceive one another in the sign of the Clinging (light); he causes them to serve one another in the sign of the Receptive. He gives them joy in the sign of the Joyous; he battles in the sign of the Creative; he toils in the sign of the Abysmal; he brings them to perfection in the sign of Keeping Still.

Here the sequence of the eight trigrams is given according to King Wên's arrangement, which is called the Sequence of Later Heaven, or the Inner-World Arrangement. The trigrams are taken out of their grouping in pairs of opposites and shown in the temporal progression in which they manifest themselves in the phenomenal world in the cycle of the year. Hereby the arrangement of the trigrams is essentially changed. The cardinal points and the seasons are correlated. The arrangement is represented as in figure 2.

The year begins to show the creative activity of God in the trigram Chên, the Arousing, which stands in the east and signifies the spring. The passage following explains more fully how this activity of God proceeds in nature.

It is highly probable that section 5 represents a cryptic saying of great antiquity that in the passage below has received an interpretation referable no doubt to the Confucian school of thought.

> All living things come forth in the sign of the Arousing. The Arousing stands in the east.

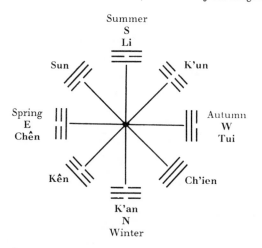

Summer
S
Li

Sun   K'un

Spring   Autumn
E   W
Chên   Tui

Kên   Ch'ien

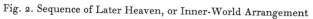

K'an
N
Winter

Fig. 2. Sequence of Later Heaven, or Inner-World Arrangement

They come to completion in the sign of the Gentle. The Gentle stands in the southeast. Completion means that all creatures become pure and perfect.

The Clinging is the brightness in which all creatures perceive one another. It is the trigram of the south. That the holy sages turned their faces to the south while they gave ear to the meaning of the universe means that in ruling they turned toward what is light. This they evidently took from this trigram.

The Receptive means the earth. It takes care that all creatures are nourished. Therefore it is said: "He causes them to serve one another in the sign of the Receptive."

The Joyous is midautumn, which rejoices all creatures. Therefore it is said: "He gives them joy in the sign of the Joyous."

"He battles in the sign of the Creative." The

> Creative is the trigram of the northwest. It means that here the dark and the light arouse each other.
>
> The Abysmal means water. It is the trigram of due north, the trigram of toil, to which all creatures are subject. Therefore it is said: "He toils in the sign of the Abysmal."
>
> Keeping Still is the trigram of the northeast, where beginning and end of all creatures are completed. Therefore it is said: "He brings them to perfection in the sign of Keeping Still."

Here the course of the year and the course of the day are harmonized. What is pictured in the foregoing passage as the unfolding of the divine is here shown as it appears in nature. The trigrams are allotted to the seasons and to the cardinal points without schematization, by cursory allusions that result in the diagram shown in figure 2.

Spring begins to stir and in nature there is germination and sprouting. This corresponds with the morning of a day. This awakening belongs to the trigram Chên, the Arousing, which streams out of the earth as thunder and electrical energy. Then gentle winds blow, renewing the plant world and clothing the earth in green; this corresponds with the trigram Sun, the Gentle, the Penetrating. Sun has for its image both wind, which melts the rigid ice of winter, and wood, which develops organically. The characteristic of this trigram is to make things flow into their forms, to make them develop and grow into the shape prefigured in the seed.

Then comes the high point of the year, midsummer, or, in terms of the day, noontide. Here is the place of the trigram Li, the Clinging, light. Creatures now perceive one another. What was vegetative organic life passes over into psychic consciousness. Thus we have likewise an image of human society, in which the ruler, turned to the light, governs the world. It is to be noted that the trigram Li occupies the place in the south that in the Primal Arrangement is held by the trigram Ch'ien, the Creative. Li consists essentially of the top and bottom lines of Ch'ien, which have taken to themselves the middle line of

K'un. To understand fully, one must always visualize the Inner-World Arrangement as transparent, with the Primal Arrangement shining through it. Thus when we come to the trigram Li, we come at the same time upon the ruler Ch'ien, who governs with his face turned to the south.

Thereupon follows the ripening of the fruits of the field, which K'un, the earth, the Receptive, bestows. It is the season of harvesting, of joint labor. Next, as evening follows day, midautumn follows under the trigram of the Joyous, Tui, which, as autumn, leads the year toward its fruition and joy.

Then follows the stern season, when proof of deeds accomplished must be forthcoming. Judgment is in the air. From earth our thoughts return to heaven, to Ch'ien, the Creative. A battle is being fought, for it is just when the Creative is coming to dominance that the dark yin force is most powerful in its external effects. Hence the dark and the light now arouse each other. There is no doubt as to the outcome of this battle, for it is only the final effect of pre-existing causes that comes to judgment through the Creative.

Now winter ensues, in the trigram K'an, the Abysmal. K'an, in the north—the place of the Receptive in the Primal Arrangement—is symbolized by the gorge. Now comes the toil of gathering the crops into the barns. Water shuns no effort, always seeking the lowest level, so that everything flows to it; in the same way, winter in the course of the year, and midnight in the course of the day, are the time of concentration.

The trigram Keeping Still, whose symbol is the mountain, is of mysterious significance. Here, in the seed, in the deep-hidden stillness, the end of every thing is joined to a new beginning. Death and life, dying and resurrection—these are the thoughts awakened by the transition from the old year to the new.

Thus the cycle is closed. Like the day or the year in nature, so every life, indeed every cycle of experience, is a continuity by which old and new are linked together. In view of this we can understand why, in several of the sixty-four hexagrams, the southwest represents the period of work and fellowship, while the northeast stands for the time of solitude, when the old is brought to an end and the new is begun.

6. The spirit is mysterious in all living things and works through them. Of all the forces that move things, there is none swifter than thunder. Of all the forces that bend things, there is none swifter than wind. Of all the forces that warm things, there is none more drying than fire. Of all the forces that give joy to things, there is none more gladdening than the lake. Of all the forces that moisten things, there is none more moist than water. Of all the forces that end and begin things, there is none more glorious than keeping still.

Therefore: Water and fire complement each other, thunder and wind do not interfere with each other, and the forces of mountain and lake are united in their action. Thus only are change and transformation possible, and thus only can all things come to perfection.

Only the action of the six derived trigrams is described here. It is the action of the spiritual, which is not a thing among things, but the force that manifests its existence through the various effects of thunder, wind, and so on. The two primary trigrams, the Creative and the Receptive, are not mentioned because, as heaven and earth, they actually are those emanations of the spirit within which, through the action of the derived forces, the visible world comes into being and changes. Each of these forces acts in a definite direction, but movement and change come about only because the forces acting as pairs of opposites, without canceling each other, set going the cyclic movement on which the life of the world depends.

CHAPTER III

The third chapter deals with the eight trigrams separately and presents the symbols with which they are associated. It is important inasmuch as the words of the text on the individual lines in each hexagram are very often to be explained against the background of these symbols. A knowledge of these associations is important as a tool in understanding the structure of the Book of Changes.

7. *The Attributes*

The Creative is strong. The Receptive is yielding. The Arousing means movement. The Gentle is penetrating. The Abysmal is dangerous. The Clinging means dependence. Keeping Still means standstill. The Joyous means pleasure.

8. *The Symbolic Animals*

The Creative acts in the horse, the Receptive in the cow, the Arousing in the dragon, the Gentle in the cock, the Abysmal in the pig, the Clinging in the pheasant, Keeping Still in the dog, the Joyous in the sheep.

The Creative is symbolized by the horse,[1] swift and tireless as it runs, and the Receptive by the gentle cow. The Arousing, whose image is thunder, is symbolized by the dragon, which, rising out of the depths, soars up to the stormy sky—in correspondence with the single strong line pushing upward below the two yielding lines. The Gentle, the Penetrating, is symbolized by the cock, time's watchman, whose voice pierces the stillness—pervasive as the wind, the image of the Gentle. Water is the image associated with the Abysmal; of the domestic animals, the pig is the one that lives in mud and water. In Li as its trigram, the Clinging, brightness, has originally the image of a pheasant-like firebird. The dog, the faithful guardian, belongs to Kên, Keeping Still. The Joyous is linked with the sheep, which is regarded as the animal belonging to the west; the two parts of the divided line at the top are the horns of the sheep.

---

1. These passages represent variants on the text of the *I Ching*, in which the Creative is symbolized by the dragon, the Receptive by the mare, and the Clinging by the cow.

9. *The Parts of the Body*

The Creative manifests itself in the head, the Receptive in the belly, the Arousing in the foot, the Gentle in the thighs, the Abysmal in the ear, the Clinging (brightness) in the eye, Keeping Still in the hand, the Joyous in the mouth.

The head governs the entire body. The belly serves for storing up. The foot steps on the ground and moves; the hand holds fast. The thighs under their covering branch downward; the mouth in plain sight opens upward. The ear is hollow outside; the eye is hollow inside. All these are pairs of opposites corresponding with the trigrams.

10. *The Family of the Primary Trigrams*

The Creative is heaven, therefore it is called the father. The Receptive is the earth, therefore it is called the mother.

In the trigram of the Arousing she seeks for the first time the power of the male and receives a son. Therefore the Arousing is called the eldest son.

In the trigram of the Gentle the male seeks for the first time the power of the female and receives a daughter. Therefore the Gentle is called the eldest daughter.

In the Abysmal she seeks for a second time and receives a son. Therefore it is called the middle son.

In the Clinging he seeks for a second time and receives a daughter. Therefore it is called the middle daughter.

In Keeping Still she seeks for a third time and receives a son. Therefore it is called the youngest son.

In the Joyous he seeks for a third time and receives a daughter. Therefore it is called the third daughter.

In the sons, according to this derivation, the substance comes from the mother—hence the two female lines—while the dominant or determining line comes from the father. The opposite holds in the case of the daughters. The child is opposite in sex to the parent who "seeks" it.

Here we note a difference between the Inner-World Arrangement and the Primal Arrangement with respect to the sex of the derived trigrams. In the Primal Arrangement the lowest line is always the sex determinant and the sons are: (1) Chên, the Arousing [☳]; (2) Li, the Clinging (the sun) [☲]; (3) Tui, the Joyous [☱]. In the arrangement shown in the diagram [fig. 1] they stand in the eastern half. The daughters are: (1) Sun, the Gentle [☴]; (2) K'an, the Abysmal (the moon) [☵]; (3) Kên, Keeping Still [☶]. They stand in the western half. In the Inner-World Arrangement, therefore, only Chên and Sun have not changed in sex. The diagram [fig. 2] shows the three sons to the left of Ch'ien, the Creative, while K'un has the two elder daughters at the right and the youngest daughter at the left between itself and Ch'ien.

11. *Additional Symbols*

The Creative is heaven. It is round, it is the prince, the father, jade, metal, cold, ice; it is deep red, a good horse, an old horse, a lean horse, a wild horse, tree fruit.

Most of these symbols explain themselves. Jade is the symbol of spotless purity and of firmness; so likewise is metal. Cold and ice are accounted for by the position of the trigram in the northwest. Deep red is the intensified color of the light principle (in the text itself, midnight blue is the color of the Creative, according with the color of the sky). The various horses denote power, endurance, firmness, strength (the "wild" horse is a mythical saw-toothed animal, able to tear even a tiger to pieces). Fruit is a symbol of duration in change.

Later commentaries add the following: it is straight, it is the dragon, the upper garment, the word.

The Receptive is the earth, the mother. It is cloth, a kettle, frugality, it is level, it is a cow with a calf,

a large wagon, form, the multitude, a shaft. Among
the various kinds of soil, it is the black.

The first of these symbols are intelligible at a glance. Cloth is
something spread out; the earth is covered with life as with a
garment. In the kettle, things are cooked until they are done;
similarly, the earth is the great melting pot of life. Frugality
is a fundamental characteristic of nature. "It is level" means
that the earth knows no partiality. A cow with a calf is a
symbol of fertility. The large wagon symbolizes the fact that
the earth carries all living things. Form and ornament are the
opposite of content, which finds expression in the Creative.
The multitude, plurality, is the opposite of the oneness of the
Creative. The shaft is the body of the tree, from which the
branches spring, as all life sprouts forth from the earth. Black
is intensified darkness. [2]

The Arousing is thunder, the dragon. It is dark yellow, it is a spreading out, a great road, the eldest son.
It is decisive and vehement; it is bamboo that is green
and young, it is reed and rush.

Among horses it signifies those which can neigh
well, those with white hind legs, those which gallop,
those with a star on the forehead.

Among useful plants it is the pod-bearing ones.
Finally, it is the strong, that which grows luxuri-
antly.

Dark yellow is a mixture of the dark heavens and the yellow
earth. A "spreading out" (perhaps to be read "blossoms") suggests the luxuriant growth of spring, which covers the earth
with a garment of plants. A great road suggests the universal
way to life in the spring. Bamboo, reed, and rush are especially
fast-growing plants. The neighing of horses denotes their relationship to thunder. White hind legs gleam from afar as the
horses run. The gallop is the liveliest gait. The seedlings of
pod-bearing plants retain the pods.

---

2. In the text of the *I Ching*, the color of the Receptive is yellow,
and its animal is the mare.

The Gentle is wood, wind, the eldest daughter, the guideline, work; it is the white, the long, the high; it is advance and retreat, the undecided, odor.

Among men it means the gray-haired; it means those with broad foreheads; it means those with much white in their eyes; it means those close to gain, so that in the market they get threefold value. Finally, it is the sign of vehemence.

The first of these meanings need no further explanation. The guideline belongs to this trigram in that it refers to a windlike dissemination of commands. White is the color of the yin principle. Here yin is in the lowest place at the beginning. Wood grows long; the wind goes up to great heights. Advance and retreat refer to the changeableness of the wind; indecision and the odor wafted by the wind belong in this same context. Gray-haired, scanty-haired people have a great deal of white in their hair. People with much white in their eyes are arrogant and vehement; those who are eager for gain are likewise vehement, so that finally the trigram turns into its opposite and represents vehemence, Chên.

The Abysmal is water, ditches, ambush, bending and straightening out, bow and wheel.

Among men it means the melancholy, those with sick hearts, those with earache.

It is the blood sign; it is red.

Among horses it means those with beautiful backs, those with wild courage, those which let their heads hang, those with thin hoofs, those which stumble.

Among chariots it means those with many defects.

It is penetration, the moon.

It means thieves.

Among varieties of wood it means those which are firm and have much pith.

The first of these attributes are again self-explanatory. Bending and straightening out are implied by the winding course of water; this leads to the thought of something bent, of bow and wheel. Melancholy is expressed by the fact that one strong line is hemmed in between two weak lines; thus also sickness of the heart. The trigram signifies toil and also the ear. Pains in the ear come from laborious listening.

Blood is the fluid of the body, therefore the symbolic color of K'an is red, though a somewhat brighter red than that of Ch'ien, the Creative. Because of its penetrating quality K'an, when applied to a carriage, is made to symbolize a broken-down[3] vehicle that serves as a wagon. Penetration is suggested by the penetrating line in the middle wedged in between the two weak lines. As a water element, K'an means the moon, which therefore appears as masculine. Persons who secretly penetrate a place and sneak away are thieves. The pithiness of wood is also connected with the attribute of penetration.

> The Clinging is fire, the sun, lightning, the middle daughter.
>
> It means coats of mail and helmets; it means lances and weapons. Among men it means the big-bellied.
>
> It is the sign of dryness. It means the tortoise, the crab, the snail, the mussel, the hawkbill tortoise.
>
> Among trees it means those which dry out in the upper part of the trunk.

Where the various symbols are not self-explanatory, they are suggested by the meaning of fire, of heat and dryness, and further by the character of the trigram, which is firm without and hollow, or yielding, within. This aspect accounts for the weapons, the fat belly, the shell-bearing creatures, and the hollow trees beginning to wither at the top.

> Keeping Still is the mountain; it is a bypath; it means little stones, doors and openings, fruits and seeds, eunuchs and watchmen, the fingers; it is the

---

3. [That is, pierced with holes.]

dog, the rat, and the various kinds of black-billed birds.

Among trees it signifies the firm and gnarled.

A bypath is suggested by the mountain path, and so are stones. A gate is suggested by the form of the trigram. Fruits and seeds are the link between the end and the beginning of plants. Eunuchs are doorkeepers, and watchmen guard the streets; both protect and watch. The fingers serve to hold fast, the dog keeps guard, the rat gnaws, birds with black beaks grip things easily; likewise, gnarled tree trunks possess the greatest power of resistance.

> The Joyous is the lake, the youngest daughter; it is a sorceress; it is mouth and tongue. It means smashing and breaking apart; it means dropping off and bursting open. Among the kinds of soil it is the hard and salty. It is the concubine. It is the sheep.

The sorceress is a woman who speaks. The trigram is open above, hence it denotes mouth and tongue. It stands in the west and is therefore connected with the idea of autumn, destruction, hence the smashing and breaking apart, the dropping off and bursting open of ripe fruits. Where lakes have dried up, the ground is hard and salty. The concubine derives from the idea of the youngest daughter. The sheep, outwardly weak and inwardly stubborn, is suggested by the form of the trigram, as already mentioned. (It should be noted that in China sheep and goats are regarded as practically the same animal and have the same name.)

Ta Chuan / The Great Treatise
[Great Commentary]¹

(also called *Hsi Tz'u Chuan*, Commentary on the Appended
   Judgments)

PART I

A. UNDERLYING PRINCIPLES

CHAPTER I. *The Changes in the Universe and in the
Book of Changes*

1. Heaven is high, the earth is low; thus the Creative
and the Receptive are determined. In correspondence with this difference between low and high, inferior and superior places are established.

Movement and rest have their definite laws;
according to these, firm and yielding lines are differentiated.

Events follow definite trends, each according to its
nature. Things are distinguished from one another in
definite classes. In this way good fortune and misfortune come about. In the heavens phenomena take
form; on earth shapes take form. In this way change
and transformation become manifest.

In the Book of Changes a distinction is made between three
kinds of change: nonchange, cyclic change, and sequent
change.² Nonchange is the background, as it were, against

---

1. [Fifth Wing, Sixth Wing. Passages of this commentary are to
be found repeated in bk. III, as "Appended Judgments."]

2. [*Umwandeln, verwandeln:* later on in his explanation Wilhelm
defines *umwandeln* as meaning, in this connection, recurrent change,
and *verwandeln* as meaning change in which there is no return to the
starting point. The words "cyclic" and "sequent" are therefore in-

which change is made possible. For in regard to any change there must be some fixed point to which the change can be referred; otherwise there can be no definite order and everything is dissolved in chaotic movement. This point of reference must be established, and this always requires a choice and a decision. It makes possible a system of co-ordinates into which everything else can be fitted. Consequently at the beginning of the world, as at the beginning of thought, there is the decision, the fixing of the point of reference. Theoretically any point of reference is possible, but experience teaches that at the dawn of consciousness one stands already inclosed within definite, prepotent systems of relationships. The problem then is to choose one's point of reference so that it coincides with the point of reference for cosmic events. For only then can the world created by one's decision escape being dashed to pieces against prepotent systems of relationships with which it would otherwise come into conflict. Obviously the premise for such a decision is the belief that in the last analysis the world is a system of homogeneous relationships—that it is a cosmos, not a chaos. This belief is the foundation of Chinese philosophy, as of all philosophy. The ultimate frame of reference for all that changes is the nonchanging.

The Book of Changes takes as the foundation for this system of relationships the distinction between heaven and earth. There is heaven, the upper world of light, which, though incorporeal, firmly regulates and determines everything that happens, and over against heaven there is the earth, the lower, dark world, corporeal, and dependent in its movements upon the phenomena of heaven. With this differentiation of above and below there is posited, in one way or another, a difference in value, so that the one principle, heaven, is the more exalted and honored, while the other, earth, is regarded as lesser and lower. These two cardinal principles of all existence are then symbolized in the two fundamental hexagrams of the Book of Changes, THE CREATIVE and THE RECEPTIVE. In the last analysis, this cannot be called a dualism. The two principles are united by a relation based on homogeneity; they do not

troduced here in anticipation of these definitions, as the types of change alluded to would not otherwise be intelligible.]

combat but complement each other. The difference in level creates a potential, as it were, by virtue of which movement and living expression of energy become possible.

This association of high and low with value differentiations leads to the differentiation of superior and inferior. This is expressed symbolically in the hexagrams of the Book of Changes, which are considered to have high and low, superior and inferior places. Each hexagram consists of six places, of which the odd-numbered ones are superior and the even-numbered ones inferior.

There is another difference bound up with this one. In the heavens constant movement and change prevail; on earth fixed and apparently lasting conditions are to be observed. On closer scrutiny, this is only delusion. In the philosophy of the Book of Changes nothing is regarded as being absolutely at rest; rest is merely an intermediate state of movement, or latent movement. However, there are points at which the movement becomes visible. This is symbolized by the fact that the hexagrams are built up of both firm and yielding lines. The firm, the strong, is designated as the principle of movement, the yielding as the principle of rest. The firm is represented by an undivided line, corresponding with the light principle, the yielding by a divided line that corresponds with the dark principle.

The fact that the character of the line (firm, yielding) combines with the character of the place (superior, inferior) results in a great multiplicity of possible situations. This serves to symbolize a third nexus of events in the world. There are conditions of equilibrium, in which a certain harmony prevails, and conditions of disturbed equilibrium, in which confusion prevails. The reason is that there is a system of order pervading the entire world. When, in accordance with this order, each thing is in its appropriate place, harmony is established. Such a tendency toward order can be observed in nature. The places attract related elements, as it were, so that harmony may come about. However, a parallel tendency is also at work. Not only are things determined by their tendency toward order: they move also by virtue of forces imparted to them, so to speak, mechanically from the outside. Hence it is not possible for equilibrium to be attained under all circumstances, for deviations may occur, bringing with them confusion and disorder. In the sphere of human affairs, the condition of harmony assures good fortune, that of disharmony predicates misfortune. These complexes of occurrences can be represented by the combinations of lines and places, as pointed out above.

Another law is to be noted. Owing to changes of the sun, moon, and stars, phenomena take form in the heavens. These phenomena obey definite laws. Bound up with them, shapes come into being on earth, in accordance with identical laws. Therefore the processes on earth—blossom and fruit, growth and decay—can be calculated if we know the laws of time. If we know the laws of change, we can precalculate in regard to it, and freedom of action thereupon becomes possible. Changes are the imperceptible tendencies to divergence that, when they have reached a certain point, become visible and bring about transformations.

These are the immutable laws under which, according to Chinese thought, changes are consummated. It is the purpose of the Book of Changes to demonstrate these laws by means of the laws of change operating in the respective hexagrams. Once we succeed in completely reproducing these laws, we acquire a comprehensive view of events; we can understand past and future equally well and bring this knowledge to bear in our actions.

> 2. Therefore the eight trigrams succeed one another by turns, as the firm and the yielding displace each other.

Here cyclic change is explained. It is a rotation of phenomena, each succeeding the other until the starting point is reached again. Examples are furnished by the course of the day and year, and by the phenomena that occur in the organic world during these cycles. Cyclic change, then, is recurrent change in the organic world, whereas sequent change means the progressive [nonrecurrent] change of phenomena produced by causality.

The firm and the yielding displace each other within the eight trigrams. Thus the firm is transformed, melts as it were, and becomes the yielding; the yielding changes, coalesces, as it were, and becomes the firm. In this way the eight trigrams change from one into another in turn, and the regular alternation of phenomena within the year takes its course. But this is the case in all cycles, the life cycle included. What we know as day and night, summer and winter—this, in the life cycle, is life and death.

To make more intelligible the nature of cyclic change and the alternations of the trigrams produced by it, their sequence in the Primal Arrangement is shown once again [fig. 3]. There are two directions of movement, the one rightward, ascending, the other backward, descending. The former starts from the low point, K'un, the Receptive, earth; the latter starts from the high point, Ch'ien, the Creative, heaven.

	North	Northeast	East	Southeast
I.	☷	☳	☲	☱
	K'un	Chên	Li	Tui
		1a	2a	3a

	South	Southwest	West	Northwest
II.	☰	☴	☵	☶
	Ch'ien	Sun	K'an	Kên
		1b	2b	3b

Figure 3

> 3. Things are aroused by thunder and lightning; they are fertilized by wind and rain. Sun and moon follow their courses and it is now hot, now cold.

Here we have the sequence of the trigrams in the changing seasons of the year, and in such a way that each is the cause of the one next following. Deep in the womb of earth there stirs the creative force, Chên, the Arousing, symbolized by thunder. As this electrical force appears there are formed centers of activation that are then discharged in lightning. Lightning is Li, the Clinging, flame. Hence thunder is put before lightning. Thunder is, so to speak, the agent evoking the lightning; it is not merely the sounding thunder. Now the movement shifts; thunder's opposite, Sun, the wind, sets in. The wind brings rain, K'an. Then there is a new shift. The trigrams Li and

K'an, formerly acting in their secondary forms as lightning and rain, now appear in their primary forms as sun and moon. In their cyclic movement they cause cold and heat. When the sun reaches the zenith, heat sets in, symbolized by the trigram of the southeast, Tui, the Joyous, the lake. When the moon is at its zenith in the sky, cold sets in, symbolized by the trigram of the northwest, Kên, the mountain, Keeping Still. Hence the sequence is (cf. fig. 3):

$$1a — 2a \qquad 1b — 2b$$
$$2a — 3a \qquad\qquad 2b — 3b$$

Thus $2a$ (Li) and $2b$ (K'an) are named twice, once in their secondary forms (lightning and rain), once in their primary forms (sun and moon).

4. The way of the Creative brings about the male.

The way of the Receptive brings about the female.

Here the beginning of sequent change appears, manifested in the succession of the generations, an onward-moving process that never returns to its starting point. This shows the extent to which the Book of Changes confines itself to life. For according to Western ideas, sequent change would be the realm in which causality operates mechanically; but the Book of Changes takes sequent change to be the succession of the generations, that is, still something organic.

The Creative, in so far as it enters as a principle into the phenomenon of life, is embodied in the male sex; the Receptive is embodied in the female sex. Thus the Creative in the lowest line of each of the sons (Chên, Li, Tui, in the Primal Arrangement), and the Receptive in the lowest line of each of the daughters (Sun, K'an, Kên, in the Primal Arrangement), is the sex determinant of the given trigram.

5. The Creative knows the great beginnings.

The Receptive completes the finished things.

Here the principles of the Creative and the Receptive are traced further. The Creative produces the invisible seeds of all development. At first these seeds are purely abstract, therefore with respect to them there can be no action nor acting upon; here it is knowledge that acts creatively. While the Creative acts in the world of the invisible, with spirit and time for its field, the Receptive acts upon matter in space and brings material things to completion. Here the processes of generation and birth are traced back to their ultimate metaphysical meanings. [3]

> 6. The Creative knows through the easy.
>
> The Receptive can do things through the simple.

The nature of the Creative is movement. Through movement it unites with ease what is divided. In this way the Creative remains effortless, because it guides infinitesimal movements when things are smallest. Since the direction of movement is determined in the germinal stage of being, everything else develops quite effortlessly of itself, according to the law of its nature.

The nature of the Receptive is repose. Through repose the absolutely simple becomes possible in the spatial world. This simplicity, which arises out of pure receptivity, becomes the germ of all spatial diversity.

> 7. What is easy, is easy to know; what is simple, is easy to follow. He who is easy to know attains fealty. He who is easy to follow attains works. He who possesses attachment can endure for long; he who possesses works can become great. To endure is the disposition of the sage; greatness is the field of action of the sage.

This passage points out how the easy and the simple take effect in human life. What is easy is readily understood, and from this comes its power of suggestion. He whose ideas are clear and easily understood wins men's adherence because he embodies love. In this way he becomes free of confusing conflicts and disharmonies. Since the inner movement is in harmony with the environment, it can take effect undisturbed and have long duration. This consistency and duration characterize the disposition of the sage.

---

3. Here the principles of the Creative and the Receptive, and the Greek principles of *logos* and *eros*, are in close approximation.

It is exactly the same in the realm of action. Whatever is simple can easily be imitated. Consequently, others are ready to exert their energy in the same direction; everyone does gladly what is easy for him, because it is simple. The result is that energy is accumulated, and the simple develops quite naturally into the manifold. Thus it grows, and the sage's mission to lead the multitude to the performance of great works is fulfilled.

8. By means of the easy and the simple we grasp the laws of the whole world. When the laws of the whole world are grasped, therein lies perfection.

Here we are shown how the fundamental principles demonstrated above are applied in the Book of Changes. The easy and the simple are symbolized by very slight changes in the individual lines. The divided lines become undivided lines as the result of an easy movement that joins their separated ends; undivided lines become divided ones by means of a simple division in the middle. Thus the laws of all processes of growth under heaven are depicted in these easy and simple changes, and thereby perfection is attained.

Hereby the nature of change is defined as change of the smallest parts. This is the fourth meaning of the Chinese word *I*—a connotation that has, it is true, only a loose connection with the meaning "change."

CHAPTER II. *On the Composition and the Use of the Book of Changes*

1. The holy sages instituted the hexagrams, so that phenomena might be perceived therein. They appended the judgments, in order to indicate good fortune and misfortune.

The hexagrams of the Book of Changes are representations of earthly phenomena. In their interrelation they show the interrelation of events in the world. Thus the hexagrams were representations of ideas. But these images or phenomena re-vealed only the actual; there still remained the problem of extracting counsel from them, in order to determine whether a line of action derived from the image was favorable or harmful, whether it should be adopted or avoided. To this extent the foundation of the Book of Changes was already in existence in the time of King Wên. The hexagrams were, so to speak, oracle pictures showing what event might be ex-pected to occur under certain circumstances. King Wên and his son then added the interpretations; from these it could be ascertained whether the course of action indicated by the images augured good or ill. This marked the entrance of free-dom of choice. From that time on one could see, in the repre-sentation of events, not only what might be expected to happen but also where it might lead. With the complex of events im-mediately before one in image form, one could follow the courses that promised good fortune and avoid those that prom-ised misfortune, before the train of events had actually begun.

2. As the firm and the yielding lines displace one another, change and transformation arise.

This brings out specifically the degree to which events in the world are represented in the Book of Changes. The hexagrams are made up of firm and yielding lines. Under certain condi-tions the firm and the yielding lines change: the firm lines are transformed and softened, the yielding lines change and become firm. Thus we have a reproduction of the alternation in world phenomena.

3. Therefore good fortune and misfortune are the images of gain and loss; remorse and humiliation are the images of sorrow and forethought.

When the trend of an action is in harmony with the laws of the universe, it leads to attainment of the desired goal; this is expressed in the appended phrase "Good fortune." If the trend is in opposition to the laws of the universe, it necessarily leads to loss; this is indicated by the judgment "Misfortune." There are also trends that do not lead directly to a goal but are rather what might be called deviations in direction. However, if a trend has been wrong, and we feel sorrow in time, we can avoid misfortune; if we turn back, we can still achieve good fortune. This situation is indicated by the judgment "Remorse." This judgment, then, contains an exhortation to feel sorrow and turn back. On the other hand, a given trend may have been right at the start, but one may become indifferent and arrogant, and heedlessly slip from good fortune into misfortune. This is indicated by the judgment "Humiliation." This judgment, then, contains an admonition to exercise forethought, to check oneself when on the wrong path and turn back to good fortune.

> 4. Change and transformation are images of progress and retrogression. The firm and the yielding are images of day and night. The movements of the six lines contain the ways of the three primal powers.

Change is the conversion of a yielding line into a firm one. This means progress. Transformation is the conversion of a firm line into a yielding one. This means retrogression. The firm lines are representations of light; the yielding lines, of darkness.[1] The six lines of each hexagram are divided among the three primal powers, heaven, earth, and man. The two lower places are those of the earth, the two middle places belong to man, and the two upper ones to heaven. This section shows the extent to which the content of the Book of Changes reproduces the conditions of the world.

> 5. Therefore it is the order of the Changes that the superior man devotes himself to and that he attains tranquillity by. It is the judgments on the individual lines that the superior man takes pleasure in and that he ponders on.

From this point on we are shown the correct use of the Book of Changes. For the very reason that the Book of Changes is a reproduction of all existing conditions—with its appended

---

1. It is to be noted that the designations yang and yin, later so much used, are not the terms chosen here. This is an indication of the antiquity of the text.

judgments indicating the right course of action—it becomes our task to shape our lives according to these ideas, so that life in its turn becomes a reproduction of this law of change. This is not the kind of idealism that artificially imposes an inflexible abstract pattern on a life of quite different mold. On the contrary, the Book of Changes embraces the essential meaning of the various situations of life: thus we are in position to shape our lives meaningfully, by acting in accordance with order and sequence, and doing in each case what the situation requires. In this way we are equal to every situation, because we accept its meaning without resistance, and so we attain peace of soul. Thus our actions are set in order, and the mind also is satisfied, for when we meditate upon the judgments on the individual lines, we intuitively perceive the interrelationships in the world.

> 6. Therefore the superior man contemplates these images in times of rest and meditates on the judgments. When he undertakes something, he contemplates the changes and ponders on the oracles. Therefore he is blessed by heaven. "Good fortune. Nothing that does not further."

Here times of rest and of action are mentioned. During times of rest, experience and wisdom are obtained by meditation on the images and judgments of the book. During times of action we consult the oracle through the medium of the changes arising in the hexagrams as a result of manipulation of the yarrow stalks, and follow according to indication the counsels for action thus supplied.

B. DETAILED DISCUSSION

CHAPTER III. *On the Words Attached to the Hexagrams and the Lines*

1. The decisions refer to the images. The judgments on the lines refer to the changes.

King Wên's decisions (judgments) refer in each case to the situation imaged by the hexagram as a whole. The judgments appended by the Duke of Chou to the individual lines refer in each instance to the changes taking place within this situation. In consulting the oracle, the judgment on the line is to be considered only when the line in question "moves," that is, when it is represented either by a nine or by a six (cf. explanation of the method of consulting the oracle in the appendix).

> 2. "Good fortune" and "misfortune" refer to gain and loss, "remorse" and "humiliation" to minor imperfections. "No blame" means that one is in position to correct one's mistakes in the right way.

This passage is an amplification of section 3 of the preceding chapter. Always making the right choice in words and acts means gain; failing in this results in loss. Slight deviations from what is right are called imperfections. When one does not know what is right and does wrong inadvertently, it is called a mistake. If we become conscious of these small lapses from the right and feel a wish to remedy them, we are moved by remorse. If we remain unaware of them, or if we have the opportunity to remedy them but are either unable or unwilling to do so, humiliation results. Mistakes are like rents in a garment; when a garment has been torn and one mends it, it is whole again. If we amend mistakes by a return to the right path, no blame remains.

> 3. Therefore the classification of superior and inferior is based upon the individual places; the equalizing of great and small is based upon the hexagrams, and the discrimination between good fortune and misfortune is based upon the judgments.

The six places in the hexagram are distinguished as follows: The lowest and the topmost are, so to speak, outside the situation. Of these, the lowest is inferior, because it has not yet entered the situation. The uppermost is superior; it is the place of the sage who is no longer involved in worldly affairs, or, under certain circumstances, of an eminent man who is without power. Of the inner places, the second and fourth are those of officials, or of sons or women. The fourth is the higher, the second inferior to it. The third and fifth are authoritative places, the former because it is at the top of the lower trigram, and the latter because it is the place of the ruler of the hexagram.

"Great" and "small" signify firm and yielding lines respectively. They are equalized in the hexagram considered as a whole. Both can be favorable and indicative of good fortune when in their proper places, but the appropriateness of the places cannot be determined in the abstract; it depends on the character of the hexagram as a whole. The situation may frequently be such that yielding is advantageous; in that case a yielding line in a yielding place will be especially favorable, while a firm line in a firm place may be unfavorable. In many cases strength is required, and then a firm place is more advantageous for a yielding line. In other cases the situation may demand that character and place coincide. In a word, the specific distribution is determined by the hexagram in question, that is to say, by the situation it reproduces. Therefore the judgments are appended, to indicate the good or ill fortune arising from the situation.

> 4. Concern over remorse and humiliation depends on the borderline. The urge to blamelessness depends on remorse.

Remorse and humiliation are the results of a deviation from the right path and consequently always require a reversal of attitude. One can avoid both by being on guard in time. The point at which concern must set in, if one is to be spared remorse and humiliation, is that point at which good or evil has begun to stir in the mind but has not yet crossed the threshold into actuality. If at this moment one takes action and directs the movement in its germinal phase toward the good, one will be spared remorse and humiliation. If, however, a mistake has already been made, remorse is the psychological force leading to repentance and improvement.

> 5. This is why there are small and great among the hexagrams, and therefore the appended judgments

speak of danger or safety. The judgments in each case indicate the trend of development.

Among the situations reproduced by the hexagrams there are some of ascending and expanding potentiality and some of descending, contracting potentiality. Accordingly, at some times one must be prepared for danger, while at others one may hope for safety and tranquillity. In order to adapt oneself completely to the given situation, it is of great value to know these conditions. This is the function of the judgments: they indicate in each case the direction in which the situation is developing.

CHAPTER IV. *The Deeper Implications of the Book of Changes*

1. The Book of Changes contains the measure of heaven and earth; therefore it enables us to comprehend the tao of heaven and earth and its order.

This chapter sets forth the mysterious connections existing between the reproductions given in the Book of Changes and reality. Since the book presents a complete image of heaven and earth, a microcosm of all possible relationships, it enables us to calculate the movements in every situation to which these reproductions apply. If we ask how the Book of Changes can be a reproduction of the cosmos, the answer is that it is the work of men with cosmic intelligence, men who have incorporated their wisdom in the symbols of this book. Hence it contains the standard of heaven and earth.

The following section explains how the fact that the Book of Changes contains the measure, the standard of heaven and earth, makes it possible for us to investigate with its help the laws of the universe. Section 3 deduces from the resemblance of the Changes to heaven and earth a complete representation of inner predispositions. The fourth section, starting from the fact that the Changes comprise all forms and situations, shows how we can attain ultimate mastery of fate.

2. Looking upward, we contemplate with its help the signs in the heavens; looking down, we examine the lines of the earth. Thus we come to know the circumstances of the dark and the light. Going back to the beginnings of things and pursuing them to the end, we come to know the lessons of birth and of death. The union of seed and power produces all things; the escape of the soul brings about change. Through this we come to know the conditions of outgoing and returning spirits.

The Book of Changes is based on the two fundamental principles of the light and the dark. The hexagrams are built up out of these elements. The individual lines are either at rest or in motion. When at rest—that is, when represented by the number seven (firm) or eight (yielding)—they build up the hexagram, When in motion—that is, when represented by the number nine (firm) or six (yielding)—they break down the hexagram again and transform it into a new hexagram. These are the processes that open our eyes to the secrets of life.

When we apply these principles to the signs in the heavens (the sun standing for light, the moon for darkness) and to the lines of direction on the earth (the cardinal points), we learn to know the circumstances concerning the dark and the light, i.e., the laws that bring about the course and alternation of the seasons and that condition the appearance and withdrawal of the vegetative life force. Thus we learn by observing the beginnings and endings of life that birth and death form one recurrent cycle. Birth is the coming forth into the world of the visible; death is the return into the regions of the invisible. Neither of these signifies an absolute beginning nor an absolute ending, any more than do the changes of the seasons within the year. Nor is it otherwise in the case of man. Just as the resting lines build up the hexagrams and produce change when they begin to move, so bodily existence is built up by the union of "outgoing" life streams of seed (male) with power (female). This corporeal existence remains relatively constant as long as the constructive forces are in the resting state, in equilibrium. When they begin to move, disintegration sets in. The psychic element escapes— the higher part mounting upward, the lower sinking to earth; the body disintegrates.

The spiritual forces that produce the building up and the breaking down of visible existence likewise belong either to the light principle or to the dark principle. The light spirits (*shên*) are outgoing; they are the active spirits, which can also enter upon new incarnations. The dark spirits (*kuei*), return home; they are the withdrawing forces and have the task of assimilating what life has yielded.[1]

This idea of returning and outgoing spirits by no means entails the notion of good and evil beings; it only differentiates the expanding and the contracting phase of the underlying life energy. These are the ebb and flow in the great ocean of life.

> 3. Since in this way man comes to resemble heaven and earth, he is not in conflict with them. His wisdom embraces all things, and his tao brings order into the whole world; therefore he does not err. He is active everywhere but does not let himself be carried away. He rejoices in heaven and has knowledge of fate, therefore he is free of care. He is content with his circumstances and genuine in his kindness, therefore he can practice love.

Here we are shown how with the help of the fundamental principles of the Book of Changes it is possible to arrive at a complete realization of man's innate capacities. This unfolding rests on the fact that man has innate capacities that resemble heaven and earth, that he is a microcosm. Now, since the laws of heaven and earth are reproduced in the Book of Changes, man is provided with the means of shaping his own nature, so that his inborn potentialities for good can be completely realized. In this process two factors are to be taken into account: wisdom and action, or intellect and will. If intellect and will are correctly centered, the emotional life takes on harmony. We have here four propositions based on wisdom and love, justice

1. [Cf. Wilhelm and Jung, *The Secret of the Golden Flower* (1962 edn.), p. 14.]

and mores, reminding us of the combination of these principles with the four words in the hexagram Ch'ien, THE CREATIVE: "Sublime success; perseverance furthers."

The effect of wisdom, love, and justice is shown in the first proposition. On the basis of all-embracing wisdom, the regulations springing from a love of the world can be so shaped that all goes well for everyone and no mistakes are made. This is what furthers. The second proposition pictures wisdom and love, excluding no person or thing; these are regulated by the mores, which do not allow one to be carried away into anything improper or one-sided, and therefore have success. The third proposition shows the harmony of mind, perfect in wisdom, that rejoices in heaven and understands its dispensations. This provides the basis for perseverance. Finally, the last proposition shows the love that acquiesces trustingly in every situation and, out of its store of inner kindness, manifests itself in good will toward all men, thereby attaining sublimity, the root of all good.

> 4. In it are included the forms and the scope of everything in the heavens and on earth, so that nothing escapes it. In it all things everywhere are completed, so that none is missing. Therefore by means of it we can penetrate the tao of day and night, and so understand it. Therefore the spirit is bound to no one place, nor the Book of Changes to any one form.

We are shown here how the individual can attain mastery over fate by means of the Book of Changes. Its principles contain the categories of all that is—literally, the molds and the scope of all transformations. These categories are in the mind of man; everything, all that happens and everything that undergoes transformation, must obey the laws prescribed by the mind of man. Not until these categories become operative do things become things. These categories are laid down in the Book of Changes; hence it enables us to penetrate and understand the movements of the light and the dark, of life and death, of gods and demons. This knowledge makes possible mastery over fate, because fate can be shaped if its laws are known. The reason why we can oppose fate is that reality is always conditioned, and these conditions of time and space limit and determine it. The spirit, however, is not bound by these determinants and can bring them about as its own purposes require. The Book of Changes is so widely applicable because it contains only these purely spiritual relationships, which are so abstract that they can find expression within every framework of reality. They contain only the tao that underlies events. Therefore all chance contingencies can be shaped according to this tao. The conscious application of these possibilities assures mastery over fate.

CHAPTER V. *Tao in Its Relation to the Light Power and to the Dark Power*

1. That which lets now the dark, now the light appear is tao.

The light and the dark are the two primal powers, designated hitherto in the text as firm and yielding, or as day and night. Firm and yielding are the terms applied to the lines of the Book of Changes, while light and dark designate the two primal powers of nature. It must be left to a later discussion to explain why up to this point the designations day and night have been used, and now suddenly the terms light and dark appear. Possibly we are dealing here with a later stratum of text. At any rate, we can observe that in the course of time the use of these expressions steadily increases.

The terms yin, the dark, and yang, the light, denote respectively the shadowed and the light side of a mountain or a river. Yang represents the south side of the mountain, because this side receives the sunlight, but it connotes the north side of the river, because the light of the river is reflected to that side. The reverse is true as regards yin. These terms are gradually extended to include the two polar forces of the universe, which we may call positive and negative.[1] It may be that these

1. Tao (*SINN*) is something that sets in motion and maintains the interplay of these forces. As this something means only a direction,

designations, which emphasize the cycle of change more than change itself, led also to the representation in circular form of the Primal Beginning, ☯ [*t'ai chi t'u*], the symbol that was later to play such an important part in Chinese thought.

> 2. As continuer, it is good. As completer, it is the essence.

The primal powers never come to a standstill; the cycle of becoming continues uninterruptedly. The reason is that between the two primal powers there arises again and again a state of tension, a potential that keeps the powers in motion and causes them to unite, whereby they are constantly regenerated. Tao brings this about without ever becoming manifest. The power of tao to maintain the world by constant renewal of a state of tension between the polar forces, is designated as good[2] (cf. Lao-tse, chap. 8).

As the power that completes things, the power that lends them their individuality and gives them a center around which they organize, tao is called the essence, that with which things are endowed at their origin.[3]

> 3. The kind man discovers it and calls it kind. The wise man discovers it and calls it wise. The people use it day by day and are not aware of it, for the way of the superior man is rare.

Tao reveals itself differently to each individual, according to his own nature. The man of deeds, for whom kindness and the love of his fellow man are supreme, discovers the tao of cosmic events and calls it supreme kindness—"God is love." The contemplative man, for whom calm wisdom is supreme,

---

invisible and in no way material, the Chinese chose for it the borrowed word tao, meaning "way," "course," which is also nothing in itself, yet serves to regulate all movements. For a discussion of the translation of the word tao, see the introduction to my translation of Lao-tse. [See p. *lv*, n. 13.]

2. This shows again to what extent the point of view of the Book of Changes is based on the principles of the organic world, in which there is no entropy.

3. This is probably the passage on which Mencius based his doctrine that man's nature is good.

discovers the tao of the universe and calls it supreme wisdom. The common people live from day to day, continually borne and nourished by tao, but they know nothing of it; they see only what meets the eye. For the way of the superior man, who sees not only things but the tao of things, is rare. The tao of the universe is indeed kindness and wisdom; but essentially tao is also beyond kindness and wisdom.

> 4. It manifests itself as kindness but conceals its workings. It gives life to all things, but it does not share the anxieties of the holy sage. Its glorious power, its great field of action, are of all things the most sublime.

The movement from within outward shows tao in its manifestations as the force of supreme kindness. At the same time it remains mysterious even in the light of day. The movement from without inward conceals the results of its workings. It is just as when in spring and summer the seeds start growing, and the life-giving bounty of nature becomes manifest: but along with it there is at work that quiet power which conceals within the seed all the results of growth and in hidden ways prepares what the coming year is to bring. Tao works tirelessly and eternally in this way. Yet this life-giving activity, to which all beings owe their existence, is something purely spontaneous. It is not like the conscious anxiety of man, who strives for the good with inward toil.

> 5. It possesses everything in complete abundance: this is its great field of action. It renews everything daily: this is its glorious power.

There is nothing that tao may not possess, for it is omnipresent; everything that exists, exists in and through it. But it is not lifeless possessing; by reason of its eternal power, it continually renews everything, so that each day the world becomes as glorious again as it was on the first day of creation.

> 6. As begetter of all begetting, it is called change.

The dark begets the light and the light begets the dark in ceaseless alternation, but that which begets this alternation, that to which all life owes its existence, is tao with its law of change.

> 7. As that which completes the primal images, it is called the Creative; as that which imitates them, it is called the Receptive.

This is based on the view expressed likewise in the *Tao Tê Ching*,[4] namely, that underlying reality there is a world of archetypes, and reproductions of these make up the real things in the material world. The world of archetypes is heaven, the world of reproductions is the earth: there energy, here matter; there the Creative, here the Receptive. But it is the same tao that is active both in the Creative and in the Receptive.

> 8. In that it serves for exploring the laws of number and thus for knowing the future, it is called revelation. In that it serves to infuse an organic coherence into the changes, it is called the work.

The future likewise develops in accordance with the fixed laws, according to calculable numbers. If these numbers are known, future events can be calculated with perfect certainty. This is the thought on which the Book of Changes is based. This world of the immutable is the daemonic world, in which there is no free choice, in which everything is fixed. It is the world of yin. But in addition to this rigid world of number, there are living trends. Things develop, consolidate in a given direction, grow rigid, then decline; a change sets in, coherence is established once more, and the world is one again. The secret of tao in this world of the mutable, the world of light— the realm of yang—is to keep the changes in motion in such a manner that no stasis occurs and an unbroken coherence is maintained. He who succeeds in endowing his work with this regenerative power creates something organic, and the thing so created is enduring.

---

4. Cf. R. Wilhelm, *Chinesische Lebensweisheit* (Darmstadt, 1922), pp. 16 ff.

9. That aspect of it which cannot be fathomed in terms of the light and the dark is called spirit.

In their alternation and reciprocal effect, the two fundamental forces serve to explain all the phenomena in the world. Nonetheless, there remains something that cannot be explained in terms of the interaction of these forces, a final why. This ultimate meaning of tao is the spirit, the divine, the unfathomable in it, that which must be revered in silence.

CHAPTER VI. *Tao as Applied to the Book of Changes*

1. The Book of Changes is vast and great. When one speaks of what is far, it knows no limits. When one speaks of what is near, it is still and right. When one speaks of the space between heaven and earth, it embraces everything.

Here the Book of Changes is brought into relation with the macrocosm and the microcosm. First the horizontal extent of its domain, its vastness, is given; its laws are valid to the utmost distance and likewise for what is nearest, as one's own inner laws. Then the vertical extent is given, the space between heaven and earth, because the fates of men come down to them from heaven.

2. In a state of rest the Creative is one, and in a state of motion it is straight; therefore it creates that which is great. The Receptive is closed in a state of rest, and in a state of motion it opens; therefore it creates that which is vast.

"The Creative" means here the trigram in the Book of Changes, and more especially the line, by which it is symbolized. When at rest, this is a simple unbroken line (———); when it is in motion, its direction is straight forward. The Receptive is symbolized by a divided line (— —); it is closed when at rest and opens when in motion. Thus that which is wrought by the Creative is designated, in accordance with its nature, as great. The Creative produces quality. That which is produced by the Receptive is designated, in accordance with its form, as broad and manifold. The Receptive produces quantity.

> 3. Because of its vastness and greatness, it corresponds with heaven and earth. Because of its changes and its continuity, it corresponds with the four seasons. Because of the meaning of the light and the dark, it corresponds with sun and moon. Because of the good in the easy and the simple, it corresponds with the supreme power.

Here the parallels between the Book of Changes and the cosmos are shown. The Book of Changes contains material multiplicity, quantity, like the earth. It contains dynamic greatness, quality, like heaven. It shows changes and closed systems like the course of the year within the four seasons. In the light principle it reveals the same meaning as that underlying the sun. The light principle is called yang. The term for the sun is *t'ai yang*, the Great Light. In the dark principle, it reveals the same meaning as that underlying the moon. The dark principle is called yin. The term for the moon is *t'ai yin*, the Great Dark.

It has been explained above that the essence of the Creative lies in the easy, the essence of the Receptive in the simple, in those seeds from which everything else develops spontaneously. This mode corresponds with the good in tao, its art of continuing life in the simplest manner (cf. chap. v, sec. 2), and thus it corresponds with the supreme power of tao (cf. chap. v, sec. 4).

CHAPTER VII. *The Effects of the Book of Changes on Man*

> 1. The Master said: Is not the Book of Changes supreme? By means of it the holy sages exalted their natures and extended their field of action.

Wisdom exalts. The mores make humble. The exalted imitate heaven. The humble follow the example of the earth.

These words are explicitly attributed to Confucius, consequently the essay of which they are a part cannot in its entirety have originated with Confucius, but is rather a product of his school. Actually the several chapters do contain commentaries of very different sorts, which probably also belong to different periods.

We are shown here how the Book of Changes, correctly used, leads to harmony with the ultimate principles of the universe. The sages exalt their natures by acquiring the wisdom preserved in this book, and thus they arrive at harmony with heaven, which is high. On the one hand, the mind gains loftiness of viewpoint; on the other hand, the field of action is widened. This comprehensiveness gives rise to the idea of mores: the individual subordinates himself to the whole. Through such humble subordination, the sages arrive at harmony with the earth, which is low. Thus the individual enlarges his field of action.

> 2. Heaven and earth determine the scene, and the changes take effect within it. The perfected nature of man, sustaining itself and enduring, is the gateway of tao and of justice.

Heaven is the scene of the spiritual, earth is the scene of the corporeal. In these worlds move the things that develop and are transformed according to the rules of the Book of Changes. So likewise the nature of man, which is perfected and endures, is the gateway through which the actions of man go in and out, and when man is in harmony with the teachings of the Book of Changes, these actions correspond with the tao of the universe and with justice. Tao, which manifests itself as kindness, corresponds with the light principle, and justice corresponds with the dark principle: the one relates to the exalting and the other to the broadening of man's nature.

CHAPTER VIII. *On the Use of the Appended Explanations*

1. The holy sages were able to survey all the confused diversities under heaven. They observed forms and phenomena, and made representations of things and their attributes. These were called the Images.

Here we are shown how the images of the Book of Changes developed out of the archetypal images that underlie the phenomenal world.

2. The holy sages were able to survey all the movements under heaven. They contemplated the way in which these movements met and became interrelated, to take their course according to eternal laws. Then they appended judgments, to distinguish between the good fortune and misfortune indicated. These were called the Judgments.

The last word, "Judgments," is actually "lines" in the text. The present translation incorporates the correction made by Hu Shih in his history of Chinese philosophy,[1] because it brings out more clearly the contrast between Image and Judgment that is found also in other passages of the Book of Changes.

3. They speak of the most confused diversities without arousing aversion. They speak of what is most mobile without causing confusion.

4. This comes from the fact that they observed before they spoke and discussed before they moved. Through observation and discussion they perfected the changes and transformations.

These two sections present again the contrast between the observation in the Image, which gives us knowledge of the diversities of things, and the discussion in the Judgment,

---

1. [See p. *lvii*, n. 16.]

which gives us knowledge of the directions of movement. We have here comments on the theory of the simple as the root of diversity in form (in conformity with the Receptive) and of the easy as the root of all movement (in conformity with the Creative), as given in chapter 1 (secs. 6 *et seq.*). The following sections (fragments of a detailed commentary on the individual lines) give examples.

5. "A crane calling in the shade. Its young answers it. I have a good goblet. I will share it with you."

The Master said: The superior man abides in his room. If his words are well spoken, he meets with assent at a distance of more than a thousand miles. How much more then from near by! If the superior man abides in his room and his words are not well spoken, he meets with contradiction at a distance of more than a thousand miles. How much more then from near by! Words go forth from one's own person and exert their influence on men. Deeds are born close at hand and become visible far away. Words and deeds are the hinge and bowspring of the superior man. As hinge and bowspring move, they bring honor or disgrace. Through words and deeds the superior man moves heaven and earth. Must one not, then, be cautious?

Compare book I, hexagram 61, Chung Fu, INNER TRUTH, nine in the second place, comment on the subject of speaking.

6. "Men bound in fellowship first weep and lament, but afterward they laugh."

The Master said:

Life leads the thoughtful man on a path of many windings.

Now the course is checked, now it runs straight again.

Here winged thoughts may pour freely forth in words,

There the heavy burden of knowledge must be shut away in silence.

But when two people are at one in their inmost hearts,

They shatter even the strength of iron or of bronze.

And when two people understand each other in their inmost hearts,

Their words are sweet and strong, like the fragrance of orchids.

Compare book I, hexagram 13, T'ung Jên, FELLOWSHIP WITH MEN, nine in the fifth place, comment on the subject of speaking.

7. "To spread white rushes underneath. No blame."

The Master said: It does well enough simply to place something on the floor. But if one puts white rushes underneath, how could that be a mistake? This is the extreme of caution. Rushes in themselves are worthless, but they can have a very important effect. If one is as cautious as this in all that one does, one remains free of mistakes.

Compare book III, hexagram 28, Ta Kuo, PREPONDERANCE OF THE GREAT, six at the beginning, comment on action.

8. "A superior man of modesty and merit carries things to conclusion. Good fortune."

The Master said: When a man does not boast of his efforts and does not count his merits a virtue, he is a man of great parts. It means that for all his merits he subordinates himself to others. Noble of nature, reverent in his conduct, the modest man is full of merit, and therefore he is able to maintain his position.

Compare book III, hexagram 15, Ch'ien, MODESTY, nine in the third place, comment on action.

9. "Arrogant dragon will have cause to repent."

The Master said: He who is noble and has no corresponding position, he who stands high and has no following, he who has able people under him who do not have his support, that man will have cause for regret at every turn.

Compare book III, hexagram 1, Ch'ien, THE CREATIVE, nine at the top, comment on action. The citation there from the *Wên Yen*[2] contains this passage, obviously from the same commentary, word for word.

10. "Not going out of the door and the courtyard is without blame."

The Master said: Where disorder develops, words are the first steps. If the prince is not discreet, he loses his servant. If the servant is not discreet, he loses his life. If germinating things are not handled with discretion, the perfecting of them is impeded. Therefore the superior man is careful to maintain silence and does not go forth.

Compare book I, hexagram 60, Chieh, LIMITATION, nine at the beginning, comment on speaking.

11. The Master said: The authors of the Book of Changes knew what robbers are like. In the Book of Changes it is said: "If a man carries a burden on his back and nonetheless rides in a carriage, he thereby encourages robbers to draw near." Carrying a burden on the back is the business of a common man; a car-

2. [Seventh Wing: Commentary on the Words of the Text.]

riage is the appurtenance of a man of rank. Now, when a common man uses the appurtenance of a man of rank, robbers plot to take it away from him. If a man is insolent toward those above him and hard toward those below him, robbers plot to attack him. Carelessness in guarding things tempts thieves to steal. Sumptuous ornaments worn by a maiden are an enticement to rob her of her virtue. In the Book of Changes it is said: "If a man carries a burden on his back and nonetheless rides in a carriage, he thereby encourages robbers to draw near." For that is an invitation to robbers.

Compare book I, hexagram 40, Hsieh, DELIVERANCE, six in the third place, comment on action.

CHAPTER IX. *On the Oracle*

1. Heaven is one, earth is two; heaven is three, earth four; heaven is five, earth six; heaven is seven, earth eight; heaven is nine, earth ten.

In the traditional form of the text, this section comes just before chapter x. It was transposed to its present position by Ch'êng Tzŭ in the Sung period and joined with the section that follows, which originally came after section 3. The two sections undoubtedly belong together, but they are only very loosely connected with what follows. They contain speculations about numbers similar to those in the section entitled *Hung Fan*[1] in the Book of History [*Shu Ching*]. Probably they represent the beginning of the connection between the number speculations of the Book of History and the yin-yang doctrine of the Book of Changes, which played an important role in Chinese thought especially under the Han dynasty. To under-

---

1. ["The Great Plan." See bk. IV of the *Shu Ching*, as translated by Legge (*The Sacred Books of the East*, III: *The Shu King*, Oxford, 1879).]

stand this connection, which can be mentioned here only in passing, we must go back to the diagram known as *Ho T'u*, the Yellow River Map, said to have originated with Fu Hsi [fig. 4]. This map shows the development out of even and odd numbers of the "five stages of change" (*wu hsing*, usually incorrectly called "elements").

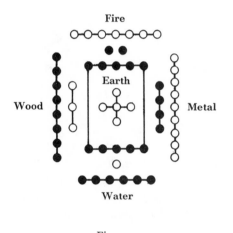

Figure 4

Water in the north has sprung from the one of heaven, which is complemented by the six of earth. Fire in the south has sprung from the two of earth, which is complemented by the seven of heaven. Wood in the east has sprung from the three of heaven, which is complemented by the eight of earth. Metal in the west has sprung from the four of earth, which is complemented by the nine of heaven. Earth in the middle (*t'u*, the soil, the earth substance as distinguished from *ti*, the earth as a heavenly body) has sprung from the five of heaven, which is complemented by the ten of earth.

The second arrangement, according to which the numbers separate again and combine with the eight trigrams, is that of the *Lo Shu*, the Writing from the River Lo [fig. 5].

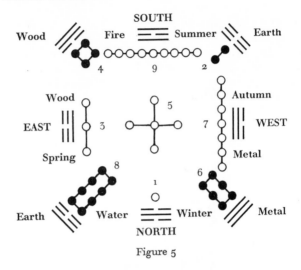

Figure 5

2. There are five heavenly numbers. There are also five earthly numbers. When they are distributed among the five places, each finds its complement. The sum of the heavenly numbers is twenty-five, that of the earthly numbers is thirty. The sum total of heavenly numbers and earthly numbers is fifty-five. It is this which completes the changes and transformations and sets demons and gods in movement.

No further comment is needed in explanation of this. Like section 1, it undoubtedly belongs to a later period.

3. The number of the total is fifty. Of these, forty-nine are used. They are divided into two portions, to represent the two primal forces. Hereupon one is set apart, to represent the three powers. They are counted through by fours, to represent the four seasons. The remainder is put aside, to represent the intercalary month. There are two intercalary months in

five years, therefore the putting aside is repeated, and this gives us the whole.

Here the process of consulting the oracle is brought into relation with cosmic processes. The procedure in consulting the oracle is as follows:

One takes fifty yarrow stalks, of which only forty-nine are used. These forty-nine are first divided into two heaps [at random], then a stalk from the right-hand heap is inserted between the ring finger and the little finger of the left hand. The left heap is counted through by fours, and the remainder (four or less) is inserted between the ring finger and the middle finger. The same thing is done with the right heap, and the remainder inserted between the forefinger and the middle finger. This constitutes one change. Now one is holding in one's hand either five or nine stalks in all. The two remaining heaps are put together, and the same process is repeated twice. These second and third times, one obtains either four or eight stalks. The five stalks of the first counting and the four of each of the succeeding countings are regarded as a unit having the numerical value three; the nine stalks of the first counting and the eight of the succeeding countings have the numerical value two. When three successive changes produce the sum $3+3+3=9$, this makes the old yang, i.e., a firm line that moves. The sum $2+2+2=6$ makes the old yin, a yielding line that moves. Seven is the young yang, and eight the young yin; they are not taken into account as individual lines (cf. the section on consulting the oracle in Appendix I, pp. 721 ff.).

4. The numbers that yield THE CREATIVE total 216; those which yield THE RECEPTIVE total 144, making in all 360. They correspond to the days of the year.

When THE CREATIVE is made up of six old yang lines, that is, of nines only, the following numbers result when the oracle is consulted.

Total number of stalks	49
Subtracted the first time	$5+4+4=13$
	$\overline{36}$

311

When this is repeated six times (for the six lines), the total of
the six remainders (36×6) is 216 stalks.

When THE RECEPTIVE consists of sixes only—that is, of
old yin lines—the following numbers result.

$$\begin{array}{lr} \text{Total number of stalks} & 49 \\ \text{Subtracted for a six (old yin)} \quad 9+8+8= & 25 \\ \hline & 24 \end{array}$$

When this has been done six times (for the six lines of a hexagram), the total of the remainders (24×6) is 144 stalks. If now
one adds together the numbers obtained for THE CREATIVE
and the numbers obtained for THE RECEPTIVE, the result is
$216+144=360$, which corresponds with the average number
of days in the Chinese year.[2]

> 5. The numbers of the stalks in the two parts amount
> to 11,520, which corresponds with the number of the
> ten thousand things.

In the whole of the Book of Changes there are 192 lines of
each kind—in all, 384 lines (64×6), of which half are yang
and half yin. As has been shown in the section above, after a
moving yang line is obtained there remain thirty-six stalks,
so that we have altogether $192 \times 36 = 6912$. Each of the moving
yin lines yields a remainder of twenty-four stalks: $192 \times 24 =
4608$. Together, $6912+4608=11,520$.

> 6. Therefore four operations are required to pro-
> duce a change; eighteen mutations yield a hexa-
> gram.

The words "change" and "mutation" are used here in the
same sense. Each line, as shown above, is composed of three
mutations or changes. The four operations are: (1) dividing
the stalks into two heaps; (2) taking up one stalk and inserting
this between the ring finger and the little finger; (3) counting
off the left-hand heap by fours and inserting the remainder
between the ring finger and the middle finger; (4) counting

2. The Chinese year is in essential agreement with the Metonic
year. [Meton, an Athenian astronomer of the fifth century B.C.,
used the phases of the moon as the basis of his calculations.]

off the right-hand heap by fours and inserting the remainder between the forefinger and the middle finger. These four operations yield one change or mutation—that is to say, the numerical value two or three (see above). When this change is carried out three times, one obtains the value of the line, either a six or a seven, an eight or a nine. Six lines (3 changes × 6 = 18 changes) produce the structure of the hexagram.

7. The eight signs constitute each a small completion.

The hexagram is made up of two trigrams. The "eight signs" are the eight primary trigrams. In a hexagram the lower trigram is also called the inner, and the upper trigram is also called the outer.

8. When we continue and go further and add to the situations all their transitions, all possible situations on earth are encompassed.

Each of the sixty-four hexagrams can change into another through the appropriate movement of one or more lines. Thus we arrive at a total (64 × 64) of 4096 transitional stages, and these represent every possible situation.

9. It reveals tao and renders nature and action divine. Therefore with its help we can meet everything in the right way, and with its help can even assist the gods themselves.

This section refers again to the Book of Changes in general. Its theme is that the book reveals the meaning of events in the universe and thereby imparts a divine mystery to the nature and action of the man who puts his trust in it, so that he is enabled to meet every event in the right way and even to aid the gods in governing the world.

10. The Master said: Whoever knows the tao of the changes and transformations, knows the action of the gods.

CHAPTER X. *The Fourfold Use of the Book of Changes*

1. The Book of Changes contains a fourfold tao of the holy sages. In speaking, we should be guided by its judgments; in action, we should be guided by its changes; in making objects, we should be guided by its images; in seeking an oracle, we should be guided by its pronouncements.

2. Therefore the superior man, whenever he has to make or do something, consults the Changes, and he does so in words. It takes up his communications like an echo; neither far nor near, neither dark nor deep exist for it, and thus he learns of the things of the future. If this book were not the most spiritual thing on earth, how could it do this?

Here the psychological basis of the oracle is described. The person consulting the oracle formulates his problem precisely in words, and regardless of whether it concerns something distant or near, secret or profound, he receives—as though it were an echo—the appropriate oracle, which enables him to know the future. This rests on the assumption that the conscious and the supraconscious enter into relationship. The conscious process stops with the formulation of the question. The unconscious process begins with the division of the yarrow stalks, and when we compare the result of this division with the text of the book, we obtain the oracle.

3. The three and five operations are undertaken in order to obtain a change. Divisions and combinations of the numbers are made. If one proceeds through the changes, they complete the forms of heaven and earth. If the number of changes is increased to the utmost, they determine all images on earth. If this were not the most changing thing on earth, how could it do this?

A great deal has been said about the "three and five" divisions, and even Chu Hsi[1] is of the opinion that the passage is no longer comprehensible. But we need only take as a basis chapter IX, section 3, which the passage above serves to explain further, in order to establish coherence in the text. The "three" operations are the division into two heaps and the special disposition of a single stalk, "to represent the three powers." After this each of the two heaps is counted through by fours, because "there are two intercalary months in five years," and thus we arrive at three plus two, i.e., five operations, which yield one change. We proceed in this way with divisions and combinations until we "complete the forms of heaven and earth," that is, until we obtain, as a first result, one of the eight primary trigrams or a "small completion" (cf. chap. IX, sec. 7). Continuing until the topmost or sixth line is reached, we obtain a complete image, which is always composed of two trigrams.

> 4. The Changes have no consciousness, no action; they are quiescent and do not move. But if they are stimulated, they penetrate all situations under heaven. If they were not the most divine thing on earth, how could they do this?

Here we have a plain statement of what has been brought out in the remarks on section 2.[2]

> 5. The Changes are what has enabled the holy sages to reach all depths and to grasp the seeds of all things.

> 6. Only through what is deep can one penetrate all wills on earth. Only through the seeds can one com-

---

1. [A.D. 1130–1200.]

2. The way in which the Book of Changes works can best be compared to an electrical circuit reaching into all situations. The circuit only affords the potentiality of lighting; it does not give light. But when contact with a definite situation is established through the questioner, the "current" is activated, and the given situation is illumined. Although this analogy is not used in any of the commentaries, it serves to explain in a few words the entire meaning of the text.

plete all affairs on earth. Only through the divine can one hurry without haste and reach the goal without walking.

Here it is shown that because the Book of Changes reaches down into the regions of the unconscious, both space and time are eliminated. Space, as the principle of diversity and confusion, is overcome by the deep, the simple. Time, as the principle of uncertainty, is overcome by the easy, the germinal.

7. When the Master said, "The Book of Changes contains a fourfold tao of the holy sages," this is what is meant.

It may be assumed that section 1 is based on a saying of Confucius that has been rhetorically elaborated and is once more summarized here.

CHAPTER XI. *On the Yarrow Stalks and the Hexagrams and Lines*

1. The Master said: The Changes, what do they do? The Changes disclose things, complete affairs, and encompass all ways on earth—this and nothing else. For this reason the holy sages used them to penetrate all wills on earth and to determine all fields of action on earth, and to settle all doubts on earth.

Here again we have a saying of the Master placed at the head of a chapter which then develops and interprets it.

2. Therefore the nature of the yarrow stalks is round and spiritual. The nature of the hexagrams is square and wise. The meaning of the six lines changes, in order to furnish information.

In this way the holy sages purified their hearts, withdrew, and hid themselves in the secret. They concerned themselves with good fortune and misfortune in common with other men. They were divine, hence they knew the future; they were wise, hence they stored up the past. Who is it that can do all this? Only the reason and clear-mindedness of the ancients, their knowledge and wisdom, their unremitting divine power.

Here the triplicity of the first section is consistently carried further. Penetration of all wills is paralleled with the spirituality of the yarrow stalks: they are round because they are symbols of heaven and of the spirit. Their basic number is seven, their total number is forty-nine (7×7). The hexagrams stand for the earth; their basic number is eight, their total number is sixty-four (8×8). They serve to determine the field of action. Finally, the individual lines are movable and changeable (their basic numbers are nine and six), in order to give information and to settle doubts pertaining to particular situations.

The holy sages were possessed of this knowledge. They withdrew into seclusion and cultivated the spirit, so that they were able to penetrate the minds of all men (penetration), so that they could determine good fortune and misfortune (the field of action), and so that they knew the past and the future (settlement of doubts). They could do this thanks to their reason and clear-mindedness (penetration of wills), their knowledge and wisdom (determination of the field of action), and their divine power (settlement of doubts). This divine power to battle (*shên wu*) acts without weakening itself (this is a better reading than "without killing").

> 3. Therefore they fathomed the tao of heaven and understood the situations of men. Thus they invented these divine things in order to meet the need of men. The holy sages fasted for this reason, in order to make their natures divinely clear.

Because these wise men knew equally well the laws of the universe and what was needful to man, they invented the use of the oracle stalks—"these divine things"—in order thus to answer the needs of men. And so they concentrated their thoughts in holy meditation for the purpose of attaining the necessary power and fullness of being. Therefore the understanding of the Book of Changes calls for a similar concentration and meditation.

> 4. Therefore they called the closing of the gates the Receptive, and the opening of the gate the Creative. The alternation between closing and opening they called change. The going forward and backward without ceasing they called penetration. What manifests itself visibly they called an image; what has bodily form they called a tool. What is established in usage they called a pattern. That which furthers on going out and coming in, that which all men live by, they called the divine.

In this passage are shown the tao of heaven and the conditions of men as recognized by the holy sages. The closing and the opening of the gates signify the alternation of rest and movement. These are likewise two conditions pertaining to yoga practice that are attainable only through individual training. Penetration is that state in which the individual has attained sovereign mastery in the psychic sphere as well and is able to move forward and backward in time. The next sentences show how the material world arises. First of all there is a pre-existent image, an idea; then a copy of this archetypal image takes shape as a corporeal form. That which regulates this process of imitation is a pattern; and the force that generates these processes is the divine principle. Many parallels to these expositions are to be found in Lao-tse.

> 5. Therefore there is in the Changes the Great Primal Beginning. This generates the two primary forces. The two primary forces generate the four images. The four images generate the eight trigrams.

The Great Primal Beginning, *t'ai chi*, plays an important role in later Chinese natural philosophy. Originally *chi* is the ridgepole—a simple line symbolizing the positing of oneness

(———). This positing of oneness implies also a positing of duality, an above and a below. The conditioning element is further designated as an undivided line, while the conditioned element is represented by means of a divided line (— —). These are the two polar primary forces later designated as yang, the bright principle, and yin, the dark. Then, through doubling, there arise the four images:

⚌ old or great yang	⚏ old or great yin
⚎ young or little yang	⚍ young or little yin

These correspond with the four seasons of the year. Through addition of another line, there arise the eight trigrams:

☰ Ch'ien	☷ K'un	☳ Chên	☲ Li
☱ Tui	☴ Sun	☵ K'an	☶ Kên

The same procedure is mentioned in chapter 42 of Lao-tse.

6. The eight trigrams determine good fortune and misfortune. Good fortune and misfortune create the great field of action.

The "great field of action" are the regulations and rules instituted by the sages in order to obtain good fortune for men and to avoid misfortune.

7. Therefore: There are no greater primal images than heaven and earth. There is nothing that has more movement or greater cohesion than the four seasons. Of the images suspended in the heavens, there is none more light-giving than the sun and the moon. Of the honored and highly placed, there is none greater than he who possesses wealth and rank. With respect to creating things for use and making tools helpful to the whole world, there is no one greater than the holy sages. For comprehending the chaotic diversity of things and exploring what is hidden, for penetrating the depths and extending influence afar, thereby determining good fortune and

misfortune on earth and consummating all efforts on earth, there is nothing greater than the oracle.

As in chapter 25 of Lao-tse, where the four great things in the universe are discussed, the great things in nature and in the world of men are here named together. Heaven and earth offer the archetypal image to be imitated. Among all things, the seasons have the most movement and the greatest degree of cohesion; the brightest are the sun and the moon.

On earth the most exalted person is the king of men, the sage on the throne, who, wealthy and noble himself, is at the same time the source of wealth and nobility. His helpers are, first, the active man of wisdom, directing and inventing, and, second, the oracle, which, corresponding with the light-giving images, the sun and moon, clarifies and illumines all conditions on earth.

> 8. Therefore: Heaven creates divine things; the holy sage takes them as models. Heaven and earth change and transform; the holy sage imitates them. In the heavens hang images that reveal good fortune and misfortune; the holy sage reproduces these. The Yellow River brought forth a map and the Lo River brought forth a writing; the holy men took these as models.

In this section the parallel between the processes in the macrocosm and the works of the holy sages is elaborated. The divine things created by heaven and earth are presumably the natural phenomena that the holy men reproduced in the eight trigrams. According to another view, tortoises and yarrow stalks are meant. The changes and transformations manifesting themselves in day and night, and in the seasons of the year, are reproduced in the character of the changes in the lines. The signs in the heavens meaning good fortune and misfortune are the sun, moon, and stars, together with comets, eclipses, and the like. They are reproduced in the appended judgments on good fortune and misfortune.

The last sentence of the section, referring to two legendary events occurring in the time of Fu Hsi and Yü[1] respectively, is a later addition and has had a disastrous effect on the exegesis of the Book of Changes. Reproductions of the two diagrams are given in the explanation of chapter IX, section 1. That this is a later addition is proven by the fact that sections 7, 8, 9 of the present chapter all deal with the threefold parallelism between nature and the world of man broached in section 1, and this addendum creates a break in the continuity of thought.

> 9. In the Changes there are images, in order to reveal; there are judgments appended, in order to interpret; good fortune and misfortune are determined, in order to decide.

The text says "four" images; this is carried over by error from section 5. Here "images" means the eight trigrams, which show situations in their interrelation. This corresponds with the archetypal images of heaven. The judgments appended to the lines indicate the changes corresponding with the changes in the seasons. Finally, the decisions about good fortune and misfortune correspond with the signs in the heavens.

CHAPTER XII. *Summary*

> 1. In the Book of Changes it is said: "He is blessed by heaven. Good fortune. Nothing that does not further."
>
> The Master said: To bless means to help. Heaven helps the man who is devoted; men help the man who is true. He who walks in truth and is devoted in his thinking, and furthermore reveres the worthy, is blessed by heaven. He has good fortune, and there is nothing that would not further.

This is a passage from the body of the commentary on the individual lines, fragments of which appear in chapter VIII,

---

1. [Like Fu Hsi, one of the legendary rulers of China. He is credited with having founded the first dynasty of China, the Hsia dynasty, said to have lasted from 2205 to 1766 B.C.]

sections 5–11. It serves to amplify the close of section 6 of chapter II, but it does not fit the context here.

> 2. The Master said: Writing cannot express words completely. Words cannot express thoughts completely.
>
> Are we then unable to see the thoughts of the holy sages?
>
> The Master said: The holy sages set up the images in order to express their thoughts completely; they devised the hexagrams in order to express the true and the false completely. Then they appended judgments and so could express their words completely.
>
> (They created change and continuity, to show the advantage completely; they urged on, they set in motion, to set forth the spirit completely.)

This section gives in dialogue form, after the manner of the *Lun Yü* [Analects], a judgment on the mode of expression of the Book of Changes. The Master has said that writing never expresses words completely and that words never express thoughts completely. A pupil asks whether one can never gain a clear view of what the sages thought and the Master uses the Book of Changes to show how it may be done. The sages set up the images and hexagrams in order to show the situations, and then appended the words: these, in conjunction with the images, may actually be taken as the complete expression of their thoughts.

The two final statements [in parentheses] have been transposed to this section from some other context, probably because of the similar rhetorical construction (cf. sec. 4, second half, and sec. 7).

> 3. The Creative and the Receptive are the real secret of the Changes. Inasmuch as the Creative and the Receptive present themselves as complete, the changes between them are also posited. If the Creative

and the Receptive were destroyed, there would be nothing by which the changes could be perceived. If there were no more changes to be seen, the effects of the Creative and the Receptive would also gradually cease.

The changes are thought of here as natural processes, practically identical with life. Life depends on the polarity between activity and receptivity. This maintains tension, every adjustment of which manifests itself as a change, a process in life. If this state of tension, this potential, were to cease, there would no longer be a criterion for life—life could no longer express itself. On the other hand, these polar oppositions, these tensions, are constantly being generated anew by the changes inherent in life. If life should cease to express itself, these oppositions would be obliterated by progressive entropy, and the death of the world would ensue.

4. Therefore: What is above form is called tao; what is within form is called tool.

We are shown here that the forces constituting the visible world are transcendent ones. Tao is taken here in the sense of an all-embracing entelechy. It transcends the spatial world, but it acts upon the visible world—by means of the images, i.e., ideas inherent in it, as is set forth more exactly in other passages—and what hereby comes into being are the objects. An object is spatial, that is, defined by its corporeal limits; but it cannot be understood without knowledge of the tao underlying it.

This section, like section 2, has an addition that reappears in large part, with a slight textual variation, in the closing section:

> (That which transforms things and fits them together is called change; that which stimulates them and sets them in motion is called continuity. That which raises them up and sets them forth before all people on earth is called the field of action.)

5. Therefore, with respect to the Images: The holy sages were able to survey all the confused diversities under heaven. They observed forms and phenomena, and made representations of things and their attributes. These were called the Images. The holy sages were able to survey all the movements under heaven. They contemplated the way in which these movements met and became interrelated, to take their course according to eternal laws. Then they appended judgments, to distinguish between the good fortune and misfortune indicated. These were called the Judgments.

This section is a literal repetition of sections 1 and 2 of chapter VIII.

6. The exhaustive presentation of the confused diversities under heaven depends upon the hexagrams. The stimulation of all movements under heaven depends upon the Judgments.

There is some connection between this passage and section 3 of chapter VIII, while the following section contains a parallel to the second half of section 4 above.

7. The transformation of things and the fitting together of them depend upon the changes. Stimulation of them and setting them in motion depend upon continuity. The spirituality and clarity depend upon the right man. Silent fulfillment, confidence that needs no words, depend upon virtuous conduct.

Here, in conclusion, the intermeshing of the Book of Changes and man is set forth. It is only through a living personality that the words of the book ever come fully to life and then exert their influence upon the world.[2]

---

2. This seems to refer to a train of thought the traces of which are scattered through chapter VIII and the present chapter. The problem

PART II

CHAPTER I. *On the Signs and Lines, on Creating and Acting*

1. The eight trigrams are arranged according to completeness: thus the images are contained in them. Thereupon they are doubled: thus the lines are contained in them.

Compare part I, chapter II, section 1. The sequence in the order of completeness is: (1) Ch'ien, (2) Tui, (3) Li, (4) Chên, (5) Sun, (6) K'an, (7) Kên, (8) K'un. The trigrams contain only the images (ideas) of the things they represent. It is only in the hexagrams that the individual lines come into consideration, because it is only in the hexagrams that the relationships of above and below, within and without, appear.

2. The firm and the yielding displace each other, and change is contained therein. The judgments, together with their counsels, are appended, and movement is contained therein.

Compare part I, chapter II, section 2. Change (as well as transformation) appears as a result of the alternation of firm and yielding lines. The judgments give their counsels through the appended oracles—"Good fortune," "Misfortune," and so on.

3. Good fortune and misfortune, remorse and humiliation, come about through movement.

---

is whether, in view of the inadequacy of our means of understanding, a contact transcending the limits of time is possible—whether a later epoch is ever able to understand an earlier one. On the basis of the Book of Changes, the answer is in the affirmative. True enough, speech and writing are imperfect transmitters of thought, but by means of the images—we would say "ideas"—and the stimuli contained in them, a spiritual force is set in motion whose action transcends the limits of time. And when it comes upon the right man, one who has inner relationship with this tao, it can forthwith be taken up by him and awakened anew to life. This is the concept of the supranatural connection between the elect of all the ages.

Compare part I, chapter II, section 3. Good fortune and misfortune, remorse and humiliation, appear only as a result of conduct of a corresponding kind.

> 4. The firm and the yielding stand firm when they are in their original places. Their changes and continuities should correspond with the time.

When the firm lines are in firm places and the yielding lines in yielding places, a state of equilibrium exists. However, this abstract state of equilibrium must yield to change and reorganization when the time demands it. The time, that is, the total situation represented by a hexagram, plays an important role in regard to the positions of the individual lines.

> 5. Good fortune and misfortune take effect through perseverance. The tao of heaven and earth becomes visible through perseverance. The tao of sun and moon becomes bright through perseverance. All movements under heaven become uniform through perseverance.

The secret of action lies in duration. Good fortune and misfortune are slow in the making. Only when a trend is followed continuously do the results of single actions gradually accumulate in such a way that they become manifest as good fortune or misfortune. Similarly, heaven and earth are the results of lasting conditions. In that all clear, luminous forces constantly rise upward, and all that is solid and turbid constantly sinks downward, the cosmos separates itself out of chaos—heaven above and earth below. So it is also as regards the course of the sun and the moon; their states of radiance are results of continuous movements and conditions of equilibrium. Thus all movements and actions continued over a long period of time channel out definite courses, which then become laws. According to this view, natural laws are not abstractions fixed once and for all, but sustained processes in which the character of law appears the more definitely the longer they are in operation.

6. The Creative is decided and therefore shows to men the easy. The Receptive is yielding and therefore shows to men the simple.

The two fundamental principles move according to the requirements of the time, so that they are continuously undergoing change. But the nature of their movements is uniform and consistent. The Creative is always strong, decided, real, hence it meets with no difficulties. It always remains true to itself; hence its effortlessness. Difficulties always indicate vacillation and lack of clarity. In the same way it is the nature of the Receptive to be consistently yielding, to follow the line of least resistance, and therefore to be simple. Complications arise only from an inner conflict of motives.

7. The lines imitate this. The images reproduce this.

Here a definition of the lines and images is given. In Chinese the word for "line" is *hsiao*; "to imitate" is also rendered by *hsiao* (written differently). "Image" and "to reproduce" (in the sense of "to represent") are expressed by *hsiang* (also written differently in each case). The lines imitate in their changes the way in which good fortune and misfortune arise in a movement by reason of its duration. The images reproduce the way in which all the changes and interrelations of the firm and the yielding issue in the easy and the simple.

8. The lines and images move within, and good fortune and misfortune reveal themselves without. The work and the field of action reveal themselves in the changes. The feelings of the holy sages reveal themselves in the judgments.

The movements of the lines and images, and of the infinitesimal germs of events symbolized by them, are invisible, but their results manifest themselves in the visible world as good fortune or misfortune. So also the changes pertaining to the work and the field of action are invisible, but are revealed by the words of the judgments.

9. It is the great virtue of heaven and earth to bestow life. It is the great treasure of the holy sage to stand in the right place.

How does one safeguard this place? Through men.[1] By what are men gathered together? Through goods. Justice means restraining men from wrongdoing by regulation of goods and by rectification of judgments.

Here the connection between the three powers is shown. Heaven and earth bestow life. The holy sage is guided by the same principle; but to carry it out he must have the position of a ruler. This position is safeguarded by the men whom he gathers under him. Men are gathered together by means of goods. The means by which goods are administered, and defended against wrong, is justice.

This presents a theory of society, based on cosmic principles, that corresponds with the views of the Confucian school.

Some commentators wish to take this section as an introduction to the next chapter. This has a certain justification, inasmuch as the next chapter gives a survey of the development of civilization, with the Book of Changes as a basis.

---

1. The reading "kindness" instead of "men" is contradicted by the context.

CHAPTER II. *History of Civilization*[1]

1. When in early antiquity Pao Hsi[2] ruled the world, he looked upward and contemplated the images in the heavens; he looked downward and contemplated the patterns on earth. He contemplated the markings of birds and beasts and the adaptations to the regions. He proceeded directly from himself and in-

---

1. [Many of the citations from the Great Commentary appearing in bk. III under the heading "Appended Judgments" are from this chapter.]

2. [Same as Fu Hsi.]

directly from objects. Thus he invented the eight trigrams in order to enter into connection with the virtues of the light of the gods and to regulate the conditions of all beings.

The *Pai Hu T'ung*[3] describes the primitive condition of human society as follows:

In the beginning there was as yet no moral nor social order. Men knew their mothers only, not their fathers. When hungry, they searched for food; when satisfied, they threw away the remnants. They devoured their food hide and hair, drank the blood, and clad themselves in skins and rushes. Then came Fu Hsi and looked upward and contemplated the images in the heavens, and looked downward and contemplated the occurrences on earth. He united man and wife, regulated the five stages of change, and laid down the laws of humanity. He devised the eight trigrams, in order to gain mastery over the world.

The name of the mythical founder of civilization is written in various ways; its meaning seems to point to a hunter or an inventor of cooking. There is a difference of opinion as to whether the sixty-four hexagrams or only the eight trigrams are to be ascribed to him. As he himself is a mythical personality, the dispute may rest where it stands. It would seem to be certain that the sixty-four hexagrams were already in use in the time of King Wên.

2. He made knotted cords and used them for nets and baskets in hunting and fishing. He probably took this from the hexagram of THE CLINGING.

This chapter tells us how all the appurtenances of civilization came into existence as reproductions of ideal, archetypal images. In a certain sense this idea contains a truth. Every invention comes into being as an image in the mind of the inventor before it makes its appearance in the phenomenal world as a tool, a finished thing. Since, according to the school represented by the *Hsi Tz'u*, the sixty-four hexagrams present,

---

3. [Written in the Han period by Pan Ku (A.D. 32–92).]

in a mysterious way, images paralleling nature, an attempt can be made here to derive from them the inventions of man that have led to the development of civilization. However, this must be understood not in the sense that the inventors simply took the hexagrams of the book and made their inventions in accordance with them, but rather in the sense that out of the relationships represented by the hexagrams the inventions took shape in the minds of their originators.

A net consists of meshes, empty within and surrounded by threads without. The hexagram Li, THE CLINGING (30), represents a combination of meshes of this sort. Furthermore, the written character means "to cling to" or "to be caught on something." For example, in the Book of Songs [4] it is frequently said that the wild goose or the pheasant was caught in the net (*li*).

> 3. When Pao Hsi's clan was gone, there sprang up the clan of the Divine Husbandman.[5] He split a piece of wood for a plowshare and bent a piece of wood for the plow handle, and taught the whole world the advantage of laying open the earth with a plow. He probably took this from the hexagram of INCREASE.

The primitive plow consisted of a bent pole with a pointed stick fastened on in front for scratching the earth. The advantage of this method over hoeing was that draft animals could be used and part of the work shifted to oxen.

The hexagram I, INCREASE (42), consists of the two trigrams Sun and Chên, both associated with wood. Sun means

---

4. [*Shih Ching*, an anthology of poems said to have been arranged by Confucius. The latest of the poems belong to the year 585 B.C.; the oldest are earlier by many centuries.]

5. [Shên Nung, who is said to have taught the people agriculture.]

penetration, Chên movement. The nuclear trigrams[6] are Kên and K'un, both associated with the earth. This led to the idea of constructing a wooden instrument that would penetrate the earth and when moved forward would turn up the soil.

4. When the sun stood at midday, he held a market. He caused the people of the earth to come together and collected the wares of the earth. They exchanged these with one another, then returned home, and each thing found its place. Probably he took this from the hexagram of BITING THROUGH.

The hexagram Shih Ho, BITING THROUGH (21), consists of Li, the sun, above and Chên, movement, below. Chên also means a great road, while the upper nuclear trigram K'an means flowing water, and the lower, Kên, small paths. Thus the connotation is of movement under the sun, a streaming together. This is hardly enough to convey the idea of a market, but the words *shih ho* when written differently can also mean food and merchandise, and the market might be suggested in this way. Evidently the hexagram formerly had the secondary meaning of market (cf. the explanation of this hexagram in bk. I).

5. When the clan of the Divine Husbandman was gone, there sprang up the clans of the Yellow Emperor, of Yao, and of Shun.[7] They brought continuity into their alterations, so that the people did not grow weary. They were divine in the transformations they wrought, so that the people were content. When one change had run its course, they altered. (Through alteration they achieved continuity.)

6. [For explanation of nuclear trigrams, see p. 358.]
7. [Yao, Shun, and Yü are the three rulers held up as models by Confucius.]

Through continuity they achieved duration. Therefore: "They were blessed by heaven. Good fortune.
Nothing that does not further."

The Yellow Emperor, Yao, and Shun allowed the
upper and lower garments to hang down, and the
world was in order. They probably took this from the
hexagrams of THE CREATIVE and THE RECEPTIVE.

In this section two different strata are to be distinguished. The
closing paragraph seems to be the older stratum. The introduction of clothes is depicted. Accordingly, Chêng K'ang Ch'êng[8]
says: "Heaven is blue-black, the earth is yellow; therefore
they made the upper garments dark blue and the lower garments yellow."

Allowing the garments to hang down was later taken to
mean that the Yellow Emperor, Yao, and Shun sat quietly
without stirring, and as a result of their inaction things automatically righted themselves. Then, from previously known
material, there was appended a description of their cultural
activity and the blessing that grew out of it. The parenthetic
sentence seems in turn to be a later addition to this description.
The meaning of the activity of the three rulers is that they
constantly carried out timely reforms.

6. They scooped out tree trunks for boats and they
hardened wood in the fire to make oars. The advantage of boats and oars lay in providing means of communication. (They reached distant parts, in order to
benefit the whole world.) They probably took this
from the hexagram of DISPERSION.

The sentence in parentheses has been questioned by Chu Hsi.
The hexagram Huan, DISPERSION (59), consists of the trigram
Sun, wood, over K'an, water. That is why it is said in the

8. [Chêng Hsüan, A.D. 127–200.]

Judgment, "It furthers one to cross the great water," and in the Commentary on the Decision, "To rely on wood is productive of merit." A boat as a means of communication across rivers and for travel to distant places is represented here. Wood over water—this is the meaning of the primary trigrams. The nuclear trigrams Kên and Chên mean large and small roads.

7. They tamed the ox and yoked the horse. Thus heavy loads could be transported and distant regions reached, for the benefit of the world. They probably took this from the hexagram of FOLLOWING.

The hexagram Sui, FOLLOWING (17), consists of Tui, liveliness, in front and Chên, movement, behind—an image of the way in which the ox and horse go ahead and the wagon moves along behind. Oxen were for heavy carts, horses for fast carriages and war chariots. The use of horses for riding was unknown to China in the earliest period.

8. They introduced double gates and night watchmen with clappers, in order to deal with robbers. They probably took this from the hexagram of EN-THUSIASM.

The hexagram Yü, ENTHUSIASM (16), consists of the trigram Chên, movement, above and K'un, the earth, below. The nuclear trigrams are K'an, danger, and Kên, mountain. K'un symbolizes a closed door, while Kên likewise means a door; hence the double gates. K'an means thief. Beyond the gates, movement, with wood (Chên) in the hand (Kên), serves as a preparation (*yü* also means preparation) against the thief.

9. They split wood and made a pestle of it. They made a hollow in the ground for a mortar. The use of the mortar and pestle was of benefit to all man-

kind. They probably took this from the hexagram of
PREPONDERANCE OF THE SMALL.

The hexagram Hsiao Kuo, PREPONDERANCE OF THE SMALL
(62), is composed of Chên, movement, wood, above and Kên,
Keeping Still, stone, below. Kuo also means transition. The
mortar was the primitive form of the mill, and signifies the
transition from eating whole grain to baking.

> 10. They strung a piece of wood for a bow and hard-
> ened pieces of wood in the fire for arrows. The use of
> bow and arrow is to keep the world in fear. They
> probably took this from the hexagram of OPPO-
> SITION.

The hexagram K'uei, OPPOSITION (38), consists of Li, the
Clinging, above and Tui, the Joyous, below. The nuclear trigrams are K'an, danger, and, again, Li. The whole hexagram
indicates strife. Li is the sun, which sends arrows from afar.
Li means weapons, K'an danger. The danger is hedged around
by weapons, therefore one is not afraid.

> 11. In primitive times people dwelt in caves and
> lived in forests. The holy men of a later time made
> the change to buildings. At the top was a ridgepole,
> and sloping down from it there was a roof, to keep off
> wind and rain. They probably took this from the
> hexagram of THE POWER OF THE GREAT.

The hexagram Ta Chuang, THE POWER OF THE GREAT (34),
has Chên, thunder, above; the upper nuclear trigram Tui,
lake, is at the top of Ch'ien, heaven, which is the lower nuclear
trigram. The lower primary trigram is also Ch'ien, heaven,

the atmosphere. Thus the hexagram as a whole means a heaven, a strong, protected space with thunder and rain above it. The trigram Chên also means wood, and as the eldest son it means the ridgepole at the top. The two yielding lines at the top are then thought of as the sloping roof.

12. In primitive times the dead were buried by covering them thickly with brushwood and placing them in the open country, without burial mound or grove of trees. The period of mourning had no definite duration. The holy men of a later time introduced inner and outer coffins instead. They probably took this from the hexagram of PREPONDERANCE OF THE GREAT.

The hexagram Ta Kuo, PREPONDERANCE OF THE GREAT (28), consists of the trigram Tui, the lake, above and Sun, wood, penetration, below. Forming the nuclear trigrams in the middle is Ch'ien, heaven, doubled. The hexagram must be taken as a whole; the two yin lines above and below mean the earth, within which the double coffin, represented by the double heaven, is inclosed. Entering (Sun) their last resting place in this way, the dead are made glad (Tui). Here we have a link with ancestor worship.

13. In primitive times people knotted cords in order to govern. The holy men of a later age introduced written documents instead, as a means of governing the various officials and supervising the people. They probably took this from the hexagram of BREAK-THROUGH.

The hexagram Kuai, BREAK-THROUGH (43), has Tui, words, above and Ch'ien, strength, below. It means giving permanence to words. The notch at the top also indicates the form of the oldest documents: cut in wood, they consisted of two halves that fitted into each other when held together. As a rule the ancient writings were scratched on tablets of smoothed bamboo. Here the significance of writing in the organization of a large community is emphasized.

NOTE. In its main features the sketch of the development of civilization given in this chapter corresponds to an extraordinary degree with our own ideas. The fundamental thought, that all institutions are based on the development of definite ideas, is likewise undoubtedly correct. It is not always easy to recognize such ideas in the complexes of ideas presented by the hexagrams, nor is it improbable that there were once certain connections that are now obliterated. There are indications that in the period preceding that of the Chou dynasty the hexagrams had meanings different from those which are traditional today. Possibly this chapter affords insight into these earliest meanings. That still another change in meaning took place later becomes evident when we compare the Judgments with the Images.

CHAPTER III. *On the Structure of the Hexagrams*

1. Thus the Book of Changes consists of images. The images are reproductions.

The hexagrams are reproductions of conditions in the heavens and on earth. Therefore they are to be applied productively; they have creative power, so to speak, in the realm of ideas, as explained above.

2. The decisions provide the material.

The Commentary on the Decision [i.e., on the Judgment],[1] which is probably what is meant here, presents the material out of which each hexagram, taken as a whole, is constructed. Thus it describes the situation as such before it undergoes change. Naturally this also applies to the Judgment itself.

3. The lines are imitations of movements on earth.

1. [First Wing, Second Wing.]

Here the lines are equivalent to the judgments appended to them; the judgments apply in the case of lines that move, that is, when they are nines or sixes. They reflect the changes within the individual situations.

> 4. Thus do good fortune and misfortune arise, and remorse and humiliation appear.

This movement reveals the direction that events are taking, and warnings or confirmations are added.

CHAPTER IV. *On the Nature of the Trigrams*

> 1. The light trigrams have more dark lines, the dark trigrams have more light lines.

The "light" trigrams are the three sons, Chên, ☳, K'an, ☵, and Kên, ☶, each of which consists of two dark lines and one light line. The "dark" trigrams are the three daughters, Sun, ☴, Li, ☲, and Tui, ☱, each of which consists of two light lines and one dark line.

> 2. What is the reason for this? The light trigrams are uneven, the dark trigrams are even.

The light trigrams are made up of the lines 7+8+8, or 7+6+8, or 7+6+6, or 9+8+8, or 9+6+6, or 9+6+8.[1] Using the relevant numbers, the numerical values of the lines in the dark trigrams can be found in the same way. Hence the sum of the values of the lines in light trigrams is always an uneven number, and the line representing the uneven number [an undivided line] is therefore the determinant of the light trigram. In the case of dark trigrams, the reverse is true.

> 3. What is their nature and how do they act? The light trigrams have one ruler and two subjects. They show the way of the superior man. The dark trigrams have two rulers and one subject. This is the way of the inferior man.

---

1. [See p. 722 for numerical values.]

Where one alone rules, unity is present, whereas when one person must serve two masters, nothing good can come of it. This truth is here more or less accidentally linked with the structure of the trigrams.

CHAPTER V. *Explanation of Certain Lines*

1. In the Changes it is said: "If a man is agitated in mind, and his thoughts go hither and thither, only those friends on whom he fixes his conscious thoughts will follow."

The Master said: What need has nature of thought and care? In nature all things return to their common source and are distributed along different paths; through one action, the fruits of a hundred thoughts are realized. What need has nature of thought, of care?

2. When the sun goes, the moon comes; when the moon goes, the sun comes. Sun and moon alternate; thus light comes into existence. When cold goes, heat comes; when heat goes, cold comes. Cold and heat alternate, and thus the year completes itself. The past contracts. The future expands. Contraction and expansion act upon each other; hereby arises that which furthers.

3. The measuring worm draws itself together when it wants to stretch out. Dragons and snakes hibernate in order to preserve life. Thus the penetration of a germinal thought into the mind promotes the working of the mind. When this working furthers and brings peace to life, it elevates a man's nature.

4. Whatever goes beyond this indeed transcends all knowledge. When a man comprehends the divine and understands the transformations, he lifts his nature to the level of the miraculous.

In this explanation of the nine in the fourth place in hexagram 31, Hsien, INFLUENCE (bk. III), a theory of the power of the unconscious is given. Conscious influences are always merely limited ones, because they are brought about by intention. Nature knows no intentions; this is why everything in nature is so great. It is owing to the underlying unity of nature that all its thousand ways lead to a goal so perfect that it seems to have been planned beforehand down to the last detail.

Then, in connection with the course of the day and the year, we are shown how past and future flow into each other, how contraction and expansion are the two movements through which the past prepares the future and the future unfolds the past.

In the two succeeding sections the same thought is applied to the man who, through supreme concentration, so intensifies and strengthens his inner being that mysterious autonomous currents of power emanate from him: thus the effects he creates proceed from his unconscious and mysteriously affect the unconscious in others, attaining such breadth and depth of influence that they transcend the individual sphere and enter the realm of cosmic phenomena.

> 5. In the Changes it is said: "A man permits himself to be oppressed by stone, and leans on thorns and thistles. He enters his house and does not see his wife. Misfortune."
>
> The Master said: If a man permits himself to be oppressed by something that ought not to oppress him, his name will certainly be disgraced. If he leans on things upon which one cannot lean, his life will certainly be endangered. For him who is in disgrace and danger, the hour of death draws near; how can he then still see his wife?

This is an example of an unfavorable pronouncement. Compare the explanation of the six in the third place in hexagram 47, K'un, OPPRESSION (bk. I).

> 6. In the Changes it is said: "The prince shoots at a

hawk on a high wall. He kills it. Everything serves to further."

The Master said: The hawk is the object of the hunt; bow and arrow are the tools and means. The marksman is man (who must make proper use of the means to his end). The superior man contains the means in his own person. He bides his time and then acts. Why then should not everything go well? He acts and is free. Therefore all he has to do is to go forth, and he takes his quarry. This is how a man fares who acts after he has made ready the means.

This is an example of a favorable line. Compare the explanation of the six at the top in hexagram 40, Hsieh, DELIVERANCE (bk. I).

7. The Master said: The inferior man is not ashamed of unkindness and does not shrink from injustice. If no advantage beckons he makes no effort. If he is not intimidated he does not improve himself, but if he is made to behave correctly in small matters he is careful in large ones. This is fortunate for the inferior man. This is what is meant when it is said in the Book of Changes: "His feet are fastened in the stocks, so that his toes disappear. No blame."

Here we have an example of a line that leads to the good through remorse. Compare the explanation of the nine at the beginning in hexagram 21, Shih Ho, BITING THROUGH (bk. I).

8. If good does not accumulate, it is not enough to make a name for a man. If evil does not accumulate, it is not strong enough to destroy a man. Therefore the inferior man thinks to himself, "Goodness in small things has no value," and so neglects it. He thinks, "Small sins do no harm," and so does not give them up. Thus his sins accumulate until they

can no longer be covered up, and his guilt becomes so great that it can no longer be wiped out. In the Book of Changes it is said: "His neck is fastened in the wooden cangue, so that his ears disappear. Misfortune."

This is an example of a line showing that misfortune follows hard upon humiliation. Compare the explanation of the nine at the top in hexagram 21, Shih Ho, BITING THROUGH (bk. I).

9. The Master said: Danger arises when a man feels secure in his position. Destruction threatens when a man seeks to preserve his worldly estate. Confusion develops when a man has put everything in order. Therefore the superior man does not forget danger in his security, nor ruin when he is well established, nor confusion when his affairs are in order. In this way he gains personal safety and is able to protect the empire. In the Book of Changes it is said: " 'What if it should fail, what if it should fail?' In this way he ties it to a cluster of mulberry shoots."

This is an example of a line showing how one remains free of blame and thus attains success. See the explanation of the nine in the fifth place in hexagram 12, P'i, STANDSTILL (bk. I).

10. The Master said: Weak character coupled with honored place, meager knowledge with large plans, limited powers with heavy responsibility, will seldom escape disaster. In the Changes it is said: "The legs of the *ting* are broken. The prince's meal is spilled, and his person is soiled. Misfortune." This is said of someone not equal to his task.

This is an example of a line showing that one meets with misfortune through being inadequate to the situation. Compare the explanation of the nine in the fourth place in hexagram 50, Ting, THE CALDRON (bk. I).

11. The Master said: To know the seeds, that is divine indeed. In his association with those above him, the superior man does not flatter. In his association with those beneath him, he is not arrogant. For he knows the seeds. The seeds are the first imperceptible beginning of movement, the first trace of good fortune (or misfortune) that shows itself. The superior man perceives the seeds and immediately takes action. He does not wait even a whole day. In the Changes it is said: "Firm as a rock. Not a whole day. Perseverance brings good fortune."

Firm as a rock, what need of a whole day?

The judgment can be known.

The superior man knows what is hidden and what is evident.

He knows weakness, he knows strength as well.

Hence the myriads look up to him.

This is an example of a line showing that foreknowledge enables one to escape misfortune in good time. Compare the explanation of the six in the second place in hexagram 16, Yü, ENTHUSIASM (bk. I).

12. The Master said: Yen Hui is one who will surely attain it. If he has a fault, he never fails to recognize it; having recognized it, he never commits the error a second time. In the Changes it is said: "Return from a short distance. No need for remorse. Great good fortune."

This is an example of a line showing that one can learn from experience. Yen Hui was the favorite disciple of Confucius. It is said in the Analects too that he never committed the same error twice. See the explanation of the nine at the beginning in hexagram 24, Fu, RETURN (bk. III).

13. The Master said: Heaven and earth come together, and all things take shape and find form.

Male and female mix their seed, and all creatures take shape and are born. In the Changes it is said: "When three people journey together, their number decreases by one. When one man journeys alone, he finds a companion."

This is an example of a line that is favorable by reason of unity. Compare the explanation of the six in the third place in hexagram 41, Sun, DECREASE (bk. III).

14. The Master said: The superior man sets his person at rest before he moves; he composes his mind before he speaks; he makes his relations firm before he asks for something. By attending to these three matters, the superior man gains complete security. But if a man is brusque in his movements, others will not co-operate. If he is agitated in his words, they awaken no echo in others. If he asks for something without having first established relations, it will not be given to him. If no one is with him, those who would harm him draw near. In the Changes it is said: "He brings increase to no one. Indeed, someone even strikes him. He does not keep his heart constantly steady. Misfortune."

This is an example of a line showing that everything depends on proper preparation. Compare the explanation of the nine at the top in hexagram 42, I, INCREASE (bk. I).

CHAPTER VI. *On the Nature of the Book of Changes in General*

1. The Master said: The Creative and the Receptive are indeed the gateway to the Changes. The Creative is the representative of light things and the Receptive of dark things. In that the natures of the dark

and the light are joined, the firm and the yielding receive form. Thus do the relationships of heaven and earth take shape, and we enter into relation with the nature of the light of the gods.

Following out what has been said in part I, chapter XII, section 3, the method of the Book of Changes is presented here. The first two trigrams, the Creative and the Receptive, are shown as representatives of the two polar primal forces. The aim is to explain that matter is the product of energy. The light and the dark are energies. The interaction of these forces gives rise to matter—that is, the firm and the yielding. Matter makes up the form, the body, of all beings in heaven and on earth, but it is always energy that keeps it in motion. The important thing is to maintain connection with these divine forces of light.

2. The names employed are manifold but not superfluous. When we examine their kinds, thoughts about the decline of an era come to mind.

The names of the sixty-four hexagrams are diverse, but they all keep within the sphere of the necessary. Actual situations, just as life brings them, are described. The situations throughout are of such a nature as to make it plain that the reference is to an era of decline, the aim being to provide the means of reconstruction. It is pointed out that the body of ideas in the hexagrams stems from a time already confronted with phenomena of decline.

3. The Changes illumine the past and interpret the future. They disclose that which is hidden and open that which is dark. They distinguish things by means of suitable names. Then, when the right words and decisive judgments are added, everything is complete.

The wording of this section, and indeed of the whole of this chapter, seems to be rather uncertain, but the general meaning is easy to understand. Here again the various connotations of the Book of Changes are pointed out: hidden things are revealed in time and space, first symbolically by means of names and relationships, then explicitly by means of the judgments.

> 4. The names employed sound unimportant, but the possibilities of application are great. The meanings are far-reaching, the judgments are well ordered. The words are roundabout but they hit the mark. Things are openly set forth, but they contain also a deeper secret. This is why in doubtful cases they may serve to guide the conduct of men and thus to show the requital for reaching or for missing the goal.

The abstract, allegorical content of the hexagrams is here pointed out. The hexagrams permit of a general extension to all sorts of situations, because they present nothing but the laws that pertain to various complexes of conditions.

CHAPTER VII. *The Relation of Certain Hexagrams to Character Formation*

> 1. The Changes came into use in the period of middle antiquity. Those who composed the Changes had great care and sorrow.

This passage refers to King Wên and his son, the Duke of Chou, who both lived through very difficult times. The writer of the lines quoted above feels himself in sympathy with them in this respect, for he too can do nothing more than preserve for posterity the framework of a perishing civilization.

> 2. Thus the hexagram of TREADING shows the basis of character. MODESTY shows the handle of character; RETURN, the stem of character. DURATION brings about firmness of character; DECREASE, cultivation of character; INCREASE, fullness of character; OPPRESSION, the test of character; THE WELL, the field of character; THE GENTLE, the exercise of character.

3. The hexagram of TREADING is harmonious and attains its goal. MODESTY gives honor and shines forth. RETURN is small, yet different from external things. DURATION shows manifold experiences without satiety. DECREASE shows first what is difficult and then what is easy. INCREASE shows the growth of fullness without artifices. OPPRESSION leads to perplexity and thereby to success. THE WELL abides in its place, yet has influence on other things. Through THE GENTLE one is able to weigh things and remain hidden.

4. TREADING brings about harmonious conduct. MODESTY serves to regulate the mores. RETURN leads to self-knowledge. DURATION brings about unity of character. DECREASE keeps harm away. INCREASE furthers what is useful. Through OPPRESSION one learns to lessen one's rancor. THE WELL brings about discrimination as to what is right. Through THE GENTLE one is able to take special circumstances into account.[1]

Here nine hexagrams are used to show the development of character. First the relations of the hexagrams to character are given, then the material of the hexagrams, and finally their effect. The movement is from within outward. What is wrought in the depths of the heart becomes outwardly visible in its effects. The nine hexagrams are as follows:

1. Lü, TREADING (10). This hexagram deals with the rules of good conduct, compliance with which is a prerequisite of character formation. This good conduct is harmonious—in conformity with the trigram Tui, the Joyous, which is inside —and hence attains its goal even under difficult circumstances ("treading upon the tail of the tiger"). Thus it brings about

---

1. [These characterizations are given again with the respective hexagrams in bk. III, under the heading "Appended Judgments."]

those harmonious forms which are a prerequisite of outward behavior.

2. Ch'ien, MODESTY (15). This hexagram shows the attitude that is necessary before character formation can be undertaken. Modesty (mountain under the earth) honors others and thereby attains honor for itself; it regulates human intercourse in such a way that friendliness evokes friendliness. To the outward forms it adds the right attitude of mind as content.

3. Fu, RETURN (24). This hexagram is characterized by the fact that a light line returns from below and moves upward. It means the root and stem of character. The good that shows itself below is at first quite insignificant, but it is strong enough to be able constantly to prevail in its own unique character against any temptation of the surroundings. In the sense of return, it also suggests lasting reform following upon errors committed, and the self-examination and self-knowledge necessary for this.

4. Hêng, DURATION (32). This hexagram brings about firmness of character in the frame of time. It shows wind and thunder constantly together; hence there are manifold movements and experiences, from which fixed rules are derived, so that a unified character results.

5. Sun, DECREASE (41). This hexagram shows a decrease in influence of the lower faculties, the untamed instincts, in favor of the higher life of the mind. Here we have the essence of character training. The hexagram shows first the difficult thing—the taming of the instincts—then the easy phase, when character is under control; thus harm is kept away.

6. I, INCREASE (42). This hexagram gives needed fullness to character. Mere asceticism is not enough to make a good character: greatness is also needed. Thus INCREASE shows an organic growth of personality that is not artificial and hence furthers what is useful.

7. K'un, OPPRESSION (47). This hexagram leads the individual of developed character finally into the field where he must prove himself. Difficulties and obstacles arise; these must be overcome, yet they often prove insuperable. He sees himself confronted by bounds that he cannot set aside and that can be surmounted only by recognizing them for what they are. In thus recognizing as fate the things that must be so taken, one

ceases to hate adversity—of what use would it be to storm against fate—and through this lessening of resentment, character is purified and advances to a higher level.

8. Ching, THE WELL (48). This hexagram represents a wellspring, which, though fixed in one spot, dispenses blessing far and wide and so makes its influence far-reaching. This shows the field in which character can take effect. We perceive the profound influence emanating from a richly endowed and generous personality, an influence that is not any the less because the person exerting it keeps in the background. The hexagram shows what is right, and thus makes it possible for the right to take effect.

9. Sun, THE GENTLE, THE PENETRATING (57). This hexagram gives the proper flexibility of character. What is needed is not rigidity that holds fast to established principles and is in reality mere pedantry, but mobility: thus one weighs things and penetrates to the needs of the time without exposing oneself to attack, so learning to take circumstances into account and to preserve a strong unity of character along with intelligent versatility.

CHAPTER VIII. *On the Use of the Book of Changes: The Lines*

1. The Changes is a book
   From which one may not hold aloof.
   Its tao is forever changing—
   Alteration, movement without rest,
   Flowing through the six empty places;
   Rising and sinking without fixed law,
   Firm and yielding transform each other.
   They cannot be confined within a rule;
   It is only change that is at work here.

2. They move inward and outward according to
      fixed rhythms.
   Without or within, they teach caution.

3. They also show care and sorrow and their causes.
Though you have no teacher,
Approach them as you would your parents.

4. First take up the words,
Ponder their meaning,
Then the fixed rules reveal themselves.
But if you are not the right man,
The meaning will not manifest itself to you.

In half rhythmic and half rhymed prose, we are here admonished to study the Book of Changes diligently. It is pointed out with praise that continuous change is the rule of the book. In conclusion, attention is called to the fact that an innate capacity is essential to an understanding of the book, otherwise it will remain locked as if with seven seals. If the person consulting the oracle is not in contact with tao, he does not receive an intelligible answer, since it would be of no avail.

CHAPTER IX. *The Lines* (continued)

1. The Changes is a book whose hexagrams begin with the first line and are summed up in the last. The lines are the essential material. The six lines are interspersed according to the meaning belonging to them at the time.

This section discusses the relation of the lines to the hexagram as a whole. With the individual lines as the material, the hexagram is built from the bottom upward. The individual lines have within this sequence the meaning imparted to them by force of the particular situation.

2. The beginning line is difficult to understand. The top line is easy to understand. For they stand in the relationship of cause and effect. The judgment on

the first line is tentative, but at the last line everything has attained completion.

Here in the first instance the reciprocal relationship between
the first and the top line is stated. Both stand, as it were, outside the essential hexagram and the nuclear trigrams. At the
first line the action is only just beginning to develop, and at
the last it is concluded.

3. But if one wishes to explore things in their manifold gradation, and their qualities as well, and to
discriminate between right and wrong, it cannot be
done completely without the middle lines.

The "things in their manifold gradation" result from the
manifold gradation of the places. Their qualities inhere in
their firm or their yielding character. Right and wrong are
distinguishable according to whether or not the lines occupy
the places appropriate to them in view of the meaning of the
time.

4. Yes, even that which is most important in regard
to surviving or perishing, in regard to good fortune
or misfortune, can be known in the course of time.
The man of knowledge contemplates the judgment
on the decision, and thus he can think out for himself the greater part.

In the Commentary on the Decision the rulers of the hexagrams are always indicated. By pondering the relationships of
the other lines to these rulers, one can gain an approximate
idea of their position and meaning in the hexagram as a whole.

5. The second and the fourth place correspond in
their work but are differentiated by their positions.
They do not correspond as regards the degree to
which they are good. The second is usually praised,
the fourth is usually warned, because it stands near
the ruler. The meaning of the yielding is that it is
not favorable for it to be far away. The important

thing, however, is to remain without blame; its expression consists in being yielding and central.

The fifth place is that of the ruler. The second and the fourth place are those of officials. The second, which stands in the relationship of correspondence to the fifth (each being centrally placed, the former in the inner, the latter in the outer trigram), is the official who, far from the court, is attending to his work in the country. The fourth place is that of the minister. Therefore the two places, both dark—that is, dependent—are not equally good, despite their correspondence with respect to their work. The second usually carries a favorable judgment, the fourth a warning one: because it is too close to the prince, it must be doubly cautious. Now it is not in the nature of the yielding to prosper when it is far from the firm, hence one would expect the second place to be less favorable than the fourth. However, an important factor is that it is centrally placed and so remains without blame.

> 6. The third and the fifth place correspond in their work but are differentiated by their positions. The third usually has misfortune, the fifth usually has merit, because they are graded according to rank. The weaker is endangered, the stronger has victory.

The fifth place is that of the ruler. The third, as the top place of the inner [lower] trigram, has at least a limited power. But it is not central; it is in an insecure position on the boundary between two trigrams. Therein, as well as in its lower rank, lie elements of weakness that in most situations show the place to be endangered. The fifth place is central and strong, the ruler of the hexagram; these are all elements of strength, promising victory.

CHAPTER X. *The Lines* (continued)

1. The Changes is a book vast and great, in which everything is completely contained. The tao of heaven is in it, the tao of the earth is in it, and the

tao of man is in it. It combines these three primal powers and doubles them; that is why there are six lines. The six lines are nothing other than the ways (tao) of the three primal powers.

2. The Way has changes and movements. Therefore the lines are called changing lines. The lines have gradations, therefore they represent things. Things are diverse; this gives rise to line characteristics. The line characteristics do not always correspond. From this arise good fortune and misfortune.

Here the places are divided according to the three primal powers. The first and the second line are the places of the earth, the third and the fourth those of man, and the fifth and the top line those of heaven; this division comes into consideration with the very first hexagram, THE CREATIVE. According to whether the lines of the different gradations are appropriate to the places, conclusions are drawn as to whether they mean good fortune or misfortune. The Chinese character for "line," *hsiao*, when written differently may also mean "to imitate." This is why the lines are here called "changing lines"—that is, lines oriented to the pattern of tao. The written character for *hsiao* consists of two sets of crossed lines, suggesting the crossing of yang and yin (爻).

CHAPTER XI. *The Value of Caution as a Teaching of the Book of Changes*

The time at which the Changes came to the fore was that in which the house of Yin came to an end and the way of the house of Chou was rising, that is, the time when King Wên and the tyrant Chou Hsin were pitted against each other.[1]

This is why the judgments of the book so fre-

---

1. [About the middle of the twelfth century B.C., according to traditional chronology.]

quently warn against danger. He who is conscious of danger creates peace for himself; he who takes things lightly creates his own downfall. The tao of this book is great. It omits none of the hundred things. It is concerned about beginning and end, and it is encompassed in the words "without blame." This is the tao of the Changes.

King Wên, the founder of the Chou dynasty, was held captive by the last ruler of the Yin dynasty, the tyrant Chou Hsin. He is said to have composed the judgments on the different hexagrams during his captivity. Because of the danger of his situation, all these judgments emanate from a caution that is intent on remaining without blame and thus attains success.

CHAPTER XII. *Summary*

1. The Creative is the strongest of all things in the world. The expression of its nature is invariably the easy, in order thus to master the dangerous. The Receptive is the most devoted of all things in the world. The expression of its nature is invariably simple, in order thus to master the obstructive.

The two cardinal principles of the Book of Changes, the Creative and the Receptive, are here once more presented in their essential features. The Creative is represented as strength, to which everything is easy, but which remains conscious of the danger involved in working from above downward, and thus masters the danger. The Receptive is represented as devotion, which therefore acts simply, but which is conscious of the obstructions inherent in working from below upward, and hence masters these obstructions.

2. To be able to preserve joyousness of heart and yet to be concerned in thought: in this way we can determine good fortune and misfortune on earth, and bring to perfection everything on earth.

In the text there appear next to the expression, "to be concerned in thought," two other characters that Chu Hsi has quite correctly eliminated as later additions. Joyousness of heart is the way of the Creative. To be concerned in thought is the way of the Receptive. Through joyousness one gains an over-all view of good fortune and misfortune, through concern one attains the possibility of perfection.

> 3. Therefore: The changes and transformations refer to action. Beneficent deeds have good auguries. Hence the images help us to know the things, and the oracle helps us to know the future.

The changes refer to action. Hence the images of the Book of Changes are of such sort that one can act in accordance with the changes and know reality (cf. also chap. II above, where inventions are traced to the images). Events tend toward good fortune or misfortune, which are expressed in omens. In that the Book of Changes interprets these omens, the future becomes clear.

> 4. Heaven and earth determine the places. The holy sages fulfill the possibilities of the places. Through the thoughts of men and the thoughts of spirits, the people are enabled to participate in these possibilities.

Heaven and earth determine the places and thereby the possibilities. The sages make these possibilities into reality, and through the collaboration of the thoughts of spirits and of men in the Book of Changes, it becomes possible to extend the blessings of culture to the people as well.

> 5. The eight trigrams point the way by means of their images; the words accompanying the lines, and the decisions, speak according to the circumstances. In that the firm and the yielding are interspersed, good fortune and misfortune can be discerned.

> 6. Changes and movements are judged according to the furtherance (that they bring). Good fortune and

misfortune change according to the conditions. Therefore: Love and hate combat each other, and good fortune and misfortune result therefrom. The far and the near injure each other, and remorse and humiliation result therefrom. The true and the false influence each other, and advantage and injury result therefrom. In all the situations of the Book of Changes it is thus: When closely related things do not harmonize, misfortune is the result: this gives rise to injury, remorse, and humiliation.

The close relationships between the lines are those of correspondence and of holding together.[1] According to whether the lines attract or repel one another, good fortune or misfortune ensues, in all the gradations possible in each case.

7. The words of a man who plans revolt are confused. The words of a man who entertains doubt in his inmost heart are ramified. The words of men of good fortune are few. Excited men use many words. Slanderers of good men are roundabout in their words. The words of a man who has lost his standpoint are twisted.

This passage summarizes the effects of states of mind on verbal expression. It becomes plain therefrom that the authors of the Book of Changes, who are so sparing of words, belong in the category of men of good fortune.

---

1. [See p. 361.]

The Structure of the Hexagrams

1. GENERAL CONSIDERATIONS

The foregoing supplies most of what is necessary for an understanding of the hexagrams. Here, however, there follows a summary regarding their structure. This will enable the reader to perceive why the hexagrams have precisely the meanings given them, why the lines have the often seemingly fantastic text that is appended to them—indicating, by means of allegory, what position the line holds in the total situation of the hexagram, and to what degree it therefore signifies good fortune or misfortune.

This substructure of explanation has been carried to great lengths by the Chinese commentators. Since the Han period[1] especially, when the magic of the "five stages of change" became associated with the Book of Changes, more and more mystery and finally more and more hocus-pocus have become attached to the book. This is what has given the book its reputation for profundity and unintelligibility. I believe that the reader may be spared all this overgrowth, and have presented only such matter from the text and the oldest commentaries as proves itself relevant.

Obviously in a work like the Book of Changes there is always a nonrational residuum. Why, in a particular instance, one given aspect is stressed, rather than some other that might just as well have been, can no more be accounted for than the fact that oxen have horns and not upper front teeth as horses have. It is possible only to give proof of the interrelations within the framework of what is posited; to sustain the analogy, it is like explaining to what extent there is an organic connection between the development of horns and the absence of upper front teeth.

---

1. [206 B.C.–A.D. 220.]

2. THE EIGHT TRIGRAMS AND THEIR APPLICATION

As has previously been pointed out, the hexagrams should be thought of not merely as made up of six individual lines but always as composed of two primary trigrams. In the interpretation of the hexagrams, these primary trigrams play a part according to the various aspects of their character—first according to their attributes, then according to their images, and finally according to their positions within the family sequence (here uniformly only the Sequence of Later Heaven[2] is taken into account):

Ch'ien	the Creative	is strong	heaven	the father
K'un	the Receptive	is devoted	earth	the mother
Chên	the Arousing	is movement	thunder, wood	the eldest son
K'an	the Abysmal	is danger	water, clouds	the middle son
Kên	Keeping Still	is standstill	mountain	the youngest son
Sun	the Gentle	is penetration	wind, wood	the eldest daughter
Li	the Clinging	is light-giving or conditioned	sun, lightning, fire	the middle daughter
Tui	the Joyous	is pleasure	lake	the youngest daughter

These general meanings, particularly when it is a question of interpretation of the individual lines, must be supplemented by the lists of symbols and attributes—at first glance seemingly superfluous—given in chapter III of the *Shuo Kua*, Discussion of the Trigrams.

In addition, the positions of the trigrams in relation to each other must be taken into account. The lower trigram is below, within, and behind; the upper trigram is above, without, and in front. The lines stressed in the upper trigram are always characterized as "going"; those stressed in the lower trigram, as "coming."

From these characterizations of the trigrams—already in use in the Commentary on the Decision—there was later constructed a system of transforming the hexagrams one into

2. [See p. 269.]

another, which has led to much confusion. This system is here left wholly out of account, since it is not in any way essential to the explanation. Nor has any use been made of the "hidden" hexagrams—i.e., the idea that basically each hexagram has its opposite hidden within it (for example, within Ch'ien is K'un, within Chên is Sun, etc.).

But it is decidedly necessary to make use of the so-called nuclear trigrams, *hu kua*. These form the four middle lines of each hexagram, and overlap each other so that the middle line of the one falls within the other. An example or two will make this clear:

The hexagram Li, THE CLINGING, FIRE (30), shows a nuclear trigram complex consisting of the four lines ☱☴. The two nuclear trigrams are Tui, the Joyous, as the upper (☱), and Sun, the Gentle, as the lower (☴).

The hexagram Chung Fu, INNER TRUTH (61), has for its nuclear trigram complex the four lines ☶☳. Here the two nuclear trigrams are Kên, Keeping Still, as the upper (☶), and Chên, the Arousing, as the lower (☳).

The structure of the hexagrams therefore shows a stage-by-stage overlapping of different trigrams and their influences:

Thus, in each case, the beginning and the top line are each part of one trigram only—the lower and the upper primary trigram respectively. The second and the fifth line belong each to two trigrams, the former to the lower primary and the lower nuclear trigram, the latter to the upper primary and the upper nuclear trigram. The third and the fourth line belong each to three trigrams—to the upper and the lower primary trigram respectively, and to both of the two nuclear trigrams. The result is that the beginning and the top line tend in a sense to drop out of connection, while a state of equilibrium, usually favorable, obtains in the case of the second and the fifth line, and the two middle lines are conditioned by the fact that each belongs to both nuclear trigrams, which disturbs the balance in all except particularly favorable cases. These relationships correspond exactly with the evaluations of the lines in the appended judgments.

3. THE TIME

The situation represented by the hexagram as a whole is called the time. This term comprises several entirely different meanings, according to the character of the various hexagrams.

In hexagrams in which the situation as a whole has to do with movement, "the time" means the decrease or growth, the emptiness or fullness, brought about by this movement. Hexagrams of this sort are: T'ai, PEACE (11); P'i, STANDSTILL (12); Po, SPLITTING APART (23); Fu, RETURN (24).

Similarly, the action or process characteristic for a given hexagram is called the time, as in Sung, CONFLICT (6), Shih, THE ARMY (7), Shih Ho, BITING THROUGH (21), and I, PROVIDING NOURISHMENT (27).

In addition, the time means the law expressed through a hexagram, as in Lü, TREADING (10), Ch'ien, MODESTY (15), Hsien, INFLUENCE (31), and Hêng, DURATION (32).

Finally, the time may also mean the symbolic situation represented by the hexagram, as in Ching, THE WELL (48), and Ting, THE CALDRON (50).

In all cases the time of a hexagram is determinative for the meaning of the situation as a whole, on the basis of which the individual lines receive their meaning. A given line—let us say, a six in the third place—can be now favorable, now unfavorable, according to the time determinant.

4. THE PLACES

The places occupied by the lines are differentiated as superior and inferior, according to their relative elevation. As a rule the lowest and the top line are not taken into account, whereas the four middle lines are active within the time. Of these, the fifth place is that of the ruler, and the fourth that of the minister who is close to the ruler. The third, as the highest place of the lower trigram, holds a sort of transitional position; the second is that of the official in the country, who nevertheless stands in direct connection with the prince in the fifth place. But in some situations the fourth place may represent the wife and the second the son of the man represented by the fifth place. Under certain circumstances the second place may be that of the woman, active within the house, while the fifth place is that of the husband, active in the world without. In short, while any of various designations may be given to a line in a specific place, the varying functions ascribed to the place are always analogous.

As regards the time of the hexagram, the lowest and the top place as a rule represent the beginning and the end. But under certain circumstances the lowest line may also stand for an individual beginning to take part in the time situation without having as yet entered the field of action, while the top line may signify someone who has already withdrawn from the affairs of the time. However, it depends on the time represented by the hexagram whether, under some conditions, these very places have a typical activity, as for example the first place in Chun, DIFFICULTY AT THE BEGINNING (3) and in Ta Yu, POSSESSION IN GREAT MEASURE (14), or the top place in Kuan, CONTEMPLATION (20), in Ta Ch'u, THE TAMING POWER OF THE GREAT (26), and in I, INCREASE (42). In all of these cases the lines in question are rulers of the hexagrams.[3] On the other hand, it may also happen that the fifth place is not that of the ruler, as when, in conformity with the situation indicated by the hexagram as a whole, no prince appears.

5. THE CHARACTER OF THE LINES

The character of the lines is designated as firm or yielding, as central, as correct, or as not central or not correct. The undivided lines are firm (or rigid), the divided lines are yielding

---

3. [Here and on the pages following, there are occasional discrepancies in regard to the examples cited.]

(or weak). The middle lines of the two primary trigrams, the second and the fifth, are central irrespective of their other qualities. A line is correct when it stands in a place appropriate to it—e.g., a firm line occupying the first, third, or fifth place, or a yielding line occupying the second, fourth, or sixth place.

Both firm and yielding lines may be favorable or unfavorable, according to the time requirement of the hexagram. When the time calls for firmness, firm lines are favorable; when the time requires giving way, yielding lines are favorable. This holds true to such an extent that correctness may not always be of advantage. When the time requires giving way, a firm line in the third place, although correct in itself, is harmful because it shows too much firmness, while conversely a yielding line in the third place can be favorable because its yielding character compensates for the rigidity of the place. Only the central position is favorable in the great majority of cases, whether associated with correctness or not. A yielding ruler in particular may have a very favorable position, especially when supported by a strong, firm official in the second place.

6. THE RELATIONSHIPS OF THE LINES TO ONE ANOTHER

Correspondence

Lines occupying analogous places in the lower and the upper trigram sometimes have an especially close relationship, the relationship of correspondence. As a rule, firm lines correspond with yielding lines only, and vice versa. The following lines, provided that they differ in kind, correspond: the first and the fourth, the second and the fifth, the third and the top line. Of these, the most important are the two central lines in the second and the fifth place, which stand in the correct relationship of official to ruler, son to father, wife to husband. A strong official may be in the relation of correspondence to a yielding ruler, or a yielding official may be so related to a strong ruler. The former is the case in sixteen hexagrams, in all of which the result is favorable. It is wholly favorable in hexagrams 4, 7, 11, 14, 18, 19, 32, 34, 38, 40, 41, 46, 50, and somewhat less favorable, owing to the time conditions, in hexagrams 26, 54, 64. The relationship of correspondence between a yielding official and a strong ruler is not nearly so favorable. Its effect is quite unfavorable in hexagrams 12, 13, 17, 20, 31. Difficulties appear in hexagrams 3, 33, 39, 63, but as these are explainable on the basis of the time, the relationship in itself can still be said to be correct. The relationship acts favorably in hexagrams 8, 25, 37, 42, 45, 49, 53.

Occasionally there is correspondence also between the first and the fourth line. It is favorable when a yielding line in the fourth place is in the relationship of correspondence to a strong first line, because this means that an obedient official seeks strong, efficient assistants in the name of his ruler (cf. hexagrams 3, 22, 26, 27, 41). On the other hand, correspondence of a strong fourth line with a yielding first line would indicate a temptation to intimacy with inferior persons, which should be avoided (cf. hexagrams 28, 40, 50). A relationship between the third and the top line hardly ever occurs—or at most only as a temptation—because an exalted sage who has renounced the world would forfeit his purity if he became entangled in worldly affairs, and an official in the third place would forfeit his loyalty if he passed by his ruler in the fifth place.

Of course when a line is a ruler of a hexagram, there occur relationships of correspondence that are independent of these considerations, and the good fortune or misfortune implied by them is determined by the time significance of the hexagram as a whole.

Holding Together

Between two adjacent lines of different character there may occur a relationship of holding together, which is also described with respect to the lower line as "receiving" and with respect to the upper as "resting upon." As regards the relationship of holding together, the fourth and the fifth line (minister and ruler) are of first importance. Here, in contradistinction to the situation respecting the second and the fifth line, it is more favorable for a yielding minister to hold together with a strong ruler, because in this closer proximity reverence is of value. Thus in sixteen hexagrams in which this type of holding together occurs, it is always more or less auspicious: it is very favorable in hexagrams 8, 9, 20, 29, 37, 42, 48, 53, 57, 59, 60, 61 and somewhat less favorable but not altogether unfavorable in hexagrams 3, 5, 39, 63. But the holding together of a strong, i.e., an incorrect line in the fourth place with a yielding ruler is generally unfavorable, as in hexagrams 30, 32, 35, 50, 51; it is somewhat less unfavorable in hexagrams 14, 38, 40, 54, 56, 62. Conversely, it is favorable in certain hexagrams in which the strong fourth line is the ruler: these are hexagrams 16, 21, 34, 55 (here the line is the ruler of the upper trigram), 64.

In addition, the relationship of holding together occurs also between the fifth and the top line. Here it pictures a ruler placing himself under a sage; in such a case it is usually a humble ruler (a weak line in the fifth place) who reveres a strong sage (a strong line above), as in hexagrams 14, 26, 27, 50. This is naturally very favorable. But when, conversely, a strong line stands in the fifth place with a weak one above it, this points rather to association with inferior elements and is undesirable, as in hexagrams 28, 31, 43, 58. The only exception to this appears in hexagram 17, Sui, FOLLOWING, because the total meaning of the hexagram presupposes that the strong element descends to a place under the weak element.

The remaining lines, the first and second, the second and third, the third and fourth, do not stand in the correct relationship of holding together. Where this occurs it always implies a danger of factionalism and is to be avoided. For a weak line, resting upon a firm line is even at times a source of trouble.

In dealing with lines that are rulers of their hexagrams, correspondence and holding together are taken into account regardless of the places of the lines. Besides the above-mentioned instances, other examples may be cited. In Yü, EN-THUSIASM (16), the fourth line is the ruler of the hexagram, the first line corresponds with it, and the third holds together with it. In Po, SPLITTING APART (23), the top line is the ruler; the third corresponds with it, the fifth holds together with it, and both these factors are favorable. In Fu, RETURN (24), the first line is the ruler; the second holds together with it, the fourth corresponds with it, and both these relationships are favorable. In Kuai, BREAK-THROUGH (RESOLUTENESS) (43), the top line is the ruler, the third corresponds with it, and the fifth holds together with it. And in Kou, COMING TO MEET (44), the first line is the ruler, the second holds together with it, the fourth corresponds with it. Here good fortune and misfortune are determined according to the trend indicated by the meaning of the hexagram.

7. THE RULERS OF THE HEXAGRAMS

Distinction is made between two kinds of rulers, constituting and governing. The constituting ruler of the hexagram is that line which gives the hexagram its characteristic meaning, regardless of whether or not the line indicates nobility and goodness of character. The weak top line in hexagram 43, Kuai, BREAK-THROUGH (RESOLUTENESS) is an example, for the idea that this line is resolutely to be cast out is the constituting factor in the hexagram.

Governing rulers are always of good character and become rulers by virtue of their position and the meaning of the time. Usually they are in the fifth place, but occasionally lines in other places may be governing rulers.

When the constituting ruler is at the same time the governing ruler, the line is certain to be good and to be in the place appropriate to the time. When it is not the governing ruler as well, it is a sure sign that its character and place do not accord with the demands of the time.

The ruler of the hexagram can always be determined from the Commentary on the Decision.[4] When the constituting ruler and the governing ruler are identical, the hexagram has one ruler; otherwise it has two. Often there are two lines constituting the meaning of the hexagram, as for instance the two advancing weak lines in hexagram 33, Tun, RETREAT; these are both rulers because they are pushing back the four strong lines. If the hexagram is produced by the interaction of the images of the primary trigrams, the two lines respectively characterizing the trigrams are the rulers.

The constituting ruler in the hexagram is designated by a

---

4. [See bk. III.]

square (□), the governing ruler by a circle (○). When the two are identical, only the circle is used. In book III, moreover, a detailed interpretation of the ruler appears in connection with each hexagram.

Book III

THE COMMENTARIES

PART I

乾

1. *Ch'ien* / *The Creative*

Nuclear trigrams[1] CH'IEN ▬▬▬ *and* CH'IEN ▬▬▬

The ruler of the hexagram is the nine in the fifth place. THE CREATIVE indicates the way of heaven, and the fifth place is the symbol of heaven. THE CREATIVE also indicates the way of the superior man, and the fifth place, as that of the ruler, is his appropriate place. Moreover, the nine in the fifth place possesses the four attributes of firmness, strength, moderation (central position in the upper trigram), and justice (correctness, the yang element being in the yang place). Hence this line possesses the character of heaven in all its perfection.

This hexagram is correlated with the fourth month (May–June), because the light-giving power is then at its zenith.

Miscellaneous Notes on the Hexagrams[2]

THE CREATIVE is strong.

Strength and firmness constitute the character of this hexagram. Its image is the trigram of heaven doubled, that is, two successive rotations or days. It is made up of positive lines only.

THE JUDGMENT

THE CREATIVE works sublime success,
Furthering through perseverance.

---

1. [For explanation, see p. 358.]
2. [*Tsa Kua:* Tenth Wing. See p. 260.]

Commentary on the Decision[3]

NOTE. This commentary, no doubt correctly ascribed to Confucius, explains the names of the hexagrams as well as the words appended by King Wên to the hexagram as a whole [the Judgment]. In general, the commentary first explains the name of the hexagram, taking into consideration as occasion demands its character, its image, and its structure. Next it elucidates the words of King Wên, either using the sources just named or else starting from the situation of the ruler of the hexagram or from the change of form that has given rise to the hexagram.

No explanation of the names of the eight primary trigrams is given, because it is assumed that this is known.

In the Chinese, the sentences in this commentary are for the most part rhymed, probably in order to make it easier to remember them. The rhymes have not been reproduced in this translation, because they are of no material significance. However, it is well to remember the circumstance, because it explains much of the abruptness in the style, which is often somewhat forced.

> Great indeed is the sublimity of the Creative, to which all beings owe their beginning and which permeates all heaven.[4]

The commentary separates the two pairs of attributes given in the Judgment into the four individual attributes of the creative power, whose visible form is heaven. The first attribute is sublimity, which, as the primal cause of all that exists, forms the most important and most inclusive attribute of the Creative. The root meaning of the Chinese word for it—*yüan*—is literally "head."

> The clouds pass and the rain does its work, and all individual beings flow into their forms.

---

3. [*T'uan Chuan:* First Wing, Second Wing. "Decision" is the equivalent of "Judgment."]

4. [See p. 4, where this passage is quoted. Here, as in a number of other instances, the phrasing differs somewhat from one book to another.]

1. *Ch'ien* / *The Creative*

This explains the expression "success." The success of the creative activity is revealed in the gift of water, which causes the germination and sprouting of all living things. The first passage tells of the beginning of all beings in general; here the separate species in their particular forms are instanced. These two passages show the attributes of greatness and success as they manifest themselves in the creative force in nature. The attributes of sublimity and success take shape correspondingly in the creative man, the sage, who is in harmony with the creative power of the godhead.

> Because the holy man is clear as to the end and the beginning, as to the way in which each of the six stages completes itself in its own time, he mounts on them toward heaven as though on six dragons.

The holy man, who understands the mysteries of creation inherent in end and beginning, in death and life, in dissolution and growth, and who understands how these polar opposites condition one another, becomes superior to the limitations of the transitory. For him, the meaning of time is that in it the stages of growth can unfold in a clear sequence. He is mindful at every moment and uses the six stages of growth as if they were six dragons (the image attributed to the individual lines) on which he mounts toward heaven. This is the sublimity and success of the Creative as it shows itself in man.

> The way of the Creative works through change and transformation, so that each thing receives its true nature and destiny and comes into permanent accord with the Great Harmony: this is what furthers and what perseveres.

Here the two other attributes, power to further and power to persevere, are explained in their relation to the creative force in nature. The mode of the Creative is not rest but continuous movement and development. Through this force, all things are gradually changed until they are completely transformed in their manifestations. Thus the seasons and all living beings change and alternate in their course. In this way each thing receives the nature appropriate to it, which, from the divine viewpoint, is called its appointed destiny. This explains the concept of furthering. With each thing thus finding its mode, a great and lasting harmony arises in the world: this is expressed in the concept of perseverance (lastingness and integrity).

> He towers high above the multitude of beings, and all lands are united in peace.

This describes the creative power of the holy man, who makes it possible for everything to attain its appropriate place, thus bringing about peace on earth, when he occupies an eminent ruling place.

In all these explanations there is an evident parallelism between the Creative in nature and the Creative in the world of man. What is said about the Creative in nature is based on the image of heaven symbolized by the hexagram. Heaven shows the strong, ceaseless movement that by its nature causes everything to happen in due time. The words about the Creative in man are based on the position of the ruler of the hexagram, the nine in the fifth place. The "flying dragon in the heavens" is the image of the sublimity and success of the holy ruler. The eminent place held by the holy man, through which peace comes to the world, has its basis in the line, "It furthers one to see the great man."

Commentary on the Images[5]

NOTE. This commentary, starting with the combination of the two trigrams, deduces from it the situation represented by the hexagram as a whole. With the attributes of the two trigrams as a basis, it then gives advice for correct behavior in this situation.

---

5. [*Hsiang Chuan:* Third Wing, Fourth Wing. In bk. I, under the heading "The Image," the reader has become familiar with the portion of this commentary known as the Great Images. It is repeated in bk. III under the same heading. The rest of the commentary, which explains the line judgments—though called Small Images (see p. 257)—appears in the passages designated *b* under the heading "The Lines." The passages designated *a* repeat the line judgments of bk. I. The German edition omits this repetition in the treatment of the first two hexagrams. However, the presence of the line itself

THE IMAGE

The movement of heaven is full of power.

Thus the superior man makes himself strong and
untiring.

The doubling of the trigram Ch'ien, the Creative, gives the
image of powerful and constantly repeated movement. The
doubling suggests that one draws strength from within oneself, and that after each action a new one follows, without
cease.

THE LINES

Nine at the beginning:

a) Hidden dragon. Do not act.

b) "Hidden dragon. Do not act." For the light-giving
force is still below.

The lowest place is as it were still wholly beneath the earth,
hence the idea of something hidden. But since the line is undivided, the image chosen is the dragon, the symbol of the
light-giving force.

Nine in the second place:

a) Dragon appearing in the field.

It furthers one to see the great man.

b) "Dragon appearing in the field." Already the influence of character reaches far.

The second place stands for the surface of the earth, hence the
idea of a field. Appearing in the field and seeing the great man
are indicated by the influential character of the line, since it
holds the center of the lower trigram and is moreover related

---

makes the commentary so much more intelligible that it has seemed
desirable here to supply the omission. Under "Six in the third place"
in K'un, a parenthetic completion of the line text under *b*, and a
sentence in the comment explaining this interpolation—both supplied by Wilhelm for elucidation in the absence of *a*—have been
omitted as superfluous.]

to the ruler of the hexagram through place and affinity of nature.

Nine in the third place:

a) All day long the superior man is creatively active.
At nightfall his mind is still beset with cares.
Danger. No blame.

b) "All day long the superior man is creatively active."
One goes to and fro on the right path.

The third place, as the place of transition from the lower to the upper trigram, is naturally unsettled and therefore frequently not exactly favorable. Here, however, owing to the uniform character of all the lines, the transition is merely a sign of tireless activity leading to and fro on the path to truth. "To and fro" means that one is only beginning to acquire moral stability.

Nine in the fourth place:

a) Wavering flight over the depths.
No blame.

b) "Wavering flight over the depths." Advance is not a mistake.

Here we reach the upper limit of what pertains to man in the hexagram. Advance on level ground is no longer possible. In order to advance, a man must dare to relinquish his foothold on earth and soar into realms of uncharted space and utter solitude. Here the individual is free—precisely because of the possibilities inherent in the position. Each man must determine his own fate.

O Nine in the fifth place:

a) Flying dragon in the heavens.
It furthers one to see the great man.

b) "Flying dragon in the heavens." This shows the great man at work.

Here the ruler of the hexagram is in the place which is preeminently that of the ruler. Hence he is symbolized by a dragon flying in the sky.

Nine at the top:

a) Arrogant dragon will have cause to repent.

b) "Arrogant dragon will have cause to repent." For what is at the full cannot last.

By the law of change, whatever has reached its extreme must turn back.

When all the lines are nines:

a) There appears a flight of dragons without heads. Good fortune.

b) "All the lines are nines." It is the nature of heaven not to appear as head.

The Creative does indeed guide all happenings, but it never becomes manifest; it never behaves outwardly as the leader. Thus true strength is that strength which, mobile as it is hidden, concentrates on the work without being outwardly visible. Since all the lines are nines, the hexagram Ch'ien changes into the hexagram, K'un, THE RECEPTIVE, which is wholly receptive; hence no head is showing.

Commentary on the Words of the Text[6]

NOTE. This wing consists of four commentaries on the first two hexagrams in the Book of Changes. Of these, two commentaries deal with the text referring to the hexagram as a whole [the Judgment] and also with the *T'uan Chuan* [Commentary on the Decision], while all four also elucidate the individual lines. [The commentaries, here designated as *a*, *b*, *c*, and *d*, contain a different number of sections each.] In the original text the sequence is arranged as follows: *a*, 1–9; *b*, 1–7; *c*, 1–7; *d*, 1–12. In the presentation below, for the sake of clarity and to avoid unnecessary repetition, the different

---

6. [*Wên Yen:* Seventh Wing.]

commentaries pertaining to the respective hexagrams have been arranged together, and are distinguishable by the classifying letters and numerals.

On the Hexagram as a Whole

a) 1. Of all that is good, sublimity is supreme. Succeeding is the coming together of all that is beautiful. Furtherance is the agreement of all that is just. Perseverance is the foundation of all actions.

Here the four fundamental attributes of the hexagram are related to the four cardinal virtues of Chinese ethics. Sublimity is correlated with humaneness, success with the mores, furtherance with justice, and perseverance with wisdom.[7]

a) 2. Because the superior man embodies humaneness, he is able to govern men. Because he brings about the harmonious working together of all that is beautiful, he is able to unite them through the mores. Because he furthers all beings, he is able to bring them into harmony through justice. Because he is persevering and firm, he is able to carry out all actions.

The four fundamental attributes of the Creative are likewise the attributes necessary to a leader and ruler of men. In order to rule and lead men, the first essential is to have humane feeling toward them. Without humaneness, nothing lasting can be accomplished in the sphere of authority. Power that influences through fear works only for the moment and necessarily arouses resistance as a countereffect.

On the basis of this conception, it follows that the mores are the instrument by which men can be brought into union. For nothing binds people more firmly together than deeply rooted social usages that are observed because they appear to each

---

7. [In the German rendering, these correlations are stated in four sentences so printed that they appear as a passage from the *Wén Yen*. Actually they do not occur in the *Wén Yen*. It is to be assumed therefore that they are part of Wilhelm's comment on *a* 1.]

member of society as something beautiful and worth striving for.

Wherever it is possible to construct a framework of mores in which each person feels content, it is easy to unify and organize the masses. Furthermore, as the foundation of social life there must be the greatest possible freedom and the greatest possible advantage for all. These are guaranteed by justice, which curtails individual freedom no more than is absolutely necessary for the general welfare. Finally, to reach the desired goals, there is the fourth requisite of wisdom, manifesting itself by pointing out the established and enduring paths that, according to immutable cosmic laws, must lead to success.

a) 3. The superior man acts in accordance with these four virtues. Therefore it is said: The Creative is sublime, successful, furthering, persevering.

d) 1. The sublimity of the Creative depends on the fact that it begins everything and has success.

d) 2. Furtherance and perseverance: thus it brings about the nature and way of all beings.

Here the attributes are again summed up in pairs. The sublimity of the Creative depends on its absoluteness, on the fact that it is the beginning of all things—for it is not itself conditioned by anything else—and that it is the active principle, i.e., it is itself the cause of all else. Furtherance and perseverance—meaning the urge to life, and the fixed laws of nature—reveal the causality of the Creative in its efficacy. The urge to life—that which furthers and is right for each being —lays the foundation of its nature, and this nature acts according to fixed laws: this is the way of all beings. In the Commentary on the Decision nature is traced back to its origin in the divine decree; here nature is shown in its mode of action.

d) 3. The Creative, by positing the beginning, is able to further the world with beauty. Its true greatness lies in the fact that nothing is said about the means by which it furthers.

377

Of the Creative it is said only that it furthers by virtue of what eternally belongs to it, by virtue of its very nature. This nature is not defined more exactly. In this lies the suggestion of the infinite possibilities and aspects of its benefits. The Receptive forms a contrast to this, because it is said: "It furthers through the perseverance of a mare." In the phenomenal world, each thing has its specific nature: this is the principle of individuation. At the same time this specific nature fixes a boundary that separates each individual being from every other.

d) 4. How great indeed is the Creative! It is firm and strong, moderate and correct, pure, unalloyed and spiritual.

Here the attributes of the whole hexagram are deduced from the nature of its ruler, the nine in the fifth place, as is frequently the case in the *T'uan Chuan*, Commentary on the Decision, to which the entire passage refers. The fifth line is firm because it is in an uneven place, strong because it is undivided (strong means movement, firm means rest); it is moderate because it is in the middle of the upper trigram, correct because it stands in its appropriate place—a strong line in a strong place. In these four attributes the four cardinal attributes of the hexagram are revealed once more. These attributes are present in pure, unalloyed, and spiritual form because the hexagram consists of strong lines only.

d) 5. The six individual lines open up and unfold the thought, so that the character of the whole is explained through its different sides.

Because of the unity of the hexagram, the individual lines stand in a continuous relationship that, as it progresses, clarifies the idea of the whole still further. In this respect the hexagram Ch'ien, THE CREATIVE, forms a contrast to K'un, THE RECEPTIVE, in which the single lines stand side by side without inner relationship. This inheres in the temporal character of THE CREATIVE as contrasted with the spatial character of THE RECEPTIVE.

d) 6. "In his own time he mounts toward heaven on six dragons. The clouds pass and the rain falls." All this means peace coming to the world.

Because of this closing remark, the corresponding passage in the Commentary on the Decision is interpreted as a reference to historical events, namely, the ordering of the empire.

On the Lines

On nine at the beginning:

a) 4. Nine at the beginning means: "Hidden dragon. Do not act." What does this signify? The Master said: This means a person who has the character of a dragon but remains concealed. He does not change to suit the outside world; he makes no name for himself. He withdraws from the world, yet is not sad about it. He receives no recognition, yet is not sad about it. If lucky, he carries out his principles; if unlucky, he withdraws with them. Verily, he cannot be uprooted; he is a hidden dragon.

b) 1. "Hidden dragon. Do not act." The reason is that he is below.

c) 1. "Hidden dragon. Do not act." The power of the light principle is still covered up and concealed.

d) 7. The superior man acts in accordance with the character that has become perfected within him. This is a way of life that can submit to scrutiny on any day.

Being hidden means that he is still in concealment and not given recognition, that if he should act he would not as yet accomplish anything. In this case the superior man does not act.

On nine in the second place:

a) 5. Nine in the second place means: "Dragon appearing in the field. It furthers one to see the great man." What does this signify?

The Master said: This means a man who has the character of a dragon and is moderate and correct. Even in ordinary speech he is reliable. Even in ordinary actions he is careful. He does away with what is false and preserves his integrity. He improves his era and does not boast about it. His character is influential and transforms men.

In the Book of Changes it is said: "Dragon appearing in the field. It furthers one to see the great man." This refers to a man who has the qualities of a ruler.

b) 2. "Dragon appearing in the field." The reason is that he is not needed as yet.

c) 2. "Dragon appearing in the field." Through him the whole world attains beauty and clarity.

d) 8. The superior man learns in order to gather material; he questions in order to sift it. Thus he becomes generous in nature and kindly in his actions.

In the Book of Changes it is said: "Dragon appearing in the field. It furthers one to see the great man." For he has the qualities of a ruler.

On nine in the third place:

a) 6. Nine in the third place means: "All day long the superior man is creatively active. At nightfall his mind is still beset with cares. Danger. No blame." What does this signify?

The Master said: The superior man improves his character and labors at his task. It is through loyalty and faith that he fosters his character. By working on his words, so that they rest firmly on truth, he makes his work enduring. He knows how this is to be achieved and achieves it; in this way he is able to plant the right seed. He knows how it is to be brought to completion and so completes it; thereby he is able to make it truly enduring. For this reason he is not proud in his superior position nor disappointed in an inferior one. Thus he is creatively active and, as circumstances demand, careful, so that even in a dangerous situation he does not make a mistake.

b) 3. "All day long he is creatively active." This is the way in which he carries out his undertakings.

c) 3. "All day long he is creatively active." He moves with the time.

d) 9. The nine in the third place shows redoubled firmness and is moreover not in a central place. On the one hand, it is not yet in the heavens above; on the other hand, it is no longer in the field below. Therefore one must be creatively active and, as circumstances demand, careful. Then, despite the danger, no mistake is made.

On nine in the fourth place:

a) 7. Nine in the fourth place means: "Wavering flight over the depths. No blame." What does this signify?

The Master said: In ascent or descent there is no fixed rule, except that one must do nothing evil. In advance or retreat no sustained perseverance avails, except that one must not depart from one's nature. The superior man fosters his character and labors at his task, in order to do everything at the right time. Therefore he makes no mistake.

b) 4. "Wavering flight over the depths." He tests his powers.

c) 4. "Wavering flight over the depths." Here the way of the Creative is about to transform itself.

d) 10. The nine in the fourth place is too rigid and not moderate. It is not yet in the heavens above, neither is it any longer in the field below nor in the middle regions of the human. Therefore it is said: "Wavering flight. . . ." To waver means that one has freedom of choice, therefore one makes no mistake.

On nine in the fifth place:

a) 8. Nine in the fifth place means: "Flying dragon in the heavens. It furthers one to see the great man." What does this signify?

The Master said: Things that accord in tone vibrate together. Things that have affinity in their inmost natures seek one another. Water flows to what is wet, fire turns to what is dry. Clouds follow the dragon, wind follows the tiger. Thus the sage rises, and all creatures follow him with their eyes. What is born of heaven feels related to what is above. What is born of earth feels related to what is below. Each follows its kind.

b) 5. "Flying dragon in the heavens." This is the supreme way of ruling.

c) 5. "Flying dragon in the heavens." This is the place appropriate to heavenly character.

d) 11. The great man accords in his character with heaven and earth; in his light, with the sun and moon; in his consistency, with the four seasons; in the good and evil fortune that he creates, with gods and spirits. When he acts in advance of heaven, heaven does not contradict him. When he follows heaven, he adapts himself to the time of heaven. If heaven itself does not resist him, how much less do men, gods, and spirits!

On nine at the top:

a) 9. Nine at the top means: "Arrogant dragon will have cause to repent." What does this signify?

The Master said: He who is noble and has no corresponding position, he who stands high and has no following, he who has able people under him who do not have his support, that man will have cause for regret at every turn.

b) 6. "Arrogant dragon will have cause to repent." Everything that goes to extremes meets with misfortune.

c) 6. "Arrogant dragon will have cause to repent." In time he exhausts himself.

d) 12. Arrogance means that one knows how to press forward but not how to draw back, that one knows existence but not annihilation, knows something about winning but nothing about losing.

It is only the holy man who understands how to press forward and how to draw back, who knows existence and annihilation as well, without losing his true nature. The holy man alone can do this.

On all the nines changing:

b) 7. When THE CREATIVE, the great, undergoes change in all the nines, the world is set in order

c) 7. When THE CREATIVE, the great, undergoes change in all the nines, one perceives the law of heaven.

NOTE. The hexagram Ch'ien, THE CREATIVE, occupies a unique position, in that it is uniformly composed of firm lines all having a certain relation to one another. They form a sequence of stages, so that a genetic development in time can be observed. For this reason the judgments attached to the individual lines in this hexagram differ from those pertaining to any of the other hexagrams. In the case of THE CREATIVE, there can be no question of relationships of correspondence and holding together[8] between firm and yielding lines, such as determine the character of the other hexagrams; instead, the judgment takes into account solely the relation of the place to the nature of the line.

A characteristic difference between the upper and the lower trigram is to be noted. The lower pictures the development of the character of the creative power; the upper, the development of the external position. The first line and the fourth each mark a beginning. The first line, at the very bottom, still within the realm of earth (first and second places), is designated as hidden, latent. The fourth line, in the lowest place of the upper trigram, likewise indicates a beginning, that is, a changing of position. In themselves, the omens for this line are not favorable. Being firm in a yielding place, the line does not fit its place, and this might well imply a defect somewhere. But because the essence of the Creative is strength, it is explicitly emphasized that there is no mistake. The divergence between the character and the place of the line manifests itself instead in the potentiality of the decision, which is still in doubt.

The middle lines in the two trigrams, the second and the fifth, are extraordinarily favorable. The second line is central and as such is immediately to be conceived as correct. Since it is still in the lower trigram, it shows the inner nature of the great man, who is already becoming known ("in the field") but does not yet hold an appropriate position. He must see the "great man" in the fifth place, with whom he is connected by kinship of character, and who, as ruler of the whole, can assign him the position suitable to him. These favorable omens hold in regard to the fifth line in a yet more marked degree. The second line shows the strong man in a weak, lowly

---

8. [See pp. 361–63.]

place; in the fifth line, however, character and position accord. It is a strong line in a strong place, in the sphere of heaven (fifth and sixth places); moreover, it is the ruler of the whole. Therefore it represents the great man whom it is worth while to see. Hence the two central lines carry no warning at all; they are altogether favorable.

It is different in the case of the two end lines, the third and the top line. Of the two, the third has the more favorable position. It is indeed too strong for the place of transition (strength of character intensified by strength of place), so that it would seem that mistakes are to be feared. However, since the whole hexagram deals with creative powers, excess of strength does no harm, for at the place of transition it can be applied to inner preparation for the new conditions. For the top line, however, matters are quite different. Here the end of the whole situation is reached. Although the place is weak, the line character is still strong. This divergence between what one wants to do and what one is able to do leads to remorse, since there is no possible way out.

坤

2. *K'un / The Receptive*

☷ *Nuclear trigrams* K'UN ☳ *and* K'UN ☶

The ruler of the hexagram is the six in the second place. K'un, THE RECEPTIVE, represents the nature of the earth; the number two symbolizes the earth. Furthermore, THE RECEPTIVE demonstrates the nature of the man who serves, and the second place is his station. In addition, this line expresses perfectly the fourfold character of the Receptive: it is yielding, devoted, moderate (i.e., central), and correct (i.e., yielding in a yielding place). For this reason, it is the ruler of the hexagram. The statements made in the Judgment all refer to the nature of an official: "If he tries to lead, he goes astray; but if he follows, he finds guidance. It is favorable to find friends in the west and south, to forego friends in the east and north."

This hexagram is linked with the tenth month (November–December), when the dark power in nature brings the end of the year.

Miscellaneous Notes

THE RECEPTIVE is yielding.

THE JUDGMENT

THE RECEPTIVE brings about sublime success,

Furthering through the perseverance of a mare.

If the superior man undertakes something and tries
    to lead,

He goes astray;

But if he follows, he finds guidance.

It is favorable to find friends in the west and south,

To forego friends in the east and north.

Quiet perseverance brings good fortune.

Commentary on the Decision

Perfect indeed is the sublimity of the Receptive. All beings owe their birth to it, because it receives the heavenly with devotion.

This is the explanation of the word "sublime" in the Judgment. The greatness of the Receptive is characterized as perfect. That which attains the ideal is perfect. This means that the Receptive is dependent upon the Creative. While the Creative is the generating principle, to which all beings owe their beginning, because the soul comes from it, the Receptive is that which brings to birth, that which takes the seed of the heavenly into itself and gives to beings their bodily form.

The Receptive in its riches carries all things. Its nature is in harmony with the boundless. It em-

braces everything in its breadth and illumines everything in its greatness. Through it, all individual
beings attain success.

This is the explanation of the word "success" in the Judgment.
Here also there is the contrasting complement to the Creative.
While the Creative shields things—that is, covers them from
above—the Receptive carries them, like a foundation that
endures forever. Infinite accord with the Creative is its essence.
This produces its success. The movement of the Creative is a
direct forward movement, and its resting state is standstill; the
movement of the Receptive is an opening out, and in its
resting state it is closed. In the resting, closed state, it embraces
all things as though in a vast womb. In the state of movement,
of opening, it allows the divine light to enter, and by means
of this light illuminates everything. This is the source of its
success, which shows itself in the success of living beings. While
the success of the Creative lies in the fact that individual
beings receive their specific forms, the success of the Receptive
causes them to thrive and unfold.

A mare belongs to the creatures of the earth; she
roams the earth without bound. Yielding, devoted,
furthering through perseverance: thus the superior
man has a direction for his way of life.

While the Creative is symbolized by the dragon flying in the
heavens, the Receptive is symbolized by the mare (combining
strength and devotion) coursing over the earth. Being yielding
and devoted must not exclude strength, for strength is necessary to the Receptive if it is to be the helper of the Creative.
This strength is expressed in the words, "furthering through
perseverance," appearing in the commentary as the model for
the way of life of the superior man. (The punctuation of the
commentary deviates from that of the Judgment. Because of
the rhyme, the commentary requires the literal translation,
"Furthering through perseverance. Thus the superior man
has somewhere to go." In the Judgment, on the other hand,
most interpreters make the last words a dependent clause

linked with what follows, and the sentence reads: "If the superior man undertakes something . . . he goes astray."[1])

> Taking the lead brings confusion because one loses his way. Following with devotion—thus does one attain his permanent place.
>
> In the west and south one finds friends, so that he proceeds with people of his own kind. In the east and north one must do without friends, so that he finally attains good fortune.

If the Receptive were to push ahead on its own initiative, it would deviate from its natural character and miss the way. By submitting to and following the Creative, it attains its appropriate permanent place.

The west and south, according to King Wên's arrangement, are the region in which the feminine trigrams are placed. Here K'un is in the midst of the daughters. But the masculine trigrams (Ch'ien and the sons) are in the east and north, so that the Receptive in this region is alone. But the very fact that it is alone with the Creative is to its advantage. Thus the earth must be alone with heaven, the official must serve only the ruler, the wife must cleave only to the husband.

> The good fortune of rest and perseverance depends on our being in accord with the boundless nature of the earth.

The earth is still. It does not act of itself but is constantly receptive to the influences of heaven. Thus its life becomes inexhaustible and eternal. Man likewise attains eternity if he does not strive vaingloriously to achieve everything of his own strength but quietly keeps himself receptive to the impulses flowing to him from the creative forces.

---

1. [The Commentary on the Decision makes two sentences of the one. "The last words" refers to the last statement in the preceding paragraph of the Commentary on the Decision, and "what follows" refers to the first sentence of the next paragraph.]

THE IMAGE

The earth's condition is receptive devotion.
Thus the superior man who has breadth of character
Carries the outer world.

Heaven moves with power; therefore it is said of it that "it moves." The earth completes within the form; hence, in reference to it, one says "condition." Earth is doubled, indicating massiveness, which is necessary in order that it may dedicate itself without forfeiting its nature. Thus man too must possess inner strength, weight of character, and breadth of view, that he may endure the world without being swayed by it.

THE LINES

Six at the beginning:

a) When there is hoarfrost underfoot,
Solid ice is not far off.

b) "When there is hoarfrost underfoot, solid ice is not far off." When the dark power begins to grow rigid and continues in this way, things reach the point of solid ice.[2]

The first line contains a warning not to minimize the beginnings of evil, because, left to itself, evil increases as inevitably as the ice of winter follows on the hoarfrost of autumn.

○ Six in the second place:

a) Straight, square, great.
Without purpose,
Yet nothing remains unfurthered.

---

2. Another reading of this line is:
    When there is hoarfrost underfoot,
    The dark [power] begins to grow rigid.
    If this continues,
    Solid ice results.

b)   The movement of the six in the second place[3] is
straight and, because of this, square.
"Without purpose, yet nothing remains unfurthered": for in the nature of the earth lies the light.

Because the Receptive in its movements adapts itself to the
Creative, these movements come to be exactly as they should
be. Thus the earth brings forth all beings, each in its own kind,
according to the will of the Creator. Square, firm, refers to
unchangingness. Each kind of living being has a fixed law of
existence, according to which it develops in a way that is
unchanging. In this lies the greatness of the earth.

For this very reason the earth has no need of a purpose.
Everything becomes spontaneously what it should rightly be,
for in the law of heaven life has an inner light that it must
involuntarily obey.

Six in the third place:

a)   Hidden lines.
One is able to remain persevering.
If by chance you are in the service of a king,
Seek not works, but bring to completion.

b)   "Hidden lines. One is able to remain persevering."
One must let them shine forth at the right time.
"If by chance you are in the service of a king. . . ."[4]
This shows that the light of wisdom is great.

To hide beauty does not mean to be inactive; it means only
that beauty must not be displayed at the wrong time. When
the right time arrives, one must reveal oneself. If one does not
boast of one's merits, but sees to it that everything is carried
out, it is a sign of great wisdom.

---

3. In the text of the commentary, the six in the second place is
explicitly named as ruler of the hexagram. [The reference here is
not to the Commentary on the Decision but to another commentary
not presented in Wilhelm's translation.]

4. [See p. 372, n. 5.]

Six in the fourth place:

a) A tied-up sack. No blame, no praise.

b) "A tied-up sack. No blame." Through caution one remains free of harm.

Here there is a yin line in a yin place; that is, the yin power is on the increase, therefore the contraction is as powerful as in the case of a tied-up sack. This naturally brings about a certain isolation, but it frees one of obligations.

Six in the fifth place:

a) A yellow lower garment brings supreme good fortune.

b) "A yellow lower garment brings supreme good fortune." Beauty is within.

This line resembles in position the six in the third place. Here also the strength inherent in the place is neutralized by the character of the line—hence, in both cases, hidden beauty.

Six at the top:

a) Dragons fight in the meadow.
     Their blood is black and yellow.

b) "Dragons fight in the meadow." The way comes to an end.

The six at the top tries to hold firm, although the situation of darkness is already at an end. At this moment the dark principle advances out of the realm of the morally indifferent and becomes positively evil. There ensues a battle with the light-giving primal power coming from without to oppose the darkness, in which both elements suffer harm.

When all the lines are sixes:

a) Lasting perseverance furthers.

b) "Lasting perseverance": it ends in great things.

The sixes change into their opposites; they become light or great lines.

Commentary on the Words of the Text

In contrast to the considerable number of commentaries on
THE CREATIVE comprised in the *Wên Yen*, there is only one on
THE RECEPTIVE.

On the Hexagram as a Whole

> The Receptive is altogether yielding, yet firm in its
> movement. It is altogether still, yet in its nature
> square.

The mare is yielding, yet strong. So likewise is the Receptive,
for only in this way can it be the peer of the Creative. It is
altogether still within, because wholly dependent, yet it is
bound immutably to definite laws in its manifestations—the
bringing to birth of the different species. "Firm in movement"
is the explanation of the text words "sublime success." "Still,
yet square" is the explanation of the text words "perseverance
furthers."

> "If he follows, he finds guidance," and thus obtains
> something enduring.
> "It embraces everything," and its power to transform
> is light-giving.

These sentences are amplifications of the Commentary on the
Decision. The reference here is to the movement of the Receptive, which corresponds with the seasons of summer and
autumn (south and west). At these times the Receptive is with
"friends," that is, obedient to the laws of heaven: it is giving
life to all varieties of beings, each according to its kind—so
sharing the eternity of heaven, embracing all things and
bringing them to maturity, and thus in bright light showing
its power to transform them.

> The way of the Receptive—how devoted it is! It
> receives heaven into itself and acts in its own time.

These two activities correspond with winter and spring (north
and east). The reference is to the solitary union with the
Creative, the receiving of the seed, and its quiet ripening to
birth.

The comments on THE RECEPTIVE are based on the character of the six in the second place, the ruler of the hexagram, just as the comments on THE CREATIVE are based on the nine in the fifth place in that hexagram.

On the Lines

On six at the beginning:

A house that heaps good upon good is sure to have an abundance of blessings. A house that heaps evil upon evil is sure to have an abundance of ills. Where a servant murders his master, where a son murders his father, the causes do not lie between the morning and evening of one day. It took a long time for things to go so far. It came about because things that should have been stopped were not stopped soon enough.

In the Book of Changes it is said: "When there is hoarfrost underfoot, solid ice is not far off." This shows how far things go when they are allowed to run on.

According to Chu Hsi the last sentence should read: "This refers to the necessary vigilance," i.e., the vigilance needed to stop in time those things which must naturally have evil consequences.

On six in the second place:

Straightness means righting things; squareness means fulfillment of duty. The superior man is serious, in order to make his inner life straight; he does his duty, in order to make his outer life square. Where seriousness and fulfillment of duty stand firm, character will not become one-sided.

"Straight, square, great. Without purpose, yet nothing remains unfurthered": because one is never in doubt as to what one has to do.

The inner life becomes right through consistent seriousness; the outer life becomes correct (square) through fulfillment of duty. Duty has a shaping influence on outer life, yet it is by no means something external. Through seriousness and fulfillment of duty, character develops richly of itself; greatness comes unsought, of its own accord. Therefore in all matters the individual hits upon the right course instinctively and without reflection, because he is free of all those scruples and doubts which induce a timid vacillation and lame the power of decision.

> On six in the third place:
>
> The dark force possesses beauty but veils it. So must a man be when entering the service of a king. He must avoid laying claim to the completed work. This is the way of the earth, the way of the wife, the way of one who serves. It is the way of the earth to make no display of completed work but rather to bring everything to completion vicariously.

It is the duty of one who subordinates himself to conceal his own worth, without craving an independent position, and to let all the merits for the completed work go to the master for whom he is working.

> On six in the fourth place:
>
> When heaven and earth are creating in change and transformation, all plants and trees flourish; but when heaven and earth close, the able man withdraws into the dark.
>
> In the Book of Changes it is said: "A tied-up sack. No blame, no praise." This counsels caution.

The six in the fourth place is near the ruler but does not receive recognition from him. In such a case, the only right thing to do is to shut oneself off from the world. This is the resting state of the dark principle, the state in which it closes (cf. above).

On six in the fifth place:

The superior man is yellow and moderate; thus he makes his influence felt in the outer world through reason.

He seeks the right place for himself and dwells in the essential.

His beauty is within, but it gives freedom to his limbs and expresses itself in his works. This is the perfection of beauty.

Yellow is the color of the middle and of moderation. Inner moderation has an outer effect, because it imbues all forms of expression with reason. The right place sought by the superior man is found in the good form that makes him yield precedence to others and stay modestly in the background. Reserved grace, unseen yet present in all movements and deeds, is the perfection of beauty.

There is a characterizing difference in what is said about the lines of THE CREATIVE and THE RECEPTIVE. In the former the emphasis is always on the real, the unfailing, while in the latter the attributes stressed are seriousness, conscientiousness, and modesty. We are dealing with the same thing seen from two sides. Only truth leads to seriousness, and only seriousness makes truth possible.

On six at the top:

When the dark seeks to equal the light principle, there is certain to be a struggle. Lest one think that nothing of the light remains, the dragon is mentioned. But to make clear that there is no deviation from their kind,[5] blood is also mentioned. Black and yellow are heaven and earth in confusion. Heaven is black and earth yellow.

This explanation is somewhat obscurely expressed. The meaning is as follows: In the tenth month, the power of the dark

---

5. [The nature of yin and yang.]

principle has completely triumphed; the last remaining light has been driven away.[6] The sun has reached its lowest position; the dark force rules unrestrained. But this is the very reason for the coming change to the opposite; the solstice takes place, and light struggles anew with darkness.

It is the same in all relationships. The dark principle cannot be the ruling one; it is in its proper place only when conditioned by the light principle, and submissive to it. If this is disregarded, and the dark principle tries to issue from its realm within and come forth upon the field of action without, the power of the light principle shows itself. The dragon, the symbol of the light-giving power, appears and drives the dark power back within its confines, as a sign that the light principle still exists. Blood is the symbol of the dark principle, just as breath is the symbol of the light principle. Since blood flows, the dark principle is injured. However, blood comes not only from the dark principle, for the light principle also suffers injury in this struggle; therefore the color is designated as black and yellow. Black, or rather dark blue, is the color of heaven, and yellow that of the earth. (It should be noted that the color symbolism here differs from that in the comments on the eight trigrams, where the Creative is said to be red and the Receptive black, i.e., dark.)

NOTE. Here, in contrast to the relationships in the hexagram of THE CREATIVE, the single lines do not have a developmental relation to one another, but stand side by side without interrelation. Each line represents a separate situation. This is in accord with the nature of the two hexagrams. THE CREATIVE represents time, producing sequence; THE RECEPTIVE represents space, which indicates juxtaposition.

With respect to the individual lines, the following is to be noted. The first and the top line, i.e., the two outside places, are unfavorable. The inner, not the outer place, is proper to the Receptive. The first line shows the dark principle taking the initiative (cf. hexagram 44, Kou, COMING TO MEET); this means danger. Therefore the dark principle is represented as something objective that must be opposed at the right time.

---

6. [The twelfth month in our calendar. See p. 3, n. 1.]

In the top place, the dark principle arrogates leadership to itself and enters into rivalry with the light principle. Here also it is represented objectively as the thing fought against (cf. hexagram 43, Kuai, BREAK-THROUGH); for these two situations are not in harmony with the nature of a superior man, and the Book of Changes is written only for superior men. Hence whatever is inferior is in every case something external or objective.

The middle lines of the primary trigrams, being central, are favorable. But in contrast to the situation in Ch'ien, the ruler here is in the second place instead of the fifth, for it is the nature of the Receptive to be below. Therefore we are here shown the way of the earth, of material, spatial nature, in which everything acts spontaneously. The fifth place shows modesty in human nature. The fact that garments are spoken of points rather to the image of a princess than to that of a prince (cf. hexagram 54, Kuei Mei, THE MARRYING MAIDEN, six in the fifth place).

The two transitional lines are neutral in meaning. The third has the possibility of entering the service of a king, for the weakness of its nature is compensated by the strength of its place. But while the third line of Ch'ien is self-contained, the third line of K'un is self-effacingly concerned only with serving others. The fourth line is too weak (a yielding line in a weak place), and moreover has no relationship with the fifth line. Hence withdrawal into itself is all that is left for it. The heightened passivity of this line corresponds with the heightened activity of the nine in the third place in Ch'ien, just as the third line in K'un corresponds in its undetermined possibilities with the nine in the fourth place of Ch'ien.

屯

3. *Chun / Difficulty at the Beginning*

⚏⚏ *Nuclear trigrams* KÊN ☶ *and* K'UN ☷

In Chun the nine at the beginning and the nine in the fifth place are the rulers. These two are the only yang lines in the hexagram. The nine at the beginning is below and means the helper who can quiet the people. The nine in the fifth place is above; it can appoint the helper for the task of quieting the people.

The Sequence of the Hexagrams[1]

After heaven and earth have come into existence, individual beings develop. It is these individual beings that fill the space between heaven and earth. Hence there follows the hexagram of DIFFICULTY AT THE BEGINNING. Difficulty at the beginning is the same as filling up.

Chun does not really mean filling up. What is meant is the difficulty that arises when heaven and earth, the light and the shadowy principle, have united for the first time, and all beings are begotten and brought to birth. This produces a chaos that fills up everything, hence the idea of filling up is associated with the hexagram Chun.

Miscellaneous Notes

Chun is visible but has not yet lost its dwelling.

---

1. [*Hsü Kua:* Ninth Wing. There is no text of this wing for the first two hexagrams.]

The grass has already pushed its tips out of the earth, that is, it is visible but still within the earth, its original dwelling place. The upper nuclear trigram, mountain, indicates visibility; the lower, earth, means dwelling.

THE JUDGMENT

DIFFICULTY AT THE BEGINNING works supreme success,

Furthering through perseverance.

Nothing should be undertaken.

It furthers one to appoint helpers.

Commentary on the Decision

DIFFICULTY AT THE BEGINNING: the firm and the yielding unite for the first time, and the birth is difficult.

The lower primary trigram is Chên, the eldest son, who comes into being when the light power and the dark power first draw together. This indicates the first union. K'an, the upper primary trigram, means difficulty, danger. This indicates the difficulty of the birth.

Movement in the midst of danger brings great success and perseverance.

The lower trigram, Chên, is movement; the upper, K'an, is danger. Hence we have movement in the midst of danger. By movement one gets out of the danger. This explains the words of the text: "Supreme success, furthering through perseverance."

The movement of thunder and rain fills the atmosphere. If chaos and darkness prevail while heaven is creating, it is fitting to appoint helpers, without being oneself thereby lulled to rest.

This too describes the filling up of the atmosphere with the difficulties that prevail up to the point when a thunderstorm breaks. The final effect, however, is presaged in the fact that the two images are not instanced in the sequence [predicated by the structure of the hexagram] of K'an (clouds) above and Chên (thunder) below; instead, thunder is mentioned first and then the clouds, dissolved, are spoken of as rain.

Just as in a storm, thunder and darkening clouds precede release, so in the affairs of men a chaotic time precedes a period of order. At such a time a ruler entrusted with bringing order out of chaos needs efficient helpers. At first, however, the situation remains serious and difficult, and he must not try to rely wholly on others. This saying is suggested by the two rulers of the hexagram. The nine at the beginning indicates the efficient helper who should be appointed in such dangerous times; the nine in the fifth place means that there are still difficulties that preclude yielding to inaction. Because of the precarious conditions, the nine in the fifth place must still await the proper solution and may not yet rest.

THE IMAGE

Clouds and thunder:
The image of DIFFICULTY AT THE BEGINNING.
Thus the superior man
Brings order out of confusion.

While in the Commentary on the Decision the sequence is that of thunder and rain, to indicate the end condition brought about by the movement, here clouds and thunder are named in the sequence they follow in the structure of the hexagram. This specifies the condition before the rain, which symbolizes danger (K'an). To overcome it, we must separate and combine, as happens when a thunderstorm breaks—first clouds above and thunder below, then thunder above and rain below.

THE LINES

○ Nine at the beginning:

a) Hesitation and hindrance.
It furthers one to remain persevering.
It furthers one to appoint helpers.

b) Although hesitation and hindrance still prevail, the aim of the work is nonetheless to carry out what is right. When an eminent man subordinates himself to his inferiors, he wins the hearts of all people.

This line is a ruler of the hexagram. It stands at the beginning, which indicates that the difficulties at the beginning remain unsolved. Here nothing can be accomplished suddenly; the confusion must be resolved gradually. The character and position of the line show the right way to this goal. It is by nature a light, firm line, hence eminent, and as such places itself below the weak yin lines, which cannot help themselves. To rule by serving is the secret of success. Thus this line is the efficient helper needed to overcome obstacles in times of difficulty at the beginning.

Six in the second place:

a) Difficulties pile up.
Horse and wagon part.
He is not a robber;
He wants to woo when the time comes.
The maiden is chaste,
She does not pledge herself.
Ten years—then she pledges herself.

b) The difficulty of the six in the second place is that it rests upon a rigid line. Pledging herself after ten years means return to the general rule.

This line stands in the midst of the difficulties at the beginning. Its normal connection is with the nine in the fifth place, with which it has a relationship of correspondence. But this relationship is disturbed by the influence of the nine at the beginning, which stands below and through its importunities (it is moreover one of the rulers of the hexagram) causes doubt and uncertainty. But since the six in the second place is central and correct, these temptations are overcome, and when the time of difficulty is at an end ("ten years" indicates a complete cycle) the general rule obtains again, and the connection with the nine in the fifth place is established.

Six in the third place:

a) Whoever hunts deer without the forester
Only loses his way in the forest.
The superior man understands the signs of the time
And prefers to desist.
To go on brings humiliation.

b) "He hunts deer without the forester," that is, he desires the game.

"The superior man understands the signs of the time and prefers to desist. To go on brings humiliation." It leads to failure.

The line is weak in character but occupies a strong place, being moreover at the top of the trigram of movement. Out of this arises the danger that its movement will be uncontrolled and disturbed by desire. Such movement must lead to failure.

In terms of the nuclear trigrams, the line belongs in one aspect to the lower nuclear trigram K'un, and in this position it has abandoned the ruler and leader and retains only movement. Here the saying in the hexagram K'un applies: "If one tries to lead, one goes astray." The forest is suggested by the upper nuclear trigram Kên, mountain, whose realm is entered here. Since the six in the third place does not have a corresponding line above, in the sixth place, it fails and does not find the game it is seeking.

Six in the fourth place:

a) Horse and wagon part.
Strive for union.
To go brings good fortune.
Everything acts to further.

b) To go only when bidden—this is clarity.

This line is in the relationship of correspondence to the nine at the beginning, and from this arises the idea of waiting until courted. The courting is expressed in the fact that the nine at the beginning subordinates itself to the six in the fourth place. This nine at the beginning is the active ruler of the hexagram; in contradistinction to this, the six in the fourth place stands for an able man wise enough not to offer his services and to wait until bidden.

○   Nine in the fifth place:

a)   Difficulties in blessing.
   A little perseverance brings good fortune.
   Great perseverance brings misfortune.

b)   "Difficulties in blessing," because the benefaction is not yet recognized.

This line is one of the rulers of the hexagram, and being central and correct, it is capable of having a beneficial influence. However, this influence is impaired in several ways. First, the line stands in the middle of the trigram K'an, gorge, and as the image implies, is shut off at both sides by steep walls. Hence, as in the case of a river between steep banks, its influence cannot benefit the surroundings. Furthermore, the six in the second place, although in the relationship of correspondence to it, is too weak, while the nine at the beginning, the other ruler of the hexagram, is not in direct relationship to it. Therefore, from the individual standpoint of the nine in the fifth place, the ruler below is to be regarded rather as a rival. Finally, the line is at the top of the upper nuclear trigram Kên, whose attribute is keeping still, and which thus also obstructs its influence.

   Six at the top:

a)   Horse and wagon part.
   Bloody tears flow.

b)   "Bloody tears flow." How could one tarry long in this!

Like the second and fourth lines, this line is symbolized by a wagon that stops and is unhitched. But while the second line is related to both the first and the fifth line, and hence needs only to avoid a false tie, and the six in the fourth place corresponds with the nine at the beginning and finds in it a suitable tie, the six at the top is entirely isolated, because there is no corresponding line in the third place. At the top of the trigram K'an, whose symbol is a defective wagon, it [the line as the traveler] is forced to unhitch. But no one comes to the rescue, and therefore the other symbols of the trigram K'an —water (tears) and blood—manifest themselves. However, the state of despair is not a lasting one. Indeed, since this top line is a six, it changes into its opposite, and out of the trigram for danger and gorge there develops the trigram Sun, which means wind, and which therefore overcomes the standstill. In this situation, therefore, one must quickly introduce a change.

NOTE. The hexagram as a whole has the character of difficulty at the beginning, and the individual lines represent different single situations at the time of this difficulty. As regards the position of the lines in relation to one another, neither their intrinsic character nor their positions in the hexagram as a whole are to be taken into account; the objective position in each case is all that matters. For instance, taking the hexagram as a whole, the nine in the fifth place and the nine at the beginning are the rulers, the former being the overlord who gives office to the latter as his vassal. But taken individually, the nine at the beginning is to be regarded not as a helper of the nine in the fifth place, but only as a rival—by virtue of its extrinsic position, deflecting the six in the second place, which has a relationship of correspondence with the nine in the fifth place. This rule for evaluating the individual lines is to be borne in mind throughout.

Another idea obtaining throughout the book is that each hexagram signifies a time situation. But the application of the hexagrams depends upon men. Here for example the time of DIFFICULTY AT THE BEGINNING is indicated. The application will vary according to whether it is a ruler, an official, or a private person who is in this time situation. The fundamental lines of direction are of course the same, but they must always be fitted to the individual case.

A survey of the individual lines shows two possible courses at the time of DIFFICULTY AT THE BEGINNING. In the case of some of the lines it is the individual's own activity, in the case of others it is external events that must overcome the difficulty at the beginning, and where these means of overcoming it fail, misfortune results. The strong places, the first, third, and fifth, represent hindrance due to one's own activity. The nine at the beginning and the nine in the fifth place are strong, hence the advice appropriate to these places is given: the nine at the beginning needs patience, stability, and helpers; the nine in the fifth place must learn to work gradually, step by step. On the other hand, the six in the third place lacks a directive, and therefore no success is augured for it.

The weak places, the second, fourth, and sixth, must fall back on outside help—"If only something would come along and take care of me!" The six in the second place and the six in the fourth place sooner or later find this help, like a girl who finds a suitor to rescue her. The six at the top, on the other hand, is too far outside and remains isolated, so that the difficulty at the beginning is not overcome. In this case it is advisable to make a complete break and to begin a new situation.

蒙

4. *Mêng* / *Youthful Folly*

☰☰ *Nuclear trigrams* K'UN ☰☰ *and* CHÊN ☰☰

The nine in the second place and the six in the fifth are the rulers. The nine in the second place has a firm and central character, and the six in the fifth corresponds with it. The nine in the second place is in a low position; it is the teacher, capable of teaching others. The six in the fifth place is in a high position; it is able to honor the teacher and thus to teach men through him.

The Sequence

When, after difficulties at the beginning, things have just been born, they are always wrapped at birth in obtuseness. Hence there follows the hexagram of YOUTHFUL FOLLY. For youthful folly means youthful obtuseness. This is the state of things in their youth.

Miscellaneous Notes

YOUTHFUL FOLLY means confusion and subsequent enlightenment.

In early life the various qualities and aptitudes are as yet undifferentiated and undeveloped. Through education everything is differentiated, and clarity takes the place of obtuseness. Obtuseness is symbolized by the inner trigram, abyss, and clarity by the outer trigram, mountain.

THE JUDGMENT

YOUTHFUL FOLLY has success.
It is not I who seek the young fool;
The young fool seeks me.
At the first oracle I inform him.
If he asks two or three times, it is importunity.
If he importunes, I give him no information.
Perseverance furthers.

Commentary on the Decision

YOUTHFUL FOLLY shows danger at the foot of a mountain. Danger and standstill: this is folly.

The image of the hexagram, a mountain with a watery abyss in front of it, as well as the attributes of the two primary trigrams, indicating a danger before which one pauses, suggests the idea of folly.

"FOLLY has success." One who succeeds hits upon the right time for his undertaking.

"It is not I who seek the young fool; the young fool seeks me." The two positions correspond.

"At the first oracle I answer," because the position is firm and central.

"If someone asks two or three times, it is importunity. If he importunes, I give no answer." To importune is folly.

To strengthen what is right in a fool is a holy task.

The ruler of the hexagram is the strong second line. It is in the middle of the lower trigram, therefore in a central position. Since the line is strong and central, it meets with success by acting at the right time. It represents a sage in a lowly position, qualified to counsel wisely a youthful and inexperienced ruler. The youthful ruler is represented by the weak fifth line, which stands in the relationship of correspondence to the strong second line. The fifth line, which is weak in a superior place, and the second line, which is strong in an inferior place, together express the fact that the strong teacher does not seek out the young fool; rather, the latter approaches the teacher as one asking a favor. This is the correct relationship in education.

Because the second line is strong and central, it can answer the questions of the fifth, keeping within definite bounds of moderation. But if these bounds are overstepped with importunate questions, the teacher in turn becomes disagreeable toward the pupil by refusing to answer.

The saying in the text, "Perseverance furthers," is amplified by the final comment, "To strengthen what is right in a fool is a holy task."

In addition to the second line, the strong line at the top is also occupied with driving out youthful folly, while the remaining four lines represent youthful fools of various kinds. The second line, which is in a central position, represents gentleness, while the strong top line stands for severity.

THE IMAGE

A spring wells up at the foot of the mountain:
The image of YOUTH.

> Thus the superior man fosters his character
> By thoroughness in all that he does.

The spring at the foot of the mountain is still small and in its youth. The superior man derives his course of action from the images of the two trigrams. In his nature he is thoroughgoing, and clear as a mountain spring. Hence he achieves a calmness in the face of danger that emulates the great calmness of a mountain on the edge of an abyss.

THE LINES

Six at the beginning:

a) To make a fool develop
   It furthers one to apply discipline.
   The fetters should be removed.
   To go on in this way brings humiliation.

b) "It furthers one to apply discipline"—that is, in order to give emphasis to the law.

The yielding line in the lower position is a youthful fool who as yet is following no settled course. He must be subjected to discipline by the strong line standing above him in the second place, in order that firm principles and good habits may be formed in him.

○ Nine in the second place:

a) To bear with fools in kindliness brings good fortune.
   To know how to take women
   Brings good fortune.
   The son is capable of taking charge of the household.

b) "The son is capable of taking charge of the household," for firm and yielding are in union.

The yielding fifth line stands in a complementary relationship to the firm second line. Therefore the compliant master of the household permits the firm son to take over. The same holds true in public life as regards the relationship between prince and official. This line is the ruler of the hexagram.

Six in the third place:

a) Take not a maiden who, when she sees a man of
bronze,

Loses possession of herself.

Nothing furthers.

b) One should not take the maiden because her conduct
is not in accord with order.

The line is yielding in a strong place; besides, it is in the place
of transition from the lower to the upper trigram. Hence it is
not able to withstand the temptation to throw itself away, and
thus it leaves the right path. An intimate union is therefore
not favorable. The emendation of the text proposed by Chu
Hsi, who wished to read "in accord with order" as "cautious,"
is superfluous.

Six in the fourth place:

a) Entangled youthful folly brings humiliation.

b) The humiliation of entangled youthful folly comes
from the fact that it of all things is furthest from
what is real.

A yielding line in a weak place, unrelated to a firm line and
surrounded by other weak lines, is through these circumstances
completely excluded from any relationship with a real, i.e.,
firm line, and therefore remains incurably entangled in its
youthful folly.

○ Six in the fifth place:

a) Childlike folly brings good fortune.

b) The good fortune of the childlike fool comes from
his being devoted and gentle.

The fifth place is that of the ruler, but since the line is yielding
and in relationship with the firm line in the second place, we
have the idea of devotion, that is, courtesy of speech, and of
gentleness, readiness to listen. The line stands at the top of the
upper nuclear trigram K'un, which is by nature devoted.

409

Nine at the top:

a)   In punishing folly
It does not further one
To commit transgressions.
The only thing that furthers
Is to prevent transgressions.

b)   "It furthers to prevent transgressions," for then those
above and those below conform to order.

This strong line is in relationship with the weak third line,
which has deviated from order and pushed ahead regardless
of circumstances. It is vigorously sent back where it belongs by
the top line, so that it conforms to order. But since the top
line acts only defensively and does not exceed its limits, it does
not itself deviate from order.

5. *Hsü / Waiting (Nourishment)*

   Nuclear trigrams   LI   *and*   TUI

The ruler of the hexagram is the nine in the fifth place. All
transactions require patient waiting, and it is particularly essential for a ruler that his plans should be brought to fruition
through continuous influence. The remark in the Commentary
on the Decision—"Occupies the place of heaven and is central
and correct in its behavior"—refers to the nine in the fifth
place.

The Sequence

When things are still small, one must not leave them
without nourishment. Hence there follows the hexa-

gram Hsü. Hsü means the way to eating and drinking.

The connection between the two meanings of the hexagram
—nourishment and waiting—lies in the fact that we must
wait to be nourished. Nourishment depends on heaven and the
rain. It does not lie within the power of man.

Miscellaneous Notes

WAITING means not advancing.

THE JUDGMENT

WAITING. If you are sincere,
You have light and success.
Perseverance brings good fortune.
It furthers one to cross the great water.

Commentary on the Decision

WAITING means holding back. Danger lies ahead.
Being firm and strong, one does not fall into it. The
meaning is that one does not become perplexed or
bewildered.

The lower trigram is Ch'ien, whose attribute is strength. The
upper trigram is K'an, the abyss, danger; but since we feel
secure in our own strength and do not act overhastily, we avoid
perplexity.

"If you are sincere, you have light and success. Perseverance brings good fortune." For the ruling line
occupies the place of heaven and is central and correct in its behavior.

"It furthers one to cross the great water." Through
progress the work is accomplished.

The fifth line, the ruler of the hexagram, has the sincerity of
water, of which it is the symbol (K'an is a watercourse between
high banks). This line corresponds in its special quality with
the meaning of the trigram Ch'ien, the Creative, heaven. In

that it is a firm line in an uneven (i.e., yang) place, its place and character correspond, hence it is correct. Moreover, it is in the middle of the upper primary trigram and therefore central. All of these are relationships of the ruler of the hexagram that point to success. Waiting does not mean giving up an undertaking, however. To defer is not to abandon. Therefore the work is accomplished.

THE IMAGE

Clouds rise up to heaven:
The image of WAITING.
Thus the superior man eats and drinks,
Is joyous and of good cheer.

In the heavens, water takes the form of clouds. Once the clouds rise, it will not be long before rain falls. While frequently the second portion of the Image separates the attributes of the two trigrams, in order to show how a given situation can be overcome, we have in this instance an explanation of how to accept and adapt to the situation. Even as rain rises to the heavens, it is preparing to fall—whereby all life is nourished and refreshed. The superior man acts in accordance with this, and so masters the second meaning of the hexagram, for Hsü signifies nourishment as well as waiting. Further, the two nuclear trigrams—Li, clarity, and Tui, pleasure, joyousness—also play a part.

THE LINES

Nine at the beginning:

a) Waiting in the meadow.
    It furthers one to abide in what endures.
    No blame.

b) "Waiting in the meadow." One does not seek out
    difficulties overhastily.
    "It furthers one to abide in what endures. No blame."
    One has not abandoned the general ground.

Because the lowest line is firm, it does not unduly press any matter in the face of a danger that is still remote (hence the

image of the meadow), but is able to remain calm and collected as if nothing extraordinary lay ahead.

Nine in the second place:

a) Waiting on the sand.
There is some gossip.
The end brings good fortune.

b) "Waiting on the sand." One is calm, for the line is
central. Although this leads to some gossip, the end
brings good fortune.

This line is even nearer to the danger symbolized in the upper
trigram than the first line, therefore the waiting on the sand.
But it is well balanced; the capability of its nature is mitigated
by the yielding character of the place, which moreover is
central. Therefore it remains calm despite minor discords (it
is not in the relation of correspondence to the ruler of the
hexagram, but rather, since the two lines are of the same
category, in the relation of mutual repulsion), hence all goes
well. Gossip is indicated by the nuclear trigram Tui.

Nine in the third place:

a) Waiting in the mud
Brings about the arrival of the enemy.

b) "Waiting in the mud." The misfortune is outside.[1]
"Brings about the arrival of the enemy." Seriousness
and caution prevent defeat.

The strong line in the strong place is too energetic. It faces
danger and plunges into it, thus inviting enemies. Only
through caution is this harm to be avoided.

Six in the fourth place:

a) Waiting in blood.
Get out of the pit.

b) "Waiting in blood." He is yielding and obeys.

---

1. [Symbolized by the outer trigram.]

This is a weak line in a weak place; consequently, although in the midst of danger and hemmed in between two strong lines (K'an means pit and blood), it does not make things worse by pressing forward. Instead, it submits, and the storm passes over.

○ Nine in the fifth place:

a) Waiting at meat and drink.
Perseverance brings good fortune.

b) "Meat and drink. Perseverance brings good fortune," because of the central and correct character.

This line is the ruler of the hexagram. As such, it occupies the center of the upper primary trigram. It has a strong place corresponding with its strong character, hence it is correct. Moreover, it is at the top of the upper nuclear trigram Li, light, which gives it enlightenment. Altogether, this gives prospect of favorable conditions.

Six at the top:

a) One falls into the pit.
Three uninvited guests arrive.
Honor them, and in the end there will be good fortune.

b) "Uninvited guests arrive. If they are honored, in the end there will be good fortune." Although the line is not in its proper place, at least no great mistake is made.

A yielding line at the high point of danger, at the very top of the hexagram, is not really in its proper place (K'an connotes a pit). Although to all appearances a weak line in a weak place is where it should be, a certain impropriety arises from the fact that it stands at the top, while the line corresponding with it, the strong third line, is below. The arrival of three uninvited guests is suggested by this third line and the two lower ones of the trigram Ch'ien, which hold together with it. Since by virtue of their strong natures they are not jealous, everything goes well, if the yin line follows its yielding nature and meets them deferentially.

Note. The situation revealed in WAITING is one in which a strong, firm nature is faced with danger. What is required of the individual here is restraint. He must await the proper time; he must be yielding and remain calm. If he does not weigh the time conditions sufficiently and presses forward, ruthless, angry, and restless, he will certainly meet defeat. The nine at the beginning is still far from danger; hence if one holds to lasting things, one can avoid mistakes. The nine in the second place is approaching closer to danger, but it too can ultimately attain good fortune by yielding and by keeping to the middle way. The nine in the third place is actually under threat of danger, therefore it is said: "Seriousness and caution prevent defeat." The six in the fourth place has been overtaken by danger, but because it is yielding and peaceful, it gets out of the pit again. The six at the top is at the peak point of danger, but through deference it too finally attains good fortune. Thus during a time of waiting, self-control and deference are the means of avoiding harm. The significance of the time of danger is great.

訟

6. *Sung / Conflict*

Nuclear trigrams SUN ☴ *and* LI ☲

The ruler of the hexagram is the nine in the fifth place. All the other lines represent persons quarreling, and the nine in the fifth place stands for the person who overhears the quarrel. This is what is referred to by the following sentence from the

Commentary on the Decision: " 'It furthers one to see the great man': thus his central and correct position is honored."

The Sequence

Over meat and drink, there is certain to be conflict. Hence there follows the hexagram of CONFLICT.

Miscellaneous Notes

CONFLICT means not to love.

THE JUDGMENT

CONFLICT. You are sincere
And are being obstructed.
A cautious halt halfway brings good fortune.
Going through to the end brings misfortune.
It furthers one to see the great man.
It does not further one to cross the great water.

Commentary on the Decision

CONFLICT: strength is above, danger below. Danger and strength produce conflict.

"The contender is sincere and is being obstructed." The firm comes and attains the middle.

"Going through to the end brings misfortune." A conflict must not be allowed to become permanent.

"It furthers one to see the great man": thus his central and correct position is honored.

"It does not further one to cross the great water," for this would lead one into the abyss.

The name of the hexagram of CONFLICT is derived from the attributes of the two trigrams Ch'ien, strength, and K'an, danger. When strength is above and cunning below, conflict is sure to arise. Similarly, a person who is inwardly cunning and outwardly strong inclines to conflict with others.

The contender, the second line, is sincere and feels himself obstructed. He is in the inner trigram, and therefore it is said, "He comes." Because the line is strong and occupies the center, it suggests sincerity, for it makes the middle "sound." It is obstructed because it is inclosed between the two yin lines. The great man is the central and correct line in the fifth place. The judge who must render the decision abides outside the dangerous situation. He can render a just decision only by remaining impartial. The abyss into which one would fall by crossing the great water is indicated by the trigram K'an, danger. Crossing of the great water is suggested by the fact that the nuclear trigram Sun, wood, is over the lower primary trigram K'an, water.

Structurally, this hexagram is the inverse of the preceding one: hence we have conflict here, forbearance there. Although the time meaning of the hexagram is that of conflict, it nevertheless teaches at every turn that conflict should be avoided.

THE IMAGE

Heaven and water go their opposite ways:
The image of CONFLICT.
Thus in all his transactions the superior man
Carefully considers the beginning.

The movement of the upper trigram, heaven, goes upward, that of the lower, water, goes downward; thus the two draw farther and farther apart, and create conflict. To avoid conflict, all transactions (nuclear trigram Sun, work, undertaking) must be well considered at the beginning (K'an means being concerned, and the nuclear trigram Li means clarity; Ch'ien is the beginning of all things).

THE LINES

Six at the beginning:

a) If one does not perpetuate the affair,
There is a little gossip.
In the end, good fortune comes.

b) Not perpetuating the affair: one must not prolong the conflict.

Although "there is a little gossip," the matter is finally decided clearly.

The six is weak and at the very bottom. Therefore, although there is a brief altercation with the neighboring nine, which comes from without, the conflict cannot continue—the place and the character of the line are too weak. Since the nuclear trigram Li, standing above it, has clarity as its attribute, everything is finally decided justly—a fortunate thing in a conflict. As the six changes, there arises the trigram Tui, speech.

Nine in the second place:

a) One cannot engage in conflict;
One returns home, gives way.
The people of his town,
Three hundred households,
Remain free of guilt.

b) "One cannot engage in conflict: one returns home, gives way." Thus one escapes. To contend from a lowly place with someone above brings self-incurred suffering.

One cannot engage in conflict, although in this hard line in the middle of the trigram K'an, the Abysmal, intention to contend with the nine in the fifth place is inherently present. This second line, being a nine, moves; that is, it changes into a yin line. Thereby it conceals itself, and with the two other yin lines it forms the town of three hundred families, who remain free of all entanglement.

Six in the third place:

a) To nourish oneself on ancient virtue induces perseverance.
Danger. In the end good fortune comes.
If by chance you are in the service of a king,
Seek not works.

b) "To nourish oneself on ancient virtue." To obey the one above brings good fortune.

Because the line is weak in a strong place, it is not correct. Above and below are strong lines hemming it in. Moreover, being in a place of transition, it is inwardly restless. All these circumstances constitute elements of danger. Still, everything goes well, provided the line rests content with what it has honorably acquired from its ancestors. It corresponds with the third line of the "mother" hexagram, K'un; hence the oracle for this line in K'un is repeated here in part.

> Nine in the fourth place:

a) One cannot engage in conflict.
One turns back and submits to fate,
Changes one's attitude,
And finds peace in perseverance.
Good fortune.

b) "One turns back and submits to fate, changes one's attitude, and finds peace in perseverance." Thus nothing is lost.

This line is neither central nor correct, and therefore originally intended to quarrel. But it cannot do so. Over it is the strong judge in the fifth place, with whom one may not quarrel. Below it is the weak line in the third place, and standing in the relationship of correspondence to it is the weak line at the beginning, neither of which gives cause for quarrel. Its position in a yielding place gives this line the possibility of being converted and of turning away from conflict.

○ Nine in the fifth place:

a) To contend before him
Brings supreme good fortune.

b) "To contend before him brings supreme good fortune," because he is central and correct.

This line is the ruler of the hexagram; it occupies the place of honor, is central, correct, and strong. All this fits it for the task of settling the quarrel, so that great good fortune comes about through it.

Nine at the top:

a) Even if by chance a leather belt is bestowed on one,
By the end of a morning
It will have been snatched away three times.

b) To attain distinction through conflict is, after all, nothing to command respect.

A strong line at the high point of CONFLICT seeks to win distinction through conflict. But this does not last.

NOTE. The nine in the fifth place is the judge, the other lines the contenders, but only the strong lines really contend. The weak lines in the first and the third place hold back. The strong lines in the second and the fourth place are inclined by nature to contend, but cannot quarrel with the judge in the fifth place, and the weak lines below them offer no resistance. Therefore they too withdraw from the conflict in good time. Only the strong top line carries the conflict through to the end and, being in the relationship of correspondence to the weak line in the third place, it triumphs and receives a distinction. Yet the line is analogous to the top line—the "arrogant dragon"—of the hexagram Ch'ien. It will have cause to rue the matter. What is won by force is wrested away by force.

師

7. *Shih* / *The Army*

Nuclear trigrams K'UN ☷ *and* CHÊN ☳

The rulers of the hexagram are the nine in the second place and the six in the fifth. The former, positioned below, is the strong man, while the latter, being above, has capacity to employ the strong man.

The Sequence

When there is conflict, the masses are sure to rise up. Hence there follows the hexagram of THE ARMY. Army means mass.

Miscellaneous Notes

THE ARMY means mourning.

THE JUDGMENT

THE ARMY. The army needs perseverance
And a strong man.
Good fortune without blame.

Commentary on the Decision

THE ARMY means the masses. Perseverance means discipline.

The man who can effect discipline through the masses may attain mastery of the world.

The strong one is central and finds response.

One does a dangerous thing but finds devotion. The man who thus leads[1] the world is followed by the people.

Good fortune. How could this be a mistake?

This hexagram consists of a mass of yielding lines in the midst of which, in a central although subordinate place, is a single strong line. As a general, not as a ruler, it holds the others under control. From this arises the idea of the mass (the many yielding lines) and of the army—a disciplined multitude. The firm line in the second place finds support, because of correspondence, in the yielding line in the fifth place, the place of the ruler. The danger of the action is indicated by the lower trigram, K'an, and devotion by the upper, K'un.

---

1. In the text, the character for "leads" is written *tu*, which means "to poison," but should be read *tan*, "to lead."

THE IMAGE

In the middle of the earth is water:
The image of THE ARMY.
Thus the superior man increases his masses
By generosity toward the people.

Owing to the compulsory military service customary in antiquity, the supply of soldiers available from the populace was as plentiful as water underground. Hence fostering the people ensured an efficient army.

Great expanse is the attribute of the earth, which also represents the masses. Water stands for serviceability; everything flows toward water.

THE LINES

Six at the beginning:

a) An army must set forth in proper order.
If the order is not good, misfortune threatens.

b) "An army must set forth in proper order."[2] Losing order is unfortunate.

This line is at the very bottom and therefore indicates the beginning, the marching forth of the army. The water trigram indicates order and the correct use of the army. If the line changes, the lower trigram becomes Tui, joyousness, whereby of course order is upset, for joyousness is not the proper frame of mind for the onset of war.

○ Nine in the second place:

a) In the midst of the army.
Good fortune. No blame.
The king bestows a triple decoration.

---

2. The word *lü*, "order," in its original sense means a reedlike musical instrument. The literal meaning would be: "The army marches forth to the sound of horns. If the horns are not in tune, it is a bad sign."

b) "In the midst of the army. Good fortune." He receives grace from heaven.

"The king bestows a triple decoration." He has the
welfare of all countries at heart.

The second place is that of the official, in this case a general,
as this is the hexagram of THE ARMY. The grace of heaven
derives from the six in the fifth place, which, occupying a
place in the sphere of heaven, stands in the relationship of
correspondence to this line. The triple decoration derives from
the three lines all of like kind composing the upper trigram
K'un.

Six in the third place:

a) Perchance the army carries corpses in the wagon.
Misfortune.

b) "Perchance the army carries corpses in the wagon."
This is quite without merit.

The upper trigram is K'un, whose image is the wagon. This
line is weak; it stands at the peak of danger, and in the middle
of the nuclear trigram Chên, agitation. All of these are circumstances suggesting a severe defeat.

Six in the fourth place:

a) The army retreats. No blame.

b) "The army retreats. No blame," for it does not deviate from the usual way.

Literally the text reads: "The army turns to the left." In war,
"to the right" is the equivalent of "in the van," and "to the
left" is the equivalent of "in the rear." The line is extremely
weak, because it is weak by nature and also in a weak place.
Yet it is in the place appropriate to it; hence retreat, for which
it is not to be censured.

○ Six in the fifth place:

a) There is game in the field.
It furthers one to catch it.

Without blame.
Let the eldest lead the army.
The younger transports corpses;
Then perseverance brings misfortune.

b) "Let the eldest lead the army," because he is central and correct.

"The younger transports corpses." Thus the right man is not put in charge.

The trigram K'an means pig; the "field" is the earth (K'un). To the inside of the trigram K'un (field) is K'an (pig, i.e., game). Therefore it furthers one to catch it. The literal rendering would be: "To explain his mistakes." This interpretation, however, is not as satisfactory.[3] The "eldest" is the strong nine in the second place, and it is this line that ought to lead the army. If some other without experience leads it (the reference is to the six in the third place), the result will be that corpses must be transported—that is to say, there will be a defeat.

Six at the top:

a) The great prince issues commands,
Founds states, vests families with fiefs.
Inferior people should not be employed.

b) "The great prince issues commands," in order to reward merit properly.

"Inferior people should not be employed," because they are certain to cause confusion in the country.

The top place shows the victorious end of war. The great prince is the six in the fifth place. Here, as occasionally elsewhere in the case of a six at the top, an additional statement concerning

---

3. The sentence *li chih yen* is best translated by taking the word *yen* (meaning "to speak," "to explain") simply as the equivalent of an exclamation point, which it frequently is in the Book of Odes. This yields the translation, "It furthers one to hold fast, to catch" (the game).

the line in the fifth place is given—from the outward, objective standpoint. The merit rewarded is that of the nine in the second place; the inferior people are represented by the six in the third place.

比

8. *Pi | Holding Together [Union]*

≡≡ *Nuclear trigrams* KÊN ≡≡ *and* K'UN ≡≡

The ruler is the nine in the fifth place, for the hexagram is so organized that it contains only one yang line, which occupies the place of honor and holds together with all the yin lines above and below it.

The Sequence

Among the masses there is surely a reason for uniting. Hence there follows the hexagram of HOLDING TOGETHER. Holding together means uniting.

Miscellaneous Notes

HOLDING TOGETHER is something joyous.

THE JUDGMENT

HOLDING TOGETHER brings good fortune.
Inquire of the oracle once again
Whether you possess sublimity, constancy, and perseverance;
Then there is no blame.
Those who are uncertain gradually join.
Whoever comes too late
Meets with misfortune.

Commentary on the Decision

"HOLDING TOGETHER brings good fortune." Holding
together means mutual help. Those below are devoted and obedient.

This hexagram is the inverse of the preceding one. In the
latter the general, the nine in the second place, is the center,
while here the center is the nine in the fifth place, the strong,
central, and correct prince. All the other lines are yielding,
hence the relationship of mutual supplementation and assistance. The yielding lines are the subordinates who obey.
Thus the name of the hexagram is explained through its
structure.

"Inquire of the oracle once again whether you possess
sublimity, constancy, and perseverance. Then there
is no blame," because of the firmness and central
position.

"Those who are uncertain gradually join." Above
and below are in correspondence.

"Whoever comes too late meets with misfortune."
His way is at an end.

The line to which everything relates is the prince in the fifth
place. All the yielding lines below correspond with it. These
five lines mutually hold together; thereby they attain power,
and it is a joyous matter. The only one that stays apart and
does not enter into the general union is the six at the top; it
insists on going its own way, which leads to nothing.

The hexagram Pi, HOLDING TOGETHER, like the hexagram
Ts'ui, GATHERING TOGETHER (45), has the trigram K'un below, but instead of Tui, the lake, here there is K'an, water,
above. There is very little difference in meaning between the
two hexagrams. "Sublimity, constancy, and perseverance"
apply here to the whole hexagram, while in Ts'ui they apply
only to the nine in the fifth place.

In the hexagram Mêng, YOUTHFUL FOLLY, there is a reference to "the first oracle," and the commentary relates it to the
firm central line. There K'an, meaning wisdom, darkness,

oracle, is below, and the firm line appears in the first trigram. Here it is said: "Inquire of the oracle once again." The explanation in the commentary points likewise to the firm central line. But here K'an is above, hence the firm line appears in the second, that is, the upper trigram.

THE IMAGE

On the earth is water:
The image of HOLDING TOGETHER.
Thus the kings of antiquity
Bestowed the different states as fiefs
And cultivated friendly relations
With the feudal lords.

The water on the earth holds together with it. From this fact a double lesson is deduced. As water penetrates and gives moisture to the earth, so should fiefs be distributed from above; and as waters flow together on the earth, so should the organization of society show union.

THE LINES

Six at the beginning:

a)   Hold to him in truth and loyalty;
       This is without blame.
       Truth, like a full earthen bowl:
       Thus in the end
       Good fortune comes from without.

b)   The six at the beginning of HOLDING TOGETHER encounters good fortune from another quarter.

This line stands at the bottom; it is weak and in no direct relation to the ruler of the hexagram. But since the attitude in the holding together is sincere—the line is at the bottom of the trigram K'un, whose attribute is devotion—it will attain what it strives for, and this unexpectedly from the outside. The earth has for its symbol the kettle, the utensil for receiving the blessing that comes from above.

Six in the second place:

a) Hold to him inwardly.
Perseverance brings good fortune.

b) "Hold to him inwardly." Do not lose yourself.

This yielding line of the inner trigram, which stands in the relationship of correspondence to the ruler of the hexagram, suggests the idea of holding together inwardly. But just because this holding together bespeaks an inner affinity and hence is inevitable, it does not depend on unworthy external maneuvers.

Six in the third place:

a) You hold together with the wrong people.

b) "You hold together with the wrong people." Is this not injurious?

The line is weak and in the place of transition, that is, restless, not central, and not correct. The lines below and above it, as well as the six at the top, with which there is a relation, are all dark lines. Here they denote evil people.

Six in the fourth place:

a) Hold to him outwardly also.
Perseverance brings good fortune.

b) Hold outwardly also to people of worth, in order thus to follow the one above.

The firm line in the fifth place is a worthy ruler, while the yielding line in the fourth place represents the minister. A minister may show outwardly his loyalty to his worthy ruler. This situation differs from that of the six in the second place, the official as yet without a post. Such a man must be reserved in order not to lose dignity, but the minister firmly established in an official relationship may safely show his attachment. Since the line is not attracted by the six at the beginning, it is free to follow the one above with undivided allegiance.

○ Nine in the fifth place:

a) Manifestation of holding together.
In the hunt the king uses beaters on three sides only
And foregoes game that runs off in front.
The citizens need no warning.
Good fortune.

b) The good fortune resulting from "manifestation of holding together" inheres in the fact that the position is correct and central.
Discarding those who resist, accepting the devoted: this is the meaning of "foregoes game that runs off in front."
"The citizens need no warning," for the one above makes them central.

This is the image of a ruler whose followers gather around him from natural instinct. He merely makes manifest what is inherent in each individual. The spontaneity of this holding together is presented in an image of the royal hunt and its customs. The quarry accepted are the lower lines, which voluntarily offer themselves. The quarry that resists and hence is not taken into consideration is the six at the top. Here again, as in the preceding hexagram, an image of the hunt is used, but in the latter the game is pursued, while here it is allowed to go free. There the lower nuclear trigram is Chên, whose movement goes upward; here the upper nuclear trigram is Kên, Keeping Still; therefore the movement, starting with the nine in the fifth place, is downward only, not upward.

Six at the top:

a) He finds no head for holding together.
Misfortune.

b) "He finds no head for holding together." Therefore he also fails to find the right end.

This line takes its position above the ruling yang line. While the lower yielding lines find their head in this yang line, the yin line at the top has no head to follow and must therefore go astray, particularly because it stands at the top of the trigram K'an, danger.

The expression "no head" occurs also in the hexagram of THE CREATIVE. There it has a favorable meaning, because the hexagram has nothing but strong lines, and thus the expression signifies humility. Here it is unfavorable, because the line is yielding. A yielding element with "no head" bodes ill, because there is nothing to steady it.

9. *Hsiao Ch'u / The Taming Power of the Small*

Nuclear trigrams   LI   and   TUI

The six in the fourth place is the constituting ruler of the hexagram, and the nine in the fifth place its governing ruler.[1] The six in the fourth place, as the only yin line, restrains the yang lines. The Commentary on the Decision refers to this as follows: "The yielding obtains the decisive place, and those above and those below correspond with it." The nine in the fifth place accords in attitude with the six in the fourth place, thus to perfect the restraint; hence it is said in the Commentary on the Decision: "The strong is central and its will is done."

The Sequence

Through holding together, restraint is certain to come about. Hence there follows THE TAMING POWER OF THE SMALL.

---

1. [See p. 364.]

Miscellaneous Notes

THE TAMING POWER OF THE SMALL is slight.

This refers to the fact that "the small" here occupies the place of the official. Compare the hexagram Ta Yu, POSSESSION IN GREAT MEASURE (14), in which the small and yielding element is in the ruler's place.

THE JUDGMENT

THE TAMING POWER OF THE SMALL
Has success.
Dense clouds, no rain from our western region.

Commentary on the Decision

THE TAMING POWER OF THE SMALL. The yielding obtains the decisive place, and those above and those below correspond with it: this is called THE TAMING POWER OF THE SMALL.

Strong and gentle: the strong is central and its will is done, therefore "success."

"Dense clouds, no rain": the movement goes still further.

"From our western region": the influence has not yet set in.

The small, yielding line in the place of the minister holds the decisive place. The firm lines above and below all correspond with it. This structure explains the name of the hexagram. Success is due to the character of the two trigrams, inner strength coupled with outer gentleness. This is the way to achievement. Moreover, the ruler is central and his will is done. The upper trigram Sun, wind, has enough strength to condense the mists rising up from the lower trigram Ch'ien, and so to form clouds, but its strength does not suffice to cause rain. "Western region" is suggested by the original position of Sun, in the west (in the arrangement of the trigrams called the Sequence of Earlier Heaven[2]; in the Sequence of Later

2. [See p. 266.]

Heaven, Tui, the lake, has the position in the west). When Tui stands over Ch'ien, we have the hexagram of BREAK-THROUGH (43); in the latter case the water vapor is already condensed and will descend easily. In the present hexagram Tui appears over Ch'ien only as a nuclear trigram, not yet separated from it. In China, the rain clouds always come from the east, from the direction of the sea, not from the west.

THE IMAGE

The wind drives across heaven:
The image of THE TAMING POWER OF THE SMALL.
Thus the superior man
Refines the outward aspect of his nature.

The wind penetrates everywhere; this means refinement. The lower trigram is heaven; this means the essence of character. The upper nuclear trigram is Li, form. This refinement of outer form, as contrasted with the carrying out of fundamental principles, is "the small."

THE LINES

Nine at the beginning:

a) Return to the way.
How could there be blame in this?
Good fortune.

b) "Return to the way." This is something that bodes well.

This strong yang line, belonging to the rising trigram Ch'ien, naturally tends upward, but it is held back by the yielding line in the fourth place. As it stands in the relationship of correspondence to the latter, it retreats again without offering opposition, so that all struggle is avoided. The good augury is based on this.

Nine in the second place:

a) He allows himself to be drawn into returning.
Good fortune.

b) Being drawn into returning derives from the central position. Also, he does not lose himself.

This line is higher than the first and likewise tends upward by nature. But because of its central and moderate position in the lower trigram Ch'ien, it attaches itself to the first line and retreats without a struggle. Thus it assumes an attitude that saves it from losing itself or throwing itself away, as would be the case if it offered itself despite its being checked by the fourth line.

Nine in the third place:

a) The spokes burst out of the wagon wheels.
   Man and wife roll their eyes.

b) When "man and wife roll their eyes," it is a sign that they cannot keep their house in order.

The idea of the spokes bursting out of the wagon wheels is suggested by the fact that Ch'ien, being round, symbolizes a wheel, and that Tui, the lower nuclear trigram, means breaking apart. Li, the upper nuclear trigram, means eyes, and Sun, the upper primary trigram, means much white in the eyes; hence the rolling of the eyes.

This line has the same upward tendency as the two preceding ones, but while the latter renounce conflict and retreat voluntarily, this line (too strong because it is strong in a strong place, unstable because it is in a place of transition) tries to push on by force. The yielding fourth line represents the wife, who allows the spokes of the wheels, belonging to the third line, her husband, to get broken. The man looks at her fiercely in his rage, and she returns the look. Inasmuch as the third line thus abandons its family (the two lower lines), it shows that it cannot maintain order.

☐   Six in the fourth place:

a) If you are sincere, blood vanishes and fear gives way. No blame.

b) "If you are sincere ... fear gives way," because the one at the top agrees in attitude.

433

This line, in the midst of the strong lines, is empty within, that is, sincere (cf. hexagram 61, INNER TRUTH). It is the middle line of the nuclear trigram Li, which is the opposite of K'an, blood and fear; hence the absence of blood and fear. The fourth place is that of the minister. It has the difficult task of controlling with weak powers the upward-striving lower lines. This is necessarily associated with danger and fear, but because the line is sincere (yielding in a yielding place, and empty within) the prince, the nine in the fifth place, stands by it and gives it the needed support.

O   Nine in the fifth place:

a)   If you are sincere and loyally attached,
      You are rich in your neighbor.

b)   "If you are sincere and loyally attached," you will not be alone in your riches.

The fifth line is in the place of honor, in the middle of the trigram Sun, riches. Sun also means a bond, and therefore the line is attached to the six in the fourth place, its neighbor. In that the two complement each other and share their wealth, they are rich indeed.

      Nine at the top:

a)   The rain comes, there is rest.
      This is due to the lasting effect of character.
      Perseverance brings the woman into danger.
      The moon is nearly full.
      If the superior man persists,
      Misfortune comes.

b)   "The rain comes, there is rest." This is the continuously cumulative effect of character.
      "If the superior man persists, misfortune comes," for there might be doubts.

Because the line moves, being a nine, the trigram Sun, wind, becomes the trigram K'an, rain and moon. The line stands at the top of Sun—gentle and devoted—which has gradually accumulated within itself the powers of the Creative, so that the desired effect has been achieved. When this effect of the Gentle is attained, it must suffice. Should it insistently presume upon its success, danger might ensue. Persistence would lead to a doubtful situation, because restraint would then turn into suppression, and this the strong Ch'ien would certainly not tolerate.

10. *Lü | Treading [Conduct]*

Nuclear trigrams SUN ☴ and LI ☲

The constituting ruler of the hexagram is the six in the third place; the nine in the fifth place is the governing ruler. The six in the third place, as the only yielding line among the numerous firm ones, enters their midst with fear and trembling. Therefore the hexagram bears the name TREADING. Whoever holds an honored place must especially be constantly mindful of danger and fear. Because of this the judgment on the nine in the fifth place couples the idea of danger with perseverance. The Commentary on the Decision says of this line: "Strong, central, and correct, he treads into the place of the ruler and remains without blame."

The Sequence

When beings are subjected to restraint the mores arise; hence there follows the hexagram of CONDUCT.

Miscellaneous Notes

That which treads does not stay.

Appended Judgments[1]

TREADING shows the basis of character. It is harmonious and attains its goal. It brings about harmonious conduct.

This hexagram is the inverse of the preceding one. The movement of the two primary trigrams is upward, hence the idea that the one strides behind the other. The youngest daughter walks behind the father.

THE JUDGMENT

TREADING. Treading upon the tail of the tiger.
It does not bite the man. Success.

Commentary on the Decision

TREADING: the yielding treads upon the firm. Joyous, and in the relationship of correspondence to the Creative; hence, "Treading upon the tail of the tiger. It does not bite the man. Success."

Strong, central, and correct, he treads into the place of the ruler and remains without blame: his light shines bright.

The yielding that treads upon the firm is the lower trigram Tui, which follows the trigram Ch'ien. Thus the forms of the two trigrams explain the name of the hexagram.

Joyousness is the attribute of Tui, the lower trigram, which moves in the same direction as the Creative, the strong; hence the image of treading upon the tail of the tiger (Tui stands in the west, which is symbolized by the tiger). The tiger's tail is mentioned because the weak line in Tui comes behind the three lines of Ch'ien. In addition, it is to be noted that the yielding line in the lower trigram stands over the two firm lines.

The comment "strong, central, and correct" refers to the ruler of the hexagram, the central line of the upper trigram,

---

1. [From chap. VII of the Great Commentary: Fifth Wing, Sixth Wing. See pp. 345–46 for the sentences quoted.]

Ch'ien; this line occupies a place in the sphere of heaven, hence the place of the ruler. Light is the primary characteristic of the trigram Ch'ien; furthermore, the nuclear trigram Li, whose attribute is light, is contained in the hexagram.

THE IMAGE

Heaven above, the lake below:

The image of TREADING.

Thus the superior man discriminates between high and low,

And thereby fortifies the thinking of the people.

Heaven represents what is highest, the lake represents what is lowest; these differences in elevation provide a rule for conduct and mores. Thus the superior man creates in society the differences in rank that correspond with differences in natural endowment, and in this way fortifies the thinking of the people, who are reassured when these differences accord with nature.

THE LINES

Nine at the beginning:

a) Simple conduct. Progress without blame.

b) The progress of simple conduct follows in solitude its own bent.

TREADING means behavior. Good behavior is determined by character. This line is at the beginning of the hexagram, hence simplicity is the right thing for it. It progresses independently. Not being related to the other lines, it goes its way alone, but since it is strong, this agrees exactly with its inclination.

Nine in the second place:

a) Treading a smooth, level course.
The perseverance of a dark man
Brings good fortune.

b) "The perseverance of a dark man brings good fortune." He is central and does not get confused.

437

This line is light, but occupies a dark place, hence the image of a dark man. However, since he walks in the middle of the road —the line is central—he does not meet with danger, but progresses along an even path and is not led astray by wrong relationships.

☐   Six in the third place:

a)   A one-eyed man is able to see,

A lame man is able to tread.

He treads on the tail of the tiger.

The tiger bites the man.

Misfortune.

Thus does a warrior act on behalf of his great prince.

b)   "A one-eyed man is able to see," but not enough for clarity.

"A lame man is able to tread," but not enough to tread with others.

The misfortune in the biting of the man is due to the fact that the place is not appropriate.

"Thus does a warrior act on behalf of his great prince," because his will is firm.

This line stands in both the nuclear trigrams, Li, eye, and Sun, leg. But since it is not correct—being weak in a strong place—its seeing and treading are defective. Furthermore, the place is in the very mouth of Tui, the lower trigram, hence the idea that the tiger bites. As a weak line it occupies a strong place and rests upon a firm line. Since it is at the high point of joyousness (Tui), it is light-minded and fails to retreat despite the danger of the situation. This suggests that it treads on the tail of the tiger and is injured. When the line changes, the lower trigram becomes Ch'ien. This suggests the warrior who pushes on ruthlessly in order to serve his prince.

Nine in the fourth place:

a)   He treads on the tail of the tiger.

Caution and circumspection

Lead ultimately to good fortune.

b) "Caution and circumspection lead ultimately to good fortune," because what is willed is done.

This line is related to the nine at the beginning, therefore it is careful when treading on the tail of the tiger. Its quality is the exact opposite of that of the foregoing line: in the latter, we have inner weakness coupled with outward aggressiveness, which leads into danger, here we have inner strength with outward caution, which leads to good fortune.

O   Nine in the fifth place:

a)   Resolute conduct.

   Perseverance with awareness of danger.

b)   "Resolute conduct. Perseverance with awareness of danger." The place is correct and appropriate.

The ruler of the hexagram, correct, central, strong, positioned in the ruler's place, is pledged to resolute action. At the same time he is aware of danger. Hence the good result announced in the judgment on the hexagram as a whole.

   Nine at the top:

a)   Look to your conduct and weigh the favorable signs. When everything is fulfilled, supreme good fortune comes.

b)   "Supreme good fortune" in the topmost place carries great blessing.

The line stands at the end of TREADING and therefore treads upon nothing further. Hence it looks back over its conduct. Since it has a strong character because of its nature (a strong line) and knows caution because of its place, good fortune is assured.

NOTE. This hexagram means conduct, with the secondary meaning of good manners. In practice, good manners depend on modesty and possession of a gracious ease. The hexagram consists of the Joyous below, related to the Creative, the strong, above. Thus the subordinate is cautious in the service of his superior.

Strange to note, although the hexagram as a whole, owing to the character of its two trigrams, contains the idea that the tiger on whose tail the man treads does not harm him, the line that evokes this idea, the six in the third place, is the very line whose individual fate it is to be bitten by the tiger. The reason is that on the one hand, when the hexagram is considered as a whole, the lower trigram as a unit is taken as joyous and obedient; on the other, however, in the judgment on the individual line, the latter is evaluated according to its unfavorable position, which bodes ill for it. Very often in the Book of Changes one can note such a difference between the judgment pertaining to the hexagram as a whole and that pertaining to an individual line.

11. *T'ai* / *Peace*

Nuclear trigrams CHÊN ☳ *and* TUI ☱

The rulers of the hexagram are the nine in the second place and the six in the fifth. The meaning of the hexagram is that what is above and what is below are united and of one will. The nine in the second place fulfills completely the duties of the official in relation to the ruler, and the six in the fifth place fulfills completely the duties of the ruler in relation to his subordinates. The two lines are the constituting as well as the governing rulers.

The Sequence

Good conduct, then contentment; thus calm prevails. Hence there follows the hexagram of PEACE. Peace means union, interrelation.

The Chinese word *t'ai* is not easy to translate. It means contentment, rest, peace, in the positive sense of unobstructed, complete union, bringing about a time of flowering and greatness. The movement of the lower trigram Ch'ien tends upward, that of the upper trigram K'un tends downward, and thus they approach each other. This hexagram is correlated with the first month (February–March).

Miscellaneous Notes

The hexagrams of STANDSTILL and PEACE stand in natural opposition to each other.

THE JUDGMENT

PEACE. The small departs,
The great approaches.
Good fortune. Success.

Commentary on the Decision

PEACE. "The small departs, the great approaches. Good fortune. Success."

In this way heaven and earth unite, and all beings come into union.

Upper and lower unite, and they are of one will.

The light principle is within, the shadowy without; strength is within and devotion without; the superior man is within, the inferior without.

The way of the superior man is waxing; the way of the inferior man is waning.

Taken as a whole and as one of the "calendar" hexagrams, this hexagram is interpreted with the idea that the strong lines entering from below are mounting, while the weak lines above are withdrawing from the hexagram. Therefore, "The small departs, the great approaches."

The movement of the two trigrams toward each other gives rise to another interpretation. The lower, ascending trigram is Ch'ien, heaven. The upper, sinking trigram is K'un, the earth. Thus the two primary powers unite, and all things enter upon union and development. This corresponds with the state of things at the beginning of the year.

In terms of the human world, with special reference to two lines—the six in the fifth place representing the prince, and the nine in the second place representing the official—the result is unity between high and low, their wills being directed to a common goal. The positions of the two trigrams—within (below) and without (above)—lead to still another reflection. The yang power is within, the yin power without. This points to a difference in rank between the ruling yang power at the center and the dependent yin power at the periphery; this is further emphasized by the respective attributes of the trigrams, strength and devotion. These relative positions are likewise favorable for both elements.

In relation to the political field, another consideration arises from the difference in value between the superior persons symbolized by the light lines and the inferior persons symbolized by the dark lines. Good men are at the center of power and influence; inferior people are on the outside, subject to the influence of the good. This likewise works for the good of the whole.

The movement of the hexagram as a whole produces finally a victorious ascendancy of the principles of the good man and a withdrawal and defeat of the principles of inferior men.

None of this occurs arbitrarily; it is born of the time. It is the season of spring, both in the year and in history, that is represented by this hexagram.

THE IMAGE

Heaven and earth unite: the image of PEACE.
Thus the ruler
Divides and completes the course of heaven and earth;
He furthers and regulates the gifts of heaven and earth,
And so aids the people.

Human activity must help nature in times of flowering. Nature must be kept within limits, as the earth limits the activities of heaven, in order to regulate excess. On the other hand, nature must be furthered, as heaven furthers the gifts of the earth, in order to make up for deficiencies. In this way the blessings of nature benefit the people. The Chinese word for "aid" means literally "being at the left and the right," which in turn derives from the fact that the movement of yang is thought of as being toward the right and that of yin toward the left.

THE LINES

Nine at the beginning:

a) When ribbon grass is pulled up, the sod comes with it.

Each according to his kind.

Undertakings bring good fortune.

b) "When ribbon grass is pulled up. . . . Undertakings bring good fortune." The will is directed outward.

The three lines of the lower trigram Ch'ien belong with one another and advance together. The lowest place suggests the idea of sod. The six in the fourth place unites with the nine at the beginning, therefore going forth—"undertakings"—brings good fortune.

O Nine in the second place:

a) Bearing with the uncultured in gentleness,

Fording the river with resolution,

Not neglecting what is distant,

Not regarding one's companions:

Thus one may manage to walk in the middle.

b) "Bearing with the uncultured in gentleness . . . thus one may manage to walk in the middle," because the light is great.

The trigram Ch'ien incloses K'un, bears the uncultured in gentleness. The line must proceed resolutely through the river because it is the lowest line in the nuclear trigram Tui, water. It must step over those that lie between, in order to

443

unite with the six in the fifth place. Those far away are symbolized by the six at the top; the friends are the two other strong lines of Ch'ien. They are not regarded because the nine in the second place unites with the six in the fifth. "Thus one may manage to walk in the middle," or according to another explanation, "Thus one obtains aid for walking in the middle," that is, from the six in the fifth place.

Nine in the third place:

a)   No plain not followed by a slope.
No going not followed by a return.
He who remains persevering in danger
Is without blame.
Do not complain about this truth;
Enjoy the good fortune you still possess.

b)   "No going not followed by a return": this is the boundary of heaven and earth.

This line is in the middle of the hexagram, on the boundary between heaven and earth, between yang and yin. This suggests the idea of a setback. But the line is extremely strong. Hence it should not be sad, but only strong, enjoying the good fortune that still remains (the nuclear trigram, Tui, in which this is the middle line, means mouth, hence enjoying, eating).

Six in the fourth place:

a)   He flutters down, not boasting of his wealth,
Together with his neighbor,
Guileless and sincere.

b)   "He flutters down, not boasting of his wealth": all of them have lost what is real.
"Guileless and sincere": he desires it in the depths of his heart.

As the three lower lines ascend together, so the three upper ones sink down together, fluttering. None wants to possess wealth for himself alone. This line has "lost what is real," that is, it has renounced material advantage such as would beckon if it should egotistically unite with the nine at the beginning.

○ Six in the fifth place:

a) The sovereign I
Gives his daughter in marriage.
This brings blessing
And supreme good fortune.

b) "This brings blessing and supreme good fortune," because he is central in carrying out what he desires.

The nuclear trigram Chên means the entrance of the ruler ("God comes forth in the sign of the Arousing"[1]). This line stands over the nuclear trigram Tui, the youngest daughter, hence the image of the daughter given in marriage to the nine in the second place, which is lower in rank. Owing to its central character, the six in the fifth place achieves the fulfillment of all its wishes.

Six at the top:

a) The wall falls back into the moat.
Use no army now.
Make your commands known within your own town.
Perseverance brings humiliation.

b) "The wall falls back into the moat." His plans fall into confusion.

The earth, in the highest place, indicates the wall. The line, like the other yin lines, tends downward; therefore it symbolizes falling into the moat. K'un means mass, the army. The nuclear trigram Tui (mouth) suggests commands.

This line is in union with the restless nine in the third place. Thus it is drawn into the confusion prophesied in relation to the latter. But if one keeps oneself inwardly free and takes care of those nearest to him, he can guard against the impending ruin—though only in silence. In general, the time fulfills itself of necessity.

---

1. [See p. 268, sec. 5.]

12. *P'i / Standstill [Stagnation]*

Nuclear trigrams SUN *and* KÊN

The rulers of the hexagram are the six in the second place and the nine in the fifth. During standstill, those above are out of union with those below. The saying associated with the six in the second place is: "Standstill brings success." The line refers to a person who takes refuge in his virtue in order to avoid difficulties. The saying associated with the nine in the fifth place is: "Standstill is giving way." This line refers to someone who transforms standstill into peace. However, the six in the second place is the ruler having the constituting function in the hexagram, while the nine in the fifth place is the ruler that governs it.

The Sequence

Things cannot remain forever united; hence there follows the hexagram of STANDSTILL.

This hexagram is the inverse of the preceding one. Therefore the movements of the trigrams diverge. The trigram Ch'ien above withdraws always farther upward, and K'un below sinks farther and farther down. The two nuclear trigrams, Sun, gentleness, and Kên, Keeping Still, also characterize the hexagram. These trigrams form the hexagram Ku, WORK ON WHAT HAS BEEN SPOILED (18), and in the latter too have the meaning of standstill. The hexagram P'i is linked with the seventh month (August–September).

Miscellaneous Notes

The hexagrams of STANDSTILL and PEACE are opposed in their natures.

THE JUDGMENT

STANDSTILL. Evil people do not further
The perseverance of the superior man.
The great departs; the small approaches.

Commentary on the Decision

"Evil people of the time of STANDSTILL do not further the perseverance of the superior man. The great departs; the small approaches."

Thus heaven and earth do not unite, and all beings fail to achieve union.

Upper and lower do not unite, and in the world, states go down to ruin.

The shadowy is within, the light without; weakness is within, firmness without; the inferior is within, the superior without. The way of the inferior is waxing, the way of the superior is waning.

Point for point, these conditions are the opposite of those in the preceding hexagram. Although we are dealing with cosmic conditions, the cause is nevertheless to be sought in the wrong course taken by man. It is man who spoils conditions—aside, naturally, from the regular phenomena of decline occurring in the normal course of life as well as of the year. When heaven and earth are disunited, life in nature stagnates. When those above and those below are disunited, political and social life stagnate. Within, at the center, there should be light; instead, the dark is there, and light is pushed to the outside. Man is inwardly weak and outwardly hard; inferior men are at the center of government, and the superior men are forced to the periphery. All this indicates that the way of the inferior man is on the increase, while that of the superior man is in decrease—just as the dark lines enter the hexagram from below and press upward, and the strong lines withdraw upward.

THE IMAGE

Heaven and earth do not unite:

The image of STANDSTILL.

Thus the superior man falls back upon his inner worth

In order to escape the difficulties.

He does not permit himself to be honored with revenue.

The way to overcome the difficulties of the time of STANDSTILL is indicated in the attributes of the two primary trigrams. K'un means frugality, retrenchment. The three strong lines of the outer trigram Ch'ien, which withdraw, symbolize escape from all the difficulties that arise from the pressing forward of the inferior men. This withdrawal also implies rejection of material rewards. While in the preceding hexagram the gifts of heaven and earth are administered by the superior man, here he stands completely aloof.

THE LINES

Six at the beginning:

a) When ribbon grass is pulled up, the sod comes with it.

Each according to his kind.

Perseverance brings good fortune and success.

b) "When ribbon grass is pulled up. . . . Perseverance brings good fortune." The will is directed to the ruler.

Here, taken singly, the yin lines are regarded not as inferior but as superior, at a time when the inferior element is triumphing. In conformity with the movement of the two trigrams, there is no relationship of correspondence between the upper and the lower lines. Hence the three lower lines hang together like ribbon grass and together withdraw downward, in order to remain loyal to the prince and to avoid association with the inferior men who are advancing.

☐ Six in the second place:

a) They bear and endure;
This means good fortune for inferior people.
The standstill serves to help the great man to attain success.

b) "The standstill serves to help the great man to attain success." He does not confuse the masses.

The inferior people ingratiate themselves with the ruler, the nine in the fifth place, which is fortunate for them, for it might enable them to improve themselves. But in order not to confuse the multitude who think as he does, the superior man does not enter into any such incorrect, sycophantic relationship.

Here as in the preceding hexagram, forbearance is meant. But in the latter a superior man bears with an inferior, while here we have servile support of influential persons who are rich and powerful.

Six in the third place:

a) They bear shame.

b) "They bear shame" because the place is not the right one.

The third line is weak in the strong place of transition. This is an incorrect place for it, hence the idea of humiliation. Because the line is at the top of the lower trigram K'un, it is the one that supports and bears with the lower ones. Here the beginning of a change for the better is indicated, just as in the preceding hexagram the beginning of failure is indicated in the nine in the third place.

Nine in the fourth place:

a) He who acts at the command of the highest
Remains without blame.
Those of like mind partake of the blessing.

449

b) "He who acts at the command of the highest remains without blame." What is willed is done.

The mid-point of the stagnation has been passed. Order is gradually being re-established. This line is strong in a yielding place, therefore not too yielding. It stands in the minister's place, hence acts under orders from above, and as a result remains free of blame. Here again, as in the preceding hexagram, minister and ruler are united.

○ Nine in the fifth place:

a) Standstill is giving way.
Good fortune for the great man.
"What if it should fail, what if it should fail?"
In this way he ties it to a cluster of mulberry shoots.

b) The good fortune of the great man consists in the fact that the place is correct and appropriate.

The fifth place is that of the ruler, and since the line has all the necessary good qualities, it brings the period of stagnation to an end. But its work is not yet finished; hence the anxious concern lest things should still go wrong. This anxiety is a good thing.

Nine at the top:

a) The standstill comes to an end.
First standstill, then good fortune.

b) When the standstill comes to an end, it reverses. One should not wish to make it permanent.

Here the end is reached. With this, change sets in actually. A strong line stands at the top of the hexagram of STANDSTILL, which indicates that the change to the opposite is at hand. Here too a parallelism—i.e., with the top line of the preceding hexagram—is to be noted.

同人

13. T'ung Jên / Fellowship with Men

Nuclear trigrams CH'IEN ☰ and SUN ☴

The rulers of the hexagram are the six in the second and the nine in the fifth place. The six in the second place, as the only yin line, is able to maintain fellowship with all the yang lines, and the nine in the fifth place corresponds with it. Therefore the Commentary on the Decision says: "The yielding finds its place, finds the middle, and the Creative corresponds with it."

The Sequence

Things cannot be at a standstill forever. Hence there follows the hexagram of FELLOWSHIP WITH MEN.

Miscellaneous Notes

Fellowship with men finds love.

The movement of both primary trigrams is upward, hence parallel. In the same way the two nuclear trigrams, Ch'ien and Sun, which together form the hexagram of COMING TO MEET (44) indicate fellowship. The lower primary trigram is Li, the sun, fire. Ch'ien, heaven, becomes especially brilliant because fire is given to it.

THE JUDGMENT

FELLOWSHIP WITH MEN in the open.
Success.

It furthers one to cross the great water.
The perseverance of the superior man furthers.

Commentary on the Decision

FELLOWSHIP WITH MEN. The yielding finds its place, finds the middle, and the Creative corresponds with it: this means fellowship with men.

FELLOWSHIP WITH MEN means: "Fellowship with men in the open. Success. It furthers one to cross the great water."

The Creative acts. Order and clarity, in combination with strength; central, correct, and in the relationship of correspondence: this is the correctness of the superior man. Only the superior man is able to unite the wills of all under heaven.

The second line is the yielding element that finds its place in the middle and with which the Creative corresponds. It is to be taken as the representative of the trigram K'un, which has established itself in the second place of Ch'ien. Therefore this line accords with the nature of the earth and of the official.

The phrase "fellowship with men in the open" is also represented by this line, which stands in the place of the field (cf. the nine in the second place in hexagram 1, THE CREATIVE). The fellowship here is brought about by the official (not by the ruler), by virtue of his character, not by virtue of the authority of his position. The kind of character capable of bringing this about is delineated in the attributes of the two primary trigrams. Order and clarity are attributes of Li, and strength characterizes Ch'ien. First knowledge, then strength —this is the road to culture.

The superior man, even when placed where he serves, fills this position correctly and unselfishly and finds the support he needs in his ruler, the representative of the heavenly principle. The will of men under heaven is represented by Li (which means enlightened will) beneath Ch'ien, heaven.

Crossing of the great water is indicated by the nuclear

trigram Sun, which means wood and gives rise to the idea of a ship.

THE IMAGE

Heaven together with fire:
The image of FELLOWSHIP WITH MEN.
Thus the superior man organizes the clans
And makes distinctions between things.

Fire has the same nature as heaven, to which it flames up. It is strengthened in this trend by the nuclear trigram Sun, wind. The wind, which blows everywhere, also suggests union and fellowship. The same thought is expressed by the sun in the sky, which shines upon all things equally.

Yet there is one thing in this fellowship that the superior man must not overlook. He must not degrade himself. Hence the necessity of organization and differentiation, which is suggested by the attribute of order in the lower trigram Li.

THE LINES

Nine at the beginning:

a) Fellowship with men at the gate.
No blame.

b) Going out of the gate for fellowship with men— who would find anything to blame in this?

This line at the beginning is light, strong without egotism. The six in the second place is a divided line, open in the center, the image of a door. The nine at the beginning, strong in a strong place, seeks fellowship, and without self-interest or egotism unites with the six in the second place, which in turn is central and correct, so that no blame attaches to such a union. Even the two envious lines in the third and the fourth place cannot find anything wrong in it.

○ Six in the second place:

a) Fellowship with men in the clan.
Humiliation.

b) "Fellowship with men in the clan" is the way to humiliation.

Clan means faction, fellowship on the basis of similarity of kind. In the sequence of the trigrams in the Inner-World Arrangement, Li is in the south, the place of Ch'ien in the Primal Arrangement. Through movement, the present line becomes a nine, and Li becomes Ch'ien. These are relationships of an intimate character. But since the meaning of the hexagram favors open relations, the fellowship represented by this line is too limited and therefore humiliating.

Nine in the third place:

a) He hides weapons in the thicket;
He climbs the high hill in front of it.
For three years he does not rise up.

b) "He hides weapons in the thicket" because he had a hard man as opponent.
"For three years he does not rise up." How could it be done?

The trigram Li means weapons, the nuclear trigram Sun means to hide, also wood, thicket. Sun, in changing, becomes Kên, mountain, hence the image of a high hill in front. This line is hard and not central. It means a rough man who seeks fellowship with the six in the second place on the basis of the relation of holding together. But the six in the second place is correct and cultivates appropriate fellowship with the nine in the fifth place. The present line tries to prevent this, but its strength is not a match for that of its opponent, and so it resorts to cunning. It peeps out at its opponent but does not dare to come forth. "Three years" is probably suggested by the three lines of Ch'ien. The place is the lowest in the nuclear trigram Ch'ien.

Nine in the fourth place:

a) He climbs up on his wall; he cannot attack.
Good fortune.

b) "He climbs up on his wall." The situation means that
he can do nothing. His good fortune consists in the
fact that he gets into trouble and therefore returns
to lawful ways.

This line also seeks the fellowship of the six in the second place.
But it is without, and the second line is within. The second
line stands in the relationship of correspondence to the nine
in the fifth place, and holds together with the nine in the
third place. Hence the nine in the third place forms the high
wall confronting this fourth line, protecting the six in the
second place from it. If the fourth line tries to contend with the
nine in the fifth place, it finds that it is in no position to do so,
because of its weak and incorrect place. But since this yielding
place softens the hardness of the line, it is moved by the
exigencies of the situation to renunciation and a return to the
right way.

○ Nine in the fifth place:

a) Men bound in fellowship first weep and lament,
But afterward they laugh.
After great struggles they succeed in meeting.

b) The beginning of the men bound in fellowship is
central and straight.
"After great struggles they succeed in meeting," that
is, they are victorious.

The fifth and the second line are in a correct, direct relationship of correspondence. At first the third and the fourth line
prevent their union and they are sad, but being central and
correct, they will eventually unite. The lower trigram Li
means weapons; the upper, Ch'ien, advances vigorously to
meet it. This points to a victory of great armies.

Nine at the top:

a) Fellowship with men in the meadow.
No remorse.

b) "Fellowship with men in the meadow." The will is
not yet satisfied.

Ch'ien means the meadow before the town. The upper line is outside the hexagram, and this also indicates the meadow. Beyond the meadow is the open country. Fellowship in the meadow, then, still falls short of the ultimate ideal. The will to fellowship in the open, which brings success, is not yet satisfied.

NOTE. This hexagram embodies the ideal of the universal brotherhood of man, which, however, is not yet attained. Its demand thus points beyond all of the situations of fellowship shown in the hexagram—none of these is wholly satisfactory. None of the individual lines attains the ideal. All seek fellowship on the basis of narrower relationships. For this reason, none of them attains the great success that the hexagram as a whole envisions.

大有

14. *Ta Yu / Possession in Great Measure*

Nuclear trigrams TUI *and* CH'IEN

The ruler of the hexagram is the six in the fifth place. This line is empty and central, occupies an honored place, and is capable of possessing all the yang lines. Therefore it is said in the Commentary on the Decision: "The yielding receives the honored place in the great middle, and upper and lower correspond with it."

The Sequence

Through FELLOWSHIP WITH MEN things are sure to fall to one's lot. Hence there follows the hexagram of POSSESSION IN GREAT MEASURE.

Miscellaneous Notes

POSSESSION IN GREAT MEASURE indicates the mass.

The two primary trigrams, Ch'ien and Li, are both ascending, and so are the nuclear trigrams, Ch'ien and Tui. All these circumstances are extremely favorable. This hexagram is the inverse of the preceding one. It is more favorable than FEL-LOWSHIP WITH MEN, because here the ruler is at the same time in the place of authority, the fifth place.

THE JUDGMENT

POSSESSION IN GREAT MEASURE.
Supreme success.

Commentary on the Decision

POSSESSION IN GREAT MEASURE: the yielding receives the honored place in the great middle, and upper and lower correspond with it. This is called POSSESSION IN GREAT MEASURE.

His character is firm and strong, ordered and clear; it finds correspondence in heaven and moves with the time; hence the words, "Supreme success."

The yielding element that receives the honored position is the six in the fifth place. As contrasted with the six in the second place in the preceding hexagram, this line occupies the "great" middle; from this vantage, possession of the five strong lines can be organized much better. The official can indeed unite people, but only the prince can possess them. In the preceding hexagram the strong lines stand only in indirect relationship to the prince; here they are directly related. Thus the structure of the hexagram gives rise to the name.

The words of the Judgment are interpreted on the basis of the attributes and structure of the hexagram. Within dwell the firmness and power of Ch'ien; to the outside, the clear and ordered form of Li appears. The six in the fifth place, the ruler to whom everything conforms, modestly conforms on his part with the nine in the second place and finds correspondence there in the center of heaven. Ch'ien, being doubled (lower primary trigram and lower nuclear trigram), indicates the

457

flow of time. The successful execution of measures demands that firm decision dwell within the mind, while the method of execution must be ordered and clear.

THE IMAGE

Fire in heaven above:

The image of POSSESSION IN GREAT MEASURE.

Thus the superior man curbs evil and furthers good,

And thereby obeys the benevolent will of heaven.

The sun in heaven, which shines upon everything, is the image of possession in great measure. Suppression of evil is indicated by the trigram Ch'ien, the trigram that metes out judgment, and that fights the evil in living beings. Furthering of the good is indicated by the trigram Li, which clarifies and orders everything. Both are the decree of benevolent heaven (Ch'ien), to which the superior man devotes himself obediently (Li means devotion).

THE LINES

Nine at the beginning:

a) No relationship with what is harmful;

There is no blame in this.

If one remains conscious of difficulty,

One remains without blame.

b) If the nine at the beginning in POSSESSION IN GREAT MEASURE has no relationships, this is harmful.

The upper trigram Li means weapons and therefore something harmful. This line is still far away from Li, hence there is no relationship with the latter. Difficulties exist, because great possession in a lowly place attracts danger. Therefore caution is fitting. However, since the line is strong, it may be assumed that it remains free of blame.

Nine in the second place:

a) A big wagon for loading.

One may undertake something.

No blame.

b) "A big wagon for loading." Accumulating in the middle; thus no harm results.

Ch'ien symbolizes a wheel and a big wagon. The load to be placed in the wagon consists of the three lines of the trigram. Since Ch'ien implies vigorous movement, undertakings are indicated. The present line is firm and central and in the relationship of correspondence to the ruler of the hexagram, therefore everything is favorable. Ordinarily, accumulation of treasure brings disaster, but here accumulating in the middle is correct and central and brings no harm. It is not earthly but heavenly treasure that is being accumulated.

Nine in the third place:

a) A prince offers it to the Son of Heaven.

A petty man cannot do this.

b) "A prince offers it to the Son of Heaven." A petty man harms himself.

This line is strong and correct and has relationships above. Being at the top of the lower trigram, it represents the prince. Since it belongs to the trigram Ch'ien and to the nuclear trigram Tui, it is ready to sacrifice. A small-minded man would give merely from a desire for gain, and this would result only in harm.

Nine in the fourth place:

a) He makes a difference
Between himself and his neighbor.
No blame.

b) "He makes a difference between himself and his neighbor. No blame." He is clear, discriminating, and intelligent.

The six in the fifth place has possession of the five yang lines. This fourth line is in the place of the minister; hence it might ignore the difference between itself and the ruler, and arrogate possession to itself. But since it is strong in a weak place, it is too modest to do this, and since it is at the beginning of Li, it

459

has Li's attribute of clear discrimination, which prevents any such confusion of "mine" and "thine."

○ Six in the fifth place:

a) He whose truth is accessible, yet dignified,
Has good fortune.

b) "He whose truth is accessible": by his trustworthiness he kindles the will of others. The good fortune of his dignity comes from the fact that he acts easily, without prearrangements.

The six in the fifth place is in the place of honor. It is modest and true, therefore it moves the other lines to confidence. Owing to its position, however, it can also impress by its dignity. This it does easily, however, and without external prearrangements, because it holds the great middle. Therefore it arouses no unpleasant feelings.

Nine at the top:

a) He is blessed by heaven.
Good fortune.
Nothing that does not further.

b) The place at the top of POSSESSION IN GREAT MEASURE has good fortune. This is because it is blessed by heaven.

The five yang lines are all in the possession of the six in the fifth place. Even the top line submits to it. Ch'ien and Li are both heavenly in nature, therefore it is said that heaven blesses this line. In the commentary on this line, as well as in that on the first line of the hexagram, special mention is made of the position, in order to emphasize the end and the beginning. For this hexagram is organized so favorably that the movement setting in at the beginning does not at the close come to standstill nor change to its opposite, but ends harmoniously.

謙

15. *Ch'ien / Modesty*

Nuclear trigrams CHÊN ☳ and K'AN ☵

The ruler of the hexagram is the nine in the third place. It is the only light line in the hexagram; it is in its proper place and stands in the lower trigram. This is the symbol of modesty, therefore the judgment on this line is the same as that on the hexagram as a whole. The commentary often attributes misfortune to third lines, but this one is very favorable.

The Sequence

He who possesses something great must not make it too full; hence there follows the hexagram of MODESTY.

Miscellaneous Notes

Things are easy for the modest person.

The movement of both primary trigrams is downward, but the sinking tendency of the upper trigram is stronger than that of the lower, and in this way the connection between the two remains assured. The lower nuclear trigram sinks, while the upper rises.

Appended Judgments

MODESTY shows the handle of character. MODESTY gives honor and shines forth. MODESTY serves to regulate the mores.

461

Good character has modesty for a handle; by means of it good character can be grasped and made one's own. Modesty is ready to honor others, and in so doing shows itself at its best. Modesty is the attitude of mind that underlies sincere observance of the mores.

THE JUDGMENT

MODESTY creates success.

The superior man carries things through.

Commentary on the Decision

MODESTY creates success, for it is the way of heaven to shed its influence downward and to create light and radiance. It is the way of the earth to be lowly and to go upward.

It is the way of heaven to make empty what is full and to give increase to what is modest. It is the way of the earth to change the full and to augment the modest. Spirits and gods bring harm to what is full and prosper what is modest. It is the way of men to hate fullness and to love the modest.

Modesty that is honored spreads radiance. Modesty that is lowly cannot be ignored. This is the end attained by the superior man.

Here the structure of the hexagram is used to explain the saying that modesty creates success. The nine in the third place is the representative of the yang force, which has sunk down. It brings light and radiance, attributes of the trigram Kên, the mountain. The upper trigram K'un shows the earth as having moved upward (the nuclear trigram Chên has a rising movement). The law governing the abasing of the proud and the elevation of the modest is set forth in four ways: (1) in heaven: when the sun reaches the zenith, it begins to decline; when the moon is full, it wanes; when dark, it begins to wax; (2) on earth: high mountains become valleys, valleys become hills; water turns toward the heights and wears them down; water turns toward depth and fills it up (the lower nuclear trigram is K'an, water); (3) in the effect of the forces of fate: powerful families draw down destruction upon themselves, modest ones become great; (4) among men: arrogance brings dislike in its train, modesty wins love.

The ultimate cause is never the outside world, which moreover reacts according to fixed laws, but rather man himself. For according to his conduct he draws upon himself good or evil influences. The way to expansion leads through contraction.

THE IMAGE

Within the earth, a mountain:
The image of MODESTY.
Thus the superior man reduces that which is too much,
And augments that which is too little.
He weighs things and makes them equal.

To bring about the conditions set forth by the hexagram, the superior man moves in harmony with the increasing and decreasing movements of the nuclear trigrams. Where the lowly stands (K'un, earth) he ascends (Chên) and augments what is too little. Conversely, where the lofty stands (Kên, mountain) he descends (K'an). Thus he equalizes things.

THE LINES

Six at the beginning:

a) A superior man modest about his modesty
May cross the great water.
Good fortune.

b) "A superior man modest about his modesty" is lowly in order to guard himself well.

Twofold modesty is indicated by the doubly yielding character of the line (a yielding line in a yielding[1] place). Crossing of the great water is indicated by the lower nuclear trigram, K'an,

---

1. [No doubt "lowly" was meant here, since the first place is always strong. See p. 361.]

situated in front of [above] the first line. Here is that modesty in a lowly place which cannot be ignored.

Six in the second place:

a) Modesty that comes to expression.
Perseverance brings good fortune.

b) "Modesty that comes to expression. Perseverance brings good fortune." He has it in the depths of his heart.

The ruler of the hexagram, who sets the tone, is the nine in the third place. The second line has a relationship of holding together with the ruler, therefore it responds to this tone, that is, expresses itself. The line is central, hence it has modesty at the center, in the heart.

O   Nine in the third place:

a) A superior man of modesty and merit
Carries things to conclusion.
Good fortune.

b) "A superior man of modesty and merit": all the people obey him.

Kên, mountain, is the trigram in which end and beginning meet. This line is at the top of Kên, and from this comes the idea of effort leading to achievement. The three upper lines belong to the trigram K'un, which means the masses and devotion. The yang line in the third place is the third line of the trigram Ch'ien, the Creative, distinguished likewise by indefatigable effort. The Master said:

When a man does not boast of his efforts and does not count his merits a virtue, he is a man of great parts. It means that for all his merits he subordinates himself to others. Noble of nature, reverent in his conduct, the modest man is full of merit, and therefore he is able to maintain his position.

Six in the fourth place:

a) Nothing that would not further modesty
In movement.

b) "Nothing that would not further modesty in movement." He does not overstep the rule.

This line is in a yielding place, at the very bottom of the trigram K'un, whose attribute is devotion; it mediates between the nine in the third place and the six in the fifth. It stands in the center of the nuclear trigram Chên, movement, hence the idea of movement (literally, "beckoning").

Six in the fifth place:

a) No boasting of wealth before one's neighbor.
It is favorable to attack with force.
Nothing that would not further.

b) "It is favorable to attack with force" in order to chastise the disobedient.

This line is central, in the place of honor, yet yielding. It combines all the virtues of the ruler. It is empty, hence not boastful of its wealth. It is in the center of the trigram K'un, signifying the masses, above the nuclear trigram K'an, danger —hence the idea of chastisement.

Six at the top:

a) Modesty that comes to expression.
It is favorable to set armies marching
To chastise one's own city and one's country.

b) "Modesty that comes to expression." The purpose is not yet attained. One may set armies marching, in order to chastise one's own city and one's country.

This line stands in the relationship of correspondence to the ruler of the hexagram, the nine in the third place; hence, for reasons analogous to those obtaining in the case of the six in the second place, "modesty that comes to expression." K'un, the upper primary trigram, and K'an, the lower nuclear trigram, together make up the hexagram Shih, THE ARMY. The trigram K'un also indicates the city and the country. The purpose is not yet achieved because the line is very far away from the nine in the third place toward which it strives; hence chastisement by means of armies, in order that the two may be united.

16. *Yü / Enthusiasm*

Nuclear trigrams K'AN and KÊN

The ruler of the hexagram is the nine in the fourth place. It is the only light line, and stands in the place of the minister. This gives the hexagram the meaning of enthusiasm. Therefore it is said in the Commentary on the Decision: "The firm finds correspondence, and its will is done."

The Sequence

When one possesses something great and is modest, there is sure to be enthusiasm. Hence there follows the hexagram of ENTHUSIASM.

Miscellaneous Notes

ENTHUSIASM leads to inertia.

Appended Judgments

The heroes of old introduced double gates and night watchmen with clappers, in order to deal with robbers. They probably took this from the hexagram of ENTHUSIASM.

Yü means preparation as well as enthusiasm. The upper trigram is movement (Chên), and also the sound of thunder: this suggests the image of the night watchman making his rounds with a clapper and encountering danger (nuclear trigram K'an). The lower nuclear trigram Kên means a closed door.

The two trigrams move in opposite directions. Thunder moves upward, the earth sinks down. Nevertheless, since the upper nuclear trigram K'an indicates downward movement, while the lower, Kên, is motionless, there is a certain coherence of structure. However, the hexagram is not as favorable in outlook as the preceding one, of which it is the inverse.

THE JUDGMENT

ENTHUSIASM. It furthers one to install helpers
And to set armies marching.

Commentary on the Decision

ENTHUSIASM. The firm finds correspondence, and its will is done. Devotion to movement: this is EN-THUSIASM.

Because ENTHUSIASM shows devotion to movement, heaven and earth are at its side. How much the more then is it possible to install helpers and set armies marching!

Heaven and earth move with devotion; therefore sun and moon do not swerve from their courses, and the four seasons do not err.

The holy man moves with devotion; therefore fines and punishments become just, and the people obey. Great indeed is the meaning of the time of ENTHUSIASM.

The trigram K'un means mass, hence army. Chên, the upper trigram, is the eldest son, the leader of the masses, hence the idea of the installment of helpers (feudal lords) and of the marching of armies. The commander of the army, whose will awakens enthusiasm and spurs to movement those devoted to him, is the nine in the fourth place, the ruler of the hexagram. The secret of all natural and human law is movement that meets with devotion.

THE IMAGE

Thunder comes resounding out of the earth:
The image of ENTHUSIASM.
Thus the ancient kings made music
In order to honor merit,
And offered it with splendor
To the Supreme Deity,
Inviting their ancestors to be present.

Chên is the sound of the thunder that accompanies the movements of reawakening life. This sound is the prototype of music. Furthermore, Chên is the trigram in which God comes forth, hence the idea of the Supreme Deity. The nuclear trigram Kên is a door, and the nuclear trigram K'an means something deeply mysterious; this leads to the idea of the temple of the ancestors.

THE LINES

Six at the beginning:

a) Enthusiasm that expresses itself
Brings misfortune.

b) The six at the beginning expresses its enthusiasm; this leads to the misfortune of having the will obstructed.

This line is analogous to the six at the top in the preceding hexagram. Consequently the idea of self-expression appears here for the same reason as it does there, namely, because of the relationship of correspondence to the strong ruler of the hexagram. The line at the beginning is weak, incorrect, isolated, and instead of being cautious, expresses its enthusiasm. This is certain to lead to misfortune.

Six in the second place:

a) Firm as a rock. Not a whole day.
Perseverance brings good fortune.

b) "Not a whole day. Perseverance brings good fortune,"
because it is central and correct.

This line is in the lowest place of the nuclear trigram Kên,
mountain, hence the comparison with a rock. The movement
of the line is directed downward rather than upward, hence
its readiness to withdraw at any time. This comes from its
prudence—indicated by its central and correct position—in
the time of ENTHUSIASM.

Six in the third place:

a) Enthusiasm that looks upward creates remorse.
Hesitation brings remorse.

b) "Enthusiasm that looks upward creates remorse,"
because the place is not the appropriate one.

This is a weak line in a strong place, and moreover in the place
of transition. It is attracted by the strong line in the fourth
place, toward which it looks up with enthusiasm, because the
relationship is that of holding together with it. Thereby,
however, it loses its independence, which is not a good thing.

○ Nine in the fourth place:

a) The source of enthusiasm.
He achieves great things.
Doubt not.
You gather friends around you
As a hair clasp gathers the hair.

b) "The source of enthusiasm. He achieves great things."
His will is done in great things.

This line is at the beginning of the trigram Chên, movement,
which strives upward; it is at the same time the only yang
line in the hexagram, and all the others conform to it. Hence
it is the source of enthusiasm. The five yin lines represent the
great thing that is attained. The excess of dark lines might
give rise to a doubt, and doubt might also be occasioned by the
nuclear trigram K'an, in which this line has the middle place.

But the five yin lines are good friends of the yang line; it unites them just as a hair clasp holds the hair together.

Six in the fifth place:

a) Persistently ill, and still does not die.

b) The persistent illness of the six in the fifth place is due to the fact that it rests upon a hard line. That it nevertheless does not die is due to the fact that the middle has not yet been passed.

This place is actually that of the ruler. But since the firm line, the nine in the fourth place, as the source of enthusiasm, unites all those around it, the fifth place is deprived of enthusiasm. The fact that the line is at the top of the nuclear trigram K'an, which suggests heart disease, accounts for the idea that the person represented is chronically ill. But since his central position keeps him from becoming desperate because of this, he lives on and on.

Six at the top:

a) Deluded enthusiasm.
But if after completion one changes,
There is no blame.

b) Deluded enthusiasm in a high place: how could this last?

A weak line at the high point of enthusiasm—this leads to delusion. But since the line also stands at the top of the upper trigram Chên, whose character is movement, a factor to be reckoned with is that this situation has no permanence.

隨

17. Sui / Following

Nuclear trigrams SUN ☴ and KÊN ☶

The rulers of the hexagram are the nine at the beginning and the nine in the fifth place. The reason why the hexagram means following is that the strong man brings himself to accept subordination to that which is weak. The first and the fifth line are both strong and stand under weak lines, hence they are the rulers of the hexagram.

The Sequence

Where there is enthusiasm, there is certain to be following. Hence there follows the hexagram of FOLLOWING.

Miscellaneous Notes

FOLLOWING tolerates no old prejudices.

Appended Judgments

The heroes of old tamed the ox and yoked the horse. Thus heavy loads could be transported and distant regions reached, for the benefit of the world. They probably took this from the hexagram of FOLLOWING.

This hexagram consists of movement below and joyousness above: it shows the Arousing (Chên) under the Joyous (Tui), suggesting rest, the more so since the nuclear trigrams Sun, the Gentle, and Kên, Keeping Still, likewise point to this idea.

Thus the domestication of the ox and the horse is to be explained as a means to labor saving. Success derives from the inner structure of the hexagram. Transportation of heavy loads is suggested by the lower nuclear trigram Kên, mountain; the ox that carries these loads is analogous to the earth (the mountain belongs to the earth). Reaching distant regions is suggested by the upper nuclear trigram Sun, wind, which reaches everywhere. The traveling cart is drawn by the horse, which, like heaven, is characterized by movement (the wind belongs to heaven).

Tui is the youngest daughter, Chên the eldest son. In the hexagram as a whole, as well as in the case of the two rulers, the strong element places itself under the weak in order to obtain a following. In their movement the two trigrams have the same upward trend.

THE JUDGMENT

FOLLOWING has supreme success.
Perseverance furthers. No blame.

Commentary on the Decision

FOLLOWING. The firm comes and places itself under the yielding.

Movement and joyousness: FOLLOWING.

Great success and perseverance without blame: thus one is followed by the whole world.

Great indeed is the meaning of the time of FOLLOWING.

First, the name of the hexagram is explained on the basis of its structure and attributes. The firm element that comes—that is, moves from above downward and places itself under the yielding—consists on the one hand of Chên, which places itself under Tui, and on the other of the two rulers of the hexagram, in the first and the fifth place, both of which place themselves under yielding lines.

Chên has movement as its attribute, Tui has joyousness. Followers readily join a movement that is associated with joyousness. The explanation of the words of the text also gives expression to the fundamental principle that one must first of all follow in the right way, if one would be followed.

THE IMAGE

Thunder in the middle of the lake:
The image of FOLLOWING.
Thus the superior man at nightfall
Goes indoors for rest and recuperation.

The trigram Chên stands in the east, Tui in the west. The time between them is night. Similarly, the image designates the time of year—between the eighth and the second month —when thunder is at rest in the lake. This gives rise to the idea of following or being guided by the laws of nature.

Such resting steels one's energy for fresh action. Turning inward is suggested by the upper nuclear trigram Sun, which means going into, and rest by the lower nuclear trigram Kên, which means keeping still.

THE LINES

○ Nine at the beginning:

a) The standard is changing.
Perseverance brings good fortune.
To go out of the door in company
Produces deeds.

b) "The standard is changing." To follow what is correct brings good fortune.
"To go out of the door in company produces deeds." One does not lose oneself.

This line is the ruler of the trigram Chên. As one in authority, it might demand that others follow it, but it changes and follows the six in the second place; since the latter line is central and correct, this exceptional procedure brings good fortune. "To go out of the door"—this is because the line is outside the lower nuclear trigram Kên, meaning door.

Six in the second place:

a) If one clings to the little boy,
One loses the strong man.

b) "If one clings to the little boy": one cannot be with
both at once.

The little boy is the weak six in the third place, the strong man
is the strong nine at the beginning. The trend expressed in
FOLLOWING implies in itself that the second line emulates the
third. But the latter is weak and untrustworthy, hence the
counsel to hold rather to the strong man below, since one
cannot have both at once.

Six in the third place:

a) If one clings to the strong man,
One loses the little boy.
Through following one finds what one seeks.
It furthers one to remain persevering.

b) "If one clings to the strong man," one's will gives up
the one below.

Here the little boy is the six in the second place, and the
strong man is the nine in the fourth place. In accord with the
movement of FOLLOWING, one ought to hold to the strong man
ahead and give up the weak man below. The strong man is in
the place of the minister, hence one obtains from him what
one seeks. But the essential thing is to remain persevering, in
order not to deviate from the right path.

Nine in the fourth place:

a) Following creates success.
Perseverance brings misfortune.
To go one's way with sincerity brings clarity.
How could there be blame in this?

b) "Following creates success": this bodes misfortune.
"To go one's way with sincerity": this brings clear-
sighted deeds.

This line is the minister who follows the strong line that is the ruler of the hexagram—the nine in the fifth place. In this way he wins the success of having people follow him—a success he cannot prevent, because he is not correct (a strong line in a weak place). Thereby he draws down misfortune upon himself. The trigram Chên means a great way. This line is over Chên, that is, on the way. The nuclear trigram Kên means brightness and light.

○ Nine in the fifth place:

a) Sincere in the good. Good fortune.

b) "Sincere in the good. Good fortune." The place is correct and central.

The six at the top symbolizes a sage in retirement. The present line, the ruler, follows him. The ruler's correct and central character safeguards him against conforming to those beneath him, from whom no good would come to him.

　　Six at the top:

a) He meets with firm allegiance
　　And is still further bound.
　　The king introduces him
　　To the Western Mountain.

b) "He meets with firm allegiance." At the top it ends.

This line is at the top, with no other line before it to be followed. Hence it withdraws from the world. But it is brought back by the firm allegiance of the ruler, the nine in the fifth place. The Western Mountain is suggested by the nuclear trigram Kên, mountain, and the upper trigram Tui, which lies in the west.

18. *Ku* / *Work on* *What Has Been Spoiled* [*Decay*]

Nuclear trigrams CHÊN ▬▬ *and* TUI ▬▬

The ruler of the hexagram is the six in the fifth place; for although all of the lines are occupied in compensating for what has been spoiled, it is only at the fifth line that the work is completed. Hence all of the other lines have warnings appended to them, and only of the fifth is it said: "One meets with praise."

The Sequence

When one follows others with pleasure, there are certain to be undertakings. Hence there follows the hexagram of WORK ON WHAT HAS BEEN SPOILED. Work on what has been spoiled means undertakings.

Miscellaneous Notes

WORK ON WHAT HAS BEEN SPOILED. Afterward there is order.

The structure of the hexagram is not favorable. The heavy Kên is above; below is the gentle, listless Sun, the eldest daughter, who is occupied with the youngest son. But this stagnation is not permanent or unalterable. The nuclear trigrams show another trend. Chên comes forth from Tui; both tend upward in movement and undertake the work of improvement energetically and joyously. This hexagram is the inverse of the preceding one.

THE JUDGMENT

WORK ON WHAT HAS BEEN SPOILED
Has supreme success.
It furthers one to cross the great water.
Before the starting point, three days.
After the starting point, three days.

Commentary on the Decision

WORK ON WHAT HAS BEEN SPOILED. The firm is above and the yielding below; gentle and standing still— that which has been spoiled.

"WORK ON WHAT HAS BEEN SPOILED has supreme success," and order comes into the world.

"It furthers one to cross the great water." On going one will have things to do.

"Before the starting point, three days. After the starting point, three days." That a new beginning follows every ending, is the course of heaven.

The name of the hexagram is explained in its structure and in the attributes of the trigrams. The preceding hexagram is here reversed: the strong, upward-striving force is above, and the weak, sinking force is below. In this way the movements diverge, and relationships are lacking. The attributes of the two trigrams are inner weakness, gentle, irresolute drifting, and, on the outside, inaction. This leads to spoiling.

At the same time, however, something thus spoiled imposes the task of working on it, with expectation of success. Through work on what has been spoiled the world is set in order once more. But something must be undertaken. Crossing of the great water is suggested by the lower trigram, which means wood (hence boat) and wind (hence progress), and by the lower nuclear trigram Tui, lake.

The phrase "before the starting point," rendered literally, means "before the sign Chia." The trigram Chên, in the east, means spring and love, and the cyclic sign[1] Chia (with I) is next to it. Chia is the "starting point." Before the three spring months, whose days taken together are called Chia (and I), lies winter; here the things of the past come to an end. After the spring months comes summer; from spring to summer is the new beginning. The words, "Before the sign Chia, three days. After the sign Chia, three days," are thus explained by the words of the commentary: "That a new beginning follows every ending, is the course of heaven." Since inner conditions are the theme of this hexagram, that is, work on what has been spoiled by the parents, love must prevail and extend over both the beginning and the end (cf. hexagram 57, Sun, THE GENTLE).

Ping
Li
SOUTH

I
Sun
SE

Ting
K'un
SW

Chia
Chên
EAST

Kêng
Tui
WEST

Kên
Kuei
NE

NORTH
K'an
Jên

Ch'ien
Hsin
NW

Figure 6

1. The ten cyclic signs are:

Chia and I	east	spring	wood	love
Ping and Ting	south	summer	fire	mores [*li*]
Mou and Chi	middle		earth	loyalty
Kêng and Hsin	west	autumn	metal	justice
Jên and Kuei	north	winter	water	wisdom

Another explanation is suggested by the order of the trigrams in the Inner-World Arrangement [fig. 6; cf. fig. 2, p. 269]. The starting point (Chia) is Chên. Going three trigrams back from this, we come to the trigram Ch'ien, the Creative; going three trigrams forward we come to K'un, the Receptive. Now Ch'ien and K'un are the father and mother, and the hexagram refers to work on what has been spoiled by these two.

THE IMAGE

The wind blows low on the mountain:
The image of DECAY.
Thus the superior man stirs up the people
And strengthens their spirit.

The wind blowing down the mountain causes decay. But the reverse movement shows work on what has been spoiled. First there is the wind under the influence of Chên, the Arousing, which stirs things up; then comes the mountain, joined with the lake, which joyously fosters the spirit of men and nourishes it.

THE LINES

Six at the beginning:

a) Setting right what has been spoiled by the father.
If there is a son,
No blame rests upon the departed father.
Danger. In the end good fortune.

b) "Setting right what has been spoiled by the father."
He receives in his thoughts the deceased father.

When the first and the top line change, this hexagram becomes T'ai, PEACE, in which the father, Ch'ien, is below and the mother, K'un, above. Hence the recurrent idea of improving what has been spoiled by the father or the mother. This line stands in an inner relationship of receiving to the strong nine in the second place.

Nine in the second place:

a) Setting right what has been spoiled by the mother.
One must not be too persevering.

b) "Setting right what has been spoiled by the mother."
    He finds the middle way.

This line is strong and central, and at the beginning of the
nuclear trigram Tui, hence joyous. Since the line is in the
relationship of correspondence to the weak six in the fifth
place, which represents the mother, strength must not be
carried to extremes by a too obstinate perseverance.

    Nine in the third place:

a) Setting right what has been spoiled by the father.
    There will be a little remorse. No great blame.

b) "Setting right what has been spoiled by the father."
    In the end there is no blame.

This line is at the beginning of the nuclear trigram Chên,
the eldest son, hence the image of work on what has been
spoiled by the father. The line is too strong to be in the strong
place of transition. Therefore it might be thought that the
situation would lead to mistakes, but good intention compensates in this case.

    Six in the fourth place:

a) Tolerating what has been spoiled by the father.
    In continuing one sees humiliation.

b) "Tolerating what has been spoiled by the father." He
    goes, but as yet finds nothing.

This line is especially weak, and at the top of the nuclear trigram Tui, the Joyous. In the given situation nothing will be
gained by letting things drift.

O   Six in the fifth place:

a) Setting right what has been spoiled by the father.
    One meets with praise.

b) "Setting right what has been spoiled by the father.
    One meets with praise." He receives him in virtue.

This line is central, in the place of honor, and yielding, hence very well fitted for rectifying mistakes of the past with forbearance, yet energetically.

Nine at the top:

a) He does not serve kings and princes,
Sets himself higher goals.

b) "He does not serve kings and princes." Such an attitude may be taken as a model.

This line is at the top, strong, and at the highest point of the trigram Kên, the mountain. Therefore it does not serve the king in the fifth place but sets its goals higher. It does not work for one era, but for the world and for all time.

19. *Lin / Approach*

 Nuclear trigrams K'UN ☷ *and* CHÊN ☳

The rulers of the hexagram are the nine at the beginning and the nine in the second place, of which the Commentary on the Decision says: "The firm penetrates and grows."

The Sequence

When there are things to do, one can become great. Hence there follows the hexagram of APPROACH. Approach means becoming great.

Miscellaneous Notes

The meaning of the hexagrams of APPROACH and CONTEMPLATION is that they partly give and partly take.

The organization of this hexagram is altogether favorable. The two lines entering from below and pushing upward give the structure of the hexagram its character. Tui below moves upward, the upper trigram K'un sinks downward; thus the two movements come toward each other. The same thing takes place to an even greater extent as regards the nuclear trigrams. The lower, Chên, is thunder, which moves upward, while the upper, K'un, moves downward.

THE JUDGMENT

APPROACH has supreme success.
Perseverance furthers.
When the eighth month comes,
There will be misfortune.

Commentary on the Decision

APPROACH. The firm penetrates and grows.

Joyous and devoted. The firm is in the middle and finds correspondence. "Great success through correctness": this is the course of heaven.

"When the eighth month comes, there will be misfortune." Recession is not slow in coming.

The name of the hexagram is explained through its structure. The firm element that penetrates and grows are the two yang lines. Joyousness and devotion are the attributes of the two trigrams. The firm element in the middle that finds correspondence is the nine in the second place. It is taken as the basis for the explanation of the words of the hexagram. The eighth month is suggested in the fact that the next hexagram, Kuan (CONTEMPLATION, VIEW), in which the retreat of the strong lines parallels their advance here, comes exactly eight months after this hexagram in the cycle of the year.

THE IMAGE

The earth above the lake:
The image of APPROACH.
Thus the superior man is inexhaustible

In his will to teach,
And without limits
In his tolerance and protection of the people.

The lake, which fructifies the earth with its inexhaustible moisture, suggests teaching, which fructifies man's inner being. The earth means the masses, hence the upholding and protection of the people.

THE LINES

○ Nine at the beginning:

a) Joint approach.
Perseverance brings good fortune.

b) "Joint approach. Perseverance brings good fortune."
His will is to act correctly.

This line advances jointly with the second, hence "joint approach." The word joint also contains the idea of stimulus, influence. Having been called in, the present line seeks to influence the weak line in the second place.[1] But its will is to act correctly, since it is strong in a strong place.

○ Nine in the second place:

a) Joint approach.
Good fortune.
Everything furthers.

b) "Joint approach. Good fortune. Everything furthers."
One need not yield to fate.

Here, coming to the upper ruler of the hexagram, we are reminded that as the joint ascent of the two strong lines is grounded in fate, so fate may in time also bring regression. But if—in accord with the nuclear trigram Chên—an upward movement is initiated in time, this movement is strong enough to counteract fate, should the consequences of fate set in before these precautions are taken.

---

1. [The line is strong, but its place is weak.]

Six in the third place:

a)   Comfortable approach.
Nothing that would further.
If one is induced to grieve over it,
One becomes free of blame.

b)   "Comfortable approach." The place is not the appropriate one. A fault that induces grief no longer exists.

The third line is at the top of the trigram of joyousness, hence "comfortable approach." Its place is not the proper one. It is a weak line in a strong place, hence nothing furthers. But because it also stands in the middle of the nuclear trigram Chên, meaning shock and terror, there is the possibility of remorse. Because of this, movement—likewise a characteristic of Chên—sets in, and thus the mistake is overcome.

Six in the fourth place:

a)   Complete approach.
No blame.

b)   "Complete approach. No blame," for the place is the appropriate one.

Here we have the most intimate mutual approach of the upper and the lower trigram. The place is appropriate—a yielding line in a yielding place. The line is in the relationship of correspondence to the nine at the beginning.

Six in the fifth place:

a)   Wise approach.
This is right for a great prince.
Good fortune.

b)   What is right for a great prince—this means that he should walk in the middle.

The wisdom lies in the fact that the weak line in the central place of the ruler knows and appreciates the strong, efficient man in the second place, with whom it has a relationship of correspondence. The bond uniting the two is their common central course.

Six at the top:

a) Greathearted approach.
Good fortune. No blame.

b) "Greathearted approach." The will is directed inward.

At first it might be assumed that the six at the top, which has no relationship of correspondence, would be drawing away from the other lines. But in the time of APPROACH its direction is inward, that is, downward, so that it remains in relation with the other lines of the hexagram.

20. *Kuan / Contemplation (View)*

 Nuclear trigrams KÊN ☶ *and* K'UN ☷

The rulers of the hexagram are the nine in the fifth place and the nine at the top. The sentence in the Commentary on the Decision, "A great view is above," refers to these.

The Sequence

When things are great, one can contemplate them. Hence there follows the hexagram of CONTEMPLA-TION.

Miscellaneous Notes

The meaning of the hexagrams of APPROACH and CONTEMPLATION is that they partly give and partly take.

This hexagram is the inverse of the preceding one: above is a tree, under it the earth. The tree on the earth is something to be viewed. The upper nuclear trigram Kên, the mountain, gives the same idea, for it too towers up and is widely visible. The hexagram has a double meaning: it "partly gives," i.e., provides a sublime view, and "partly takes," i.e., contemplates, seeks to attain something by contemplation.

THE JUDGMENT

CONTEMPLATION. The ablution has been made,
But not yet the offering.
Full of trust they look up to him.

Commentary on the Decision

A great view is above. Devoted and gentle. Central and correct, he is something for the world to view.

"Contemplation. The ablution has been made, but not yet the offering. Full of trust they look up to him."

Those below look toward him and are transformed. He affords them a view of the divine way of heaven, and the four seasons do not deviate from their rule. Thus the holy man uses the divine way to give instruction, and the whole world submits to him.

The great view above consists of the two lines in the fifth and the top place. The lower trigram K'un is devoted, the upper, Sun, is gentle. The nine in the fifth place, the ruler of the hexagram, is central and correct. The nuclear trigram Kên, mountain, appears twice in the make-up of the hexagram, the one trigram intermeshed with the other.

$$\left(\text{Instead of} \ \equiv\equiv \ \text{there is} \ \begin{array}{c}\rule{1.2em}{0.5pt}\\[-2pt]\rule{0.5em}{0.5pt}\ \rule{0.5em}{0.5pt}\\[-2pt]\rule{0.5em}{0.5pt}\ \rule{0.5em}{0.5pt}\end{array}. \right)$$

Kên indicates gates and palaces; these bring to mind the temple of the ancestors, mysteriously locked. Kên is the hand, Sun means pure, hence washing of the hands. Kên means pausing, hence the uncompleted sacrifice. The rite of sacrifice is shown to the people and contemplated by them. The holy man knows the laws of heaven. He reveals them to the people, and his predictions come true. Just as the seasons of the year move under divine and immutable laws, so events do not deviate from the course he prophesies. Thus he uses his knowledge of the divine ways to teach the people, and the people trust him and look up to him.

THE IMAGE

The wind blows over the earth:
The image of CONTEMPLATION.
Thus the kings of old visited the regions of the world,
Contemplated the people,
And gave them instruction.

The wind blows everywhere on earth and reveals all things. Thus the journeys of the kings of antiquity are symbolized by the trigram Sun, wind, and the regions of the world by the trigram K'un, earth. The contemplation is the taking and the instruction is the giving for which the hexagram stands.

THE LINES

Six at the beginning:

a) Boylike contemplation.
For an inferior man, no blame.
For a superior man, humiliation.

b) The boylike contemplation of the six at the beginning is the way of inferior people.

The six in the first place pictures a small (because it is a yin line) boy (because it is in a yang place). He is very far away from the object of everyone's gaze, i.e., the prince in the fifth place, with whom he has no relationship; hence the idea of a boyishly inexperienced way of looking about.

Six in the second place:

a) Contemplation through the crack of the door.
Furthering for the perseverance of a woman.

487

b) "Contemplation through the crack of the door" is humiliating even where there is the perseverance of a woman.

The nuclear trigram Kên indicates a door, the trigram K'un a closed door, hence the crack of the door. The six in the second place indicates a girl. This line is in the relationship of correspondence to the nine in the fifth place, hence a connection exists, although it is greatly impeded.

Six in the third place:

a) Contemplation of my life
Decides the choice
Between advance and retreat.

b) "Contemplation of my life decides the choice between advance and retreat." The right way is not lost.

Here a weak line in the place of transition is undecided whether to go forward or backward. It is at the bottom of the nuclear trigram Kên, mountain. Hence the backward look over its life, hence also the idea of the right way.

Six in the fourth place:

a) Contemplation of the light of the kingdom.
It furthers one to exert influence as the guest of a king.

b) "Contemplation of the light of the kingdom." One is honored as a guest.

This line is at the top of the nuclear trigram K'un, which means kingdom, and also in the middle of the nuclear trigram Kên, meaning light. Furthermore, it is near the strong, central ruler, the nine in the fifth place, and stands in a receiving relationship to it. Hence the idea of its being treated as a guest.

O Nine in the fifth place:

a) Contemplation of my life.
The superior man is without blame.

488

b) "Contemplation of my life," that is, contemplation of the people.

Here the ruler of the hexagram is in the honored place, central and correct, at the top of the nuclear trigram Kên, mountain, hence the viewing of life as from a mountain. He who is the object of general contemplation here contemplates himself, especially with regard to the influence he has exerted upon the people.

○ Nine at the top:

a) Contemplation of his life.
The superior man is without blame.

b) "Contemplation of his life." The will is not yet pacified.

Here one ruler of the hexagram looks from the vantage of the greatest height upon the nine in the fifth place. He has not yet forgotten the world and is therefore still concerned with its affairs.

噬 嗑

21. *Shih Ho* / *Biting Through*

Nuclear trigrams K'AN ☵ and KÊN ☶

The ruler of the hexagram is the six in the fifth place. The Commentary on the Decision says of it: "The yielding receives the place of honor and goes upward."

The Sequence

When there is something that can be contemplated, there is something that creates union. Hence there follows the hexagram of BITING THROUGH. Biting through means union.

Miscellaneous Notes

BITING THROUGH means consuming.

Appended Judgments

When the sun stood at midday, the Divine Husbandman held a market. He caused the people of the earth to come together and collected the wares of the earth. They exchanged these with one another, then returned home, and each thing found its place. Probably he took this from the hexagram of BITING THROUGH.

The hexagram is here explained in the light of the meaning of the two trigrams Li and Chên. Li represents the sun high above, while Chên represents the turmoil of the market below. The inner structure of the hexagram is by no means as favorable as the outer form might lead one to conclude. It is true that clarity and movement are present, but between them, as opposing elements, there stand the nuclear trigrams K'an, danger, and Kên, Keeping Still—both formed by reason of the one fateful line in the fourth place.

THE JUDGMENT

BITING THROUGH has success.
It is favorable to let justice be administered.

Commentary on the Decision

There is something between the corners of the mouth. This is called BITING THROUGH.

"BITING THROUGH, and moreover, success." For firm and yielding are distinct from each other.

Movement and clarity. Thunder and lightning are united and form lines. The yielding receives the place of honor and goes upward.

Although it is not in the appropriate place, it is favorable to let justice be administered.

The name of the hexagram is here explained on the basis of its structure. The top line and the lowest are the jaws. The nine in the fourth place stands between the two as an obstacle to be removed by biting through. This points to the necessity of using force. The firm yang lines and the yielding yin lines are clearly set apart one from the other, without falling asunder. This is the substance of the hexagram. In the same way, innocence and guilt are clearly distinguishable in the eyes of a just judge.

Movement is the attribute of Chên, clarity that of Li; both tend upwards, thus uniting and forming clearly visible lines. The movements are separate, the coming together occurs in the heavens, whereupon the line of the lightning appears.[1]

The ruler of the hexagram is yielding by nature, a quality desirable in legal proceedings, because it prevents cruelty. However, this yielding quality is compensated by the firmness of the place, hence does not turn into weakness.

THE IMAGE

Thunder and lightning:

The image of BITING THROUGH.

Thus the kings of former times made firm the laws

Through clearly defined penalties.

Thunder and lightning follow upon each other invariably. The phrase is "thunder and lightning," not "lightning and thunder," because the movement starts from below (however, the text according to Hsiang An Shih[2] on an old stone tablet reads, "Lightning and thunder"). The penal severity that serves to make men avoid transgressions should be as clearly defined as lightning. "Penalties" corresponds with the upper nuclear trigram K'an, danger. The strengthening of the laws, in order to intimidate the heedless, should ensue with the decisiveness

---

1. Today one would speak here of the coming together of positive and negative electricity, the resultant discharge producing lightning.

2. [Author of a treatise on the *I Ching*; died A.D. 1208.]

of thunder. The laws are stable and stand rooted like a mountain (lower nuclear trigram Kên).

THE LINES

Nine at the beginning:

a)   His feet are fastened in the stocks
So that his toes disappear.
No blame.

b)   "His feet are fastened in the stocks, so that his toes disappear. No blame." He cannot walk.

Chên is foot; here it is below, hence toes. Chên also stands for the stocks. The line at the beginning is hard and stubborn, and must therefore be punished. But since it is seized at its first movement, it will improve under light punishment, hence there is no blame.

Six in the second place:

a)   Bites through tender meat,
So that his nose disappears.
No blame.

b)   "Bites through tender meat, so that his nose disappears." He rests upon a hard line.

The nuclear trigram Kên means nose. This is a yielding line in a yielding place, and it rests on the hard nine at the beginning; hence it goes a little too far in punishment.

Six in the third place:

a)   Bites on old dried meat
And strikes on something poisonous.
Slight humiliation. No blame.

b)   "Strikes on something poisonous." The place is not the appropriate one.

The nuclear trigram K'an means poison. The place is not appropriate—a weak line is in a strong place at a time of transition. Because of the lack of power, decisions are allowed to hang fire indefinitely.

> Nine in the fourth place:
>
> a) Bites on dried gristly meat.
>   Receives metal arrows.
>   It furthers one to be mindful of difficulties
>   And to be persevering.
>   Good fortune.
>
> b) "It furthers one to be mindful of difficulties and to be persevering. Good fortune." He does not yet give light.

Firmness in a yielding place points to meat with bones. This is dried by the sun (Li, in which this is the beginning line). The nuclear trigram K'an means arrows. The line is in the place of the official. It is strong, but in view of the weakness of its place, remains aware of the difficulties, hence the augury of good fortune. Although it is at the beginning of Li, the line does not yet give light, because it is in the middle of the nuclear trigram K'an.

> ○ Six in the fifth place:
>
> a) Bites on dried lean meat.
>   Receives yellow gold.
>   Perseveringly aware of danger.
>   No blame.
>
> b) "Perseveringly aware of danger. No blame." He has found what is appropriate.

The line is yielding, hence "lean" meat, and in the middle of Li, hence "dried" meat. When it changes, the upper trigram becomes Ch'ien, which means metal. As the middle line of K'un, its color is yellow—hence "yellow gold." By reason of its mildness in the place of honor, it succeeds in biting through and receives yellow gold, the symbol of firmness and loyalty. Therefore in its verdict it hits upon what is right and appropriate, so that everything turns out properly.

Nine at the top:

a) His neck is fastened in the wooden cangue,
So that his ears disappear.
Misfortune.

b) "His neck is fastened in the wooden cangue, so that his ears disappear." He does not hear clearly.

The top line indicates the head; the trigram Li, fetters. The nuclear trigram K'an means ear. The line is too hard, places itself arrogantly over the ruler of the hexagram, and does not heed him. It therefore does not heed the just sentence passed upon it, and because of this meets with the misfortune of being unable to hear any longer, even if it should desire to do so.

22. *Pi / Grace*

Nuclear trigrams CHÊN ☳ *and* K'AN ☵

The rulers of the hexagram are the six in the second place and the nine at the top. The Commentary on the Decision refers to these when it says: "The yielding comes and gives form to the firm, the firm ascends and gives form to the yielding."

The Sequence

Things should not unite abruptly and ruthlessly; hence there follows the hexagram of GRACE. Grace is the same as adornment.

Miscellaneous Notes

GRACE means being undyed.

The most perfect grace consists not in external ornamentation but in allowing the original material to stand forth, beautified by being given form. The upper trigram Kên, the mountain, is disposed to remain still; fire, Li, blazes up from below and illumines the mountain. This movement is strengthened by the nuclear trigram Chên, which likewise moves upward, while the resting weight of the mountain is activated to a falling movement by the lower nuclear trigram K'an. Thus the inner structure of the hexagram shows a harmonious equalization of movement, giving no excess of energies to the one side or the other. This hexagram is the inverse of the preceding one.

THE JUDGMENT

GRACE has success.
In small matters
It is favorable to undertake something.

Commentary on the Decision

"GRACE has success." The yielding comes and gives form to the firm; therefore, "Success." A detached firm line ascends and gives form to the yielding; therefore, "In small matters it is favorable to undertake something." This is the form of heaven. Having form, clear and still: this is the form of men. If the form of heaven is contemplated, the changes of time can be discovered. If the forms of men are contemplated, one can shape the world.

The text of the commentary does not appear to be intact. There seems to be a sentence missing before, "This is the form of heaven." Wang Pi[1] says: "The firm and the yielding unite alternately and construct forms: this is the form of heaven." This was taken as the original text, now missing, but Mao Ch'i Ling[2] takes another view and sees in it only an explanation of the foregoing sentence. But something of the sort must in fact be presupposed.

1. [A.D. 226–249.]
2. [A.D. 1623–1716.]

The yielding element that comes is the six in the second place. It places itself between the two firm lines and gives them success, gives them form. The strong element that detaches itself is the nine at the top. It places itself at the head of the two upper yielding lines and gives them the possibility of attaining form. In each case, the yang principle is the content, the yin principle the form. In the first case it is the yin line that bestows form directly and therefore brings about success, whereas the ascending yang line, by lending content, only indirectly provides the material on which the otherwise empty form of the yin lines can work itself out. Hence the effect is that it is favorable for "the small" to undertake something.

The form of heaven is symbolized by the four trigrams constituting the hexagram. The lower primary trigram Li is the sun, the lower nuclear trigram K'an is the moon; the upper nuclear trigram Chên by its movement represents the Great Bear, and the upper primary trigram Kên by its stillness represents the constellations. If one observes the rotation of the Great Bear, one knows the course of the year; through contemplation of the course of the sun and the phases of the moon, one recognizes the time of day and the periods of the month.

The form of human life results from the clearly defined (Li) and firmly established (Kên) rules of conduct, within which love (light principle) and justice (dark principle) build up the combinations of content and form. Here too love is the content and justice the form.

THE IMAGE

Fire at the foot of the mountain:
The image of GRACE.
Thus does the superior man proceed
When clearing up current affairs.
But he dare not decide controversial issues in this
    way.

This hexagram is the inverse of the preceding one. In the latter we find brightness and movement; these indicate a swift carrying out of penalties according to clearly understood laws. Here we have standstill (Kên) outside and clarity (Li) inside, and this means a theoretical, not a practical turn of mind. This attitude suffices for the application of the established rules of everyday affairs, but not for extraordinary things. One ruler of the hexagram is too weak, the other too far outside to be capable of taking hold of the situation.

THE LINES

Nine at the beginning:

a) He lends grace to his toes, leaves the carriage, and walks.

b) "He leaves the carriage and walks," for it accords with duty not to ride.

Being lowest, this line corresponds to the toes. The nuclear trigram K'an means a carriage. But the present line is below this trigram, hence does not ride. The six in the second place is the ruler of the hexagram; the nine in the beginning has no relationship with this ruler, so that it is not fitting for the line to ride. On the other hand, as a yang line, it possesses sufficient inner strength to be reconciled to the fate thus imposed.

○ Six in the second place:

a) Lends grace to the beard on his chin.

b) "Lends grace to the beard on his chin": that is, he ascends with the one above.

The third line is the chin and the second is, as it were, merely its appendage. The upward movement that evokes grace takes place in the two lines together. The yielding element can adorn the strong, but cannot add to it any independent quality. This line has significance only in the hexagram taken as a whole; in its individual aspect it is not especially important.

Nine in the third place:

a) Graceful and moist.
Constant perseverance brings good fortune.

b) The good fortune of constant perseverance cannot, in the end, be put to shame.

497

The nine in the third place has content, because it is a strong line in a strong place; the six in the second place is in the relationship of holding together with it and adorns it. Hence grace. The nuclear trigram in which this line occupies the middle place is K'an, water, hence moistness. Moistness is the height of grace, and the line moreover stands at the highest point of the trigram Li, clarity. But since it also stands in the middle of the nuclear trigram K'an, the abyss, there is a danger that it may be submerged. Hence the praise of constant perseverance as a protection against this danger.

Six in the fourth place:

a) Grace or simplicity?

A white horse comes as if on wings.

He is not a robber,

He will woo at the right time.

b) The six in the fourth place is in doubt; this accords with its place.

"He is not a robber, he will woo at the right time."

In the end, one remains free of blame.

The six in the fourth place stands outside the lower trigram and at the beginning of the upper one; hence, because of its weakness, some uncertainty arises. This is resolved by the quickly advancing first line, which is in the relationship of correspondence to it. The trigram Chên means a white horse, hence the image. White is the color of simplicity. In itself the intention of the approaching line is not quite clear, because the weak six in the fourth place is at the top of the nuclear trigram of danger. However, there is nothing to fear, because the inner relation to the oncoming line preponderates. It helps in warding off the danger of exaggerated grace and in returning to simplicity.

Six in the fifth place:

a) Grace in hills and gardens.

The roll of silk is meager and small.

Humiliation, but in the end good fortune.

b)   The good fortune of the six in the fifth place has joy.

The upper trigram Kên means a large hill; the nuclear trigram Chên means a grove. By a change in the line, there arises Sun, meaning a roll of silk. The fifth place really depends on the second, but in this instance there is no relationship with the line in that place, because it too is weak. Hence the alliance with the strong line at the top, in order to enjoy grace with it.

○   Nine at the top:

a)   Simple grace. No blame.

b)   "Simple grace. No blame." The one above attains his will.

The top line stands outside, at the top of the trigram Kên, mountain. Its strong nature allows it to forego all ornament. It chooses plain white. With the six in the fifth place joining it, it succeeds in carrying out its wish for simplicity.

NOTE. The relationships of correspondence and holding together appear in this hexagram. The six in the fourth place and the nine at the beginning are in the relationship of correspondence; the nine at the beginning leaves the carriage and goes toward the six in the fourth place, which sees it approaching as a winged horse. The second line holds together with the third, so also the fifth with the top line. Thus all of the lines are related in one way or another, and in such a manner that it is always a reciprocal relationship between a firm and a yielding line that produces grace. Also to be noted is a tendency throughout the hexagram to counteract overemphasis of form by means of content.

剝

23. *Po* / *Splitting Apart*

Nuclear trigrams K'UN ☷ *and* K'UN ☷

The ruler of the hexagram is the nine at the top. Although the dark force splinters the light, the light principle cannot be wholly split apart; therefore it is the ruler of the hexagram.

The Sequence

When one goes too far in adornment, success exhausts itself. Hence there follows the hexagram of SPLITTING APART. Splitting apart means ruin.

Miscellaneous Notes

SPLITTING APART means decay.

The thought here, taken together with that in the next hexagram, shows the connection between decay and resurrection. Fruit must decay before new seed can develop.

The sinking tendency of the hexagram is very strong. Both nuclear trigrams as well as the lower primary trigram are K'un, whose movement is downward. In contrast with this the upper primary trigram Kên stands still, without motion. This leads to a loosening of the structure. The tendency of the five yin lines is to bring about the downfall of the yang line at the top, in that they sink down and thus take the ground from under it. Here too the fundamental trend of the Book of Changes is expressed: the light principle is represented as invincible because in its sinking it creates new life, as does a grain of wheat when it sinks into the earth.

THE JUDGMENT

SPLITTING APART. It does not further one
To go anywhere.

Commentary on the Decision

SPLITTING APART means ruin. The yielding changes
the firm.

"It does not further one to go anywhere." Inferior
people increase.

Devotion and keeping still result from contemplating the image. The superior man takes heed of
the alternation of increase and decrease, fullness and
emptiness; for it is the course of heaven.

The yielding element changes the strong by imperceptible
gradual influence. The yin lines are about to increase. This
gives us the attitude of the superior man in such times, an
attitude that derives from the two trigrams. In accordance
with the attribute of the trigram K'un, he is devoted; in accordance with that of Kên he is calm, which means that he
undertakes nothing, because the time is not yet come. Thus
he submits to the course of heaven, which alternates between
decrease and increase, in that whatever is full decreases and
whatever is empty increases.

THE IMAGE

The mountain rests on the earth:
The image of SPLITTING APART.
Thus those above can ensure their position
Only by giving generously to those below.

The broader the base of the mountain, the less is it liable to
splitting apart. Here it is not so much the condition of splitting
apart that is set forth as the condition that can prevent it.
Hence also it is not the waning of the light principle and the
waxing of the shadowy that are to be considered, but the
solidity of the foundation. Through generous giving, such as

lies in the nature of the earth (K'un), an assured calm, such as lies in the nature of the mountain (Kên), is attained.

THE LINES

Six at the beginning:

a)   The leg of the bed is split.
Those who persevere are destroyed.
Misfortune.

b)   "The leg of the bed is split," in order to destroy those below.

The position at the beginning, as the lowest place, means the leg. What is split is the resting place, hence the image of a bed. The splitting begins below. Therein lies the danger.

Six in the second place:

a)   The bed is split at the edge.
Those who persevere are destroyed.
Misfortune.

b)   "The bed is split at the edge," because one has no comrade.

The splitting apart mounts upward from the leg of the bed. Now the edge is splitting. This line is isolated; it is neither in the relationship of correspondence to the lines around it nor in that of holding together. Already the attack is emerging from concealment into the open.

Six in the third place:

a)   He splits with them. No blame.

b)   "He splits with them. No blame." He loses the neighbor above and the one below.

This line is in the relationship of correspondence to the nine at the top and quarrels with its environment because it remains loyal to these original ties. Because of this relation with the nine at the top, the line becomes separated from the two neighboring lines, with which there is no relationship of holding together.

Six in the fourth place:

a) The bed is split up to the skin.
Misfortune.

b) "The bed is split up to the skin. Misfortune." This is
a serious and immediate misfortune.

The trigram K'un below represents the bed, the resting place.
The trigram Kên above represents the person resting. Here
the splitting spreads from the resting place to the person resting
on it; therefore misfortune is directly at hand.

Six in the fifth place:

a) A shoal of fishes. Favor comes through the court
ladies.

Everything acts to further.

b) "Favor comes through the court ladies." In the end
this is not a mistake.

When this line changes, the upper trigram becomes Sun,
which means fish (the fish is associated with the shadowy
principle). The line is in the ruler's place. Here, however,
since the activity of the yin power becomes clearly manifest, it
represents a queen, not a prince. The line stands in the relationship of holding together with the top line, hence there
is no hostile activity; on the contrary, at the peak of its influence
it subordinates itself to the yang line, which it approaches
while leading the other four yin lines as though they were a
shoal of fishes. These friendly relationships are represented in
terms of the ruler's relationship to the court ladies and his
queen.

○ Nine at the top:

a) There is a large fruit still uneaten.
The superior man receives a carriage.
The house of the inferior man is split apart.

b) "The superior man receives a carriage." He is carried
by the people.

"The house of the inferior man is split apart": he ends up as useless.

The one strong line at the top, containing the seed of the future, is seen in the image of a large fruit. K'un means a carriage. The collapse of the line through its change into a yin line is compared to the collapse of an inferior man's hut. The line is, so to speak, the roof of the whole hexagram. When it falls apart the whole collapses.

復

24. *Fu / Return (The Turning Point)*

Nuclear trigrams K'UN ☷ and K'UN ☷

The ruler of the hexagram is the nine at the beginning. This is the line referred to by the Commentary on the Decision in the statement, "The firm returns."

The Sequence

Things cannot be destroyed once and for all. When what is above is completely split apart, it returns below. Hence there follows the hexagram of RETURN.

Miscellaneous Notes

RETURN means coming back.

Appended Judgments

RETURN is the stem of character. RETURN is small, yet different from external things. RETURN leads to self-knowledge.

The hexagram of RETURN, applied to character formation, contains various suggestions. The light principle returns: thus the hexagram counsels turning away from the confusion of external things, turning back to one's inner light. There, in the depths of the soul, one sees the Divine, the One. It is indeed only germinal, no more than a beginning, a potentiality, but as such clearly to be distinguished from all objects. To know this One means to know oneself in relation to the cosmic forces. For this One is the ascending force of life in nature and in man.

This hexagram is the inverse of the preceding one, and the movement tends very strongly upward from below—from the trigram Chên—going through the sinking trigram K'un.

THE JUDGMENT

RETURN. Success.

Going out and coming in without error.

Friends come without blame.

To and fro goes the way.

On the seventh day comes return.

It furthers one to have somewhere to go.

Commentary on the Decision

"RETURN has success." The firm returns.

Movement and action through devotion. Therefore, "Going out and coming in without error."

"Friends come without blame. To and fro goes the way. On the seventh day comes return." This is the course of heaven.

"It furthers one to have somewhere to go." The firm is on the increase.

In the hexagram of RETURN one sees the mind of heaven and earth.

This hexagram expresses the idea that the light force is the creative principle of heaven and earth. It is an eternal cyclic movement, from which life comes forth again just at the moment when it appears to have been completely vanquished. Through the re-entrance of the yang line into the hexagram below, movement develops (Chên, the lower trigram), and this movement acts through devotion (K'un, the upper trigram). Going out and coming in are without error. The yang force has indeed gone (cf. the foregoing hexagram, Po), but like a fruit falling to earth, it has not disappeared without a trace; it has left an effect behind. This effect shows itself in the re-entrance of the yang line. The friends who come are either the other yang lines about to enter the hexagram after this first line (according to Ch'êng Tzŭ), or the five yin lines, which meet the yang line cordially. The way of yang goes to and fro, up and down. After the light force begins to diminish in Kou, COMING TO MEET (44), it returns again in the hexagram Fu, after seven changes.

"It furthers one to have somewhere to go," that is, to undertake something. Both this sentence and the image of the friends occur in the text of the second hexagram, K'un, THE RECEPTIVE.

THE IMAGE

Thunder within the earth:
The image of THE TURNING POINT.
Thus the kings of antiquity closed the passes
At the time of solstice.
Merchants and strangers did not go about,
And the ruler
Did not travel through the provinces.

The hexagram is associated with the month of the winter solstice. From this are drawn the conclusions resulting in the right behavior at the time when the returning yang force is still weak and must therefore be strengthened by rest.

THE LINES

○ Nine at the beginning:

a) Return from a short distance.
No need for remorse.
Great good fortune.

b) "Return from a short distance": thus one cultivates one's character.

The strong line at the bottom turns back at once. The first line of Chên is very mobile; hence the immediate turnabout before going too far. Confucius says about this line:

Yen Hui is one who will surely attain it. If he has a fault, he never fails to recognize it; having recognized it, he never commits the error a second time. In the Book of Changes it is said: "Return from a short distance. No need for remorse. Great good fortune."

Six in the second place:

a) Quiet return. Good fortune.

b) The good fortune of a quiet return depends on subordination to a good man.

This line is central and modest (yielding), and stands in the relationship of holding together with the ruler of the hexagram, the nine at the beginning. The good fortune depends on the resulting subordination to this good man.

Six in the third place:

a) Repeated return. Danger. No blame.

b) The danger of repeated return is, in its essential meaning, deliverance from blame.

This line is at the peak of movement. This points to a repeated turning back. The first turning back is from good to bad. The second is from bad to good once more. This line likewise turns as a friend to the nine at the beginning.

Six in the fourth place:

a) Walking in the midst of others,
One returns alone.

b) "Walking in the midst of others, one returns alone," and so follows the right way.

The fourth line is in the middle of the upper nuclear trigram K'un; it is moreover the top line of the lower nuclear trigram K'un and the lowest line of the upper primary trigram K'un. In a word, it is in the midst of weak lines, and is itself compliant and in a weak place. One might infer a lack of initiative. But this line is in the relationship of correspondence to the strong nine at the beginning, hence solitary return.

Six in the fifth place:

a)   Noblehearted return. No remorse.

b)   "Noblehearted return. No remorse." Central, therefore he is able to test himself.

This line is actually very far away from the nine at the beginning. But it is central; therefore it is possible for it to test itself and thus to find a way of turning back from all mistakes. The relationship with the nine at the beginning is not suggested by any external ties, hence it represents noblehearted free decision.

Six at the top:

a)   Missing the return. Misfortune.
Misfortune from within and without.
If armies are set marching in this way,
One will in the end suffer a great defeat,
Disastrous for the ruler of the country.
For ten years
It will not be possible to attack again.

b)   The misfortune in missing the return lies in opposing the way of the superior man.

This line is at the end of the yin lines, hence there is no turning back for it. In refusing to turn back it defiantly seeks to attain its objective by force; thereby, however, owing to inner and outer misfortune, it loses for a long time all possibility of recuperating. The top line in the hexagram K'un, THE RECEPTIVE, has a similar judgment.

The trigram Chên means a general, K'un means crowd, hence "to set armies marching." K'un means nation, Chên means ruler. Ten is the number belonging to the earth.

NOTE. Missing the return (six at the top) is the opposite of return from a short distance (nine at the beginning). The first line is not far off and comes back. Quiet return (six in the second place) and solitary return (six in the fourth place) resemble each other; both lines are related to the ruler of the hexagram. Repeated return (six in the third place) and noble-hearted return (six in the fifth place) are opposites: in the one there is going back and forth, the other shows calm consistency.

无妄

25. *Wu Wang / Innocence (The Unexpected)*

Nuclear trigrams SUN ☴ and KÊN ☶

The rulers of the hexagram are the nine at the beginning and the nine in the fifth place. The nine at the beginning is the first movement of the light principle as well as the first movement of the sincere heart of man. The nine in the fifth place symbolizes the essence of the Creative, as well as the tireless-ness of the supremely sincere. Therefore it is said in the Commentary on the Decision: "The firm comes from without and becomes the ruler within." This refers to the first line. And further: "The firm is in the middle and finds correspondence." This refers to the fifth line.

The Sequence

By turning back one is freed of guilt. Hence there follows the hexagram of INNOCENCE.

Miscellaneous Notes

THE UNEXPECTED means misfortune from without.

Innocence frees itself of mistakes, so that no misfortune of internal origin can overtake it. When misfortune comes unexpectedly, it has an external origin, therefore it will pass again.

The hexagram has a very strong ascending tendency; both the upper and the lower trigram have an upward movement. This fact suggests movement in harmony with heaven, which is man's true and original nature. The two nuclear trigrams, Kên, Keeping Still, mountain, and Sun, the Gentle, wind (tree), yield the idea of the functioning and development of the primal trends.

THE JUDGMENT

INNOCENCE. Supreme success.

Perseverance furthers.

If someone is not as he should be,

He has misfortune,

And it does not further him

To undertake anything.

Commentary on the Decision

INNOCENCE. The firm comes from without and becomes the ruler within. Movement and strength. The firm is in the middle and finds correspondence.

"Great success through correctness": this is the will of heaven.

"If someone is not as he should be, he has misfortune, and it does not further him to undertake anything." When innocence is gone, where can one go? When the will of heaven does not protect one, can one do anything?

The firm element coming from without is the lowest line, a yang line. It comes from heaven (Ch'ien). The Receptive, in approaching the Creative for the first time, receives the first line of Ch'ien and gives birth to Chên, the eldest son. Applied to man, this means that he receives the primal divine spirit as his guide and master. The attribute of the lower trigram, Chên, is movement, that of the upper, Ch'ien, is strength. The firm line in a central position that finds correspondence is the upper ruler of the hexagram, the nine in the fifth place, and the six in the second place corresponds with it. This all leads to success, because it shows man in the proper relationship to the divine, without ulterior designs and in primal innocence. Thus man is in harmony with heavenly fate, the will of heaven, just as the lower trigram harmonizes in movement with the upper.

But where the natural state is not this state of innocence, where desires and ideas are astir, misfortune follows of inner necessity. This hexagram differs from P'i, STANDSTILL, only in having a firm line at the beginning. If this should lose its firmness, the whole situation would change.[1]

THE IMAGE

Under heaven thunder rolls:
All things attain the natural state of innocence.
Thus the kings of old,
Rich in virtue, and in harmony with the time,
Fostered and nourished all beings.

"Under heaven thunder rolls: all things attain the natural state of innocence." This image is explained by the saying in the Discussion of the Trigrams: "God comes forth in the sign of the Arousing." This is the beginning of all life. Here we have the Creative above in association with movement. The upper nuclear trigram is wood, the lower is mountain.

"Rich in virtue" refers to the strength of the Creative. "The time" derives from the trigram Chên (east and spring)—the trigram in which life comes forth. Fostering and nourishing are indicated by the nuclear trigram Kên, mountain. The fact that this influence extends to everything is symbolized by the nuclear trigram Sun, meaning wind and universal penetration.

---

1. In this hexagram there appear ideas that correspond with the mystical interpretations of the legends of Paradise and the fall of man.

THE LINES

O   Nine at the beginning:

a)   Innocent behavior brings good fortune.

b)   Innocent behavior attains its will.

Innocence is symbolized by the light character of the line, which enters as ruler below the two dark lines. Coming from heaven, it bears within itself the warrant of success. It attains its goal with intuitive certainty.

Six in the second place:

a)   If one does not count on the harvest while plowing,
Nor on the use of the ground while clearing it,
It furthers one to undertake something.

b)   Not plowing in order to reap: that is, one does not seek wealth.

The trigram Chên means wood, hence a plow, and the second place is that of the field. The nuclear trigram Kên means hand, hence the image of clearing a field.

This line is central and correct. On the one hand, it is in the relationship of holding together with the nine at the beginning; on the other, it is in the relationship of correspondence to the nine in the fifth place. But being central and correct, it does not allow itself to be deflected by these relationships. It is the lowest line in the nuclear trigram Kên, Keeping Still, hence it keeps a calm mind; but it is also in the middle of the trigram Chên, movement, hence may undertake something.

Six in the third place:

a)   Undeserved misfortune.
The cow that was tethered by someone
Is the wanderer's gain, the citizen's loss.

b)   If the wanderer gets the cow, it is the citizen's loss.

This line stands at the high point of movement and at the beginning of the nuclear trigram Sun, wind. Therefore it is in its movements not in harmony with the time. It is equally far from both rulers of the hexagram and hence does not find the right connection anywhere. Through change in this line, the trigram Li, meaning cow, develops below.

Nine in the fourth place:

a) He who can be persevering
Remains without blame.

b) "He who can be persevering remains without blame," for he possesses firmly.

The nine in the fourth place is originally neither correct nor central. However, as the lowest line in the trigram Ch'ien, it is able to preserve the firmness belonging to the Creative. By this means it remains free of the blame otherwise to be feared.

○ Nine in the fifth place:

a) Use no medicine in an illness
Incurred through no fault of your own.
It will pass of itself.

b) One should not try an unknown medicine.

Medicine is suggested by the two nuclear trigrams, wood and stone (mountain). The illness is innocently incurred because this line, as the middle line of the Creative, represents a person by nature free of illness; that he appears ill comes from his way of taking the illnesses of others upon himself. His central, correct, and ruling position predisposes him to allow the ills of others, vicariously taken upon himself, to work themselves out in him.

Nine at the top:

a) Innocent action brings misfortune.
Nothing furthers.

b) Action without reflection brings about the evil of bewilderment.

This line is related to the weak, restless six in the third place. Thoughtless action brings misfortune. The line is at the end,

513

in a time when action is no longer appropriate. To go on thoughtlessly leads to bewilderment. The line describes a situation similar to that of the top line of THE CREATIVE.

NOTE. In this hexagram the six lines are all innocent, that is, naïve, without ulterior motives. The nine at the beginning is in its appropriate place and is the ruler of the trigram of movement; this indicates that the time has come to act. Hence action brings good fortune. The nine at the top is not in the right place and stands outermost in the trigram Ch'ien. The time to act has already passed. Hence action, even though innocent, brings misfortune. Everything depends on the time. The line at the beginning has good fortune, the second is favorable; this is due to the time. The third line bears an augury of misfortune, the fifth of illness, the top line of misfortune. All this does not happen by plan, but is likewise the result of the time conditions. It is possible for the first and second lines to advance. The time has come for them to move. The fourth should remain steadfast, the fifth should use no medicine, the top line has misfortune if it acts: all this indicates that for these lines the time has come to remain quiet.

大畜

26. *Ta Ch'u / The Taming Power of the Great*

Nuclear trigrams CHÊN ☳ *and* TUI ☱

The rulers of the hexagram are the six in the fifth place and the nine at the top. These are the lines referred to when it is said in the Commentary on the Decision: "The firm ascends and honors the worthy."

The Sequence

When innocence is present, it is possible to tame.
Hence there follows THE TAMING POWER OF THE
GREAT.

Holding fast to heavenly virtue is the prerequisite for innocence. On the other hand, innocence is the indispensable
condition for being able to hold fast to pristine heavenly virtue.

Miscellaneous Notes

THE TAMING POWER OF THE GREAT depends on the
time.

The movements of the two trigrams are toward each other.
The Creative below presses powerfully upward, and Keeping
Still above holds it fast. The nuclear trigrams Chên and Tui
also have a tendency to rise, the upper more so than the lower.
These are the latent forces that are intensified by the holding
fast. The two weak lines occupying the ruler's and the minister's place restrain the strong lines below, while showing
recognition and liberality toward the strong line above. This
hexagram is the inverse of the preceding one.

THE JUDGMENT

THE TAMING POWER OF THE GREAT.
Perseverance furthers.
Not eating at home brings good fortune.
It furthers one to cross the great water.

Commentary on the Decision

THE TAMING POWER OF THE GREAT. Firmness and
strength. Genuineness and truth. Brilliance and
light. Daily he renews his virtue.

The firm ascends and honors the worthy. He is
able to keep strength still; this is great correctness.

"Not eating at home brings good fortune," for
people of worth are nourished.

> "It furthers one to cross the great water," because
> one finds correspondence in heaven.

The upper trigram Kên is firm, the lower, Ch'ien, is strong; the upper is genuine, the lower is true: the upper is brilliant, the lower light. Thus the two trigrams complement each other. Through keeping still (Kên), the powers of character (Ch'ien) are so strengthened that a daily renewal takes place. This refers to the effect of the personality. Here the first meaning of the hexagram is given—keeping still and collecting oneself.

The firm element that ascends is the nine at the top. It mounts above the six in the fifth place—the place of the ruler —and this ruler honors it in its ascent because it is worthy. The upper trigram Kên, Keeping Still, is able to hold fast the lower, Ch'ien, the strong. This explains the words of the Judgment: "Perseverance furthers." Here we have the second meaning of the hexagram—holding fast and keeping still.

Not eating at home, that is, entering public service, brings good fortune, because the six in the fifth place represents a ruler who nourishes people of worth. This gives the third meaning—holding fast and nourishing.

"It furthers one to cross the great water." This idea is suggested by the two nuclear trigrams—Chên, which also means wood, over Tui, lake. This dangerous action is possible because the ruler of the hexagram, the six in the fifth place, is in the relationship of correspondence to the nine in the second place, the central line of the lower trigram, heaven (Ch'ien).

THE IMAGE

Heaven within the mountain:
The image of THE TAMING POWER OF THE GREAT.
Thus the superior man acquaints himself with many
    sayings of antiquity
And many deeds of the past,
In order to strengthen his character thereby.

Heaven (Ch'ien) points to character, virtue. Strengthening is suggested by the mountain (Kên). The means to this strengthening of character are hidden in the nuclear trigrams: the

lower, Tui, mouth, suggests words; the upper, Chên, movement, suggests deeds.

THE LINES

Nine at the beginning:

a)   Danger is at hand. It furthers one to desist.

b)   "Danger is at hand. It furthers one to desist." Thus
one does not expose oneself to danger.

This strong line, which is in its proper place, would like to
advance. But it is in the relationship of correspondence to the
six in the fourth place, which is one of the two obstructing
lines. This indicates danger that would hold it back if it should
try to advance; but since the line is still just at the beginning,
it allows itself to be held back and so escapes the danger.

Nine in the second place:

a)   The axletrees are taken from the wagon.

b)   "The axletrees are taken from the wagon." In the
middle there is no blame.

Ch'ien is round, hence the image of the wheel. Tui, the nuclear
trigram, indicates breaking. The nine in the second place is
central, hence able to control itself. It is held back by the six
in the fifth place, to which it is related.

Nine in the third place:

a)   A good horse that follows others.
Awareness of danger,
With perseverance, furthers.
Practice chariot driving and armed defense daily.
It furthers one to have somewhere to go.

b)   "It furthers one to have somewhere to go." The will
of the one above is in agreement.

Ch'ien is a good horse; the nuclear trigram Chên, in which this
is the beginning line, is movement, hence advance. This line
stands in the relationship of congruity to the nine at the top,

517

hence the agreement in will between them. But the fourth and the fifth line still create separation and danger, which must be borne in mind. The chariot is suggested by the trigram Ch'ien, the weapons by the nuclear trigram Tui, meaning metal and breaking.

Six in the fourth place:

a) The headboard of a young bull.
   Great good fortune.

b) The great good fortune of the six in the fourth place consists in the fact that it has joy.

This line constitutes the horns of the nuclear trigram Tui, which to be sure means sheep and not horned cattle. The line easily restrains the nine at the beginning before it has begun to be dangerous, hence the joy.

O   Six in the fifth place:

a) The tusk of a gelded boar.
   Good fortune.

b) The good fortune of the six in the fifth place consists in the fact that it has blessing.

Another interpretation reads: "The tethering post of a young pig." The meaning is doubtless that of an indirect check before the danger grows formidable. An old commentary connects the pig of this line, as well as the bull of the preceding line, with sacrificial rites, hence the good fortune and the blessing. In any case, the blessing comes from the relationship of this line to the middle line of the lower trigram, heaven.

O   Nine at the top:

a) One attains the way of heaven. Success.

b) "One attains the way of heaven." Truth works in the great.

The top line is honored as a sage by the six in the fifth place. It stands in the relationship of congruity to the nine in the third place, which is, however, the top line of the trigram Ch'ien, heaven. The upper trigram Kên means a way.

NOTE. In this hexagram, the relationships between the yin and the yang lines are not those of correspondence and furtherance, but, in accordance with the character of the hexagram, those of obstruction. The lines of the lower trigram are obstructed, those of the upper trigram are the obstructors. Only the third and the top line, which, as two yang lines, are in harmony, are free of the idea of obstruction.

The persons represented by the first two lines are still eating at home and still obstructed in crossing the great water. The fourth and fifth lines operate by obstructing the two misbehaving lines—this is easy for the one, more difficult for the other. The third line advances, though with caution and under difficulties. The top line alone has a clear path ahead, and the obstacles disappear. It stands for the person of worth who can achieve great things and who is nourished.

27. *I* | *The Corners of the Mouth* (*Providing Nourishment*)

Nuclear trigrams K'UN ☷ *and* K'UN ☷

The rulers of the hexagram are the six in the fifth place and the nine at the top. These are the lines referred to in the Commentary on the Decision: "He provides nourishment for men of worth and thus reaches the whole people."

The Sequence

When things are held fast, there is provision of nourishment. Hence there follows the hexagram of

THE CORNERS OF THE MOUTH. "The corners of the mouth" means the providing of nourishment.

Miscellaneous Notes

THE CORNERS OF THE MOUTH means providing nourishment for what is right.

The two primary trigrams are opposed in movement. Kên, the upper, stands still; Chên, the lower, moves upward. This suggests the jaws and teeth. The upper jaw is immobile, the lower moves; hence the designation of the hexagram as THE CORNERS OF THE MOUTH. In contrast to Hsü, WAITING (5), which also deals with provision of nourishment but emphasizes man's dependence on nourishment, the theme of the hexagram I is rather the human role in the providing of nourishment. A secondary meaning is that of providing nourishment first for men of worth, in order that thereby the people also may be nourished. The two hexagrams therefore present provision of nourishment as a natural process (Hsü, WAITING) and as a social problem (I, THE CORNERS OF THE MOUTH). A similar contrast obtains between the two hexagrams denoting nourishment in itself—Ching, THE WELL (48), the water necessary for nourishment, and Ting, THE CALDRON (50), the food necessary for nourishment.

THE JUDGMENT

THE CORNERS OF THE MOUTH.
Perseverance brings good fortune.
Pay heed to the providing of nourishment
And to what a man seeks
To fill his own mouth with.

Commentary on the Decision

"THE CORNERS OF THE MOUTH. Perseverance brings good fortune." If one provides nourishment for what is right, good fortune comes.

"Pay heed to the providing of nourishment," that is, pay heed to what a man provides nourishment for.

"To what he seeks to fill his own mouth with,"

that is, pay heed to what a man nourishes himself with.

Heaven and earth provide nourishment for all beings. The holy man provides nourishment for men of worth and thus reaches the whole people. Truly great is the time of PROVIDING NOURISHMENT.

As an image the hexagram is conceived as a whole—as the image of an open mouth; consequently there is no need of explaining how it came to mean provision of nourishment. But it stresses the idea that as regards the manner of providing nourishment, everything depends on its being in harmony with what is right. In accord with the character of the two trigrams—movement and keeping still—there is no relation of correspondence between the relevant lines of the lower and the upper trigram. The lower trigram seeks nourishment for itself, the upper affords nourishment for others.

THE IMAGE

At the foot of the mountain, thunder:
The image of PROVIDING NOURISHMENT.
Thus the superior man is careful of his words
And temperate in eating and drinking.

Thunder is the trigram in which God comes forth; the mountain is the trigram in which all things are completed. This is the image of PROVIDING NOURISHMENT. From the hexagram as a whole, as representing an open mouth, are derived the movements of the mouth, speech and the taking in of food. This movement corresponds with the character of the trigram Chên. It must be moderated if it is to be correct. This is in correspondence with the character of the trigram Kên.

THE LINES

Nine at the beginning:

a) You let your magic tortoise go,
 And look at me with the corners of your mouth drooping.
 Misfortune.

b) "You . . . look at me with the corners of your mouth
   drooping": this is really not to be respected.

Structurally the whole hexagram recalls the trigram Li, the
Clinging, hence the image of a tortoise.

The hexagram contains three ideas—nourishing oneself,
nourishing others, and being nourished by others. The strong
line at the top, the ruler of the hexagram, provides nourishment for others. The weak middle lines are obliged to depend
on others to provide them with nourishment. The strong line
below should indeed be able to provide nourishment for itself
(the magic tortoise needs no earthly food but can nourish itself
on air). Instead, however, it too moves toward the general
source of nourishment and wants to be fed with the rest. This
is contemptible and disastrous. "You" is the nine at the beginning, "me" is the nine at the top.

Six in the second place:

a) Turning to the summit for nourishment,
   Deviating from the path
   To seek nourishment from the hill.
   Continuing to do this brings misfortune.

b) If the six in the second place continues to do this, it
   brings misfortune, because in going it loses its place
   among its kind.

The six in the second place could seek nourishment from its
peer, the nine at the beginning. Instead, it turns aside from
this path and seeks nourishment at the summit, that is, from
the upper ruler of the hexagram (the upper trigram is Kên,
mountain). This brings misfortune.

Another interpretation reads: "To seek to be provided with
nourishment the other way round (by the nine at the beginning) or, leaving the path, to seek nourishment from the hill
(the nine at the top) brings misfortune."

Six in the third place:

a) Turning away from nourishment.
   Perseverance brings misfortune.

Do not act thus for ten years.

Nothing serves to further.

b) "Do not act thus for ten years," because it is all too contrary to the right way.

This line also, standing at the top of the trigram Chên, movement, seeks nourishment from the nine at the top instead of from the nine at the bottom. "Ten years" is implied by the nuclear trigram K'un, whose number is ten. The reason why this behavior is so severely criticized is that the line seeks personal advantages on the basis of its relationship of correspondence, which is not valid in this hexagram.

Six in the fourth place:

a) Turning to the summit
For provision of nourishment
Brings good fortune.
Spying about with sharp eyes
Like a tiger with insatiable craving.
No blame.

b) The good fortune in turning to the summit to be provided with nourishment inheres in the fact that the one above spreads light.

This line likewise turns to the nine at the top to be provided with nourishment, but because it belongs to the same trigram as the latter, this brings good fortune, in contrast to the fate of the six in the second place. "Spying about with sharp eyes" derives from the form of the hexagram, which is reminiscent of Li. The trigram Li also means eye.

○ Six in the fifth place:

a) Turning away from the path.
To remain persevering brings good fortune.
One should not cross the great water.

b) The good fortune in remaining persevering comes from following the one above devotedly.

This line is in the place of the ruler, but as a yielding, submissive line, it stands in the relationship of receiving to the strong line above it. Hence it devotedly places itself below the latter. (When the hexagram changes into the next one, the upper trigram Kên becomes Tui, lake. The fifth line then gets into the middle of the water, hence it is not favorable to cross the great water.)

○ Nine at the top:

a) The source of nourishment.

Awareness of danger brings good fortune.

It furthers one to cross the great water.

b) "The source of nourishment. Awareness of danger brings good fortune." It has great blessing.

The danger comes from the responsibility of the position at the top of the hexagram and from the fact that, in addition, the line receives authority and honor from the yielding ruler in the fifth place. But in this position it dispenses great blessing. Being thus aware of the danger, it is able to undertake great enterprises, such as crossing the great water. (When the hexagram changes into the following one, this line is on the surface of Tui, the lake, hence, unlike the preceding line, not in danger of drowning.)

大過

28. *Ta Kuo / Preponderance of the Great*

Nuclear trigrams CH'IEN ☰ *and* CH'IEN ☰

The rulers of the hexagram are the nine in the second place and the nine in the fourth. The nine in the second place is firm, central, and not too heavy. The nine in the fourth place is a beam that does not sag to the breaking point.

The Sequence

Without provision of nourishment one cannot move; hence there follows the hexagram of PREPONDERANCE OF THE GREAT.

Nourishing without putting to use finally evokes movement. Movement without end leads finally too far, to overweighting.

Miscellaneous Notes

PREPONDERANCE OF THE GREAT is the peak.

The peak refers to the image of the ridgepole mentioned in the Judgment. The hexagram shows great strength within. Both the nuclear trigrams are Ch'ien, whose attribute is strength. But underneath is the gentle Sun, penetrating indeed, but ethereal as well, while above is the joyous Tui, the lake. Thus the outer ends are not equal to the weight of the strong structure within; hence the great in preponderance. This hexagram is the opposite of the preceding one.

Appended Judgments

In ancient times the dead were buried by covering them thickly with brushwood and placing them in the open country, without burial mound or grove of trees. The period of mourning had no definite duration. The holy men of a later time introduced inner and outer coffins instead. They probably took this from the hexagram of PREPONDERANCE OF THE GREAT.

The hexagram represents wood that has penetrated below ground water; this gives the coffin image. Another explanation holds that the two yin lines (above and below) represent the earth and trees of the burial place, while the yang lines between indicate the coffin. When the dead are thus well cared for, they enter (Sun) the earth and are happy (Tui). This hexagram is the opposite of the preceding one in this further respect, that the former shows the provisions of nourishment

525

for the living, and the present one shows the care provided for the dead.

THE JUDGMENT

PREPONDERANCE OF THE GREAT.
The ridgepole sags to the breaking point.
It furthers one to have somewhere to go.
Success.

Commentary on the Decision

PREPONDERANCE OF THE GREAT. The great preponderates. The ridgepole sags to the breaking point
because beginning and end are weak.

The firm preponderates and is central. Gentle and
joyous in action: then it furthers one to have somewhere to go, then one has success.

Great indeed is the time of PREPONDERANCE OF
THE GREAT.

The name is explained on the basis of the structure. The great,
that is, the yang element, outnumbers with its four lines the
two lines of the yin element. This by itself would not mean
preponderance, but the great is within, although it belongs
without. Similarly, the small preponderates (cf. hexagram 62)
when weak lines are in the majority and without, for by their
nature they belong within. As representing preponderance of
the great, the hexagram suggests the image of a ridgepole, the
top beam of a house, on which the whole roof rests. Since
beginning and end are weak, there arises the danger of a too
great inner weight and of consequent sagging to the breaking
point.

Despite this extraordinary situation, action is important. If
the weight were to remain where it is, misfortune would arise.
By means of movement, however, one gets out of the abnormal
condition, chiefly because the ruler in the lower trigram is
central and strong. The attributes of the trigrams, joyousness
and gentleness, also indicate the right behavior for successful
action.

THE IMAGE

The lake rises above the trees:
The image of PREPONDERANCE OF THE GREAT.
Thus the superior man, when he stands alone,
Is unconcerned,
And if he has to renounce the world,
He is undaunted.

The ideas of standing alone and of renunciation of the world are derived from the situation indicated by the hexagram as a whole. Standing alone unconcerned is suggested by the symbol of Sun, the tree, and undauntedness by the attribute of Tui, joyousness.

THE LINES

Six at the beginning:

a) To spread white rushes underneath.
No blame.

b) "To spread white rushes underneath": the yielding is underneath.

The yielding line under the strong ruler of the hexagram, the nine in second place, indicates that the load is set down with caution. Confucius says about this line:

It does well enough simply to place something on the floor. But if one puts white rushes underneath, how could that be a mistake? This is the extreme of caution. Rushes in themselves are worthless, but they can have a very important effect. If one is as cautious as this in all that one does, one remains free of mistakes.

○   Nine in the second place:

a) A dry poplar sprouts at the root.
An older man takes a young wife.
Everything furthers.

b) "An older man takes a young wife." The extraordinary thing is their coming together.

The trigram for wood stands under the trigram for water, hence the image of the poplar, which grows near water. This line, the ruler of the hexagram, has the relationship of holding together with the six at the beginning. On the one hand, this produces the image of a root sprouting afresh from below and so renewing the life process; on the other hand, it represents an older man (the nine in the second place) who takes a young girl to wife (the six at the beginning). Although this is something out of the ordinary, everything is favorable.

Nine in the third place:

a) The ridgepole sags to the breaking point. Misfortune.

b) The misfortune of the sagging and breaking of the ridgepole is due to its finding no support.

The third and the fourth line, occupying the middle of the hexagram, represent the ridgepole. The nine in the third place is a firm line in a firm place, which gives too much firmness for an exceptional time, hence the misfortune of bending and breaking threatens. For through obstinacy one cuts oneself off from the possibility of support.

O   Nine in the fourth place:

a) The ridgepole is braced. Good fortune.
   If there are ulterior motives, it is humiliating.

b) The good fortune of the braced ridgepole lies in the fact that it does not sag downward and break.

This line is in better state than the preceding one. It does not sag down and break. While the nine in the third place is too strong and restless, the firmness of the nine in the fourth place is modified by the yieldingness of its position. While the nine in the third place is exposed to the danger of breaking because it is the top line of the trigram Sun, which is open underneath and hence weak, the nine in the fourth place rests at the bottom of the trigram Tui, which is open at the top; hence its security. "Ulterior motives" is implied by the fact that this line is related by correspondence to the six at the beginning, but here no conclusions may be drawn from that fact, because the chief thing to be considered about this line is its position, as minister, in relation to the ruler in the fifth place.

Nine in the fifth place:

a) A withered poplar puts forth flowers.
An older woman takes a husband.
No blame. No praise.

b) "A withered poplar puts forth flowers." How could this last long?
"An older woman takes a husband." It is nevertheless a disgrace.

This line stands in contrast to the nine in the second place. In the latter an older man marries a young girl, here an older woman takes a husband. There the poplar puts forth sprouts at the root; here it puts forth flowers. There the relation of correspondence is with the line below, hence a sprouting root; here it is with the line above, hence the flowers. There the strong nine in the second place is the man who marries a young girl (the six at the beginning); here the six at the top is the old woman who marries the nine in the fifth place.

Six at the top:

a) One must go through the water.
It goes over one's head.
Misfortune. No blame.

b) One should not join blame to the misfortune of going through the water.

The upper trigram Tui is a lake, hence the water. The nuclear trigram is Ch'ien, the head. The upper nuclear trigram ends with the nine in the fifth place; thus the six at the top shows water reaching above the head. However, one ought not to join blame to the misfortune, because it is due to the time, and the intention is good. This oracle, "Misfortune. No blame," is among the noblest thoughts possible about the overcoming of fate.

NOTE. As in the hexagrams I (27), Chung Fu (61), and Hsiao Kuo (62), the relationship of correspondence is not valid in this hexagram; instead, the upper and lower lines, reckoned from the middle, stand in contrast to one another. Thus the third and the fourth line both symbolize the ridgepole. But the third, a firm line in a firm place, is unlucky, and the ridgepole sags and breaks, while the fourth, a firm line in a yielding place, is lucky; the ridgepole is braced. The second and the fifth line are both old poplars. The second, a firm line in a yielding place, is lucky; it "sprouts at the root." The fifth, a firm line in a firm place, is unlucky; it begins to blossom and consumes its last remnant of strength. The lowest line, which is yielding in a firm place, is lucky by dint of great caution; the top line, which is yielding in a yielding place, is unlucky by reason of courage and stubborn tenacity. All the lines standing in places opposed to their natures are lucky, because place and character complement each other. All the lines standing in places that accord with their natures are unlucky, for this creates overweighting.

坎

29. K'an / The Abysmal (Water)

Nuclear trigrams KÊN ☶ *and* CHÊN ☳

The rulers of the hexagram are the two yang lines in the second and the fifth place. The fifth, however, is ruler in a more marked degree; it represents water, which flows on when it has filled up a given place.

The Sequence

Things cannot be permanently in an overweighted state. Hence there follows the hexagram of THE ABYSMAL. The Abysmal means a pit.

Miscellaneous Notes

THE ABYSMAL is directed downward.

Water moves from above downward; it comes from the earth, but here it is in the heavens, hence its tendency to return earthward.

This hexagram is one of the eight formed by doubling of a trigram. The trigram K'an contains the middle line of the Creative (in the Inner-World Arrangement this trigram has shifted to the north, the place occupied by the Receptive in the Primal Arrangement[1]). Therefore this hexagram and the next following one, Li—which bears the same relation to the Receptive that K'an bears to the Creative—stand together at the end of part 1, which begins with THE CREATIVE and THE RECEPTIVE.

THE JUDGMENT

The Abysmal repeated.
If you are sincere, you have success in your heart,
And whatever you do succeeds.

Commentary on the Decision

The Abysmal repeated is twofold danger. Water flows on and nowhere piles up; it goes through dangerous places, never losing its dependability.

"You have success in your heart," for the firm form the middle.

"Whatever you do succeeds": advancing brings about achievements.

The danger of heaven lies in the fact that one cannot climb it. The dangers of earth are the

---

1. [See p. 266.]

mountains and rivers, hills and heights. The kings and princes make use of danger to protect their realms.

The effects of the time of danger are truly great.

This hexagram is explained in two ways. First, man finds himself in danger, like water in the depths of an abyss. The water shows him how to behave: it flows on without piling up anywhere, and even in dangerous places it does not lose its dependable character. In this way the danger is overcome. The trigram K'an further means the heart. In the heart the divine nature is locked within the natural inclinations and tendencies, and is thus in danger of being engulfed by desires and passions. Here likewise the way to overcome danger is to hold firmly to one's innate disposition to good. This is indicated by the fact that the firm lines form each the middle in one of the trigrams. Hence action results in good. Second, danger serves as a protective measure—for heaven, earth, and the prince. But it is never an end in itself. Therefore it is said: "The effects of the time of danger are great."

THE IMAGE

Water flows on uninterruptedly and reaches its goal:
The image of the Abysmal repeated.
Thus the superior man walks in lasting virtue
And carries on the business of teaching.

Water is constant in its flow; thus the superior man is constant in his virtue, like the firm line in the middle of the abyss. And just as water flows on and on, so he makes use of practice and repetition in the business of teaching.

THE LINES

Six at the beginning:

a) Repetition of the Abysmal.
   In the abyss one falls into a pit.
   Misfortune.

b) "Repetition of the Abysmal." One falls into the abyss because one has lost the way; this brings misfortune.

This line stands at the bottom and is divided, i.e., in the bottom of the abyss there is still another pit. This repetition of danger leads to habituation to danger. Being weak, the line does not possess the inner strength to withstand such temptation. Hence at the very start it falls away from the right path.

○ Nine in the second place:

a) The abyss is dangerous.

One should strive to attain small things only.

b) "One should strive to attain small things only." For the middle has not yet been passed.

This line is strong and central and could therefore of its own nature accomplish something great. But it is still hemmed in by danger, hence there is nothing to be done. And its strength lies in the very fact that it does not seek the impossible but knows how to adapt itself to circumstances.

Six in the third place:

a) Forward and backward, abyss on abyss.

In danger like this, pause at first and wait,

Otherwise you will fall into a pit in the abyss.

Do not act in this way.

b) "Forward and backward, abyss on abyss": here any effort ends up as impossible.

This line is weak, and not in its proper place. It is in the midst of danger and moreover stands in the middle of the nuclear trigram Chên, movement; hence it is not only surrounded by danger but also full of inner disquiet. Hence the warning not to act, as the nature of the line suggests.

Six in the fourth place:

a) A jug of wine, a bowl of rice with it;

Earthen vessels

Simply handed in through the window.

There is certainly no blame in this.

b) "A jug of wine, a bowl of rice with it." It is the boundary line between firm and yielding.

The trigram K'an means wine. The nuclear trigram Chên means ritual vessels. The whole is conceived as a simple sacrifice. K'an stands in the north and is often coupled with the idea of sacrifice. Despite its simplicity, the sacrifice is accepted, because the attitude is sincere. The fourth line is in the relationship of holding together with the upper ruler of the hexagram —hence the close relationships that can dispense with ceremonious outer form.

○ Nine in the fifth place:

a) The abyss is not filled to overflowing.
   It is filled only to the rim.
   No blame.

b) "The abyss is not filled to overflowing," for the central line is not yet great.

The ruler of the hexagram, being moreover strong and in a strong place, might easily feel himself to be great and powerful. But his central position prevents this; therefore it is enough for him merely to extricate himself from the danger. This is the line referred to by the sentence in the Commentary on the Decision: "Water flows on and nowhere piles up."

   Six at the top:

a) Bound with cords and ropes,
   Shut in between thorn-hedged prison walls:
   For three years one does not find the way.
   Misfortune.

b) The six at the top has lost the way. This misfortune continues for three years.

In contrast to the six at the beginning, which is caught in a pit within the abyss, this line is at the top, hence inclosed by a wall behind thorn hedges (prison walls in China are arranged in this way to prevent escape). Thorns are indicated by the trigram K'an. The unfortunate situation of the line is due to the fact that it rests upon a hard line, the nine in the fifth place. For minor offenses, where repentance was shown, pardon was granted after a year, for more serious ones after two years, and for very grave ones after three years, so that here it is question of an extremely serious entanglement.

NOTE. The whole hexagram of THE ABYSMAL is based on the idea that the light lines are inclosed by the dark lines, and thus endangered. This idea of danger not only gives the hexagram its character, but also dominates the individual lines. It appears that the two strong lines (the second and the fifth) fare better than the others and have the prospect of getting out of danger, while the six at the beginning and the six in the third place fall into abyss after abyss, and the six at the top sees no way out for three years. Thus the danger threatening the dark lines is even greater. It often happens, however, that the idea of a given hexagram as a whole is differently expressed in some of the lines.

30. *Li* | *The Clinging, Fire*

Nuclear trigrams TUI ☱ *and* SUN ☴

The rulers of the hexagram are the two yin lines in the second and the fifth place; of these, the line in the second place is ruler in a more marked degree, for fire is brightest when it first flames up.

The Sequence

In a pit there is certain to be something clinging within. Hence there follows the hexagram of THE CLINGING. The Clinging means resting on something.

535

Miscellaneous Notes

THE CLINGING is directed upward.

Appended Judgments

Fu Hsi made knotted cords and used them for nets and baskets in hunting and fishing. He probably took this from the hexagram of THE CLINGING.

This hexagram, divided within and closed without, is an image of the meshes of a net in which animals remain snared.[1] It is the opposite of the preceding hexagram, not only in structure but also in its entire meaning.

THE JUDGMENT

THE CLINGING. Perseverance furthers.

It brings success.

Care of the cow brings good fortune.

Commentary on the Decision

Clinging means resting on something. Sun and moon cling to heaven. Grain, plants, and trees cling to the soil.

Doubled clarity, clinging to what is right, transforms the world and perfects it.

The yielding clings to the middle and to what is right, hence it has success. Therefore it is said: "Care of the cow brings good fortune."

Here the co-operation of the two world principles is shown. The light principle becomes visible only in that it clings to bodies. Sun and moon attain their brightness by clinging to heaven, from which issue the forces of the light principle. The plant world owes its life to the fact that it clings to the soil (the Chinese character here is *t'u*, not *ti*[2]), in which the forces of life express themselves. On the other hand, bodies are like-

---

1. [Literally, "clinging."]
2. [*Ti* means the earth.]

wise needed, that the forces of light and of life may find expression in them.

It is the same in the life of man. In order that his psychic nature may be transfigured and attain influence on earth, it must cling to the forces of spiritual life.

The yielding element in Li is the central line of the Receptive, hence the image of the strong but docile cow.

THE IMAGE

That which is bright rises twice:

The image of FIRE.

Thus the great man, by perpetuating this brightness,

Illumines the four quarters of the world.

Fire flames upward, hence the phrase, "That which is bright rises." Twice is implied by the doubling of the trigram. In relation to the spiritual realm, brightness means the innate light-imbued predispositions of man, which through their consistency illumine the world. The trigram Li stands in the south and represents the summer sun, which illumines all earthly things.

THE LINES

Nine at the beginning:

a) The footprints run crisscross.

If one is seriously intent, no blame.

b) Seriousness when footprints run crisscross serves in avoiding blame.

The first line means the morning. The fire at first burns fitfully—an image of the restless confusion of daily business. The line is firm, hence the possibility of seriousness.

○ Six in the second place:

a) Yellow light. Supreme good fortune.

b) The supreme good fortune of yellow light lies in the fact that one has found the middle way.

This line is the middle one of the lower trigram, hence "the middle way." Yellow is the color of the middle, here specially mentioned because the line originates as the middle line of the trigram K'un, the Receptive.

Nine in the third place:

a) In the light of the setting sun,
  Men either beat the pot and sing
  Or loudly bewail the approach of old age.
  Misfortune.

b) How can one wish to hold for long the light of the setting sun?

The third line ends the lower trigram, hence the image of the setting sun. The line is simultaneously in the nuclear trigram Tui, which indicates autumn, and in the nuclear trigram Sun, meaning growth. But Tui also means joyousness and Sun also means sighing.

Nine in the fourth place:

a) Its coming is sudden;
  It flames up, dies down, is thrown away.

b) "Its coming is sudden." Yet in itself it has nothing that would cause it to be accepted.

The fourth line is restless at the point of intersection of the two nuclear trigrams. It is oppressed from below and rejected from above.

O Six in the fifth place:

a) Tears in floods, sighing and lamenting.
  Good fortune.

b) The good fortune of the six in the fifth place clings to king and prince.

The fifth place is that of the ruler. Since the line is yielding, it is not arrogant but humble and sad (it is at the top of the nuclear trigram Tui, mouth, hence the lament). Therein lies its good fortune.

Nine at the top:

a) The king uses him to march forth and chastise.
Then it is best to kill the leaders
And take captive the followers. No blame.

b) "The king uses him to march forth and chastise": in order to bring the country under discipline.

The ruler of the hexagram, the six in the fifth place, is the king. He uses the top line to lead the armed forces (the trigram Li has weapons for its symbol). Since it is at the top and strong, the line is correct, and therefore does not push the business of war too far. It shows the light at its height.

PART II

咸

31. *Hsien / Influence* (*Wooing*)

Nuclear trigrams CH'IEN ——— *and* SUN ———

The nine in the fourth place is in the place of the heart. The heart holds mastery in influence, hence the fourth line is here a ruler of the hexagram. The nine in the fifth place is in the place of the back and therefore means keeping still in the midst of the influence. In the midst of movement, it is able to remain quiet and is therefore ruler of the hexagram to a still greater degree.

The Sequence

After there are heaven and earth, there are the individual things.

After individual things have come into being, there are the two sexes.

After there are male and female, there is the relationship between husband and wife.

After the relationship between husband and wife exists, there is the relationship between father and son.

After the relationship between father and son exists, there is the relationship between prince and servitor.

After the relationship between prince and servitor exists, there is the difference between superior and inferior.

After the difference between superior and inferior
exists, the rules of propriety and of right can operate.

Miscellaneous Notes

INFLUENCE fulfills itself quickly.

THE JUDGMENT

INFLUENCE. Success.
Perseverance furthers.
To take a maiden to wife brings good fortune.

Commentary on the Decision

INFLUENCE means stimulation. The weak is above,
the strong below. The forces of the two stimulate
and respond to each other, so that they unite.

Keeping Still and joyousness.[1] The masculine subordinates itself to the feminine. Hence it is said:
"Success. Perseverance furthers. To take a maiden
to wife brings good fortune."

Heaven and earth stimulate each other, and all
things take shape and come into being. The holy
man stimulates the hearts of men, and the world
attains peace and rest. If we contemplate the outgoing stimulating influences, we can know the nature of heaven and earth and all beings.

Hsien differs from the character *kan*, "to stimulate," in that
the heart is not a constituent part of it, as it is of the latter.
Hence it represents an influence that is unconscious and involuntary, not one that is conscious and willed. It is a matter of
objective relationships of a general kind, not those of a subjective, individual character.

The "weak above" is the trigram Tui, the youngest daughter; its attribute is joyousness, its image is the lake. The
"strong below" is Kên, the youngest son; its attribute is keeping still, its image is the mountain.

---

1. [Tui.]

The explanation of the Judgment is based on the organization of the hexagram (the weak element above, the strong below), the attributes, and the symbols (the youngest son, the youngest daughter).

THE IMAGE

A lake on the mountain:
The image of INFLUENCE.
Thus the superior man encourages people to approach him
By his readiness to receive them.[2]

The mountain lake gives of its moisture to the mountain; the mountain collects clouds, which feed the lake. Thus their forces have a reciprocal influence. The relation of the two images shows how this influence comes about: it is only when a mountain is empty at its summit, that is, deepened into a hollow, that a lake can form. Thus the superior man receives people by virtue of emptiness. The superior man is compared to the mountain, the people to the lake. The relation is formed through the initiative of the mountain, the superior man.

THE LINES

The stimulation here shows itself step by step. The individual lines denote the respective parts of the body: the three lower lines are the legs, including toe, calf, and thigh; the three upper lines are the trunk, with the heart, the back of the neck, and the organs of speech.

Six at the beginning:

a) The influence shows itself in the big toe.

b) Influence in the big toe: the will is directed outward.

This line is related to the nine in the fourth place in the outer trigram. The image of the toe is chosen because it denotes the lowest part of the body. The will is directed outward, though

---

2. Literally, "Thus the superior man receives people by virtue of emptiness."

this does not become manifest, because the movement of the toe is invisible from outside.

Six in the second place:

a) The influence shows itself in the calves of the legs. Misfortune.

Tarrying brings good fortune.

b) Even though misfortune threatens, tarrying brings good fortune. One does not come to harm through devotion.

This line is related to the nine in the fifth place. If it does not move in unison with the six at the beginning, but tarries until stimulated from above by the nine in the fifth place, it does not come to harm. The possibility of tarrying is open to it because its position is central.

Nine in the third place:

a) The influence shows itself in the thighs. Holds to that which follows it.

To continue is humiliating.

b) "The influence shows itself in the thighs." For he cannot keep still.

When the will is directed to things that one's followers hold to, this is very base.

Since the two lower lines are weak by nature, it is not surprising that they let themselves be influenced by others. But this strong line could easily master itself and not yield to every stimulus from below. It makes itself contemptible by conforming to the aims of the two lower lines, its followers.

○ Nine in the fourth place:

a) Perseverance brings good fortune. Remorse disappears.

If a man is agitated in mind,

And his thoughts go hither and thither,

Only those friends

On whom he fixes his conscious thoughts
Will follow.

b) "Perseverance brings good fortune. Remorse disappears." Because in this way one does not stir up anything injurious.

Thoughts going hither and thither in agitation: by this one shows that one has as yet no clear light.

This is a strong line in a weak place, hence it has a twofold possibility. It can remain firm and, resisting the temptation to use special influence, quietly make itself felt as one of the rulers of the hexagram, by virtue of its character; in this case it does not stimulate anything injurious, since it is in harmony with the right. Or it can instead yield to the influence of the six at the beginning, to which it is related. Thereby it limits its influence; everything is shifted to the conscious plane, and the inner light darkens. This possibility is suggested by the fact that the line is the lowest in the trigram Tui, hence deepest within the realm of the shadowy (Tui is a yin trigram, therefore dark). Confucius says of this line:

What need has nature of thought and care? In nature all things return to their common source and are distributed along different paths; through one action, the fruits of a hundred thoughts are realized. What need has nature of thought, of care?

O   Nine in the fifth place:

a)   The influence shows itself in the back of the neck. No remorse.

b)   "The influence shows itself in the back of the neck." The will is directed to the ramifications.

The back of the neck is immobile. The influence is sound at the root. And where the root is sound the ramifications are also sound. Therefore the influence is good. The line is strong and central and ruler of the hexagram, hence it influences through the perfect calm of inner equilibrium. At the same time the will is not inert; by controlling the chief organic processes, it achieves order in particulars as well.

Six at the top:

a) The influence shows itself in the jaws, cheeks, and tongue.

b) "The influence shows itself in the jaws, cheeks, and tongue." He opens his mouth and chatters.

This is a weak line that in itself has little influence. The trigram Tui means the mouth. The top line is divided; hence opening of the mouth.

恒

32. *Hêng | Duration*

Nuclear trigrams TUI and CH'IEN

Duration means that which always is. What is in the middle abides always. In the hexagram the second and the fifth place are middle positions. But the six in the fifth place, although central, is weak, whereas the nine in the second place is central and strong as well. Hence the second line is the ruler of the hexagram.

While in the preceding hexagram the correspondence of the lines comes into account as more of a hindrance than a help, here the fact that all the lines correspond is proof of a firm inner organization of the hexagram that guarantees duration. The strong second line stands in the relationship of correspondence to the weak six in the fifth place.

The Sequence

The way of husband and wife must not be other than long-lasting. Hence there follows the hexagram of DURATION. Duration means long-lasting.

Miscellaneous Notes

DURATION means that which lasts long.

Appended Judgments

DURATION brings about firmness of character. DU-
RATION shows manifold experiences without satiety.
DURATION brings about unity of character.

THE JUDGMENT

DURATION. Success. No blame.
Perseverance furthers.
It furthers one to have somewhere to go.

Commentary on the Decision

DURATION means that which lasts long. The strong
is above, the weak below; thunder and wind work
together.

Gentle and in motion. The strong and the weak
all correspond: this signifies duration.

"Success. No blame. Perseverance furthers": this
means lasting perseverance in one's course. The
course of heaven and earth is enduring and long
and never ends.

"It furthers one to have somewhere to go." This
means that an end is always followed by a new
beginning.

Sun and moon have heaven and can therefore
shine forever. The four seasons change and transform, and thus can forever bring to completion.
The holy man remains forever in his course, and the
world reshapes itself to completion. If we meditate
on what gives duration to a thing, we can understand the nature of heaven and earth and of all
beings.

The organization of the hexagram shows the strong Chên above and the weak Sun below; this is the enduring condition in the world. Here the eldest son and the eldest daughter are united in marriage, in contrast to the situation in the preceding hexagram, which represents entering into marriage.

The images show thunder, which is carried still farther by the power of wind, and wind, which is strengthened by the power of thunder. Their combined action imparts duration to both. The attribute of the trigram Sun is gentleness, that of Chên is movement. The outer movement, supported within by devotion, is likewise such that it is capable of duration.

Finally, the hexagram is given inner firmness by the correspondence between the individual lines. The six in the first place corresponds with the nine in the fourth; the nine in the second place with the six in the fifth; the nine in the third place with the six at the top.

All this serves to explain the name of the hexagram.

On the basis of the Judgment, the conditions necessary for duration are then set forth. They consist in perseverance in the right course, that is to say, continuity in change. This is the secret of the eternity of the universe.

Perseverance in a course leads to the goal, the end. However, since the course is cyclic, a new beginning is joined with every end. Movement and rest beget each other. This is the rhythm of all happening. The operation of this principle in specific instances, in relation to the macrocosm and the microcosm, is then pointed out.

THE IMAGE

Thunder and wind: the image of DURATION.
Thus the superior man stands firm
And does not change his direction.

Thunder is that which is mobile, wind is that which is penetrating—the most mobile of all things that have duration under the law of motion. Wood is an attribute of both Chên and Sun, hence the idea of standing firm. Sun is within and penetrates, Chên is without and moves; hence the idea of a fixed direction.

THE LINES

Six at the beginning:

a)   Seeking duration too hastily brings misfortune persistently.

Nothing that would further.

b)   The misfortune of seeking duration too hastily arises from wanting too much immediately at the outset.

The first line is the ruler of the trigram Sun, penetration. The line seeks to penetrate too hastily and too deeply. This impetuosity interferes with the influence, otherwise good, of the strong line in the fourth place, whose affinity with the first line is thus prevented from having effect.

O   Nine in the second place:

a)   Remorse disappears.

b)   Remorse disappears for the nine in the second place, because it is permanently central.

A strong line in a weak place might in itself produce occasion for remorse. But since the line is strong and central and in correct relation to the six in the fifth place, there is no danger of overstepping the limits of moderation, and thus no occasion for remorse.

Nine in the third place:

a)   He who does not give duration to his character
Meets with disgrace.
Persistent humiliation.

b)   "He who does not give duration to his character" meets with no toleration.

The line is at the point of transition from the lower to the upper trigram, hence excited and superficial. In the forward direction, it has not yet entered into the movement of the trigram Chên; in the backward direction, it has already passed beyond the gentleness of Sun (because it is a strong line in a strong place). Therefore it does not come to rest anywhere.

Nine in the fourth place:

a) No game in the field.

b) When one is forever absent from one's place, how can one find game?

Chên is represented by a horse ranging the field, likewise by a highroad, where there is no game; hence the image.

The line is at the beginning of the trigram Chên, i.e., not yet central. It is a strong line in a weak place, hence not correct. Thus it bestirs itself unceasingly where it should not, and therefore finds nothing. The third line has character (a strong line in a strong place) but no duration; the present line has duration but no character (a strong line in a weak place).

Six in the fifth place:

a) Giving duration to one's character through perseverance.

This is good fortune for a woman, misfortune for a man.

b) Perseverance brings good fortune for a woman, because she follows one man all her life. A man must hold to his duty; if he follows the woman, the results are bad.

This line is yielding but central and in direct relation to the strong nine in the second place, which is ruler of the hexagram. Hence these relations are enduring. However, the law that the weak unswervingly follows the strong reflects a virtue of woman. Things are different in the case of a man.

Six at the top:

a) Restlessness as an enduring condition brings misfortune.

b) Restlessness as an enduring condition in a high position is wholly without merit.

Chên has movement for its attribute. Here a weak line is at the high point of the trigram of movement. It cannot control itself and therefore falls prey to a restlessness that is harmful because it is in opposition to the meaning of the time. The line is the opposite of the six at the beginning; there we have movement too hasty to endure, here movement that endures but accomplishes nothing.

33. *Tun / Retreat*

Nuclear trigrams CH'IEN ☰ *and* SUN ☴

The constituting rulers of the hexagram are the two yin lines in the first and the second place. They show the dark principle pressing forward, with the light principle in retreat. The ruler of the action is the strong, central line in the fifth place, which finds correspondence in the weak, central line in the second place. This is the line referred to in the Commentary on the Decision: "The firm is in the appropriate place and finds correspondence. This means that one is in accord with the time."

The lower trigram is Kên, Keeping Still, hence the three lower lines show themselves hampered in retreating. The upper trigram is Ch'ien, strong movement, hence the retreat of these three lines is free and unhampered.

The Sequence

Things cannot abide forever in their place: hence there follows the hexagram of RETREAT. Retreat means withdrawing.

Miscellaneous Notes

RETREAT means withdrawing.

THE JUDGMENT

RETREAT. Success.
In what is small, perseverance furthers.

Commentary on the Decision

"RETREAT. Success": this means that success lies in
retreating.

The firm is in the appropriate place and finds correspondence. This means that one is in accord with
the time.

"In what is small, perseverance furthers": this
means that it is pressing forward, and on the increase.

Great indeed is the meaning of the time of
RETREAT.

Success lies in being able to retreat at the right moment and in
the right manner. This success is made possible by the fact
that the retreat is not the forced flight of a weak person but the
voluntary withdrawal of a strong one, as is implicit in the nature of the strong ruler of the hexagram, the nine in the fifth
place, which finds correspondence in the weak six in the second
place. Strength is shown in that one does not attempt to force
anything but shows perseverance in small matters alone, because the dark element, represented by the two yin lines below,
is pressing forward and on the increase.

The meaning of the time of RETREAT is great; that is, it is
vitally important to hit upon the moment when retreat is called
for.

THE IMAGE

Mountain under heaven: the image of RETREAT.
Thus the superior man keeps the inferior man at a
distance,
Not angrily but with reserve.

The question is to what extent the mountain under heaven
suggests the image of RETREAT. One interpretation is that the
mountain under heaven is so high and steep that men cannot

come near to it. However, the other interpretation—that heaven represents the superior man, the mountain the inferior man—is more in harmony with the movement of the trigrams. Heaven has a strong upward movement and therefore automatically retreats from the mountain, whose character is immobility. An even greater divergence occurs in the hexagram P'i, STANDSTILL (12), in which the movements are directly opposed.

What the situation in the present hexagram teaches is, as in the case of P'i, deduced from the attributes of the trigrams taken separately. The superior man keeps the inferior at a distance by being as reserved and inaccessible as heaven; thus he brings the inferior man to a standstill (this is the attribute of the lower trigram, Kên, mountain).

THE LINES

☐ Six at the beginning:

a) At the tail in retreat. This is dangerous.
   One must not wish to undertake anything.

b) If one undertakes nothing while exposed to the danger of the retreating tail, what misfortune could befall one?

The two lower lines are those before which the four upper ones retreat, therefore they are the constituting rulers. As in the hexagram Lü, CONDUCT (10), in which the youngest daughter follows the trigram Ch'ien, so likewise here, where the youngest son is under Ch'ien, the tail is used as the image of the first line. The interpretation does not take into account the fact that in the hexagram as a whole, this line represents the inferior man, because the Book of Changes gives counsel not for inferior men but only for the superior. Instead, the counsel focuses on the situation as such, which is retreat, particularly retreat at the tail—the rear. To be at the rear in a retreat is dangerous. The danger is avoided by keeping still.

☐ Six in the second place:

a) He holds him fast with yellow oxhide.
   No one can tear him loose.

b) "He holds him fast with yellow oxhide": this means
a firm will.

Here also the retreat is hampered. This line occupies the middle
of the trigram Kên, Keeping Still. Yellow is the color of the
middle. The line is near the nine in the third place, hence
holds it fast. Here we have the perseverance of the inferior,
the small, referred to in the Judgment.

Nine in the third place:

a) A halted retreat
Is nerve-wracking and dangerous.
To retain people as men- and maidservants
Brings good fortune.

b) The danger of a halted retreat is nerve-wracking;
this brings fatigue.
"To retain people as men- and maidservants brings
good fortune." True enough, but one cannot use
them in great things.

The line is strong in itself, and it might therefore be expected to have the strength to retreat. What makes this impossible is the fact, first, that it is at the top of the trigram Kên,
Keeping Still, and, second, that the two weak lines below
cling to it. This is tiring. It can of course use the lower lines as
men- and maidservants, because in the trigram Kên the top
line has the mastery. This provides a way out, to the extent
that the immediate danger is thereby avoided. However, with
such a following it is not possible to attain great ends.

Nine in the fourth place:

a) Voluntary retreat brings good fortune to the superior
man
And downfall to the inferior man.

b) The superior man retreats voluntarily; this brings
downfall for the inferior man.

Here the entrance into the upper trigram is completed. Since
heaven is strong, all three of the upper lines can retreat

unhindered. This is the line of demarcation. The superior man retreats upward and the inferior man remains alone below. This is bad for him—though not for the superior man—because he cannot rule himself.

O Nine in the fifth place:

a) Friendly retreat. Perseverance brings good fortune.

b) "Friendly retreat. Perseverance brings good fortune," because the will thereby reaches a correct decision.

The will here is related to the will of the six in the second place, because the two lines correspond. The one shows a strong will to hold on firmly (a good thing for inferior men), the other an unwavering will to remain persevering and not to submit to being held.

Another explanation, from the *Chou I Hêng Chieh*,[1] deserves mention, namely, that it is a question only of an inner retreat here, while outwardly one remains at one's post in order to prepare a countermove.

Nine at the top:

a) Cheerful retreat. Everything serves to further.

b) "Cheerful retreat. Everything serves to further," because there is no longer any possibility of doubt.

Here one knows exactly what to do. Under such circumstances the carrying out of the decision is not difficult.

---

1. [See p. 665.]

大壯

34. *Ta Chuang / The Power of the Great*

Nuclear trigrams TUI ☱ and CH'IEN ☰

The ruler of the hexagram is the yang line in the fourth place, because the four yang lines are the basis of the power of the hexagram, with the fourth at their head.

The Sequence

Things cannot retreat forever, hence there follows THE POWER OF THE GREAT.

Miscellaneous Notes

The meaning of THE POWER OF THE GREAT shows itself in the fact that one pauses.

Appended Judgments

In the most ancient times people dwelt in caves and lived in forests. The holy men of a later time made the change to buildings. At the top was a ridgepole, and sloping down from it there was a roof, to keep off wind and rain. They probably took this from the hexagram of THE POWER OF THE GREAT.

The four strong lines taken together are regarded as a ridgepole, as also in the hexagram Ta Kuo, PREPONDERANCE OF THE GREAT (28). The two divided lines at the top represent rain and wind.

The hexagram can be thought of as formed by the lines of Tui taken twice each. Tui has the sheep (or goat) for its animal, hence the goat is used as an image in several of the lines. The two upper lines are the horns.

It is the contrast between power and violent force that is expressed in the meaning of the hexagram. In structure it is the inverse of the preceding one.

THE JUDGMENT

THE POWER OF THE GREAT. Perseverance furthers.

Commentary on the Decision

THE POWER OF THE GREAT means that the great are powerful. Strong in movement—this is the basis of power.

"THE POWER OF THE GREAT. Perseverance furthers," for what is great must be right.

Great and right: thus we can behold the relations of heaven and earth.

☷☰ The hexagram linked with the first month is T'ai, PEACE (11). Although in it the light lines are advancing, they are not yet in the majority.

☱☰ The hexagram correlated with the third month is Kuai, BREAK-THROUGH (43). In this instance the light lines are markedly in the majority, but downfall is already imminent.

Neither of these situations can be said to denote power.

But the presence of four yang lines [in Ta Chuang] indicates power. Strength is the attribute of the inner trigram, the Creative, and movement that of the outer, the Arousing. Strength makes it possible to master the egotism of the sensual drives; movement makes it possible to execute the firm decision of the will. In this way all things can be attained. This is the foundation upon which power rests. When the statement is made that what is great must be right, it means not that great and right are two different things, but that without rightness there is no greatness. The relations of heaven and earth are never other than great and right.

THE IMAGE

Thunder in heaven above:
The image of THE POWER OF THE GREAT.
Thus the superior man does not tread upon paths
That do not accord with established order.

The upper trigram is Chên, thunder; the lower is Ch'ien, heaven. Thunder in the heavens shows the power of something great in full expansion. The trigram Chên also has as its image the foot, and the attribute of Ch'ien is "great and right." Thus the foot treads upon the great and right and takes its way thereon. The strength of the trigram Ch'ien imparts to the movement of the trigram Chên the force resolutely to do what is good, and this is the basis of great power.

THE LINES

Nine at the beginning:

a) Power in the toes.
Continuing brings misfortune.
This is certainly true.

b) "Power in the toes." This certainly leads to failure.

The first line, as is often the case (cf. hexagram 31), means the toes, while the upper lines mean the horns.

Nine in the second place:

a) Perseverance brings good fortune.

b) The nine in the second place finds good fortune through perseverance because it is in a central place.

A nine, being a strong line, is not ordinarily correct in the second place, which is weak, and it might therefore be expected that perseverance would not be recommended here. But the place is central and moreover in the center of the trigram Ch'ien, heaven, hence inherently strong. Further, the line has a firm relationship of correspondence with the six in the fifth place. All this indicates that in the place here occupied by the line, perseverance acts favorably.

Nine in the third place:

a) The inferior man works through power.
The superior man does not act thus.
To continue is dangerous.
A goat butts against a hedge
And gets its horns entangled.

b) The inferior man uses his power. This the superior
man does not do.

These words explain the first sentence of the oracle. The
image for this line is a goat butting against a hedge and
entangling its horns. This is due to the fact that the line is the
lowest in the upper nuclear trigram Tui, whose animal is the
sheep or goat. Since a strong line is in front of it, this suggests
the idea that the goat butts against a hedge and is caught fast
by the horns.

O Nine in the fourth place:

a) Perseverance brings good fortune.
Remorse disappears.
The hedge opens; there is no entanglement.
Power depends upon the axle of a big cart.

b) "The hedge opens; there is no entanglement." It can
go upward.

This line, as the uppermost of the four advancing light lines, is
the ruler of the hexagram. It finds before itself a divided line
that does not hinder further advance. Hence it can advance
upward unchecked.

Six in the fifth place:

a) Loses the goat with ease.
No remorse.

b) "Loses the goat with ease," because the place is not
the appropriate one.

The place is strong, it is in fact the place of the prince, but the
nature of the line is yielding, hence the outer place does not

correspond with the inner nature. Therefore the line easily rids itself of its obstinate disposition.

Six at the top:

a) A goat butts against a hedge.
It cannot go backward, it cannot go forward.
Nothing serves to further.
If one notes the difficulty, this brings good fortune.

b) "It cannot go backward, it cannot go forward." This does not bring luck.
"If one notes the difficulty, this brings good fortune."
The mistake is not lasting.

This line is at the height of the movement (Chên), topping the figure of the goat, the symbol of the nuclear trigram Tui; this suggests the idea of butting with horns. But since it has reached the end it can go no farther; hence confusion and difficulties. However, the line is yielding in character; therefore, instead of stiffening in its obstinacy, it yields, and in this way the mistake does not become a lasting one.

晉

35. *Chin | Progress*

☷ *Nuclear trigrams* K'AN ☵ *and* KÊN ☶

This hexagram is characterized by light rising out of the earth. The six in the fifth place is the ruler of the trigram Li (light), because it is in the middle place of heaven. Hence it is the ruler of the hexagram, referred to in the sentence of the Commentary on the Decision: "The weak progresses and goes upward."

The Sequence

Beings cannot stay forever in a state of power; hence there follows the hexagram of PROGRESS. Progress means expansion.

Miscellaneous Notes

PROGRESS means the day.

The hexagrams Chin, Shêng, PUSHING UPWARD (46), and Chien, DEVELOPMENT (53), all mean progress. Chin has for its image the sun mounting over the earth. It is the finest of these three hexagrams. Shêng is symbolized by wood rising above the earth. Chien shows the still more gradual development of a tree on a mountain. It is true that a too rapid expansion has its dangers, as the next hexagram shows.

In terms of human society, the present hexagram indicates a wise ruler with obedient servitors at his side.

THE JUDGMENT

PROGRESS. The powerful prince
Is honored with horses in large numbers.
In a single day he is granted audience three times.

Commentary on the Decision

PROGRESS means making advance. Clarity rises high over the earth. Devoted, and clinging to this great clarity, the weak progresses and goes upward. Hence it is said: "The powerful prince is honored with horses in large numbers. In a single day he is granted audience three times."

The structure of the hexagram points to progress—indeed, to progress on all sides, to expansion. Devoted refers to the lower trigram K'un, here meaning servitor. The great clarity is the upper trigram Li, here meaning the ruler. The weak element that progresses is the middle line of K'un, which occupies the middle place in the upper trigram, originally Ch'ien, the father; hence it is the ruler of the hexagram, the wise prince.

The ruler needs the loyalty of his servitors, and being possessed of great wisdom, he knows how to reward them fittingly. This explains the words of the Judgment.

THE IMAGE

The sun rises over the earth:
The image of PROGRESS.
Thus the superior man himself
Brightens his bright virtue.

The Image is directly explained through the relative positions of the two trigrams: Li, light, stands above K'un, the earth. Here we have a model for a philosophy of life: what is innately light rises over that which darkens. It can do this of its own power because it is not obstructed by the earth, which is devoted and compliant in its nature.

THE LINES

Six at the beginning:

a) Progressing, but turned back.
Perseverance brings good fortune.
If one meets with no confidence, one should remain calm.
No mistake.

b) "Progressing, but turned back." Solitary, he walks in the right. Composure is not a mistake. One has not yet received the command.

A standstill is imposed upon the lowest line, weak in itself, by the nuclear trigram Kên forming above it. Hence it is stopped in its tendency to progress. Nevertheless it goes its solitary way on the path of duty and calmly awaits the time that will surely come.

Six in the second place:

a) Progressing, but in sorrow.
Perseverance brings good fortune.

Then one obtains great happiness from one's ancestress.

b) "One obtains great happiness," because of the central and correct position.

This line is similar in character to the ruler of the hexagram, the six in the fifth place. The latter appears under the image of the ancestress, because according to ancient custom the grandson was associated with the grandfather, not with the father. Both lines being weak, the images here are feminine— the grandson's wife and the ancestress. The line is at the base of the nuclear trigram Kên, Keeping Still, hence likewise hindered in its advance.

Six in the third place:

a) All are in accord. Remorse disappears.

b) "All are in accord," because there is a will to go upward.

This line is quite close to the upper trigram Li, clarity, hence misunderstandings are cleared up. Since it is at the head of others of the same mind, progress is possible for it.

Nine in the fourth place:

a) Progress like a hamster.
Perseverance brings danger.

b) A hamster gets into danger through perseverance; the place is not appropriate.

This line is at the top of the trigram Kên, with which the rat and other rodents are associated. Rats and hamsters hide themselves by day and are active only by night. But the line is already in the trigram of the sun, whose light it cannot endure. Since it is a time of progress, the line mingles with the crowd and joins in what is going on. However, this is not its proper place (a strong line in a weak place); therefore going on in this way brings danger (the line is also the middle line of the upper nuclear trigram K'an, danger).

○ Six in the fifth place:

a) Remorse disappears.
Take not gain and loss to heart.
Undertakings bring good fortune.
Everything serves to further.

b) "Take not gain and loss to heart." Undertaking brings
blessing.

A yin line in a yang place should really cause remorse, but
since it is here in the center of the great light,[1] there is no need
for remorse. Furthermore, the line is empty, that is, divided
in the middle. This is an indication that it does not take gain
and loss to heart, because it is not dependent on external things.
Fire has no definite form, it flames up and goes out; hence the
image of gain and loss. Moreover, although the line is the uppermost one in the nuclear trigram K'an, the Abysmal, which
suggests sorrow, it is the ruler of the hexagram, hence sorrow
is not necessary.

Nine at the top:

a) Making progress with the horns is permissible
Only for the purpose of punishing one's own city.
To be conscious of danger brings good fortune.
No blame.
Perseverance brings humiliation.

b) "Permissible only for the purpose of punishing one's
own city." The way is not yet in the light.

The line at the top is strong. This suggests the image of horns.
Since it is a time of progress, there is shown here at the end an
attempt to progress by means of force. But the line stands
isolated, because under it the Abysmal (upper nuclear trigram)
sinks into the depths, leaving it forsaken. It is thrown back
upon itself and is able to discipline only its own city.

---

1. [Li, the sun.]

36. *Ming I / Darkening of the Light*

Nuclear trigrams CHÊN ☳ *and* K'AN ☵

This hexagram has for its characterizing image the sun sunk below the earth. The six at the top stands for the greatest accumulation of earth, hence it is the line that damages and darkens the light of the others. It is the ruler determining the meaning of the hexagram. Both the six in the second place and the six in the fifth place have the attributes of central and devoted character, and it is they that are injured. They are the rulers governing the hexagram. Hence it is said in the Commentary on the Decision: "King Wên experienced this, Prince Chi experienced this."

The Sequence

Expansion will certainly encounter resistance and injury. Hence there follows the hexagram of DARK-ENING OF THE LIGHT. Darkening means damage, injury.

Miscellaneous Notes

DARKENING OF THE LIGHT means injury.

The whole hexagram has a historical background. For at the time when King Wên wrote the judgments on the hexagrams, conditions in China were just as this hexagram pictures them. In the judgments on the lines, the Duke of Chou refers to Prince Chi as exemplifying the situation. Confucius carries this further in the Commentary on the Decision by adding the example of King Wên.

Later on—quite in keeping with the meaning—historical personages came to be linked with each of the lines. The evil ruler was Chou Hsin,[1] the last king of the Yin dynasty. He is symbolized by the six at the top. Under him the most able princes of the realm were all made to suffer severely, and their fates are mirrored in the individual lines. The highminded Po I withdrew into hiding with his brother, Shu Ch'i. He is represented by the nine at the beginning. The six in the second place pictures King Wên, who, as the foremost of the feudal princes, was long held prisoner by the tyrant, with constant danger to his life. The nine in the third place represents his son, afterward King Wu of Chou, who overthrew the tyrant. The six in the fourth place depicts the situation of Prince Wei Tzǔ, who was able to save himself by timely flight abroad. Finally, the six in the fifth place depicts the situation of Prince Chi, who could save his life only by dissembling.

This hexagram is the inverse of the preceding one.

THE JUDGMENT

DARKENING OF THE LIGHT. In adversity
It furthers one to be persevering.

Commentary on the Decision

The light has sunk into the earth: DARKENING OF THE LIGHT. Beautiful and clear within, gentle and devoted without, hence exposed to great adversity —thus was King Wên.

"In adversity it furthers one to be persevering": this means veiling one's light. Surrounded by difficulties in the midst of his closest kin, nonetheless keeping his will fixed on the right—thus was Prince Chi.

The inner trigram is Li, light, whose attributes are beauty and clarity; the outer trigram is K'un, the Receptive, whose attributes are yieldingness and devotion. King Wên, in whom

1. [Overthrown *ca*. 1150 B.C.]

these attributes are seen united, is depicted in one of the rulers of the hexagram, the six in the second place.

Prince Chi is depicted by the six in the fifth place. He too is in difficulties; these are represented by the nuclear trigram K'an, the Abysmal, danger. King Wên is as it were hidden by this nuclear trigram over him. For the six in the fifth place the difficulties lie within, that is, below. It is not overcome by them because it is at the top of the upper nuclear trigram Chên, movement. By movement it gets clear of the difficulties, and the light, although jeopardized, cannot be extinguished.

THE IMAGE

The light has sunk into the earth:

The image of DARKENING OF THE LIGHT.

Thus does the superior man live with the great mass:

He veils his light, yet still shines.

The upper trigram K'un means the mass. Amid the multitude are the two dominating rulers of the hexagram, as the superior men. Their behavior is explained on the basis of the relative positions of the two trigrams: Earth stands over light, and this suggests a veiling of the light. But the lower trigram Li is not injured in its character by this combination. Its light is only veiled, not extinguished.

THE LINES

Nine at the beginning:

a) Darkening of the light during flight.

He lowers his wings.

The superior man does not eat for three days

On his wanderings.

But he has somewhere to go.

The host has occasion to gossip about him.

b) It is the obligation of the superior man to refrain from eating during his wanderings.

The animal symbol belonging to the trigram Li is the pheasant, hence the idea of flying. The line, being strong, is about to advance. But the nuclear trigram over it is K'an, danger; hence it is hindered in its flight. It renounces the idea of sacrificing its principles in order to secure a livelihood; it prefers going hungry to eating without honor.

○ Six in the second place:

a) Darkening of the light injures him in the left thigh.
He gives aid with the strength of a horse.
Good fortune.

b) The good fortune of the six in the second place comes from its devotion to the rule.

One might expect misfortune from the situation, yet the oracle is, "Good fortune." This is because the line, being yielding, correct, and in the proper place, is equal to the demands of its position. The first half of the Commentary on the Decision, which uses the example of King Wên, has reference to this line.

Nine in the third place:

a) Darkening of the light during the hunt in the south.
Their great leader is captured.
One must not expect perseverance too soon.

b) The purpose of the hunt in the south has great success.

The aim is centered on the hunt. That success comes, that the great leader of the darkening is captured, is not something premeditated, hence the success is all the greater. King Wu had no intention of acquiring personal power and seizing empire for himself; it fell to him because of his character. The line is a strong one in a strong place, hence it carries out its intention. The upper nuclear trigram Chên is linked with the horse, the lower, K'an, with the chariot, hence the idea of a hunt. Li, in which this is the top line, is the south.

Six in the fourth place:

a) He penetrates the left side of the belly.
One gets at the very heart of the darkening of the light,
And leaves gate and courtyard.

b) "He penetrates the left side of the belly," that is, he finds out the inmost sentiment of the heart.

K'un, the upper primary trigram, means the belly, and Chên, the upper nuclear trigram, means the left side—hence the left side of the belly. The line stands near the lord of darkness; thus it finds out his inmost sentiment and can take itself out of danger in good time. Staying on would mean sacrificing oneself to no purpose.

○ Six in the fifth place:

a) Darkening of the light as with Prince Chi.
   Perseverance furthers.

b) The perseverance of Prince Chi shows that the light cannot be extinguished.

The second half of the Commentary on the Decision refers to this line, which is central and yielding. Prince Chi concealed his perseverance but maintained it inwardly. Similarly, the light of the sun is veiled from time to time, but it cannot be extinguished. The upper nuclear trigram Chên, in which this is the top line, means being aroused, pressing forward. Thus the light cannot be permanently held below but presses forward powerfully when the time has come.

□ Six at the top:

a) Not light but darkness.
   First he climbed up to heaven,
   Then he plunged into the depths of the earth.

b) "First he climbed up to heaven." Thus he might have been able to illumine the lands of all the four quarters of the earth.
   "Then he plunged into the depths of the earth," because he had lost the rule.

First he held a position through which he might have been able to enlighten all the people of the realm. Instead, however, he made it his business to injure men, and thus transgressed the rule that binds one who governs; as a result, he prepared his own downfall.

The line stands at the top, where the earth veils the sun most heavily; but it is also the first to be unmasked in its sinister character when the sun reappears.

家人

37. *Chia Jên / The Family [The Clan]*

Nuclear trigrams LI ☲ *and* K'AN ☵

The rulers of the hexagram are the nine in the fifth place and the six in the second, hence it is said in the Commentary on the Decision: "The correct place of the woman is within; the correct place of the man is without."

The Sequence

He who is injured without, of a certainty draws back into his family. Hence there follows the hexagram of THE FAMILY.

Miscellaneous Notes

THE FAMILY is inside.

The upper trigram Sun means influence, the lower, Li, means clarity; accordingly the hexagram points to the outgoing influence that emanates from inner clarity.[1]

---

1. As these relationships indicate, the Chinese family is the patriarchal clan, which forms the nucleus of the patriarchal state. This trend of thought is developed still further in the Great Learning [*Ta Hsüeh*].

THE JUDGMENT

THE FAMILY. The perseverance of the woman furthers.

Commentary on the Decision

THE FAMILY. The correct place of the woman is
within; the correct place of the man is without.
That man and woman have their proper places is
the greatest concept in nature.

Among the members of the family there are
strict rulers; these are the parents. When the father
is in truth a father and the son a son, when the
elder brother is an elder brother and the younger
brother a younger brother, the husband a husband
and the wife a wife, then the house is on the right
way.

When the house is set in order, the world is
established in a firm course.

While the Judgment speaks only of the perseverance of
woman, because of the fact that the hexagram consists of the
two elder daughters, Sun and Li, who are in their proper
places—the elder above, the younger below—the commentary
is based on the two rulers of the hexagram, the nine in the
fifth place and the six in the second, and speaks accordingly of
both man and woman, whose proper places are respectively
without and within. These positions of man and woman correspond with the relative positions of heaven and earth, hence
this is called the greatest concept in nature (literally, heaven
and earth).

The proper positions of the individual lines have been discussed above. The action of the family on the world corresponds with the action of fire, which creates the wind.

THE IMAGE

Wind comes forth from fire:
The image of THE FAMILY.

Thus the superior man has substance in his words
And duration in his way of life.

Wind is an effect of fire. Similarly, the effect of order within
the family is to create an influence that brings order into the
world. It is achieved when the head of the family has substance in his words, just as flame must rely upon fuel, and
duration in his way of life, just as the wind blows without cease.

THE LINES

Nine at the beginning:

a) Firm seclusion within the family.
Remorse disappears.

b) "Firm seclusion within the family": the will has not
yet changed.

The line is at the beginning, in the lowest place; hence it
represents the time when the will of an individual has not yet
changed for the worse. Here is the point at which to intervene
and prevent change.

○ Six in the second place:

a) She should not follow her whims.
She must attend within to the food.
Perseverance brings good fortune.

b) The good fortune of the six in the second place depends upon devotion and gentleness.

Devotion and gentleness are mentioned three times—in the
hexagram of YOUTHFUL FOLLY (4) as attributes necessary in
serving a teacher, in the hexagram of DEVELOPMENT (53) as
attributes necessary in serving a ruler, and in the present
instance as attributes necessary in serving a husband.

The middle line in the trigram Li means devotion and correctness, which seek nothing for themselves. One of the nuclear
trigrams, K'an, means wine and food, and the other, Li, means
cooking and baking; hence the preparation of food is said to be
the duty of woman.

Nine in the third place:

a)   When tempers flare up in the family,
    Too great severity brings remorse.
    Good fortune nonetheless.
    When woman and child dally and laugh,
    It leads in the end to humiliation.

b)   "When tempers flare up in the family," nothing is as yet lost.
    "When woman and child dally," the discipline of the house is lost.

This line is at the top of the lower primary trigram Li, flame, and likewise at the beginning of the upper nuclear trigram, which is also Li; hence it implies too much heat. Although this is a mistake, such behavior is still to be preferred in the case of a strong line between two weak ones. If the line changes and becomes yielding, the discipline of the house is lost.

Six in the fourth place:

a)   She is the treasure of the house.
    Great good fortune.

b)   "She is the treasure of the house. Great good fortune."
    For she is devoted and in her place.

The fourth line is the yielding lowest line in the upper primary trigram Sun, gentleness. It is the middle line of the upper nuclear trigram Li; when the line changes, it remains within the lower nuclear trigram Sun thus formed. Sun means work, silk, a near-by market—all things that promise wealth. As a yielding line in its proper place, it means great good fortune.

○   Nine in the fifth place:

a)   As a king he approaches his family.
    Fear not.
    Good fortune.

b)   "As a king he approaches his family": they associate with one another in love.

The line is correct, strong, central; hence the image of a king. As a ruler of the hexagram, it influences the other lines. Being central, it does not effect its ends by means of severity.

Nine at the top:

a) His work commands respect.
In the end good fortune comes.

b) "Commands respect" and "good fortune": this indicates that one makes demands first of all upon
oneself.

This line is at the end of the hexagram. It is strong and stable, hence does not turn to others but only to itself; from this finally good fortune comes.

38. *K'uei* / *Opposition*

Nuclear trigrams K'AN *and* LI

The rulers of the hexagram are the six in the fifth place and the nine in the second. Therefore it is said in the Commentary on the Decision: "The yielding progresses and goes upward, at-tains the middle, and finds correspondence in the firm."

The Sequence

When the way of THE FAMILY draws to an end, misunderstandings come. Hence there follows the hexagram of OPPOSITION. Opposition means misun-derstandings.

Miscellaneous Notes

OPPOSITION means estrangement.

Appended Judgments

The men of ancient times strung a piece of wood for a bow and hardened pieces of wood in the fire for arrows. The use of bow and arrow is to keep the world in fear. They probably took this from the hexagram of OPPOSITION.

The upper primary trigram Li means weapons; the lower, Tui, is associated with the west, metal, and killing; hence the idea of bow and arrow to keep the world in fear and alarm.[1] The correspondences between the lines are of great importance in this hexagram. In all the lines the situation is that of opposition; throughout, however, the tendency is toward smoothing out misunderstandings. This is why at the first line no search is made for the horse, which returns of its own accord, and why at the fourth line one meets a person of like mind. At the second place it is said, "One meets his lord," and correspondingly at the fifth place, "The companion bites his way through the wrappings." Again, the pronouncement at the third place, "Not a good beginning, but a good end," is related to that at the topmost place: "As one goes, rain falls." This hexagram is the inverse of the preceding one.

THE JUDGMENT

OPPOSITION. In small matters, good fortune.

Commentary on the Decision

OPPOSITION: fire moves upward, the lake moves downward. Two daughters live together, but their minds are not directed to common concerns.

Joyousness and dependence upon clarity: the yielding progresses and goes upward, attains the middle,

---

1. Cf. the arrows of Helios.

and finds correspondence in the firm. This is why there is good fortune in small matters.

Heaven and earth are opposites, but their action is concerted. Man and woman are opposites, but they strive for union. All beings stand in opposition to one another: what they do takes on order thereby. Great indeed is the effect of the time of OPPOSITION.

The name of the hexagram is derived from the relationships developing out of the movement of the two trigrams. Fire flames upward, water seeps downward: when they are quiescent, their movements can unite; when they are in motion, they draw farther and farther apart. The two daughters are originally together in the parental house. Their ways part as they grow up and marry into different families. Thus the movement leads more and more to opposition. However, since this movement is a natural one, it comes of itself to a turning when it has reached an extreme.

The trigram Tui has joyousness as an attribute; the trigram Li, dependence upon clarity. Joyousness unites, clarity finds the right way for this. Furthermore, the relations of the two rulers of the hexagram are favorable, so that there is a possibility of success at least in small matters.

However, Confucius goes still further. He shows that opposition is actually the natural prerequisite for union. As a result of opposition, a need to bridge it arises; this is true as regards heaven and earth, man and woman. Similarly, it is the individual differences between things that enable us to differentiate them clearly and hence to classify them. This is the effect of the phase of opposition—a phase that must be transcended.

THE IMAGE

Above, fire; below, the lake:
The image of OPPOSITION.
Thus amid all fellowship
The superior man retains his individuality.

The images belonging to the trigrams, whose tendencies combat each other, create the condition of opposition, while their attributes lead to its being overcome. The joyousness of Tui symbolizes fellowship; the clarity of Li symbolizes clearly recognizable individuality.

The reason why the two daughters tend to opposition is that the eldest, whose authority would maintain order, is absent.

THE LINES

Nine at the beginning:

a) Remorse disappears.
If you lose your horse, do not run after it;
It will come back of its own accord.
When you see evil people,
Guard yourself against mistakes.

b) "When you see evil people," avoid mistakes.

As long as an opposition has not become poisoned, it can be smoothed out. A mistake arises only in letting it go too far. This line is in relationship with the fourth, which stands in the nuclear trigram K'an, meaning horse, but does not correspond with it; hence the horse gets lost. The first line is firm and can control itself, and so it does not run after the horse. The horse comes back of its own accord when the opposition has run its course. The fourth line, which belongs both to the nuclear trigram K'an, danger, and to Li, excitement, symbolizes the evil man. Through the joyousness of the trigram Tui, a sharpening of the opposition, and the mistakes that would ensue, are avoided.

O Nine in the second place:

a) One meets his lord in a narrow street.
No blame.

b) If one meets his lord in a narrow street, one has not lost his way.

Attempting to attain something by crooked paths is to lose one's way. But this line is firm and central, hence not set on a meeting at all costs. The meeting, although informal—that is, not quite according to rule—is accidental, or brought about by the lord, so that there is no reason for reproaching oneself.

Six in the third place:

a) One sees the wagon dragged back,
The oxen halted,
A man's hair and nose cut off.
Not a good beginning, but a good end.

b) "One sees the wagon dragged back": this happens because the place is not the right one.
"Not a good beginning, but a good end": this happens through meeting one that is firm.

The place is not the right one, because a weak six is in the strong third place. Moreover, the weak line is placed between the strong lines in the second and the fourth place; these dare encroach because they also are not in their proper places. The nuclear trigram K'an means a wagon; the nuclear trigram Li, in the center of which the line stands, is associated with the cow. The fact that a good end is attained is due to the relations with the strong line at the top, which resolves the misunderstandings.

Nine in the fourth place:

a) Isolated through opposition,
One meets a like-minded man
With whom one can associate in good faith.
Despite the danger, no blame.

b) Association in good faith, without blame: this means that the will effects its purpose.

The companion found is the strong line at the beginning, which is of the same character as the nine in the fourth place. Both have the will to overcome the misunderstandings, and thus succeed. This line is isolated because of outer circumstances; for it is placed between two dark lines representing inferior persons. Here there is no relationship of correspondence with the first line, but rather that of similarity of kind.

○   Six in the fifth place:

a)   Remorse disappears.
The companion bites his way through the wrappings.
If one goes to him,
How could it be a mistake?

b)   "The companion bites his way through the wrappings." If one goes to him, it brings blessing.

The companion is the nine in the second place. The present
line stands in the upper primary trigram Li, the nine in the
second place stands in the lower nuclear trigram Li; thus they
are of like kind. Change of the nine in the second place
produces the hexagram of BITING THROUGH (21), whose second
line similarly bites through the skin. This describes the leader
who finds a capable assistant to help in clearing up misunderstandings. The person in the superior position must go out
to meet the companion. The rule demands this. A man of
ability will not take the initiative and offer himself.

Nine at the top:

a)   Isolated through opposition,
One sees one's companion as a pig covered with dirt,
As a wagon full of devils.
First one draws a bow against him,
Then one lays the bow aside.
He is not a robber; he will woo at the right time.
As one goes, rain falls; then good fortune comes.

b)   The good fortune of the rainfall means that all
doubts disappear.

The nuclear trigram is K'an, meaning pig as well as wagon,
cunning, danger, also robbers. The trigram Li means a bow.
But since the third line, to which all this refers, is in the relationship of correspondence to the present line, this is all illusion. It is not a hostile assault, but a well-meant approach,
for the purpose of a mutual relation. As soon as this is recognized, doubts disappear and misunderstandings are cleared up.

39. *Chien / Obstruction*

Nuclear trigrams LI *and* K'AN

The ruler of the hexagram is the nine in the fifth place. Therefore it is said in the Commentary on the Decision: "He goes and attains the middle." The reference to "the great man" in the Judgment always relates to the fifth place.

The Sequence

Through opposition difficulties necessarily arise. Hence there follows the hexagram of OBSTRUCTION. Obstruction means difficulty.

Miscellaneous Notes

OBSTRUCTION means difficulty.

The idea of obstruction is expressed by danger without (K'an), in the face of which one keeps still within (Kên). This distinguishes the hexagram from YOUTHFUL FOLLY (4), where K'an is within and Kên is without. The obstruction is not a lasting condition, hence everything in the hexagram is centered on overcoming it. It is overcome in that the strong line moves outward to the fifth place and from there initiates a countermovement. The obstruction is overcome not by pressing forward into danger nor by idly keeping still, but by retreating, yielding. Hence the text alludes to the words of the hexagram K'un, THE RECEPTIVE (2). K'un is in the southwest, it is the earth, that which is level; friends are there. Kên is in

579

the northeast, it is the mountain, that which is steep; there it is lonely. For overcoming danger one has need of fellowship, hence retreat. The great man is seen because he stands at the top of the nuclear trigram Li, which means light and the eye. The movement indicated is expressed also in the individual lines.

THE JUDGMENT

OBSTRUCTION. The southwest furthers.

The northeast does not further.

It furthers one to see the great man.

Perseverance brings good fortune.

Commentary on the Decision

OBSTRUCTION means difficulty. The danger is ahead. To see the danger and to know how to stand still, that is wisdom.

In OBSTRUCTION "the southwest furthers," because he goes and attains the middle.

"The northeast does not further," because there the way comes to an end.

"It furthers one to see the great man," because he goes and wins merits.

In the right place, "perseverance brings good fortune," because through it the country comes into order.

The effect of a time of OBSTRUCTION is great indeed.

Danger, the trigram K'an, is in front. To see the danger (upper nuclear trigram Li, light, eye) and to stop short in time (inner trigram Kên, Keeping Still) is true wisdom, in contrast to the situation in YOUTHFUL FOLLY, where the positions of danger and standstill are reversed. In order to overcome the danger it is important to take the safe road, the road toward the southwest, where one attains the middle, that is, sees oneself surrounded by helpers. The nine in the fifth place does this. When the ruler of the hexagram is in the outer trigram it is said, "He goes," and when it is in the inner trigram, "He comes." In the northeast (north means danger, northeast means mountain) one comes to an impassable road, leading no farther. It is favorable to see the great man—the nine in the fifth place, standing at the top of the nuclear trigram Li. Through going something is achieved: in that the ruler of the hexagram "goes," he takes part in the downward movement of the trigram K'an, water, which flows toward the earth and thus accomplishes something. Abiding in the right place brings good fortune, because one's activity is directed not outward but inward, to one's own country. Turning inward is achieved through obstructions, and the improvement brought about by this turning inward ("conversion") is the great value inhering in the effect of a time of obstruction.

THE IMAGE

Water on the mountain:
The image of OBSTRUCTION.
Thus the superior man turns his attention to himself
And molds his character.

Water on the top of a mountain cannot flow down in accordance with its nature, because rocks hinder it. It must stand still. This causes it to increase, and the inner accumulation finally becomes so great that it overflows the barriers. The way of overcoming obstacles lies in turning inward and raising one's own being to a higher level.

THE LINES

Six at the beginning:

a) Going leads to obstructions,
Coming meets with praise.

b) "Going leads to obstructions, coming meets with praise," because it is right to wait.

Going, as this weak line at the beginning would be inclined to do, would lead into danger. Coming back is in accord with the trigram Kên, Keeping Still.

Six in the second place:

a) The king's servant is beset by obstruction upon obstruction,

But it is not his own fault.

b) "The king's servant is beset by obstruction upon obstruction." But in the end there is no blame in this.

This line is in the relationship of correspondence to the ruler of the hexagram, the nine in the fifth place. The ruler stands in the very center of the danger (upper primary trigram K'an). His servant hastens to his aid, but since his path leads through the nuclear trigram K'an, he meets with one obstruction after another. However, this situation is not due to his own position; the line is in the trigram Kên, Keeping Still, hence it is not inherently necessary for it to go into these dangers. It is only duty, arising from the relation to the ruler, that leads it into peril. Therefore it remains free of fault even in the most dangerous situation.

Nine in the third place:

a) Going leads to obstructions;

Hence he comes back.

b) "Going leads to obstructions; hence he comes back." Those within rejoice over it.

This strong line is the ruler of the trigram Kên and has two weak lines depending on it. Its strength might induce it to move outward, but there it encounters the trigram of danger (K'an). Hence it turns back, and the six in the second place, which has a relationship of holding together with it, rejoices.

Six in the fourth place:

a) Going leads to obstructions,

Coming leads to union.

b) "Going leads to obstructions, coming leads to union." In the appropriate place one finds support.

The six in the fourth place is related to the six at the top, but should it wish to go there, it would find a weak line at the pinnacle of danger. Return to its own place leads to union. The fourth place is that of the minister, who serves the strong ruler above, the nine in the fifth place, and who is supported from below by the strong assistant, the nine in the third place. In the appropriate place (the dark fourth place is the proper one for a yielding line), it achieves union with these two strong lines.

○ Nine in the fifth place:

a) In the midst of the greatest obstructions,
Friends come.

b) "In the midst of the greatest obstructions, friends come." For they are ruled by the central position.

The fifth line is the ruler of the hexagram. As the middle line of the upper trigram K'an, it is in the center of danger—that is, in the midst of the greatest obstructions. However, it is related to the six in the second place, to the six in the fourth place, and also to the six at the top, and these come as friends to help it, because it rules them by virtue of its central position.

Six at the top:

a) Going leads to obstructions,
Coming leads to great good fortune.
It furthers one to see the great man.

b) "Going leads to obstructions, coming leads to great good fortune," for the will is directed to inner things.
"It furthers one to see the great man." For thus does one follow a man of rank.

If the weak line at the top should try to go forth and overcome the obstacles alone, it would meet with failure. Its nature, its will, direct it toward the great, i.e., strong nine in the third place, which has a relationship of correspondence with it. It furthers one to see the great man because the nine in the fifth place, the great man of the hexagram, stands at the top of the nuclear trigram Li, eye, light. He is seen in the sense that the present line, together with the nine in the third place, follows him as the man of rank under whose leadership the obstructions are overcome.

解

40. *Hsieh / Deliverance*

Nuclear trigrams K'AN ☵ *and* LI ☲

The rulers of the hexagram are the nine in the second and the six in the fifth place. Therefore it is said in the Commentary on the Decision, "By going he wins the multitude," this referring to the fifth place, and further, "He wins the central position," this referring to the second place.

The Sequence

Things cannot be permanently amid obstructions. Hence there follows the hexagram of DELIVERANCE. Deliverance means release from tension.

Miscellaneous Notes

DELIVERANCE means release from tension.

The idea of release and deliverance is expressed in the fact that the trigram Chên, movement, stands above (without) and moves away from the lower (inner) trigram K'an, danger. In one aspect, this hexagram is a further development of the situation described in Chun, DIFFICULTY AT THE BEGINNING (3): in the latter, there is movement within danger, here movement brings deliverance from danger. In another aspect, this hexagram is the inverse of the preceding one. The obstruction is removed, deliverance has come.

In terms of the Image, thunder—electricity—has penetrated the rain clouds. There is release from tension. The thunderstorm breaks, and the whole of nature breathes freely again.

THE JUDGMENT

DELIVERANCE. The southwest furthers.
If there is no longer anything where one has to go,
Return brings good fortune.
If there is still something where one has to go,
Hastening brings good fortune.

Commentary on the Decision

DELIVERANCE. Danger produces movement. Through movement one escapes danger: this is deliverance.

During deliverance "the southwest furthers": by going he wins the multitude.

"His return brings good fortune," because he wins the central position.

"If there is still something where one has to go, hastening brings good fortune." Then going is meritorious.

When heaven and earth deliver themselves, thunder and rain set in. When thunder and rain set in, the seed pods of all fruits, plants, and trees break open.

The time of DELIVERANCE is great indeed.

Danger incites to movement, and this movement leads out of the danger: this explanation of the name of the hexagram is derived from the attributes of the two primary trigrams. The southwest is the place of the trigram K'un, the Receptive. Its opposite, the northeast, is no longer mentioned, because here the difficulties have already been overcome. K'un also means the multitude. This refers to the six in the fifth place. When deliverance has only just come, a certain protection is needed, a quiet nurturing under the maternal care of the Receptive. By returning when there is nothing more to be attended to, the nine in the second place attains the center of the lower trigram. If there is still something to be done, it brings good fortune to do it as quickly and carefully as possible, because the movement is then crowned with success; it is not a purposeless, futile effort. Lastly there is mentioned, as an analogy, the release from atmospheric tension that comes with a thunderstorm, which clears the air and causes all seed pods to burst open. Thus the time of DELIVERANCE also has its greatness.

THE IMAGE

Thunder and rain set in:
The image of DELIVERANCE.
Thus the superior man pardons mistakes
And forgives misdeeds.

K'an means lawsuits and transgressions. Chên moves upward and lets the mistakes sink down behind it. In life this brings a release from tension similar to that produced in nature by the clearing of the air after a thunderstorm.

THE LINES

Six at the beginning:

a) Without blame.

b) On the border between firm and yielding there should be no blame.

This line is in a strong place, but yielding by nature. It stands in the relationship of correspondence to the nine in the fourth place, which occupies a weak place but is strong by nature. The joint action of these balanced opposites brings order into the whole situation, and naturally everything goes well.

○ Nine in the second place:

a) One kills three foxes in the field
And receives a yellow arrow.
Perseverance brings good fortune.

b) The good fortune of the perseverance of the nine in the second place is due to its attaining the middle way.

The trigram K'an denotes a fox, Li denotes bow and arrow. The second place, as the upper of the two lowest places, is the place of the field (cf. the nine in the second place in hexagram 1, Ch'ien, THE CREATIVE). The three foxes are three of the four yin lines, omitting the six in the fifth place.

Six in the third place:

a) If a man carries a burden on his back
And nonetheless rides in a carriage,
He thereby encourages robbers to draw near.
Perseverance leads to humiliation.

b) "If a man carries a burden on his back and nonetheless rides in a carriage," he should really be ashamed of himself.
When I myself thus attract robbers, on whom shall I lay the blame?

This line is at the place where the lower primary trigram K'an and the upper nuclear trigram K'an come in contact. K'an means carriage and robbers. The structure of the hexagram is such that this six, a yin line and weak by nature, seeks to occupy the top place in the lower trigram. Its strength being insufficient for this, it carries a heavy burden. In this untenable position it necessarily attracts robbers. Persisting in this state naturally leads to humiliation.

Nine in the fourth place:

a) Deliver yourself from your great toe.
Then the companion comes,
And him you can trust.

b) "Deliver yourself from your great toe": for the place is not the appropriate one.

The trigram Chên means foot; the six in the third place is under Chên and so gives rise to the image of the big toe. The present line and the nine in the second place are friends of kindred nature, jointly rendering loyal help to the ruler in the fifth place. But to do this it is necessary first to exclude the interfering six in the third place, to which the present line stands in the relationship of holding together. The place is not appropriate, because this is a yin place, while the line is a yang line.[1]

○ Six in the fifth place:

a) If only the superior man can deliver himself,
   It brings good fortune.
   Thus he proves to inferior men that he is in earnest.

b) The superior man delivers himself, because inferior men then retreat.

The fifth place is that of the ruler. In times of deliverance, the yielding disposition of this line is appropriate, because it is in the relationship of correspondence to the strong assistants. But it is important to liberate oneself from inferior men who are also yielding in temperament. When they notice this attitude, they retreat of their own accord. The line delivers itself, as does the preceding line, by moving upward in accord with the trigram Chên.

Six at the top:

a) The prince shoots at a hawk on a high wall.
   He kills it. Everything serves to further.

b) "The prince shoots at a hawk": thereby he delivers himself from those who resist.

The dark line at the top is injurious. With the exception of the six in the fifth place, all the yin lines in the time of DE-LIVERANCE tend to have a negative influence, in so far as this

---

1. According to another interpretation, the big toe from which one is to liberate oneself is the six at the beginning; with this line there is a relationship of correspondence from which one must free oneself.

is not neutralized by relationships with yang lines. This highly placed evildoer is shot from below, where the trigram K'an (arrow) is situated, because the movement is upward, and thus deliverance from the last obstacle is achieved.

損

41. *Sun / Decrease*

Nuclear trigrams K'UN ☷ *and* CHÊN ☳

The hexagram Sun is based on the idea that the top line of the lower trigram is decreased in order to increase the top line of the upper trigram; hence it is the six in the third place and the nine at the top that are the constituting rulers of the hexagram. But, since the ruler is the one who is enriched through decrease of what is below and increase of what is above, the governing ruler of the hexagram is the six in the fifth place.

The Sequence

Through release of tension something is sure to be lost. Hence there follows the hexagram of DECREASE.

Miscellaneous Notes

The hexagrams of DECREASE and INCREASE are the beginning of flowering and of decline.

This hexagram consists of Tui below and Kên above. The depth of the lake is decreased in favor of the height of the mountain. The top line of the lower trigram is decreased in favor of the top line of the upper trigram. In both cases, what is below is decreased in favor of what is above, and this means out-and-out decrease.

When decrease has reached its goal, flowering is sure to begin. Hence DECREASE is the beginning of flowering, as INCREASE, through fullness, ushers in decline.

Appended Judgments

DECREASE shows the cultivation of character. It shows first what is difficult and then what is easy. Thus it keeps harm away.

THE JUDGMENT

DECREASE combined with sincerity
Brings about supreme good fortune
Without blame.
One may be persevering in this.
It furthers one to undertake something.
How is this to be carried out?
One may use two small bowls for the sacrifice.

Commentary on the Decision

DECREASE. What is below is decreased, what is above is increased; the direction of the way is upward.

"DECREASE combined with sincerity brings about supreme good fortune without blame. One may be persevering in this. It furthers one to undertake something. How is this to be carried out? One may use two small bowls for the sacrifice."

"Two small bowls" is in accord with the time. There is a time for decreasing the firm, and a time for increasing the yielding. In decreasing and increasing, in being full and being empty, one must go with the time.

The firm top line of the lower trigram is decreased, that is, replaced by a yielding line; at the same time, the yielding top line of the upper trigram is increased, that is, replaced by a strong line, and this strong line makes its way upward. The upper element is enriched at the expense of the lower. Those below bring a sacrifice to the ruler. If this sacrifice is offered sincerely it is not wrong; rather, it results in success and all things desirable. Nor is thrift then a disgrace. All that matters is that things should happen at the right time.

THE IMAGE

At the foot of the mountain, the lake:
The image of DECREASE.
Thus the superior man controls his anger
And restrains his instincts.

The lake evaporates; its waters decrease and benefit the mountain's vegetation, which thereby is furthered in its growth and enriched. Anger rises mountain high; the instincts drown the heart like the depths of a lake. Inasmuch as the two primary trigrams represent the youngest son and youngest daughter, passions are especially strong. The anger aroused must be restrained by keeping still (upper trigram Kên), and the instincts must be curbed by the confining quality of the lower trigram Tui, as the lake confines its waters within its banks.

THE LINES

Nine at the beginning:

a) Going quickly when one's tasks are finished
Is without blame.
But one must reflect on how much one may decrease others.

b) "Going quickly when one's tasks are finished": this is right because the mind of the one above accords with one's own.

The lowest line stands for people of the lower classes. Though strong itself, it stands in the relationship of correspondence to the weak six in the fourth place, which represents an official. The one above needs help from the one below, and it is readily offered by the latter. Instead of the word for "finished" the word for "through" or "with" appears in old texts (cf. the *Shuo Wên*,[1] where the wording is cited); thus the sentence would read: "Going quickly with services"—i.e., to help the one above—"is without blame." This means self-decrease on the part of the one below for the benefit of the one above. The second half of the line, which reads literally, "One must weigh how much one may decrease him," refers to the one above, who claims the services of the one below. It is his duty to weigh in his mind how much he may require without injuring the one below. Only when this is the attitude of the one above does it fit in with the self-sacrifice of the one below. If the one above should make inconsiderate demands, the joy in giving felt by the one below would be decreased.

Nine in the second place:

a) Perseverance furthers.
   To undertake something brings misfortune.
   Without decreasing oneself,
   One is able to bring increase to others.

b) That the nine in the second place furthers through perseverance is due to the fact that it has the correct mean in its mind.

The nine is strong and stands in a central place. Hence perseverance in this attitude serves to further. The line stands at the beginning of the nuclear trigram Chên, the Arousing. This would suggest that it might of its own initiative go to the six in the fifth place, with which it has a relationship of correspondence. If it did this, however, it would demean itself somewhat. It is in keeping with its central position to increase the other without decreasing itself.

☐ Six in the third place:

a) When three people journey together,
   Their number decreases by one.
   When one man journeys alone,
   He finds a companion.

---

1. [A dictionary compiled *ca.* A.D. 100.]

b) If a person should seek to journey as one of three, mistrust would arise.

The text says that three persons journeying together are decreased by one, but one man journeying alone finds a companion. This refers to the change that has taken place within the lower trigram. At the outset it consisted of the three strong lines of the trigram Ch'ien, the Creative. They have been journeying together. Then one leaves them and goes up to the top of the upper trigram. The weak line entering the third place in its stead is lonely in the company of the two other lines of the lower trigram. But it stands in the relationship of correspondence to the strong line at the top, hence finds its complement in the latter. Through this separation, three become two; further, through the union one becomes two. Thus what is excessive is decreased, and what is insufficient is increased. Through this process of interchange between the trigrams Ch'ien and K'un of the original hexagram, there come into being the two youngest children, Kên and Tui.

On the other hand, the present line, the six in the third place, which is lonely in the lower trigram, should not again consider going along with the other two, for this would give rise to misunderstandings. Confucius says about this line:

Heaven and earth come together, and all things take shape and find form. Male and female mix their seed, and all creatures take shape and are born. In the Book of Changes it is said: "When three people journey together, their number decreases by one. When one man journeys alone, he finds a companion." This refers to the effect of becoming one.

Six in the fourth place:

a) If a man decreases his faults,
It makes the other hasten to come and rejoice.
No blame.

b) "If a man decreases his faults," it is indeed something that gives cause for joy.

The fault of the six in the fourth place is excessive weakness. A weak line in a weak place, it is inclosed above and below by weak lines. However, through its relationship of correspondence to the strong first line, these faults are compensated. Through elimination of these faults, the six in the fourth place hastens the helpful coming of the nine at the beginning, which brings joy to both and is not a mistake.

○ Six in the fifth place:

a) Someone does indeed increase him.
Ten pairs of tortoises cannot oppose it.
Supreme good fortune.

b) The supreme good fortune of the six in the fifth place comes from its being blessed from above.

If he is enriched, ten pairs of tortoise shells cannot oppose it, and supreme good fortune comes. The number ten is suggested by the nuclear trigram K'un. The tortoise belongs to the trigram Li—which of course can be read into this hexagram only by straining the point considerably. A large tortoise used for fortune telling costs twenty cowrie shells. A double cowrie shell is called a pair. Accordingly, one explanation takes the line to mean a tortoise worth ten pairs of cowrie shells. Another explanation reads it as referring to ten pairs of tortoise shells. Blessing from above is suggested by the strong top line covering the hexagram protectively.

☐ Nine at the top:

a) If one is increased without depriving others,
There is no blame.
Perseverance brings good fortune.
It furthers one to undertake something.
One obtains servants
But no longer has a separate home.

b) Without decreasing, he is increased; that is, he attains his will in great measure.

The top line is enriched by the six in the third place. It accepts this increase, but in such a way that the other is not decreased by it. Therefore the relationship here is the opposite of that represented by the nine in the second place, which increases others without decreasing itself. Hence the outlook is favorable throughout, because harmony is maintained between those above and those below.

Kên, mountain, denotes a house. As the line changes, the upper primary trigram Kên turns into the trigram K'un, which knows no house, i.e., no mountain, its place being the southwest; hence there are loyal helpers, but not for promoting family interests.

42. *I / Increase*

Nuclear trigrams KÊN ☶ and K'UN ☷

The idea of increase is here expressed through the fact that the lowest line in the upper trigram is decreased, whereby the lowest line of the lower trigram is increased. Hence the six in the fourth place and the nine in the first place are the constituting rulers of the hexagram. But since the decrease above is at the hands of the prince, and the increase below is received by the official, the nine in the fifth place and the six in the second place are the governing rulers of the hexagram.

The Sequence

If decrease goes on and on, it is certain to bring about increase. Hence there follows the hexagram of IN-CREASE.

Miscellaneous Notes

The hexagrams of DECREASE and INCREASE are the beginning of flowering and of decline.

The two hexagrams with which part II begins, namely, IN-
FLUENCE (31) and DURATION (32), after ten changes become the
hexagrams of DECREASE (41) and INCREASE (42)—just as the
first two hexagrams of part I, THE CREATIVE and THE RECEPTIVE,
after ten changes become the hexagrams of PEACE (11) and
STANDSTILL (12). PEACE and STANDSTILL have an inner connection with DECREASE and INCREASE, because through the
transference of a strong line from the lower to the upper trigram, DECREASE develops from PEACE, and through the transference of a strong line from the upper to the lower trigram,
INCREASE develops from STANDSTILL. Thus when in P'i, STAND-
STILL,

the lowest line of the upper trigram is transferred to the
bottom, the resultant new hexagram is I, INCREASE:

The fact that continuous decrease finally leads to a change into
its opposite, increase, lies in the course of nature, as can be
perceived in the waning and waxing of the moon and in all of
the regularly recurring processes of nature.

The hexagram consists of the primary trigrams of wind and
thunder, which increase each other. The decrease above and
the strengthening below produce a stability that means increase for the whole. This hexagram is the inverse of the
preceding one.

Appended Judgments

When Pao Hsi's clan was gone, there sprang up the
clan of the Divine Husbandman. He split a piece of
wood for a plowshare and bent a piece of wood for
the plow handle, and taught the whole world the
advantage of laying open the earth with a plow. He
probably took this from the hexagram of INCREASE.

Both parts of the hexagram have wood for a symbol. The outer
trigram means penetration, the inner means movement.

Movement combined with penetration has brought the greatest increase to the world.

> INCREASE shows fullness of character. INCREASE shows the growth of fullness without artifices. Thus INCREASE furthers what is useful.

THE JUDGMENT

INCREASE. It furthers one
To undertake something.
It furthers one to cross the great water.

Commentary on the Decision

INCREASE. Decreasing what is above
And increasing what is below;
Then the joy of the people is boundless.
What is above places itself under what is below:
This is the way of the great light.
And it furthers one to undertake something:
Central, correct, and blessed.
It furthers one to cross the great water:
The way of wood creates success.
INCREASE moves, gentle and mild:
Daily progress without limit.
Heaven dispenses, earth brings forth:
Thereby things increase in all directions.
The way of INCREASE everywhere
Proceeds in harmony with the time.

The name of the hexagram is explained on the basis of its structure: increase of what is below at the cost of what is above is out-and-out increase, because it benefits the whole people. The fourth line, in descending from the upper trigram to the lowest place in the lower trigram, shows a self-abnegation that gives proof of great clarity. In times of INCREASE it is favorable to undertake something, for the rulers of the hexagram, the nine in the fifth place and the six in the second, are centrally placed and correct—a strong line in a strong place and a weak line in a weak place. Crossing of the great water is suggested by the upper trigram, Sun, which means wood and so gives the idea of a ship, while the lower trigram guarantees the movement of the ship. The attributes of the trigrams Chên, movement, and Sun, gentleness, guarantee lasting progress.

The idea of increase in the cosmic sphere is expressed through the fact that the first line of heaven (Ch'ien) places itself below the earth (K'un); this gives rise to the trigram Chên, in which all beings come into existence. This process of increase also is bound up with the right time, within which it comes to consummation.

THE IMAGE

Wind and thunder: the image of INCREASE.

Thus the superior man:

If he sees good, he imitates it;

If he has faults, he rids himself of them.

Wind and thunder generate and reinforce each other. Thunder corresponds in its nature with the light principle, which it sets in motion; wind is connected in its nature with the shadowy principle, which it breaks up and dissolves. What is light corresponds to the good, which is attained by moving toward it, in accordance with the trigram Chên. The shadowy corresponds to evil, which is destroyed by being broken up and dissolved, as Sun, wind, breaks up clouds. Both principles further increase, for in the moral realm the good is the equivalent of the light, the positive, and furthering of this principle signifies increase.

THE LINES

☐ Nine at the beginning:

a) It furthers one to accomplish great deeds.
Supreme good fortune. No blame.

b) "Supreme good fortune. No blame." Those below do not use it for their own convenience.

The nine at the bottom stands for the common people. In that the six in the fourth place, the minister, descends (it stands in the relationship of correspondence to the first line), it enables the lower line to accomplish great things, because it does not selfishly retain for itself the grace bestowed on it from above. This line is at the bottom of the trigram Chên and therefore moves upward. Hence the great good fortune.

○ Six in the second place:

a) Someone does indeed increase him;
   Ten pairs of tortoises cannot oppose it.
   Constant perseverance brings good fortune.
   The king presents him before God.
   Good fortune.

b) "Someone does indeed increase him." This comes from without.

The increase of the inner trigram comes from without. Therefore it is regarded as being unexpected, a spontaneous happening. The hexagram I is the hexagram Sun inverted, hence the text of this line corresponds with that of the six in the fifth place of the preceding hexagram. Increase comes because its prerequisites are provided in the line's own correctness, central position, and yielding nature, and because the strong nine in the fifth place is in the relationship of correspondence to it. The admonition to constant perseverance is necessary because the yielding quality of the line, in combination with the yielding place, might lead to a certain weakness, which must be balanced by firmness of will. The increase here is threefold—through men, through gods (indicated by the tortoises, through which the will of the gods is revealed), and through the supreme Lord of Heaven, who graciously receives the man brought to him at the sacrifice. The hexagram I refers to the first month, in which the rites of sacrifice were carried out in the meadow.

Six in the third place:

a) One is enriched through unfortunate events.
   No blame, if you are sincere

> And walk in the middle,
> And report with a seal to the prince.

b) "One is enriched through unfortunate events." This
is something that certainly is one's due.

This is a weak line in a strong place, at the high point of
excitement (lower trigram Chên), and furthermore not central. All this points to misfortune. But since it is the time of
INCREASE, even this misfortune, which is not accidental but
comes upon one from inner causes, must serve to good ends.
The line is in the center of the lower nuclear trigram K'un and
at the same time at the top of the lower primary trigram Chên,
movement, which gives rise to the idea of movement, of walking the middle path. The seal is a round jade piece that was
bestowed as a badge of office.

One interpretation explains the line of thought as follows:
If in the time of INCREASE heaven sends disaster, such as crop
failure and the like, a sympathetic prince will ease the burden
of those affected by granting them remission of taxes and other
relief, and the official who announces this remission carries the
jade insignia as a mark of his authority.

☐ Six in the fourth place:

a) If you walk in the middle
And report to the prince,
He will follow.
It furthers one to be used
In the removal of the capital.

b) "If you report to the prince, he will follow," because
his purposes are thereby increased.

The fourth place is that of the minister. The six in the fourth
place is the lowest line of the trigram Sun, wind, penetration.
The line has influence in correspondence with this. However,
since it is in the middle of the upper nuclear trigram Kên, it
does not use this influence for personal ends, for this is the line
whose decrease increases the lower trigram. It therefore represents a man who, as mediator between the prince and the

people, is in a position to make the will of the former clear to the latter. Persons of this kind are of great importance in dangerous and decisive undertakings (crossing the great water —here the moving of the capital, which took place five times under the Shang dynasty).

O Nine in the fifth place:

a) If in truth you have a kind heart, ask not.
Supreme good fortune.
Truly, kindness will be recognized as your virtue.

b) "If in truth you have a kind heart, ask not." If kindness is recognized as your virtue, you have attained your purpose completely.

The ruler of the hexagram, strong and central in a correct, strong place, has a truly kind heart and seeks to give increase to those below. Here there is no question: the effect is inevitably favorable, and because the good intention is recognized, all is well.

Nine at the top:

a) He brings increase to no one.
Indeed, someone even strikes him.
He does not keep his heart constantly steady.
Misfortune.

b) "He brings increase to no one." This is a saying that pictures one-sidedness.
"Someone even strikes him." This comes from without.

This line is obdurate and not consistently concerned with bringing increase to those below. Despite its relation to the six in the third place, the latter shows no sign of being influenced by it. Thus the line is one-sided and aloof. Without intent on the part of anyone, this wrong position automatically provokes misfortune, because the attitude of the line is not stable, that is, not in harmony with the demands of the time.

夬

43. *Kuai / Break-through (Resoluteness)*

Nuclear trigrams CH'IEN and CH'IEN

The meaning of the hexagram is based on the fact that a dark line is at the top, in the outermost place, hence the six at the top is the constituting ruler. But the five light lines turn resolutely against the dark one. The fifth line is at their head, and furthermore in the place of honor; therefore the nine in the fifth place is the governing ruler of the hexagram.

The Sequence

If increase goes on unceasingly, there is certain to be a break-through. Hence there follows the hexagram of BREAK-THROUGH. Break-through means resoluteness.

Miscellaneous Notes

BREAK-THROUGH means resoluteness. The strong turns resolutely against the weak.

Appended Judgments

In primitive times people knotted cords in order to govern. The holy men of a later age introduced written documents instead, as a means of governing the various officials and supervising the people. They probably took this from the hexagram of BREAK-THROUGH.

The hexagram Kuai actually means a break-through as when a river bursts its dams in seasons of flood. The five strong lines are thought of as mounting from below, resolutely forcing the weak upper line out of the hexagram. The same idea evolves from the images. The lake has evaporated and mounted to the sky. There it will discharge itself as a cloudburst. Here again we have the idea of a break-through.

The hexagram consists of the trigram Tui, words, above, and Ch'ien, whose attribute is strength, below. Thus the hexagram indicates that words should be made strong and enduring.

THE JUDGMENT

BREAK-THROUGH. One must resolutely make the
   matter known
At the court of the king.
It must be announced truthfully. Danger.
It is necessary to notify one's own city.
It does not further to resort to arms.
It furthers one to undertake something.

Commentary on the Decision

BREAK-THROUGH is the same as resoluteness. The firm resolutely dislodges the yielding. Strong and joyous—this means resolute and harmonious.

"One must make the matter known at the court of the king." The weak rests upon five hard lines.

Truthful announcement is fraught with danger. However, this danger leads to the light.

"It is necessary to notify one's own city. It does not further to resort to arms." What that man holds high comes to nothing.

"It furthers one to undertake something," because the firm grow and lead through to the end.

In forcing out the dark line at the top it is essential that it be done in the right spirit. For the issue of this struggle is not in doubt. What happens is inevitable, therefore a serenely cheerful and calm resoluteness is the correct attitude of mind, as denoted by the character of the two trigrams (Tui, the Joyous, without, and Ch'ien, the Creative, strength, within). One must make the truth known at the court of the king: the weak six at the top stands over five strong lines, of which the uppermost occupies the place of the prince. The weak line symbolizes an inferior man in a high position. The trigram Tui means mouth; hence the making known, announcing. Ch'ien also means battle and danger; Ch'ien and Tui both mean metal, hence the image of weapons. But since the situation in itself promises success, there is no need of using weapons against outside forces.

THE IMAGE

The lake has risen up to heaven:
The image of BREAK-THROUGH.
Thus the superior man
Dispenses riches downward
And refrains from resting on his virtue.

The lake has evaporated and its waters are gathering high in the heavens as mist and clouds: this points to an imminent break-through, in which the water will come down again as rain. In order to avoid a violent break-through, it is necessary to take advantage of the attributes of the two trigrams. Tui means pleasure; therefore, instead of piling up wealth in dangerous places and thus inviting a breach, one will be continuously giving and thus causing joy. In self-education we should be mindful of the stern judgment meted out by Ch'ien. Then we shall never be self-satisfied, which would also lead to catastrophe, but shall always retain a sense of awe. When joy has mounted high, as a lake mounts to the heavens, it easily leads to excessive pride; hence it must be supplemented by the beneficent way of heaven. When strength perceives weakness above it, as does heaven under the lake, it leads easily to defiance; hence it must be moderated by the friendly way of Tui.

THE LINES

Nine at the beginning:

a) Mighty in the forward-striding toes.
When one goes and is not equal to the task,
One makes a mistake.

b) When one goes without being equal to the task, it
is a mistake.

Toes are suggested by the lowest line. The hexagram of BREAK-
THROUGH is the next stage after the hexagram of THE POWER
OF THE GREAT (34). This is why the pronouncement on the
lowest line is the same in both, except that here it is moderated
somewhat, because the situation has developed further.

Nine in the second place:

a) A cry of alarm. Arms at evening and at night.
Fear nothing.

b) Despite weapons, no fear—because one has found
the middle way.

Tui, the upper trigram, means mouth, hence the cry of alarm.
Tui is in the west, which indicates evening; Ch'ien is in the
northwest, which indicates night. Metal is associated both with
Tui and with Ch'ien, and this indicates weapons. But there is
nothing to fear, because the line is strong and central and in
the middle of the lower trigram Ch'ien, heaven.

Nine in the third place:

a) To be powerful in the cheekbones
Brings misfortune.
The superior man is firmly resolved.
He walks alone and is caught in the rain.
He is bespattered,
And people murmur against him.
No blame.

b) "The superior man is resolutely resolved." Ultimately this is not a mistake.

Ch'ien is the head. The third place is at the top of this trigram, hence the image of the cheekbones. This line belongs to the strong primary trigram Ch'ien and also stands in the middle of the lower nuclear trigram Ch'ien, hence the redoubled resolution. It is solitary because it alone is in the relationship of correspondence to the dark line at the top. Tui, as water, suggests the idea of rain bespattering the line. The strength of its nature protects it from contamination by the dark line above, hence despite evil appearances there is no mistake.

Nine in the fourth place:

a) There is no skin on his thighs,
And walking comes hard.
If a man were to let himself be led like a sheep,
Remorse would disappear.
But if these words are heard
They will not be believed.

b) "Walking comes hard." The place is not the appropriate one.
"If these words are heard they will not be believed."
There is no clear comprehension.

This line is in the lowest place of the upper trigram, hence the image of the thighs. The fact that the line is hindered in its forward push by the strong line in the fifth place suggests the idea that walking is impossible. A symbol of Tui is the sheep, hence the advice to let oneself be led like a sheep. As the line changes, the upper trigram will turn into the trigram K'an, which means ear; but since the line is neither correct nor in its proper place, it pays no heed to what is said.

○ Nine in the fifth place:

a) In dealing with weeds,
Firm resolution is necessary.

Walking in the middle
Remains free of blame.

b) "Walking in the middle remains free of blame." The
middle is not yet in the light.

The line is the ruler of the hexagram. It is this line that must
lead the resolute struggle against the six at the top, which
symbolizes the inferior man. But while the nine in the third
place is in the relationship of correspondence to the six above,
the nine in the fifth place is in the relationship of holding
together with it. This makes the struggle more difficult. But
the line can be resolute. It is on the one hand the ruler of the
hexagram, and moreover ruler in the most distinguished place;
on the other hand it is the top line of the vigorous upper
nuclear trigram Ch'ien. Furthermore, it is in the middle of
the upper primary trigram; thus there is a hope that it will
succeed in remaining consistent.

☐ Six at the top:

a) No cry.
In the end misfortune comes.

b) The misfortune of not crying out should in the end
not be allowed to persist.

This line is the representative of the evil that is to be rooted
out. The undertaking requires caution. It appears easy, because there are five strong lines as against only one weak line;
but the dark nature of the present line suggests that it knows
how to silence those who would raise the warning. However,
its kind must not be tolerated; otherwise it is to be feared that
from the neglected solitary yin line, evil will sprout forth as
from a seed.

44. *Kou / Coming to Meet*

Nuclear trigrams CH'IEN *and* CH'IEN

The hexagram of COMING TO MEET takes its meaning from the one dark line that develops at the bottom; therefore this first line is the constituting ruler of the hexagram. But the five yang lines have the duty of restraining the yin power. Among the five, the second and the fifth have a strong and central character. The one stands near to the yin power in order to restrain it, the other holds the place of honor and comes down from above to restrain it. Therefore the nine in the fifth place and the nine in the second are the governing rulers of the hexagram.

The Sequence

Through resoluteness one is certain to encounter something. Hence there follows the hexagram of COMING TO MEET. Coming to meet means encountering.

Miscellaneous Notes

COMING TO MEET means encountering.

Coming to meet means encountering. The lower trigram is Sun, wind, which drives along beneath Ch'ien, heaven, the upper trigram, and hence encounters all things. Furthermore, a yin line develops below, so that the dark principle thus unexpectedly encounters the light. The movement is initiated by the dark principle, the feminine, which advances to meet the light principle, the masculine. This hexagram is the inverse of the preceding one.

THE JUDGMENT

COMING TO MEET. The maiden is powerful.

One should not marry such a maiden.

Commentary on the Decision

COMING TO MEET means encountering. The weak advances to meet the firm.

"One should not marry such a maiden." This means that one cannot live with her permanently.

When heaven and earth meet, all creatures settle into firm lines.

When the firm finds the middle and the right, everything under heaven prospers splendidly.

Great indeed is the meaning of the time of COMING TO MEET.

Sun is the eldest daughter. A yin line develops within and rules the hexagram, while the yang lines stand aside as guests. In this way the yin element becomes increasingly powerful. This is the line of the trigram K'un of which it is said: "When there is hoarfrost underfoot, solid ice is not far off." Hence the gradual expansion must be checked in time, for the way of inferior people increases only because superior men entrust them with power. If this is avoided when the inferior element first appears, the danger can be averted.

When the strong element appears for the first time in the midst of yin lines, the hexagram is called RETURN. The superior man always stays where he belongs. He comes only into his own domain. When the weak element first appears in the midst of yang lines, the hexagram is called COMING TO MEET (or ENCOUNTERING). The inferior man always has to depend on a lucky chance.

Marriage is an institution that is meant to endure. But if a girl associates with five men, her nature is not pure and one cannot live with her permanently. Therefore one should not marry her.

However, things that must be avoided in human society have meaning in the processes of nature. Here the meeting of earthly and heavenly forces is of great significance, because at the moment when the earthly force enters and the heavenly force is at its height—in the fifth month—all things unfold to the high point of their material manifestation, and the dark force cannot injure the light force. The two rulers of the hexagram, the nine in the fifth place and the nine in the second, likewise symbolize such a fortunate meeting. Here a strong and central assistant meets a strong, central, and correct ruler. A great flowering results, and the inferior element below can do no harm. Thus it is an important time, the time of the meeting of the light with the dark.

THE IMAGE

Under heaven, wind:

The image of COMING TO MEET.

Thus does the prince act when disseminating his commands

And proclaiming them to the four quarters of heaven.

The prince is symbolized by the upper trigram Ch'ien, heaven. His commands are symbolized by the lower trigram Sun, wind, whose attribute is penetration. The spreading to the four quarters of heaven is symbolized by the wind driving along under heaven.

THE LINES

☐ Six at the beginning:

a) It must be checked with a brake of bronze.
   Perseverance brings good fortune.
   If one lets it take its course, one experiences misfortune.
   Even a lean pig has it in him to rage around.

b) To check with a brake of bronze. This means that it is the way of the weak to be led.

The brake is below. K'un, in which this is the first line, means a wagon; Ch'ien is metal, by means of which the wagon is to be braked underneath. This braking brings good fortune, because it accords with the truth that a weak thing unable to guide itself must be led. If we give it free rein, misfortune befalls us. This shows the trend of the whole hexagram. The line is compared to a pig that is as yet weak and lean but that will later tear about: this likewise refers to the yin nature of the line. The pig belongs to water, in particular to the yin aspect of water. It is worth noting that this line comes into account only as an object acted upon.

○ Nine in the second place:

a) There is a fish in the tank. No blame.
   Does not further guests.

b) "There is a fish in the tank." It is a duty not to let it reach the guests.

The fish likewise belongs to the yin principle. The reference is to the six at the beginning. This six is in the relationship of correspondence to the nine in the fourth place, the "guest." But through this relationship the yin element would penetrate too far into the hexagram. Therefore the six at the beginning is held captive, like a fish in a tank, by the nine in the second place, the loyal official, who has a relationship of holding together with it. As a result all goes well. It is to be noted that the word here rendered by "tank" includes the idea that the yin element is treated in a perfectly friendly way.

Nine in the third place:

a) There is no skin on his thighs,
   And walking comes hard.
   If one is mindful of the danger,
   No great mistake is made.

b) "Walking comes hard." He still walks without being led.

Since this hexagram is structurally the inverse of the preceding one, the present line corresponds with the nine in the fourth place in Kuai. Hence the similarity in text. But the inner attitudes are different: in the former there is a resolute intention to press upward in order to throw out the dark line above, here a desire to meet the dark line below. But this dark line has already been taken into custody by the nine in the second place, so that a meeting—which indeed would be disastrous— is not possible. The proximity of the line to the upper trigram Ch'ien makes it possible to recognize the danger, but desire remains unsatisfied. Hence the unsatisfactoriness of the situation, although serious mistakes are avoided.

Nine in the fourth place:

a) No fish in the tank.
   This leads to misfortune.

b) The misfortune inhering in the fact that there is no fish in the tank comes from his having kept aloof from the people.

The fourth place is that of the minister. The six at the beginning stands here for the inferior, lowly people. There is a relationship of correspondence between the two lines. Furthermore, it would be the duty of the official to keep in touch with the people. But this has been neglected. The line belongs to the trigram Ch'ien, hence strives upward, away from the people below. By doing this it attracts misfortune to itself. The corresponding nine in the third place of the preceding hexagram is also isolated, but there the inner attitude is correct, here it is not.

O Nine in the fifth place:

a) A melon covered with willow leaves.
   Hidden lines.
   Then it drops down to one from heaven.

b) The nine in the fifth place hides its lines, for it is in the middle and correct.
   "Then it drops down to one from heaven," because the will does not give up what has been ordained.

This line is the ruler of the hexagram, standing as a prince in its correct and honored place in the middle, and referred to by the words of the Commentary on the Decision: "When the firm finds the middle and the right." Ch'ien is round, hence symbolizes a round fruit. Here the fruit is a melon; it represents the yin line at the beginning and so belongs to the dark principle. It is protected and covered with willow leaves. No forcible interference takes place. The regulative lines of the laws upon which the beauty of life depends are covered over. We entrust the fruit in our care entirely to its own natural development. Then it ripens of its own accord. It falls to our lot. This is not contrived but is decreed by our accepted fate.

Nine at the top:

a) He comes to meet with his horns.
Humiliation. No blame.

b) "He comes to meet with his horns." At the top it comes to an end, hence humiliation.

Ch'ien is the head, here the highest place, which is moreover hard, hence the image of horns. The orientation of the line is quite different from that of the first line, which it should go to meet. It meets the first line with harshness, hence an understanding is extremely difficult. This leads to humiliation. But one does not try to force a meeting, hence one withdraws without blame.

45. Ts'ui / Gathering Together [Massing]

Nuclear trigrams SUN ☲ and KÊN ☶

The rulers of the hexagram are the nine in the fifth place and, secondarily, the nine in the fourth. Only these two yang lines are in high places. They gather all the yin lines around them.

The Sequence

When creatures meet one another, they mass together. Hence there follows the hexagram of GATHERING TOGETHER. Gathering together means massing.

Miscellaneous Notes

GATHERING TOGETHER means massing.

In the two light lines, of which one is in the place of the prince or father, and the other in the place of the minister or son, the hexagram has a strong focus for gathering together the other lines, all of which belong to the dark principle. While the two primary trigrams, K'un and Tui (crowd and joyousness), indicate the basis of the gathering together, the two nuclear trigrams have the meaning of standing still (Kên) and exerting influence (Sun), which likewise indicates gathering together.

THE JUDGMENT

GATHERING TOGETHER. Success.
The king approaches his temple.

It furthers one to see the great man.
This brings success. Perseverance furthers.
To bring great offerings creates good fortune.
It furthers one to undertake something.

Commentary on the Decision

GATHERING TOGETHER means massing. Devoted and at the same time joyous.

The strong stands in the middle and finds correspondence. Therefore the others mass around it.

"The king approaches his temple." This brings about reverence and success.

"It furthers one to see the great man. This brings success." The massing takes place on a correct basis.

"To bring great offerings creates good fortune. It furthers one to undertake something," for that is devotion to the command of heaven.

By observing what they gather together, one can behold the relationships of heaven and earth and of all creatures.

The strong line in the fifth place represents the king, the great man, whom it is favorable to see. Below him is the nuclear trigram Kên, meaning mountain and house. By his side there stands moreover the strong line in the fourth place, that of the minister. The mountain indicates perseverance. Mountain and temple are both places where great offerings are brought. Wind, the upper nuclear trigram Sun, means the influence of what is above, as a result of which works begun will meet with success.

The name of the hexagram is explained in the Commentary on the Decision in a number of ways: (1) the attributes of the two trigrams are devotion and joyousness, on the basis of which gathering together takes place; (2) a gathering needs a head, a center of crystallization, and this is provided in the nine in the fifth place, around which the other lines gather. In order to gather the people together, the ruler above needs joyousness (Tui); the people below show themselves devoted (K'un).

There is in addition a reference to religion as the basis of gathering together in a community. Heaven is the bond of union in nature, as the ancestors are the bond of union among men. If one knows these forces, all relationships become clear.

THE IMAGE

Over the earth, the lake:
The image of GATHERING TOGETHER.
Thus the superior man renews his weapons
In order to meet the unforeseen.

The juxtaposition of the two trigrams provides the image of GATHERING TOGETHER. In that the lake is over the earth and therefore threatens to overflow, the danger connected with gathering together is also indicated. The primary trigrams and the nuclear trigrams, taken individually, show how these dangers are to be met. Tui means metal, hence weapons. K'un means renewal (earth produces metal). The nuclear trigram Sun means the penetrating, the unforeseen. The nuclear trigram Kên means keeping still, obstruction.

THE LINES

Six at the beginning:

a) If you are sincere, but not to the end,
   There will sometimes be confusion, sometimes gathering together.
   If you call out,
   Then after one grasp of the hand you can laugh again.
   Regret not. Going is without blame.

b) "Sometimes confusion, sometimes gathering together." The will is in confusion.

The weak line at the beginning is not yet stabilized. To be sure, there is a relationship of correspondence with the nine in the fourth place—indicating sincerity—but since the line is associated with the two other weak lines of K'un, it allows itself to be influenced by these, so that its natural relations with the nine in the fourth place are disturbed. This brings confusion. But a call (Tui is mouth, hence call) suffices to do away with the misunderstanding, and laughter comes again (Tui is joyousness). It is important, however, to hold to the upward direction.

Six in the second place:

a) Letting oneself be drawn
Brings good fortune and remains blameless.
If one is sincere,
It furthers one to bring even a small offering.

b) "Letting oneself be drawn brings good fortune and remains blameless." The middle is still unchanged.

Here there is a strong inner relationship of correspondence with the nine in the fifth place, the ruler of the hexagram. Therefore this line is naturally attracted by the strong line. Since it is central, it does not permit itself to be wrongly influenced by its environment. Hence this inner influence takes effect.

Six in the third place:

a) Gathering together amid sighs.
Nothing that would further.
Going is without blame.
Slight humiliation.

b) "Going is without blame." The Gentle is above.

This line has no relationship of correspondence, hence the sighs, the forlornness and helplessness. Since the line belongs to the lower trigram, the relationship of holding together with the nine in the fourth place does not become effective, for the latter line belongs to the upper trigram. However, a connection is established through the upper nuclear trigram Sun, the Gentle, for the six in the third place forms the lowest line in this nuclear trigram, of which the nine in the fourth place is the center. Thereby going, as well as a connection, becomes possible without blame, even though some humiliation remains.

○ Nine in the fourth place:

a) Great good fortune. No blame.

b) "Great good fortune. No blame," for the place demands nothing.[1]

This line occupies the place of the minister, who brings about the gathering together on behalf of his prince, the nine in the fifth place. But he does not claim the merit of it for himself; hence great good fortune.

○ Nine in the fifth place:

a) If in gathering together one has position,
This brings no blame.
If there are some who are not yet sincerely in the work,
Sublime and enduring perseverance is needed.
Then remorse disappears.

b) If in gathering together one has only position, the will does not yet shine forth sufficiently.

Essentially the requisite position for effecting the gathering together is at hand. But there are difficulties. The nuclear trigram Kên, Keeping Still, works in such a way that the effects on the lower lines do not immediately make themselves felt. Therefore an enduring influence is needed. To the influence of the position must be added the influence of personality. This line according to its character belongs to Ch'ien, hence it is sublime. This character must needs acquire enduring form; hence remorse disappears.

Six at the top:

a) Lamenting and sighing, floods of tears.
No blame.

1. [The Chinese text reads literally, "The place is not correct." Wilhelm's translation follows suggestions of the Chinese commentators.]

b) "Lamenting and sighing, floods of tears." He is not tranquil at the top.

The top line has no relationship of correspondence (cf. the six in the third place), hence the lamenting and the tears. However, there is no blame; for though the line is not tranquil in its exalted yet solitary position, it conforms to the relationship of holding together and turns downward toward the ruler of the hexagram, the nine in the fifth place. The gathering together is achieved because the idea that it is favorable to see the great man accords with the meaning of the hexagram as a whole.

46. *Shêng | Pushing Upward*

Nuclear trigrams CHÊN ≡≡ *and* TUI ≡≡

The ruler of the hexagram is the six in the fifth place. The Commentary on the Decision refers to it as follows: "The yielding pushes upward with the time." The six in the fifth place is the most honored line among those pushing up. However, the pushing up certainly begins at the bottom. The hexagram pictures wood growing within the earth. But the six at the beginning is the ruler of the trigram Sun and the root of wood; therefore it is at least a constituting ruler of the hexagram.

The Sequence

Massing toward the top is called pushing upward. Hence there follows the hexagram of PUSHING UPWARD.

Miscellaneous Notes

That which pushes upward does not come back.

On the face of it this hexagram is very favorably organized. The movement of the upper trigram K'un is downward, hence the lower trigram Sun (penetration, wood) strives unhindered toward the top. However, the pushing upward is neither as easy nor as extensive as the rising of the sun in the hexagram of PROGRESS (35). The upward movement is furthermore reinforced by the nuclear trigrams, Chên and Tui, both of which tend upward. This hexagram is the inverse of the preceding one.

THE JUDGMENT

PUSHING UPWARD has supreme success.

One must see the great man.

Fear not.

Departure toward the south

Brings good fortune.

Commentary on the Decision

The yielding pushes upward with the time. Gentle and devoted.

The firm is in the middle and finds correspondence, hence it attains great success.

"One must see the great man. Fear not," for it brings blessing.

"Departure toward the south brings good fortune." What is willed is done.

The yielding element that, borne by the time, pushes upward, is the yielding line at the beginning; it stands for the root of wood, the lower trigram. The lower trigram is gentle, the upper devoted. These are preconditions of the time that make it possible for the strong line in the second place—which finds correspondence in the weak line in the place of the ruler—to achieve great success. It is said, "One must see the great man," and not, "It furthers one to see the great man," as is usually the case. For the ruler of the hexagram is not the great man;

it is, on the contrary, a yielding line. The reason for success is not an earthly but a transcendental one. Therefore it is said further, "Fear not," and, "It brings blessing." The favorableness of the conditions comes from the invisible world; we must make the most of them, however, through work. Departure toward the south means work. The south is the region of the heavens between Sun and K'un, the two components of the hexagram.

THE IMAGE

Within the earth, wood grows:
The image of PUSHING UPWARD.
Thus the superior man of devoted character
Heaps up small things
In order to achieve something high and great.

The heaping up of small things—steady, imperceptible progress—is suggested by the gradual and invisible growth of wood in the earth. "Devoted character" corresponds with the trigram K'un; "something high and great" corresponds with Sun, whose image is a tree.

THE LINES

☐ Six at the beginning:

a) Pushing upward that meets with confidence
Brings great good fortune.

b) "Pushing upward that meets with confidence brings great good fortune": those above agree in purpose.

The yielding line at the beginning agrees in nature with the yielding lines of the upper trigram K'un. Therefore it meets with confidence and has success in its pushing upward, just as the hidden root connects the tree with the earth, and through this connection makes growth possible.

Nine in the second place:

a) If one is sincere,
It furthers one to bring even a small offering.[1]

---

1. [See p. 179, where this line includes the augury, "No blame."]

b) The sincerity of the nine in the second place brings joy.

This line is the lowest in the nuclear trigram Tui, meaning joy. The oracle is the same as that pertaining to the second line in the preceding hexagram. In the latter a weak line is intimately connected with the king in the fifth place; here a strong line has an equally intimate relation with the weak line in the fifth place. In each case the spiritual affinity is so close that gifts may be small in extrinsic value without disturbing mutual confidence.

Nine in the third place:

a) One pushes upward into an empty city.

b) "One pushes upward into an empty city": there is no reason to hesitate.

This is a strong line in a strong place; it is moreover at the beginning of the upper nuclear trigram Chên, movement. Furthermore, before it are the divided lines of the trigram K'un, as though empty and open, so that they offer no obstruction to progress. This easy progress might cause hesitation, but as it accords with the time, the main thing is to press forward and take advantage of the time.

Six in the fourth place:

a) The king offers him Mount Ch'i.
Good fortune. No blame.

b) "The king offers him Mount Ch'i." This is the way of the devoted.

This is a weak line in a weak place. It stands at the top of the trigram Tui, which means the west, and so may suggest Mount Ch'i. The king is the six in the fifth place; the present line represents the minister. The king is like-minded, and therefore makes it possible for him to work effectively.

○ Six in the fifth place:

a) Perseverance brings good fortune.
One pushes upward by steps.

b) "Perseverance brings good fortune. One pushes upward by steps." One achieves one's will completely.

From the first line to this, the pushing upward proceeds step
by step. The first line meets with confidence, the second needs
small sacrifices only, the third pushes up into a deserted city,
and the fourth finally gains admittance even to realms beyond:
these are steps of a progress all summed up in the ruler of the
hexagram. At this point, with such brilliant success achieved,
it is of the greatest importance to remain persevering.

Six at the top:

a) Pushing upward in darkness. It furthers one
To be unremittingly persevering.

b) "Pushing upward in darkness." At the top is decrease
and not wealth.

This line is at the top of the trigram K'un and cannot advance
farther. Culmination of the shadowy indicates darkness. When
one can no longer distinguish things, one must hold fast that
perseverance which lies below consciousness, in order not to
lose one's way.

田

47. *K'un | Oppression (Exhaustion)*

Nuclear trigrams SUN ☴ *and* LI ☲

The rulers of the hexagram are the nine in the second place
and the nine in the fifth. The idea of the hexagram is based
on the penning in of the firm element. The second and the

fifth line are by nature firm and central, and each is inclosed between dark lines. Hence both these lines are constituting as well as governing rulers of the hexagram.

The Sequence

If one pushes upward without stopping, he is sure to meet with oppression. Hence there follows the hexagram of OPPRESSION.

Miscellaneous Notes

OPPRESSION means an encounter.

Oppression is something that happens by chance. The fact that there is no water in the lake is due to certain exceptional conditions.

Appended Judgments

OPPRESSION is the test of character. OPPRESSION leads to perplexity and thereby to success. Through OPPRESSION one learns to lessen one's rancor.

The hexagram is full of danger in its structure—a lake, with an abyss opening under it, through which the water flows off downward. Wind and fire, as the nuclear trigrams, are likewise at work, oppressing the water from within. The forces trend in opposite directions. K'an, the lower trigram, sinks downward, while Tui, the upper, evaporates upward. As regards the lines, the yang element is oppressed by the yin element. The two upper strong lines are hemmed in by two weak ones, and so likewise is the middle line of the lower trigram.

THE JUDGMENT

OPPRESSION. Success. Perseverance.
The great man brings about good fortune.
No blame.
When one has something to say,
It is not believed.

624

Commentary on the Decision

OPPRESSION. The firm is hemmed in. Danger and joyousness. The superior man alone is capable of being oppressed without losing the power to succeed.

"Perseverance. The great man brings about good fortune," because he is firm and central.

"When one has something to say, it is not believed." He who considers the mouth important falls into perplexity.

The name of the hexagram is explained in its structure, because in various ways the firm lines are hemmed in between dark ones. Success is achieved in the time of OPPRESSION by maintaining cheerfulness (upper trigram Tui) in face of danger (lower trigram K'an). The firm and central lines that in each case indicate the great man are the rulers of the hexagram in the second and the fifth place. The trigram Tui also suggests speech. But one gets no hearing; the trigram K'an means earache, hence disinclination to listen.

THE IMAGE

There is no water in the lake:
The image of EXHAUSTION.
Thus the superior man stakes his life
On following his will.

The Image derives from the relative positions of the two primary trigrams: water is under the lake, therefore drained off. The trigrams individually yield advice for conduct in the time of EXHAUSTION: K'an, abyss, danger, indicates staking one's life; Tui, joyousness, indicates following one's own will.

THE LINES

Six at the beginning:

a) One sits oppressed under a bare tree
And strays into a gloomy valley.
For three years one sees nothing.

b) "One strays into a gloomy valley." One is gloomy and
   not clear.

The trigram K'an stands in the north, where gloom prevails.
The nuclear trigram is Li, clarity. The line stands outside of
clarity. In other cases the first line images the foot, the toes.
But in times of oppression a man sits; therefore the first line
here represents the buttocks. The gloomy valley is the first line
in the trigram K'an, the pit in the abyss.

O   Nine in the second place:

a)   One is oppressed while at meat and drink.
      The man with the scarlet knee bands is just coming.
      It furthers one to offer sacrifice.
      To set forth brings misfortune.
      No blame.

b)   "Oppressed while at meat and drink." The middle
      brings blessing.

K'an is wine, Tui food. The man with the scarlet knee bands
is the nine in the fifth place, the ruler (the nuclear trigram
Sun, in which the nine in the fifth place is the top line, means
leg). Between the two rulers of the hexagram—the prince, the
nine in the fifth place, and the official, the nine in the second
place—the significant relationship is that of congruity rather
than that of correspondence. Accordingly, it is a matter not of
natural but of supranatural relationships, and therefore the
religious act of sacrifice is mentioned. Since it accords with the
time, going to the prince who is kindred in spirit is in itself not
a mistake, but it cannot be done, because the six in the third
place obstructs the way and makes it dangerous.

      Six in the third place:

a)   A man permits himself to be oppressed by stone,
      And leans on thorns and thistles.
      He enters his house and does not see his wife.
      Misfortune.

b) "He leans on thorns and thistles": he rests on a hard line.

"He enters his house and does not see his wife": this bodes misfortune.

The oppression that afflicts this line is due to the hard line below it and to the hard line above, which is like a stone over it. Thus it can neither progress nor retreat. It represents a man holding the wrong office and hence in an untenable position. The appended judgments therefore allude directly to imminent death; this is what the text under *b* refers to in the words "bodes misfortune."

Nine in the fourth place:

a) He comes very quietly, oppressed in a golden carriage.

Humiliation, but the end is reached.

b) "He comes very quietly": his will is directed downward. Though the place is not appropriate, he nevertheless has companions.

K'an is a carriage, Tui metal. This line is in the minister's place and therefore has the task of relieving the oppression. The minister allows himself to be influenced by the honor of having received a golden carriage at the hands of the prince, so that he does not fulfill his task as quickly as he should. This is humiliating; yet in the end all goes well. The line is not in its proper place (the place is yielding, the line firm), but it is in the relationship of correspondence to the six at the beginning, toward which its will is directed, and therefore it has a companion that induces it to act.

O   Nine in the fifth place:

a) His nose and feet are cut off.

Oppression at the hands of the man with the purple knee bands.

Joy comes softly.

It furthers one to make offerings and libations.

b)   Cutting off of the nose and feet means that he does not yet attain his will.

"Joy comes softly," because the line is straight and central.

"It furthers one to make offerings and libations." Thus one attains good fortune.

The line is hemmed in by dark lines. Above it is a dark line. When it tries to do away with this line, the effect is as though its nose were being cut off. When it tries to turn downward, it finds there another obstructing line, the six in the third place; when it tries to remove this line, the effect is as though its feet were being cut off. Therefore it cannot carry out its purpose. Nor is the official, with whom it has a relationship of congruity, in a position to come to its help, because the latter also is penned in and oppressed by dark lines. However, the strong nature of both guarantees final success. Here too, as in the case of the nine in the second place, sacrifice is mentioned.

Six at the top:

a)   He is oppressed by creeping vines.

He moves uncertainly and says, "Movement brings remorse."

If one feels remorse over this, and makes a start, Good fortune comes.

b)   "He is oppressed by creeping vines." That is, he is not yet suitable.

"Movement brings remorse." If there is remorse, this is an auspicious change.

A weak line at the peak of oppression—this is not yet the suitable way. But through movement and the awakening within of the requisite insight, one frees oneself from oppression. Hence the prospect of good fortune when the time of OPPRESSION comes to an end.

卅

48. *Ching / The Well*

Nuclear trigrams LI ☲ and TUI ☱

The ruler of the hexagram is the nine in the fifth place. The influence of the well depends on water, and the nine in the fifth place is the ruler of the trigram K'an, water. The meaning of the hexagram is nourishment of the people, and the nine in the fifth place is the prince who provides them with nourishment.

The Sequence

He who is oppressed above is sure to turn downward. Hence there follows the hexagram of THE WELL.

Miscellaneous Notes

THE WELL means union.

Appended Judgments

THE WELL shows the field of character. THE WELL abides in its place, yet has influence on other things. THE WELL brings about discrimination as to what is right.

The well remains in its place; it has a firm, never-failing foundation. Similarly, character must have a deep foundation and a lasting connection with the springs of life. The well itself does not change, yet through the water that is drawn from it, it exerts a far-reaching influence. The well is the image of a tranquil dispensing of bounty to all who approach it. Character

629

likewise must be tranquil and clear, so that ideas of what is right can become clear. This hexagram refers to nourishment, like Hsü, WAITING (5), I, THE CORNERS OF THE MOUTH (27), and Ting, THE CALDRON (50). THE WELL refers to the water necessary for nourishment, as indispensable to life.

The two nuclear trigrams tend to rise. Hence the text lines indicate, from the first line upward, ever increasing clarification and auspiciousness in the situations, in contrast to the danger indicated in the judgment on the hexagram as a whole.

THE JUDGMENT

THE WELL. The town may be changed,
But the well cannot be changed.
It neither decreases nor increases.
They come and go and draw from the well.
If one gets down almost to the water
And the rope does not go all the way,
Or the jug breaks, it brings misfortune.

Commentary on the Decision

Penetrating under water and bringing up the water:
this is THE WELL.

The well nourishes and is not exhausted.

"The town may be changed, but the well cannot be
changed," because central position is combined with
firmness.

"If one gets down almost to the water and the rope
does not go all the way," one has not yet achieved
anything.

"If the jug breaks": this brings misfortune.

It seems as though the text at the beginning of the commentary were somewhat incomplete. Yet nothing of the essential meaning has been lost. The first half of the Judgment refers to the nature of the well. It is the unchangeable within change. The upper trigram K'an indicates a well, and the lower trigram Sun symbolizes a town. The ruler of the hexagram is in the

upper trigram, hence the idea of no change. The second half of
the text refers to the dangers connected with using the well.
The trigram Sun means a rope, the nuclear trigram Li a hollow
vessel, the nuclear trigram Tui means to break in pieces. In
this way the danger of breaking the jug is indicated.

The hexagram also contains a symbolic meaning. Just as
water in its inexhaustibility is the basic requisite of life, so
the "way of kings"—good government—is the indispensable
foundation of the life of the state. Place and time may change,
but the methods for regulating the collective life of the people
remain forever the same. Evil conditions arise only when the
right people are not at hand to execute the plan. This is
symbolized by the shattering of the jug before it has reached
the water.

THE IMAGE

Water over wood: the image of THE WELL.
Thus the superior man encourages the people at
their work
And exhorts them to help one another.

The well symbolism is here again applied to government, the
well itself being regarded as the center of the social structure.
There is likewise an allusion to the agrarian system ascribed
to remotest antiquity. In this system the fields were so divided
that eight families with their fief lands were grouped around
a center that held the well and the settlement, and that had to
be cultivated in common for the benefit of the central government. The form of the settlement was suggested in the ideo-
gram for *ching*, 井. The fields were divided as follows:

1	4	6
2	9	7
3	5	8

Fields 1 to 8 were used by the individual families; field 9
contained the well, together with the settlement and the
lord's fields. Under this arrangement, the members of the
settlement naturally had to rely on co-operative work.

The influence of the government on the people is suggested
by the two trigrams. Encouragement of the people at their

work corresponds with the trigram K'an, which symbolizes work or drudgery (*lao*). Exhortation corresponds with the trigram Sun, which denotes dissemination of commands.

THE LINES

Six at the beginning:

a) One does not drink the mud of the well.
No animals come to an old well.

b) "One does not drink the mud of the well": it is too far down.
"No animals come to an old well": time forsakes it.

The line is weak and at the very bottom, hence the idea of mud in the well. It is hidden by the firm line in the second place, hence the idea that no animals come. It remains quite outside the movement. Time passes it by.

Nine in the second place:

a) At the wellhole one shoots fishes.
The jug is broken and leaks.

b) "At the wellhole one shoots fishes": he has no one to do it with him.

This line in itself is strong and central, but it is not in the relationship of correspondence to the ruler of the hexagram. The trigram Sun means fishes. The upper nuclear trigram Li means jug; the lower, Tui, means to break in pieces, hence the broken jug.

This line is so to speak the antithesis of the ruler of the hexagram. It is the place referred to in the second half of the Judgment (concerning the broken jug).

The phrase, "At the wellhole one shoots fishes," here translated in accordance with the old commentaries, was later also interpreted to mean: "The water of the wellspring bubbles only for fishes." The Chinese character *shê*, shooting, also means figuratively the shooting forth of a ray. In any case, the meaning is that the water is not used by human beings for drinking.

Nine in the third place:

a) The well is cleaned, but no one drinks from it.
This is my heart's sorrow,
For one might draw from it.
If the king were clear-minded,
Good fortune might be enjoyed in common.

b) "The well is cleaned, but no one drinks from it." This
is the sorrow of the active people.
They beg that the king may be clear-minded, in
order to attain good fortune.

This line is strong and at the top of the lower trigram, therefore the well is cleaned. No relationship exists between the
lower and the upper trigram, hence the isolation. Within,
however, there are unifying tendencies, because both nuclear
trigrams in their movement indicate upward direction: hence
the regret of the active people (represented by these nuclear
trigrams) and the hope that the king may become clear-minded. The king is the ruler of the hexagram, the nine in the fifth
place, which is connected with the present line through the
upper nuclear trigram Li, clarity.

Six in the fourth place:

a) The well is being lined. No blame.

b) "The well is being lined. No blame," because the well
is being put in working order.

The line has a relationship of holding together with the ruler
of the hexagram in the fifth place, hence the idea that the
well is being reconditioned, made fit to receive the spring
water from the nine in the fifth place. Here the minister is
in immediate proximity to the prince, who works together with
him for the good of all.

○ Nine in the fifth place:

a) In the well there is a clear, cold spring
From which one can drink.

b) Drinking from the clear, cold spring depends on its central and correct position.

Here we have the ruler of the hexagram. It is the light line between the two dark ones in the upper trigram and represents the water within the well rim; hence the idea of the clear, cold spring. As ruler of the hexagram, it stands at the disposal of the others because of its central, correct position.

Six at the top:

a) One draws from the well
Without hindrance.
It is dependable.
Supreme good fortune.

b) "Supreme good fortune." In the top place, this means great perfection.

The line is at the top, that is, where the well water can be used by people. The rising of the water to the top makes it possible to use the well. Because of this, the line marks the completion of the hexagram; this is why the augury of great good fortune is added.[1]

---

1. Since the image is based on the idea of the drawing up of water, the meaning of the individual lines grows the more favorable, the higher the line stands.

汉

49. *Ko / Revolution (Molting)*

Nuclear trigrams CH'IEN ☰ *and* SUN ☴

The ruler of the hexagram is the nine in the fifth place, for a man must be in an honored place in order to have the authority to bring about a revolution. One who is central and correct is able to bring out all the good of such a revolution. Therefore it is said of this line: "The great man changes like a tiger."

The Sequence

The setup of a well must necessarily be revolutionized in the course of time. Hence there follows the hexagram of REVOLUTION.

A well must be cleaned out from time to time or it will become clogged with mud. Therefore the hexagram Ching, THE WELL, which means a permanent setup, is followed by the hexagram of REVOLUTION, showing the need of changes in long-established institutions, in order to keep them from stagnating.

Miscellaneous Notes

REVOLUTION means removal of that which is antiquated.

The hexagram is so constructed that the influences of the two primary trigrams are in opposition; hence a revolution develops inevitably. Fire (Li), below, is quickened by the nuclear trigram Sun, meaning wind or wood. The upper nuclear trigram Ch'ien provides the necessary firmness. The entire movement of the hexagram is directed upward.

THE JUDGMENT

REVOLUTION. On your own day
You are believed.
Supreme success,
Furthering through perseverance.
Remorse disappears.

Commentary on the Decision

REVOLUTION. Water and fire subdue each other.
Two daughters dwell together, but their views bar
mutual understanding. This means revolution.

"On your own day you are believed": one brings
about a revolution and in doing so is trusted.

Enlightenment, and thereby joyousness: you
create great success through justice.

If in a revolution one hits upon the right thing,
"remorse disappears."

Heaven and earth bring about revolution, and
the four seasons complete themselves thereby.

T'ang and Wu[1] brought about political revolutions because they were submissive toward heaven
and in accord with men.

The time of REVOLUTION is truly great.

Molting depends on fixed laws; it is prepared in advance. The
same is true of political revolutions. The expression "on your
own day" points—as in the case of the hexagram Ku, WORK
ON WHAT HAS BEEN SPOILED (18)—to one of the ten cyclic signs.
These ten cyclic signs are: (1) Chia, (2) I, (3) Ping, (4) Ting,
(5) Wu,[2] (6) Chi, (7) Kêng, (8) Hsin, (9) Jên, (10) Kuei. As
noted earlier in connection with hexagram 18, the eighth
of these signs, Hsin [metal, autumn], has also the secondary
meaning of renewal, and the seventh, Kêng, means change.
Now the sign before Kêng is Chi, hence it is on the day before

1. [T'ang the Completer (see p. 51); Wu Wang, son of King Wên.]
2. [Wu=Mou. See p. 478 for a discussion of the cyclic signs.]

the change takes place that one is believed (therefore the rendering "your own day"; *chi* also means "own"). If the cyclic signs are combined with the eight trigrams as correlated with the cardinal points in the Sequence of Later Heaven [Inner-World Arrangement], it will be found that K'un stands for Chi—which means earth—in the southwest,[3] midway between Tui in the west and Li in the south, that is, between the two trigrams that combat and subdue each other. The earth in the middle balances their influences, so that the clarity of fire (Li) and the joyousness of water (Tui) can manifest themselves separately. Hence the need of enlightenment and joyousness in gaining the popular confidence necessary for a revolution.

As revolutions in nature take place according to fixed laws and thus give rise to the cycle of the year, so political revolutions —these can become necessary at times for doing away with a state of decay—must follow definite laws. First, one must be able to await the right moment. Second, one must proceed in the right way, so that one will have the sympathy of the people and so that excesses will be avoided. Third, one must be correct and entirely free of all selfish motives. Fourth, the change must answer a real need. This was the character of the great revolutions brought about in the past by the rulers T'ang and Wu.

THE IMAGE

Fire in the lake: the image of REVOLUTION.
Thus the superior man
Sets the calendar in order
And makes the seasons clear.

Fire in the lake causes a revolution. The water puts out the fire, and the fire makes the water evaporate. Arrangement of the calendar is suggested by Tui, which means a magician, a

---

3. [Mou and Chi do not appear in the diagram showing the cyclic signs in relation to the trigrams in the Inner-World Arrangement (see p. 478), since this pair of cyclic signs stands for the center, not for one of the cardinal points. K'un is connected with Mou and Chi, since it too symbolizes the center. The cyclic signs and the primary trigrams represent two different systems of speculation, the one based on the "five stages of change," the other on the dualism of yin and yang. Therefore the two systems cannot coincide point for point.]

calendar maker. Making clear is suggested by Li, whose attribute is clarity.

THE LINES

Nine at the beginning:

a) Wrapped in the hide of a yellow cow.

b) "Wrapped in the hide of a yellow cow." One should not act thus.

One of the animals belonging to the trigram Li is the cow. The hide (*ko*) is suggested by the name of the hexagram, which means hide or molting. Yellow is the color of the second (middle) line, by which this first line is held fast. The present line is strong, and the trigram Li, to which it belongs, presses upward; thus it might be tempted to start a revolution. But the nine in the fourth place has no relationship with it, nor has the six in the second place, so that the moment for action has not yet come.

Six in the second place:

a) When one's own day comes, one may create revolution.

Starting brings good fortune. No blame.

b) "When one's own day comes, one may create revolution." Action brings splendid success.

This line is correct, central, and clear. The place is that of the official. As to connections above, it is in the relationship of correspondence to the ruler of the hexagram, the nine in the fifth place, and therefore has the potentiality of successful action. This is the moment indicated by the Judgment as being right for winning confidence (as regards the meaning of "one's own day," *chi jih*, cf. above). Here the configuration is especially clear: the trigram Li suggests day, while the middle line holds the place representing the earth, which stands in the southwest next to Li (south).

Nine in the third place:

a) Starting brings misfortune.

Perseverance brings danger.

> When talk of revolution has gone the rounds three
>   times,
> One may commit himself,
> And men will believe him.

b) "When talk of revolution has gone the rounds three
times, one may commit himself." If not, how far
are things to be allowed to go?

This line is strong and clear and in the place of transition, but
these very circumstances suggest danger of too great haste.
Hence one should wait until the time is ripe. The relationship
with the top line is not taken into account, because the latter
is already bound to the fifth line. Therefore going prematurely
would bring danger. If fire is to be effective against water, it
must act with absolute determination. Success is possible only
if all three lines form a single unit.

> Nine in the fourth place:

a) Remorse disappears. Men believe him.
>   Changing the form of government brings good for-
>   tune.

b) The good fortune in changing the form of government is due to the fact that one's conviction meets
with belief.

As a strong line in a yielding place, this line is harmoniously
balanced. It is like in kind to the ruler of the hexagram and in
alliance with him, hence it meets with belief. Here the time
for change has come. When the text speaks not only of revolution but also of change and alteration, it means that while
revolution merely does away with the old, the idea of change
points at the same time to introduction of the new.

> ○ Nine in the fifth place:

a) The great man changes like a tiger.
>   Even before he questions the oracle
>   He is believed.

b) "The great man changes like a tiger": his marking is distinct.

This line is related to the six in the second place and therefore has the clarity of Li at its disposal. The trigram Tui, in which this is the central line, stands in the west, the place of the white tiger. The season of the year corresponding with this trigram is autumn, when animals change their coats.

Six at the top:

a) The superior man changes like a panther.
The inferior man molts in the face.
Starting brings misfortune.
To remain persevering brings good fortune.

b) "The superior man changes like a panther." His marking is more delicate.
"The inferior man molts in the face." He is devoted and obeys the prince.

This line has a relationship of holding together with the ruler of the hexagram, therefore is assigned the work of carrying out specific details. The markings of the panther are more delicate than those of the tiger. The inferior man changes externally at least through the preponderating influence of superior men.

鼎

50. *Ting / The Caldron*

Nuclear trigrams   TUI ☱   *and*   CH'IEN ☰

The rulers of the hexagram are the six in the fifth place and the
nine at the top. The idea on which the hexagram Ting is based
is that of the nourishing of worthy men. The six in the fifth
place honors the venerable man represented by the nine at the
top. The image is derived from the way in which the rings and
ears of the *ting*[1] fit into each other.

The Sequence

Nothing transforms things so much as the *ting*.
Hence there follows the hexagram of THE CALDRON.

The transformations wrought by Ting are on the one hand the
changes produced in food by cooking, and on the other, in a
figurative sense, the revolutionary effects resulting from the
joint work of a prince and a sage.

Miscellaneous Notes

THE CALDRON means taking up the new.

The hexagram is structurally the inverse of the preceding one;
in meaning also it presents a transformation. While Ko treats
of revolution as such in its negative aspect, Ting shows the
correct way of going about social reorganization. The two
primary trigrams move in such a way that their action is

---

1. [See p. 193, n. 1.]

mutually reinforcing. The nuclear trigrams Ch'ien and Tui, which mean metal, complete the idea of the *ting* as a sacred ceremonial vessel. These old bronze vessels—as still occasionally found in excavations—have been connected throughout all time with the loftiest expressions of Chinese civilization.

THE JUDGMENT

THE CALDRON. Supreme good fortune.
Success.

Commentary on the Decision

THE CALDRON is the image of an object. When one causes wood to penetrate fire, food is cooked. The holy man cooks in order to sacrifice to God the Lord, and he cooks feasts in order to nourish the holy and the worthy.

Through gentleness the ear and eye become sharp and clear. The yielding advances and goes upward. It attains the middle and finds correspondence in the firm; hence there is supreme success.

The whole hexagram, with its sequence of divided and undivided lines, is the image of a *ting*, from the legs below to the handle rings at the top. The trigram Sun below means wood and penetration; Li above means fire. Thus wood is put into fire, and the fire is kept up for the preparation of the meal. Strictly speaking, food is of course not cooked in the *ting* but is served in it after being cooked in the kitchen; nevertheless, the symbol of the *ting* carries also the idea of the preparation of food. The *ting* is a ceremonial vessel reserved for use in sacrifices and banquets, and herein lies the contrast between this hexagram and Ching, THE WELL (48), which connotes nourishment of the people. In a sacrifice to God only one animal is needed, because it is not the gift but the sentiment that counts. For the entertainment of guests abundant food and great lavishness are needed. The upper trigram Li is eye, the fifth line stands for the ears of the *ting;* thus the image of eye and ear is suggested. The lower trigram Sun is the Gentle, the adaptive.

Thereby the eye and ear become sharp and clear (clarity is the attribute of the trigram Li).

The yielding element that moves upward is the ruler of the hexagram in the fifth place; it stands in the relationship of correspondence to the strong assistant, the nine in the second place, hence has success. In ancient China nine *ting* were the symbol of sovereignty, hence the favorable oracle.

THE IMAGE

Fire over wood:

The image of THE CALDRON.

Thus the superior man consolidates his fate

By making his position correct.

Fire over wood is the image not of the *ting* itself but of its use. Fire burns continuously when wood is under it. Life also must be kept alight, in order to remain so conditioned that the sources of life are perpetually renewed. Obviously the same is true of the life of a community or of a state. Here too relationships and positions must be so regulated that the resulting order has duration. In this way the decree of fate whereby rulership falls to a particular house becomes established.

THE LINES

Six at the beginning:

a) A *ting* with legs upturned.

Furthers removal of stagnating stuff.

One takes a concubine for the sake of her son.

No blame.

b) "A *ting* with legs upturned." This is still not wrong. "Furthers removal of stagnating stuff," in order to be able to follow the man of worth.

The line at the bottom means the legs of the *ting*.[2] Since the line is weak and stands at the beginning, the implication arises

---

2. The *ting* of ancient China had either three legs or four. Since the divided line at the beginning touches the earth as it were at only two points, it suggests the idea of a *ting* upturned.

that before cooking one must turn the *ting* upside down to throw out the old food remnants. The line has a connection by position with the central and strong line next to it; hence the idea of a concubine (weak and subordinated).

Nine in the second place:

a) There is food in the *ting*.
My comrades are envious,
But they cannot harm me.
Good fortune.

b) "There is food in the *ting*." Be cautious about where you go.
"My comrades are envious." This brings no blame in the end.

This line is firm and central, hence it symbolizes the contents of the *ting*. It forms a unit with the third and fourth lines, but as it stands in the relationship of correspondence to the ruler of the hexagram, it must go its own ways as prescribed for it by these relationships. This leads on the other hand to envy from its comrades, the two lines from which it is separated by inner relationships. But being quite free of possible entanglements and shielded by the strong relationship to the ruler, it need fear nothing.

Nine in the third place:

a) The handle of the *ting* is altered.
One is impeded in his way of life.
The fat of the pheasant is not eaten.
Once rain falls, remorse is spent.
Good fortune comes in the end.

b) "The handle of the *ting* is altered." He has missed the idea.

This line is the lowest in the upper nuclear trigram Tui, whose top line means mouth. It might therefore be assumed that the contents, indicated by the upper trigram Li, which means pheasant, are eaten, but this is not the case. The vessel is not portable, because the handle has been altered. This is suggested by the fact that the present line, which ordinarily would be related to the top line, representing the carrying rings, is itself firm [not hollow] and therefore cannot receive the carrying rings (cf. on the other hand the six in the fifth place). There is a promise for the future. As the line changes, K'an, meaning rain, takes shape as the lower primary trigram and upper nuclear trigram. The situation is made easier by this. The stoppage ceases, and the movement leads to the goal.

Nine in the fourth place:

a) The legs of the *ting* are broken.
The prince's meal is spilled
And his person is soiled.
Misfortune.

b) "The prince's meal is spilled." How can one still trust him?

This line stands in the relationship of correspondence to the six at the beginning, the line suggesting the upturned legs of a *ting*. The latter situation is not of grave import, for the *ting* is still empty; here, however, the matter is serious, since the *ting* contains food. It is therefore not simply an overturning: the legs of the *ting* are broken, and the prince's meal is spilled. In conformity with the place, there should be a relationship with the ruler of the hexagram, the six in the fifth place, either that of holding together or that of receiving. But the relationship with the six at the beginning interferes. This points to a disastrous split between character and position, between knowledge and aspirations, between strength and responsibility.

O Six in the fifth place:

a) The *ting* has yellow handles, golden carrying rings. Perseverance furthers.

b) The yellow handles of the *ting* are central, in order to receive what is real.

This line is centrally placed in the upper trigram Li; it is moreover the middle line of the trigram K'un, which is associated with the color yellow. The carrying rings are of metal because the upper nuclear trigram Tui means metal. The carrying rings (which in ancient Chinese vessels are usually linked together) are no doubt represented by the strong line at the top. This line is in contrast with the nine in the third place: the handle is hollow and can therefore receive the "real" (i.e., firm) carrying rings, and the vessel can be carried.

In the language of symbols this means a great deal. The line is the ruler of the hexagram and has over it a sage (the nine at the top), with whom it is connected by position and complementary relationship. The ruler is "hollow" [receptive], hence capable of receiving the power, that is, the teachings of this sage ("handle," *erh*, is represented by the same character as "ear"). Thereby he makes progress.

○　Nine at the top:

a)　The *ting* has rings of jade.
Great good fortune.
Nothing that would not act to further.

b)　The jade rings in the highest place show the firm and the yielding complementing each other properly.

This situation is the same as that of the six in the fifth place, except that here it is seen from the standpoint of the sage who bestows. What appears in the six in the fifth place as the firmness of metal manifests itself here as the soft sheen of jade. It is possible for the sage to impart his teaching because the six in the fifth place meets him halfway with the proper receptivity.

51. *Chên / The Arousing (Shock, Thunder)*

Nuclear trigrams K'AN ═══ *and* KÊN ═══

The rulers of the hexagram Chên are the two light lines. But since it is implicit in the idea of the hexagram of SHOCK that the light element is moving upward from below, the fourth line is not regarded as a ruler, and only the line at the beginning is so considered.

The Sequence

Among the custodians of the sacred vessels, the eldest son stands first. Hence there follows the hexagram of THE AROUSING. The Arousing means movement.

Miscellaneous Notes

THE AROUSING means beginning, arising.

This hexagram is one of the eight in which a primary trigram is doubled. It is formed by doubling of the trigram Chên, which symbolizes the eldest son, the beginning of things in the east—the spring. This is also suggested by the Image, which shows the upward movement of electricity, thunder, making itself heard again in the spring.

THE JUDGMENT

SHOCK brings success.
Shock comes—oh, oh!
Laughing words—ha, ha!

The shock terrifies for a hundred miles,
And he does not let fall the sacrificial spoon and
chalice.

Commentary on the Decision

"SHOCK brings success. Shock comes—oh, oh!" Fear
brings good fortune.

"Laughing words—ha, ha!" Afterward one has a
rule.

"The shock terrifies for a hundred miles." If one
causes fear far and wide and has concern for what is
near by, one may come forth and protect the temple
of the ancestors and the altar of the earth, and be
the leader of the sacrifice.

"Shock comes—oh, oh": the exclamatory words mean first a
frightened tiger, then a lizard running in fright hither and
thither on the wall. Thus the meaning of fear became attached
to the two onomatopoeic characters. The fear thus aroused
makes one cautious, and caution brings good fortune. "Laughing words—ha, ha": the words are suggested by the sound of
thunder, which sounds like "ha, ha." They are a symbol of
inner calm in the midst of the storm of outer movement.

"The shock terrifies for a hundred miles": this is the sound
of thunder, which is at the same time the symbol of a mighty
ruler (suggested by the idea of the eldest son) who knows how
to make himself respected by all those about him, yet is careful
and exact in the smallest detail. The concluding sentence also
refers to this. The lord of the sacrifices is at the same time the
lord of the house or of the realm. In this regard also the eldest
son had his special task. The trigram Chên means the coming
forth of God in the spring and also the reawakening of the life
force, which stirs again from below.

THE IMAGE

Thunder repeated: the image of SHOCK.
Thus in fear and trembling

The superior man sets his life in order
And examines himself.

The phrase is "thunder repeated" because the trigram Chên is doubled. The first thunder denotes fear and trembling, the second denotes shaping and exploring.

THE LINES

O   Nine at the beginning:

a) Shock comes—oh, oh!
Then follow laughing words—ha, ha!
Good fortune.

b) "Shock comes—oh, oh!" Fear brings good fortune.
"Laughing words—ha, ha!" Afterward one has a rule.

A part of the Judgment, and of the commentary on it, is given here word for word, as is occasionally done in the case of the ruler of a hexagram. The strong line at the beginning initiating the movement from below shows the quintessence of the whole situation.

Six in the second place:

a) Shock comes bringing danger.
A hundred thousand times
You lose your treasures
And must climb the nine hills.
Do not go in pursuit of them.
After seven days you will get them back again.

b) "Shock comes bringing danger." It rests upon a firm line.

Since the first line presses upward with powerful shock, there can be no thought of a relationship of holding together between it and this weak line in a weak place. But the line is central and correct, and is therefore affected only externally by the threatening danger, just as a thunderstorm causes only momentary shock. Danger is indicated by the nuclear trigram K'an, under which the line stands. Flight to the hills is suggested by the lower nuclear trigram Kên, mountain. Seven is the number

649

indicating return, which restores the old conditions after the situations of all of the six lines have changed.

Six in the third place:

a) Shock comes and makes one distraught.
If shock spurs to action
One remains free of misfortune.

b) "Shock comes and makes one distraught." The place is not the appropriate one.

The word *su*, here rendered by "distraught," denotes literally the reviving movements of insects still numb and stiff after their winter sleep. The place is not the proper one, for the place is strong and the line weak; therefore it is not equal to the shock of the position. Hence it must allow itself to be set in motion by the shock. Through movement a weak line becomes a strong line. Thus one becomes equal to shock.

Nine in the fourth place:

a) Shock is mired.

b) "Shock is mired." It is not yet brilliant enough.

The line itself is strong, but its strength is impaired by the weakness of the place. Furthermore, it is in the nuclear trigram K'an, just where the pit lies, and also at the top of the nuclear trigram Kên, Keeping Still. Thus the strong nature of the line cannot become effectual; it does not show enough brilliance, hence is caught fast in the mire.

Six in the fifth place:

a) Shock goes hither and thither.
Danger.
However, nothing at all is lost.
Yet there are things to be done.

b) "Shock goes hither and thither. Danger." One walks in danger.
The "things to be done" are in the middle, hence nothing at all is lost.

The line is central, like the six in the second place. But while in the latter case danger threatens (nuclear trigram K'an), here it has been overcome and one is already on the hill (nuclear trigram Kên). Hence one loses nothing. The point is to hold firmly to the central position and thus to conserve for oneself the strength inherent in it—the fifth place being the place of the ruler. The six in the second place is the official. An official may lose his property temporarily, but all of it can be replaced. The six in the fifth place, however, is the ruler, and his possessions consist of land and people. These must not be lost. Such loss can be prevented if one maintains a central position and behaves correctly.

Six at the top:

a) Shock brings ruin and terrified gazing around.
Going ahead brings misfortune.
If it has not yet touched one's own body
But has reached one's neighbor first,
There is no blame.
One's comrades have something to talk about.

b) "Shock brings ruin." He has not attained the middle. Misfortune, but no blame. One is warned by the fear for one's neighbor.

This line is related to the third, which is the comrade who has something to say. The fifth line is the neighbor. Here a weak line stands at the climax of shock and is therefore inherently not equal to it. The shock threatens ruin as in an earthquake, hence the terrified gazing around. Trying to undertake something under such conditions would lead to misfortune. But if one takes warning from the experience of one's neighbor—in this case the fifth line—and remains calm, mistakes are avoided. The third line, the comrade, is forced by the situation to move, hence cannot understand why the sixth line stays calm. However, the difference in behavior is the result of the difference in place. Therefore one must be wholly independent in one's actions.

52. *Kên / Keeping Still, Mountain*

Nuclear trigrams CHÊN ☳ *and* K'AN ☵

Here also, strictly speaking, the two light lines are the rulers of the hexagram. But since the meaning of the hexagram of KEEPING STILL is based on the fact that the light element stands still, the third line does not count as a ruler, and only the line at the top is so regarded.

The Sequence

Things cannot move continuously, one must make them stop. Hence there follows the hexagram of KEEPING STILL. Keeping Still means stopping.

Miscellaneous Notes

KEEPING STILL means stopping.

This hexagram is the inverse of the preceding one. It is formed by doubling of the trigram Kên, the youngest son, the mountain. The place of Kên is in the northeast, between K'an in the north and Chên in the east. It is the mysterious place where all things begin and end, where death and birth pass one into the other. The attribute of the hexagram is keeping still, because the strong lines, whose trend is upward, have attained their goal.

THE JUDGMENT

KEEPING STILL. Keeping his back still
So that he no longer feels his body.

He goes into his courtyard
And does not see his people.
No blame.

Commentary on the Decision

KEEPING STILL means stopping.
When it is time to stop, then stop.
When it is time to advance, then advance.
Thus movement and rest do not miss the right time,
And their course becomes bright and clear.

Keeping his stopping still[1] means stopping in his place. Those above and those below are in opposition and have nothing in common. Therefore it is said: "He does not feel his body. He goes into his courtyard and does not see his people. No blame."

The nature of the hexagram predicates a separation of the upper and the lower trigram. This is indicated also by the divergent movements of the nuclear trigrams, the upper going upward and the lower downward. Keeping still is the meaning of the hexagram itself, movement is the meaning of the nuclear trigrams. Therefore it is explained that movement and stopping, each at the right time, are both features of rest: the one is continuance in a state of movement, the other continuance in a state of rest. The hexagram Kên has an inner brilliance, because the light line at the top is above the two dark ones and so is not darkened; hence the saying: "Their course becomes bright and clear."

The back is that part of the body which is invisible to oneself; keeping the back still symbolizes making the self still. The lower primary trigram indicates this keeping still of the back, so that one is no longer aware of one's body, that is, of one's personality. The upper primary trigram means courtyard. The

1. This phrase, "Keeping his stopping still" (*kên ch'i chih*), is a textual mistake persisting from Wang Pi's time [A.D. 226–249]; it should read as the Judgment has it: "Keeping his back still" (*kên ch'i pei*). A comparison of the older explanations makes this evident.

individual lines of the upper trigram have no relation to the corresponding lines of the lower trigram, hence the upper and the lower trigram turn their backs on each other, as it were. Hence one does not see the other persons in the court-yard.

THE IMAGE

Mountains standing close together:
The image of KEEPING STILL.
Thus the superior man
Does not permit his thoughts
To go beyond his situation.

The corresponding lines of the upper and the lower trigram do not stand in the relationship of correspondence in any of the hexagrams formed by doubling of a trigram. But only in the hexagram of KEEPING STILL is it expressly noted that the mountains have merely an outward connection; in the case of the other hexagrams so formed, a reciprocal movement [of the trigrams] is always presupposed. In KEEPING STILL the opposite of movement and interchange is represented. Accordingly, the lesson taught by the Image is that of restriction to what is within the limits of one's position.

THE LINES

Six at the beginning:

a)   Keeping his toes still.
No blame.
Continued perseverance furthers.

b)   "Keeping his toes still": what is right is not yet lost.

With respect to their images, the individual lines in this hexagram are reminiscent of the lines of Hsien, INFLUENCE (31). Thus the lowest line is again the symbol of the toes. The line is weak, therefore keeping still accords with the time and is not a mistake. It is important only that a weak nature of this sort should not become impatient but should possess enough perseverance to keep still.

Six in the second place:

a) Keeping his calves still.
He cannot rescue him whom he follows.
His heart is not glad.

b) "He cannot rescue him whom he follows." Because
this one does not turn toward him to listen to him.

The line that is followed by the six in the second place is the
nine in the third place. The six in the second place is correct
and central and would like to save not only itself but also the
one it follows. But the nine in the third place is a strong line in
the place of transition, and it is the lowest line of the nuclear
trigram Chên, the Arousing; hence it is extremely restless. At
the same time it is in the nuclear trigram K'an, the Abysmal,
which means earache, hence the failure to hear. K'an is also
the symbol of the heart; hence, "His heart is not glad."

Nine in the third place:

a) Keeping his hips still.
Making his sacrum stiff.
Dangerous. The heart suffocates.

b) "Keeping his hips still." There is danger that the
heart may suffocate.

This line is in the middle of the nuclear trigram K'an, hence
the allusion to the heart. At the same time it is the one light
line between dark lines, and this indicates danger and confine-
ment. Keeping still in this situation is dangerous. When the
back is kept still one gains control over the whole body. The
hips, however, form the boundary between the movements
of the light and the dark forces. If rigidity occurs here, the
heart will move aimlessly, the nerve paths will thereby be
interrupted, and a suffocation of the heart is to be feared.

Six in the fourth place:

a) Keeping his trunk still.
No blame.

b) "Keeping his trunk still." He stops within his own body.

The fourth place is the trunk. It is very weak, and a weak line stands over it. In the time of KEEPING STILL it is altogether correct if one knows how to restrain oneself at the right time.

Six in the fifth place:

a) Keeping his jaws still.

The words have order.

Remorse disappears.

b) "Keeping his jaws still," as a result of central and correct behavior.

While in INFLUENCE (31) the image of the jaws does not appear until the topmost place is reached, it comes in the fifth place here, because in this hexagram the ruler occupies the sixth place.

The present line is in a central place and also correct. But since it belongs simultaneously to the trigram Kên, Keeping Still, and to the nuclear trigram Chên, movement, it suggests the possibility of movement of the jaws and of speaking like thunder. But this is avoided through the central behavior of the line and the fact that it belongs to the upper trigram, Keeping Still.

O Nine at the top:

a) Noblehearted keeping still.

Good fortune.

b) The good fortune of noblehearted keeping still comes from the fact that there is an ample end.

This line ending the hexagram is strong, hence it is thought of as ample. The ruler of the hexagram is at the top of the mountain, in the place where the layers of earth are most amply (most densely) piled upon one another. As the highest line it has light intrinsically; this can be fully effectual precisely because of the calm keeping still of the line. Hence good fortune is attained here. Since this strong line does not strive further upward but stays quietly in its place, it is, in contrast to other strong lines at the top, not unfavorable.

漢

53. *Chien / Development (Gradual Progress)*

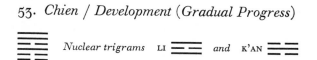

Nuclear trigrams LI ☲ *and* K'AN ☵

The basic idea of the hexagram of DEVELOPMENT is the marriage of a girl. Only the six in the second place stands in the relationship of correspondence to the nine in the fifth. It represents the girl who is to be married. Hence the six in the second place is a ruler of the hexagram. However, development also connotes progress, and the nine in the fifth place has progressed, occupies a high position, and has a firm and central character; hence it also is a ruler of the hexagram.

The Sequence

Things cannot stop forever; hence there follows the hexagram of DEVELOPMENT. Development means to progress.

Miscellaneous Notes

DEVELOPMENT shows how the maiden is given in marriage and in this must await the actions of the man.

Like the hexagrams Chin, PROGRESS (35), and Shêng, PUSHING UPWARD (46), this hexagram pictures progress. But while PROGRESS is like the rising sun spreading light over the earth, and Shêng shows a tree pushing up through the earth, what is meant here is slow growth such as that of a tree on a mountainside. In another aspect the hexagram is one of those dealing with the relation of man and woman, and therefore most closely related to the hexagram Hsien, INFLUENCE (31). In the latter the youngest daughter is being influenced by the youngest son. The effect is quick and mutual, expressing the natural attraction between the sexes. In the present hexagram, the mature elder daughter is being influenced by the youngest son; hence in this instance the emphasis is rather on the mores with their restraining effect. Thus we are reminded here of the gradual development in the case of marriage, which in the course of time came to require the carrying out of six different rites (cf. the next hexagram).

THE JUDGMENT

DEVELOPMENT. The maiden
Is given in marriage.
Good fortune.
Perseverance furthers.

Commentary on the Decision

The progress of DEVELOPMENT means the good fortune of the maiden's marriage.

Progressing and thereby attaining the right place: going brings success.

Progressing in what is right—thus one may set the country in order.

His place is firm, and he has attained the middle.

Keeping still and penetrating: this makes the movement inexhaustible.

The meaning of the name of the hexagram is explained in terms of the first part of the Judgment, the rest of which is elucidated on the basis of the structure of the hexagram. The two rulers of the hexagram, the second and the fifth line, show a progressing and therefore attain their correct and natural places. Attainment of a proper place bespeaks a correct attitude of mind; thereby undertakings meet with success, and the state can be set in order. The emphasis here is on the combination of personal moral effort and such strength as is required to set the state in order. The ruler of the hexagram, standing in the fifth place—that of command—combining strength and central correctness, is especially well qualified for achieving successful results of this kind. The latter part of the commentary deals with the two primary trigrams and points out that the inexhaustible source of progress is inner calm combined with adaptability to circumstances. Calm is the attribute of the inner trigram, Kên, adaptability that of the outer trigram, Sun.

THE IMAGE

On the mountain, a tree:
The image of DEVELOPMENT.
Thus the superior man abides in dignity and virtue,
In order to improve the mores.

The tree on the mountain grows larger slowly and imperceptibly. It spreads and gives shade, and thus through its nature influences its surroundings. Thus it is an example of the active power by which an individual improves the mores of his environment through consistent cultivation of his own moral qualities. The tree on the mountain, like the tree on the earth in Kuan, VIEW (20), represents influence by example. The keeping still of the mountain is a symbol for abiding in dignity and virtue. The penetrating attribute of wood (or wind) is a symbol of the positive influence emanating from a good example.

THE LINES

The hexagram as a whole refers to the contracting of marriage, and consequently the image common to all the lines is the wild goose, symbol of conjugal fidelity.

Six at the beginning:

a) The wild goose gradually draws near the shore.
The young son is in danger.
There is talk. No blame.

b) The danger besetting the little son implies no blame.

The nuclear trigram Li means a flying bird, hence the image of a wild goose. The first line stands next to the nuclear trigram K'an, the Abysmal, hence the shore as an image. Kên, the lower trigram, symbolizes the youngest son. It contains the nuclear trigram K'an, danger. The "talk" comes perhaps from the upper trigram Sun, wind, which soughs and resounds.

This is a yielding line in a lowly[1] place. Therefore it is not impetuous in pressing forward; it is conscious of the danger. Hence, though others talk about it, it remains blameless.

O   Six in the second place:

a) The wild goose gradually draws near the cliff.
      Eating and drinking in peace and concord.
      Good fortune.

b) "Eating and drinking in peace and concord": he does
      not merely eat his fill.

Kên is the mountain, hence the image of a cliff. The nuclear trigram K'an indicates eating and drinking. When the wild goose finds food, it calls its comrades. This line is yielding and related to the nine in the fifth place, which it calls. It does not eat to satisfy itself alone but takes thought at once of others as well.

    Nine in the third place:

a) The wild goose gradually draws near the plateau.
      The man goes forth and does not return.
      The woman carries a child but does not bring it
         forth.
      Misfortune.
      It furthers one to fight off robbers.

b) "The man goes forth and does not return." He leaves
      the group of his companions.
      "The woman carries a child but does not bring it
      forth." She has lost the right way.

---

1. ["Yielding" in the German, but this is assumed to be a slip of the pen. See p. 463, n. 1.]

"It furthers one to fight off robbers." Devotion and
mutual protection.

This line, as the uppermost one in the trigram Kên, indicates
a high place, hence the plateau. It is a strong line in a strong
place, hence not moderate in movement. It pictures a man who
never desists from his course and who therefore proceeds without ever turning back. It stands in relationship to the two
strong lines at the top, but there is no correspondence. Further,
it is in the middle of the nuclear trigram of danger and is
therefore separated from its own kind (a dark line above,
another below it). Since the line does not return, the trigram
K'un, forming below as a result of its departure, is left behind
without a child. Thus the woman has lost her way. Only in so
far as this strong line protects the two weak ones under it from
robbers, does it have any furthering quality.

Six in the fourth place:

a) The wild goose gradually draws near the tree.
Perhaps it will find a flat branch. No blame.

b) "Perhaps it will find a flat branch." It is devoted and
gentle.

This line has entered the upper trigram Sun, wood, hence the
image of its gradually approaching a tree. The tree itself affords no foothold for the wild goose, whose feet are not made
for clutching; but through adaptability and devotion it may
find a flat branch. This is a weak line in a weak place, hence
correct. It is therefore adaptable and cautious, and thus temporarily finds a resting place.

O   Nine in the fifth place:

a) The wild goose gradually draws near the summit.
For three years the woman has no child.
In the end nothing can hinder her.
Good fortune.

b) In the end nothing can hinder good fortune. One
attains one's wish.

This line is the upper ruler of the hexagram, hence it is the summit to which the wild goose draws near. It stands in relationship to the lower ruler of the hexagram, the six in the second place; the correspondence between the two places is analogous to the relation of husband and wife. Hence the idea that union finally takes place. But this takes three years, for the line is separated from the six in the second place by the nuclear trigram K'an, danger. However, the union is based on natural affinity; hence it can be delayed but not permanently prevented.

> Nine at the top:
>
> *a)* The wild goose gradually draws near the cloud heights.
>
> Its feathers can be used for the sacred dance.
>
> Good fortune.
>
> *b)* "Its feathers can be used for the sacred dance. Good fortune." He is not to be disconcerted.

The place at the top is the region of the clouds, and here the character *lu*, really meaning a plateau (cf. the nine in the third place) has mistakenly been written in place of another character meaning "highest heights."

The trigram Sun means wind. This suggests flight through the clouds. The line is strong and already outside the affairs of the world. It is regarded by the others solely as an example and thus exerts a beneficent influence. It no longer enters into the confusion of mundane affairs.

The dances mentioned were sacred pantomimes in which feathers of a special sort were used. The idea inhering in this line recalls that of the top line of Kuan, VIEW (20). In the latter too the line as such stands outside the affairs of the world, taking part only as a spectator.

葺 妹

54. Kuei Mei / The Marrying Maiden

Nuclear trigrams K'AN ☵ and LI ☲

The hexagram of THE MARRYING MAIDEN is based on the idea that the girl is marrying on her own initiative. Her character is not good, therefore the Commentary on the Decision says: " 'Nothing that would further.' The yielding rests upon the hard." This refers to the six in the third place and to the six at the top, which are thus the constituting rulers of the hexagram. The six in the fifth place, on the other hand, is in the place of honor and associates with those below; thus it changes what is not good into good and transforms misfortune into good fortune. Because of this the six in the fifth place is the governing ruler of the hexagram.

The Sequence

Through progress one is sure to reach the place where one belongs. Hence there follows the hexagram of THE MARRYING MAIDEN.[1]

Miscellaneous Notes

THE MARRYING MAIDEN shows the end of maidenhood.

This hexagram is judged in very different ways. In later times it was considered immoral for a girl to marry on her own initiative. The mores demanded that the girl wait for the

---

1. Literally, "the maiden who passes into ownership."

man to take the lead, as set forth in the preceding hexagram. This goes back to patriarchal times. But the present hexagram has also so to speak a cosmic meaning. For, according to the arrangement of the eight trigrams by King Wên [Inner-World Arrangement[2]], the upper trigram Chên belongs in the east and denotes spring, the beginning of life; the lower trigram Tui belongs in the west and denotes autumn, the end of life, and the two nuclear trigrams K'an and Li represent the north (winter) and the south (summer) respectively. Consequently the whole cycle of life is contained in this hexagram.

THE JUDGMENT

THE MARRYING MAIDEN.
Undertakings bring misfortune.
Nothing that would further.

Commentary on the Decision

THE MARRYING MAIDEN describes the great meaning of heaven and earth. If heaven and earth do not unite, all creatures fail to prosper.

THE MARRYING MAIDEN means the end and beginning of humanity.

Joyousness in movement: she who marries is the young girl.

"Undertakings bring misfortune." The places are not the appropriate ones.

"Nothing that would further." The yielding rests upon the hard.

In the sequence of the trigrams in the Primal Arrangement,[3] which corresponds with the world of the idea, Ch'ien is in the south and K'un in the north; Li is in the east as the sun and K'an in the west as the moon. In the Inner-World Arrangement, which corresponds with the phenomenal world, the action is transferred to the four trigrams Chên (east), Li (south),

2. [See p. 269.]
3. [See p. 266.]

Tui (west), and K'an (north). Sun and moon here take the place of heaven and earth as active forces. Heaven, Ch'ien, has withdrawn to the northwest, and the eldest son, Chên, in the east, is the originator of life. The earth, K'un, has withdrawn to the southwest, and the youngest daughter, Tui, in the west, presides over harvest and birth. Thus the present hexagram indicates the cosmic order of the relations of the sexes and the cycle of life.

The interpretation given by Liu Yüan[4] in the *Chou I Hêng Chieh* is significant. He sees in the hexagram not the maiden (Tui) following an older man (Chên), but the elder brother (Chên) leading his younger sister to her husband. A certain basis for this view is afforded by the words accompanying the fifth line. We are dealing here with reminiscences of matriarchal times disseminated in popular romance by the story of how Chung K'uei gave his sister in marriage.

THE MARRYING MAIDEN means the beginning and end of humanity, as Chên in the east means spring, ascent, and Tui in the west means autumn, decline. The commentary then explains the name of the hexagram by citing the attributes of the two trigrams—Tui, joyousness, and Chên, movement. The judgment on the hexagram, "Undertakings bring misfortune," is derived from the position of the four middle lines, none of which is in its proper place. "Nothing that would further" results from the position of the six in the third place (one of the rulers of the hexagram), which is over the hard nine in the second place, and from the positions of the other two rulers, the six in the fifth place and the six at the top, both over the hard nine in the fourth place.

THE IMAGE

Thunder over the lake:
The image of THE MARRYING MAIDEN.
Thus the superior man
Understands the transitory
In the light of the eternity of the end.

---

4. [A writer of the Ch'ing dynasty. The work named is an explanation of the *I Ching*.]

In the autumn everything comes to its end. When thunder is over the lake, this end is near. The eternity of the end is suggested by the trigram Chên, which comes forth in the east (spring) and reaches the end of its activity in the west (autumn), in accordance with fixed laws. At that moment the death-dealing power of autumn, which destroys all transient beings, becomes active. Through knowledge of these laws, one reaches those regions which are beyond beginning and end, birth and death.

THE LINES

Nine at the beginning:

a)   The marrying maiden as a concubine.
A lame man who is able to tread.
Undertakings bring good fortune.

b)   "The marrying maiden as a concubine," because that gives duration.
"A lame man who is able to tread. Good fortune," because they receive each other.

This line is at the bottom, in an inferior position. Furthermore, it is in the trigram Tui, the youngest daughter; hence the idea of a concubine. Tui, the youngest daughter, is weak in relation to the eldest son (just as Tui is weak in relation to Ch'ien in hexagram 10, Lü, TREADING, in which the image of a lame, one-eyed man likewise occurs). The lowest line stands for the foot, hence the idea of a lame man, because there is no relationship with the fourth line. "Receive each other" means that the first line is in the relationship of receiving to the second, serving the latter line as well as the fifth; therefore it is able to accomplish something indirectly at least, and advances.

Nine in the second place:

a)   A one-eyed man who is able to see.
The perseverance of a solitary man furthers.

b)   "The perseverance of a solitary man furthers." The permanent law is not changed.

666

This line is in the lowest place of the nuclear trigram Li, which means eye. It stands in the relationship of correspondence to the fifth line, which is weak; hence the image of a one-eyed man.

Since the line is strong and central, it is not changed, although the line that belongs to it is weak and not good. It is true that this brings it into darkness and loneliness—it is under the nuclear trigram K'an, abyss, that is, a gloomy valley—but it does not change its attitude toward the law and remains faithful to its duty.

☐ Six in the third place:

a) The marrying maiden as a slave.
   She marries as a concubine.

b) "The marrying maiden as a slave": she is not yet in
   the appropriate place.

This is a weak line in a strong place, hence not in the appropriate position. Moreover, it stands at the high point of pleasure, hence throws itself away as the lowest type of slave, merely in order to achieve marriage at any cost. In following the nine in the second place, it finds shelter as a concubine.

   Nine in the fourth place:

a) The marrying maiden draws out the allotted time.
   A late marriage comes in due course.

b) The state of mind that leads to drawing out of the
   allotted time indicates a desire to wait for something
   before going.

Of the lines of the upper and the lower trigram, only the fifth and the second line stand in relationship. But while the other two lines in Tui, being in the trigram of pleasure, also seek a marital connection (although by a detour around the second line), the lines of the upper trigram that are not bound by the relationship of correspondence move away from the idea of marriage. The present line, besides having no correspondence in the lower trigram, is not in the proper place (a strong line in a weak place) and is in the center of the nuclear trigram K'an, danger. Hence it holds back from marriage and waits for

667

conditions to change before it undertakes anything—the danger being eventually surmounted by movement (Chên). But the new situation begins only after the present cycle of events has come to an end.

○ Six in the fifth place:

a) The sovereign I gave his daughter in marriage.
The embroidered garments of the princess
Were not as gorgeous
As those of the servingmaid.
The moon that is nearly full
Brings good fortune.

b) "The sovereign I gave his daughter in marriage. Her embroidered garments were not as gorgeous as those of the servingmaid." The place is in the middle, hence action has value.

The place is central and honored. Nevertheless, the line is yielding and condescends to the strong nine in the second place like a princess marrying an inferior. Therefore because of her nobility she pays no attention to outer appearance, and the servingmaid, in the lowest place, is more gorgeous than she. The image of the moon appears because this line is at the top of the nuclear trigram K'an (moon).

☐ Six at the top:

a) The woman holds the basket, but there are no fruits in it.
The man stabs the sheep, but no blood flows.
Nothing that acts to further.

b) The reason why the six at the top has no fruits is because it holds an empty basket.

The weak six at the top, at the high point of movement (Chên) and without relationship to a strong line, no longer has a chance of marrying. Hence the attempts at sacrifice are empty and unavailing—the upper trigram symbolizes an empty basket, and the lower trigram Tui has the sheep for its animal.

55. *Fêng / Abundance [Fullness]*

Nuclear trigrams   TUI ☱   *and*   SUN ☴

The ruler of the hexagram is the six in the fifth place. When it is said in the Judgment, "The king attains abundance. Be not sad. Be like the sun at midday," the reference is to this line, for this is the king's place. The line is yielding and in the center —the character of the sun at midday.

The Sequence

That which attains a place in which it is at home is sure to become great. Hence there follows the hexagram of ABUNDANCE. Abundance means greatness.

Miscellaneous Notes

ABUNDANCE means many occasions.

This hexagram is composed of Chên, which strives upward, and Li, which also moves upward. The nuclear trigrams are Tui, the Joyous, the lake, and Sun, the Penetrating, the wind. Hence wind and water, and thunder and lightning, are together here and all this points to great power. Something of a climax is indicated in that Chên, which is the more vigorous in movement, is above. While Shih Ho, BITING THROUGH (21) deals with the problem of surmounting a hindrance, here the hindrance is already surmounted. Still, greatness at a pinnacle suggests the danger of regression. The light is darkened in varying degree by the nuclear trigram Sun, wood, contained within the hexagram. The hexagram is one of those referring

669

to the mutability of all earthly things. This is most likely also the meaning of the saying, "ABUNDANCE means many occasions," that is, occasions for care and sorrow.

THE JUDGMENT

ABUNDANCE has success.
The king attains abundance.
Be not sad.
Be like the sun at midday.

Commentary on the Decision

ABUNDANCE means greatness. Clarity in movement, hence abundance.

"The king attains abundance." In this way greatness is emphasized.

"Be not sad. Be like the sun at midday." One should give light to the whole world.

When the sun stands at midday, it begins to set; when the moon is full, it begins to wane. The fullness and emptiness of heaven and earth wane and wax in the course of time. How much truer is this of men, or of spirits and gods!

Fêng represents a time when clarity and progress bring about greatness and prosperity in public life. To achieve these, there is needed a strong and leading personality, drawing to itself others of like nature. Therefore it is not the relation of correspondence but that of congruity between the lines which must be taken into account (cf. the nine at the beginning and the nine in the fourth place, as well as the six in the second place and the six in the fifth place). But such a time of very great culture also carries hidden dangers. For according to the universal law of events, every increase is followed by decrease, and all fullness is followed by emptiness. There is only one means of making foundations firm in times of greatness, namely, spiritual expansion. Every sort of limitation brings a bitter retribution in its train. Abundance can endure only if ever larger groups are brought to share in it, for only then can the movement continue without turning into its opposite.

THE IMAGE

Both thunder and lightning come:
The image of ABUNDANCE.
Thus the superior man decides lawsuits
And carries out punishments.

The Image is immediately intelligible, especially in association with the hexagram of BITING THROUGH (21). The trigrams Li, clarity, and Chên, shock, terror, give the prerequisites for a clearing of the atmosphere by the thunderstorm of a criminal trial.

THE LINES

Nine at the beginning:

a) When a man meets his destined ruler,
They can be together ten days,
And it is not a mistake.
Going meets with recognition.

b) "They can be together ten days, and it is not a mistake." More than ten days is harmful.

The line is strong and clear. The destined ruler that it meets, and that is of like kind, is the nine in the fourth place. The Chinese word *hsün* means a space of ten days, a complete cycle. Despite the situation in ABUNDANCE, one may spend a full cycle of time with a friend of kindred spirit without fear of making a mistake. One may therefore go unhesitatingly and seek him out, if he is in a high position. Nonetheless, the commentary warns against overstepping this time limit and against clinging to him after completion of the task. This is harmful. One must be able to stop at the right moment especially in times of abundance.

The Sung interpreters take the word *hsün* in the sense of "similar," so that it would be an additional emphasizing of *p'ei*—"of like kind, destined for someone."

Six in the second place:

a) The curtain is of such fullness
That the polestars can be seen at noon.
Through going one meets with mistrust and hate.
If one rouses him through truth,
Good fortune comes.

b) "If one rouses him through truth"—that is, one must
rouse his will through trustworthiness.

The nuclear trigram Sun, wood, darkens the lines it covers, but
the darkening here and as regards the nine in the fourth place
is less marked than in the case of the nine in the third place,
the center, where it is particularly strong. Because this second line
is weak, it meets only with doubt and hatred when it turns
toward the prince who belongs to it, the six in the fifth place,
which is also weak. But since it is central and correct, the
power of inner truth will enable it to overcome the separation
and to arouse the will of the ruler.

Nine in the third place:

a) The underbrush is of such abundance
That the small stars can be seen at noon.
He breaks his right arm. No blame.

b) "The underbrush is of such abundance" that one can
carry out no great transactions.
"He breaks his right arm": in the end, one must not
try to do anything.

Here the darkening is at its height. The nuclear trigram Sun
is joined with the nuclear trigram Tui, lake, which limits the
inherent possibility of accomplishing great things. Tui means
to break. The right arm is denoted by the weak six at the top,
which, in accordance with the relations in this hexagram, is
not to be taken into account as an aid to the strong nine in the
third place. If one refrains from action, recognizing that it is
impossible, one remains blameless.

The word *p'ei*, rendered as "underbrush," means also a

body of water, and the word *mo*, rendered as "small stars," means also foam, drizzle. However, the interpretation given above seems to suit the context better.

Nine in the fourth place:

a) The curtain is of such fullness
That the polestars can be seen at noon.
He meets his ruler, who is of like kind.
Good fortune.

b) "The curtain is of such fullness": the place is not the appropriate one.

"The polestars can be seen at noon." He is dark and not light-giving.

"He meets his ruler, who is of like kind. Good fortune." This means action.

The first sentence here is the same as in the case of the six in the second place; the latter is the beginning and the present line the ending of the nuclear trigram Sun, wood. The place is not appropriate, because this is a hard line in a yielding place. The line is no longer in the trigram Li, hence no longer light-giving by nature. Light is below. However, movement enables it to meet the first line, which is of like kind, i.e., likewise strong. Thus light comes through action (the first line is light, because it is in the trigram Li), and with it good fortune.

O Six in the fifth place:

a) Lines are coming,
Blessing and fame draw near.
Good fortune.

b) The good fortune of the six in the fifth place comes from the fact that it bestows blessing.

This line is related to the six in the second place. In the latter case the expression is "going," here it is "coming." The lines are the light, clear force just approaching by reason of the trigram Li, light—whose central line is the six in the second place—and thus making possible blessing and fame.

Six at the top:

a) His house is in a state of abundance.
He screens off his family.
He peers through the gate
And no longer perceives anyone.
For three years he sees nothing.
Misfortune.

b) "His house is in a state of abundance." He flutters
about at the border of heaven.
"He peers through the gate and no longer perceives
anyone." He screens himself off.

The weak line at the high point of movement goes too far. Thus
it seems to rise continually higher, but precisely through this
it loses its hold increasingly and moves ever farther from the
light—all the more so as it is itself darkening the nine in the
third place. Hence the six at the top falls into a hopelessly
isolated state, for which it has only itself to blame.

旅

56. *Lü / The Wanderer*

Nuclear trigrams TUI ☱ *and* SUN ☴

The ruler of the hexagram is the six in the fifth place. Therefore it is said in the Commentary on the Decision, "The yielding attains the middle outside," and also, "Keeping still and
adhering to clarity." The fifth line is in the outer trigram; this
symbolizes the wanderer in foreign parts. It is in the middle
place as ruler of the trigram Li; this symbolizes attainment of
the mean and adherence to clarity.

The Sequence

Whatever greatness may exhaust itself upon, this much is certain: it loses its home. Hence there follows the hexagram of THE WANDERER.

Miscellaneous Notes

He who has few friends: this is THE WANDERER.

This hexagram is so organized that the two primary trigrams tend to pull apart. Li, flame, goes upward, Kên, the mountain, presses downward; their union is only temporary. Kên (mountain) is a hostel, Li (fire) is the wanderer who does not tarry there long but must push on. This hexagram is the inverse of the preceding one.

THE JUDGMENT

THE WANDERER. Success through smallness.
Perseverance brings good fortune
To the wanderer.

Commentary on the Decision

"THE WANDERER. Success through smallness": the yielding attains the middle outside and submits to the firm.

Keeping still and adhering to clarity; hence success in small things.

"Perseverance brings good fortune to the wanderer." The meaning of the time of THE WANDERER is truly great.

The ruler of the hexagram is the six in the fifth place. It is yielding, hence it represents reserve and unpretentiousness. It is in the middle, hence it cannot be humiliated, though it is outside, in a strange land. It submits to the strong lines above and below, hence does not provoke misfortune. The lower trigram Kên indicates keeping still, inner reserve, while the upper trigram Li indicates clinging to outside things. A wanderer in a foreign country cannot easily find his proper place, hence it is a great thing to grasp the meaning of the time.

THE IMAGE

Fire on the mountain:
The image of THE WANDERER.
Thus the superior man
Is clear-minded and cautious
In imposing penalties,
And protracts no lawsuits.

Usually, it is a question of criminal cases when clarity and movement come together (hexagrams 21, BITING THROUGH, and 55, ABUNDANCE). Here also we have clarity, in the upper trigram; the calm of the mountain signifies caution in imposing penalties. Dispatch in the settlement of criminal cases is moreover indicated in the mutual relationship of the trigrams. Fire does not linger on the mountain, but passes on rapidly.

THE LINES

Six at the beginning:

a) If the wanderer busies himself with trivial things,
       He draws down misfortune upon himself.

b) "If the wanderer busies himself with trivial things":
       thereby his will is spent, and this is a misfortune.

This is a weak line at the very bottom of the trigram Kên, hence the suggestion of unworthy, trivial things. Kên denotes standing still. The line is far away from the trigram Li, clarity, hence it has no breadth of vision and consumes its will power on trivialities. For this reason its connection with the nine in the third place has not an enlightening but a harmful effect— just as throughout the hexagram, fire is regarded chiefly as a consuming, injurious force.

Six in the second place:

a) The wanderer comes to an inn.
       He has his property with him.
       He wins the steadfastness[1] of a young servant.

_____
1. [Literally, "perseverance."]

b) "He wins the steadfastness of a young servant." This is not a mistake in the end.

This line is yielding and central, in the middle of the trigram Kên, which means door and hut; hence the image of an inn. The nuclear trigram Sun means market and gain; hence, "He has his property with him." The young servant is the six at the beginning.

Nine in the third place:

a) The wanderer's inn burns down.
He loses the steadfastness of his young servant.
Danger.

b) "The wanderer's inn burns down." This is a loss for him personally.
If he deals like a stranger with his subordinate, it is only right that he should lose him.

The line is too hard, since it is hard in a strong place. Hence it does not show devotion to its superior, therefore the latter does not help it, and its dwelling burns down. Owing to its hardness, it is unfriendly toward its subordinates and so loses their loyal affection, which naturally means danger. The line is at the top of the trigram Kên, meaning hut, and Li, fire, is immediately above it, hence the idea of the hut burning down. The servant is the six at the beginning.

Nine in the fourth place:

a) The wanderer rests in a shelter.
He obtains his property and an ax.
My heart is not glad.

b) "The wanderer rests in a shelter." He has not yet obtained his place.
"He obtains his property and an ax." But he is not yet glad at heart.

The shelter is only temporary, because the line is outside the trigram Kên. It rests only briefly, because it has not yet reached

677

its true place (the line is strong, the place is weak). Although it has property, it also needs an ax for defense (Li means weapons, and the nuclear trigram Tui means both metal and injury). Hence it is not yet glad at heart.

○　Six in the fifth place:

a)　He shoots a pheasant.

It drops with the first arrow.

In the end this brings both praise and office.

b)　In the end he rises through praise and office.

This line, which is yielding, and in the central place outside,[2] is the wanderer. Being central and devoted, it succeeds in gaining friends below (the nine in the fourth place) and an official position above (nine at the top); thus it rises.

The trigram Li denotes pheasant and weapons. The nuclear trigram Tui is metal, hence the idea of shooting. Tui is also the mouth, hence praise.

Chu Hsi interprets the second sentence as follows: "An arrow is lost." Grammatically this version is of course also possible.

Nine at the top:

a)　The bird's nest burns up.

The wanderer laughs at first,

Then must needs lament and weep.

Through carelessness he loses his cow.

Misfortune.

b)　Being at the top as a wanderer rightly leads to being burnt up.

"Through carelessness he loses his cow." In the end he hears nothing.

The strong line at the top, whose movement moreover tends upward, loses its foundations. Thus all gaiety leads only to losses, because the line neglects all too much the duties of a wanderer, and even injury does not make it the wiser.

---

2. [In the outer trigram Li.]

Li is bird and also flame. The place is high up, over the nuclear trigram Sun, hence the image of a nest. The idea of laughing derives from the nuclear trigram Tui, meaning gaiety and mouth. The idea of lamenting derives from the destructive force lurking in Tui. Li is cow; it is lost because of gaiety and carelessness in a high place. There is no hope for this line; it never comes to its senses, because it merely goes on striving further upward, giving no thought at all to return.

巽

57. *Sun* / *The Gentle* (*The Penetrating, Wind*)

Nuclear trigrams LI and TUI

Although this hexagram is conditioned by the two yin lines, there is only one feminine hexagram, namely Li, THE CLING-ING, in which the yin lines are the rulers. They are rulers because they occupy middle places. The two yin lines here are the constituting rulers of the hexagram but cannot be re-garded as the governing rulers. The governing ruler is rather the nine in the fifth place, for only one who is in an honored place can "spread his commands abroad and carry out his undertakings." When therefore it is said in the Commentary on the Decision, "The firm penetrates to the middle and to the correct, and its will is done," the reference is to the fifth line.

The Sequence

The wanderer has nothing that might receive him; hence there follows the hexagram of THE GENTLE, THE PENETRATING. The Gentle means going into.

This means that the wanderer in his forlornness has no place to stay in, and that hence there follows Sun, the hexagram of homecoming.

Miscellaneous Notes

THE GENTLE means crouching.

The dark line is below, it crouches down beneath the light lines, and through this gentle crouching succeeds in penetrating among the strong lines.

Appended Judgments

THE GENTLE shows the exercise of character. Through THE GENTLE one is able to weigh things and remain hidden. Through THE GENTLE one is able to take special circumstances into account.

Gentle penetration makes the character capable of influencing the outside world and gaining control over it. For thus one can understand things in their inner nature without having to step into the forefront oneself. Herein lies the power of influence. In this position, one is able to make the exceptions demanded by the time, without being inconsistent.

Among the eight trigrams, Sun occupies the southeast, between spring and summer. It means the flowing of beings into their forms, it means baptism and giving life.

THE JUDGMENT

THE GENTLE. Success through what is small.

It furthers one to have somewhere to go.

It furthers one to see the great man.

Commentary on the Decision

Penetration repeated, in order to spread commands abroad.

The firm penetrates to the middle and to the correct, and its will is done.

Both of the yielding lines submit to the strong; therefore it is said: "Success through what is small. It furthers one to have somewhere to go. It furthers one to see the great man."

This hexagram is constituted by a doubling of the trigram Sun, which means on the one hand gentleness, adaptability, on the other penetration. In the issuing of commands, it is all-important that they really penetrate the consciousness of the subordinates. This is effected by adaptation of the commands to their understanding. A twofold penetration is required: first penetration of a command to the feeling of the vassals, scattering the evil hidden in secret recesses, as the wind scatters clouds; second, a still deeper penetration, to the depths of consciousness, where the hidden good must be awakened. To obtain this effect, commands must be given repetitively.[1]

The text is further explained in the light of the structure of the hexagram. The strong line that has penetrated to the center—the correct place for it—is the nine in the fifth place; therefore its will is done, and it is favorable to undertake something. The yielding lines in the first and the fourth place obey the firm ruler of the hexagram above them. Hence success is connected with the small, which is furthered by seeing the great man (the nine in the fifth place).

THE IMAGE

Winds following one upon the other:
The image of THE GENTLY PENETRATING.
Thus the superior man
Spreads his commands abroad
And carries out his undertakings.

Of the two winds the first disperses resistances, "spreads his commands abroad," and the second accomplishes the work, "carries out his undertakings."

THE LINES

☐ Six at the beginning:

a) In advancing and in retreating,
The perseverance of a warrior furthers.

---

1. Cf. the modern theories on the nature of suggestion.

b) "In advancing and in retreating": the will wavers.
"The perseverance of a warrior furthers." The will is
controlled.

This line is yielding and at the very bottom of the hexagram
of THE GENTLE, hence the indecision. But in subordinating
itself to the strong line over it, it is sustained by military
discipline.

Nine in the second place:

a) Penetration under the bed.
Priests and magicians are used in great number.
Good fortune. No blame.

b) The good fortune of the great number is due to the
fact that one has attained the middle.

The line is strong but central, hence indicates good fortune.
The trigram Sun means wood, and the divided line below
stands for legs; hence the image of a bed. The nuclear trigram
Tui means mouth and magician. By submitting to the strong
ruler of the hexagram, who is of like kind, the line is able to
aid the ruler in spreading his commands, because it penetrates
to the most secret corners. Priests are the intermediaries between men and gods; magicians serve as the intermediaries
between gods and men. Here we have penetration of the
realms of the visible and the invisible, whereby it becomes
possible for everything to be set right.

Nine in the third place:

a) Repeated penetration. Humiliation.

b) The humiliation of repeated penetration comes from
the fact that the will exhausts itself.

The third place is intermediate in the relation of the two Sun
trigrams: one trigram is at its close, the other just beginning;
hence penetration repeated. The nine in the third place is too
hard and not central. Although this character is not suitable
for gentle penetration to the core of things, it is attempted
nonetheless. No result is achieved. Everything remains in a
state of irresolute vacillation.

☐ Six in the fourth place:

a) Remorse vanishes.
During the hunt
Three kinds of game are caught.

b) "During the hunt three kinds of game are caught."
This is meritorious.

The nuclear trigram Li means weapons, hence the hunt. The six in the fourth place is correct, submits to the ruler, and brings the three lower lines to him. In this way it acquires merit, and averts the remorse that might be occasioned by too much weakness.

○ Nine in the fifth place:

a) Perseverance brings good fortune.
Remorse vanishes.
Nothing that does not further.
No beginning, but an end.
Before the change, three days.
After the change, three days.
Good fortune.

b) The good fortune of the nine in the fifth place inheres in the fact that the place is correct and central.

This line, the ruler of the hexagram, is central in the upper trigram; hence it is the source of that influencing through commands which is the characteristic action of the hexagram. In contrast to the situation in Ku, WORK ON WHAT HAS BEEN SPOILED (18), where it is question of compensating for what the father and mother have spoiled, it is work on public matters that is described here. Such work is characterized not so much by love that covers up defects as by impartial justice, as symbolized by the west (metal, autumn), with which the eighth cyclic sign, Kêng[2] (rendered as "change"), is associated.

---

2. [For a discussion of the cyclic signs or time divisions, see p. 478. There this sign is listed as the seventh, therefore "eighth" must be assumed to be a slip.]

In order to enforce commands, it is necessary first to abandon a wrong beginning, then to attain the good end; hence the saying: "No beginning, but an end." This saying is elaborated in the words: "Before the sign Kêng, three days. After the sign Kêng, three days." The problem turns therefore on a decisive elimination of something that has developed as a wrong beginning. Three "days" before Kêng the summer draws to a close; then comes its end. Three "days" after Kêng comes winter, the end of the year. Therefore, although one has not achieved a beginning, at least the end is attainable. (This situation differs from that in hexagram 18, Ku, which lies in the middle between end and beginning.)

Nine at the top:

a) Penetration under the bed.
He loses his property and his ax.
Perseverance brings misfortune.

b) "Penetration under the bed." At the top, the end has come.
"He loses his property and his ax." Is this right? It brings misfortune.

By penetration under the bed, the second line establishes connection between what is above and what is below, and so sets everything in order. Here, however, the penetration signifies merely dependence and instability. Thus the line loses what it possesses of firmness (the line, strong in itself, loses its strength because it is at the top of the hexagram of gentleness), together with its ax (the nuclear trigram Tui means metal), so that it is no longer capable of any decision. Persistence in this attitude is definitely harmful.

兑

58. *Tui / The Joyous, Lake*

☱ *Nuclear trigrams* SUN ☴ *and* LI ☲

The two yin lines are the constituting rulers of the hexagram but are incapable of acting as governing rulers. The second and the fifth line are the governing rulers. Therefore it is said in the Commentary on the Decision: "The firm is in the middle, the yielding is without. Joyousness and perseverance further."

The Sequence

When one has penetrated something, one rejoices. Hence there follows the hexagram of THE JOYOUS. The Joyous means to rejoice.

Miscellaneous Notes

THE JOYOUS is manifest.

Tui is the lake, which rejoices and refreshes all living things. Furthermore, Tui is the mouth. When human beings give joy to one another through their feelings, it is manifested by the mouth. A yin line becomes manifest above two yang lines; this indicates how these two principles give joy to each other and how this becomes manifest outwardly. On the other hand Tui is linked with the west and with autumn. Its "stage of change"[1] is metal. The cutting and destroying quality is the other side of its meaning. This hexagram is the inverse of the preceding one.

1. [See p. 309.]

THE JUDGMENT

THE JOYOUS. Success.
Perseverance is favorable.

Commentary on the Decision

THE JOYOUS means pleasure. The firm is in the
middle, the yielding is without. To be joyous—and
with this to have perseverance—furthers; thus does
one submit to heaven and accord with men.

When one leads the way for the people joyously,
they forget their drudgery; when one confronts difficulty joyously, the people forget death. The greatest
thing in making the people joyous is that they keep
one another in order.[2]

The firm in the middle are the two lines in the second and the
fifth place, while the yielding without are the six in the third
place and the six at the top. That is the right kind of joy which
is inwardly firm and outwardly gentle. This joy is also the
best means of government.

THE IMAGE

Lakes resting one on the other:
The image of THE JOYOUS.
Thus the superior man joins with his friends
For discussion and practice.

Tui means lake, also mouth. The repetition of mouth means
general discussion, the repetition of lake means practice.

THE LINES

Nine at the beginning:

a) Contented joyousness. Good fortune.

b) The good fortune of contented joyousness lies in the
fact that one's way has not yet become doubtful.

---

2. [Another possible rendering here is "encourage one another."]

Firmness and modesty are the prerequisites of harmonious joy. Both are fulfilled in this strong line in a lowly place. When the light principle is bound to the shadowy, there are many doubts and scruples that interfere with joyousness. The line at the beginning is still far from all such complications, hence sure of good fortune.

○ Nine in the second place:

a) Sincere joyousness. Good fortune.
Remorse disappears.

b) The good fortune of sincere joyousness consists in having faith in one's own will.

This line is in close relationship with the dark third line, hence doubt and remorse could set in. However, because it is central and firm, the sincerity of its nature and of its position prove stronger than the relationship. It trusts itself, is sincere toward others, and therefore meets with belief.

□ Six in the third place:

a) Coming joyousness. Misfortune.

b) The misfortune of coming joyousness lies in the fact that its place is not the proper one.

A weak line in a strong place, at the high point of joyousness— here control is lacking. When a man is open to distractions from without, they stream toward him and force their way in. Misfortune is certain, because he allows himself to be overwhelmed by the pleasures he has attracted.

Nine in the fourth place:

a) Joyousness that is weighed is not at peace.
After ridding himself of mistakes a man has joy.

b) The joy of the nine in the fourth place brings blessing.

This line holds the middle between the strong ruler, the nine in the fifth place, with which it has a relationship of receiving, and the yielding six in the third place, which is in the relationship of holding together with it and is trying to seduce it. Although the person represented has still not altogether attained peace in this situation, he possesses enough inner strength both to decide whom he wishes to follow and to sever the relation with the six in the third place. From this, good fortune and blessing result both for him and for others.

○   Nine in the fifth place:

a) Sincerity toward disintegrating influences is dangerous.

b) "Sincerity toward disintegrating influences": the place is correct and appropriate.

The disintegrating influences are represented by the six at the top. The nine in the fifth place, which is strong and correct, is inclined to place confidence in the line above. This is dangerous. However, the danger is avoidable, because by nature and position the present line is strong enough to overcome these influences.

☐   Six at the top:

a) Seductive joyousness.

b) The reason why the six at the top seduces to pleasure is that it is not bright.

This line is similar to the six in the third place. But while the latter is in the inner trigram and draws pleasures to itself through its desire, the six at the top is in the outer trigram and tempts others to pleasure. "Seductive joyousness" does not pertain to the person consulting the oracle but shows a situation confronting him. It rests with him whether he will let himself be seduced. It is, however, important to be on one's guard in face of such dubious situations.

There is a somewhat different interpretation for the *a* text, likewise based upon the Chinese literature on the *I Ching*.

汉

59. *Huan / Dispersion [Dissolution]*

Nuclear trigrams KÊN ☶ *and* CHÊN ☳

The ruler of the hexagram is the nine in the fifth place, because only a person occupying an honored place can bring
order into world-wide dispersion. However, the nine in the
second place is within, in order to strengthen the foundations,
and the six in the fourth place is in the relationship of receiving
to the nine in the fifth place, in order to complete the work of
the latter. Consequently these two lines also have important
functions within the hexagram. This is why it is said in the
Commentary on the Decision: "The firm comes and does not
exhaust itself. The yielding receives a place without, and the
one above is in harmony with it."

The Sequence

After joy comes dispersal. Hence there follows the
hexagram of DISPERSION. Dispersion means scattering.

Miscellaneous Notes

DISPERSION means scattering.

Appended Judgments

They scooped out tree trunks for boats and they
hardened wood in the fire to make oars. The advantage of boats and oars lay in providing means of
communication. They probably took this from the
hexagram of DISPERSION.

This hexagram has a double meaning. The first is suggested by the image of wind over water, indicating the breaking up of ice and rigidity. The second meaning is penetration; Sun penetrates into K'an, the Abysmal, indicating dispersion, division. As against this process of breaking up, the task of reuniting presents itself; this meaning also is contained in the hexagram.

The image of wood over water gives rise to the idea of a boat.

THE JUDGMENT

DISPERSION. Success.

The king approaches his temple.

It furthers one to cross the great water.

Perseverance furthers.

Commentary on the Decision

"DISPERSION. Success." The firm comes and does not exhaust itself. The yielding receives a place without, and the one above is in harmony with it.

"The king approaches his temple." The king is in the middle.

"It furthers one to cross the great water." To rely on wood is productive of merit.

"Comes" refers to position within the inner, i.e., lower trigram, while "goes" refers to position in the outer, i.e., upper trigram. The firm element that comes is therefore the nine in the second place. Occupying the middle place in the lower trigram, it creates for the light principle placed in the midst of dark lines a basis of activity as inexhaustible as water (K'an). The yielding line that receives a place without and acts in harmony with the one above is the six in the fourth place, the minister. The action connoted by the hexagram is based upon the reciprocal relationships between the three lines in the fifth, the fourth, and the second place.

The king in the middle is the nine in the fifth place. His central position denotes the inner concentration that enables him to hold together the elements striving to break asunder.

The temple is suggested by the upper nuclear trigram Kên, mountain, house. The idea of crossing the great water derives from Sun (wood) and K'an (water).

THE IMAGE

The wind drives over the water:
The image of DISPERSION.
Thus the kings of old sacrificed to the Lord
And built temples.

This again indicates an inward striving to hold together, through the fostering of religion, elements outwardly falling asunder. The task is to preserve the connection between God and man and between the ancestors and their posterity. Here likewise the image of the temple is suggested by the nuclear trigram Kên. Finally, the idea of entering is suggested by Sun, and the idea of the dark by K'an.

THE LINES

Six at the beginning:

a) He brings help with the strength of a horse.
Good fortune.

b) The good fortune of the six at the beginning is based on its devotion.

The strong horse is the nine in the second place. K'an means a strong horse with a beautiful back. The six at the beginning is weak and in a lowly place, and does not itself possess the strength to stop the dissolution. But since the line is only at the beginning of the dissolution, its rescue is relatively easy. The strong, central nine in the second place comes to its aid, and the six submits and joins with it in service to the ruler in the fifth place.

☐ Nine in the second place:

a) At the dissolution
He hurries to that which supports him.
Remorse disappears.

b) "At the dissolution, he hurries to that which supports him" and thus attains what he wishes.

The nuclear trigram Chên means foot and rapid running. The support upon which this line can count is that of the like-minded strong ruler, the nine in the fifth place. Because the man represented by the nine in the second place seeks out the prince on his own initiative, it might be surmised that he would have occasion to regret it. But he is strong and central, and his unusual behavior is caused by the unusual time. He does not act from egotistic motives, but wishes to put a stop to the dissolution, and this he finally achieves in fellowship with the nine in the fifth place.

Six in the third place:

a) He dissolves his self. No remorse.

b) "He dissolves his self." His will is directed outward.

This is a weak line in a strong place, hence remorse could be expected. But it is the only line of the inner trigram that stands in the relationship of correspondence to a line of the outer trigram. Hence its will is directed outward. At the top of the trigram of water, it is in direct contact with the trigram of wind, hence the idea of dissolution in connection with one's own self, and, consequently, the absence of remorse.

☐ Six in the fourth place:

a) He dissolves his bond with his group.
   Supreme good fortune.
   Dispersion leads in turn to accumulation.
   This is something that ordinary men do not think of.

b) "He dissolves his bond with his group. Supreme good fortune." His light is great.

The lower trigram is to be regarded as a transformed K'un. K'un denotes a group of people. In that its middle line has detached itself and moved into the fourth place, it has dissolved its bond with its group and dissolved the group, for its place is now taken by the strong nine in the second place.

Thus through dispersion there comes accumulation (nuclear trigram Kên, mountain). This yielding line, the six in the fourth place, stands in the relationship of receiving to the ruler, the nine in the fifth place, and has won the strong official, the nine in the second place, as its assistant, so that accumulation does in fact follow upon dispersion.

○ Nine in the fifth place:

a) His loud cries are as dissolving as sweat.
    Dissolution! A king abides without blame.

b) "A king abides without blame." He is in his proper place.

Wind meeting water dissolves it as sweat is dissolved.[1] The trigram Sun, wind, which reaches everywhere, signifies loud cries. The king is in his proper place, hence without blame.

    Nine at the top:

a) He dissolves his blood.
    Departing, keeping at a distance, going out,
    Is without blame.

b) "He dissolves his blood." Thus he keeps at a distance from injury.

K'an is blood. Wind dissolves. Thus occasion for bloodshed is removed. Not only does the line itself surmount the peril, but it also helps the six in the third place, to which it is related.

---

1. [See the explanation of this line on p. 230.]

節

60. *Chieh / Limitation*

☷ *Nuclear trigrams* KÊN ☶ *and* CHÊN ☳

The ruler of the hexagram is the nine in the fifth place. Only a man who is honored, and who possesses the necessary spiritual power for the task, can establish measure and mean for holding the world within bounds. Hence it is said in the Commentary on the Decision: "In the appropriate place, in order to limit; central and correct, in order to unite."

The Sequence

Things cannot be forever separate. Hence there follows the hexagram of LIMITATION.

Miscellaneous Notes

LIMITATION means stopping.

This hexagram is the inverse of the preceding one, but the inner structure and the interrelationships of the nuclear trigrams are the same in both. Here water is held together by the lake, while in the preceding hexagram water is dispersed by the wind.

THE JUDGMENT

LIMITATION. Success.
Galling limitation must not be persevered in.

Commentary on the Decision

"LIMITATION. Success." The firm and the yielding are
equally divided, and the firm have attained the
middle places.

"Galling limitation must not be persevered in,"
because its way comes to an end.

Joyous in passing through danger; in the appropriate place, in order to limit; central and correct, in
order to unite.

Heaven and earth have their limitations, and the
four seasons of the year arise.

Where limitation is applied in the creation of
institutions, property is not encroached upon, and
people are not harmed.

There are three yang lines and three yin lines symmetrically
distributed—first two yang lines, then two yin lines, then one
of each. Hence there are strong lines in the two central places,
the second and the fifth.

To persist in galling limitation would lead to failure. But
owing to the central and moderate behavior of the ruler of
the hexagram, the nine in the fifth place, this danger is overcome. Joyousness is the attribute of the lower trigram Tui, and
danger that of the upper trigram K'an. The limitation of the
ruler of the hexagram is brought about by the two yin lines
between which it stands. But owing to its central and correct
position, it attains an all-pervading influence.

Limitation—division into periods—is the means of dividing
time. Thus in China the year is divided into twenty-four
chieh ch'i, which, being in harmony with atmospheric phenomena, make it possible for man to arrange his agricultural
activities so that they harmonize with the course of the
seasons. The limitation or suitable division of production and
consumption was one of the most important problems of good
government in ancient China. Fundamental principles pertaining to this problem are also indicated in the present hexagram.

THE IMAGE

Water over lake: the image of LIMITATION.
Thus the superior man
Creates number and measure,
And examines the nature of virtue and correct con-
    duct.

The idea of number and measure is indicated by the reciprocal relationship between water and lake. Creating corresponds with the trigram K'an, and examining, literally "discussing," corresponds with the trigram Tui, mouth. The idea of number and measure—the resting, firm—corresponds with the upper nuclear trigram Kên. The idea of virtue and conduct—the mobile, active—corresponds with the lower nuclear trigram Chên.

THE LINES

Nine at the beginning:

a) Not going out of the door and the courtyard
    Is without blame.

b) "Not going out of the door and the courtyard" is a
    sign that one knows what is open and what is closed.

This line stands at the very beginning. Kên, the nuclear trigram above, means gate, and we are still far away from it; we are not yet concerned with the outer double gate, but only with the inner single door. We see locked doors ahead and therefore hold back. Not going out of the door and the courtyard indicates discretion, essential in beginning any work that is to succeed.

Nine in the second place:

a) Not going out of the gate and the courtyard
    Brings misfortune.

b) "Not going out of the gate and the courtyard brings
    misfortune," because one misses the crucial moment.

Here the situation is different. Before us are two divided lines imaging an open double courtyard gate. It is now high time to go forth and not to hold back selfishly with the hoarded provisions (the nuclear trigram Chên, which begins with this line, indicates movement, therefore hesitation brings misfortune).

Six in the third place:

a) He who knows no limitation
Will have cause to lament.
No blame.

b) Lament over neglect of limitation—who is to blame for this?

The six in the third place is weak and stands at the top of the trigram Tui, joyousness; it therefore neglects necessary limitation. The trigram Tui means mouth, the nuclear trigram Chên means fear, and K'an means mourning, hence the idea of lament. But one has oneself to blame for this result.

Six in the fourth place:

a) Contented limitation. Success.

b) The success of contented limitation comes from accepting the way of the one above.

This correct, yielding line is in the relationship of receiving to the ruler. It adapts itself contentedly to its position, hence gains success by joining with the line above, the nine in the fifth place, which it follows.

○ Nine in the fifth place:

a) Sweet limitation brings good fortune.
Going brings esteem.

b) The good fortune of sweet limitation comes from remaining central in one's own place.

The central, strong, and correct attitude of the ruler of the hexagram makes even holding back easy for it (it is at the top of the nuclear trigram Kên), and by its example it makes limitation sweet for the others. The mountain, Kên, is composed chiefly of earth, the taste of which is sweet.

Six at the top:

a) Galling limitation.
Perseverance brings misfortune.
Remorse disappears.

b) "Galling limitation. Perseverance brings misfortune." Its way comes to an end.

Here at the end of the time of LIMITATION one should not attempt forcibly to continue limitation. This line is weak and at the top of the trigram K'an, danger. Anything attempted here by force has a galling effect and cannot be continued. Hence a new direction must be taken, and thereupon remorse will disappear.

中孚

61. *Chung Fu / Inner Truth*

Nuclear trigrams KÊN ☶ *and* CHÊN ☳

The center of this hexagram is empty: this is its determining feature. Therefore the six in the third place and the six in the fourth place are the constituting rulers of the hexagram. However, truth depends in another aspect on the fact that the center has substance; therefore the nine in the second place and the nine in the fifth place are the governing rulers. Since, furthermore, the basic idea is that a whole realm is transformed by the strength of inner truth, the place of honor is necessary for this undertaking. Hence the actual ruler of the hexagram is the nine in the fifth place.

The Sequence

Through being limited, things are made dependable. Hence there follows the hexagram of INNER TRUTH.

Miscellaneous Notes

INNER TRUTH means dependability.

This hexagram, like the two that precede it, has a closed-off inner structure; it differs from them in the fact that its two outermost lines are strong. The eldest and the youngest daughter are together here in their appropriate positions, hence mutual trust is not disturbed. The attributes of the trigrams are well harmonized: gentleness is above, joyousness below, and the nuclear trigrams are rest and movement. Moreover, the entire structure of the hexagram is very harmonious and symmetrical: the yielding lines are within and the firm without. These are all highly favorable circumstances; therefore a highly favorable judgment goes with the hexagram.

THE JUDGMENT

INNER TRUTH. Pigs and fishes.
Good fortune.
It furthers one to cross the great water.
Perseverance furthers.

Commentary on the Decision

INNER TRUTH. The yielding are within, yet the strong hold the middle. Joyous and gentle: thereby truly the country is transformed.

"Pigs and fishes. Good fortune." The power of trust extends even to pigs and fishes.

"It furthers one to cross the great water." One makes use of the hollow of a wooden boat. Inner truth, and perseverance to further one: thus man is in accord with heaven.

The yielding within are the third and the fourth line. The strong in the middle in the two trigrams are the second and the fifth line. The yielding lines in the middle of the hexagram create an empty space. This emptiness of heart, this humility, is necessary to attract what is good. However, central firmness and strength are needed to assure the essential trustworthiness. Thus the foundation on which the hexagram is built is an intermingling of yieldingness and strength.

Joyousness and gentleness are the attributes of the two primary trigrams: Tui means joyousness in following the good, and Sun means penetration into the hearts of men. Thus one establishes the foundation of trust that is necessary in transforming a country.

Pigs and fishes are the least intelligent of all creatures. When even such creatures are influenced, it shows the great power of truth.[1] Wood and water, wood and a hollowed cavity, are interpreted as the image of a boat with which the great stream can be crossed.

THE IMAGE

Wind over lake: the image of INNER TRUTH.
Thus the superior man discusses criminal cases
In order to delay executions.

Tui is the image of the mouth—hence discussion. Sun is the Gentle, the hesitating—hence delay of executions. In other hexagrams, Sun also means commands. Killing and judging are attributes of Tui.[2]

---

1. The *Chou I Hêng Chieh* [see p. 665, n. 4] gives another interpretation. There the two words are read together as meaning pig-fishes, i.e., dolphins: "Dolphins originate in the ocean (Tui) and warn boats (Sun) when a wind is coming up. They are reliable harbingers of storm, hence the symbol of inner truth. The approaching wind is heralded by definite signs, causing the dolphins to rise to the surface. Thus inner truth is the means of understanding the future."

The idea is very ingenious, except for the fact that the Book of Changes goes back to a time when the ocean was still unknown to the Chinese.

2. [As the symbol of the west and of autumn, the place and time of death.]

THE LINES

Nine at the beginning:

a) Being prepared brings good fortune.
    If there are secret designs, it is disquieting.

b) The preparedness of the nine at the beginning
    brings good fortune: the will has not yet changed.

The character translated as "prepared" originally meant the
sacrifice offered on the day after a funeral, and from this it
acquires the meaning of preparation. The character *yen*,
"quiet" (in "disquieting"), really means the swallow, but
from ancient times on it has also been used in combinations in
the sense of *an*, "quiet." This line is strong and dependable,
inwardly serene and prepared. Its will is not influenced from
without. Secret designs are suggested by its relationship of
correspondence to the six in the fourth place. But in the
hexagram of INNER TRUTH no secret exclusive relationships
should occur.

Nine in the second place:

a) A crane calling in the shade.
    Its young answers it.
    I have a good goblet.
    I will share it with you.

b) "Its young answers it": this is the affection of the in-
    most heart.

The crane is a lake bird whose cry is heard in the autumn.
Tui means lake and autumn. The nuclear trigram Chên denotes inclination to call, hence the image of a calling crane.
It is under the nuclear trigram Kên, mountain, in the shadow
of two yin lines, in the middle of Tui, the lake, hence "in the
shade." Its son is the nine at the beginning, which is of like
kind and belongs to the same body (the lower trigram). According to another interpretation, its relationship is with the
nine in the fifth place. This suggestion—of influence at a
distance—gains added weight from the explanation given by

Confucius (cf. pp. 237–38). Goblet and drinking are derived from Tui, mouth.

☐ Six in the third place:

a) He finds a comrade.
   Now he beats the drum, now he stops.
   Now he sobs, now he sings.

b) "Now he beats the drum, now he stops." The place is
   not appropriate.

A yielding line in a firm place at the high point of joyousness suggests a lack of self-control. The line is attracted by the nine at the top but finds no footing there, because attractions are contrary to the spirit of the hexagram. It also fails to attach itself to the neighboring six in the fourth place (no doubt the comrade referred to), which is of like kind.

Drumming in ancient China was the signal for advance; a retreat, or cessation of an attack, was indicated by the striking of a metal gong. This line stands in the two nuclear trigrams Chên (the Arousing) and Kên (Keeping Still). The alternation of sobbing and laughing is derived from the primary trigram Tui and the nuclear trigram Chên.

☐ Six in the fourth place:

a) The moon nearly at the full.
   The team horse goes astray.
   No blame.

b) "The team horse goes astray." It separates from its
   kind and turns upward.

The team horse is the six in the third place. But the fact that there is similarity in kind has no determining effect. The line is correct in its place and has a receiving relationship to the ruler of the hexagram, the nine in the fifth place, whom it serves as minister. Hence the turning away from its mate of like kind toward what is above.

○ Nine in the fifth place:

a) He possesses truth, which links together.
   No blame.

b) "He possesses truth, which links together." The place
is correct and appropriate.

The image of linking together derives from the meaning of
the upper trigram Sun, rope, and that of the upper nuclear
trigram Kên, hand. For the rest, the influence of this line as
ruler of the hexagram is shown by the correct, central, and
honored position it occupies.

Nine at the top:

a) Cockcrow penetrating to heaven.
Perseverance brings misfortune.

b) "Cockcrow penetrating to heaven." How could such
a one last long?

The cock is associated with the trigram Sun. It wants to fly to
heaven, but that it cannot do. Hence only the cry issues forth
(Sun means a shouting that penetrates everywhere, like the
wind). This means an exaggeration: the expression is stronger
than the feeling. It creates false pathos, because it is not to be
reconciled with inner truth. In the long run misfortune results.
The line is too strong in its exposed position and is therefore no
longer carried by the strength of the hexagram, hence this
misfortune.

小過

62. *Hsiao Kuo / Preponderance of the Small*

Nuclear trigrams TUI and SUN

The rulers of the hexagram are the second and the fifth line,
because they are yielding and hold the middle. They are in a
time when a transition must be made, but without going too far.

The Sequence

When one has the trust of creatures, one sets them in motion; hence there follows the hexagram of PREPONDERANCE OF THE SMALL.

Miscellaneous Notes

PREPONDERANCE OF THE SMALL signifies a transition.

Appended Judgments

The rulers split wood and made a pestle of it. They made a hollow in the ground for a mortar. The use of the mortar and pestle was of benefit to all mankind. They probably took this from the hexagram of PREPONDERANCE OF THE SMALL.

The Chinese word *kuo* cannot be translated in such a way as to render all its secondary meanings. It means to pass by, and then comes the idea of excessiveness, preponderance; in fact, it means everything that results from exceeding the mean. The hexagram deals with transitional states, extraordinary conditions. It is so constructed that the yielding elements are on the outside. When, given such a structure, strong lines predominate, the hexagram of PREPONDERANCE OF THE GREAT (28) results; but when the weak lines are in the majority, we have PREPONDERANCE OF THE SMALL. The nuclear trigrams of the present hexagram produce the same structure as the primary trigrams of hexagram 28. This hexagram is the opposite of the preceding one.

THE JUDGMENT

PREPONDERANCE OF THE SMALL. Success.

Perseverance furthers.

Small things may be done; great things should not be done.

The flying bird brings the message:

It is not well to strive upward,

It is well to remain below.
Great good fortune.

Commentary on the Decision

PREPONDERANCE OF THE SMALL. The small preponderate and have success. To be furthered in transition by perseverance: this means going with the time.

The yielding attains the middle, hence good fortune in small things.

The hard has lost its place and is not in the middle: hence one should not do great things.

The hexagram has the form of a flying bird.

"The flying bird brings the message: It is not well to strive upward, it is well to remain below. Great good fortune." Striving upward is rebellion, striving downward is devotion.

In exceptional times exceptional measures are necessary for re-establishing the norm. The point here is that the time demands a restraint that would appear to be excessive. It is a time like that of King Wên and the tyrant Chou Hsin, and this restraint, which might appear exaggerated, is exactly what the time calls for. Preponderance of the small is indicated by the fact that yielding, i.e., small lines hold the middle places and thus are rulers of the hexagram, while the strong lines have been forced out of key positions outside into places inside, without being central.

PREPONDERANCE OF THE GREAT is like a beam; its danger lies in excessive weight, therefore it must be supported in the middle from below. PREPONDERANCE OF THE SMALL is like a bird; the danger for it lies in mounting too high and losing the ground under its feet.

THE IMAGE

Thunder on the mountain:
The image of PREPONDERANCE OF THE SMALL.

Thus in his conduct the superior man gives preponderance to reverence.

In bereavement he gives preponderance to grief.

In his expenditures he gives preponderance to thrift.

Thunder rising from the plain to the heights becomes gradually fainter in transition. From this is taken the idea of overweighting, of doing a little too much in the right way. For it is precisely by doing a little too much in the direction of the small that we hit the mark as to what is right. It is thus that we attain the right degree of reverence in our conduct, the right degree of mourning at a burial, and the right degree of economy in expenditures. Conduct is suggested by the upper trigram Chên, movement, and burial by the position of the nuclear trigrams—Tui, the lake, over Sun, wood (cf. hexagram 28, in which the idea of burial is likewise represented by this combination). Thrift in spending is suggested by the trigram Kên, mountain, which indicates limitation.

THE LINES

Six at the beginning:

a) The bird meets with misfortune through flying.

b) "The bird meets with misfortune through flying."
Here there is nothing to be done.

This line is in the lowest place in the trigram Kên, mountain. It ought to keep still, but since according to the meaning of the hexagram, the weak preponderates, and since there is a secret relationship between it and the nine in the fourth place, it will not suffer restraint, but seeks to soar like a flying bird. But in doing so it willfully endangers itself; for if a bird flies up when it is time for it to keep still, it is sure to fall into the hands of the hunter.

O   Six in the second place:

a)   She passes by her ancestor
And meets her ancestress.
He does not reach his prince

And meets the official.
No blame.

b) "He does not reach his prince." The official should
not wish to surpass (the prince).

The nine in the third place is the father, the nine in the fourth
place the grandfather, the six in the fifth place the grandmother. Congruity relates the present line to the six in the
fifth place. But because it is presupposed in this hexagram that
the small passes by and surmounts the great, and because
furthermore the six in the fifth place is the ruler of the hexagram, the image of the ancestress is chosen. In another aspect,
the present line represents an official who does not surpass the
yielding prince, the six in the fifth place, because he himself is
yielding in nature. In the nine in the third place he meets with
an official with whom he is united through the relationship of
holding together.

Nine in the third place:

a) If one is not extremely careful,
Somebody may come up from behind and strike him.
Misfortune.

b) "Somebody may come up from behind and strike
him." What a misfortune this is!

This line is strong, it is true, but the six in the second place is in
a more favorable position, because it is not only central but
also a ruler of the hexagram. The nine in the third place, being
at the top of the primary trigram Kên, can guard itself against
unexpected accidents. If it fails to do this, disaster comes from
behind.

Nine in the fourth place:

a) No blame. He meets him without passing by.
Going brings danger. One must be on guard.
Do not act. Be constantly persevering.

b) "He meets him without passing by." The place is not
the appropriate one.

707

"Going brings danger. One must be on guard." One must on no account continue thus.

The strength of the nine in the fourth place is modified by the weakness of the place. It is the place of the minister. He does not seek to surpass his prince but meets him, so that all is well. However, as ruler of the upper trigram Chên, the line is too readily inclined to be drawn into excessive movement, which would be dangerous. Hence the warning against action.

○   Six in the fifth place:

a)   Dense clouds,
No rain from our western territory.
The prince shoots and hits him who is in the cave.

b)   "Dense clouds, no rain": he is already above.

The oracle, "Dense clouds, no rain," appears also in THE TAMING POWER OF THE SMALL (9), which deals with a somewhat similar situation. There, however, it is the strong lines at the top that finally cause the clouds to condense to rain. Here, where the small passes by the great, the six in the fifth place is too high up. There is no strong line above it that could condense the clouds. The upper trigram Tui is the west. It also means metal, hence the image of shooting. The man in the cave is the six in the second place. The word for shooting means shooting with an arrow attached to a line for the purpose of dragging in the game that has been shot. The connection arises from the fact that the present line and the six in the second place are related through similarity of kind.

Six at the top:

a)   He passes him by, not meeting him.
The flying bird leaves him.
Misfortune.
This means bad luck and injury.

b)   "He passes him by, not meeting him." He is already arrogant.

The six at the top really stands in the relationship of correspondence to the nine in the third place, but at a time when
the small passes by the great, this relationship does not apply.
The six at the top is directed upward only. Thus the image of
the bird appears again. In the case of the six at the beginning,
disaster results from impatience; here it comes from the fact
that the line is too high, too arrogant, and unwilling to come
back. As a result, it loses its way, leaves the others, and draws
disaster upon itself from both gods and men.

旣濟

63. *Chi Chi | After Completion*

Nuclear trigrams LI ☲ *and* K'AN ☵

The ruler of the hexagram is the six in the second place. The
hexagram of AFTER COMPLETION means that at first good fortune prevails and in the end disorder. The six in the second
place is in the inner trigram just at the time when good fortune
begins. Therefore it is said in the Commentary on the Decision: " 'At the beginning good fortune'; the yielding has attained the middle."

The Sequence

He who stands above things brings them to completion. Hence there follows the hexagram of AFTER
COMPLETION.

Miscellaneous Notes

AFTER COMPLETION means making firm.

This hexagram is the only one in which all the lines stand in
their proper places. It is the hexagram of transition from T'ai,

PEACE (11) to P'i, STANDSTILL (12). It contains the two primary trigrams K'an, water, and Li, fire, which likewise, in the reverse order, constitute its nuclear trigrams. K'an strives downward and Li upward; hence the outer and the inner organization of the hexagram create a state of equilibrium that is obviously unstable.

THE JUDGMENT

AFTER COMPLETION. Success in small matters.
Perseverance furthers.
At the beginning good fortune,
At the end disorder.

Commentary on the Decision

"AFTER COMPLETION. Success." In small matters there is success.

"Perseverance furthers." The firm and the yielding are correct, and their places are the appropriate ones.

"At the beginning good fortune": the yielding has attained the middle.

If one stands still at the end, disorders arise, because the way comes to an end.

The ruler of the hexagram is the six in the second place; although weak, it has success because it stands in the relationship of correspondence to the strong nine in the fifth place. Perseverance furthers because all the lines are in their appropriate places, and therefore any deviation brings misfortune. At the beginning all goes well, because the yielding six in the second place occupies the middle in the trigram Li, clarity. It is a time of very great cultural development and refinement. But when no further progress is possible, disorder necessarily arises, because the way cannot go on.

THE IMAGE

Water over fire: the image of the condition
In AFTER COMPLETION.

Thus the superior man
Takes thought of misfortune
And arms himself against it in advance.

In one aspect, fire and water counteract each other, whereby an equilibrium is created; in another aspect, however, fear of a collapse is also suggested. If the water escapes, the fire goes out; if the fire flames high, the water dries up. Hence precautionary measures are necessary. The trigram K'an suggests danger and disaster, Li suggests clarity, foresight. The taking thought occurs in the heart, the arming in external actions. The danger still lurks unseen, hence only reflection enables one to perceive it in time and thus avert it.

THE LINES

Nine at the beginning:

a) He brakes his wheels.
   He gets his tail in the water.
   No blame.

b) "He brakes his wheels." According to the meaning, there is no blame in this.

K'an denotes wheel, fox, hindering. The first line is at the rear of the fox, hence the tail. Because it has a connection with the lowest line of the upper primary trigram, K'an, it gets wet. Since the lower nuclear trigram is likewise K'an, the symbols of the fox and the wheel occur here at the very beginning. The possibility of overcoming the danger by holding back firmly arises from the strong nature of the line.

○ Six in the second place:

a) The woman loses the curtain of her carriage.
   Do not run after it;
   On the seventh day you will get it.

b) "On the seventh day you will get it," as a result of the middle way.

The primary trigram Li, in which this is the middle line, is the middle daughter, hence a woman as the symbol. The same idea is suggested by the fact that the line is yielding and in the relationship of correspondence to the husband, the nine in the fifth place. K'an means wagon, Li means curtain. K'an also means robbers, hence the theft of the curtain. "After seven days" means the complete cycle of change in the six lines of the hexagram; at the seventh change the starting point recurs. The line is yielding and stands between two strong lines; it can be compared to a woman who has lost her veil and is consequently exposed to attack. But since she is correct, these attacks do her no harm. She remains true to her husband and also obtains her veil again.

Nine in the third place:

a)   The Illustrious Ancestor
      Disciplines the Devil's Country.
      After three years he conquers it.
      Inferior people must not be employed.

b)   "After three years he conquers it." This is exhausting.

Li means weapons. The Devil's Country is the territory of the Huns in the north. North is the direction of K'an. This line is in the middle of the nuclear trigram K'an. It is a strong line in a strong place. "The Illustrious Ancestor" is the dynastic title of Wu Ting, the emperor who gave a new impetus to the Yin dynasty. The warning against employing inferior people is suggested by the secret relation of this line to the weak six at the top.

Six in the fourth place:

a)   The finest clothes turn to rags.
      Be careful all day long.

b)   "Be careful all day long." There is cause for doubt.

This is a yielding line in a yielding place at the beginning of danger. Hence the warning that even the finest clothes turn to rags. Cause for doubt comes from the trigram K'an, danger, which we enter here.

. Chêng Tzŭ gives another explanation. He employs the

image of a boat, and says: "It has a leak, but there are rags for plugging it up."

Nine in the fifth place:

a) The neighbor in the east who slaughters an ox
Does not attain as much real happiness
As the neighbor in the west
With his small offering.

b) The eastern neighbor, who slaughters an ox, is not as much in harmony with the time as the western neighbor. The latter attains true happiness: good fortune comes in great measure.

Li is the ox. K'an represents the pig slaughtered in the small sacrifice. The second line, which is in the nuclear trigram K'an, is the western neighbor, because in the Sequence of Earlier Heaven, K'an is placed in the west. The fourth line, which is in the nuclear trigram Li, is the eastern neighbor, because Li stands opposite to K'an. The nine in the fifth place presides over the sacrifice. The six in the second place is central; it brings the intrinsically lesser offering of a pig at the right time and therefore has greater happiness than the six in the fourth place, which, though it brings the relatively greater offering of an ox, is not central.

Six at the top:

a) He gets his head in the water. Danger.

b) "He gets his head in the water." How can one endure this for long?

While the nine at the beginning is the tail of the fox, the six at the top is its head. It gets into the water because it is a weak line at the top of K'an, water, danger. While crossing the water it turns back and so incurs the danger of drowning. These are the disorders prophesied by the hexagram as the final outcome.

未濟

64. *Wei Chi / Before Completion*

Nuclear trigrams K'AN ☵ and LI ☲

The ruler of the hexagram is the six in the fifth place, because BEFORE COMPLETION implies a time in which at first disorder prevails, then finally order. The six in the fifth place is in the outer trigram and initiates the time of order. Therefore it is said in the Commentary on the Decision: " 'BEFORE COMPLETION. Success.' For the yielding attains the middle."

The Sequence

Things cannot exhaust themselves. Hence there follows, at the end, the hexagram of BEFORE COMPLETION.

Miscellaneous Notes

BEFORE COMPLETION is the exhaustion of the masculine.

This hexagram is at once the inverse and the opposite of the preceding one. K'an and Li, both as nuclear and as primary trigrams, have changed places. The hexagram depicts the transition from P'i, STANDSTILL (12) to T'ai, PEACE (11). Outwardly viewed, none of the lines appears in its proper place; but they are all in relationship to one another, and order stands preformed within, despite the outward appearance of complete disorder. The strong middle line has come down from the fifth place to the second and has thus established a connection. It

714

is true that K'un is not above nor Ch'ien below, as in the hexagram T'ai, but their representatives, Li and K'an, are in these positions. Li and K'an represent K'un and Ch'ien in spirit and influence (because of their respective middle lines). In the phenomenal world (Sequence of Later Heaven) they are the representatives of K'un and Ch'ien, and stand in the regions of the latter—Li in the south and K'an in the north.

THE JUDGMENT

BEFORE COMPLETION. Success.

But if the little fox, after nearly completing the crossing,

Gets his tail in the water,

There is nothing that would further.

Commentary on the Decision

"BEFORE COMPLETION. Success." For the yielding attains the middle.

"The little fox has nearly completed the crossing": he is not yet past the middle.

"He gets his tail in the water. There is nothing that would further." Because the matter does not go on to the end.

Although the lines are not in their appropriate places, the firm and the yielding nevertheless correspond.

K'an has the fox as its symbol, and also denotes water. There is hope of success because the firm and the weak lines all correspond. The ruler of the hexagram, the six in the fifth place, has reached the middle, and this insures the right attitude for bringing about completion. The nine in the second place, on the other hand, has not yet passed the middle, and in its case this is dangerous. It is a strong line hemmed in between two yin lines. Like the incautious young fox that runs rashly over the ice, it relies too much on its strength. Therefore it gets its tail wet; the crossing does not succeed.

THE IMAGE

Fire over water:
The image of the condition before transition.
Thus the superior man is careful
In the differentiation of things,
So that each finds its place.

Fire flares upward, water flows downward; hence there is no completion. If one were to attempt to force completion, harm would result. Therefore one must separate things in order to unite them. One must put them into their places as carefully as one handles fire and water, so that they do not combat one another.

THE LINES

Six at the beginning:

a) He gets his tail in the water.
Humiliating.

b) "He gets his tail in the water." For he cannot take the end into view.

Here we have the same images as in the preceding hexagram, though somewhat differently distributed. The first line is the tail. It is weak and stands at the bottom in a dangerous position, hence does not perceive the consequences of its actions. It rashly tries to cross and fails.

Nine in the second place:

a) He brakes his wheels.
Perseverance brings good fortune.

b) The nine in the second place has good fortune if it is persevering. It is central and hence acts correctly.

Here the image of the wheel and of braking, which in the preceding hexagram is associated with the first line in virtue of its strength, is transferred to the strong second line. The strength and correctness of the latter make the outlook favorable.

Six in the third place:

a) Before completion, attack brings misfortune.
It furthers one to cross the great water.

b) "Before completion, attack brings misfortune." The
place is not the appropriate one.

The place is at the end of the lower primary trigram K'an,
danger, so that completion would be possible. But since the
line is too weak for this decisive position, and since it stands at
the beginning of the nuclear trigram K'an, a new danger
arises. One should not attempt to force completion but should
try to get clear of the whole situation. A change of character is
necessary. Owing to the fact that the line changes from a six
into a nine, the trigram Sun develops below; this, together
with the primary trigram K'an, results in the image of a boat
over water, hence the crossing of the great water.

Nine in the fourth place:

a) Perseverance brings good fortune.
Remorse disappears.
Shock, thus to discipline the Devil's Country.
For three years, great realms are awarded.

b) "Perseverance brings good fortune. Remorse disappears." What is willed is done.

As this hexagram is the inverse of the preceding one, the
disciplining of the Devil's Country, there mentioned in connection with the third place, appears here in connection with
the fourth. Here the result is more favorable—there three
years of fighting, here three years of rewards. The present line
is a strong official who assists the gentle ruler in the fifth place
and therefore carries out his will.

O Six in the fifth place:

a) Perseverance brings good fortune.
No remorse.
The light of the superior man is true.
Good fortune.

b) "The light of the superior man is true." His light
   brings good fortune.

This line is in the middle of the trigram Li, light, hence everything is favorable for accomplishing the transition to a new
period.

   Nine at the top:

a)   There is drinking of wine
      In genuine confidence. No blame.
      But if one wets his head,
      He loses it, in truth.

b)   When one wets his head while drinking wine, it is
      because he knows no moderation.

The top line is strong and inherently favorable. The image of
wine comes from the trigram K'an; the present line is in
relationship with the top line of K'an. As in the preceding
hexagram, the image of a head-wetting occurs. But here it is
only a possibility, an avoidable danger.

Thus at its close the Book of Changes leaves the situation
open for new beginnings and new formations. The same idea
indeed finds expression in the *Tsa Kua*, Miscellaneous Notes
on the Hexagrams, in which Kuai, BREAK-THROUGH (43), is
placed at the end, with these closing words:

> BREAK-THROUGH means resoluteness. The strong
> turns resolutely against the weak. The way of the
> superior man is in the ascendant, the way of the
> inferior man leads to grief.

APPENDIXES

I. On Consulting the Oracle

1. THE YARROW-STALK ORACLE

The oracle is consulted with the help of yarrow stalks. Fifty stalks are used for this purpose. One is put aside and plays no further part. The remaining 49 stalks are first divided into two heaps [at random]. Thereupon one stalk is taken from the right-hand heap and put between the ring finger and the little finger of the left hand. Then the left-hand heap is placed in the left hand, and the right hand takes from it bundles of 4, until there are 4 or fewer stalks remaining. This remainder is placed between the ring finger and the middle finger of the left hand. Next the right-hand heap is counted off by fours, and the remainder is placed between the middle finger and the forefinger of the left hand. The sum of the stalks now between the fingers of the left hand is either 9 or 5. (The various possibilities are 1+4+4, or 1+3+1, or 1+2+2, or 1+1+3; it follows that the number 5 is easier to obtain than the number 9.) At this first counting off of the stalks, the first stalk—held between the little finger and the ring finger—is disregarded as supernumerary, hence one reckons as follows: 9 = 8, or 5 = 4. The number 4 is regarded as a complete unit, to which the numerical value 3 is assigned. The number 8, on the other hand, is regarded as a double unit and is reckoned as having only the numerical value 2. Therefore, if at the first count 9 stalks are left over, they count as 2; if 5 are left, they count as 3. These stalks are now laid aside for the time being.

Then the remaining stalks are gathered together again and divided anew. Once more one takes a stalk from the pile on the right and places it between the ring finger and the little finger of the left hand; then one counts off the stalks as before. This time the sum of the remainders is either 8 or 4, the possible combinations being 1+4+3, or 1+3+4, or 1+1+2, or 1+2+1, so that this time the chances of obtaining 8 or 4 are equal. The 8 counts as 2, the 4 counts as 3.

The procedure is carried out a third time with the remaining stalks, and again the sum of the remainders is 8 or 4.

Now, from the numerical values assigned to each of the three composite remainders, a line is formed.

If the sum is 5 (= 4, value 3) +4 (value 3) +4 (value 3), the resulting numerical value is 9, the so-called old yang. This becomes a positive line that moves and must therefore be taken into account in the interpretation of the individual lines. It is designated by the symbol ⊖ or ○.

If the sum of the composite remainders is 9 (= 8, value 2) +8 (value 2) +8 (value 2), the final value is 6, the so-called old yin. This becomes a negative line that moves and is therefore to be taken into account in the interpretation of the individual lines. It is designated by the symbol — ✕ — or ✕.

If the sum is

$$\left. \begin{array}{l} 9 \ (2) \ +8 \ (2) \ +4 \ (3) \\ \text{or } 5 \ (3) \ +8 \ (2) \ +8 \ (2) \\ \text{or } 9 \ (2) \ +4 \ (3) \ +8 \ (2) \end{array} \right\} = 7$$

the value 7 results, the so-called young yang. This becomes a positive line that is at rest and therefore not taken into account in the interpretation of the individual lines. It is designated by the symbol ————.

If the sum is

$$\left. \begin{array}{l} 9 \ (2) \ +4 \ (3) \ +4 \ (3) \\ \text{or } 5 \ (3) \ +4 \ (3) \ +8 \ (2) \\ \text{or } 5 \ (3) \ +8 \ (2) \ +4 \ (3) \end{array} \right\} = 8$$

the value 8 results, the so-called young yin. This becomes a negative line that is at rest and therefore not taken into account in the interpretation of the individual lines. It is designated by the symbol — —.

This procedure is repeated six times, and thus a hexagram of six stages is built up. When a hexagram consists entirely of nonmoving lines, the oracle takes into account only the idea represented by the hexagram as a whole, as set down in the Judgment by King Wên and in the Commentary on the Decision by Confucius, together with the Image.

If there are one or more moving lines in the hexagram thus obtained, the words appended by the Duke of Chou to the given line or lines are also to be considered. His words therefore carry the superscription, "Nine in the xth place," or "Six in the xth place."

Furthermore, the movement, i.e., change[1] in the lines, gives rise to a new hexagram, the meaning of which must also be taken into account. For instance, when we get hexagram 56

showing a moving line in the fourth place

we must take into account not only the text[2] and the Image belonging to this hexagram as a whole, but also the text that goes with the fourth line, and in addition both the text and the Image belonging to hexagram 52:

Thus hexagram 56 would be the starting point of a development leading, by reason of the situation of the nine in the fourth place and the appended counsel, to the final situation, i.e., hexagram 52.

In the second hexagram the text belonging to the moving line is disregarded.

2. THE COIN ORACLE

In addition to the method of the yarrow-stalk oracle, there is in use a shorter method employing coins: for this as a rule old Chinese bronze coins, with a hole in the middle and an

---

1. By movement or change a yielding line develops out of a strong line, and a strong line out of a yielding line.
2. [Judgment and Commentary on the Decision.]

inscription on one side, are used. Three coins are taken up and thrown down together, and each throw gives a line. The inscribed side counts as yin, with the value 2, and the reverse side counts as yang, with the value 3. From this the character of the line is derived. If all three coins are yang, the line is a 9; if all three are yin, it is a 6.

Two yin and one yang yield a 7, and two yang and one yin yield an 8. In looking up the hexagrams in the Book of Changes, one proceeds as with the yarrow-stalk oracle.

There is yet another kind of coin oracle, employing, besides the hexagrams of the *I Ching*, the "five stages of change," the cyclic signs, etc. This oracle is used by Chinese soothsayers, but without the text of the hexagrams of the *I Ching*. It is said to be a perpetuation of the ancient tortoise oracle, which was consulted in antiquity in addition to the yarrow-stalk oracle. In the course of time it was gradually supplanted by the *I Ching*, in the more rational form imparted to it by Confucius.

II. *The Hexagrams Arranged by Houses*

≡≡ the Creative has three whole lines.

☷ the Receptive has six half lines.

☳ the Arousing is like an open bowl.

☶ Keeping Still is like an inverted bowl.

☵ the Abysmal is full in the middle.

☲ the Clinging is empty in the middle.

☱ the Joyous has a gap at the top.

☴ the Gentle is divided at the bottom.

THE EIGHT HOUSES

1. *The House of the Creative*

1. THE CREATIVE is Heaven (1)
2. Heaven with Wind is COMING TO MEET (44)
3. Heaven with Mountain is RETREAT (33)
4. Heaven with Earth is STANDSTILL (12)
5. Wind with Earth is CONTEMPLATION (20)
6. Mountain with Earth is SPLITTING APART (23)
7. Fire with Earth is PROGRESS (35)
8. Fire with Heaven is POSSESSION IN GREAT MEASURE (14)

2. *The House of the Abysmal*

1. THE ABYSMAL is Water (29)
2. Water with Lake is LIMITATION (60)
3. Water with Thunder is DIFFICULTY AT THE BEGINNING (3)
4. Water with Fire is AFTER COMPLETION (63)
5. Lake with Fire is REVOLUTION (49)
6. Thunder with Fire is ABUNDANCE (55)
7. Earth with Fire is DARKENING OF THE LIGHT (36)
8. Earth with Water is THE ARMY (7)

3. *The House of Keeping Still*

1. KEEPING STILL is Mountain (52)
2. Mountain with Fire is GRACE (22)
3. Mountain with Heaven is THE TAMING POWER OF THE GREAT (26)
4. Mountain with Lake is DECREASE (41)
5. Fire with Lake is OPPOSITION (38)
6. Heaven with Lake is TREADING (10)
7. Wind with Lake is INNER TRUTH (61)
8. Wind with Mountain is DEVELOPMENT (53)

4. *The House of the Arousing*

1. THE AROUSING is Thunder (51)
2. Thunder with Earth is ENTHUSIASM (16)
3. Thunder with Water is DELIVERANCE (40)
4. Thunder with Wind is DURATION (32)
5. Earth with Wind is PUSHING UPWARD (46)
6. Water with Wind is THE WELL (48)
7. Lake with Wind is PREPONDERANCE OF THE GREAT (28)
8. Lake with Thunder is FOLLOWING (17)

5. *The House of the Gentle*

1. THE GENTLE is Wind (57)
2. Wind with Heaven is THE TAMING POWER OF THE SMALL (9)
3. Wind with Fire is THE FAMILY (37)
4. Wind with Thunder is INCREASE (42)
5. Heaven with Thunder is INNOCENCE (25)
6. Fire with Thunder is BITING THROUGH (21)

726

7. Mountain with Thunder is THE CORNERS OF THE MOUTH (27)
8. Mountain with Wind is WORK ON WHAT HAS BEEN SPOILED (18)

6. *The House of the Clinging*

1. THE CLINGING is Fire (30)
2. Fire with Mountain is THE WANDERER (56)
3. Fire with Wind is THE CALDRON (50)
4. Fire with Water is BEFORE COMPLETION (64)
5. Mountain with Water is YOUTHFUL FOLLY (4)
6. Wind with Water is DISPERSION (59)
7. Heaven with Water is CONFLICT (6)
8. Heaven with Fire is FELLOWSHIP WITH MEN (13)

7. *The House of the Receptive*

1. THE RECEPTIVE is Earth (2)
2. Earth with Thunder is RETURN (24)
3. Earth with Lake is APPROACH (19)
4. Earth with Heaven is PEACE (11)
5. Thunder with Heaven is THE POWER OF THE GREAT (34)
6. Lake with Heaven is BREAK-THROUGH (43)
7. Water with Heaven is WAITING (5)
8. Water with Earth is HOLDING TOGETHER (8)

8. *The House of the Joyous*

1. THE JOYOUS is Lake (58)
2. Lake with Water is OPPRESSION (47)
3. Lake with Earth is GATHERING TOGETHER (45)
4. Lake with Mountain is INFLUENCE (31)
5. Water with Mountain is OBSTRUCTION (39)
6. Earth with Mountain is MODESTY (15)
7. Thunder with Mountain is PREPONDERANCE OF THE SMALL (62)
8. Thunder with Lake is THE MARRYING MAIDEN (54)

INDEXES

An Index of The Hexagrams

The page references pertain to Book I, where each hexagram is first treated. (For an explanation of this and other sequences, see H. Wilhelm, *Change*, pp. 89–91.)

General Index

The name of each hexagram is followed by its number, in parentheses. The text for each hexagram in Books I and III is shown by page references in boldface type; the text for the Ten Wings is shown likewise. Small capitals are used for the English names of the hexagrams. Proper names are indexed fully, but subjects are treated selectively.